Lincoln's
Banner Regiment

MW00785455

# Lincoln's Banner Regiment

*The 107th New York Volunteer Infantry*

## George R. Farr

McFarland & Company, Inc., Publishers
*Jefferson, North Carolina*

LIBRARY OF CONGRESS CATALOGUING-IN-PUBLICATION DATA

Names: Farr, George R., 1935– author.
Title: Lincoln's banner regiment : the 107th New York Volunteer Infantry / George R. Farr.
Other titles: 107th New York Volunteer Infantry
Description: Jefferson, North Carolina : McFarland & Company, Inc., Publishers, 2023 |
Includes bibliographical references and index.
Identifiers: LCCN 2023015993 | ISBN 9781476689777 (paperback : acid free paper) ∞
ISBN 9781476648019 (ebook)
Subjects: LCSH: United States. Army. Infantry Regiment, 107th. | United States—History—
Civil War, 1861–1865—Regimental histories. | New York (State)—History—Civil War, 1861–1865—
Regimental histories. | BISAC: HISTORY / Military / United States | HISTORY / United States /
Civil War Period (1850–1877)
Classification: LCC E523.5 107th .F37 2023 | DDC 973.7/447—dc23/eng/20230404
LC record available at https://lccn.loc.gov/2023015993

BRITISH LIBRARY CATALOGUING DATA ARE AVAILABLE

ISBN (print) 978-1-4766-8977-7
ISBN (ebook) 978-1-4766-4801-9

Front cover image: Banner given to the 107th NY by President Lincoln
and Secretary of State Seward in recognition of the 107th
as the first regiment to answer the president's call for additional troops;
background oil painting "Scene behind the breastworks on Culps Hill,
morning of July 3rd 1862." Artist Edwin Forbes, created between 1870 and 1884
(Library of Congress)

Printed in the United States of America

McFarland & Company, Inc., Publishers
Box 611, Jefferson, North Carolina 28640
www.mcfarlandpub.com

To my parents,
Ralph Cummings Farr and Ada Florence Wingrave;
to my wife and first love,
Teresa Marie Carozza;
and to our children,
Diane Christine and Daryl Robert

# Table of Contents

# Acknowledgments

A number of people were of great help to me while I was researching and writing this book. It was a book in the local library, however, that proved the greatest single source of information about the 107th NY. That book was *A Civil War Courtship* by William Walton. Walton was a descendant of Edwin Weller and his then-fiancée Antoinette Watkins. Weller wrote to Nettie (as he called her) all during his service with the 107th NY during the war. In the late 1970s Walton obtained those letters from his cousin and used them as a source for his book. In the book Walton also made reference to a *History of the 107th New York Volunteers,* replete with detailed, first person accounts written soon after the war. In addition, the Elmira and Havana newspapers over the next few decades gave generous space to regimental reunions when the veterans gathered to reminisce, refight old battles, and crack old jokes. Walton did not specifically identify the source of this history, but it made sense to examine the newspapers, especially the Havana Journal, which had been microfilmed and was available at the local library. I spent the following month searching until I found the beginning of it in the November 6, 1869, issue. It continued for 35 chapters until May 14, 1870. It was written by a former officer in the regiment named Harvey Denniston, and the articles covered the entire service period of the regiment. While the accounts were not greatly detailed, they did provide major highlights and a chronology of the regiment's service.

In May of 1996, the Chemung County Historical Society received a letter from Sue Hackett-Ernst who was planning a trip from Lyons, Colorado, to visit Montour Falls (formerly Havana) to see where her great-grandparents Edwin and Nettie Weller lived. She asked if there was a local historian who could help her tour the area. Fortunately, I was available and helped her during her stay. As a result of our friendship, she later gave me copies of parts of letters that Walton did not include in the book as well as a full copy of a journal that Edwin Weller kept about his service in Tennessee through the end of the war. She continued her travels relative to the service of the 107th NY and for two years continued to send me material that she thought may be helpful for the book.

The newspapers in the counties of Chemung, Steuben, and Schuyler covered the activities of the 107th NY beginning with the raising of the regiment in great detail, and every effort was made to keep the public informed of its progress through the many campaigns and battles until the end of the war. Coverage continued of its annual reunions through the early 1930s. Copies of the issues were available on microfilm for most of the local newspapers, and in some cases, articles were available from national newspapers. This material is available at local libraries such as the Steele Memorial Library in Elmira, NY. Additional libraries include the Montour Falls Library and Museum; Davenport Memorial Library in Bath, NY; Hornell Public Library in Hornell, NY; and Southeast Steuben County Corning Library in Corning, NY. University collections include William L. Clements Library at the University of Michigan; Olin Library at Cornell University Ithaca, NY; the New York State Library in Albany, NY; Duke University in Durham, NC; and Dartmouth College in Hanover, NH.

The Chemung County Historical Society was the most significant local source of 107th NY material. They had a number of collections that served as tremendous sources of material. Arthur Fitch was a member of the regiment who kept a journal and wrote many letters, copies of which were available. He was an exceptional writer and with articles published in national newspapers. He wrote a piece called "The Bronze Soldier" that had the 107th NY memorial statue enter into a conversation with Fitch and another veteran, Frank Frost, as they passed by it one evening. Fitch also gave many speeches at the annual reunions. The society also has the scrapbook of Frank Frost, an exceptionally active member of the regimental association, containing many obituaries of 107th soldiers. The director of the society during the 1990s was Connie Barone, and she did an outstanding job in aiding my search for material pertinent to the history of the 107th NY. I would like to thank the current director Bruce Whitmarsh for allowing a photograph of the regiment's banner. In addition, I would also like to thank the archivist Rachel Dworkin for her help over the years.

Captain John Orr was another member of the 107th whose letters and journal provided a great deal of information about his regiment. His material was found in Cooperstown at the New York State Historical Association Library and in a book called *Mr. Tubbs' War* by Nat Brandt. This book contains letters written by Charles Tubbs and his friends, all students at Alfred University in New York State. The author gave credit to Peter Conners Andrews, whose grandfather John Tuttle Andrews was the author of three of the letters in the collection on which the book is based. The book contains references to thirteen letters written by Orr. A copy of the book was given to me by Andrews.

Lt. Col. William Freeman Fox of the 107th was the primary author of *Slocum and His Men*, *Regimental Losses in the Civil War* and the three-volume *New York at Gettysburg*. Both books furnished a great deal of material relevant to the service of the 107th NY. Fox was New York Superintendent of Forestry for 22 years.

Over the course of researching this book, it was very important to investigate what records the government might have. I found that Record Group 94 of the National Archives in Washington, D.C., was the place to start. However, I didn't know how long that would take or where could I stay. Fortunately, I had been in contact with a gentleman named Lathel Duffield, an employee of the Board of Indian Affairs, and he offered to let me stay at his home in Falls Church, VA, while I did research at the National Archives. Every day I would take the train into Washington, where I was able to gather the entire available records for the 107th New York Volunteer Infantry.

In December of 1995, I received an email from a Steve Ross of Birmingham, AL, who said that he had heard my name mentioned at a Civil War Show in Nashville, TN. He was originally born and raised in Syracuse, NY, and his mother's maiden name was Brayton. His interest in the 107th stemmed from a second cousin of hers named Sweet Brayton, a corporal in Company K of the 107th. Thus began a series of communications between us leading to his providing me with an enormous amount of 107th material for my book.

In January of 1994, I began correspondence with William Hughes, who edited "The Civil War Papers of Lt. Colonel Newton T. Colby, New York Infantry." Colby was a member of the 107th NY Vol. Infantry. We corresponded for a long period of time and shared information about the regiment. Bill referenced our communications in his book, and I share his good feelings about our sharing of information.

During the summer of 1997, I communicated with George C. Bradley, an attorney in Carlisle, PA, and also a writer who was devoting time to the study and writing of Civil War history. He was also a contributor to the *Gettysburg Magazine*. He offered to host me while I was in the area to do research at Gettysburg, Chancellorsville, and the Carlisle U.S. Army Military Institute, where I could research the records and photographs of the 107th NY. I accepted his offer, and my time at the institute and the battlefields proved to be very fruitful. One of the major items that I found at Carlisle was a large collection of letters (transcripts) written by 2nd Lt John Hill of Co. F. who was killed at the battle of New Hope Church.

Brian Saxton of Boston University provided me with the pension papers of Private Levi H. Saxton of Co. C along with affidavits from his captain, Charles J. Fox, and four other members of his company.

The story about Nathan Dykeman's theft of the Dunker bible was told in print many times, and portions of it were always in error. It wasn't until I received a copy of his mother's application for a pension from James H. Harkin of Beaver Dams, NY, in the spring of 1997 that I discovered the true story of his death. In 2011, I forwarded the correct information on Dykeman's death to the Park Service at the Antietam National Battlefield. Mr. Harkin also provided me with additional postwar information about Frank Frost.

After my health crisis of the early 1990s, I worked a short while at the Chemung County Historical Society where I did research and corresponded with people asking questions about local history. Russ Hunley of Hampton, VA, wrote inquiring about his ancestors who fought in the Civil War and were from Elmira. He subsequently furnished me with information about 107th NY.

As was the case with many of those who communicated with me during my early research efforts, Benedict Maryniak, an employee of Niagara Mohawk Power near Buffalo, was a contributor to my efforts in 1995–96. He was a Civil War buff, and we exchanged information numerous times.

Leland L. Crane of St. Petersburg, FL, was likewise very knowledgeable about the history of the 107th NY. He helped me in several different ways and a number of times.

Roger Sturcke of Woodbridge, VA, corresponded with me from August 1997 until September 2000. During that time, he sent me twenty packages of information that referenced the 107th NY. While the material was extensive and accurate, it did not relate well with the overall content of the book.

Gerald Tomlinson was a local high school history teacher who, along with another teacher, had written an article about the regiment for the local historical society booklet that described, in part, the regiment's participation in the battle at Antietam. The article was inaccurate, and we met and discussed the discrepancies.

Steve Ross of Birmingham AL, originally from Syracuse, NY, is a descendant of Sweet Brayton, a member of the 107th NY. He had done considerable research about Brayton and the regiment. We corresponded extensively, and he shared his research with me as I did with him.

Jeffery Sauter of Scotia, NY, was another researcher of the 107th NY with whom I corresponded. He was tremendously interested in the 107th NY, and although he did not furnish me with material for the book, we did maintain communications via email for a couple of years.

Lowell C. Newvine, the Hannibal Town and Village Historian, provided me with letters written by Solomon R. Reniff and other material related to his service with the 107th NY.

Russ Hunley of Hampton, VA, a graduate of West Point and a volunteer at the local historical society, provided me with material on Charles Terwilliger. His great, great uncle was a member of the 107th NY.

Phyllis Bratt of Walnut Creek, CA, is the great granddaughter of Private Thomas Gilmore of Co. I, an Irish immigrant who was wounded and lost a leg at the battle of New Hope, GA, and went on to live a productive life. She graciously provided me with information about his experiences as well as a photograph taken during his later life.

Rock Thomas of Rising Fawn, GA, is a lifelong resident of the state. We had a brief correspondence during which he discussed the general area near the battlefield of New Hope Church.

Joseph Husted of Knoxville, PA, was the great grandson of George Husted, a sergeant in Co. F who was discharged because of chronic diarrhea. Joseph sent me various documents pertaining to his situation.

I want to thank everyone that I came in contact with during my journey to uncover the history of this regiment.

# Preface

In 1992 at age 57, I required a heart operation. It didn't go well, and it took two years for my health to return to some level of normalcy. As a result, I went on social security. During those two years, I began to study local history, as I had graduated from college with a major in history even though I never had plans to make any specific use of it. However, I had done many local history lectures, and some years earlier I had been asked by the local Chemung County Historical Society to participate in the re-dedication of the banner of the 107th NY Volunteer Infantry; that had sparked a further interest in that regiment. I discovered through further study that while all the regiments in its brigade had histories written, the 107th had not. For the next several years, I gathered up material on the regiment's service during the American Civil War. The 107th had been raised from three local counties, and I began scouring all possible sources for material in each county as well the National Archives in Washington, DC, many universities, and several state historical archives. I began writing the book in 2001. The writing did not progress very well as my wife was ill with an incurable disease. It was not until after she died in 2011 that I made a concerted effort to complete the book.

The source that identified the general chronological activity of the regiment during the the war came from the very first book that I found: *A Civil War Courtship: The Letters of Edwin Weller from Antietam to Atlanta* by William Walton. However, it wasn't the story covered in the book that provided the material. Walton referenced a history of the regiment that was published in a local newspaper, but he didn't identify the newspaper or the date. I had several local newspapers to choose from and was fortunate enough to choose the right one first, the *Havana Journal*. I searched through the microfilm of that newspaper covering a period of several years until I found the history, which had been serially published from November 6, 1869, through May 15, 1870, with one or more of its 36 chapters published in each consecutive bi-weekly edition. It had been written by a former officer of the regiment, Lieut. Harvey Denniston. I subsequently contacted the owner of the letters, Sue Ann Hackett-Earnst, a cousin of William Walton. She also had Weller's original journal from the war that had not been included in Walton's book. She subsequently gave me a copy of the journal.

This is the only book that fully describes the service of the regiment that was the first to answer President Abraham Lincoln's call for additional troops at a critical point in the American Civil War. It describes the arrival of the regiment in Washington and the presentation of a banner to the regiment by President Lincoln and Secretary of State Seward. That banner never saw battle and was preserved by Seward from that time until the end of the war when it was returned to the regiment. When the regiment organized a veterans' association in 1867, the banner was displayed at its annual meetings. After the association was dissolved in the mid–1930s, the banner was held in private hands until it was given to the Chemung County Historical Society, where it was hung in a frame on the 2nd floor. It was photographed for the first time for this book.

While three books have been published that relate to the regiment, they are primarily about individual officers and do not present a broad and detailed representation of the regiment's overall experiences and contribution to the success of the Union army. The regiment served with 12th and 20th Army Corps at the battles of Antietam, Chancellorsville, and Gettysburg, as well as the lesser-known battles of Resaca, New Hope Church, Kennesaw Mountain, and Peach Tree Creek during Sherman's campaign in Georgia that resulted in the capture of Atlanta.

Following the capture of Atlanta, the men of the 107th NY participated in the March to the Sea that resulted in the capture of Savannah. Lastly, they marched north through the Carolinas, where they participated in the battles of Bentonville and Averasboro. The war ended while they were in Raleigh, NC. They then marched north through Virginia to Washington, DC, to participate in the Grand Review. Following the review, they returned home to Elmira, where they were welcomed with a celebration.

Starting in 1867, annual celebrations occurred on September 17, the anniversary of the regiment's first action, which was with the 12th Army Corps at the battle of Antietam. It was always an occasion when memories both joyful and sad further expressed their many personal experiences during the war.

# Introduction

In the writing of this work, I have attempted to search out as much material as I could that would both identify the military campaigns of this regiment and present to the reader some flavor of the circumstances in which these men found themselves during their great adventure. That adventure was a source of great learning to some, a terrible hardship for others, and an unfortunate death and burial far from home for so many. And as is the case in all wars, the end of the fighting did not mean the end of suffering. Many of these men came home broken in health and met with untimely deaths. Such was the case of my great-uncle who, although he survived the loss of his arm at Antietam, died of a heart attack while still in his thirties. His widow was granted a pension due to the circumstances of his death, which was thought to have been brought on by the rigorous march from Washington to Sharpsburg prior to the battle of Antietam. Her pension request documentation points out the discrepancy.

Much of the language you find may be in the style prevalent during the times. I have made no effort to update the style of writing, hoping to give you a better impression of how these expressed themselves during these years of great danger to our country. I believe that almost all of them had strong feelings regarding their duty toward the preservation of this nation.

In July of 1862, this country was facing a great crisis. The Civil War had been in progress for over a year, and it had not gone well for the North. President Lincoln felt it necessary to raise more troops. It was in answer to his call for 300,000 more men that the 107th New York Volunteer Infantry was raised.

The 107th was composed of men from the counties of Chemung, Steuben, and Schuyler. Each township was given a quota of men based on its population. To aid in the raising of the regiment, so called "war meetings" were held almost every day for over a month. Several meetings would be held during a given day with the speakers and other participants riding by horse or wagon from town to town. The men who were to be the regiment's officers, both regimental and company commanders, gave patriotic speeches urging the men to volunteer. They were joined by elected officials, ministers, and other civic leaders.

The speech making was often interspersed with patriotic songs and music by local bands. People in attendance were not limited to potential volunteers. Women and children and men not of military age also attended, and they were encouraged to donate money to be used to pay bounties to the men who did volunteer. Meetings were often begun with a firing of a cannon if one could be had. Sometimes the meeting hall could not hold the crowd, and it was necessary to hold a second meeting simultaneously outside on the hall steps.

As the effort progressed, the men were sworn in and shipped off to the Elmira Military Rendezvous to receive their uniforms and equipment. There they would train until the regiment was full, and then they would be shipped off to Washington, DC.

The 107th was the first regiment from the North to reach Washington in response to the president's call. For this honor, they were presented a regimental banner by President Lincoln with Secretary of State Seward, a New Yorker, at his side. That banner was kept by Secretary Seward until after the war when it was returned to the regiment and placed in a large frame. When the regimental association was no more, it was donated to the Chemung County Historical Society along with other memorabilia of the regiment. At the time, the society had no place to store the banner in its enormous frame, and it was put in temporary storage in the carriage house of Elmira mayor Mooers' home on the south-west corner of Washington Ave. and College Ave. in Elmira, NY. It was later restored and re-rededicated and now resides at the Chemung County Historical Society's home in Elmira, NY. The author was proud to have been asked to speak at its re-dedication.

This is the story of that regiment, which brought a certain measure of fame and honor to itself during its service. It may not have been one of the better-known regiments in the war, but the men who served with it, and the people at home who supported them, felt a great deal of pride in what it was able to accomplish. This division was commanded by General A.S. Williams. He was its only commander, the only instance in which a division had one commander for the duration of the war. The Twelfth Army Corps, and later the Twentieth, had the reputation of never having lost a color or a gun.

If a regiment that fought in that terrible conflict can be called fortunate, the 107th was in the sense that it participated in some of the most memorable campaigns of the war. It saw its first action, as a member of the Twelfth Army Corps' First "Red Star" Division, north of Sharpsburg, MD, in the battle of Antietam, the single bloodiest day of the war. Following a winter of picket duty, guarding against Confederate incursions along the Potomac River, it participated in the battle of Chancellorsville.

Not long after Chancellorsville, it marched up to Pennsylvania where it met another invasion of the North by General Robert E. Lee at Gettysburg. The 107th was not involved in the repulsing of "Pickett's Charge," but it did help fight off the Confederate charge against Culp's Hill earlier that day. The Rebel charge that took place at the break of day on Culp's Hill has gone largely unnoticed by all but the learned scholars of the war. If that charge had succeeded, the Rebels would have broken through to the rear of the Union troops who fought off Pickett. Who knows what the result might have been.

Following Gettysburg, the regiment was re-assigned and sent to Tennessee to guard railroads during the winter of 1863–64. It was a welcome change from their previous duty, and for the most part the men thoroughly enjoyed their stay there. Little did they know that their hardest fighting and greatest loss of life lay in front of them in bloody Georgia.

Early in 1864, they were brought together in the Twentieth Army Corps, a consolidation of the 11th and the 12th that took place on April 4, 1864, by General William T. Sherman to form an army of over 70,000, which would become of one of the most famous armies in the history of warfare. They were to be part of his plan to devastate the underbelly of the Confederacy. The 107th fought hard in the many skirmishes and battles on its way to Atlanta, losing a great many men in the battle of New Hope Church, also known as Dallas. They were among the first troops to enter Atlanta, and they were part of its provost guard while Sherman chased after Hood's army.

They left Atlanta in mid–November and began the "March to the Sea." Only three days out of the city, over forty of them were captured and sent off to Confederate prison camps. A week later, a sergeant of the 107th raised the American flag over the state capitol at Milledgeville, and his picture appeared on the cover of *Harper's Weekly*. They continued southward and participated in the capture of Savannah. After resting there a while, they began their last campaign, one that would take them north through the Carolinas where they participated in the battles of Averasboro and Bentonville. Finally, at the end of this campaign, their army would receive the surrender of General Joseph Johnson, which for all practical purposes ended the war.

There was one last march for them before they could go home. Onward to Washington they marched, where they would parade in the "Grand Review" of the Union Army on May 24, 1865, in front of the newly sworn-in President Andrew Johnson. After the review, they remained in camp near Bladensburg until June 5 when they were mustered out. They arrived home in Elmira on June 8 to the cheers of the of the local populace and were formally discharged from the service on June 18.

However, this was not the end of the 107th. Two years later, they organized their regimental association. Thereafter, as long as they were alive and able, the members of the regiment would meet on September 17, the date of their first battle, to remember their fallen comrades and to reminisce about their experiences in the war.

# 1

# Raising the Regiment

CAMPBELL GUARDS TO ARMS
THE CALL IS TO EVERY ABLE-BODIED MAN
The undersigned having determined to raise another full company for the war,
make an earnest appeal to the **Young Men and Firemen of Elmira.**
To step forward and volunteer in response to the President's urgent call for
**300,000 MEN**
To complete the overthrow of the rebellion, *THE COMPANY MUST BE FILLED AT ONCE!!*
**Extraordinary Inducements to every volunteer the following liberal offer is made:**
**$2.00 PREMIUM AND $25 BOUNTY IN CASH** when he enlists in the service, and
ONE MONTHS PAY IN ADVANCE when the regiment is mustered in!
Pay and clothing from the day of enlistment.————Clothing, food, transportation and
medical attendance free by the government. Terms of service three years or during the war.
The disabled from wounds and other causes draw pensions for life.
Recruiting office in Judge Gray's new store on Water St. opposite Baldwin St.

H.M. Stocum
O. N. Smith
O. D. Reynolds[1]

The common thread that ran through the postwar reunions and outings of the men who fought with the 107th New York Volunteer Infantry was that the regiment saw its birth when two New York congressmen, Alexander S. Diven and Robert Van Valkenburgh, were summoned by President Lincoln to Secretary of State Seward's home in Washington to ask them to go back to their home state to raise a regiment. That story is for the most part true, and it always made for good listening at the regimental reunions. However, the real beginnings of this regiment go back several weeks before that to the latter part of May when Elmira, Chemung County, and the surrounding counties of Steuben and Schuyler were already involved in seeking volunteers for the army.

In Elmira, Colonel Elliott F. Shepard, the recently appointed commander of the military depot under General Order No. 31 issued by Adjutant General Thomas Hillhouse on May 23, 1862,[2] had been contacting prominent local men to ask for their help in raising more troops. On May 27, he wrote to attorney Hull Fanton in Havana requesting his help and giving him authorization to enroll volunteers. At the time, Mr. Fanton was not enthusiastic about the possibility of raising another volunteer company in Schuyler County, and he advised Col. Shepard of local sentiment.[3]

Schuyler County had already raised three full companies.[4] It would take the call by the president for 300,000 more men, and the leadership of congressmen Van Valkenburgh, Diven, and many others, including Hull Fanton, to overcome this sentiment.

One of the men most active in the early recruiting was Captain William L. Morgan. In the May 29 issue of the *Elmira Weekly Gazette* in the column titled "Local Facts and Fancies," he was noted as having a need for two lieutenants and several sergeants and corporals. In the same issue, he placed an advertisement calling for volunteers to join the new regiment. Captain Morgan had formerly held the rank of Second Lieutenant in the 50th New York Engineers and now, commissioned as a captain in the new regiment, he had taken an office opposite the Brainard House with R.H. Ransom. There he and Ransom advertised that they would be happy to accept new volunteers.

The following day a meeting was held at the Elmira town hall. Its stated purpose was to discuss the raising of companies for a new regiment. All Elmirans were invited, and the primary speaker was advertised as the Attorney General for New York State,[5] the Hon. Daniel S. Dickenson from Binghamton. The meeting was well attended, and some of the more prominent attendees were J.A. McWilliams, the Reverend Mr. Curtis, the Reverend Mr. Beecher, and M.C. Wilkinson, who previously was a lieutenant in the 23rd Regiment. It was decided to hold a "War Meeting" to encourage enlistments in a new "Southern Tier Regiment" the following Monday at Ely's Hall on Baldwin Street.[6]

On Monday evening, June 2, Ely's Hall was thoroughly filled, and the crowd was very enthusiastic. Daniel F. Pickering chaired the meeting and, R.R.R. Dumars and C.G. Freeman were chosen secretaries. The Rev. Thomas K. Beecher submitted the following resolutions, and they were unanimously adopted.

> **Resolved:**
> That the rebellion which the government and loyal people of the United States are now engaged in suppressing, though greatly weakened by important and multiplied victories of arms, is nevertheless still of formidable proportions and purpose, and therefore impose the duty of unabated prosecution of the war.
> That a ready people will make a short war, while to the feeble hearted even victories are worthless.
> That the call of our rulers for more men, satisfies us that we have more work to do.
> That Chemung County is ready to meet the call.
> That if adjacent counties agree, a new Southern Tier Regiment can be enrolled at once.

Speeches of an eloquent nature were made by the Reverend Beecher, Col. Shepard, Wm. Smith Esq. of the *Owego Times*, M.C. Wilkinson, and Major Atkins of the Illinois 11th Infantry, whose ranks had been terribly decimated at the siege of Fort Donelson. Major Atkins, a former resident of the town of Southport just south of Elmira and the son of Mrs. Adna Atkins, made a speech that carried the audience by storm. The audience showed a great deal of curiosity and contempt for a large "Secession" flag that was exhibited from the stage. The flag had been captured at New Bern, NC, by the 51st "Shepard Rifles" New York Volunteer Infantry.[7]

The following day, it was reported that Newton T. Colby, a resident of Corning, had received authority from Col. Shepard to enlist a company of men and report to the Elmira Depot.[8] That same day Col. Shepard issued General Order No. 5 from the headquarters of the Elmira Depot.

> I. The Barracks on Lake and William Streets will hereafter be known as the "Arnot Barracks." Those on Washington Avenue as the "Post Barracks." Those on Water Street as the "Rathbun Barracks." Those at Southport as the "Robinson Barracks."
> II. The following transportation companies have generously and patriotically agreed to issue return tickets to volunteers leaving this depot on furlough upon exhibiting their furlough documents at the respective ticket offices and paying fare one way to wit: The Erie Railway, Buffalo and N.Y., Erie R.R. Co. Syracuse, Binghamton and N.Y., R.R. Co., New York Central R.R. Co.
> III. Major G.L. Smith, Inspector of the 20th Brigade, pursuant to instructions received from General Headquarters, is appointed Military Examiner at this Depot. He will report in writing on Saturday the 7th of June at 3 o'clock p.m. a list of applicants passed or rejected by him, and thereafter will continue such report weekly.
> IV. Dr. Wm. C. Wey having been appointed surgeon of the Post, will report daily at these Headquarters with his morning report before two o'clock p.m.
> V. Capt. Wm. L. Morgan is assigned to the command of the Rathbun Barracks. His morning report will be sent to these Headquarters before 9 o'clock daily.
> VI. Lieut. Jacob M. Covell is appointed acting Adjutant to the Commandant, and will be obeyed and respected accordingly.
> VII. Charles M. Backman is appointed Lance Sergeant and Ezekiel Smith Lance Corporal of Captain Morgan's company Campbell Guards, new Southern Tier Regiment. George Goldsmith is appointed Lance Sergeant and William Wheeler Lance Corporal of Captain Wilkinson's company same regiment. Harlan P. Boyd is appointed Lance Sergeant and Benjamin F. Newman Lance Corporal of Captain Davis' company same regiment. Seth M. Mitchell is appointed Lance Sergeant of Captain Warwick's company same regiment.
> VIII. The General Hospital is established for the sick and wounded at the Arnot Barracks.[9]

During the next two weeks, recruiting continued to progress. Captain Morgan had a squad or two of men enlisted and mustered into the service. They had been furnished with uniforms and were housed in the #3 "Rathbun" barracks. To facilitate a speedier enlistment of men, Captain Morgan, from his recruiting office opposite the Brainard House, offered two dollars' bounty and a month's pay in advance to any man joining his company. Captain Wilkinson had also made good progress towards filling up his company. In other towns, men were also being enlisted for the new regiment. Lt. Newton P. Colby, also formerly of the 23rd NY, had begun recruiting in Corning. In Kanona, Steuben County, Captain John J. Lamon was at work, and Hull Fanton of Havana in Schuyler County had also begun to recruit.[10]

On June 28, the *Bath Courier* reported the Capt. Laman was progressing rapidly toward filling up his company. As of that date, he had recruited 31 of the 100 men he required to fill the company.

By the end of June, the setbacks in the Peninsula Campaign and the Shenandoah Valley had made Washington fearful of imminent attack by Confederate forces. This fear was not totally unfounded for McClellan had taken most of the combat forces from northern Virginia and transported them by sea to Yorktown. It would take him until almost the end of August to get them back to Washington. This situation led to a requisition upon New York State to send all available National Guard regiments into service for a period of three months. Within a matter of days, 8,588 such troops were transported to Washington and the vicinity. These regiments consisted of the 5th Artillery, 7th, 8th, 11th, 22nd, 25th, 27th, and 71st N.Y. Militia Infantry.[11]

On June 26, the following letter was sent by Congressman Robert R. Van Valkenburgh in Washington to Col. E.F. Shepard:

> We need more troops, McClellan has not enough. His force is not equal to the force of rebels at Richmond. We may, and will proceed in taking that city, but it will be with the terrible loss of life. I visited Fair Oaks a few days ago; went to the advance lines and saw some of the enemy's pickets. I was there when Lieut. Palmer, Gen. Sickles aid [sic] was killed, and Major Dereulaux was wounded. Our pickets were partially driven in, but soon succeeded in repulsing the rebels. I hoped to have an opportunity of in part avenging my brother, but the advance was stayed and no general fight came off-we had a very pretty little skirmish. The men of Western New York should turn out. The government needs at least 150,000 more troops, and that soon I hope the New Southern Tier will fill up.[12]

The congressman was probably not aware that McClellan was shortly to be called back to Washington, but it was apparent that he knew that a new regiment was being recruited in Elmira. His reference here was to the Southern Tier Rifles, a home guard unit that saw its beginnings shortly after Chemung County was organized in 1836. This unit made its first formal appearance in a parade held prior to early settler and Revolutionary War soldier Colonel John Hendy's funeral in 1840. The original unit was disbanded in 1854, and a new unit was formed shortly afterwards and took the name "Southern Tier Rifles." It was at its height in 1858 when it was commanded by H.C. Hoffman and 1st Lt. Nat B. Fowler. In an answer to President Lincoln's initial call for troops on April 15, 1861, a meeting was held in the Concert Hall on Lake Street just below Water where many men from the "Rifles" helped form the 23rd New York Volunteer Regiment. These men formed Company K in that regiment, and most of the regiment's officers were also from the "Rifles" including Colonel H.C. Hoffman and Lieut. Colonel Nirom Crane, who later would command the 107th. The 23rd was mustered into service on May 16, 1861, for two years.[13]

The setbacks of the Campaign prompted action to be taken by the governors of the northern states. On June 28, 1862, the governors of sixteen states and the President of the Military Board of Kentucky met and signed a letter to President Lincoln which asked him to "call upon the States for such numbers of men as may be required to fill up all military organizations in the field and add to the armies heretofore organized such additional number of men as may in your judgment be necessary to garrison and hold all of the cities and military positions that have been captured by our armies, and speedily crush the rebellion that still exists in several of the southern states."

In answer to this request, President Lincoln issued the following on July 1:

> Gentlemen, fully concurring in the wisdom of the views expressed to me in so patriotic a manner by you in the communication of the twenty-eighth day of June, I have decided to call

into service an additional force of THREE HUNDRED THOUSAND men. I suggest and recommend that the forces should be chiefly of infantry. Each state will have a quota according to population. I trust that they may be enrolled without delay, so as to bring this unnecessary and injurious civil war to a speedy and satisfactory conclusion. An order fixing the quotas of the respective states will be issued by the War Department. Signed, Abraham Lincoln.

The very next day Governor Edwin D. Morgan of New York issued a proclamation in answer to the president's call:

The President of the United States has duly called upon the country for an additional Three Hundred Thousand Volunteers to serve for three years or for the war. The wisdom of this is obvious to all. Our army in the field has been reduced by the ordinary casualties of the service and must be recruited; and the positions captured by our arms must be held by military authority. The people appreciate these facts. They fully estimate the magnitude of the great struggle, and necessity of exerting a power that will speedily quell the rebellion, restore the rightful authority of the Government and give peace to the country.

This appeal is to the State of New York; it is to each citizen. Let it come to every fireside. Let the glorious example of the Revolutionary period be our emulation. Let each feel that the commonwealth now counts on his individual strength and influence to meet the demands of the Government. The period has come when all must aid. New York has not thus far stood back. Ready and more than willing, she has met every summons to duty. Let not her history be falsified, nor her position be lowered. We cannot doubt that the insurrection is in its death throes; that a mighty blow will end its monstrous existence. A languishing war entails vast losses of life, of property, the ruin of business pursuits, and invites the interference of foreign powers. Present happiness and future greatness will be secured by responding to the present call. Let the answer go back to the President and to our brave soldiers in the field, that in New York the patriotic lists of the country's defenders is being augmented. It will strengthen the hands of one, and give hope and encouragement to the other.

An order fixing the quota of this State, as with others, will be immediately issued from the war department. The details of organization will be in accordance with orders from the Adjutant General of New York. The state will be districted, local committees will be appointed, and Regimental camps established.[14]

Discussions on how to improve past methods of enrollment were held, resulting in a plan that would hopefully stimulate local pride and engage the active assistance of eminent and influential men in every part of the state. There were thirty-two state senatorial districts in New York; in each of these a district military committee composed of twelve or more prominent citizens from both political parties was to be established. On July 7, General Order No. 52 was issued prescribing the details of enlistment and organization of the troops under the president's call. The quotas were soon established for each of the counties in the 27th District. From Chemung County the call was for 244 men and from Schuyler County a total of 171 men. Steuben, the largest county in size and population, had a quota of 605 men. This came to a total of 1,020 men and was equivalent to a fully manned regiment.[15]

On Sunday evening, July 6, 1862, Congressman Alexander S. Diven was sitting on his porch at his residence in Washington, DC. It was a sultry night, and he was anxiously reflecting on the condition of the country. Around midnight a man came up to his porch with a message from President Lincoln, who was at Secretary Seward's home. The president wished to see him immediately. Irrespective of the late hour and never having received so distinguished a summons, Congressman Diven went to Secretary Seward's home. Arriving at the house, he found only the secretary, Mr. Van Valkenburgh of Bath, and Mr. Pomeroy of Auburn. The secretary came right to the point: "Will you go home, and raise a regiment in your district? Pomeroy is going, Van Valkenburgh is going, and you must go. I mean to invite every member of Congress to do so." Without any hesitation, Congressman Diven said yes to the request even though he had little knowledge of military matters and had never entertained New York ambitions of a military nature. Seward thanked him very warmly and told him that the president had been with him until a late hour. They had sent for many New York members of Congress, whom the president had asked to raise regiments. Their request had not met with much encouragement, little more than a promise to think of it, but Pomeroy and Van Valkenburgh had agreed to go home and try. They had suggested to Seward, even though the hour was very late and the president was leaving, that he send for Diven. Van Valkenburgh and Pomeroy had waited to see what Diven would say. Seward closed the conversation by saying that Diven's promptness was somewhat of a surprise, but nothing could have gratified him more. He wished that they would leave by the first train available.

As they were about to leave, it occurred to Diven that it would be helpful if the secretary would give him a letter for New York State Senator Charles Cook of Havana, whose help Diven felt was absolutely necessary for the raising of troops in Schuyler County. Seward agreed and sat down and wrote the following:

My Dear Cook,

You must help Diven, and Van Valkenburgh raise men. All is well, if we instantly show our strength. I send him home for that purpose.

Faithfully yours,
William H. Seward.

The three men left Seward's house and went to Pomeroy's rooms. They concluded that Diven would stay, but the other two would leave in the morning as promised. Diven remained for the next day's session of the House of Representatives, where he asked for a leave of absence for the three of them, stating that they desired to return to their respective districts to use their influence in raising troops for the service of the country. In addition, he wanted to submit to Congress a bill on which he had been working. The bill called for the enlistment of Black troops to be used for entrenching, siege services, etc., and it would also guarantee them their freedom. He stated that about ten thousand such persons were now maintained at the expense of the government. The leaves of absence were granted, and Diven gave the bill to Thaddeus Stevens, who submitted it after making several revisions to it. Van Valkenburgh and Pomeroy left for home on that morning, Monday, July 7th. Diven arrived home on the evening of Tuesday the 8th and forwarded Seward's letter to Cook with a letter of his own. Diven's letter read as follows:

Dear sir,

I shall be with you in a day or two. Don't say you CAN'T. Don't say that we must resort to drafting. We have not the time to draft. We must end this war soon or fight the world. We can end it now. We cannot fight the world successfully—you know we cannot. As I am to see you soon., no more now.

In haste now, A.S. Diven

Diven's comments about "fighting the world" referenced the fact that the Confederacy was hoping that their recent strong showings in the war might induce either or both England and France to recognize them as an independent country.

It so happened at that time that there was a redistricting in the state, and Diven and Van Valkenburgh were left in one district; the 27th was to consist of Chemung, Steuben, and Schuyler counties. When the next election was held, they both might be running for the same seat. Previously Diven's district had included Chemung, Schuyler, Tioga, and Tompkins counties while Van Valkenburgh's had included Steuben and Livingston counties. In preparing for their tasks ahead, it was arranged between them that since Van Valkenburgh was in the state militia, he would devote himself to organizing and fitting out the men for the field; Diven was to go about raising the men for the regiment.

They were initially met with a great deal of discouragement when they arrived home. It was generally thought that troops could not be raised by volunteering, and that there must be a draft so that the burden would fall equally upon all. However, they felt that the draft would take too long, and the army was in perilous need of more troops now. This was the reason for Secretary Seward's letter to Mr. Cook of Schuyler County, who up until this time had been a proponent of the draft. The letter changed his mind, and he participated vigorously in a war meeting held the following Saturday in Havana.[16]

During that same week, the Rev. Thomas K. Beecher of Park Church, along with several other prominent men such as E.F. Crane, Stephen McDonald, H. Boardman Smith, Archibald Robertson, and G.L. Smith, volunteered to attend the war meetings in any part of Chemung County and address the people about the war. The Reverend Beecher was a member of the well-known Beecher family, being the brother of author Harriet Beecher Stowe and the nationally known minister Henry Ward Beecher.

At the same time, Lathrop Baldwin of the *Elmira Advertiser*, George Swain, Esq. of Chemung, George Beers of the *Elmira Free Press*, and M.V.B. Backman, Esq. of Horseheads announced that they had joined together to raise a company of volunteers.[17]

The events of the past several weeks prompted the *Elmira Advertiser & Republican* to publish the following editorial on Saturday July 12:

### The Great Duty of The People

Within the last ten days the startling fact has become shown to the people that the American Union cannot be saved except at the cost of raising and equipping a new Army of Three

Hundred Thousand Men. We say this fact has become known to the people. The President has issued his Proclamation and the Governors of the loyal states have issued theirs. This had made the fact known, but its immense and overwhelming importance has not yet been impressed upon their minds. Scores and hundreds of able-bodied men, with no family's [sic] dependent on their daily earnings for support, walk the streets unconcerned for the life of the country, or at least not sufficiently concerned to volunteer their personal services to save it from destruction.

This ought not be the case. The Nation needs the sustaining arm of all her children. No mere question of personal comfort ought to detain any man from the wars. These are times that are once again to try men's souls. We must sacrifice our ease, our business, our social relations, our ambitions. We must give up all, and serve only one mother, our common country.

But all cannot go personally to the field of battle, nor is it necessary that all should do so. The exigency calls for but fifty thousand men from this state, while there are eight hundred thousand capable of bearing arms. A draft so comparatively small ought to be promptly honored. The entire number of men that are wanted ought to spring to arms at once. The recruiting offices ought to be overwhelmed with the applications of patriotic citizens flying to the rescue of the nation from its perils. Governor Morgan ought to be able to respond to the President in ten days time that "New York is ready. Fifty thousand of her sons are marching, armed and equipped to the seizure of Richmond, and to the certain downfall of the Rebellion."

How quick shall the be the response of the state depends altogether upon the spirit of her people. If they shall rise in their majesty, and act as becomes a state which ought to surpass all others in patriotism as is does in wealth and population, our gallant fellows on the banks of the James will soon "hear the Slogan." Who will hold back in such an emergency? Who will fail to lay at least some small sacrifice upon the alter of his country? It cannot be possible that there is such a man in all the free North. If there be, he is not a patriot, he is not a lover of his country and does not deserve to enjoy the blessing of the government under which he lives. We assume that every man is ready to "do or die."—that those who cannot give themselves, will give their money, and that freely. Let the riches of your purse flow freely like water, if thereby men can be had to put down this rebellion. Give your last cent of money to him who goes to give what is still more precious, his last drop of blood.

Let us come home to the work that must be done here. The draft upon the counties of Chemung, Steuben and Schuyler is for a regiment of a thousand men. In this county must be raised a little more than one fifth of the number, or not to exceed three hundred men. Is that a draft to appall a community of thirty thousand people? Is anything needed but the will and the determination? And will any man be laggard or mean, or parsimonious in contributing all in his power? If any, speak, for him have I offended.

Let a public meeting be called at once—Let means be taken to procure the contribution from the surplus of abundance of the people of this county a sum of ten thousand dollars, to which shall be added the public riches from both the County and the Village in whatever amount shall be necessary to give to each man, in addition to that received from the government, a bounty of Fifty Dollars, and to pay the necessary and proper expenses of searching out and bringing the men together.

Are there not two hundred men who will cheerfully give fifty dollars each in such a cause at such a time? Or four hundred who will give half that amount? Is there a taxpayer who will hesitate to pay the small proportion which would come to him to supply the balance of the fund? We will not believe that there is or can be. Rather let us feel that EVERY MAN WILL DO HIS DUTY!

Citizens of Chemung County! We earnestly entreat that this matter may not be neglected even for a day. Every hour that we slumber is a crime against the country. Let every person bring this subject home to himself. Resolve from this moment henceforth to act and cease not to labor until the great work is accomplished. The blessings of providence will be the reward of those who rise in their might and decree the salvation of the country."

In the same paper, the editors went further and spoke directly to the leaders of the community, naming them individually and seeking out their leadership with the following editorial, titled "The Call for Men:"

We yet hear no movement which looks like concerned, earnest work to raise the quota of Chemung County for the new Army of the Union. Where are our leading and influential citizens? Where are our men who ought to be first and foremost in stimulating the patriotism of the People? Does nobody suppose this call is to *him*? Does every man imagine that his neighbor is meant and not himself? When will the great fact be felt and appreciated that in this emergency *all* are invited and none excused?

Fellow citizens of Chemung County, it is your duty to AROUSE AT ONCE! If you have time to give, money to bestow, or a life to risk in the service of your country, *to-day is the appreciated hour.* We beseech the people of this County that they not be laggard in the cause of the Union. We have spoken heretofore in general terms, and the response has been as general as the speech. We now make our appeal to individuals. We call upon Hiram Gray, upon John Arnot, upon Judge Thurston, Judge Brooks, Stephen Mac Donald, John T. Rathbun, John I. Nicks, Asher Tyler, Colonel Hathaway, Boardman Smith, Wm. T. Post, James Dunn. Gentlemen, you are men of property and influence. You are men who have much at stake in the direful contest now waging. You are men whose duty it is to act, and that promptly. We have selected you because your names happen to occur to us. You are the types of hundreds more in like circumstances, and of like power and influence. If you will start the ball, the masses will keep it rolling. Come forward, then, to the front and show your appreciation of the crisis. Devote your time and subscribe your money to advance the work. Depend upon it there are men enough to go and fight the battles. But they want some kind of support and encouragement.

Will you not unite, then, in calling a public meeting, and will you not see to it that the meeting when held has a well defined and definite purpose, and that all proper arrangements are perfected for making it effectual? Let this be done and done at once. Whatever may be neglected elsewhere, let it not be said that Chemung County has failed in her duty to free institutions. Let there be no necessity within her borders for resort to an odious draft, which *will* come, which *ought* to come, if her quota is not otherwise filled.

Our entreaty is to all citizens that they join freely and promptly in this work. "A long pull, a strong pull, and a pull together" will lift the nation out of her peril and *nothing else will.* This is the solemn fact, and he who will not act upon it is neither a good patriot nor a good citizen.

These two editorials appeared to have roused the citizens of Chemung County, for the recruiting of volunteers began in earnest. They undoubtedly had a similar effect on the counties of Steuben and Schuyler whose newspapers often repeated, if not exactly, the general spirit of the articles appearing in the Elmira newspapers. And to be sure, there was a great deal of competition between the three counties. What was to follow was a whirlwind of activity that fostered an almost daily occurrence of war meetings in the villages and the various towns in the three counties. Prominent citizens, local bands, and a singer by the name of Kate Dean accompanied the men responsible for raising companies for the new regiment from village to village.

On Thursday, July 10, a number of the citizens of Havana held a meeting at the courthouse. It was chaired by Major William Skellenger. The letters from Secretary of State Seward and the Honorable A.S. Diven were read, and after a short discussion, it was decided to hold a war meeting the following Saturday evening.

That Saturday at 7 p.m.[18] a war meeting was held in the second-floor hall of the Havana courthouse. A great crowd of people attended, and there was standing room only. Major Skellenger was selected chairman and the Hon. Charles Cook as secretary. Miss Kate Dean of Tompkins County did her part by singing several patriotic songs.[19] Introduced by Colonel E.H. Downs and accompanied by Miss Merinda McMillen on the Melodeon, she sang "Where Liberty Dwells, There Is My Country." The meeting was addressed by the Hon. A.S. Diven, the Rev. Thomas K. Beecher, and several other speakers. Mr. Diven began the speaking and stated that he had come home to his district at the request of the secretary of state with the approval of the president. Other members of Congress had gone home, and still others were now going to their respective districts upon the same duty. Each and all were to frankly and truthfully lay before the people the present necessities of the government: that the Army of the Potomac must be reinforced, and the rebellion put down speedily, or there was great danger of foreign intervention, particularly by France or England; that the administration desired all the facts to be fully and fairly laid before the people; that this government was established by the people and for the people, and it was for the people to determine whether they would protect and defend it. The president had called for 300,000 troops, of which 50,000 were expected to come from this state, and the governor had made each of the Senate districts a military district, with each district raising one full regiment. The balance was hoped to be raised by the large cities. After Mr. Diven concluded his speech, Miss Dean sang "The Rebel Flags."[20]

Miss Dean had previously conceived of the idea of singing to the soldiers in Washington, DC, and as a result had been introduced to President Lincoln by Congressman Diven. Diven explained her wishes to the president, who received her kindly. He commended her purpose to Gen. McClellan, who at once furnished her the necessary passes and protection within the lines. It was said that the effect of her singing was electrical and inspiring. Nothing else could have so greatly delighted and animated the soldiers confined to the tedious routine of the camps associated with the training of the new troops and the manning of the many forts around the capitol. Among the songs she sang were "The Red, White, and Blue," "We are going on to Richmond," and "Marching down to Dixie."[21] She, being home for a short visit, spent much of her time singing at many of the war meetings and giving concerts locally, one being given at Ely's Hall in Elmira. At these concerts she was dressed in a costume as a "daughter of the regiment." The price of attendance was twenty-five cents, and it was noted as only half the usual price of first-class concerts.[22]

Following Miss Dean's second song, Mr. Cook read off the quota of men required from each county, and for Schuyler County, the quota for each township. He said that, based on the full strength of a regiment being 1020 men, the quota for Schuyler was 165 men. It was immediately resolved that meetings would be held in each of the townships for the purpose establishing a committee whose duty it would be to take all necessary measures to furnish as quickly as possible their quota of volunteers. The quotas for each of the towns were as follows: Catherine 16, Cayuta 6, Dix 25, Hector 50, Montour 17, Orange 21, Reading 12, and Tyrone 18.

The next speaker to address the crowd was the Rev. Thomas K. Beecher. He was described as a vigorous public speaker, with what he said coming directly from his heart. He announced his willingness to attend the meetings in the various towns wherever the people would assemble. He said that if he could arouse two good men to go instead of one, he would continue, but if he failed in that, he declared his intention to take the musket upon his own shoulder and march to the field of duty. He closed by saying that next to his maker, his duty was to his country.

Following the Reverend Beecher's speech, Miss Dean sang "We are Marching Down to Dixie Land." Brief and earnest speeches were then made by the Reverend Mr. Howe, Hon. S.L. Hood of Watkins, Major G.L. Smith of Elmira, C.G. Tuthill of Burdett, and Colonel Van Deventer of Dix. The latter said that although he was over sixty years of age, he had been out to Elmira, was examined by the proper military board, and pronounced by them a hale, strong man with a good constitution and would be received into the service. He said that he was ready and willing to serve his country in any capacity.

The schedule for the meetings to be held in the various towns was announced, along with the scheduled speakers for each. Mr. C.G. Tuthill then offered a resolution tendering thanks to Miss Dean for kindly consenting to sing some of the national songs before and during the meeting, and that she be requested to sing the "Star Spangled Banner." The Reverend Beecher asked that the audience be permitted to join in the chorus, to which Miss Dean gracefully assented. Following this last song, the meeting was adjourned.[23]

That same day, the *Havana Journal* printed as an extra to its regular Saturday edition the letters of Secretary Seward and Colonel Diven in the form of a handbill.[24] In the same edition, a notice was printed from S.F. Griffeth, the clerk of the Schuyler County Board of Supervisors. It stated that the list of men residing in the county who were eligible for military duty had been completed and filed in the offices of the various town clerks. Anyone who claimed he was exempt for any reason was required to file a written statement of exemption accompanied by an affidavit of verification by the fifteenth day of August.

Two days after the War Meeting in Havana, copies of its proceedings were distributed to the various towns in the county. In addition to calling for similar meeting in each town, there was a passionate appeal made. It stated:

> It was impossible to believe that there are any considerable number of persons in the county that would claim or enjoy the privileges and protection of their government to their persons and property without at least sharing in the responsibilities of defending that government when attacked; and particularly when attacked by rebels who have heretofore enjoyed more of its blessings and privileges than all other portions of the Union put together. We trust that no town nor election district in this county will be followed by the humiliation and disgrace

of neglecting or refusing to send its full share of men to defend the government in this hour of its greatest necessity and peril.

The appeal closed by asking that it would be very desirable that the enlistments for this Senate district be completed, and the troops mustered into the United States service at Elmira within the next twenty days.[25]

It wasn't immediately apparent to everyone why the congressmen had taken a leave of absence from Washington. On July 12, 1862, the *Elmira Advertiser & Republican*, which never missed a chance to be critical of Diven, ran an article with the headline, "A CONGRESSMAN SKEDADDLED." The newspaper was questioning Congressman Diven's reason for leaving Congress and used the term *skedaddled* to compare him to persons who were avoiding the draft by whatever means they could. The article was very suspicious of the Congressman's actions, and concluded, "We are in favor of enlisting all men who will serve under the banner of the nation, without distinction of faith, color, birth or position. We would allow the followers of the Pope and the disciples of Martin Luther, the skedaddling Congressman and the loyal Negro to shoulder the musket and march side by side to the defense of a common country. Let us wait therefore, and see the purpose of Mr. Diven. It may be that he will yet be useful to the country." The actions of Mr. Diven gave quick response to this article when he spoke at the war meeting in Havana that same day and began in earnest his efforts to raise the troops, as he had been requested to do by President Lincoln.

The same edition of the *Advertiser & Republican* printed the story of Congressmen Diven and Van Valkenburgh making their application to be excused from Congress for the remainder of the session. They explained that they desired to return to their respective districts to use their influence in raising troops for the service of the country. Diven, the article stated, asked his fellow members to remain in their positions and provide for the maintenance of the troops. It was apparent here that even though the newspaper knew the truth about Diven's leave of absence, it couldn't waste the opportunity to cast some doubts about the reasons for his actions.[26]

**100 MEN WANTED**
for the
CAMPBELL GUARDS REG'T!

In response to the call of President Lincoln and under authority of the Governor of the State, the undersigned will open an office at

**No. 18 LAKE STREET**

TO-DAY for the purpose of recruiting the above number of patriotic soldiers for a company to be attached to the Campbell Guards.

The following extraordinary inducements are offered to volunteers.

**$27 Bounty** *WILL BE PAID TO EACH RECRUIT AS SOON AS SWORN IN,*
AND
ONE MONTH'S PAY IN ADVANCE WHEN THE COMPANY
IS MUSTERED INTO THE REGIMENT.

The remainder of the bounty $75 will be paid at the close of the war, and if wounded each volunteer will be entitled to a liberal pension. We ask the patriotic young men of Chemung to call at our Recruiting Office, No. 18 Lake Street, and join in this last great effort to do something for the country.

> L. Baldwin
> George Swain
> M.V.B. Backman
> Geo. A. Beers[27]

On July 15 Alexander S. Diven received a letter from the New York State Adjutant General Thomas Hillhouse informing him that he had been appointed to the Military Committee of the 27th District. This committee's purpose was to aid in the organization of a regiment of volunteers under the recent call of the president. The committee was requested to assemble at the earliest practicable moment.[28] The very next day, the committee met at the Brainard House. Lieutenant Governor Campbell, chairman of the committee, called the meeting to order, and Col. C.C.B. Walker of Steuben County was appointed secretary. The following members of the committee were present from their respective counties. From Steuben: Lieut. Gov. Robert Campbell, Hon R.B. Van Valkenburgh, S.M. Alley, Hon. Henry Sherwood, Dr. L.A. Ward, and Col. C.C.B. Walker. From Chemung: Hon. A.S. Diven, Major G.L. Smith, and Charles Hulett, Esq. From Schuyler: Hon. Charles Cook and Hon. S.L. Rood.

The following resolutions were passed:

1. That the chairman and Secretary of this Committee appoint three persons in each town of this senatorial district, whose duty it shall be to canvass their respective towns, and assist in securing volunteers, and correspond with this committee and do such other duties as may be deemed necessary, and that the Supervisor of each town be chairman of each town committee. The committee was instructed to select the town committees without delay, and announce them through the newspapers published in the district.

2. That the call for three hundred thousand additional volunteers meets our cordial approbation; and we feel assured that this fresh appeal to the patriotism of the people will be met with the same spirit that has responded to other calls.

3. That our brave men in the field must not be left to an unequal contest; that we have the men and the resources to reinforce them and crush this rebellion; and we recognize in this call a determination the part of the government to meet promptly this emergency.

4. That this is a war for the existence of our government; that no man enjoying its protection has any right to withhold his aid; that those who have money are called on to contribute, and those who have strength are called on to fight; and every man performing his duty will make this a short struggle and a sure victory.

5. That this is no time to contend among ourselves over differences of opinion. Before everything we must conquer the armies of rebellion. To this object there should be, and we believe will be, a single will and united effort. We call upon every man who loves his government and desires its perpetuity, laying aside all excuses, to end this war, and secure a speedy and sure peace.

R.B. Van Valkenburgh was unanimously recommended for colonel of the regiment, and by the same vote Hon. A.S. Diven was recommended for lieutenant colonel. The regiment, once it was fully manned, would be formally known as Campbell's Guards after the lieutenant governor. However, through the years that name would fall into disuse, and the regiment was hardly ever referred to by it. The Committee adjourned and scheduled their next meeting at the Brainard House on Friday, July 25, at 10 a.m.[29] The Brainard House, a popular hotel of the day, was located on the northwest corner of Water and Baldwin Streets in Elmira.

The following day, State Senator Cook wrote Colonel Shepard and advised him that Mr. Fanton would accept the responsibility for raising a company in Schuyler County for the new regiment. He did this irrespective of the fact that Fanton had commenced doing so several weeks before.

Only fifteen days would pass before the company from Schuyler County would arrive at #3 "Rathbun" barracks in Elmira. On Friday, July 18, Mr. Fanton and James H. Miles were examined for their ability to be officers of a company in the regiment. They were examined by Captain Gabriel L. Smith, the military examiner of the Elmira Depot. The questions put to them were not so much about military matters as they were about intelligence, common sense, and leadership. Both men were found acceptable and were given documents certifying to Colonel Shepard that they were competent for the position of company officer. Fanton immediately went to work and developed a formal plan for enrolling volunteers as quickly as possible. He began to develop a network of young men to help him cover Schuyler County. On that same day, he convinced H.D. Donnelly, a law student from Burdett, and Lewis O. Sayler of Mecklenburg to help him enroll volunteers. These men were given the responsibility for the town of Hector, and as a reward for their work, would begin their service in the army as 1st and 2nd lieutenants respectively. On Saturday, Samuel Lawrence was given the responsibility for raising volunteers in the town of Catherine. On Monday, Edwin Weller, a store clerk from Havana, joined the group, and also Lorenzo Webber, who was given the responsibility for the Town of Orange. Weller would be given the rank of 1st sergeant for his effort. Fanton's law office, which was in the west basement of the Montour House under the Bank of Havana, became the company's headquarters for the purpose of recruiting volunteers. Some years later, he would become president of this bank, which then would be located in the current library building.

To bring attention to the location of the recruiting office, a garrison flag was obtained from the Military Depot in Elmira and placed at the entrance. The flag later accompanied the Company to the battlefield, and it was brought back to Havana when Fanton resigned his commission. Mr. Webber's efforts in the town of Orange brought in the first quantity of recruits of any considerable size on Tuesday. The next few days saw them coming from all sections of the county, and on Thursday, sixty-four were taken to Elmira for a medical inspection and muster. Forty-two of these were accepted into service. Fanton continued to build his recruiting organization, and on Saturday, July 26, Frank M. Cronkrite of Tyrone was given the responsibility for recruiting there. He later became a sergeant in the Schuyler County company. On Tuesday July 29, the second squad of recruits, fifteen in number, were accompanied to the depot in Elmira. All but one was accepted and, including six others that had been enrolled and mustered in the interval, a total of fifty-six men from Schuyler County were at the barracks. The following day, all others that had enlisted were asked to present themselves for muster, and all who were already mustered in received a bounty payment of $27.

Ultimately ninety-eight men were paid a bounty from this company for a total of $2,646. On Thursday, July 31, the third squad of recruits from Schuyler County were received at Elmira, and six were accepted. By the sixth of August, another twenty-seven more men were enrolled. With ninety-five men now in the company, elections for commissioned officers were scheduled for the next day, Thursday, at 7:30 a.m. The evening before the election, Mr. Fanton spoke to the men about his friend, E.C. Clark, who previously had been in the employ of Congressman Cook and had been a member of the Utica Citizen's Corps, a militia organization. Fanton had talked to Cook about recommending Clark to command the company. The congressman, reflecting on the time Clark was in his employ, thought that he would be an excellent choice. The men of the company also agreed with Fanton, and Clark was subsequently elected captain of the company. On the day of the election, three more men were mustered in, and two musicians were added the following week, bringing the company total to one hundred men.

When all of the companies were assigned their letters of identification, the one from Havana would become Company H of the 107th New York State Volunteer Infantry Regiment. It had been a tremendous effort by Hull Fanton and the people of Schuyler County. In addition to those already identified, Fanton publicly gave credit to Peter and Daniel Tracy, William H. and Nathan Skellenger, Joseph M., Horace V. and Mason N. Weed, Dr. George T. Hinman, Peter and Alpheus Keyser, Albert O. Whittemore, Adam G. and John Campbell, John Fitzpatrick, Joseph Giles, Moses S. Weaver, and Amasa H. Decker, all of Havana, Hon. Samuel Lawrence of Catherine, Hon. A.V. McKeel of Hector, Isaac H. Hill of Tyrone, and Col. Eli C. Frost and his father Thomas L. Fanton.[30]

On the evening of July 16, a very large and enthusiastic audience assembled in Union Hall in the village of Horseheads "for the purpose of creating interest in and facilitating enlistments throughout the county." The meeting was organized by the selection of the following officers: President—Hon. Charles Hulett; Vice Presidents— Cyrus Barlow, Grover Leavens, George Bennett, J.B. Mosher, A.C. McCumber, John Ross, Wm. H. Van Duzer, Orrin Eddy, Samuel C. Smith, John N. Barbour, Civilian Brown, Samuel D. Westlake, Increase Mather, and Joseph Rodburn; Secretaries—S.C. Taber, D.C. Curtis, and J.H. Osmer.

On motion, Captain Charles E Barbour was invited to a seat on the stage, and the following were appointed to a committee on resolutions: S.C. Taber, J.H. Osmer, D.C. Curtis, Cyrus Barlow, and W.S. Daily.

Resolutions were offered and unanimously approved. Directly after, the Hon. A.S. Diven was introduced to the audience, and he made a very stirring and patriotic speech, urging the people to respond to the president's call for additional men. After the singing of a song by the Horseheads Glee Club, the Hon. R.B. van Valkenburgh was introduced. His speech was cited as one "that electrified the audience with one of the most eloquent appeals to which they had ever had the good fortune to listen." Major G.L. Smith was universally called by the audience and made a speech that seemed to please everybody and increase the patriotism and enthusiasm of the audience. The DeWitt Avengers, a young military company newly organized in that village and named after the late and lamented Captain DeWitt of the previous company raised in Horseheads, and the Martial Band of Breesport added much to the interest of the meeting. Additional brief, but stirring appeals were made, and a military committee for the town was established to solicit subscriptions of money to aid in procuring volunteers.[31]

The following day, a War Meeting was held at Baldwin in the church at Hammond's Corners. The attendance was quite large, and the meeting was addressed by Captain Crane. Resolutions were drawn up and passed. By the time the meeting had adjourned, nine men had enrolled in the new regiment.[32]

On Friday evening, July 18, a great war meeting was held at Ely's Hall in Elmira. As was the custom, local community leaders were chosen officers of the meeting. The Honorable Hiram Gray, a prominent lawyer and judge, was selected president. In addition to the president, there were sixteen vice presidents selected: John Arnot (banker and businessman), Simeon Benjamin (real estate and railroads), Samuel Partridge (lumber), William Foster (farmer), Robert Covell (merchant), William Hoffman (farmer), Benjamin Vail (undertaker), Uriah Smith (doctor), John Sexton (community leader), Asher Tyler (rolling mill), B.P. Beardsley (manufacturer), S.L. Gillette (merchant), J.B. Clark (lumber), J.T. Rathbun (real estate), Tracy Beadle (doctor), and Stephen McDonald (merchant). The names of the prominent Elmirans who were identified in the newspaper editorial of a week before are easily found as attendees of this meeting.

Three secretaries, all newspapermen, were also selected: C.G. Fairman, Horton Tidd, and R.R.R. Dumars. A Committee on Resolutions, which included James Dunn (lawyer), F.A. De Voe (newspaperman), J.B. Clark, John I. Nicks, (manufacturer), and D.F. Pickering (postmaster), was appointed. The committee reported the following resolutions, which were unanimously adopted with an accompanying loud applause.

Resolved, That we heartily approve the call recently made the President for additional force of 300,000 men to reinforce our armies now in the field-believing that an overwhelming force and its vigorous use in prosecuting active hostilities against the enemy is the only way to obtain a speedy and successful termination of the war.

Resolved, That in the recent terrible conflicts with the enemy near Richmond our officers and soldiers fought with a courage, devotion and heroism worthy the glorious cause in which they are engaged and have justly won the applause and gratitude of a powerful and magnanimous people.

**Resolved,** That the Union of all the States of this Republic can alone protect us against domestic and foreign wars in the future, and that a dissolution of the Union would be followed with the destruction of our commercial prosperity, and ere long by the overthrow of Republican institutions; that we owe it to the present generation and to posterity to put down this rebellion at any and every cost and sacrifice, and that it is the duty of the Government in carrying on the war to avail itself of all the means recognized by the law of nations to bring it to a successful issue.

**Resolved,** That any intervention or interference with the domestic troubles of this country by France or England should be met with the stern and united hostility of all loyal citizens; that a recognition by any foreign power of the so-called Confederate States should be treated by our Government as an act of hostility- as an attempt to intimidate us into a disgraceful consent to a dissolution of the Union, and the ultimate destruction and overthrow of popular governments throughout the civilized world.

**Resolved,** That forbearance and charity toward the rebels has ceased to be a virtue; that henceforth the Government should treat them with the rigor and severity due to the great crimes they have committed; that experience has shown that the capture of rebel cities and towns and the defeat of their armies has failed to humiliate them-no offers of peace having as yet come from their leaders-no disposition to come to an amicable arrangement has been manifested-on the contrary, they carry on the war with a cruelty and barbarity unexampled in the history of civilized nations.

**Resolved,** That Chemung County will do her whole duty in the present emergency; that her gallant and patriotic young men, emulating the example of the lamented Captain DeWitt, will rush to the field, and if need be, perish in bearing aloft the glorious flag of their country.

**Resolved,** That Hon. Tracy Beadle, John Arnot, Jr., Stephen McDonald, Hon. John T. Rathbun, F.A. De Voe, C.G. Fairman, J. Davis Baldwin, J.I. Nicks, Hon. Hiram Gray, L.J. Stancliff, J.M. Robinson and Erastus P. Hart be a committee to make arrangements for providing for the families of soldiers enlisting under this call, and to make such arrangements as they may deem expedient and proper to provide for advancing the bounty to be paid by the United States to soldiers enlisting; and for raising additional bounties if they shall think best; to raise money by subscription or otherwise; to provide for the distribution of and to distribute the same; and to make any other financial arrangements which they shall deem necessary and expedient for the furtherance of enlistments.

The quota for each town in Chemung County was arrived at according to their current population.

| TOWN | POPULATION | QUOTA |
|---|---|---|
| Baldwin | 918 | 8 |
| Big Flats | 1,853 | 17 |
| Catlin | 1,308 | 12 |
| Chemung | 2,128 | 19 |
| Elmira | 8,682 | 79 |
| Erin | 1,339 | 12 |
| Horseheads | 2,277 | 20 |
| Southport | 4,733 | 43 |
| Van Etten | 1,508 | 14 |
| Veteran | 2,171 | 20 |
| TOTAL | 26,917 | 244 |

From Steuben County, with a population of 66,689, the quota was 605, and from Schuyler County with a population of 18,840, the quota was 171 men, making the total number of men for the 27th district 1,020.[33]

At the rear of the Brainard House, later known as the Rathbun Hotel, and almost directly across from Ely's Hall at No. 5 Baldwin Street[34] was the headquarters of the Elmira Military Depot, where applications for authorization to raise volunteers were received. Next to the headquarters was a separate military warehouse. It was from this warehouse that uniforms and equipment for the volunteers were distributed. This depot was one of three established in New York State on April 16, 1861, the other two being in New York City and Albany. Military stores for the volunteer regiments raised by the state were received at the New York City depot and distributed to Albany and Elmira. The first depot commander was Robert B. Van Valkenburgh of Bath who was a Brigadier General in the New York State Militia. He was appointed commander of the Elmira Depot on July 30, 1861, and held this position as well as being a member of Congress.[35]

The crisis brought on by the war not only increased awareness in the county of the need for more volunteers but was also manifested in the organizing other much needed groups. That same Friday evening, a large number of the most influential ladies and gentlemen of Elmira assembled at Ely's Hall for the purpose of organizing a Soldiers' Relief Association. Ely's Hall was of fairly new construction and provided Elmira with an exceptionally good facility for theatrical presentations, meetings, and other events. It was located on the northeast corner of Baldwin and Carroll Streets. The meeting was held in response to a call published in the village papers to take the right steps toward forming an association for the relief of sick and wounded soldiers. It was called to order by the appointment of Mayor Reynolds as chairman and William F. Corey as secretary.

The Chairman briefly explained that several other towns, smaller than Elmira, had already formed such an association, and it was time for Elmira to do the same. On a motion, the chairman appointed a committee of three to draft resolutions and submit them for approval. The committee presented the following:

**Resolved,** That we hereby form an association for the benefit of sick and wounded soldiers, to be called the Elmira Army Relief Association.

**Resolved,** That the following Ladies and Gentlemen are hereby elected managers of this Association:

| | | |
|---|---|---|
| Miss Mariana Arnot | Miss Mary B. Tuthill | Dr. H.S. Chubbuck |
| Mrs. N.W. Gardiner | Mrs. James H. Rutter | Rev. Thomas K. Beecher |
| Mrs. Dr. F.H. Squires | Miss Mary M. Rathbun | Samuel G. Hathaway, Jr. |
| Mr. Charles B. Stuart | Miss Diven | Edward Covell |
| Mrs. W.W. Ballard | Miss Anna Beadle | Riggs Watrous |
| Miss Sarah Hart | Mrs. Dr. H. Sayles | Samuel Conkey |
| Miss Tyler | Mrs. William P. Corey | John Arnot, Jr. |

A general debate and interchange of opinions and views was followed by the introduction of several more resolutions, and all were finally adopted.

The desire of these people to organize a "Relief Association" for the soldiers was so great that they met again the following morning at the rooms of the Y.M.C.A. The Reverend Dr. Lincoln chaired the meeting with William F. Corey again acting as secretary. They voted to make the society's official name the "Soldier's Relief Association of Elmira." Dr. Lincoln was elected president, and Miss Marianna Arnot, Mrs. N.W. Gardener, and Miss Sarah Hart vice presidents. William F. Corey was elected permanent secretary and the following as his assistants: Mrs. T.K. Beecher, Theodore W. Crane, W.W. Ballard, C.B. Stuart, Mrs. Wm. F Corey, Miss Ella Diven, Mrs. W.H. Maxwell, Mrs. W.H. Stark, James H. Rutter, Miss Mary B. Tuthill, Mrs. C. Preswick, and Miss Mary McDonald. Mr. John Arnot, Jr. was elected treasurer. The committee on finances was to be made up of Miss Mariana Arnot, Mrs. W.W. Ballard, and Mrs. C.B. Stuart.

A motion was made and carried to choose a committee consisting of Dr. Lincoln, the Rev. T.K Beecher, and Riggs Watrous to confer with the government authorities in regard to securing the establishment of a hospital camp in Elmira and to have discretionary powers as to the amount and nature of the service to be offered by the association. In addition, the secretaries were directed to inquire whether a suitable room for the use of the association could be obtained near the depot.[36]

During that week, new recruits for the regiment were filling up barracks #3 on Water Street between Hoffman and Foster Streets. These were the same barracks that were later used to house Confederate prisoners of war in 1864-65. The new volunteers were drilling to the manual of arms each day, usually for two hours at a time, and doing guard duty. On Wednesday, they drilled from 10 a.m. until 12 noon, and their supper that day consisted of pudding, bread and butter, cold beef, and coffee. The next day, there were 150 men in the regiment, and enlistments were brisk.[37]

The new recruits were immediately introduced to the daily regimen of the camp. Reveille was sounded at 5 a.m. when the men fell in for roll call without arms under the 1st sergeants superintended by a company officer. Immediately afterwards the beds were made, and the barracks cleaned. "Peas upon a Trencher," the signal for breakfast, was sounded or beaten at 6 a.m., and at 6:30 a.m. all those sick were conducted to the hospital. At 8 a.m. the "Troop" was sounded or beaten for the purpose of assembling the men. Immediately afterwards, guard duty was assigned, and following that the men were drilled by company or as a regiment until 11:20 a.m. "Roast Beef," the signal for dinner, was sounded or beaten at 12 noon, and a roll call of companies was taken by the 1st sergeants. Drilling commenced again at 1:30 p.m. and continued until 4:30 p.m. Supper was served as directed by the regimental officers. "Retreat" was sounded or beaten at such a time as ordered by the regimental officers, and at that time, a dress parade was held, followed by a roll call. At 9:30 p.m., "Tattoo" was beaten, and all men were to be in the barracks unless on guard or other duty or on special leave. Three taps were beaten on a drum at 10 p.m.. as the signal for the lights to be out except in the officers' quarters.

The camp guard consisted of two sergeants, three corporals, two drummers and enough men to man the required guard posts and patrols. The guards carried their arms, but they were not loaded and could not be loaded without special order of the commanding officer of the barracks. The designated officer of the day made frequent visits to the guards on duty to make sure that the men were carrying out their duties properly.[38]

Regulations were somewhat unrealistic about furloughs, stating that not more than five men could be on furlough at any one time. This regulation was tempered greatly by what the regimental officers felt was prudent; on weekends the barracks, especially in the beginning, were nearly empty.

That Thursday their supper consisted of mush and milk, and they were pleased with it. Drilling and guard duty were the order of the day. The men drilled without rifles, and they would not be issued to them until they were in camp near Washington a month later. On Friday, July 18, Capt. L. Baldwin and Capt. E.F. Crane each mustered fourteen men into service. That evening the men in camp #3 had a supper of rice and molasses. Saturday would bring the first real excitement in camp. The breakfast, as the men described it, consisted in part of "poor meat and alive." One of the men, John Morgan, protested having to eat it, and he became so loud and boisterous that guards were sent into the mess to subdue and arrest him. Things calmed down quickly, and Morgan was not arrested. Afterwards, the officer of the day and the food contractor reviewed the situation and declared that the men were right about the meat being unfit to eat. That same day, the men enjoyed a good dinner and supper. Some other soldiers were not so fortunate, and three were put in the guardhouse for various offenses.

On Sunday, most of the recruits obtained passes for the day despite it raining all morning. They were expected back in camp before nightfall. Some went to church, others to their homes, and the boys from further away took the opportunity to tour Elmira. Monday saw more volunteers arriving and finally a greater number of officers. The regiment was filling up, and some companies were almost full. Keeping track of the men became more of a problem, and on some days, patrols were sent out to bring the tardy ones back to camp.[39]

That same day, July 21, Col. Van Valkenburgh, in an effort to maintain the momentum of the call for volunteers, issued a letter to be printed in the newspapers of the 27th district. It read:

PATRIOTS TO ARMS! Citizens of the 27th Senatorial District, N.Y. The governor of this state having, in pursuance of the recommendation of the Military Committee of this district appointed the undersigned Colonel of a regiment to be raised herein, he appeals to its citizens to respond with alacrity to the call of the president for more troops.

Rally to the support of our gallant brothers already in the field! Rally to the defense of our common country! Rally to the destruction of the rebellion, wicked in its inception, and barbarous in its execution! Rally to the support of our flag, beneath whose ample folds we had became rich, prosperous and happy! Let there be no laggards. The spirit of Liberty calls to you, let it not call in vain.

Citizens of Steuben and Schuyler! Emulate the patriotic spirit and the noble bearing of those brave men whose names your respective counties bear. Let your hills and your valleys teem with the rushing crowd of young men, anxious to do battle for our glorious Union.

Citizens of Chemung! Patriot bands have trod your plains, and patriot blood has watered your fields. Forget not your historic memories. Cowards cannot live upon your soil.

Come all! Leave the cradle and the scythe; quit the counting house, the workshop and the office, and come with one united, determined purpose, let us;

Strike! till the last armed foe expires,
Strike! for our altars and our fires,
Strike! for the green graves of our sires,
God, and our native land!"

R.B. van Valkenburgh[40]

The war meetings continued to be held at a rapid pace in all three counties, and the primary speakers were making trips by horse and buggy on a daily basis. The largest meeting ever held in Hornellsville, for any purpose, was assembled in Canisteo Hall that evening. Hon. W.M. Hawley and a number of secretaries chaired the meeting, and vice presidents were appointed. A committee reported a number of resolutions, and they were unanimously adopted. Messrs. Van Valkenburgh, Diven, Beecher, Beadle, and Major Smith addressed the meeting. The "celebrated American Songstress," Miss Kate Dean, assisted by Miss Johnson on the piano, enlivened the meeting with well-chosen patriotic songs that elicited "hearty and protracted applause." The music of the Almond Band was also greatly appreciated. Many men came forward and signed their names to the regimental roll. In addition, Mrs. Woolsey and Mrs. Phillips, on behalf of a society of patriotic ladies, came forward and placed in the hands of Harlow

Colonel Robert Van Valkenburg of the regiment was a member of the House of Representatives, a general in the New York State Militia, and the commander of the Elmira military camp (Library of Congress).

Hakes, chairman of the Finance Committee, the sum of fifteen dollars to be used for the benefit of Capt. Sill's company. Alonzo Graves of Howard also generously donated five dollars for the same purpose.[41]

The next evening, Tuesday, July 22, a war meeting was held in Wellsburg, and like those held in every other community, it was successful. S. McDonald, Tracy Beadle, T.C. Cowen, Judge J. Dunn, L. Baldwin, and others addressed it.[42]

That same evening, a "Patriotic Demonstration" was held in Chemung. Wm. Holbeck, Esq. presided over the meeting, which was addressed by Hon. A.S. Diven, S.M. McDonald, Esq., G.L. Smith Esq., Judge McDowell, and others with marked and happy effect. Liberal contribu-

Lt. Colonel Alexander S. Diven of the regiment was a member of the House of Representatives and a prominent Elmiran (Library of Congress).

tions of money were subscribed on the spot—enough to guarantee to each and every recruit volunteering from the village a town bounty of $25, in addition to state and government bounty. Characterized by a hearty enthusiasm and earnest working zeal and feeling throughout, the War Meeting at Chemung was deemed a grand success and highly creditable to the good people of the locality.[43]

The following evening, a war meeting was held in the village of Weston of Tyrone Township in Schuyler County. Church pastors had spread the notice of the meeting. The meeting was held in the Baptist Church and was attended by an overflowing crowd of people, most of whom arrived well before the speakers. The meeting was called to order on motion of Edward Kernan. I.H. Hill was chosen chairman and D.G. Weaver secretary. The crowd was so great that it was deemed advisable to open the Presbyterian Church in that village. A spirited Military Band then escorted the overflow crowd to the church. Even with two churches in use, a large number of people were still outside. The next night, a meeting was held in the Wayne Hotel. Each meeting resulted in the enrolling of twenty volunteers, a total of forty men for the new regiment.[44] That same evening, a meeting was held in the Presbyterian Church in Canisteo. N.C. Taylor was appointed chairman, and Judge Hawley and Messrs. H. Hakes, H. Bemis, and E.C. Grover addressed the meeting. It was reported that about twenty-five men had been enrolled from Canisteo.[45]

Still another meeting was held that evening, this one on Elmira's East Hill at the Red School House. An enthusiastic and earnest feeling pervaded the gathering, which was ably addressed by Hon. Tracy Beadle, Stephen Mac Donald Esq., and Judge Dunn. The people were viewed as being "alive and aroused, and their patriotism and energies were stimulated by the meeting, and they will answer it by a squad or two of likely recruits."[46]

*The Owego Gazette* reported that Miss Kate Dean, the celebrated vocalist, was doing a most efficient service in the Union cause by attending the enlistment meetings and rousing the enthusiasm of the people by singing patriotic songs. The paper wrote, "She is a splendid singer, and her whole soul being in the cause, she sings with tremendous effect. Indeed, we have no hesitation in saying that the songs, We're marching down to Dixie's Land, The Star-Spangled Banner or The Red White and Blue as sung by Kate Dean, will procure more recruits for the army than all the eloquence of which our best orators are capable."

### NOTICE

Is hereby given, that the enrollment of persons liable to military duty in the several company districts of this County, have been completed, and filed in the offices of the several town clerks therein, and that any person who claims that he is for any reason exempt, shall on or be-fore the 15th day of August next, file a written statement of such exemption, in such office verified by affidavit, in default of which, he shall lose the benefit of such exemption.

**C.H. BOUTON**
Clerk of the Board of Supervisors of Steuben
Dated Bath, July 7th, 1862[47]

On Thursday morning, July 24, Captain Lathrop Baldwin made an announcement for the election of non-commissioned officers in his company, Company B. The elections were to be held at his recruiting office at number 18 Lake Street at 3 p.m. The company was to march from their barracks to his office at 2:30 p.m.[48]

That evening, a great war meeting was held in at the Concert Hall in Corning. Prior to the start of the meeting, several rounds were fired from the cannon, and the Martial Band played several stirring airs. S.T. Hayt called the meeting to order and nominated Hon. T.A. Johnson for president. He was unanimously chosen, and the following men were selected as vice presidents: Hon. A.C. Morgan, Lindley; A.H. Erwin, W.C. Bronson, and Samuel Adams of Erwin; Col. N.B. Stanton, Hon. Asem Eddy, and Daniel Rogers of Hornby; Dr. J.B. Graves, Alex Olcott, Capt. Colby, and Capt. Creamer. George B. Bradley and C.H. Thompson were selected as secretaries. Judge Johnson stated the purpose of the meeting and introduced Hon. A.S. Diven, who made an earnest appeal for the immediate enlistment of an army to save the government, which was threatened not only by Rebels, but also by foreign powers who were waiting for a reasonable excuse to interfere.

After Diven came Hon. R.B. Van Valkenburgh, who asked the young men of

Steuben to follow him and give aid to the government and to the brave volunteers who enlisted last year but were now in danger unless additional troops were made available. He was followed by the Rev. Thomas K. Beecher, Hon. Tracy Beadle, and H.M. Hyde, each of whom made earnest and effective speeches. At the conclusion of each address, Miss Kate Dean, the "American Prima Donna," sang a patriotic song. Soon after the meeting had commenced, the Patterson's Cornet Band and a large delegation of citizens from Painted Post arrived. The band added much to the enthusiasm of the crowd with their fine music. Not more than half of the people present could gain admittance to the hall, and a second meeting was organized in front of the Dickinson House. Col. Bostwick presided, and speeches were made by Maj. Smith and Messrs. Diven and Beecher. The results of the meeting were very successful with enlistments receiving a fresh impetus and a fund of $2,700 being collected to pay for bounties and further enlistments in the company.[49]

That same evening, a spirited, enthusiastic War Meeting was held in the town of Erin. The meeting was addressed by Cyrus Barlow, E.H. Osmere, A. Robertson, and G.M. Diven, Esq. At the close of the meeting, Mr. Joseph Rodburn, the highly successful local businessman whose patriotic efforts and zeal resulted in the success of the meeting, came forward and headed a subscription paper. He stated, "For the purpose of sustaining the families of Volunteers who may volunteer from the town of Erin as soldiers of the United States of America, we the subscribers, mutually agree to pay the sum set opposite our names, as the same may be called for by those in whose hands the disbursement of such funds may be placed, or to the Supervisor of the Town of Erin." Mr. Rodburn's contribution of $25 was matched by Messrs. A.H. McDowell, David Parks, and Elisha Harding. A total of over $150 was collected from twenty-seven townspeople.[50] That same evening, a War Meeting was held in Millport where over $500 was raised, and about twelve men volunteered.[51]

Additional war meetings were scheduled in Steuben County by the Military Committee at its meeting in Elmira on Friday, July 25. The meeting schedule listed Prattsburgh, July 31, 8 p.m.; Hammondsport, Aug. 1, 8 p.m.; Campbelltown, Aug. 1, 8 p.m.; and Troupsburgh Center, Aug. 4, 8 p.m.[52] During that same day, two companies arrived in the afternoon from out of town. The new recruits were finding guard duty monotonous, especially at night when it was very difficult to stay awake.

The next day, an election of officers was held. There was considerable electioneering going on with some rivalry among the candidates. Colonel Van Valkenburgh took command of the regiment. Saturday and Sunday were quiet; many of the officers were not in camp, and Sunday saw the camp mostly deserted.[53] *The Elmira Advertiser and Republican* reported in its Saturday, July 26, issue:

> The quota of Chemung County for the new regiment to be raised from this Senatorial District is now full-more than full. Our portion is two hundred and forty-eight men. We are already three hundred, and yet there is scarcely any abatement in the rush of volunteers. Two companies, Capt. Baldwin's and Capt. Crane's, have reached the maximum of one hundred each and the other two, Capt. Morgan's and Capt. Stocum's are nearly up to the minimum number. Both will be completed. There is every prospect now that Chemung County will furnish for the regiment

four full companies of one hundred men each-nearly double its proper proportion-and have them all ready before either of the other counties shall furnish a single company.

Chemung County became the first county in the state to raise her quota under the new call, and this fact was publicized in Albany and New York City. The July 25 edition of the *Albany Journal* carried a small article about it and closed it with the accolade, "A shout for little Chemung." *The Elmira Advertiser and Republican* also reported the appointment of Dr. Patrick H. Flood of Elmira to the position of surgeon of the new regiment. Dr. Flood was known to be "satisfactorily educated, and with many years of practical experience."

During the week, Captain Fox of Steuben County mustered 85 men into his company, the minimum number required. This was the first complete company for the regiment coming from outside of Chemung County. Enlistments in Steuben and Schuyler were progressing nicely. Three companies were complete, two others lacked but a half dozen each, and the others were filling up rapidly.[54]

On Friday, July 25, a War Meeting was held in Mecklenburg in Schuyler County where a crowd of 2,500 people was addressed by Mr. Stephen McDonald, Hon. A.S. Diven, the Rev. Thomas K. Beecher, and A.C. George, all of Elmira. Miss Kate Dean, assisted by Miss Libbie Yobe on the melodeon, sang several patriotic songs. The meeting adjourned at a late hour with three rousing cheers for the flag. After the meeting, many young men signed up for the new regiment.[55] That same evening, a meeting was held in the hall in Greenwood in Steuben County. The hall was overflowing with both men and women. The chairman was Israel Brundage, and the meeting was addressed by Messrs. H. Bemis and E.C. Grover. The quota of men for this small hamlet was met.[56]

In Chemung County that evening, in the "Town of Big Flatt," a rousing meeting was held, prominent citizens spoke, and many came forward promptly with generous donations of money.[57]

WAR MEETING
AT ADDISON ON
**Saturday, July 26, at 3 P.M.**
**Gen. Van Valkenburgh**
**Cols. A.S Diven**
**and G.L Smith**
And other distinguished speakers
are to be present.
**FARMERS**
Leave your work for one day and
attend your country's call.
Military Committee
E.J Horn
Capt. Jas. H. Miles
John Dininny[58]

A war meeting was scheduled in Addison on Saturday, July 26, at 3 p.m. The speakers were to be Gen. Van Valkenburgh, Col. A.S. Diven, and G.L. Smith. The meeting broadside called for the farmers to "Leave your work for one day and attend your country's call." The military Committee in Addison was composed of E.J Horn, Capt. James H. Miles, and John W. Dininny. The meeting was held in the public square where seats had been erected, and the crowd that attended was estimated to be about two thousand. William R. Smith officiated as chairman, and the meeting was opened with a prayer by the Rev. D.F. Judson. The "Turk family" of Addison sang a beautiful, patriotic song. The Hon. A.S. Diven then riveted the audience with a patriotic, soul-stirring, and eloquent speech. He was followed by American song-stress Miss Kate Dean, who was accompanied on the melodeon by Miss Johnson. Miss Dean's rendition of a patriotic song received great applause from the audience. The meeting was also addressed by Dr. Beadle of Elmira, Adjutant G.L. Smith of the new regiment, Gen. Van Valkenburgh (New York State Militia), and Capt. Miles. Miss Dean and the Turk family enlivened the audience with their song during the intervals. The Elkland Band, from Elkland, PA, was also present and took part in the entertainment.

During the progress of the speeches, 30 men stepped to Capt. Miles' recruiting table at the rear of the speaker's platform and signed their name to the register of the new regiment. Members of the audience were very generous when a collection was taken up for the purpose of bounty payments. Sums of $2, $5, $10, and as high as $40 were given.[59]

An example of the strong tide of patriotism felt in Steuben County was evidenced by the actions taken by Mr. Josiah Curtis of the firm D. Curtis & Son of Addison Mills. Mr. Curtis stated that every volunteer who had a family and enlisted in Captain Miles' Company last week had received a barrel of flour for his family.[60]

Three other war meetings were scheduled that same day: one at Avoca at 8 p.m., and the others at Adrien and Peach Orchard. A large crowd began to gather in Avoca, and when the meeting began, there were between one and two thousand loyal citizens convened together. S.D. Lewis was selected president, Salmon Waterbury, Matthias Fox, James Silsbee, and S.H. Palmer vice presidents, and A.M. Waterbury and F.H. Guiwitte secretaries. After a few appropriate remarks by the president, Captain Crane of Elmira was introduced. The captain, who was a minister as well, appealed to the loyalty and patriotism of those people present to come to the aid of their country, which was involved in battling a Godless rebellion. He was followed by A.M. Spooner of Avoca and George S. Ellias of Bath. During the intervals between speeches, the Bath Cornet Band played excellent and patriotic music. Captain Laman of Avoca was on hand to enroll the names of those desiring to enlist. A number of young men promptly responded to the call and were sworn in on the spot.

In Adrien the schoolhouse was filled to overflowing, and Mr. Hallett, the town supervisor, presided. The crowd sat for over an hour listening intently to the address by E.C. Grover. Capt. Sill was also present and made some timely remarks. The people in attendance seemed determined not to be outdone by any other community.[61]

The War Meeting at Peach Orchard in Hector Township, Schuyler County, was called to order by R.S. Smith. John A. Gillett was elected president; Capt. E. Curry, D.P. Budd, Hector Ely, George Howell, Zalmon Ellis, and Dr. N. Nichols, vice presidents; Dr. M.D. Hawes, secretary. The meeting was addressed by Mr. McDonald, Esq. of Elmira in firm, truthful facts and also by the Rev. Thomas K. Beecher in his usual impressive, home-sending words. While he stood pleading for volunteers to help in this great struggle, the tears of many were seen to fall.

An interesting incident took place at a war meeting in Wayland in Steuben County. Lieut. Col. Diven was standing by after speaking when the men were called to the recruiting table to sign up. He noticed a bright looking young man step up, take up the pen, lay it down, take it up again, and exhibit very plainly other evidence of hesitation. An older lady standing by asked him, "Are you afraid?" "No," said the youth, "not for myself, mother, but for you," and then he signed his name.[62]

As can be seen by the enormous number of war meetings being held, every township was making a tremendous effort to reach its quota. There was a great competition going on between the three counties of the 27th election district, and although Schuyler County had developed a strong organization for the recruiting of volunteers, its size and smaller population put it at a disadvantage. In addition, there were several practices taking place which further complicated its task. This was illustrated in the public letter from Charles Cook and S.L. Root published in the July 26 edition of the *Havana Journal*:

> It is well known to most of our citizens that our quota of volunteers is two full companies, and as this county was among the first, if not the first county in the state to respond to the call of the President, the feeling among our citizens is general; that our government shall be protected and defended at every hazard no matter from what source the attacks may come. This general feeling pervading the public mind of this county early brought out our people on the side of the government, and that feeling has not changed and we trust it will not change: "Our Government first, last, and always should ever be our motto."
>
> Remembering the early stand which this county has taken and that we have two more full companies of troops to raise, we wish to call the attention of our people, and of each one of them, to the practice which has lately grown up among us, of individuals, for pay or otherwise, taking squads of men to recruiting stations out of the county, and there enlisting these men into companies organized by other counties.
>
> If this practice is continued, or even carried to a much greater extent, we shall fail in raising our two full companies, and in that event, we will stand self-disgraced before the public for we get no credit for volunteers who enlist in companies armed outside of our county.
>
> Another practice which is still more reprehensible is carried on by aspirants to a captaincy in other counties, that of hiring persons to enlist for them in this county, at a given sum of money per head which in reality is selling the services of our citizens as the services of slaves are sold in the market, and it may be into the hands of a man so unworthy that he cannot raise a company in the county where he is known.
>
> Practices so vile and dishonorable, we trust that all of our citizens will discourage and discountenance; but encourage all of our volunteers to enlist in their own county, under their chosen officers and go to the field of duty together, and if need be, there die together or together return home after a glorious triumph.

On Monday, July 28, it rained very hard, turning the camp into a sea of mud. More new recruits came into camp, and the guards were doubled.[63] Capt. Miles of

Addison, because of the great success at the war meeting on Saturday, arrived by train. He brought 65 men for their physicals, and 60 of them passed. At the train depot in Addison, he made a short speech and thanked the citizens for their perservering and generous assistance in recruiting his men.[64] The following day, drilling began in earnest again, as the camp was fairly dried out. The regiment now had 550 men in its ranks. That evening, the men sat around the fire after dark. One of them played a guitar, and the others joined in singing patriotic and other songs. This was a major change from other nights when it was difficult to sleep because of the great amount of noise in the camp.[65]

On Tuesday evening, July 29, a War Meeting was held at the Court House in Bath. D. Rumsey was selected president and O. Seymour, John Ostrander, James Moore, D.C. Howell, Samuel Balcom, Willia Snell, and Joseph Carrier were appointed vice presidents. E.R. Kasson and George S. Ellas were appointed secretaries. An immense crowd of people gathered, filling the Court House completely, and it was necessary to erect a stand in the street outside to organize a separate meeting. The meetings were ably and eloquently addressed by Hon. A.S. Diven, the Rev. T.K. Beecher, Hon. Tracy Beadle, Capt. E.F. Crane, and Gen. R.B. Van Valkenburgh. Miss Kate Dean favored the inside audience with patriotic songs. The crowd was very enthusiastic and gave generously to the War Fund. In a short time, as much as two thousand dollars were raised for volunteer purposes.[66]

Uniforms were distributed to the men on that same day.[67] While there is no absolute proof, it is most probable that the regiment was issued New York State regulation uniforms. The jacket was park blue in color, waist length with eight buttons down the front and three buttons on the sleeve. The pants were of a lighter "sky blue" color. The hat was the standard kepi, dark blue with a leather visor, and the regiment number and company letter on the top.[68] Later, when the Corps were given individual insignias, a red star signifying first the First Division of the 12th and later the 20th Army Corps was added. The red star was worn on the kepis or officers' hats, and also on the arm or breast of their jackets.[69]

The items issued to each man consisted of the following: Overcoat, Frockcoat, Pants, Cap, Wool Shirts (2), Flannel Drawers (2), Wool Socks (2),[70] Shoes, Blanket, Bed Sack, Knapsack, Haversack, Canteen, and Straps (2).

Organizations continued to be formed for the purpose of providing aid and comfort to the sick and wounded soldiers. In Bath, Steuben County, through the invitation of the Reverend Mr. Jones, a large number of ladies convened at the courthouse on Wednesday afternoon, July 30, to consult about organizing such a group. Jones called the meeting to order and stated its purpose. Officers were elected and the group decided to call themselves "The Ladies' Aid Society of Bath, NY." The following persons were chosen as officers of the society: President—Mrs. Henry Brother, Vice Pres.—Mrs. Dr. De Wolfe, Secretary—Miss Addie Church, and Treasurer—Miss Jennie Wilkes.[71]

The prompt response which the 27th Senatorial District, consisting of the counties of Steuben, Chemung and Schuyler, is giving to the call for volunteers, is worthy of imitation throughout the whole state. Meetings have been held in almost every school district, and the most influential men in each town have been appointed to personally urge everyone whom they consider likely to enlist and see that they do so at once. In Elmira, 200 men were sworn in on Wednesday and Thursday of last week, and in the little town of Dix, in Schuyler County, whose quota is only 27, 19 men were enlisted in three days. The 27th leads the state.[72]

In the August 2 edition of the *Havana Journal*, Hull Fanton had a letter headed "Attention Volunteers," printed under his name and directed to the men who were enrolled but not yet mustered into his company. He instructed them to report forthwith to the company headquarters at his law office to be sworn in, and they would then proceed to Elmira and the regimental barracks. Each man would then be paid the U.S. federal bounty of $27 and one half of the $50 state bounty as soon as possible.[73]

The weather in August started out very warm, and over two-thirds of the regiment was in camp. The company from Schuyler County arrived in camp on Friday, August 1. There was more drilling, the barracks had to be scrubbed, and the first dress parades were held. Talk in the camp centered on the possibility of a draft if the quota of volunteers was not reached.

On Monday, August 4, seven hundred men were present for a dress parade.[74] The next day, the morning report stated that 308 men were present for duty, 13 were sick, 363 absent with leave, and 6 absent without leave. Later that day, 150 men under Captain Laman arrived at camp from Steuben County. On Wednesday, an announcement was made that the regiment would probably leave Elmira in the latter part of the following week. Colonel Van Valkenburgh moved his headquarters from the Brainard House to the Regimental Camp at the Rathbun #3 Barracks. He announced that henceforth he proposed to be "at home" with the men under his command.[75]

There was a large and enthusiastic War Meeting at Caton Centre on Tuesday evening. The speakers were Capt. Newton T. Colby, Dr. Ingersoll, and George R. Graves of Corning and the Rev. Allen R. Woodworth of Newfield. Dr. Ingersoll and C. Minier, Esq. of Caton each gave a $10 bounty, and others gave smaller sums to those who volunteered. Eight or ten good, able-bodied citizens volunteered, and as many more promised to do so the following week. The Baptist church was crowded to overflowing, and the meeting did not break up until nearly midnight.[76]

Finally, on Thursday, the order came in the form of a telegram from the War Department that the president would like to see the regiment in Washington as early as possible. There was a great deal of discussion in the camp that the regiment would be the first to answer the president's call for 300,000 men, and what a feather in their cap that would be. The next day, to celebrate, Colonel Van Valkenburgh bought a "family" ticket at his own expense to "Russell's Panorama of the War," which was showing in Elmira at Ely's Hall, and he took the entire regiment to see it. They marched from their barracks on West Water Street to the hall. It was the first time that the regiment had paraded in public.[77]

The following day, the men's knapsacks, haversacks, and canteens arrived, and a great many of the men were given furloughs until Monday.[78] The knapsacks were hot and ill-fitting affairs that would eventually be replaced in the field by blanket rolls. The blanket was rolled up with just the bare necessities in it, slung over the left shoulder, and tied with a string on the right hip. Haversacks were white canvas bags about a foot square with a long strap used to carry them over the right shoulder. They hung on the left hip and were used to carry daily rations. They usually were waterproof and had a flap that pulled over the top. The man's name, his company letter, and regiment number typically were stenciled on the flap.

On Thursday, August 7, a war meeting was held in Coopers Plains. Mr. W.K. Logie in his address sought last minute volunteers for the regiment and defended General McClellan against those who were criticizing his tactics during the Peninsula Campaign. Other speakers were the Reverend De Boise of Elmira, Col. Van Valkenburgh, Capt. Crane, Lt. Knox of Campbell and of Capt. Mile's company. Patriotic songs were sung by Master Crane, the son of Capt. Crane.

On Saturday, the father of Private Edwin Sherman of Company A showed up to bring his son back home. It seemed that young Sherman was not yet 18. He was promptly turned over to his father after it was proven that he was underage and there without his parents' consent.[79]

That evening, a war meeting was held at the Baptist Church in the village of Savona. Speakers at the meeting included Gen. R.B. Van Valkenburgh and Mr. Coon of Burdett.[80] *The Havana Journal* printed an article that same day comparing volunteering to being drafted. It stated that those who volunteered would receive a $27 bounty advance, $13 advance of monthly pay, $75 guarantee of mustering out pay, 160 acres of bounty land, and pecuniary assistance to one's family during the enlistment period. If drafted, one would receive only the pay of $11 per month. That same day, the rolls of the regiment were tallied up, and all of the companies were full.

On that Sunday, August 10, the Reverend Beecher's sermon at Park Church urged, "It is the duty of every man in the land to constitute himself a police officer, to come forth not in wrath, but calmly, sternly resolved to put down this wicked rebellion at once and restore peace." He also offered consolation to those who were grieving at the parting of wife from husband and son from parents, showing very clearly that there never was a better chance for a Christian to show forth his patriotism and his Christianity than at the present time.[81]

On Monday, Col. Van Valkenburgh received the following communication dated August 9 from Col. Henry P. Casey, the acting Quartermaster of New York:

Sir, the balance of all the clothing, camp and garrison equipage for your regiment has this day been forwarded to your Quartermaster with exception of the flag. It was necessary to have the number of your regiment printed on the Regiment Color; what that should be, we did not know until last evening. The U.S. had no National Color to give us, I therefore purchased from Messrs. Tiffany & Co. a very handsome one, which will together with your Regimental Color be forwarded to you on Monday. I would also respectfully state that his Excellency Gov. Morgan has purchased, and will have forwarded to you immediately, a very beautiful Regimental Color in honor of your regiment being the first ready for the field, under the President's call. I regret to say that Genl. Arthur is absent from the city, and therefore cannot express to you the high appreciation, His Excellency Gov. Morgan entertains for the patriotic zeal manifested by yourself and the officers under your command, which has been so signally crowned with success. I am very respectfully your obedient servant, Henry P. Casey Colonel Commander and Acting Quarter Master State of New York.[82]

The regimental banner purchased by Gov. Morgan was the banner that gave this regiment the name "The Banner Regiment." Prior to this honor, the regiment was called and is still officially referred to as Campbell's Guards, after the then Lieutenant Governor of New York State, Robert Campbell. This banner survived the war and was passed along through the years to different people for safe keeping. The banner ended up, years later, in the Mooers' family museum in Elmira. It was given to the Chemung County Historical Society in 1988, restored to its original condition, and rededicated at a ceremony held at the historical society.

Monday, August 11 saw the first muster rolls written out.[83] The following day, the regiment was visited by W.E. Dodge, Jr., a United States Allotment Commissioner, and $50 was paid to each man. Commissioner Dodge was also there to decide with the soldiers on the amount of money that each might feel disposed to set apart from his wages for the benefit of his family or friends, to be paid directly to them by the authorities, on the certificate of the proper officers.[84]

During this last week, many of the officers of the regiment were presented gifts from their friends and admirers. Colonel Van Valkenburgh was presented a horse by his friend Colonel C.C.B. Walker. It was said that the horse had come from Montgomery, AL, and was surely the horse to carry the colonel into war against the southern troops. The ladies of Horseheads presented their Lieutenant Backman with a fine sword, and he also received a pistol and other accoutrements form his "legal" friends.[85] One officer, Adjutant Hull Fanton, took a bride. On Tuesday, August 12, he and Miss Louise Tracy, the eldest daughter of Peter Tracy, were married at the bride's home by the Reverend Chester.[86]

The regiment was ready to leave, but unavoidable delays in the preparation of company papers would prevent them from leaving until the following evening.[87] The regiment was made up twelve staff officers and non-commissioned officers and ten companies of officers, non-commissioned officers, and enlisted men. Each company had one hundred and one men, with the exception of Companies C and E, which had 100, and Company I, which had one hundred and two. This came to a total of one thousand and twenty-one men shown on the first muster roll. Companies A, B, C, D, and E were principally made up of men from Elmira and other villages and towns in Chemung County. Company F was from Addison, Cameron, and Campbell in Steuben County; Company G from Elmira, Bath, and Hammondsport of Steuben County; Company H from Havana and other villages and towns in Schuyler County;

Company I from Corning, Wayland, and West Union in Steuben County; and Company K from Elmira, Hornellsville, Howard, and Canisteo of Steuben County.[88] The mustering was completed on Wednesday, August 13.

On Wednesday at 10 p.m., they marched from the barracks on West Water Street to the train station.[89] Men from the fire department of Elmira accompanied the regiment and lighted their way with a torch light procession.[90] Leading the regiment was a band from Painted Post that they had hired especially for the occasion. The band would accompany them to their camp near Washington.[91] A large crowd, waving flags and handkerchiefs, gathered along the way, and many gathered at the Erie Depot to see the regiment off. Tearful good-byes were said, but a brass band cheered everyone up with its playing of patriotic songs.[92] God's blessing was invoked, and prayers were said for the welfare and safety of these men and boys going off to war.[93] Several hours passed, and the crowd thinned out considerably. When the special Northern Central train made up of twenty-seven cattle cars left the station at 3 a.m. on August 14, there was only a small crowd of people remaining to see the regiment off.[94]

The staff officers[95] of the 107th when they left Elmira were as follows:

| | |
|---|---|
| Colonel | R.B. van Valkenburgh, Bath |
| Lieut. Colonel | A.S. Diven, Elmira |
| Major | G.L. Smith, Elmira |
| Adjutant | Hull Fanton, Havana |
| Surgeon | Dr. P.H. Flood, Elmira |
| Asst. Surgeon | Dr. J.D. Hewett, New York |
| Chaplain | Rev. E.F. Crane, Elmira |
| Quarter Master | E.P. Graves, Corning |
| Quarter Master Sgt. | L.B. Childsey, Hornellsville |
| Commissary Sgt. | Henry Inscho, Corning |
| Sutler | Isaac H. Reynolds, Elmira |

Quartermaster Edward P. Graves previously had held the position of quartermaster's clerk with the rank of captain under Colonel Walker at the Elmira Rendezvous.[96]

*The Steuben Courier* of Bath in its August 13 edition carried the following article in tribute to the 107th:

We feel a just pride in announcing that Col. R.B. Van Valkenburgh's regiment is fully organized and was the first full regiment from the Empire State to respond to the late call for 300,000 troops. All honor to the 27th Senatorial District, and to the gallant and persevering Colonel of the 107th. Great credit is also due to the other officers of the regiment who have worked with a will to hasten enlistments. We challenge the State to raise another body of officers and men who will compare with the one just organized at Elmira. The Colonel and Lieut. Colonel of the 107th Regiment are men of commanding influence, who have held high positions in the councils of the state and nation, and who now leave their business and professional pursuits to take up the sword in defense of their country.

The regiment has already received marching orders and will probably leave Elmira for Washington today. The men are to be armed with Springfield rifles and will receive every comfort that can be possibly secured. Officered by men of peculiar fitness and unquestioned ability, and composed of the hardy sons of old Steuben, Chemung and Schuyler Counties, we predict that the gallant 107th will make its mark high, and rank among the first of the many Regiments that have gone forth to battle in the cause of Liberty and Union.

The regiment was truly destined to make its mark, but there would also be times when some members did not live up to the lofty expectations expressed in the article. When the regiment left in the early morning hours of August 14, there were six men absent at the roll call. In all, nine men who had enrolled in the regiment were not there when the train pulled out. Three had deserted early enough so that they had been replaced, but six additional men were missing just prior to embarkation.[97] It is sufficient to state that desertion was a problem throughout the war in all regiments and on both sides.

# 2

# In Camp Near Washington, DC

We are coming, Father Abraham, three hundred thousand more,
From Mississippi's winding stream and from New England's shore.
We leave our plows and workshops, our wives and children dear,
With hearts too full for utterance, with but a silent tear;
We dare not look behind us, but steadfastly before:
We are coming, Father Abraham, three hundred thousand more.

J. S. Gibbons

The 107th was on its way to the training ground for the Union Army. The capitol of Washington was surrounded by fifty-nine forts and seventeen other smaller defense facilities that were manned largely by newly formed regiments.[1] It was here that the untried soldiers would spend hour upon hour learning discipline, drilling, taking care of and firing their weapons, living in the field, and doing picket duty. Many of them would spend only a few weeks learning the soldier's way of life. For the most part, they would be trained by their own officers, men who didn't know much more about being a soldier than they did. There was hardly enough time to make them understand what was expected of them or how to carry out their duties. The strategy of battle, however, hadn't changed much since the time of Napoleon. These men, when advancing against the enemy, would be marching exposed, in straight lines, directly at Confederate troops, who would be employing similar tactics. The result was usually a dreadful slaughter on both sides.

The train arrived in Williamsport, PA, at about seven o'clock in the morning. Troop trains did not run on a regular schedule, and the 107th clearly was not expected at such an early hour. Over one thousand men departed from the train amidst a great deal of confusion. However, as soon as it was apparent that they were hungry, the people at the station scurried around and provided them with some food. The train remained there for about forty-five minutes while the ladies passed out bread and butter, pie, cake, and hot coffee, much of which found its way into the men's haversacks. The train was soon moving again; heading south, it stopped at Harrisburg on the west side of the river and for a little while at York just above the Pennsylvania and Maryland border. At both places, the citizens displayed the same kind of generous spirit. The men, many of them farmers, were very impressed with the rich farming land between Williamsport and Harrisburg. After passing into

Maryland, they saw Union pickets at intervals along the railroad. When the train was about twenty miles from Baltimore, guards were posted to make sure that the men did not get off and to ward off any possible attempts to cause harm to the train or its occupants. Trains traveling down this line in the past had been fired on after they passed into Maryland, most recently at a bridge crossing by some "secession prowlers." Men selected from the regiment acted as guards; they were very nervous, but the trip passed without incident.[2]

The train reached Baltimore at ten o'clock Friday evening. The men remained uneasy because of the trouble other troops had experienced from Rebel sympathizers in this city. They were very pleasantly surprised to find ladies congregated in groups, cheering, waving flags and handkerchiefs. After they departed the train, they enjoyed an excellent supper provided for them by the Eutaw Relief Association[3] at the Union Hall.[4] After they finished their meal, it was too late to make the trip to Washington, so they moved to a nearby open area where they spent the night sleeping on the ground. For many of them, this was probably the first night they had spent out in the night air, and it would be the first of many nights through fair weather and foul that the men of the 107th New York Volunteers would spend together. However, their sleep would not be a long one, for it was not too long after midnight when they were awakened for their trip to Washington.

The regiment departed Baltimore by train for Washington at approximately 3 a.m. It was a slow and tedious ride with much stopping and starting. Several times other trains were allowed to pass them. They arrived at the small, wood frame depot of the Baltimore and Ohio Railroad located at New Jersey Avenue and C Street[5] between 10 and 12 noon on Saturday, August the 16.[6] After departing the train, they crossed over the railroad tracks to the building called the "Soldier's Rest," which was located to the east of the depot on North Capitol Street. Here they were served what was supposed to pass for dinner. The meal consisted mainly of very tough, cold boiled beef, which was very salty. It was so bad that they said it must be "horse flesh." Besides the beef, they had bread and coffee[7] served from pails.[8] The bread was good enough, but they complained that the coffee was not fit to drink. After dinner, they moved outdoors, and at approximately 2 p.m., they were briefly addressed and reviewed by President Lincoln and Secretary of State Seward along with Colonel Van Valkenbergh, Lt. Colonel Diven, and Major G.L. Smith.

The president, whom the men thought looked very homely, was dressed in black pants and a coat that looked like it was made from alpaca. He went down the lines with a good-natured grin on his face and said that it was the best appearing regiment that he had ever seen in the service except for one, the Ellsworth Regiment. Secretary Seward praised the regimental officers for having raised so splendid a regiment in such a short time. He said that he was entirely satisfied with it, except for the fact that it had arrived ahead of the Cayuga regiment, which he had hoped would be the first from the Empire State.[9] The Secretary was from Auburn, NY, and had previously been a senator from New York State. He was a leader of the anti-slavery faction, and he and President Lincoln, though close friends now, had been opponents in the Republican primary for the presidential election of 1860.

The soldiers were obviously very excited and pleased with their audience with "Old Abe," and gave him and Seward six rousing cheers. The banner that Governor Morgan had purchased for the 107th, in honor of their being the first regiment to answer the call of the president, had preceded them to Washington, where it had been on display for a short while. The banner was presented to them by the president during the review.[10]

*Author's note: The banner did not go with the regiment but was believed to have remained at Secretary Seward's residence in Washington during the war. There is no record of when it was returned to the regiment, but it was given to the former colonel of the regiment, A.S. Diven, when the war was over. After Diven died, it was passed along to Colonel Gabriel Smith, then to Layman W. Babcock, and finally to Frank Frost, who was the last surviving member of the regiment. After the war, it was displayed at the regimental association celebrations and hung at the New York State Armory on Church Street where the association held its meetings. Later a frame was made for it by a local cabinet maker, Lafayette Brown of Wellsburg. Mr. Brown was so highly regarded as a cabinet maker that he was sent to Europe with two other men by the Pullman Company to do the interior woodwork of a railroad car for King Victor Emmanuel of Italy. "Lafe," as Mr. Brown was called, was well known throughout the local schools for his story of the Civil War and what the American flag stood for. He was often seen at parades holding the flag aloft, leading the way with his "Zouave" color guard of small boys.[11] When the association presented its artifacts and books to the Chemung County Historical Society, the flag was temporally housed in the coach house of Edward T. Mooers because the society did not have room for so large an object. Later it was restored, placed back in the frame, and hung at the historical society's new facilities in the old Chemung Canal Trust Bank on Water Street in Elmira.[12]*

After the ceremonies, the men were allowed to do a little sightseeing, and at four o'clock, they sat down to a supper of more cold beef, bread, and coffee. Following their meal, they formed their companies and began their march toward Pennsylvania Avenue and their final destination at Fort Albany near Arlington, Virginia. Colonel Van Valkenburgh rode at the head of the column, and at his side in an open carriage was Secretary Seward accompanied by two ladies. Immediately following them were several other carriages containing other distinguished persons, and directly behind them was the regiment's band. The rear was brought up by a long train of baggage wagons.

As the troops moved on toward their destination, the band was playing, and they saw flags displayed from many buildings. Ladies in horse-driven street cars and others on the sidewalks greeted them by waving their handkerchiefs.[13] They were able to view many of the sights including the Capitol, Washington's Monument, and the Smithsonian Institution.[14] In 1862, the dome on the Capitol was under construction, and Washington's Monument was less than half finished because funds for it had run out. As they continued up the avenue toward the White House, Private John Ten Broeck of Company B staggered and fell unconscious. Captain Baldwin ordered him to be placed in an ambulance and taken to the hospital. Several days later, he was released and sent back to the regiment. His problem was too much drink. A great deal of whiskey had been consumed by the regiment during the train ride from Elmira, and Ten Broeck obviously had more than his share. It was common knowledge that he had been drinking steadily for the past four weeks, so his accident did not come as a surprise to many in the regiment. This incident was reported in the Elmira newspapers, stating that Ten Broeck was the first casualty of the regiment and that he had died.[15] No one knew how serious his condition was at the time. Many of the men found it very amusing that when he passed out; it was directly in front of one of several coffin shops on the avenue.[16] There were a great number of coffin shops in Washington owing to the large number of army hospitals and the many deaths among the citizens from typhoid and smallpox. During this time, the business of undertaking was very profitable. In fact, one undertaker was arrested for creating a public nuisance because his premises were overly full of bodies waiting to be embalmed.

The city of Washington in the summer 1862 was much different than one might expect. The only buildings of any real consequence were the Capitol with its dome partially finished, the White House, the partially completed Treasury building, and the Smithsonian Institution. All of them could be seen from almost any part of the city. Washington had been formally laid out, but very little other major construction had taken place.[17] The men of the 107th always spoke proudly of their march up Pennsylvania Avenue, which was then the only paved street in Washington. An article in the August 23 edition of the *Elmira Advertiser and Republican* indicated the regiment's route for its march through Washington. The article was reprinted from the *Washington National Republican*. They began near the railroad terminal, marched down North Capitol Street, west on B Street to 1st Street, and south on 1st Street to the Capitol. At the Capitol, they turned right onto Pennsylvania Avenue, marching northwest toward the White House. At 14th Street they turned left, getting their first view of Virginia, and marched directly to the Long Bridge, which crossed the Potomac River to Arlington, Virginia.

When they saw Virginia, the regiment let out cheer after cheer and crossed the Long Bridge into "Secession Land" with the band playing "Dixie." Once over the bridge, they marched along the Columbia Turnpike past Fort Jackson and the very imposing Fort Runyon, the largest fort in Washington's defenses. They continued on the turnpike, crossing over the Chesapeake and Ohio Canal. After a short while, they came to the Old Alexandria and Georgetown Road. There they turned left and marched past Fort Albany and up the hill behind it. Beyond them on a hill to the southwest, they could see Fort Richardson, a fort where Rebel prisoners were confined.[18] This piece of ground between the two forts was to be their first camp. It was between 9:30 and 10 p.m. Saturday evening when they arrived. The evening was warm and pleasant, but the march of approximately five miles had completely exhausted them. They had no tents nor the energy to pitch them if they did have them. They rolled themselves up in their blankets on the hard ground and fell asleep under the stars.[19] Most of them had slept very little since they left Elmira. In honor of the secretary of state, they named their camp Camp Seward. While they were based in this area, whatever piece of ground the regiment occupied was called Camp Seward.

The next morning, each man was given rations of a loaf of bread. They spent the rest of the day laying out the camp and putting up their temporary tents. The tents were small; they held two men and were open at both ends. After they were finished leveling the camp streets, some of them took the opportunity to bathe in a small stream that ran nearby. Nearby Fort Albany, with a perimeter of 429 yards, had 12 guns in place[20] and was manned by two companies of the 14th Massachusetts. Fort Cass, which had been built mostly by the 23rd New York, the first Elmira regiment, was just north of them. The city of Washington and the Potomac River, to the northeast and east, provided a magnificent view from their camp, but the land around the fort had been cleared of trees and was very desolate. At 10 p.m., after a long hard day, they fell in for roll call, and afterwards turned in for a good night's sleep.

On Sunday morning, they had a breakfast of coffee, bread, and beef. The night had been quite cold, and the morning was very chilly. In the afternoon, Chaplain Crane held Sunday services for the men who sat on the ground in the nearby peach orchard. After the service, discussions were held regarding the starting of a non-denominational church, and Major Smith read aloud the articles of war and General Order number 4 as issued by Colonel Van Valkenburgh. This general order specified the name of their camp as "Camp Seward" after the secretary of state. In addition, it specified that individual companies would mess together with two men from each company detailed as cooks. These men were to be exempt from any other duty. The order also contained rules of conduct for the men, such as only three passes at a time to be allowed for each company, gambling and swearing were prohibited along with no drunkenness, no destruction of private property including fences, trees, shrubbery, or fruit.[21] Sutlers were located near the camp, and additional provisions or snacks such as crackers and ginger cookies were available from them. Watermelons were also available, and the largest could be bought for 10 or 15 cents. The weather during the day was comfortable but not as warm as they had expected. A dress parade was held late in the day, and the men were advised that General Halleck would be reviewing them in a day or two. At this parade, the companies were assigned their respective positions for the first time. Capt. Baldwin's Company B took the right of the regiment and Captain Morgan's Company E the left. The other companies were also positioned according to their captain's commission date. During the day, two regiments, the 35th Massachusetts and the 125th Pennsylvania, pitched camps on either side of them. That made five new full regiments near them since Saturday morning. That evening, the campfires of the other regiments could be seen in all directions and made for a magnificent sight. New and larger tents were distributed to the men on Monday. They were called Sibley tents and held six men each. They were erected immediately in neat rows and were found to be very comfortable. Some of the officers, including Captain Brigham of

Company H, invested some money in furniture, thinking that they would be at their present location for some time. They found out soon enough that it was a bad investment. The furniture was eventually left behind, and any future needs were satisfied by "right of possession."[22] More grading was done to the streets to make sure that the rainwater would be carried away from the tents. Each Company occupied its own street, and the street for Company B was named Baldwin Street after its captain, Lathrop Baldwin. That same day, the men finally received their weapons. Each was issued a fine Springfield rifle and the other necessary accoutrements.[23] The regiment had been there only three days, and in that time ten more regiments had arrived, making their camps all around the 107th. News from home was plentiful because the Elmira newspapers were mailed to them and were always available in camp.

There were orchards on both sides of the camp: peach on one side and an apple on the other. The men, however, were cautioned not pick any fruit. Rations were getting better; they now included fresh beef, salt pork, rice, beans, and coffee. Some of the companies hired a man to do their cooking for them, and each man paid him two dollars a month. However, each man washed his own dishes, which consisted of a tin plate, cup, knife, fork, and spoon. Soap and candles were distributed every day. Water was scarce, and most were careful not to waste it.[24]

On Tuesday, August 19, the first battalion drill was held under the direction of Captain Carroll Potter of General Casey's staff. General Casey was in charge of the regiments located around the 107th. The daily regimen in the camp was similar to what it had been in Elmira. The men were up at 5 a.m. for roll call, drill until breakfast at 7 a.m., guard assignments or other duty given out at 8 a.m., company drill from 10 until 12 noon, and then dinner. Battalion drill was held for two or three hours in the afternoon, and supper was at 6 p.m. A dress parade was held at sundown, and roll call taken at 9 p.m. The "remainder" of the day belonged to the men. To say the least, their days were fully occupied. Drilling was always a large part of every day, and a German officer was assigned to their regiment to teach them how to do it properly. A typical German officer type, he had the men wondering if he owned the Union Army, or if maybe they had been transferred into the German Army. When he wasn't drilling them, he told them stories about Germany, and he introduced them to lager beer.[25] There was always talk about getting marching orders soon, and they expected to be in front of the enemy in less than a month. Little did they know how right they were. They felt very proud of their accomplishments. Colonel Van Valkenburgh told them that the president said, "They are the best regiment as regards to eveness in size and physique that I ever reviewed." After being in camp for a week, the men all remained in good health.

On Thursday, for first time since the regiment arrived, it rained a little. Regiments continued to come over the Long Bridge and make camp around them. In all there were about fifteen or twenty regiments, most of them from Pennsylvania.[26] Some of them, because their enlistment term was only seven or nine months, had already moved out to join General Pope at Manassas. Firing was heard every day from the different forts located nearby as artillery practice was held.

Peddlers were a common sight in the camp, selling the newspapers from Baltimore, Philadelphia, and Washington. Photographers visited the camps often, taking pictures of the soldiers. There were usually long lines of men waiting to have their pictures taken. On Friday, the regiment was again visited by Secretary of State Seward, and he was accompanied by General Bartlett of General Slocum's division. During that same day, the regiment received forty rounds of ammunition and marching orders to occupy Fort Lyon.

The next morning, Saturday, August 23, they packed their knapsacks and struck their tents. At about 7 a.m., they left their camp near Fort Albany to move to a location near Fort Lyon, where they would relieve the 69th New York State Militia who were going home.[27] Fort Lyon was the second largest fort in defense of Washington. It had a perimeter of 937 yards and was one of the southernmost forts guarding the capital. While thirty-eight guns were mounted, it had capacity for a total of forty-six. The fort covered about nine acres and had encasements sufficient to protect two thousand men.[28] The march to the new camp seemed to be by a very circuitous route; even though they were told it would be only six or seven miles, it turned out to be more like ten or twelve. The march was by Bailey's Crossroads[29] through countryside that once was beautiful but now contained farmhouses going to ruin and large barns with the boards stripped off. The woodlands were cut down, and no crops were planted. In some places, crowds of people came to the roadside to watch them go by. They even passed several troop encampments that provided them with pails of water.

It was a very warm day, and the march was much worse than the one from the train depot in Washington. Fred Wagner of Company F, along with several others, had to give up and ride on a baggage wagon. Benjamin Kimball, also of Company F, gave out just as he reached the new camp.[30] In Kimball's defense, it must be noted that he was forty-four years old, while Wagner was only a boy of twenty.[31] Some of the men hired someone to carry their knapsacks or guns, but that was against the rules unless they were sick.[32] More than one man was seen to pour some the water from his canteen over his head.

They arrived at Fort Lyon at about 3 p.m., worn out, faces dirty and uniforms covered with dust. Even so, some of the men, after eating and resting two or three hours, went down to Alexandria to see the sights. They felt that Alexandria was as large as Elmira, although not near so pleasant. It was said to be full of secessionists, and that it was dangerous to be out after dark. They were told that a Union soldier had been shot and killed from a window of one of the houses just the night before. They saw the Marshall House, which was where Colonel Ellsworth, the first casualty of the war, was shot and killed when he took down the Rebel flag. The Star-Spangled Banner flew there now, and the building, which looked very gloomy, was being used for a hotel. While in town, they passed by some New Jersey troops, who appeared hard and battle toughened. The dust was thrown up in the street when about thirty pieces of artillery rolled through the town. When the sightseers returned to camp, they found that their tents would be coming in the second trip of the wagons, so they turned in wherever they could, some in tents and others outside.[33]

The next day was Sunday, and they were able to rest all day. In addition to the Sabbath, church services were now held two or three times during the week. Chaplain Crane was liked by all the men, and they enjoyed listening to his sermons. In addition to being the regiment's chaplain, he was also captain of Company A. Among his duties as chaplain was attending to the mailing and receiving of letters and packages each day. That day church services were held at 11 a.m. in front of the regimental hospital.[34] After church services, about twenty men from Company G, which had been raised in Bath, decided to venture down to Alexandria to visit Kennedy's artillery battery. This battery had been raised by Captain Stocum and was made up of men mostly from Bath. A big shout went up when the artillery men saw them. The artillery men, in stark contrast to their 107th buddies, looked like they had been through some tough times. Only thirty remained of the one hundred and one originally raised. They all sat around, reminiscing about home and friends, some of whom wouldn't be going back.

The men felt that it was a great honor for their colonel and themselves to be assigned to man this installation, largely because Fort Lyon was to be under the command of Colonel Van Valkenburgh. The fort was located on the east side of the Shenandoah Valley about two miles southwest of Alexandria. The men still had a good view of Washington and Georgetown, which was some ten miles to the north of them, as well as Alexandria and the Potomac River. In fact, they could watch steamboats and other vessels going up and down the river all day. The railroad to Manassas was also visible for three miles. The land around the fort was completely bare of vegetation. The fort was built on high ground just southwest of Hunting Creek. This creek, which should have been more correctly described as an inlet, bordered the southwestern part of Alexandria with the Potomac River flowing east of the city. The magnificent oaks that had once stood on the George Mason estate had been cut down to provide firing space for the artillery. These forts and campsites had been carved out of the timber-clad countryside. Fort Ellsworth, one of the nearby forts, was situated across the valley about one and a half miles away. The men felt the new camp was much better situated than their previous one. Many regiments were nearby, their white tents gleaming in the sun. Halfway between the two forts flowed Cameron Run, a creek that ran into the that body of water referred to as Hunting Creek.

Two companies were sent immediately into the fort to clean and fix it up.[35] Four companies from the regiment, D, F, G, and K, were detailed for artillery practice in the fort, with two of them on duty at a time. The first two companies sent in were companies D and G. This was probably because they had done the best job of maintaining their ranks during the march. It was the men's first experience with cannons, and they were very excited about it. The noise of the solid projectile was particularly startling to them, as was the thought of the damage it would do to friend and foe alike. Other companies were detailed to cut down trees in front of the fort. Companies B, F, D, and K were detailed to be ready to leave camp at 7 a.m. on Monday and take one day's rations. They spent the day cutting trees on the north and northeast side of Fort Lyon, returning to camp at 6 p.m. They were excused from further duty for the rest of the day.[36] Others were assigned picket duty.[37] The pickets were assigned posts northwest to Fairfax Seminary for two miles and east to the Potomac River. With so many men assigned to the fort for picket duty and for the felling of trees, their camp was fairly deserted most of the time.[38]

Picket duty for the 107th called for one hundred and forty men to be sent out for a period of thirty-six hours. The men were warned to watch their step, especially if they were out after dark. Some of them, still being unaccustomed to firearms, experienced accidents with their weapons. Emmet Crane of Company F had just been relieved from picket duty and was resting his gun against a stone. The gun slipped off the stone, striking the hammer and firing. The ball passed through his hand, which was over the muzzle at the time. Another accident was more humorous than serious. George Wombough of the same company had his face blackened when his pistol discharged while it was in his belt.[39]

Picket duty had other hazards besides the mishandling of weapons. There was always the chance that one might run into the enemy. Two men from Company B had the misfortune to encounter a Rebel patrol and barely escaped. The incident was reported in the *Elmira Weekly Advertiser* on September 13, 1862. Privates Edward A. Carl and Seldon M. Averill exchanged fire with the patrol, and Carl was wounded. They both escaped, but Carl was transported to a hospital in Philadelphia and later discharged for disability on December 1, 1862.

Troop movements continued, and up to forty regiments of McClellan's men had moved west to support General Pope. The men of the 107th observed these troops and saw that they were a hard-looking bunch who were probably veterans of many campaigns. The thought of fighting so nearby prompted the hired band from Painted Post to leave the camp in great haste, so much so that one of the wives was left behind; she was off on the next train to catch up to her fleeing husband.[40] A Rebel was caught nearby, poisoning a spring that was the water supply for another regiment. He was brought to the fort and put in jail. It was thought that he would probably be shot.[41] The regiment continued the same regimen at Fort Lyon, and the men thought that the drilling was hard work. By now they were all tanned, and felt they were becoming more effective soldiers. After the last roll call, they very often sat around the watchfires during the evening to sing or listen to the band.

On the morning of Wednesday, August 27, the 50th and 15th New York Engineers and the 27th New York Infantry took up positions near the 107th, and many old acquaintances were renewed. Many of the 50th engineers were from Chemung County. At 3 p.m. that day, the long roll was sounded, and the regiment was quickly formed. The men were told that Pope's army had been defeated, and all his guns taken. The regiment was then marched into the fort and then out again, brought back to camp, and formed again. They received the news that Stonewall Jackson was within five miles of the fort, and between Pope and them. Major Smith came along the lines and told them to keep cool, and that in all probability before morning, they would be in battle. He urged them not to spill their powder or waste their lead and said that even though they might not be the best on the drill field, they could show the old regiments they had courage. "Boys," he said, "for God's sake don't run before the old regiments do! If I do, shoot me!" All of the regiments nearby were in position. They all were kept in line until sundown when they were dismissed but told to be ready to spring to their posts should the long roll sound again. The men spent a fitful night without much sleep. Knapsacks were packed and farewell letters written; most laid down with their musket and cartridge box close at hand.[42]

The next day, Colonel Van Valkenburgh invited General Bartlett to take command of the 107th dress parade. The general began his career as a captain of a Binghamton company in the 27th NYV regiment at Elmira, He rose to the rank of colonel of the 27th and fought at Bull Run and the Peninsula Campaign with McClellan. Gen. Bartlett was camped nearby with his regiment, which was a member of General Slocum's division of McClellan's army. The men of the 107th viewed Bartlett's troops during their drills and felt extremely humble in their presence. They were veterans of several campaigns and looked it, uniforms less than perfect, the men begrimed with powder and darkly tanned.[43]

The night passed with no Rebel attack, but in the morning, Friday, August 29, cannon fire could be heard in the distance. They couldn't tell if it was enemy troops or the other forts practicing. Major Smith told them that the next twenty-four hours would determine whether or not they would be attacked. He said, "I don't think they can get any nearer Washington than they are now. If they do, it will be through blood and fire." The rest of the day, the situation was calmer, and they went through their regular routine of drills. During the afternoon, several of the men from the 50th Engineers came over to visit with their buddies in the 107th.

On Saturday and Sunday, they continued to hear the roar of cannons from the battlefield at Bull Run, which was only sixteen miles away. They expected to be ordered out any minute in support of Pope. On Saturday, Richardson's division of McClellan's army marched past them on their way to aid him. Among them were the 64th and 84th New York regiments. Only a handful of the 64th were left, having suffered many casualties in its recent battles. This division numbered some twelve thousand, all hardened veterans just returned from the Peninsula Campaign against Richmond. Their colors were torn and riddled, uniforms faded and ragged. It made the blood of the men of the 107th tingle, not with excitement, but with shame that they were not going, and these men, who had already been through so much, were again exposing themselves to more death and hardship.[44]

Colonel Diven was the officer of the day in charge of the brigade. General

French came along with his division and asked him if this was enemy country. He also asked what those things were, referring to the boys who were on picket duty but had their coats unbuttoned and were lying in the grass with their cartridge boxes besides them. Lieutenant Brigham overheard him, hustled over the hill, and told the men to button up and get in shape. The general came around the hill for a closer look, and they saluted him smartly. He raised his hat in salute, and said, "Now I know we are protected by soldiers. Who commands that line?" "Colonel Diven, sir," replied Lieutenant Brigham.[45]

On Sunday, the regiment received orders to leave Fort Lyon and march back to the vicinity of Fort Craig. This fort was north of their old campground at Fort Albany. They were being replaced at Fort Lyon by McClellan's veteran troops. This move more than likely came as the result of the loss at 2nd Bull Run and the fear that Confederate troops might attack Washington. The 107th struck their tents and soon were on the march. They reached their new camp that evening and began to settle in. Fort Craig was located a mile or so northwest of Fort Albany and was situated on an estate of about one thousand acres that belonged to George W. Parke Custis, the adopted son of George Washington. The original mansion was intact, but the once beautiful grounds and groves of trees had disappeared. They had all been replaced by tents, ditches, entrenchments, rifle pits, ramparts, and cannons. Some of the men found relaxation at a spring down near the river.[46] The next day the regular routine was begun again. The regiment was progressing favorably in drill, considering the marching and counter-marching to which it had been subjected. The men were all in good shape, and no amount of significant sickness had been experienced. The quartermaster, E.P. Graves, was highly praised by the men for the fine care he was taking of them. This was especially true of Colonel Van Valkenburgh, who was presented with a fine field glass by the quartermaster.[47]

On Monday, the weather was cool, and during the night there were high winds and a thunder shower. The wind blew down many of the tents in camp, and during that day, time had to be taken to put the camp in order. Companies as usual were assigned to their duties. From the orders read at the dress parade, they learned that they had been assigned to the 5th Brigade of Whipple's Division of the Reserve Corps, along with the 35th Massachusetts and two Pennsylvania regiments, the 124th and the 125th. This brigade was to be under the command of Colonel van Valkenburgh and was to be part of the defenses of Washington. They were to guard the chain of forts from Fort Tillinghast to Fort Blenker. On September 1, Colonel Van Valkenburgh appointed 107th Adjutant Hull Fanton as adjutant of the newly formed 5th Brigade.[48]

News came of Pope's defeat by Jackson at Bull Run, and how Pope had pulled back to Centerville where he had taken a strong defensive position. It was hoped that Jackson would not escape and return to Richmond. They didn't yet realize that it wasn't the fear of Jackson's escaping that should worry them, but more the possibility that he might push on toward them and Washington. The first muster rolls were made out for the regiment's pay, but they had no idea when they would actually receive it. The next day, a practice long roll call was sounded in order to see how quickly the regiment could fall into ranks and be ready for action.

That afternoon, the regiment was practicing loading and firing when Captain Smith spoke to Van Valkenburgh, who suddenly ordered, "Parade dismissed." The men were sent back to their quarters with the instructions to be ready to fall in at a minute's warning. No sooner were they in their camp when the order came to form their lines. They rushed back, formed their ranks, and double quick marched just across from camp. They were broken down into smaller units and positioned behind a hill where they expected to remain all night. After ten or fifteen minutes had elapsed, they returned to the grounds for a dress parade. The colonel told them that he was very satisfied with their performance and that it had been just a test of their abilities.

The engineers had been busy marking out the lines for breastworks that extended in both directions for over a mile in front of their camp. On Wednesday, September 3, most of the regiment was assigned to work on the breastworks. The men knew how important this work was. They realized that these forts might be the only thing that would prevent the Capitol from being captured by the Rebels. Everyone was very discouraged about the current state of the war. Talk was that Jackson appeared to be ready to move into Maryland. During the day, the road was filled with the debris of Pope's army. They saw thousands of troops on foot, cavalry, and artillery interspersed with four or five hundred baggage wagons and ambulances carrying the wounded pass by in great disarray on their way to the Long Bridge.

The next day, some companies were excused from duty, and they passed the time in the morning by drilling on their own. In the afternoon, they struck their tents and moved their camp closer to Fort Albany, nearer where their first camp had been located. Their new camp was located next to that of the 13th New Jersey, a regiment that would eventually be in the same brigade as they for the remainder of the war. That same day, a small group of volunteer doctors and nurses from Elmira were in camp to help care for sick and wounded soldiers. Among the visitors were Edward French and John Laidlaw. Many of the men sought their company, very glad to see someone from home.

Friday was a warm and pleasant day. Most of the regiment spent the day working on the breastworks. Otherwise, it was quiet and peaceful with no hint of what the next day would bring.

### Headquarters, Washington, September 6, 1862, Special Orders, No. 3.

I. The following mentioned new regiments are distributed as herein indicated, and will proceed forthwith to join their respective corps and stations, viz.:

By command of Major General McClellan, S. Williams Asst. Adjutant General Banks Corps.

| | | |
|---|---|---|
| 24th Michigan | 13th New Jersey | 107th New York |
| 128th New York | 124th Pennsylvania | 125th Pennsylvania |

On Saturday, September 6, marching orders were announced early in the day. The men were ordered to stow their knapsacks in the baggage wagons, fill their haversacks with three days of rations, and to be prepared to march at 7 p.m. Their tents were to be left behind. Their destination was Rockville, MD, some twenty miles away. Rumors were that the Rebels had indeed crossed the Potomac River into Maryland and were threatening Washington. At last, they were going into battle. They loaded their bulging knapsacks into the wagons and carried their haversacks with rations of hard bread and meat. They carried their overcoats, blankets, and small tents with them.[49] As the sun sank, throwing the red light of the sunset over the tented hills, the 107th filed slowly out of Camp Seward.[50] Every man felt that their time had come, into battle at last, not knowing who among them would not return.

During the time the regiment spent at Camp Seward, four men decided that they had had enough of army life. In fact, on their very last day there, as the regiment prepared to march off to what was going to be their first battle, these four deserters stole off into the night.[51]

# 3

# Antietam

From sunrise to sunset the waves of battle ebbed and flowed. Men wrestled with each other in lines of regiments, brigades, divisions; while regiment, brigade, division faded away under a terrible fire, leaving long lines of dead to mark where stood the living. Fields of corn were trampled to shreds, forests were battered, and scathed, huge limbs sent crashing to the earth, rent by shell or round shot; grape and canister mingled their hissing scream in this hellish carnival, yet within all this and through it all the patriots of the North wrestled with hearts strong and nerves unshaken. Wrestled with the rebel hordes that thronged and pressed upon them as to destruction; never yielding though sometimes halting to gather up their strength, then with one mighty bound throwing themselves upon their foes to drive them into their protecting forest beyond. Thus, terminated a bloody and obstinate contest. We slept upon the bloody field of our victory.

—Brig. General George H. Gordon
Comm. 3rd Brigade, 1st Div., 12th Army Corps

The 107th NY marched over the Aqueduct Bridge, crossing the Potomac River at Georgetown. Directly behind them came the 13th New Jersey Volunteers, another "green" regiment.[1] Once over the bridge, they turned northwest and marched along the highway in the general direction of Harper's Ferry. The night was beautiful, and there was a full moon shining down on the moving mass of soldiers. At the summit of each hill, the moon could be seen reflecting on the gun barrels. For a long time in the beginning, the different regiments moved on with laughter and song, up and down the line. As the night wore on, the men grew weary and still; only the sound of the march could be heard. When the steps became less certain, the colonels gave the order, "Rout step. Arms at will." Muskets were shifted to the most comfortable position, but the rhythm of the march became still more irregular. Officers checked their watches and found that Sunday had come; it was one a.m. Silently the vast army moved on with no sound save the shuffling of the many dusty feet and the dull rumbling of the wagons. A long time had passed since Private Charlie Golden of Company C told one of his Irish jokes. Another hour passed: two o'clock. The men begin to lag, and one called out, "Captain, how long before they let us rest?" "Can't say, stick to it, and we'll have a halt soon," replied the officer. Before long the order came, "Halt, Rest." The men, many nearly exhausted, laid down in the road; a few who were less tired made it to the roadside and laid in the grass.

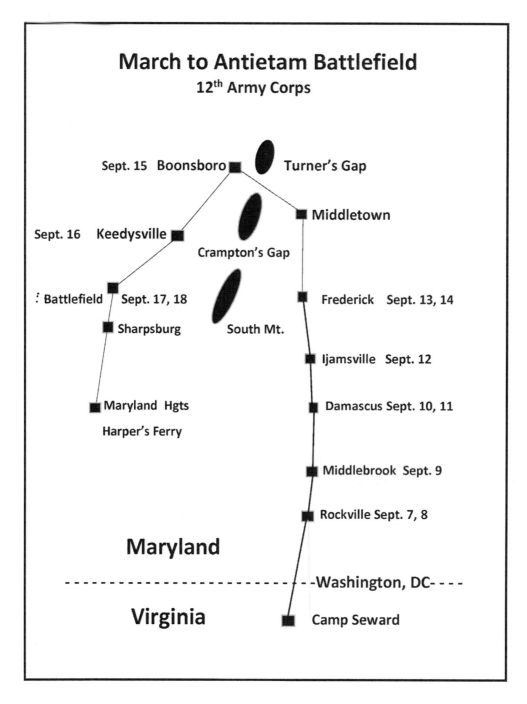

# March to Antietam Battlefield
## 12<sup>th</sup> Army Corps

Sept. 15 Boonsboro ■ Turner's Gap

■ Middletown

Sept. 16 Keedysville ■

Crampton's Gap

⋮ Battlefield / Sept. 17, 18 ■ Frederick Sept. 13, 14

■ Sharpsburg South Mt.

■ Ijamsville Sept. 12

■ Damascus Sept. 10, 11

■ Maryland Hgts

Harper's Ferry

■ Middlebrook Sept. 9

■ Rockville Sept. 7, 8

**Maryland**

- - - - - - - - - - - - - - - - - - - -Washington, DC- - - -

**Virginia** ■ Camp Seward

Map showing the route that 107th New York took from northern Virginia to the Antietam battlefield.

They had rested no longer than an hour when there was the tooting of horns and the beating of drums, accompanied by the order, "Attention battalion, forward march." Silently the weary men fell into line and moved on, passing artillery in great quantities posted on either side of the road. They marched through the night until the glowing in the eastern sky gave notice of the coming day. Day broke, and still on they marched. Soon the sound of church bells reached their ears.[2] At 6 a.m. they halted a short while for breakfast but were quickly on the march again by 7 a.m. At 11 a.m. they arrived at Rockville and stopped, very much fatigued. They halted near a beautiful grove of trees that bordered the Montgomery County[3] fairground. There they stacked their arms and lay down in the grass to rest. It was a beautiful setting for a camp with a splendid spring nearby, and firewood was very plentiful. Most of the other troops did not arrive until later that afternoon, allowing the 107th to have their pick of a campground.[4]

Word was passed around that they would camp there overnight unless the enemy, which was just to the north, began to stir things up. Some of the men went into a neighboring field and brought back some green corn. They boiled it and had it for dinner. Later a report came down the line that there were no Rebels this side of the Potomac, and that the regiment was to march back to their old camp near Washington. The men didn't believe the report, thinking maybe they have been fooled, and there will be no battle. In any case, they were now much rested and looked forward to a good night's sleep in their beautiful surroundings.

The evening passed peacefully, and they were up early for breakfast. Immediately after eating, they were on the road again. Marching through Rockville, they commented on how much it looked like Horseheads, one of the villages back home, a pretty little place that looked quite thrifty. Much of the country they had passed through since crossing the river was nice farming country and looked more inviting than the Virginia countryside they had seen. This could have been easily true, for the Virginia they had seen was much devastated by Union and Confederate forces fighting back and forth while Maryland was just beginning to experience the effects of war. They marched some two miles past Rockville and made camp. How lucky they were again, for this camp was in a pleasant spot on the side of a hill. The camp was nearly surrounded by woods with a cool breeze helping to lessen the heat. A small stream ran nearby, and along its banks they found apples and large juicy grapes in abundance.[5] Word came that the 107th and the 13th New Jersey were, by Special Order No. 3 issued by General McClellan on September 6, put into Gordon's 3rd Brigade of William's 1st Division, Bank's 2nd Army Corps of the Army of the Virginia.[6] They were confused about what this meant: was it temporary and were they to be a reserve unit? One thing was for sure: they weren't marching back to Washington, and they weren't going to settle any place soon.

The next day, Tuesday, September 9, orders were given at noon to strike tents and be prepared to march. They were soon underway, sharing the road with artillery, ambulances, and other infantry units. They were put through a quick step, and because of the congestion on the road, soon left it to march through cornfields, woods, and farmyards. At 3:30 p.m. they stopped at Middlebrook, having marched ten miles without rest. It had been a tough march, and many men had fallen out, but some did well, having by now become more accustomed to the marching. Whether it was only for practice, or the officers thought the enemy was near, the troops were, without notice, formed into a line of battle. The men in the 107th had never seen such an imposing sight, twenty thousand men, by their estimates, drawn up into a long line ready for battle. Even the ambulances were in readiness to carry off any wounded. Here, along with the 13th New Jersey, they joined the rest of the regiments in their new brigade: the 27th Indiana, the 3rd Wisconsin, and the 2nd Massachusetts. They were now in General Gordon's 3rd Brigade of General A.S. Williams' 1st Division of the 12th Army Corps. The Rebels never appeared, and the men went into camp and built fires for supper. Mutton was fried and eaten, and with hardtack washed down with coffee, it made a good supper.[7]

During the march, the men suffered from the suffocating clouds of dust, and the march had been a severe test for them. The sun at times shown with intense heat, and the sweat ran in streams from their faces. Two men in the 13th New Jersey were so overcome by the heat that they died. As the day progressed, men began falling out one by one and were carried into the hospitals, which began to line the road along which the army marched. Many of the men were too proud and spirited to own up that they were tired out and would keep up as long as they could, but now and then one would reel blindly forward and fall senseless in the road. Covered with sweat and dust, the man would be dragged to the side of the road, a comrade left with him.[8]

The veteran regiments of their brigade were quite amused by the green soldiers of the 13th New Jersey and the 107th New York. These two fully manned regiments had almost twice as many men as the other three older regiments combined. Their new uniforms, enormous knapsacks, and excess of equipment were in stark contrast to the well-worn uniforms and half empty knapsacks of their newfound comrades.[9]

Roasted corn was added to the breakfast menu the next morning. The men were pleased at getting accustomed to camp life and providing for themselves. They were well satisfied with their regular fare and how they were able to supplement it through foraging. After breakfast they took up their march at 9 a.m. Rumors said that Frederick City was their destination. They marched all day and camped that night in a field near Damascus, having done by their estimate a march of twelve miles. Much of their march this day was through forests of chestnut trees. All in all, the whole regiment was totally exhausted.

On Thursday morning, September 11, they were up early, had their breakfast, and were on the march. They had gone only two miles when they halted and were ordered to rest. The farmers along the way suffered much because of the advancing troops. Any crops growing near their path of march, fowls, and an occasional pig were stowed away by them. This was against orders, and the men of the 107th resisted the temptation, though they could not blame others for adding to their food supply.[10] A short time later, they turned into the woods that lined the road and formed a line of battle. It was obvious that the Rebels were not too far off. Colonel Diven told the men that they were nearer a fight than they had yet been. As they held their line of battle, large numbers of artillery and infantry passed hurriedly by. Corporal Arthur Fitch of Company B counted forty-four pieces of artillery. Once the traffic had passed, they moved up the road another half mile and went into camp. Shortly thereafter their mail was delivered, but otherwise the rest of day and night passed uneventfully.

When morning came, they were off again, marching towards Frederick. They had only gone three or four miles when they halted and formed a line of battle; again, a false alarm. There was no doubt, however, that they were getting closer to the Rebel forces and a possible confrontation.[11] During that day, September 12, 1862, General Order 129 was issued by the Adjutant General's Office, changing the designation of the Second Army Corps of Virginia to the Twelfth Army Corps of the Potomac.[12] The regiment passed through a small village, probably Mt. Airy, and after a halt of an hour moved on. During the halt, two men in another regiment were caught trying to steal some ducks. They were arrested and placed at the rear of the column with guards made up of men from the 107th. The troops were now marching along the railroad tracks of the Baltimore and Ohio Railroad. Off in the distance to the south-east, they could see Sugar Loaf Mountain. Again, it was a very fatiguing march, and many of the men were hard pressed to keep up. They halted just east of Ijamsville, some ten miles from Frederick, and went into camp.

The night was calm, and after a good sleep, they were up early in the morning. They marched through Ijamsville at about 8 a.m., still following the railroad tracks. For the first time they could hear the reports of artillery in the west; a battle was not too far off.[13] They marched rapidly toward the Monocacy River, and because there was no bridge, were forced to ford it. The water was warm and only knee-deep, so it was no hardship. Some in the older regiments, even with badly worn shoes and tattered pants, did not flinch,[14] but to the 107th New York and the 13th New Jersy, it was not welcomed. Again, they heard the firing of the advanced units of Burnside's Corps as they were driving the rear guard of the retreating enemy from the passes of the Catoctin Mountains about five miles west of the city.[15] In the distance they could see puffs of smoke rise over the hills at each discharge. On they marched, straight into the southern fringe of Frederick with the 107th band playing "Hail Columbia" and "Yankee Doodle." The music received uproarious cheers from the citizens. At noon they halted for an hour or two. They thought that it was a very pretty place, somewhat larger than Elmira. Union sentiment was obvious with Union flags flying from many houses.[16]

The ground on which the Twelfth Corps made its camp that day was the same that had been occupied by Confederate General A.P. Hill's troops the day before. During the time they were making camp, two members of the 107th's brigade, Private W.A. Mitchell and First Sergeant John M. Bloss of Company F of the 27th Indiana, found a piece of paper wrapped around three cigars. After examining it, they decided to take it to Colonel Colegrove, commanding officer of their regiment. He examined it and saw that it was a copy of a general order dated September 10, 1862 issued by General Lee of the Confederate Army to General D.H. Hill detailing the movements of the Rebel army over the next few days. Colegrove immediately delivered it to Colonel Pitman, General Williams' adjutant general. The order had been signed by Colonel Chilton, General Lee's adjutant general. Ironically Pitman recognized the signature as Chilton's because he had served with Pitman prior to the war and was familiar with his handwriting. Pitman, accompanied by Colegrove, took the order directly to General McClellan.[17] Within an hour, troops began moving toward the Rebel army. However, the Twelfth Corps, which was to remain in reserve, spent the night at their present camp.[18]

The next morning, Friday, September 14, was a memorable day. The weather was beautiful, and they passed through a delightful countryside. The regiment, although ready to march at four, didn't move with the rest of the Corps until eight a.m. because of the congestion on the road.[19] Heavy firing was heard again to the west over the mountains in the direction toward which they began to march.[20] The road west from Frederick was wide enough for two or three wagons abreast, but it was now completely choked with the ammunition and provision wagons of the advance regiments. Consequently, they left the main road and marched through cornfields, across meadows, and over fields of full-grown wheat, trampling down acre after acre of bountiful crops. Nearing the top of the mountains, they heard the artillery and musketry on the mountain ridge beyond. Occasionally they could catch a glimpse of the lines of the Union troops as they moved up the slopes to assault the position of the enemy. Quickly they marched down one mountain and turned off by a circuitous route to the right, hoping to strike the enemy on the left flank. Before they could reach their position, it had already been carried by assault, and the enemy had disappeared into the darkness. The battle of South Mountain was over, and they moved on, counter marching west to the turnpike near Middletown, never stopping until after midnight.

It was a tedious and trying march; a slight rain fell almost constantly. There was much stopping and starting because the darkness made it difficult to know where they were going. This was more wearisome than steady marching would have been.[21] Before darkness fell, they passed by a log house that had been used as a hospital. In its yard were several soldiers' bodies, and a heap of arms and legs were stacked beneath a window where they had been thrown out after amputation.[22] The hard marching began to take its toll; officers and enlisted men fell out of the ranks in squads. They had been on the road for twenty-two consecutive hours, most of the time climbing over rocks and through brush on the mountainside. At one a.m., the regiments, very much fatigued, moved off to the sloping mountain side near the turnpike east of where it passes the summit of South Mountain and were soon asleep.

Two thirds of the 107th, also greatly fatigued from marching all day and most of the night, had fallen out during the night's march. In small groups they made their own camps, building fires, drying themselves out, and making supper. Afterwards they stretched out their blankets and went to sleep. The next morning, they rose at four o'clock, ate their breakfast and were soon on their way to rejoin the rest of the regiment. It took them a good hour's march to catch up, and on the way, they passed a great many Rebel prisoners who had been captured during the previous day's battle. The prisoners looked very dirty, and their clothes were ragged. They found the main camp of the 107th surrounded by many other regiments. By eight a.m., the stragglers had all appeared, and the regiment, now intact, was on the march again toward Turner's Gap. They marched in the direction the Rebels had retreated, crossing over the battlefield. The wagon trains again occupied the road while they marched in the field next to it. For the first time, they saw dead Rebels lying along the road, covered by old clothes and leaves. The sight left a strong impression on the men, one that would soon be made worse by the fighting they would experience in the next several days.

The Rebels must have left the area in a terrific hurry, for large quantities of blankets, clothes, and knapsacks had been left along the road. Their wounded occupied every house and barn along the way. Further along, they passed a good many more prisoners, all looking very tough. About three p.m., they began to hear a continuous cheering along the line behind them. Word passed along the ranks that General McClellan was coming. He soon overtook them, and as he rode by with numerous other officers and his bodyguards, they got a good look at him. No question it was he; he looked just like his picture. Their route that day took them through Crampton's Gap and Pleasant Valley. They were very much impressed with the beauty of the valley. Soon they marched into the town of Boonsboro, where the citizens told them that the Rebels had gone through in a hurry on their retreat. They marched about eight miles and went into camp to the west of Boonsboro.[23] Their camp was on the Philip Pry Farm, near the junction of the Boonsboro-Keedysville-Hagerstown Pike, which was the road that led to the "upper" bridge over Antietam Creek.[24] In Boonsboro the churches and barns had been converted into hospitals. They were filled with the wounded of Reno's and Hooker's corps who had been engaged at Turner's Gap. There were also hospitals with Rebel doctors caring for their wounded.

While they were in camp, General Burnside rode by, trailed by his numerous and showy cavalcade. As was the custom whenever senior officers appeared, the men cheered loudly. A little later, General McClellan appeared again, and the men went wild. They were glad to see these officers, and also glad because of the small victory that had been won the day before.[25]

That evening Dr. Flood bandaged Colonel Van Valkenburgh's feet, as he had been doing for the past week. The colonel's feet were badly swollen from fatigue and hours in the saddle. That evening the swelling was so severe that the Colonel could not stand up. The slower pace of the next day allowed the swelling to subside, and he would not be so terribly troubled by it during the violent activity of the 17th.[26]

The next day, Tuesday, September 16, the 107th was still in camp at ten a.m. when they were suddenly told to fall in and prepare for battle. During their breakfast, several Rebel shells had fallen into the nearby camp of the 23rd New York, another Elmira area regiment. No one was hurt, but one of the shells did destroy a stack of guns.[27] In the distance they could hear the sounds of cannon and musketry very plainly. They moved rapidly in the direction of those sounds, crossing a hill from where they could see on the plain below some 30,000 or 40,000 Union troops ready for battle. The regiment was placed in line with the rest of the brigade and remained stationary. The momentary rest was welcome as the heat of the day had become oppressive. The battle seemed to be just three or four miles in front of them, and they could see where balls and shells had fallen that morning on the ground where they now stood. A dead color bearer was carried past them to the rear. Still, they remained motionless with their guns loaded. After a while they were on the march again, and late in the day they made camp on the former campsites of the 1st Army Corps near the Cost farm close to the "upper" bridge.[28] It was in the Cost farmhouse that General Mansfield had his supper that evening.[29]

At about ten o'clock, an hour or so after it had begun to rain, the officers went among the tents and in subdued tones woke their men. The regiment was given orders to march and told not to do any loud talking or to make a fire. They marched through a slow and steady drizzle in the direction of the firing heard earlier that day.[30] Lt. Benjamin Wilson, Co. I, who was ill and had been under the care of Surgeon Flood for several days, was resting in a nearby house when the regiment moved out, and he was not aware until the next morning that they had moved.[31]

They marched about two hours, crossed over the upper bridge spanning Antietam Creek, and soon heard the scattered rattle of musketry in the darkness to the south of them. At midnight, just southwest of Smoketown, they turned into a field on the George Line farm and lay down in the damp clover on their arms. They, along with the rest of the 12th Corps, lay in front of a narrow strip of woods that ran east to west parallel to their line and were but only a short distance to the north of the Rebel regiments who were to confront them in the morning. General Hooker's troops lay on the other side of the woods off to the west but a short distance.[32] A cold rain chilled them and threw a gloom over their spirits, already sober at the prospect of the bloody scenes that awaited them in the morning. Still, dead tired, and the rain having stopped, they fell fast asleep.[33]

The jarring sound of cannon fire roused them at daybreak. The morning brought a sky absent of clouds but with a foggy mist present. As the morning wore on, the mist would break up and the sun would shine brightly. It was approaching six a.m. when General Hooker's I Corps began the attack on the Rebel army by advancing south down between Hagerstown Pike and the Smoketown Road. The 107th regiment, along with others of the Third Brigade and the remainder of the Twelfth Corps, formed quickly, and there was no time for breakfast. It was after six a.m. when they were placed in column by company and moved forward in quick time. Their brigade was in the center, with Crawford's brigade on the right and Greene's division on the left. The firing in front was very sharp both from infantry and artillery. They moved across an open field, past the George Line Farm on their left and then through a corn field. Once through the cornfield, the 107th came to a fence along the Smoketown Road. The fence had an opening, but it was only big enough to allow a column of four

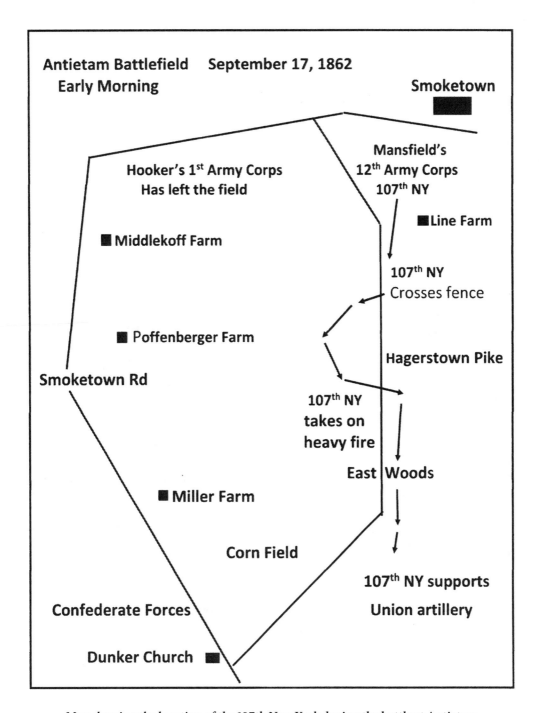

**Antietam Battlefield September 17, 1862**
**Early Morning**

**Smoketown**

**Hooker's 1st Army Corps**
**Has left the field**

**Mansfield's**
**12th Army Corps**
**107th NY**

**Line Farm**

**Middlekoff Farm**

**107th NY**
**Crosses fence**

**Poffenberger Farm**

**Hagerstown Pike**

**Smoketown Rd**

**107th NY**
**takes on**
**heavy fire**

**East Woods**

**Miller Farm**

**Corn Field**

**107th NY supports**

**Union artillery**

**Confederate Forces**

**Dunker Church**

Map showing the location of the 107th New York during the battle at Antietam.

abreast to pass through. The regiment was ordered to pull down the fence to make the opening larger. However, the fence was very strong, and it resisted their efforts. Colonel Diven then ordered the men to climb over the fence. They were nearly across when they were ordered to face left march to the edge of woods in front of them and form a line of battle. They marched south, half of the regiment on either side of the fence. When they reached the lower edge of the woods, there was an opening in the fence. At this point they were about 450 yards north and slightly west of the famous "East Woods" through which the Smoketown Road passed. To their right was the 13th New Jersey, and beyond them almost to the Hagerstown Pike was the J. Poffenberger farm. In front of them advancing toward the "Cornfield" were, from left to right, the 27th Indiana, the 3rd Wisconsin, and the 2nd Massachusetts.[34]

Here they were halted and took their positions in reserve of the veteran regiments of their brigade. Shells flew over their heads taking limbs from the trees, and they moved nervously around trying to avoid the screaming missiles. Then they were ordered to lie down and remained so for 15 minutes.[35] At that time, General Mansfield came back toward them from the front where he had gone to observe the position of Hooker's men. As he rode to the head of the regiment, he said to the men, "Boys, we have got them where we want them; stick to them today and we will drive them into the Potomac." Every man gripped his gun a little tighter and resolved to stand by the old general. General Mansfield and a portion of his staff rode forward to a rise of ground about one hundred and fifty yards in front of the regiment. Almost immediately, he was struck and fell from his horse. It appeared that he might have been struck by a bullet fired by a sniper concealed in David Miller's barn west of the Hagerstown Pike.[36] Colonel Van Valkenburgh called to Lt. Colonel Diven that General Mansfield had been shot and to send Dr. Flood to his aid. Dr. Flood reached the general, south of them at the north end of the "East Woods." He knelt beside Mansfield, cut open his coat, inserted his finger in the wound, and found that the bullet had lodged deep in his body. The general was carefully placed on two blankets and carried from the field through the ranks of Company F of the 107th by six soldiers of the 125th Pennsylvania Regiment. They took him to the Line house in the rear with Dr. Flood walking along beside him.[37]

The men laid down behind the fence with the fire from muskets and artillery in the front of them. Colonel Diven's sleeve was torn by a shell fragment, but the regiment was not in any immediate danger. At this time, the Rebels had been driven from the "East Woods" in front of them and beyond the cornfield. The Rebels continued to retreat in a southwest direction and retreated into the "West Woods," which were on the other side of the Hagerstown Pike and at whose southern tip was located the Dunker Church. Wounded Union soldiers in great numbers began to file back past them. As the enemy left the wood, General Gordon told the men to begin cheering and advance.

With Colonel Van Valkenburgh in the lead, waving his hat and cheering the men on,[38] they entered a ploughed field and moved double quick through it. They raced across the cornfield and into the meadow beyond it. Sergeant Jessie Lewis of Company C carried the regimental banner as they passed through the meadow and were subjected to a galling fire from the "West Woods." The men, whether from fright or not being used the fast pace, became winded. They moved straight toward the "East Woods" and entered them as the Rebel artillery found them in their sights. Two shells exploded within the regiment's lines as they passed into the woods.

Captain Colby at the head of his company heard the scream of the men and saw them fall but pressed on toward the woods not knowing who had been hit or what became of them.[39] The second shell struck Private Cyrus Covill in the head, killing him instantly. It had exploded as it passed Private Stephen Edwards, causing a horrible wound on the back of his neck and head. Edwards would survive his injuries and re-enlist in the regiment just before the Atlanta Campaign. Ironically, he would die of chronic diarrhea at Savannah, GA.

Fragments from the first shell did the most damage. A large fragment struck Willie Everett of Company G, a lad of only sixteen, in the legs.[40] He collapsed to the ground and began to scream in a demonical way. His screaming could be heard by others in the regiment above the roaring of the artillery and the rolling of the musketry.[41] He was even heard by men in the nearby 13th New Jersey. None of them had ever heard such unearthly yelling. To them it sounded as if it came from a lost soul in purgatory, and it made their blood run cold. Several of them hurried over to the edge of the woods where he lay. What they saw almost turned their stomachs. Both of Willie's legs had been torn off near the knees. His feet and ankles were gone completely, and the bones of his legs protruded from the lacerated flesh. They turned quickly away with pallid faces, but one of them asked Willie what he could do for him. "Water, water, water!" moaned Willie. The soldier reached for his canteen and handed it to him. "No, no," he said, in a weak voice, as the soldier held it to his lips. "No, not—drink. Pour—head——." Willie's head was bursting with the fever of the terrible anguish he was suffering, but he managed to thank the soldier for the water. It was obvious to everyone there that the young boy did not have much longer to live. At that point, the 13th New Jersey was ordered to advance into the woods. As they did so, it occurred to one of them that the poor boy that they had just left would probably be buried in the battlefield cemetery in an unknown grave.[42] To this day, poor Willie Everett's final resting place is known only but to God.

Others killed by fragments of the same shell included John Kallahar, who died from the loss of his foot, and Jesse Stevens, whose right leg was badly mangled. Alonzo Johnson from Thurston in Steuben County was wounded badly in the leg and would die after it was necessary to amputate it. Following the operation, he went into shock and developed lockjaw. During his ordeal, a friend, Ambrose Mosher who was a fifer in Company G, tried to comfort him. Mosher had also been wounded in the right arm below the elbow.[43] Nelson Robinson, badly wounded by the same shell, would linger on until December 13, when he would die in the hospital at Smoketown, just north of the battlefield. Others who were badly wounded included Amos Fisk whose arm was broken, Rufus Henderson who was wounded in the left leg and shoulder, and Volkert Benedict who was sent home and remained sick in a hospital in Elmira from October 29, 1862, until after the end of the war. Tyler Paris was one of the lucky ones. His wounds were minor, and he returned to service.

Lt. Ezra Gleason suffered a leg wound from the shell. After being hit, he crawled away as far as he could and sat down behind a large white oak. While he was sitting there, a cannon ball made a direct hit on the tree, and it shivered from its roots to its top. Years later, upon visiting the battlefield, he was able to locate this very tree and spot the scar where the nearly overgrown cannonball had imbedded itself in the trunk.[44]

The 107th passed through the "East Woods" in a north to south direction. Emerging from the woods, they found themselves on the edge of the Smoketown Road just north of Dunker Church. They crossed over the fence along the side of the road and lay down in the road behind the fence on the other side. They immediately came under fire from an artillery battery. Musket and artillery fire were flying briskly over their heads. Quickly they began to return fire, being somewhat protected by a small knoll. A shell struck their banner while it was lying on the ground and tore it to pieces.[45] Afterwards the color bearer Sergeant Jesse Lewis, who was injured by the same shell, raised it to show the rest of the regiment, knowing well that they were watching it.[46]

While in this position, Corporal Asa Brownell of Company F was wounded in the hand,[47] and Private Theodore Smith of the same company was hit by a solid shot that tore away his ankle and foot. Smith lay there some time before being carried back through the woods. The rest of the regiment remained in the Smoketown Road for fifteen or twenty minutes, and then were ordered back in front of and toward the southern tip of the "East Woods" where they would protect their brigade's left flank. Next to them in line was the 27th Indiana, then the 3rd Wisconsin, 2nd Massachusetts, and finally the 13th New Jersey on the other flank. They were facing directly across the open field toward the Hagerstown Pike and the "West Woods" to where the Confederates had previously retreated. By this time, Hooker's 1st Corps had left the field and moved north, and Sumner's 2nd Corps was advancing from behind them through the "East Woods" toward the enemy in the "West Woods."

While they had been in the road, three batteries of artillery had been placed in their vicinity and in front of the "East Woods." They were ordered to support Capt. George W. Cothran's Battery M of the New York 1st Light Artillery. Amid heavy fire, they counter marched to in front of it and positioned themselves. They lay there flat on their faces and awaited the possibility of Confederate forces attempting to overrun the battery. They were in a defensive position, unable to fire their weapons. Much of the time, shell and shot flew rapidly over them, and occasionally one struck close to them. Capt. Colby said that he "laid rather close, in fact tried to get as thin as possible."[48] At times the musketry was fearful over their heads, and the men received injuries. It wasn't just them men who were in danger; three artillery horses standing near the battery were killed either by shell or mini ball.[49]

There are conflicting reports regarding regiment's support of the batteries in front of the woods. The formal reports place them in support of Cothran at his rear. Other reports place half of them in his front and half in his rear, and still another version places their left half in his rear with another battery behind their right half not more than 15 rods away.[50] None of the battle maps show them any place other than in the rear of Cothran's battery. However, what was unofficially reported in letters by several officers and enlisted men illustrates that the damage done to the men by artillery fire is undisputed.

Colonel Van Valkenburgh ordered Lieutenant Colonel Diven to search out General Gordon, commander of their brigade, and inform him as to their present position. General Gordon was not aware of the circumstances that brought them to support Cothran's battery. Diven found Gordon, who was in the process of reforming their brigade into a new position. He told Diven that he desired that the 107th be included. When Diven returned to the regiment's position, he found that a battery of Napoleon guns had been positioned to the rear and right of them. However, the fire of this battery was carrying over a portion of the regiment and Cothran's battery. Under these circumstances, the regiment could not move, and Diven hastened back to inform General Gordon. Diven found Gordon amid a great deal of artillery fire with the tree bark flying as though lightning was striking the trees. Gordon advised Diven to let the regiment remain where it was.

When Diven returned to the regiment, he found that it had moved off to one side thus avoiding the fire of the Napoleon guns.[51] Diven was told that the movement was necessary because several of the men had been hit by a defective charge from the Napoleons. In fact, a shell from these guns had exploded prematurely right over men in Companies F and B, which were positioned next to each other.[52] The explosion terribly wounded Private Harvey Harrington in the left side. He would die early the next day, just past midnight in a field hospital. Private John E. Hoag and Corporal William Hurd of Elmira were both wounded in the thigh by the same shell. Hurd, Private George Davis, and Private James Mitchell were also hit by fragments from the same shell and ended up in the Frederick hospital. Others who received minor wounds were Privates Charlie Terwilliger, Elijah Coles, Amos Decker, and George Kilmer.

After a while, the action quieted down. It was during this time that Capt. William Fox called out to a sergeant of his company, Michael Cowley, and asked him how he liked the fight. In his Irish brogue, Cowley replied, "Och murther captain, I woould rather be sittin in your father's kitchen a talkin wid Mary, that I wud."[53]

As the enemy troops in the "West Woods" had nearly ceased firing, General Greene, who was situated to the left of the 107th's line, sent for Colonel Van Valkenburgh. He commanded the colonel to send two companies of skirmishers into the "West Woods" to determine the enemy's position. The colonel asked for volunteers from companies I and E, the only companies that had ever drilled in skirmish. The captains of these companies, Captain Colby of I Company and Captain Morgan of E Company, asked that all who desired to go to "Fall in." About one third of each company responded, making about 60 in the line, with Company E on the right. The field in front of them was thickly strewn with the dead, both blue and gray. "Forward, quick time march!" was the order given and up through the field as they went to the Hagerstown Turnpike.[54] As the companies moved past the remainder of the regiment, they were loudly cheered.[55] They moved quickly toward the nearly quiet woods, not knowing what to expect. Would they awaken the fire of the enemy? The road ahead had been cut through the hill and was about ten feet deep. The dead were piled so thickly in this cut that that they could not reach the opposite side without stepping on them. Once on the other side of the road, they formed their line again and received the order "Double quick." They started for the woods about 60 rods away. Along the edge of the woods were piles of fence rails, but the men did not realize their significance. Forward they rushed until they were 20 rods from the rail piles. Suddenly thunder and lightning erupted from behind them. "Fall back!" was the order from Capt. Morgan as the bullets began to whistle around them. The men turned and quickly began to retrace their steps back to their lines. Stumbling over bodies, they crossed the road and raced down the hill toward their batteries. When the terrible firing had begun, it seemed that the whole Confederate army was concentrated behind those rail fences. The men who were left behind guarding the battery were about to give the skirmishers up for lost, when they appeared out of the cut of the road and moved quickly back to their starting point. When they had almost reached their guns, they were told to lie down, and they did so with amazing haste. Immediately the two batteries opened fire on the Johnnies who had followed them across the road. The roar of the guns and the screech of the shot and shell, grape and canister were indescribable. When the guns became so hot that it was dangerous to load them, the men ceased firing. As the smoke cleared, they could see no live Johnnies but many more dead ones than when they were out there. Amazingly they had not lost a man, killed or wounded, during their excursion. Private Robert Ganoung rose to his feet and discovered that his hearing was gone. Further investigation showed two bullet holes in his cap and several in his dress coat, which was also missing its left skirt. The stock of his Springfield was gone, and looking around, all he could find was an Enfield of which he quickly took possession. Lieutenant Rutter's sword had been bent by a mini ball. Some of the Rebel firepower reached the men who had remained behind. Sergeant Amos Rogers of Company F had to replace his rifle because one of the Rebel bullets had hit its lock and made it unfit for firing.[56] The rebel artillery had opened up once the union batteries had begun. A Rebel shell landed in the midst of Company I, which had just returned, killing Daniel Corwin and wounding Sergeant Johnny Brown, taking away part of his foot. A fragment of the shell also destroyed the blade of Capt. Colby's sword. The injured men were carried off the field and through to the other side of the "East Woods."[57]

During this part of the battle, the regiment was in awe of Captain Cothran, who directed the fire of his battery in full view of the enemy. Bullets flew all around, but none came close to him or his horse. Lieutenant Colonel Diven and Colonel Van Valkenburgh had left their horses in the rear as they were advised to do by their superior officers. However, they wished they had their mounts with them, seeing what a great, though dangerous, sight the mounted officers presented.

Captain Clark of Company H was hit in the chest by a mini ball, and it was feared to be a mortal wound. He was moved back into the "East Woods," and eventually north of the battlefield to a hospital on the George Line farm.[58] Other men from the regiment remained closer to the battlefield in a hospital set up at the home of Samuel Poffenberger. This farm was located behind the "East Woods" and a substantial spring flowed there.[59] This hospital is thought to have been the place where Clara Barton, of Red Cross fame, nursed soldiers during and after the battle.[60] Pvt. Theodore Smith, who had lost the lower part of his leg, was taken there. Smith was carried into the house already filled to capacity with wounded. To make room for him, the stove was dumped out of doors, and he was given a bed on the brick floor in front of the old-fashioned brick fireplace. He was next moved to the barn of E.H. Hoffman, just east of the Line farm. Three days after his injury, his lower leg was amputated to prevent further infection and allow for proper healing.[61]

Later in the afternoon, at about 3 p.m., the battery's guns became much too heated to continue, and their ammunition was exhausted. Because of this, the men retired to the rear of the "East Woods." The 107th followed behind them and located themselves in the vicinity of the Samuel Poffenberger house.[62] It was the first opportunity that the regiment had to relax and to fix themselves a well-deserved meal. However, they were prepared to return to the field if it were necessary, as they remained close behind the "East Woods." They had left a great number of Rebels lying dead and wounded on the field. Many were begging to be removed from the field, but there was little that could be done for them. Captain Colby observed one Rebel with the side of his face, including one eye and one ear, blown off trying to eat a hard cracker with the uninjured side of his face.[63]

While the regiment was there behind the "East Woods," they were found by Lieut. Wilson of Company I. He had awakened that morning to find them gone and had hitched a ride in an ambulance to the upper part of the battlefield. He had searched for them but was unable to find them until they were pulled off the line late in the afternoon. On his arrival, Captain Colby, who by now was totally fatigued, turned over command of the company to Wilson until the next morning.[64]

Early in the evening Adjutant Hull Fanton was looking for the wounded Captain Clark of Company H, the company that he had raised. He came across Private Patrick Callaghan of Company D in a hospital on the George Line farm near where the 107th had halted the night before.[65] He was lying in front of the farmhouse surrounded by perhaps two hundred severely wounded men. One of Callaghan's legs had been shot away, and he was in great pain. He recognized Adjutant Fanton, and in his agony appealed for help. Fanton stopped and attempted to comfort him, but there was little that he could do. Continuing his search, Fanton found Captain Clark who, though badly wounded, looked likely to survive. A bullet remained in the left side of his chest but had not punctured his lung.[66] Fanton continued to check on poor Callaghan and at about 6 o'clock found that he was dead.

On the porch the surgeons were busy with their work. A little footpath led from the pump to one of the entrances of the house. Down this footpath coursed a stream of blood from the many amputations and operations being performed, and next to the operating table was a pile of arms and legs reaching almost to its top. In another part of the yard, the adjutant found the body of Private Jesse Stevens of Company G, who had also died that afternoon. All through that night, the wounded were brought to the hospital. In this same hospital lay Private Harvey Harrington of Company B, who had been struck in the left side by an artillery fragment. Very late that evening, Private Patrick Traynor of the same company went to visit his comrade. Traynor tried to comfort Harrington, who recognized him and said, "Pat, I can't live." Traynor tried to keep up his courage, telling him that he would live. It would be after midnight when Traynor left his comrade, and later he was told that it was only five minutes after they both said goodbye that Harrington had passed away.[67]

That evening the regiment remained in the vicinity of the battlefield at the rear of the "East Woods" where they had retired that afternoon. Most of the men lay without any shelter or blankets to cover them.[68] They were ready to resume the fight if called upon. Captain William F. Fox slept in a nearby barn that was also being used as a hospital. The barn was full of the wounded, and there was no one to tend to the wounded and dying men. Amid the groans of so many, no one heeded nor saw the dying men whose lives ebbed slowly away. In the morning, the surgeon walked among the sufferers, and now and then he would stop and shake his head as he came upon another body of one who no longer needed his help.[69]

During that first night, Adjutant Fanton, having an occasion to go down to the pump, counted over fifty ambulances waiting to be unloaded at the Line farm hospital. The cries and groans of anguish that ascended from them would never leave his memory. The next day he was again searching for the dead and wounded of the regiment. Walking through the "East Woods," he came upon the body of Cyrus Covill. Fanton attached a piece of paper to his coat giving his name, company, and regiment. Afterward while the regiment was encamped at Antietam Ford south of the battlefield, Fanton looked for his place of burial. He found none and assumed correctly that Covill was resting among the unknown dead.[70]

After a rainy night, the sun rose bright the next morning, and the Confederates put out a flag of truce under the pretext of collecting their wounded and dead. They kept out their pickets to prevent any close inspection of their lines and were preparing to move their army back across the Potomac into Virginia. At the time, some men of the 107th had an opportunity to survey the battlefield. What they saw were former fields of grain and corn now piled high with the carcasses of dead horses and hundreds of human bodies, the stench from which was unbearable.[71]

The rain and hot sun had caused rapid decomposition of the dead; bodies bloated to unnatural and frightful proportions in every shape and posture, their mouths open, their eyeballs glaring wildly, their countenances presenting every phase of feeling and passion predominant at death. One grasped a musket as if intent on killing; another with uplifted eyes and hands seemed to be invoking God's mercy on his soul. Many were torn into shreds by bursting shells; some were headless, limbless, with every conceivable manner of wound. Many of the wounded still lay upon the field crying for water, while others begged to be killed so as to end their suffering.[72]

Corporal Nathan Dykeman wandered down through the southern tip of the "East Woods" to where the Smoketown Road met the Hagerstown Pike. In front of him lay the Dunker Church that was to become a famous landmark of the battle. In the clearing around it lay remnants of the battle. Dykeman ventured inside the church and found his souvenir of this battle. He removed the large bible from its resting place, placed it under his coat, and returned to camp. It would be over thirty years before the bible would return to its rightful place.

Other souvenirs were collected that day. One of the cavalry men who was part of the party showing the Union flag of truce brought back a Rebel cavalry saber and presented it to Captain Colby, who also picked up a saber bayonet from the battlefield. Colby was able to send them home to his father with a civilian friend of Lt. Rutters of the same company. In addition to the sabers, Capt. Colby took possession of a young horse in poor condition; it could eventually be restored to good health. It was his intention to send the horse back to Corning for his own private use. Colby also was repulsed by the awful sights to be seen after the battle: Rebel soldiers who after day or two in the hot sun had turned so dark that they could be mistaken for Black soldiers. Corpses were everywhere, so much so that the men became so used to their presence that lying down to sleep among them would not have been a concern.[73]

In the afternoon of the 18th, General A.S. Williams received orders to march the 12th Army Corps from the battlefield and to occupy Maryland Heights.[74]

The following day, dead Confederates still lay in piles where they had been cut down by the Union artillery. When buried, they were placed in long trenches that contained 50 to 100 men. The Union regiments also went about burying their dead comrades. A hasty trench not over two feet deep was all the grave they could give them. They would place the body in the grave with the head resting on the dead soldier's cartridge box and his blanket as a shroud. With a rough tenderness, they would shovel the hard, gravelly soil over the upturned face of the soldier with comment and remarks upon his life or fate. A piece of board was driven into the ground for a head stone with his name and regiment painted on it. Officers usually fared somewhat better, being buried in a rude coffin in a larger, more carefully dug grave.[75]

The scene at the Line farm had not changed from the previous day. People from the nearby, small country towns continued to arrive with food and other items to help in the care of the wounded. These good people, both Confederate and Union, had been advised that government supplies had failed to reach the army, and there was a great need. Foods such as mashed potatoes, fried ham, and chicken and beef sandwiches were collected and loaded into wagons. The roads leading to the battlefield were filled with all types of vehicles carrying needed goods to the hospitals that had been set up in the various farms adjacent to the battlefield. The Line farm was a stark contrast from its status prior to the battle. What had been a large farmhouse surrounded by a beautiful lawn, garden, barns, carriage houses, corn cribs, and haystacks was now a home deserted by its owners, heavy furniture removed, and every available space occupied by wounded and dying Union and Confederate soldiers. The house was used for operating purposes, and wo tables were set up in the yard with piles of severed hands, arms, and legs accumulating alongside of them. Local people went among the wounded still waiting for care and distributed sandwiches, which were quickly devoured.

Captain Clark was being attended to by Corporal Duryea of his company when one of the locals, a Mrs. Davis from nearby Funkstown but originally from Batavia in western New York, stopped to inquire how he was doing. Duryea identified the captain for Mrs. Davis and told her that he had been wounded in his left lung, and they feared mortally. She asked if there was anything she could do for him, and Captain Clark, able to speak, replied, "No." The ladies had given him a cup of tea, which was very refreshing, and he was now anxious to get to Hagerstown. Mrs. Davis replied that even if the captain could get to Hagerstown, it would be impossible to find a room because the hotels were overflowing with people from the North.

At that moment, Adjutant Fanton came by, and was told of Mrs. Davis' offer. He said to her that if it were possible, he would see that Captain Clark would be brought to her house the next day. He also informed her that she would be amply remunerated for anything she could do for his friend Chalmers Clark as he was the only child of very devoted parents who lived in Utica, N.Y. Mrs. Davis replied that remuneration of any kind was out of the question and seeing Mr. Davis off in the distance, waved to him to approach. She introduced him to Adjutant Fanton and told him of her invitation to Captain Clark, to which he gave immediate approval. The Davises then prepared to leave, taking with them about a hundred letters written by the soldiers.[76]

That same day in a little orchard just in the rear of the house, Adjutant Fanton had a trench dug. With the assistance of Chaplain Crane, he laid the two soldiers of the 107th to rest. They marked the spot with boards at the head and foot of the trench. Before their work was complete, the trench was enlarged, and a score or more were laid in it. Fanton would visit the farm in November 1864, and when he made an inquiry as to the grave, he was told that no disinterments had been made. He saw that the area had been ploughed and sown with some sort of grain.[77] To this day there is no record of where Stevens is buried, but there is a record of not one but two Patrick Callaghans from the 107th buried in the Antietam National Cemetery. One of the records lists a Patrick Collihan, but it undoubtedly was meant to be Callihan.[78]

Near Captain Clark, who was lying to the east of the house in the shade of a small shelter tent, Fanton found little John H. French, a private in Company A. He had a horrible wound in his back, and his cries had been heard through the last two nights and days, constantly calling for his mother. Early that morning, his cries grew fainter and fainter, and his suffering came to an end as he became yet another casualty of the 107th. Fortunately, his body was properly identified, and today his grave can be found in the National Cemetery. Howard Castor, a private in Company I, suffered a concussion resulting from a nearby shell explosion, and was unable to speak. His injuries would result in his discharge.

The regiment's losses on September 17 included 12 killed or mortally wounded, 29 wounded and later discharged, four deserted, and two captured. Eighteen men were wounded but able to return to duty. There were also other instances of desertion from the time they left near Fort Craig until after, but not including, the day of the battle. During this time through the day after the battle of Antietam, an additional eleven men deserted.

From the time the regiment started its march to Antietam until after the battle when it left for Maryland Heights, there were a total of thirteen desertions, two captured, fifty-one wounded, and nine dead, either killed in action or from wounds. Later three more men would die of wounds received at Antietam. These figures do not necessarily agree with the official count but were arrived at independently from analyzing other records.

Major Gabriel Smith, third in command of the regiment, wrote home about the battle and let it be known that even though his name was not mentioned anywhere in the official reports, "it must not be supposed that I failed in my duty." He went on to say that General Gordon mentioned no regimental officers except colonels in his report, unless they were killed or members of Congress. The *Elmira Weekly Gazette* repeated Major Smith's sentiments with the following statement: "Who so bloweth not his own horn, the same shall not be blowed, except he be a colonel or member of Congress."[79]

That afternoon the regiment marched from the battlefield, heading south through Sharpsburg. They left behind many wounded and dead, and a small number of officers and men to help care for them.

The next morning, as promised, Adjutant Fanton had Captain Erastus Clark of Company H transported in a wagon to the Davis house in Funkstown. Fanton had borrowed the wagon, complete with blankets and pillows, from a nearby farmer. On his arrival at the Davis home, Captain Clark appeared weak and could hardly speak above a whisper. He was given some brandy, which revived him. Mr. Davis had come straight home from his store to help in bringing the captain into the house. At that moment, an officer riding by dismounted and suggested that they carry the captain in a bed quilt if a stretcher could not be procured.

A cot had been set up in the parlor because Mrs. Davis had thought that it would be impossible to have him taken upstairs. However, the four men easily carried him into the house, and it was decided to carry him on up to the guest room. That afternoon, Adjutant Fanton, accompanied by his orderly, came by to check on Captain Clark's condition. Afterwards he went over to Hagerstown to telegraph the captain's father but was unable to do so because of the office was under army control and would not allow any private messages to be sent.

The Davis' family physician along with Surgeon Hewitt of the 107th kept a close watch on the captain's condition. His wound was probed for the mini ball, but neither was successful in extracting it.

On Tuesday evening, Mrs. Davis had a visitor. He told her that a friend, while at the Doyle's Hotel in Hagerstown, had met a lady from New York who was looking for her son who had been in the battle. She and her husband, a doctor, had visited various hospitals in the city but had been unsuccessful and now were heading to the battlefield to search for him. The visitor asked Mrs. Davis if she thought this couple might be the parents of Captain Clark. Mrs. Davis did not think so because the captain had told her that his father was not a physician and was too unwell to have made the journey to Maryland.

When Mr. Davis came home that evening, his wife told him of the incident. She stated that she could not get the lady out of her mind and wished that she could help her. She told her husband that they should invite her to stay at their house while she searched for her son. Adjutant Fanton was visiting Captain Clark that evening and overheard the Davis' conversation. He offered the use of his horse if Mr. Davis could get a buggy. Accordingly, they started out at about 8 p.m. The night was dark, and lightning flashed, and thunder rolled as they rode the two miles to the hotel. With the weather threatening, they had second thoughts about their errand but decided to continue.

When they arrived at the hotel, Adjutant Fanton asked to see the register. The desk clerk replied that they did not keep a register in times such as these. Fanton then asked if there were a gentleman and a lady from New York staying at the hotel who were looking for their son who had been in the Battle of Antietam. Mr. Doyle, the proprietor replied, "Yes, but I do not know their names. They came in the previous night and the doctor has gone to Sharpsburg as he could not find him in any of the city's hospitals. However, the lady did not go with him and is still in the hotel."

Following the proprietor's directions, they went up the stairs to the lady's room but received no answer to their knock. Then they went to the hotel's parlor where they saw a lady writing. As they entered, she looked up and to Mrs. Davis' amazement, the adjutant exclaimed, "Why, Mrs. Clark, is it possible this is you?"

"Hull Fanton! Where did you come from?" Rushing to him she threw her arms around his neck. "Oh, where is Chalmers? Is he badly wounded and dying on the battlefield?"

Mrs. Davis stood there dazed and blinded by tears running down her cheeks. She burst out, "No, no Mrs. Clark, he is at our house, in a bed, as comfortable as you could expect under the circumstances." Fanton introduced the two and explained that Mrs. Davis had played a major role in saving the captain's life.

Mrs. Clark was asked who, if not her husband, was traveling with her, and she replied that it was Dr. Trowbridge, their family physician from Syracuse. She added that he had gone to Sharpsburg to look for Chalmers. Although she didn't know when he might return, she would like to return with them immediately to Mrs.

Davis' home. They left for Funkstown, leaving a message behind for Dr. Trowbridge.

During their trip back to Funkstown, Mrs. Clark explained how she had heard the dreadful news about her son. As they drove up to the house, Mr. Davis met them at the door and was introduced to Mrs. Clark. Mr. Davis told them that he had told the captain that they had gone to Hagerstown to meet with a doctor and a lady that might be his mother. Because of this warning, the meeting between the captain and his mother did not excite him as much as they had feared.

The next morning while they were at breakfast, Dr. Trowbridge was announced. He examined the captain, who still could not speak above a whisper, and found him to be weak but in better health than he had expected.

On the following Friday, September 26, the adjutant, Mrs. Davis, Mrs. Clark, and Dr. Trowbridge drove over to the general hospital at Antietam, also visiting the battleground, Sharpsburg, General McClellan's headquarters, Keedysville, and Boonsboro before completing the circuit of thirty miles and returning home. They found many soldiers in the hospitals suffering from the necessities of life. Many were still lying on the ground with nothing but a shelter tent over them. They were suffering from the cold and the lack of good substantial food.

The battlefield was still littered with dead horses. They viewed the burnt out Mumma farm and the results of fighting in Sharpsburg. They returned home about 8 p.m. and found the captain, although a little impatient with their tardiness, had been entertained for several hours by Dr. Hewitt of the 107th.

The next day, Adjutant Fanton approached Mrs. Davis with a roll of money in his hands, saying that he would like to know what their bill was. Mrs. Davis refused to accept anything for the kindness she had shown the captain and his mother. In a few minutes, Mrs. Clark came to Mrs. Davis with tears in her eyes, expressed her gratitude, and asked if she could at least make a little present to Mrs. Davis' servant Sarah. Mrs. Davis replied that she could, and Mrs. Clark gave Sarah three one-dollar Greenbacks.

On Saturday morning, Adjutant Fanton and Dr. Hewitt left for the camp of the 107th at Harper's Ferry. The next evening, Mrs. Clark, the captain, and Dr. Trowbridge went to Hagerstown to stay overnight in a hotel before taking the early train for the North the next morning. Mr. and Mrs. Davis made the trip to Hagerstown the next morning and arrived just as they were leaving for the train station. All were delighted to see each other one last time. The next day, Tuesday, September 30, the Clarks and Dr. Trowbridge arrived in Havana (Montour Falls), NY. The captain was transported to the home of Major Skellenger, where he would continue his recovery.[80]

## Battle of Antietam Near Sharpsburg, MD, September 17, 1862

*Summary of Casualties, Captured and Missing*

COMPANY A:

Broas, William—Left hand, Discharged December 4, 1862, Elmira, NY

Brown, Francis—Wounded, Discharged November 17, 1862, Elmira, NY

Egbert, John—Left arm amputated, Discharged January 6, 1863, Hospital Philadelphia, PA

French, John—Back, Died September 19, 1862, Field Hospital, Antietam battlefield

Goldsmith, Robert—Mouth, Discharged January 5, 1863, Hospital Philadelphia, PA

Harden, Rufus—Missing, Returned to duty

Wilkinson, Capt. Melville—Concussion from shell explosion, Returned to duty

COMPANY B:

Coles, Elijah—Left leg, Transferred to Co. F, 16th Regt. Veteran Reserve Corps Nov. 15, 1863

Davis, George—Left leg and thigh, Discharged January 11, 1863, Hospital Frederick, MD

Decker, Amos—Wounded, Returned to duty

Harrington, Harvey—Left side, Died September 18, 1862, Field Hospital, Antietam battlefield

Hurd, William—Left thigh, Discharged November 22, 1862, Hospital Frederick, MD

Kilmer, George—Left arm, Returned to duty

Mitchell, James—Wounded, Discharged December 23, 1862, Hospital Frederick, MD

Terwilliger, Charles—Wounded, Returned to duty

COMPANY C:

Bagley, Abel—Round shot contusion, Discharged February 19, 1863, Hosp. Harper's Ferry, VA

Brazee, Abram—Contusion shell, Deserted September 18, 1862, Antietam battlefield

Austin, Peter—Face, Discharged February 19, 1863, Elmira, NY

Fay, (first name not given, Edwin or Francis)—Breast and side, Returned to duty

Fox, William F.—Concussion from Shell explosion, Returned to duty

Herrick, Joseph—Missing, Deserted September 17, 1862

Leavenworth, David—Hip, Discharged February 5, 1863, Hospital Philadelphia, PA

Osburn, Lawrence—Left hand, Returned to duty

COMPANY D:

Beardsley, Beach—Hand slight, Returned to duty

Birmingham (also Bradenburg), Michael—Wounded, Discharged November 20, 1862

Burris, George—Hand slight spent ball, Returned to duty

Callaghan, Patrick—Killed in action

Churchill, Jackson—Thigh slight, Returned to duty

Rogers, (Benjamin or Nelson)—Back slight, same ball that hit Burris, Returned to duty

Slawson, Isaac—Missing, Captured, Died July 18, 1863, Richmond, VA Prison.

Smith, Robert—Wounded, Returned to duty

Vredenburg, Francis—Hand slight, Deserted, no date from hospital

COMPANY E:

Bennett, Sylvester—Wounded, Discharged March 6, 1863

Crow, David—Ankle, Discharged May 15, 1863, Hospital Antietam, MD

Crum, Clark -Wounded, Captured, Reported Deserted, September 18, 1862, Antietam battlefield

Lalor, John—Wounded, Returned to duty

Tongue, Eli—Wounded, Returned to duty

COMPANY F:

Brownell, Asa—Wounded, Transported to New York in Oct., Returned to duty March 2, 1864

Hoag, John—Missing, Wounded, Discharged March 27, 1863

Hovey, Howe, Peter?—Missing, Captured and paroled no dates, Mustered out June 1865, Hicks

Hosp., Baltimore, MD

Smith, Theodore—Leg amputated in a farmhouse hospital behind the East Woods, struck by a shell (supposedly while the regiment was supporting Cothran's battery), Discharged December 6, 1862

COMPANY G:

Benedict, Volkert—Wounded, Sick in hospital at Elmira, NY since Oct. 29, 1862 & at muster out

Everett, William—Lost both legs from artillery shell fragments, Died Sept. 17, 1862

Gleason, David—Knee shell wound, Discharged Oct. 27, 1862

Fisk, Amos—Right arm broken, Discharged Dec. 17, 1862, Hospital Frederick, MD

Henderson, Rufus—Left leg and shoulder, Discharged October 24, 1864, Elmira, NY

Johnson, Alonzo—Leg amputated, Died Sept. 17, 1862

Kallahar, John—Foot, Died Sept. 17, 1862

LeRoy, Nicholas—Missing, Returned to duty

Mosher, Ambrose—Right Arm, Discharged April 29, 1863, Convalescent Camp, Alexandria, VA

Paris, Tyler—Leg, Returned to duty

Robinson, Nelson—Wounded, Died Dec.13, 1862, Hospital Smoketown, MD

Stevens, Jesse—Right Leg, Died Sept. 17, 1862

COMPANY H:

Callahan, Patrick—Thigh, leg amputated, Died September17, 1862

Clark, Erastus Chalmers—Mini ball left breast, Discharged Dec. 24, 1862

Covell, Cyrus—Killed instantly by musket fire in action, Sept. 17, 1862

Durfee, Stephen—Fingers shot off, Deserted Sept. 17, 1862, Antietam, MD

Dawson, Matthew—Leg, Died Oct. 1, 1862, Hospital Frederick, MD

Eumans (also Youmans), Jason—Left hand, Returned to duty

Edwards, Stephens—Discharged Jan. 13, 1863, Hospital Washington, DC

Gardiner, Owen—Shoulder, Returned to duty

Gregory, Josiah—Abdomen, Discharged Nov. 30, 1862, Hospital Philadelphia, PA

Hall, Eugene—Shell injury, Discharged Mar. 6, 1863, Frederick, MD

COMPANY I:

Brown, John—Right foot, Discharged April 3, 1863, Convalescent Camp
   Alexandria, VA

Castor, Howard—Contusion, discharged no date given.

Corwin, Daniel—Thigh, Died Sept. 17, 1862

COMPANY K:

Babcock, Enoch—Left arm, Returned to duty

Cole, Sylvester—Right hand, Discharged March 6, 1863, Washington, DC

Japhet, James—Right hand, Discharged April 10, 1863, Baltimore, MD

# 4

# Maryland Heights
# and Antietam Ford

Harper's Ferry, October 1862; scenes of waste everywhere, everybody
on the move and nobody knowing anything or able to tell you anything. Through the elegant cast iron sash of the arched windows is seen
the long-drawn vacancies of the old armory buildings burned with fire.
Deserted, door less and sash less houses. Horses eating hay in parlors.
Enterprising photographers set up their cameras in ownerless houses.
Aetna insurance plates stand over doors long since burned. Sutlers
peddle soft bread, tobacco and sausages from deserted dwelling houses
where children played, hospitals fill with sick breaths, rooms where
beaux have visited, and sweethearts charmed. Cavalry horses gnaw in
the young orchards. And over all floats and clings the grime and dust
where 10,000 feet each day do the pulverizing and constant winds the
distribution.

> —Chaplain Thomas K. Beecher, 141st New York,
> observations on Harper's Ferry while visiting the camp
> of the 107th New York on Maryland Heights.1

The regiment marched from the battlefield at 4 p.m. on the 19th of September,
going south through a dirty and dilapidated Sharpsburg. Along the way, they passed
many unburied Confederate dead, giving evidence to the havoc their artillery had
done. They crossed over "Burnside's Bridge" and traveled beyond Sharpsburg, where
the road became very rough. Upwards they moved through a range of mountains,
and long after darkness fell, they passed through a narrow mountain cut. The way
was made more difficult by rocks and other obstructions. Downward they trod, soon
reaching a regular road. Toward 11 p.m., many fell out of ranks, exhausted and their
feet suffering from worn out shoes. Those who could not go on silently limped into
the fields, falling quickly into a deep sleep. The remains of the regiment moved on a
mile or so until reaching Pleasant Valley, where they bivouacked.

The following morning, September 20, the stragglers caught up to the main
body who were eating breakfast. Their brief meal completed, they filed onto the road
and resumed the march. Their route took them to the summit of a mountain along
a steep rocky lumber road. They continued on through the woods for six or eight
miles along the side and summit, sometimes up hill and then down. In some places,
the Rebels had cut down trees to impede their progress. The going was tough, and

they stopped every so often to rest.[2] Along the way, they saw numerous knapsacks and blankets that had been discarded by the retreating Rebels and a great number of graves where their dead had been hastily buried.[3] As the day worn on, it became oppressively hot, and the men, loaded down with their own heavy baggage, collapsed from sheer exhaustion.[4] At noon they reached their destination, a good eighteen miles from their starting point. Here they rested for about three hours while stragglers slowly caught up with the main body. Moving on, they descended into a beautiful valley and a place called Sandy Hook,[5] where the men encamped in an apple orchard.

The regiment was suffering greatly. The march to Antietam and fighting of the 17th had taken its toll on their once neat and bright uniforms. Many of the men were in rags, some almost shoeless, and almost all were covered with vermin. Sickness, which had spared the regiment up until now, was appearing among the men in the form of diarrhea.[6] That evening they were able to rest and have their first good meal since before the battle. They dined on bread, bacon, crackers, and coffee and even had peaches for dessert.

The next day, Sunday, was a pleasant day, and the regiment was allowed to rest even more. Many of them took the opportunity to have their hair cut and still more to bathe in the nearby creek. They had time to think about their experiences of the past several weeks. They were quite proud of themselves and felt they had sustained the good name of the "Banner Regiment." The next afternoon, orders were given to fall in and prepare to march. No sooner than they had done so when the order was countermanded, and they remained at Sandy Hook another night.[7]

On Tuesday the 23rd, along with the other regiments of the 1st Division, 3rd brigade, they marched to Maryland Heights, overlooking the Potomac River and Harper's Ferry.[8] They had taken the road from Sandy Hook to Harper's Ferry, following the ruin around the hill. They ascended the heights on the Maryland side of the Potomac River and found themselves nearly opposite the village.[9] They arrived at the summit of the heights at 10 in the morning.[10] On the summit, they saw the still unburied remains of Confederate soldiers who had died during the assault on Harper's Ferry. There was not enough soil on the rocky surface to bury them. Attempts were made to burn them but were only partially successful.[11] From the summit they moved further down the mountain to a location from where they had a spectacular view of the surrounding country.[12] The camp was described as "pitched high upon the mountainous bluffs whose base was washed by the Potomac. In fact it was located along with its own and another brigade from the 1st division halfway down the heights on a considerable plateau surrounded by trees, except toward the river, where in the next week an installation would be made of artillery pieces consisting of big ship Dahlgren guns of one hundred pound caliber and a quantity of thirty pound Parrotts."[13] The fortifications where these guns were be installed would be built from trees cut down over a period of ten days by the woodchoppers of the 107th, under the command of Capt. Stocum of Co. D,[14] and the other regiments camped nearby.[15] From the 107th camp the eye could range over a vast territory of singular beauty and loveliness in which the wild and picturesque was finely mingled with pleasing valleys. To the north could be seen South Mountain, the Blue Ridge which lined the Shenandoah and the tortuous hills which girt the Potomac as it passed over its rocky bed to the Atlantic."[16]

The regiment was without most of its tents and blankets, as were all of the regiments in their brigade, and did the best they could to settle into their new camp. Their equipment, including their tents, had been left behind when they marched from near Washington, and what they did have with them at Antietam was left behind when they went into battle. Those without made some cover from bushes and rails, anything they could find. The sun did not reach their camp until 9 or 10 in the morning, and when it did, it was very hot.[17] The days were mostly pleasant, but the nights got quite cold, although there was not yet any frost.[18]

They went about their usual routine of company drills, and when the chance appeared, they watched the hot air balloon "Atlantic" with its daily ascensions to spy on Confederate troop movements. And at night they sat around their campfires, telling stories and sometimes singing, while off in the distance a thousand lights gleamed brightly from the surrounding camps.[19]

Once settled in, Captain Colby, commander of Company I, took the opportunity to send home some souvenirs that he had acquired on the Antietam battlefield: a saber bayonet and a cavalry saber. The saber was given to him by one of Union cavalrymen who accompanied the flag of truce at the meeting that took place with the Confederates when they asked permission to bury their dead. He had the items sent home by a wealthy friend, Mr. Lloyd Paxton, of his subordinate Lieut. Rutter. Because his sword was destroyed during the charge against the "West Woods" at Antietam, Colby had borrowed the sword of the quartermaster Graves until he purchased a new one. Lieut. Rutter's sword was badly damaged during the battle, but he had been promised by friends at home that they would buy him a new one. On his way to Elmira, a guard in Washington stopped Mr. Paxton, and took the bayonet and saber from him.[20] Several days later, Capt. Colby and Lieut. Rutter were surprised to receive a package by express from Mr. Paxton. In the package they found new swords for each of them. Colby's had a bronze scabbard and was beautifully trimmed.[21]

On Thursday, September 25, Colonel Ruger of the 3rd Wisconsin was temporarily placed in command of the brigade.[22] In that capacity, he held the temporary rank of Brig. General. The regiment was under very strict orders at the "Heights." There were five roll calls a day, at which at least one regimental officer, major or above, had to be in attendance; anyone absent without excuse was to be placed under arrest. Soldiers of each company had to remain on their street until a report of absentees was compiled and turned in. Pickets were to be stationed so that a man could not go a half-mile from camp without a pass. This meant that no one could visit nearby farms to purchase pies, bread, milk, or any other necessities.[23]

The camp of the 107th was located near a small creek in which the men were able to bathe and wash their clothes. While at the camp, the quartermaster issued new shoes to all that needed them. It was none too soon, for many of the men were without them, and the regiment was to drill that day. During the drill, the ranks were very depleted from the loss of men at Antietam, those still injured, and the many who were on the sick list. Some men tried to drill but were forced to return to camp because of weakness.[24] Diarrhea had become very prevalent in camp. Because of the general poor condition of the men and the fear of it worsening, the drills only lasted for about two hours each day.

Colonel Van Valkenburgh and Lt. Colonel Diven were not in camp, having traveled to Washington on Sept. 27.[25] There was a rumor in camp that their purpose was to seek easier duty for the regiment.[26]

The sutlers, as usual, were available to the camp, and those that had any money were able to supplement their diet or purchase other necessities. Cheese cost $2 per pound, soft bread 15 cents per loaf, butter 40 cents per pound, and ginger cakes 20 cents per dozen.[27]

Colonel Van Valkenburgh and Lieut. Col. Diven returned from their trip to the Capitol on the first of October.[28]

The weather was now turning much colder, and the men of the 107th NY still did not have the proper tents and other equipment to protect them from the weather. In addition, the site of their current camp could not have been worse. The site was on a slope facing west and gave the men limited exposure to the sun. The site also was too small to house the thousands of men assigned there, and the soil was shallow and rocky, making it impossible to dig proper latrines. All of this was made worse by their water supply. The only close supply of what appeared to be good water was a spring on the southwest side of the Heights. However, it contained extremely high levels of magnesium. Though magnesium is an essential element for the body, elevated levels can irritate the bowels and cause extreme diarrhea. After continued drinking of it, thousands on the Heights became sick before the spring was abandoned as a source of water. From then on, the men had to go down to the Potomac River, which made it labor intensive to bring water up to the camp on a daily basis. Because of the multitude of problems that the location of the camp presented to the men, a great number of them became ill. The illnesses became worse over time and the potential for death appeared to be growing.

The first deaths experienced by the regiment since the battle of Antietam and its immediate aftermath occurred on October 1. Corporal Joseph Couse of Company H, who had suffered from an exploding shell, died of what was then determined to be congestion of the brain.[29] However, Couse's cause of death was actually typhoid fever. He died near noon in an outhouse that was being used as a workshop. His body was buried in the garden behind Mr. Russell's house that stood near the camp, and Corporal Edward Kendall of the same company commanded the burial squad. Couse was buried by Sgt. Abram Whitehorn. Whitehorn, who was a carpenter by trade, made him a coffin from old fence boards. A private from Company F, the Rev. Enos P. Barnes, conducted the services at the grave. This was the regiment's first military funeral and made a profound impression throughout the regiment. Ironically, several weeks later, the Rev. Barnes would also succumb to typhoid.[30] Two other deaths took place that same day. Private Gilbert Sticker of Company F died of typhoid fever at a hospital in Frederick, MD. Private Matthew S. Dawson of Company H died from a foot injury he had suffered during the battle of Antietam.

Back home people were beginning to hear of the privations of the men, and in Havana, Schuyler County, the ladies had formed a soldiers' relief society. They met every Tuesday afternoon at the courthouse, a building that still stands in the center of Montour Falls. Their first project resulted in sending a box to the men containing lint, bandages, garments for hospital use, and dried fruit. They urged that those who could not attend the meetings should prepare items at home and have them delivered to a member of the society. At their last meeting, two gentlemen each donated $10 to buy material for garments.[31]

On Thursday morning October 2, President Lincoln reviewed the regiment along with others in their corps. In the company of the president were Major General Halleck, Major General Sumner, and General Thomas Francis Meagher. The men loudly cheered the cortege, and the cannon upon the surrounding hills echoed and re-echoed their thunder. The president rode along the front of the regiment, then back, passed to the rear, then came around the front again. Turning to General Halleck, he said, "Well general, I reckon we may as well be going." The regiment then marched in review before him, after which he rode off to review the next regiment. The men felt that he was making observations as to the position and morale of the army. He didn't look any different than when he reviewed them at the train depot, but they certainly were not the same, being able to muster only 500 men for the review.

The regiment drilled that afternoon and afterwards mail was delivered, including a number of boxes. The men eagerly opened them but found that many of the articles had spoiled because the boxes had been held in Washington for a number of weeks.[32] The mail delivery was badly disorganized because of Chaplain Crane had been in a Washington hospital since the battle of Antietam. He was mostly missed because of the sickness in the regiment. The officers did not avoid the sick bed either, and both Lt. Col. Diven and Capt. Wilkinson were confined with the fever. Mrs. Diven had traveled from Elmira to the camp to help care for her husband during his illness.[33]

The next day at dress parade, Major Smith informed the regiment of Colonel Van Valkenburg's nomination by the Republican Party to represent the 27th Congressional District in the next session of Congress. The men, upon hearing the report, gave their colonel a loud cheer, and that evening the entire regiment turned out at his headquarters. Adjutant Hull Fanton addressed Van Valkenburgh on behalf of the officers and the men of the 107th, congratulating him on his nomination. The colonel replied that whatever position he might hold in the future, he would always think of their welfare as he had in the past, and that he was very proud of the regiment.[34] He spoke in a trembling voice as he responded to their congratulations, referring to them as his children.[35]

On Saturday, Private Martin Sage of Company K died. His was the third death since the regiment had arrived at Maryland Heights. However, the worst was yet to come.

That same day, Company B was detailed to do guard duty for 48 hours at the pontoon bridge that crossed the Potomac River at Harper's Ferry.[36] A squad of 50 men was turned out, and while on duty, they were quartered at a house near the bridge. The house was located directly opposite the engine house in which John Brown barricaded himself and his men during their raid on Harper's Ferry. While on duty, they guarded the bridge, examined the passes of the crossing soldiers, picked up stragglers, and prevented the baggage, munitions, and supply trains from clogging up the thoroughfare. With all of the traffic passing over the bridge, it was to be expected that they would meet some familiar faces. Among them were Capt. Henry Baldwin of the 34th NY, Lieut. James Flynn of the 145th NY, and U.S. Lowe, Quartermaster.[37] Being in such close proximity to civilians and the railroad and canal, they felt as if they were back in civilization again.

Some had the opportunity to cross the bridge into the village and view the ruins of the arsenal and other government buildings that were destroyed at the beginning of the war to prevent their use by the Rebels. The buildings had been extensive, and a lot of money must have been wasted to destroy them. While they were not actually on duty, some of the men in the detail bathed in the river. On Monday evening, a company from the 2nd Massachusetts relieved a 107th NY company from guard duty. That same day, orders were issued at the evening dress parade that from then on, drills would be by battalion. The size of a battalion was arbitrarily set during the Civil War. It could contain anywhere from four to eight companies, and often a regiment was split into two battalions.

An unpleasant and controversial story came out of the battle at Antietam that concerned Captains Morgan and Colby. Capt. Morgan wrote a letter to an Elmira newspaper accusing Capt. Colby of allowing his men to advance only halfway to the "West Woods" before they skedaddled back-to-back to the regiment. Colby was supported by the other officers of the regiment who stated that they did not see anything regarding Colby's actions that could be construed as cowardice. In fact, Capt. Fox of Company C wrote a letter to the *Corning Journal* on October 10 stating that he observed the whole maneuver, and the squad under Colby's command accomplished their task of locating the enemy and retired from the field in good order. Fox further stated that the colonel thanked Colby and his men on the spot in front of the regiment.

On Tuesday, October 7, the men were glad to see that their knapsacks had arrived. However, many of the men found that much of the contents were missing. It appeared that they had been emptied of everything but the clothes, and the clothes then stuffed back inside. Capt. Colby found that he was missing three flannel shirts and a blanket.[38] The knapsacks had been left at Camp Seward in the care of Sergeant Bernard Curran of Company G.[39] Another note of dismay that day was the death of Sergeant Amos Rogers of Company F from typhoid fever. As it turned out, his death signaled the beginning of a terrible cycle.

That same day Colonel Van Valkenburgh tendered his letter of resignation as shown below. Major Smith made the announcement of his resignation to the troops at dress parade.[40]

> HeadQuarters 107th Reg. N.Y.V.
> Sandy Hook, Md. 7th Oct. 1862
>
> Brig. Genl. L. Thomas
>     Adjutant General U.S.A
>
> General. I hereby respectfully tender my resignation as Colonel of the 107th Reg. N.Y. Vols. To take effect on the 21st inst.
>
> My constituents have seen fit to re-nominate me for Congress, thereby expressing their desire that I should serve them in congress instead of the field. The prospect of my election is reasonably certain.
>
> Believing that votes cast for me for congress, while I should be acting as an officer duly mustered into the military service of the United States, would be invalid. I deem it my duty to resign, and quit the service before the election which takes place about 1st prox.
>
> Hoping you may approve my action; I have the honor to be
>
> Your Very Obedient Servant
>
> R.B. Van Valkenburgh
>
> Col Comg 107th Reg NYV[41]

With the resignation of the colonel, there would be a shift upwards of the officers, and among the captains there was a certain amount of competition to obtain the promotion to major. Diven would naturally become the new colonel. The new lieutenant colonel would be former Major Gabriel L. Smith, but below Smith things were uncertain.[42] There was a captain in each company, and all were eligible to be promoted to major. It was not beyond the officers to seek the help of potentially influential friends in their quest for promotion. However, the rank of major was left vacant for the time being and would not be filled until December 31, 1862.[43] It should be pointed out here that there is ample evidence that the higher-ranking officers—captains and above—did not all agree on the merits of their peers as officers. Lieut. Col. Smith was considered by at least one officer to be a conceited ass. Diven was regarded, and to some degree rightfully so, to be lacking in experience in military matters. It must be said of Diven that despite his lack of military training and his advanced age, he lasted longer at his post than one might reasonably expect. And no one ever said anything negative about his performance at either Antietam or Chancellorsville.

The resignation of Colonel Van Valkenburgh provided a great deal of material for the Democratic-leaning newspapers in Elmira and nearby towns. The *Corning Democrat* in its October 30 edition urged those with sons in the service to vote against him because he had deserted their sons. Ironically, Van Valkenburgh's opponent in the election was Colonel Hathaway, commander of the 141st NY. Colonel Hathaway in his letter of October 22 in the same *Corning Democrat*, advised those who nominated him that because his duty was first to his regiment, he would be unable to campaign but would accept the position should he be elected.

Other notable jabs at the "*Ex-Colonel*," which is the title he was given, included two short pieces appearing in the same edition of the *Corning Democrat*. One article referred to the passing through Bath of the horse recently presented to Van Valkenburg by a resident of Corning, Colonel C.C.B. Walker. The horse was described as looking emaciated and worn down, doubtless by grief at the desertion of the regiment by the brave and patriotic *Ex*-Colonel. Another article was entitled "How Have the Mighty Fallen." It related Van Valkenburgh's statement prior to his election two years prior. He had "declared his ability to drive the South into the Gulf of Mexico with a dozen oyster women armed with broom sticks." It went on to say that "the smoke of one battle cured him of any desire to follow the Rebels to the Gulf." And it concluded, "He prefers an easy armchair in the halls of Congress. We don't know, but it is all right. He ain't fit to lead the brave boys of the 107th anywhere but may be competent to command a dozen old women with broomsticks."

There were also rebuttals to these attacks, including one from Lt. Alonzo Howard of Company K, 107th NY. The lieutenant stated that no officer ever treated his men better than did the colonel. Howard told of how during the first leg of the march from Camp Seward, Van Valkenburgh walked most of the way rather than ride. That he, at every halt, would pass up and down the column, cheering up the men who were nearly exhausted, and by those actions he gained the love and esteem of every man in the regiment. Howard went on to say, "The regiment has been left in the good hands of Colonel Diven, and if any man chooses to condemn Van Valkenburgh let him set an example by spending his time, money and talents to raise a regiment, lead it into battle and return home with half the honors to himself and his regiment."

In the *Corning Journal*, a Republican newspaper, another defense was published at the same time as the *Corning Democrat* attack. A letter from Doctor J.S. Dolson, a neighbor of the colonel, advised all of the fact that Mrs. Van Valkenburgh had been ill and bedridden for several weeks before his return and that her recovery had seemed doubtful. He himself had contacted the colonel and urged him to hasten home if he expected to see his wife alive.

With sickness becoming rampant in the camp, some officers, who were ill, asked for and were granted leave to go home and recuperate. They included Lt. Bachman and Capt. Sill, both of whom were granted leave for health reasons: Bachman for 14 days and Sill for 20 days.[44] That evening at 8 o'clock, one of the designated battalions turned out for drill, but only 90 men and officers appeared, the rest being on duty or in the hospital. As a result, the drill was canceled. The next day, battalion drills were held in the morning and afternoon with Colonel Ruger, commander of the brigade, drilling the troops.

The rest of the week passed uneventfully except for the cycle of deaths. On Thursday the mail arrived in the evening. The weather was hot one day and cool the next. Some drilling was done, and on Saturday, October 11, some of the camp streets, each one belonging to a company, were cleaned up. Sunday was a quiet, cool day with no drilling.[45]

Private William R. Kelly of Company K died on Thursday, Private Francis Wheaton of Company G on Friday, Private Augustus Daniels of Company A on Sunday, and on Monday the 13th, a cold, wet and drizzly day, there were four deaths in the regimental hospital: Privates Abraham Decatur and Henry P. Smith of Company A, van Buren Stage of Company B and Charles Matthews of Company H, all from typhoid fever.

During this period of sickness, in the middle of October, over one fourth of the regiment was on the sick list. From Company F at one point, there were many men in the hospital suffering from typhoid fever. They included Sgt. George Husted, Private William Hatch, Private Daniel Hathaway (died), Private Samuel Phoenix, Private Ira Smith, Private George Stickler, Private Mark Dickerson, Private Charles Titus, Private Walter Crandall, Private Daniel Rosencrans, Corporal John Deuel, Private John Brewer, and Private Ralph Stevens; none of whom were thought to be in serious danger.[46]

Most cases were generally referred to as "Camp Fever," but in reality, as was stated by the camp surgeon Dr. Flood, it was typhoid fever. The first symptom was severe diarrhea and then prostration of the system and a great fever. It was equally present in both the new and the old regiments. Many believed their location to be an unhealthy one; others did not think that possible. Some thought that the men were careless and indifferent in taking care of their health, half cooking their food and eating too much. In addition, it was felt that the severity of the weather was a factor and more of a problem because most of the men had thrown away their shelter tents, overcoats, blankets, and even their undercoats. The regiment had actually been ordered to leave behind most of this when they went into battle at Antietam.[47]

The troops continued cutting down trees at a fast pace, and by October 14, it was estimated that over 500 acres had been cut to be used for building fortifications. The cutting moved from Maryland Heights to further up the river and also across from the heights. The high ground made these places almost impregnable, and the addition of the fortifications made them a second "Gibraltar."[48]

On Tuesday, death took a brief holiday, but it was back at work on Wednesday when Private Charles B. Terwilliger of Company B died. The next day Privates Abraham Miller of Company F and Henry Brewer Company K died, supposedly all of typhoid fever. It had been said of Private Terwilliger that he was one of the best men in Company B.

Despite the medical staff working night and day to overcome the terrible sickness, they lacked most of the medicine, stimulants, and proper food to combat the sickness.[49] The hospital facilities provided for the regiment were described as "inadequate and miserable. An old barn was fitted up for the purpose, and the sick were placed on pallets of straw, but surrounded by filth." However, "everything was done to stay disease and promote good health; new tents were furnished, new clothing provided, and good rations given out."[50] There had been ample evidence that the food rations were not what they should be. Bread could be broken open to reveal worms, and beef had been issued that was alive with maggots.[51]

All together there were about six thousand troops camped on Maryland Heights. This included all of the regiments in the 107th's brigade. Sickness was rampant through the whole brigade, and scarcely a day went by that one did not see three or four funerals. Soldiers were buried in their everyday uniforms. The coffins were made from boards from the hardtack boxes, and poles were tied to their sides so that the pallbearers could carry them. The soldier's company was mustered, and the chaplain said a short prayer over the body. Then followed the parade to the grave with the lowest in rank marching first. The music was always Pleyal's "Dead March" played on the fife and drum. At the grave, six soldiers fired three shots over the body before it was placed in the grave and covered over. A piece of board from either a barrel stave or hardtack box was marked with the name and regiment of the deceased and stuck in the ground at the head of the grave. On the way back to camp, the band played the liveliest tune in its repertoire.[52]

On October 15 by order of the War Department, Major General Henry W. Slocum was assigned to command the 12th Army Corps. The news was heartily received by the men in this corps as Slocum had a magnificent record that had most recently been embellished by his assault at Crampton's Gap during the battle of South Mountain.[53]

On Thursday, it rained very hard, making picket duty difficult for the men. However, all of the men's spirits were heightened somewhat by the arrival of mail. There was a visitor in camp that day, a Mr. N.S. Lowe from Elmira. Heavy firing from across the river broke the sound of the rain.[54] Friday brought the arrival of shelter tents and an extra supply of blankets and clothing.[55]

During the weekend, even though the men were off duty, an unusual amount of activity was evident as the men were busy cutting down trees to build huts. The trees were plentiful even though they were a considerable distance from the camp. The logs were cut to size and dragged to the camp. Each hut required about 20 logs, and it took the entire day for three men to cut them down and bring them to camp. The next day the logs were laid up about four feet high, and then sticks were set up for the canvas tent to be laid on for the roof. The canvas was firmly tied down and the cracks in the logs filled with a mud plaster. When finished, the hut was 7 by 9 feet and about 10 feet high. Some of the men did not like to be so engaged in work during the Sabbath, but it was the only time they were free from duty. Rain fell later in the day, but by that time, the roofs of the huts were in place. The men had been ordered to get their company street in order, and thus the effort made to erect huts, but they were fearful that it might all be for nothing as there was a rumor going around that they would be moving within a week.[56]

Their feelings about the inactivity of camp life were aptly described in the following letter composed for publication in the *Steuben Courier* by Prattsburg native 2nd Lieut. Harvey G. Denniston.

Maryland Heights, Md.
October 26th, 1862
Editors Courier,

Gents: Still encamped on Maryland Heights, and like a certain "Wilkin Micawber, Esq." The 107th is waiting for something to turn up. Of all lives in the world which men are doomed to live, that of the camp is the most monotonous and presents the least varying phases.

The reveille awakens you from dreams of dislocated bones to the aching reality of answering the roll call, doled out by a sleepy orderly. Then came the sick call at the tapping of which the lame, the halt and the blind wend their weary way to the surgeons to be doctored at imminent danger of crippling a lot of shirks who are expecting to escape drill.

Then comes the drill call in which commissioned officers lead out their companies to go through the evolutions and gyrations of Hardee or Casey. After drilling is effectually disposed of, comes the "breakfast taps"; a summons to which all answer with alacrity. Then we have the "guard mounting" and "picket duty" and "wood chopping" and "dinner call" and "battalion drill" and "dress parade" and "supper call" and "home to quarters" and "lights out." All of which is done in true soldier like precision, especially the eating part. Thus, is day-by-day doled off in the same manner, and you can wonder Mr. Editor we get tired of camp life and want to move. And why should we not move? That's the question.

In these valleys of Maryland, running down to Harper's Ferry, upon every hilltop as far as the eye can see, are thousands of loyal men, fresh men ready to move and eager to do so. And the supply trains are without stint and number, enough to curse the movement of any army where promptness and dispatch is necessary, and the sight of which to one unaccustomed would cause a feeling of wonderment as to where all the money was coming from. While speaking of these supply trains, Mr. Editor, they are a nuisance to the army when on the march. They block up the way, cause unnecessary travel and act as obstacles to our columns when they are needed most.

In our Maryland campaign, to protect these encumbrances, we were marched for miles unnecessarily, and led into battle fatigued and worn out. The enemy had none—we thrashed them—they fled and we followed with our supply trains. All that the soldier wants is his blanket, his haversack, his gun and ammunition, and then he can move with celerity, as occasion requires. Let the supply trains follow by all means, but let the cakes be hurried up with this rebellion.

At present everything indicates a move. How do I know it? I don't, but I can't help hoping so. I know that reconnaissance's have been made daily for some time past, and these you know are precursors to a move. I know that the command of the forces have been altered, and that the 107th is now of Burnside's corps, and this looks like a move. Knowing ones say that the Army of the Potomac is to be divided equally, that McClellan is to lead the front and Burnside the flank and this in all conscience would foreshadow a move of some kind. I hope we will move. I'm tired of this dilly-dallying upon this cold, bleak hill where the four winds of heaven plays the deuce with your tent and to keep comfortable is impossible.

Col. Diven has assumed the Eagles and now has command of the 107th. He is a favorite with our boys; they have all confidence that he will be a true friend to the regiment. He is fast recovering from his recent indisposition and is very assiduous to the wants and requirements of all. We all of us felt very sad to have Col. Van Valkenburgh leave us, and it was hard to become reconciled thereto, but the feeling is wearing away as we become better acquainted and learn to know our present colonel. Let me add right here that if the 27th Congressional District don't give Col. Van a rousing majority it will be because his loyal friends at home do not do their duty. The 107th would be a unit in his support had they an opportunity of voting—mark that.

Yours hurriedly, H.G.D.

P. S. A comrade at my elbow says that the paymaster will be here the latter part of the month. If so, I agree with him in saying, "we will be sure to move" before that personage makes his appearance. The 107th is confident of this, every man of it.

Co-incidentally, the Rev. Thomas K. Beecher, who was visiting the 107th NY's camp, also wrote to the *Elmira Advertiser & Republican* that same day and expressed his observations of the regiment's situation on Maryland Heights.

Dear Fairman,

I've just been spending an hour in Captain Lathrop Baldwin's tent, and of course we have been talking about you and the Advertiser, and so very naturally I write to you.

With twenty or more of Elmira boys of my acquaintance here in the regiment. There is a press of information for my pencil. I heard that this regiment was having a hard time of it and getting rather blue so as our colonel is proverbial generous, he detailed the chaplain to come over and do what deeds of comfort he might compass. The boys have been having a gloomy time, but the sky is brighter now.

There have been twenty-two or twenty-three deaths and sick ones in far larger numbers. In my judgment the sickness has been due to over-marching and over-eating combined. Few men know the ravenous appetite that is bred by an outdoor life. And fewer still are ever wise enough to "stop hungry." But experience is a very faithful teacher, and if God please the Chaplain will dispense good counsel tomorrow morning touching the same subject.

As I said before the skies are brighter now. No one of my acquaintances need feel any present anxiety for the boys in this regiment. Young Munson is the sickest one of my acquaintances and he is convalescent. Though it is easy to see on the dull faces of scores like him that camp fever is an ugly customer. Dr. Beadle and Mrs. Diven are untiring in their labors for the sick and it is really surprising to see how much comfort their presence in camp seems to the boys. I hear talking and laughter among the tents. But Mrs. D tells me it was not so a week ago.

And so, this is Harper's Ferry, and these are Maryland Heights. Yonder is the battery so shamelessly surrendered a few weeks ago. Over the valley like a great city shines the camp lights on Bolivar, a little to the left I see the thousands encamped on Loudoun. Yes, this is an army—a very big thing. One man, and he a chaplain feels small. Afternoons, I look over and see the black patches on Bolivar, brigades of men, and seen upon the grand bare mountain they seem only as lice on some leaf—patches of vermin infesting nature. They move very slowly hither and thither on drill or parade, and in their multitude seem insignificant and too numerous to seem men. Too small to rival the grandeur of nature.

This afternoon in company with Dr. Beadle, the chaplain experimented with Col. Diven's black horse a riding. I insist that equestrianism is a most unnatural and semi-barbarous accomplishment. It is a shame to put upon a dumb beast such duty and a greater shame to put men to such uses. Call the human frame divine a log, the horse a wedge and mother earth a beetle or maul, and you have the essentials of horseback performances, he would have been created with angle irons to withstand the strain. But war creates necessities, and necessities are their own law.

Round the mountain roads men must ride who never rode before—and behold the chaplain wandering forth in search of the 64th regiment. We found it, and found young Lincoln busy like his father, improving a hospital tent by constructing an underground stove and pipe. Lieut. Fassett hailed us and many times this chaplain had to stop his horse and chat with unexpected friends.

He found that to stop one's horse is easier than to stop oneself. The rider is apt to go on after the horse is halted dead. If he goes on too recklessly, he is sure to go off. I overheard the chaplain ask Dr. Beadle how he looked and whether anybody was laughing. It is a great pity that he did not bring with him a certain faithful little nag with a low neck and active tail which use to haul him through Elmira streets. She was a war horse and looms large in the distance.

Harper's Ferry is familiar to all who see the pictorials. But they cannot sketch into woodcuts scenes which cover miles, scenes of waste, confusion and destruction. If you want to feel friendless just alight as I did in the wagon crowded thoroughfares of Harper's Ferry. Everybody on the move and nobody knowing anything or able to tell you anything.

It is my trade to use words, but words can't tell you of the scenes we see here. For miles below the river is thickly strewn with wrecks of pontoons—successive bridges destroyed. On every rock or two is stranded the carcass of a dead horse. In the riverbed at the ford, I noted ton after ton of pig iron cast away. Across the river stands the extemporized trussle bridge, between the piers that once held up the iron viaduct. There through the elegant cast iron sash of the arched windows may be seen the long-drawn vacancies of the old armory building, burned with fire

My letter is waxing long and my candle is short. Major Smith is clean gone in. He won't stir till morning. Let me cut off short and turn in too.

Yours ever, Chaplain

Monday, October 27, brought a cold and raw morning, but the newly constructed huts warmed the men during that night and through the morning until the sun shone later in the day. They finally heard the news of General Slocum being assigned to command the 12th Army Corps. The next day proved to be cold and windy, but the shelter provided by the huts greatly protected the men. The weather was also somewhat forgotten because the mail arrived, and the men all enjoyed hearing from home a line or two. That day command of the regiment passed from Colonel Van Valkenburgh to now Colonel Alexander S. Diven. Although Colonel Diven had gained his health back, his wife remained in camp and was present daily at the hospital helping to care for the sick.[57]

Wednesday was clear but cold, and the wind blew a perfect gale. Still the men were out on picket duty, and drills were held. Thirty men from Company H and a like number from Company I under the command of Capt. Colby were assigned picket duty that day, and a most unfortunate incident occurred. Lieut. Lewis Saylor and Private John Lane, both of Company H and part of the picket detail, took a boat and crossed over the Potomac ostensibly to get some food. While they were in a house, three Confederate cavalrymen captured them. The women of the house ran down to the bank and screamed to the other guards to come over and rescue the two men, but unfortunately there had only been the one boat. Saylor had disobeyed his orders that forbid him to cross to the other side of the river. Both soldiers were eventually exchanged, and Lane returned to the regiment. However, while Saylor was being held captive, he was by General Order 195 issued November 23, 1862, by the Adjutant General's Office, War Department, Washington, "dismissed from the service for being captured when across the Potomac contrary to orders."[58]

On Friday a general inspection was held, and rumors again were heard that the regiment was to move soon. A visitor in the camp pleasantly surprised many of the men. The Reverend Thomas K. Beecher, chaplain of the 141st NY was visiting for a few days.[59] Also in camp from Elmira was Doctor Tracy Beadle and his son Ralph.[60]

Company F was on picket on Saturday, and Private E. Crane was accidentally wounded in the hand. The wound was sufficient to cause his discharge for disability.

1st Lieut. M.V.B. Bachman of Company B was given 14 days leave of absence for health reasons and left camp on Oct. 20. Nine days later, he wrote to the Adjutant General in Washington, D.C., to have his leave extended for another thirty days. No record could be found as to whether or not his leave was extended.

On Tuesday, 2nd Lieut. Irving Bronson and Capt. William F. Fox, both of Company C, and Capt. James H. Miles of Company F were each given 20 days leave of absence for the benefit of their health. Below is the letter of application by Capt. Miles and the supporting medical certificate authored by Surgeon Flood.

> To the Adjutant General
>
> I hereby respectfully apply for a leave of absence for twenty days for the purpose of visiting my home and obtaining the care and treatment necessary to the restoration of my health.
>
> > Very Respectfully
> > Your Obedient Servt
> > James H Miles
> > Capt Co F 107th Reg N.Y.V.
>
> > Maryland Heights Md. Oct 23[d] 1862
>
> Captain James H Miles Co F 107th Regiment N.Y.V.
>
> having applied for a certificate on which to ground an application for leave of absence. I do hear by certify that I have carefully examined this officer and find that he has been suffering from typhoid fever the effects have left him in that debilitated state that a change of climate and the careful attention of friends at home are absolutely necessary for his recovery. And in consequence thereof he is unfit for duty. I further declare my belief that he will not be able to resume his duties in a less period of twenty days, and further, that if he remains here, he will not recover, and the change is absolutely necessary to prevent permanent disability.
>
> D. G. Himrod
>
> > Asst & Act Surgeon
> > 107th NY Vol
>
> > Approved
> > Francis Leland
> > Surg. 2nd Regt Mass. Vol. Senior Surg. 3rd Brig[61]

Surgeon Flood of the 107th traveled home to Elmira the week of October 20 to collect food that would improve the men's diets and help fight scurvy. To aid in his endeavor, he wrote a letter to the newspapers in the three counties from which the 107th men came. His letter specified that there was a necessity for vegetables to combat sickness and scurvy. He sought contributions of potatoes, onions, and black pepper for the camp and ground mustard, cayenne pepper, and pure whiskey for the hospital. In Elmira Mr. W.F. Corey, the secretary of the Soldiers Relief Association, headed the effort to gather up the needed items, and the friends of the regiment were asked to bring their contributions to J.M. Robinson's store on Lake Street.[62] The letter published in the *Havana Journal* referred to the companies of Capt. Clark and Capt. Morgan, two companies raised mostly from Schuyler County, in its appeal to the people of that county. The letter included directions for packaging the goods. The potatoes and onions were to be put into barrels, well headed up, and the hoops securely nailed. The black pepper was to be placed into boxes 1½ to 2 by 3 to 4 inches with a tin cover on each so that any member of a mess could put it into his pocket and carry it with him to use on his food and soups during marches. All contributions were to be delivered to the railroad depot at Havana or Watkins. Those in charge of handling the items delivered were Mr. Risdon in Havana and Mr. J.M. Coddington in Watkins. Since there were no distilleries of pure whiskies known to be in the county, it was suggested that the Chemung County War Committee could obtain the whiskey required by the regiment from a copper still recently erected by a German in Southport.[63] Dr. Flood successfully procured a large quantity of the and also mustard and whiskey for medicinal purposes.[64] The reported weight of the goods collected was said to be from eight to ten tons. Cash contributions of $150 were used to pay the freight costs and to purchase additional goods that were deemed necessary but not included in the contributions.[65]

The month of October wreaked havoc on the entire regiment. Private Ethan Worden of Company H and Gideon Beman of Company I died of scarlet fever on October 22. The men in Worden's company walked three miles to find suitable lumber for his coffin. They found wood from a dooryard fence. In Company H, the prevailing diseases were listed as diarrhea, rheumatism, and fevers. The company reported thirty-six men answering the sick call and being given quinine; allowing for the men on special duty and those confined to their beds or in the hospital, only forty men were able to do duty.[66] The next day, Private John B. Arnot of Company A also died of scarlet fever.

Colonel Diven, mindful of the conditions adversely affecting his regiment, wrote a letter to Brig. General George W. Gordon, the contents of which were as follows.

> HeadQuarters 107th Regiment N.Y. Vols.
> Maryland Heights October 23$^d$ 1862

General,

I am constrained by the deplorable sanitary conditions of my regiment. To report the facts. We have averaged for the past three weeks about one hundred men in hospital and from 100 to 150 sick in quarters. I enclose you report of Asst. Surgeon for yesterday from which you will see we had three deaths between yesterdays and day before yesterday's report, and I know we have had three deaths since the last report. The 26 returned to duty would indicate an improvement. Our sergeant's returns for this morning shows 230 sick in hospital and quarters. We have since in the camp lost from sickness twenty-one men.

Reference to our report of this morning shows but 471 reported for duty. Add to this 74 on extra duty, mostly in hospital waiting, and it gives 545 men for duty. Of these I know a great number are only fit for light duty. I don't believe we have 250 men who could perform a march similar to that through Maryland. This is true of a regiment that entered the service the middle of August with 1024 strong.

On our arrival at this camp our men gave evidence of much exhaustion. They had thrown away their tents, blankets and overcoats in battle and were much exposed. I attributed their sickness at first to this cause, but it is now two weeks since we were supplied with all we could ask, and yet I discover no abatement in the sickness.

Our Surgeons appear diligent in their efforts to allay the malady. We at first had no hospital save an old log barn. Through the exertions of our Surgeon, we procured houses at Harper's

Ferry for hospital purposes. Our sick still occupy most of these houses they have been made Brigade Hospitals.

I beg the advice and cooperation of the Brigade Surgeon or any other means that may occur to you to stay this sickness and death. The spirits of our men are giving way and desertions are frequent. I have done all in my power to encourage them, they have nearly all built log huts, their sinks are kept in good condition and their streets clean, still the sickness is in my judgment increasing.

I have the honor to be<br>
Your Obt Servt

A. S. Diven Lt. Col.

Commanding

This letter was forwarded from brigade headquarters to the headquarters of the Army of the Potomac where the medical director was ordered by command of Maj. Gen. McClellan to make a medical inspection of the regiment. The medical director's office responded accordingly.

On Saturday, October 25, General Order No. 12 was issued and gave warning that a move of the regiment was forthcoming. It advised that ammunition was to be examined to make sure that it was good, and that each man was to have forty rounds. In addition, it stated that any articles not to be carried by the men where to be neatly packed.[67] Corporal Albert V. Borden of Company G and Private Enos P. Barnes of Company F died of typhoid fever.[68]

Unfortunately for the men, it rained the next day, and they did not have the benefit of the Reverend Beecher's sermon on how to keep healthy. They were truly disappointed. However, the good reverend decided to stay over an extra day and gave his sermon to the soldiers on Monday afternoon. He gave only a short talk, but it was enough to remind the men of home and church, especially some of the Elmira men who had previously attended his services. Arthur Fitch thought of being seated with his mother and father, his brother and sister in the choir, listening to the Reverend Beecher's "eloquent voice." The memory of it brought tears to his eyes as he wondered if he would ever be "permitted again to enjoy those sacred privileges." He questioned his decision to leave the comfort of his life at home but knew that it was his duty "towards putting down the unholy rebellion."[69]

Corporal Charles Willover of Company D died of scarlet fever on October 26, 1862, and two days later, Private Marcus Dayton of Company D died of the same disease. That same day, Private Jacob W. Jackson of Company B died in a Philadelphia hospital of consumption.[70]

On Tuesday, October 28, the Reverend Beecher returned to the camp of the 141st New York. There was unusual activity near the 107th's camp as two Pennsylvania regiments who had been encamped near them for some time dismantled their camp and marched away. The weather, while comfortable during the day, was turning colder at night as evidenced by the frost that covered their huts that morning.[71]

That week the Army of the Potomac moved into Virginia, following Lee's forces southward and occupying the passes of the Blue Ridge Mountains. Slocum's forces were left at Harper's Ferry to remain on guard until operations to the south would make its further occupation unnecessary.[72]

On Wednesday, it was again the turn of Company B to do picket duty, leaving their street in the camp totally deserted. However, after supper they were ordered back to the camp to pack up their belongings and with the rest of the regiment prepare to leave their present camp. Orders were given to march to a location below Sharpsburg on the north side of the Potomac River where they would take the place of General Fitz Hugh Porter's command in the 5th Army Corps.[73] Except for their brigade, the 12th Army Corps was to remain at Harper's Ferry.[74] They fell in at about 8 p.m. and headed out on the road to Sharpsburg. It was a beautiful moonlight night, very similar to the night when they left Camp Seward on their way to the Battle of Antietam. The road was good, and they kept a brisk pace, halting now and then to catch their breath. They arrived at the east side of Antietam Creek above where it flows into the Potomac at about midnight and within an hour were situated in their camp. The night brought a frost, but they had built large fires, and even without their tents erected, slept well under their blankets.

The next day they were on the march by 8 a.m., crossed the creek and proceeded to within three miles of Sharpsburg. Upon arriving there, the rest of their brigade marched directly south to the river while they counter marched over the road they had just arrived on to the place where they had spent the previous night. They were told that they were to do picket duty along the canal and the river in place of the regiments that they found there.[75]

During the period the regiment was at Maryland Heights, up until when they arrived at Antietam Ford, there were eleven desertions. Their names, company, and date of desertion can be found in the rear of the book.

While the regiment had moved from Maryland Heights to Antietam Ford, the hospital of the 3rd Brigade 1st Division of the 12th Army Corps was still in operation at its Maryland Heights location. The *Addison Advertiser* published this story of the aid civilian doctors provided during the typhoid fever crisis. The 1st Asst. Surgeon of the hospital, James D. Hewitt, a member of the 107th, wrote a letter to the newspaper extolling the virtues of Dr. W.H. Sheffield of Greenwood in Steuben County for his tremendous effort in treating the soldiers stricken with the fever. The newspaper went on to say that Dr. Sheffield, feeling the effects of his great effort, decided to return home. Before he was able to reach his home, he himself was stricken with the fever, and he was forced to lie prostate for over four weeks until the fever broke. He then told those around him that once he was on his feet again, he would return to the hospital of the 107th if he was needed.

The hospital had remained functioning when the regiment left their camp on Maryland Heights for good reason. From the day the regiment left on October 29, until November 8, eight more men of the regiment died, and all but two deaths occurred in the hospital at the "Heights." The following deaths were recorded in the hospital: Private David Abel, Company C, October 29; Private Samuel Johnson,

Company I, October 30; Private Erastus Baskins, Company E, November 3; Private Andrew Van Camp, Company E, November 3; Private Daniel Hathaway, Company F, November 3; Private Edward Sherman, Company E, November 8; all of scarlet fever. Private Parley S. White of Co. F died of scarlet fever at home in Campbell, Steuben County, and Private Josiah Hand of Co. E died of scarlet fever in a Wilmington, Delaware, military hospital on Nov. 7.[76]

An interesting analysis has been made regarding the death rate from typhoid fever in the 107th New York and that of the 13th New Jersey. It has been concluded that because the 13th New Jersey was composed of urban soldiers and the 107th New York of rural soldiers, the much lower death rate from typhoid in the New Jersey regiment was from living in a more congested area where resistance to diseases had been built up over time.[77]

The regiment erected their small shelter tents and began to settle down immediately in their new camp at Antietam Ford. Only 275 men were in line at the morning roll call. With the withdrawal of the regiments who were previously doing picket, they expected to have plenty of boards, old tents, and other materials to make themselves a comfortable camp. Three companies were sent out on picket duty that first night. The men all had their knapsacks with them in camp, not making the mistake of leaving them behind as they had when they marched from Camp Seward to Antietam. That made the march of twelve miles a bit tougher, but few fell out.

Friday, October 31 brought another fine day. The brigade that had previously been there moved out during the night, and the 107th moved to their campground,[78] which was located on in the rear of a bluff on the east side of the river about three miles below Sharpsburg.[79] The men immediately began to construct more permanent structures that were often a combination of huts and tents. The huts were similar to those constructed at Maryland Heights, but boards were used in place of logs. Water wasn't as close as they would have liked, but it was one of the few inconveniences in an otherwise very acceptable situation. As it was last day of the month, the company clerks were busy writing up the muster and payrolls.[80]

The weather continued to be excellent, which made it easier for the men on picket. They were closer to the enemy than they had been since Antietam. General Order 23 gave specific rules to the 107th and the other regiments in the brigade regarding picket duty.

 

    I. No one passes through the lines without proper authority. Do not inform anyone of the size of the guard force.

    II. Hucksters will be allowed no closer than one mile of the line of guards.

    III. Watch all houses for signals.

    IV. Strictly observe all rules.

    V. Guards cannot sit down while on duty.

    VI. Penalty for neglect of duty will be arrest.

    VII. All communications with the other side will be by use of flags of truce and with the bearer crossing the canal at the ruins of the Shepardstown Bridge and passing along the canal to and over the ford.

    VIII.  Arrest all persons found at the canal or riverbank.

    IX.  Strangers in camp will not be permitted to visit the camps or guards.

    X.  No communicating with the other side.

    XI.  Persons attempting to cross the river will be shot, all boats seized and destroyed.

    XII.  Sentinels will arrest all civilians without proper passes.

    XIII.  Fire on any parties on the other side.

    XIV.  It is the regiment and company commander's responsibility for the above.

    XV.  Officers are to respect Alfred Spats Esq. President of the C & O Canal and are prohibited from hindering the operation of the canal.[81]

On Saturday the men put the finishing touches on their new huts and tidied up the camp streets while heavy firing was heard from across the river. Nothing could be seen, but all assumed a battle was taking place. The men on picket sent in a Rebel taken prisoner, and Mr. Samuel Reynolds of Elmira arrived to visit the camp.[82]

Sunday was another pleasant day, and the noise of battle was heard all day. Orders read at dress parade included promotions and appointments. General Order 14 named Leroy Swartwood and Henry Drummond of Company H as the principal musicians of the regiment. Each regiment was allowed two musicians per company for a total of twenty to make up the regimental band. Corporal Arthur Fitch was promoted to 4th sergeant of Company B.

A court martial was held Wednesday that resolved the theft from the knapsacks left behind when the regiment left Camp Seward on its march to Antietam. Sgt. Bernard Curran of Company G, sergeant of the guard who had been left behind to guard the equipment, was convicted of stealing a shirt from James Van Vleet and a pair of boots and two dollars from another soldier. There had been many other items stolen, but these were the only ones stated in the court martial. Curran's penalty was forfeiture of all pay, having his head shaved, and being drummed out of camp. His penalty was scheduled to be carried out on November 9.[83]

President Lincoln replaced General McClellan, because of his inactivity, with General Burnside as the commander of the Army of the Potomac.

As the week progressed, the weather turned colder, and the days became very windy. It was anticipated that a major advancement was going to made against the Rebels, but nothing came of it. Thursday, November 6 brought a general inspection by the brigade commander Brig. General Gordon. He reviewed the troops and inspected their arms and equipment.[84] General Order 17 was issued instructing company commanders to establish a schedule for picket duty with the proviso that no man was to have the duty more than once every four days.[85]

The following report was issued on November 7 by the Adjutant of the regiment identifying the enlisted men and officers available for duty.

| Company | Enlisted | Officers | Total |
|---------|----------|----------|-------|
| A | 33 | 1 | 34 |
| B | 62 | 2 | 64 |
| C | 47 | 1 | 48 |
| D | 49 | 3 | 52 |
| E | 49 | 3 | 52 |
| F | 57 | 1 | 58 |
| G | 46 | 2 | 48 |
| H | 45 | 1 | 46 |
| I | 41 | 2 | 43 |
| K | 47 | 2 | 49 |
| Total | 476 | 18 | 494 |

Out of the 1021 men that left Elmira in August 1862, now less than three months later, the regiment was unable to have even half that number available for duty. The report listed 179 present but sick and 156 absent and sick, making a total of 811 accounted for. The remainder had either been killed, died of disease, wounded, discharged because of disability, or deserted. The latter figure was a significant number. The above numbers do not include the field officers.

That same day, Colonel Diven wrote home and asked the people of the three counties to send him 800 pairs of mittens for his men. In his letter he wrote,

> The special duty of our regiment while remaining here is to guard the fords and crossings from the Virginia to the Maryland side of the Potomac. It is now an outpost, and our men have to walk as sentinel's night and day along the riverbank. The sentinel, while on guard, must always be on his feet and always carry his gun. The government furnishes no mittens. You can imagine the hardships of walking in a cold night or day, the bare hand always upon the gun which cannot be supported except by keeping the hand in contact with the iron of the barrel or the mountings.[86]

In response to Diven's letter, the Soldier's Relief Association in Elmira invited all those who wished to knit mittens for the regiment to call at Mrs. Ballards' on the corner of Church and Baldwin streets where they could procure the necessary materials free of charge.[87]

On Friday the colder weather was accompanied by a fierce snowstorm that began in the morning and was reminiscent of those so often experienced in New York. Whether or not it prompted Colonel Diven to issue an order calling for the building of substantial log cabins is not known. In addition to his order for the commencement of the building of the log cabins, Diven also issued an order stating that the material to be used in building the cabins was not to include any taken from fences or other buildings in the vicinity.[88] In any case, the men began immediately to cut and draw logs to the campsite to build not only huts, but also cook houses. They rushed to complete their new quarters before the weekend was over.[89] The snow also brought out the boy in many of the soldiers as they took time out for some snowballing fun.[90]

On Sunday, November 9, the snowstorm was all but forgotten when a carload of vegetables arrived from Elmira. They had been toted from Harper's Ferry by Quartermaster Graves. The food was distributed in equal proportions to each of the companies. In addition to potatoes and onions, there were also beets and turnips. Some of the men had not had six potatoes since leaving Elmira. They had looked often on many a forbidden field, and some had not resisted the temptation. They had even seen them for sale by the sutlers but did not have the money to purchase even one.

Accompanying the food were boxes sent by the families or loving friends to individual soldiers. And more than one of those boxes could not be accepted by the designated soldier, for unbeknownst to the sender, the soldier had died.

The men were eternally grateful for Surgeon Flood's effort to improve their diet and were even more pleased when it was announced that he had been appointed brigade surgeon. Colonel Diven and Mrs. Diven welcomed his return to the regiment from Elmira because the colonel had been ill for several days. During this period, Lt. Colonel Smith took over his responsibilities. For the past five or six weeks, Smith had been president of a court martial.[91]

Later that day, the court martial sentence of Sgt. Curran was carried out. This was the first incident of its kind to be witnessed by the regiment. The regiment had finished its usual dress parade in the evening and was in line when the prisoner, under guard, was brought out and placed at the right of the regiment. The sentence was read to Curran, who once had a luxurious growth of hair but was now shaved clean. At the order, he was marched to the front of the line closely behind the drum corps playing the "Rogue's March." Following directly behind him was the guard at "fixed bayonets," urging him on. He passed the whole line of the regiment and beyond the boundaries of the camp. Shunned by his comrades, he lingered in the vicinity a day or two and then left. He was not seen afterwards.[92]

It was at this time that Lt. Colonel Smith's wife Frances arrived in camp from Elmira, accompanied by Mrs. Blossum and Mrs. W.H. Frost. She found her husband in command due to the illness of Colonel Diven. Along with the 107th, he also had temporary command of the 3rd Wisconsin because Col. Ruger had temporary command of the brigade. The ladies found the scenery beautiful and took notice of the old, abandoned blast furnace that was part of the iron works. The principal furnace was made of brick and the source of the material used to build the fireplaces and chimneys in the men's huts.

Lt. Col. Smith had his headquarters in a large storehouse near the Potomac River. It was close enough to the river to be easily observed from the Rebel side. One night while there was a large fire burning in the fireplace, shots were fired from across the river. Bullets came crashing through the windows, attracted by the glow of the fire. From then on, they hung blankets over the windows at night. After Col. Diven recovered from his illness, he and his wife came to visit Lt. Col. Smith's headquarters, and the two couples enjoyed the evenings in front of the huge fires made from scented red cedar wood.

The ladies would go out into the countryside whenever they could get an officer from the regiment to go with them. However, they were cautioned by their husbands not to interfere with the men's drilling by taking officers away with them. Thereafter they could not go out riding unless a willing officer was off duty.[93] Mrs. Diven and Mrs. Smith often rode up toward the Antietam battlefield. There they saw huge newly dug graves, some of which they were told contained five hundred bodies. During their first ride to the battlefield, the landscape was covered with dead horses, and the odor was awful. The battlefield itself was a scene of great destruction: trees torn by shot and shell, brick walls knocked through by cannon shells, bloody and splintered fences, and all over newly made graves without headstones. They even rode down to Harper's Ferry, hoping to see where John Brown had made his raid. While they were there, they visited the small building where he carried out his fight and the schoolhouse where he had stored some of his arms. They were truly affected, and tears came to Mrs. Smith's eyes, standing there where Brown's small band of men fought to bring notice to the issue of slavery.

In addition to the load of food brought by Quartermaster Graves, there were also other shipments, one delivered by Mr. Simon van Etten of Corning and another by Andrew Hathorn of Elmira.[94] With the availability of more and better-quality food, Diven took the opportunity to make a change in the way the men of the regiment were to be fed. He ordered the company commanders to appoint three men as cooks. The cooks were to be excused from drills, guard duty, and picket duty. Food was to be delivered at each drumbeat: breakfast, dinner, and supper. After eating the men were to return their vessels to the cooks, who would wash them. Each company was to provide its own firewood and water. A company tent was to be designated as the kitchen. Men were not allowed to keep food in their tents, and all remains from the meals were to be buried. Other measures taken by Diven included placing guards at the wheat stacks of Mr. Wade's field just north of the camp until the wheat was thrashed and joining forces with the 3rd Wisconsin to procure wood required for fuel and other purposes.[95]

On Wednesday, November 12, the regiment was awakened at midnight and formed in line because of a report that Rebels were in their rear. Pickets were sent out but returned having seen no signs of the enemy. Two nights later there was a similar alarm, but again nothing came of it. On Friday Chaplain Crane returned after a lengthy sickness and on Sunday held services for the first time in many weeks. It rained continually for several days, making the camp muddy and gloomy, but the men were snug and warm in their sturdy log huts. There were rumors of an impending invasion by Stonewall Jackson, but everything remained quiet for the remainder of that week and the next.[96]

In an attempt to further organize the regiment and control many aspects of their personal habits a 17-point order was issued on November 25. Each company was to be divided into four squads, with each squad under a non-commissioned officer. This officer was to be responsible for the squad's cleanliness and order, including the men, their equipment, their tents, and special cleaning details. Dirty clothes were to be segregated from clean clothes in their knapsacks; nothing was to be placed underneath their bed ticking. Men were to wash their feet twice a week, keep their hair short and their beards trimmed. They were also to wash their hands and face daily, comb their hair, and have themselves and their equipment always ready for parades.

Other points included in the order covered the men's mess. Cooks were to deliver the meals to the men on clean plates with the nearest squad served first. Breads were to be thoroughly baked and not eaten until cold, soup had to be boiled at least five hours, beans were to be soaked overnight in cold water, and vegetables cooked until soft and digestible. Only cooks were to be allowed in the kitchen, but they were not to sleep there. Company commanders were responsible for seeing that the individual company streets were kept free of garbage, and sinks were to be dug at the end of each street to dispose of the kitchen refuse.[97]

On November 16, Private Henry B. Aldrich, Company F, died of typhoid fever.[98]

As the end of November approached, the health of the regiment had improved greatly. Serious illnesses were reduced to only a few cases of rheumatism. Chaplain Crane observed that there were a few who he thought would be completely cured if they could only get home, entirely exempt from any further army duty. An honorable discharge, he felt, would do more to cure them than "Kennedy's Medical Discovery or the present mode of applying electricity." It was his opinion that the "terrible marches with salt junk and hardtack for food, and the damp earth for a bed of rest laid the foundation for a disease in some that won't be cured."

At this point in time, there were still about two hundred men absent from the regiment in various hospitals and in the regimental hospital. It was estimated that about one in four would not return. Still, while many had recovered, there were those who didn't. On Wednesday, November 26, Private Edwin M. Reynolds, Company F from Tuscarora in Steuben County, died in the regimental hospital of typhoid fever.[99]

On November 20, Governor Morgan of New York State issued General Order 24 ordering the men to observe Thanksgiving.[100] All drill and work was suspended at 11 a.m.,[101] and the regiment gathered with Chaplain Crane for a "thanksgiving" service that was accompanied by singing.

At the regimental headquarters, it was a very social occasion hosted by Mrs. Diven, ably assisted by Mrs. Smith, the lieutenant colonel's wife, and Mrs. Blossom, the sutler's wife. They prepared puddings, two roasted turkeys, and stewed chickens for the occasion. The ladies and their husbands were seated at the table along with their guests, who included General Jackson of the 12th Army Corps, his adjutant general, Brigade Quartermaster U.S. Lowe from Elmira, Adjutant Hull Fanton, and Chaplain Crane.

Colonel Diven, who was seated at the head of the table, did the honors of carving the larger turkey, while at the other end of the table, the smaller turkey was carved by Lt. Col. Smith. At the same time, the enlisted men were furnished with some "extras" for the occasion and seemed to enjoy themselves very well.[102] For their main course they were served bean soup, pork, and hardtack.[103]

Col. George S. Elias,    Bath N.Y.

Dear sir,

Your kind favor of the 19th inst is just recd. We are certainly grateful for the good opinion we have obtained in the minds of the people at home. Yet I do not think it entirely uninvited. The 107th has gained a good name not only in the 27th district of New York, but Old Abe did us the honor of calling us his "Fighting Regiment" and consequently placed us in a brigade with the 2nd Massachusetts, 3rd Wisconsin & 27th Indiana. All of which have been through at least 7 or 8 hard fought battles & seen 15 or 18 months service & this to without sufficient drilling to make a respectable appearance at a general training & my opinion is this was the great cause of the resignation of Col. Van. There were at least 2 colonels who outranked him & made his chances for a Brigadier ship rather uncertain.

[This references the fact that three of the other regiments in their brigade were veteran regiments, and their colonels would outrank Colonel Van Valkenburgh of the 107th for promotion. Next, he talks about the common practice of politicking for promotions.]

Speaking of resignation reminds me that that the field office of Major is still vacant. If you can assist me any by your influence with Gov. Campbell & others to obtain that position, you will do me a kindness & and a favor to the 107th. What is done must be immediately. Gov. Campbell has written me favorably. Yet a strong recommendation from the military committee of the 27th District won't give me the appointment. I am the fourth Captain in the Reg't & those preceding me are all inexperienced men & only one aspires for it & even I am told has withdrawn his claims. Another reason, Steuben furnished 605 men of the Reg't and now has not a representative either in Field or Staff except Quarter Master & he is from Corning.

There is not much news in camp. We are having rather easy & monotonous times except in picketing. Our line is about 3 miles on the east side of the Potomac extending from the mouth of Antietam [Creek] towards Shepardstown. Occasionally we have a "big scare" when a report comes to camp the Rebs are crossing. Two or three times such has been the case & the whole Reg't by command of the Lt. Col [A.S. Diven]. Turned out in deep dark midnight hours to drive them back or ourselves to skedaddle over the mountains out of sight. All of these have proved to be visions of someone scared out of his wits. At one time the Lt. Col. Got us out frightened to death of a flock of sheep on the hills of Virginia 3 miles off. Oh, what delectable officers. Not long since I was sent for by this gallant officer in great haste. Knowing the heated and vivid imagination he possesses I quietly finished my little work & exactly at 11 o'clock p.m. called at the Headquarters. Trembling with fear yet he tried to conceal it. I was ordered to take company G & patrol the east bank of the Potomac until daylight. Thinking I alone could keep the Rebs at bay, I left Co. G & went alone over the lines found "all Quiet on the Potomac" consequently came back to quarters & cooly went to sleep. These false alarms maybe all right to put raw troops in a watchful way. Yet there is a chance for him to lose the confidence of his men. It is certainly very bad policy. Co. G is no. 1 in drill, discipline & evolutions of the regiment.

[At this point in time, the colonel of the regiment was Alexander S. Diven, who replaced Robert Van Valkenburgh when he resigned to seek re-election to the House of Representatives. While Van Valkenburgh had been a general in the New York militia, Diven, an attorney in private life, had no previous military experience. Diven's lack of military experience was very often evident, and he was heavily criticized by the other officers behind his back. He did lead the regiment at Chancellorsville but resigned following the battle after first having persuaded Nirom Crane, late of the 23rd New York, took take over the colonelcy of the 107th. Following his resignation, Diven was commissioned adjutant general with a rank of major and put in charge of the Elmira Rendezvous. On August 30, 1864, he was brevetted Brigadier General and assigned to special duty as assistant provost marshal general of the western military district of New York. He was subsequently put in command of the Northern and Western districts of New York, a post he held until the end of the war.]

Harvey G. Denniston of my Co. has been promoted to the 2nd Lieut. In the place of Ezra Gleason resigned. Harvey is a good soldier, brave & generous, in fact fully equal to his predecessor. Gleason is a fine fellow very popular among the men, yet military life did not agree with him.

[Company G was made up primarily of men from Elmira. Harvey Denniston entered the service as a corporal and became an excellent officer but would be forced to resign after an unfortunate incident with alcohol while the regiment was in Tennessee guarding railroads during the spring of 1864. He subsequently wrote a 35-chapter history of the regiment that was published in the *Geneseo Valley Times* newspaper after the war.]

Myron Fletcher is with us & doing much good in the Hospital. He brought us many delicacies from our good friends at home, which were equally divided among the different Companies of the Reg't, Co. G getting its share. We were glad to see Myron & hope he will remain with us until we have another fight. The health of the regiment is much improved. My Co. now numbers 45 fit for duty.

[Fletcher was a civilian from back home who had brought donations and was helping out in the regimental hospital. There was a significant amount of sickness present. Many soldiers died, who were then buried on the heights.]

Some parts of this detached letter are strictly confidential. Yet you ought to know what kind of field officers we have.

[Lamans wants the letter's recipient to know that his comments about Diven should remain secret.]

I am told Eleazer J. Mowers who left us on the 14th of Sept is at home. If such be the case, I wish Marshall Breck would arrest him & send him back to the Reg't. David Sanford who lives near Savona & Frazier McCarty who lives at Wallace Station are also deserters & Frank Stryker at Mitchellville. All of these I want the Marshall to arrest & send back. These constitute all the deserters in my company. Some of the companies in the 107th have lost as many as 30 by desertion.

[Eleazor J Mowers deserted the regiment on September 12, 1862, as it passed through Frederick, MD, on its way to Antietam. He was returned to the regiment and was killed August 17, 1864, during the siege of Atlanta. David Sanford deserted the regiment the day of the battle of Antietam, September 17, 1862. He was returned to the regiment and was killed May 25, 1864, during the battle of New Hope Church near Dallas, GA. Frazier McCarty deserted the regiment on October 29, 1862. On that day, the regiment began its move from Maryland Heights opposite Harper's Ferry to Antietam Ford. He was returned to the regiment and fined $10 per month from his $13 per month pay. He was mustered out on June 5, 1865, at Bladensburg with the rest of the regiment. Frank Stryker deserted along with McCarty on October 29, 1862. I have no record of what happened to him.]

Please let me hear from you as often as possible. Lieut. Brigham makes a capital officer and is quite popular among the men. I have no fault to find in my Co. either with officers or men. All with 2 or 3 exceptions are brave, good soldiers.

[Gustavus Henry Brigham entered the service as 1st Lieutenant of Company G and later was made captain of Company H, a company originally raised in Schuyler County and captained by E. Chalmers Clark.]

John Cummings who was so well soaked in whiskey around Bath has not touched a drop since we left Elmira & is one of the best & most faithful men in the regiment. You would hardly know him now; he is so changed. He is a fine noble looking soldier & says he "will never leave his captain until me legs fall off."

[John Cummings entered the service at age 43, and he was discharged because of disability, no date given. At his age, army life was probably very difficult.]

Very truly yours,<br>J.J. Lamans

Please Direct to 107th Regt, N.Y. Vol. Harpers Ferry Va.[104]

On December 1, Col. Diven issued General Order 27 advising officers that a school for their instruction was to be held on Monday, Wednesday, and Friday at 7 p.m. Officers were warned that failure to attend would bring a penalty.[105] It was during this time that the regiment's quartermaster, 1st Lt. Edward Graves, was promoted to quartermaster for the brigade.[106]

The following Thursday, a platoon of Rebels was seen on the other side of the river. Neither side fired a shot, and the calm that had accompanied their stay at Antietam Ford continued.

Snow had begun falling during the first week in December, and by the 8th, some four inches had fallen. It was accompanied by intense cold, reminding all of the winters they experienced in the North. It had become very difficult for the men on guard and picket duty. They were required to walk back and forth over a distance of 125 paces for a period of 24 hours with two-hour reliefs. Otherwise, the men were very comfortable in their huts with the aid of a good fire. The following day, orders came that they were to march and to be ready to start in the morning on Wednesday, December 10. No destination was given, but they were to start off south in the direction of Harper's Ferry.

Meanwhile, back in Havana, there was a wedding announcement in the *Havana Journal* on December 6; "In this village on the 2inst [sic] by Rev. Sidney Wilbur, Captain E.C. Clark and Miss Harriet A. Skellenger daughter of Major Wm. Skellenger all of this village". However, the following week there was another announcement in the same newspaper: "Died of consumption in this village, Saturday Dec. 13th at the home of her father William Skellenger, Mrs. Harriet A. Skellenger Clark, wife of Captain E.C. Clark aged 25 years, 11 months and 26 days."

# 5

# The Mud March
# and Hope Landing

By sheer determination, they slogged forward toward the enemy at Fredericksburg. They were the soldiers of the Union's Army of the Potomac, and they did not give up. Just weeks earlier, they had been dispatched in an assault on the Confederates at the battle of Antietam. Now they were advancing again. The weather caused the roads to be churned into an ocean of mud. It was "an indescribable chaos of pontoons, vehicles, and artillery," a federal officer would later recall, "wagons upset by the roadside, guns stalled in the mud—horses and mules buried in the liquid mud." Even so, the battle-hardened soldiers of the Army of the Potomac did not give up. However, the weather ultimately proved to be an obstinate foe, and they were forced to seek out a new camp.

On December 10, the regiment was up early and spent the morning preparing for the march. There was snow on the ground, but it was a sunny and pleasant day. By 2 o'clock they, along with the rest of the regiments in their brigade, were on the road, marching in the direction of Harper's Ferry. The march was uneventful, and as darkness fell, they bivouacked in a stand of trees and ate their supper. Large fires were built to keep them warm.

The next morning, reveille was beaten at half past three; after breakfast they started out at about 5 o'clock. By dinnertime they had reached Harper's Ferry. They halted to the rear of Louden Heights and ate their dinner.[1] It was at this point that Brigadier General Alpheus S. Williams joined their brigade on the march. He had been relaxing with his daughter at Harper's Ferry, and she had left him to return home.[2] It was three o'clock before the 107th was on the road again, moving on into Virginia. It was after dark when they finally halted after a very difficult march over muddy roads. Hay was provided to make very comfortable beds for them that night. On Friday, December 12, they did not begin their march until 2 p.m. They passed through the small village of Hillsborough, marching until well after dark.[3] Here Williams ordered them into camp because their wagons had not kept pace with them.[4] It was almost 10 p.m. when they finally stopped. Their destination was Leesburg, but because of their late start, they were only able to reach a spot four miles north of it.

The next day, on the road at 5 a.m., they continued on but at a very slow pace. Rebel guerrillas who were attempting to capture wagons from their supply train were continually harassing them. At one point, one of their sutler wagons was captured, but their cavalry was able to drive the Rebels off and recapture the wagon. They passed through Leesburg, marched all day, and stopped 14 miles beyond at Chantilly. It was a hard march with many men falling out. They were now marching on the pike, which led to Fairfax Court House. The countryside appeared to be excellent for farming, and there was no denying, from the people's attitude, that they were in "secesh" country. Unbeknownst to them, the objective of their march, Fredericksburg, was already a scene of bloody fighting of which they would not be a part. That same day, private Nelson A. Robinson of Company G died of disease in the hospital at Smoketown.

On Sunday the 14th, they stopped to rest several times during the morning. The going was slow, and there was much evidence of Seigel's corps being there before them.[5] Warmer weather had caused the snow and frost to thaw and left the roads almost impassable. Many trains passing over them had cut up deeply what never was very good. General Williams wrote in a letter to his daughter: "You cannot imagine the difficulties of marches at this season, on short rations, short forage, bad roads, bad preparations and the like. Think of moving a force of 10,000 men with all its supplies in wagons over a stripped country in the month of December. The thing looks impossible, and yet we have done it so far and I have no doubt I shall get through with a fagged command."[6] They had finally caught up with the rest of their division. They passed through Fairfax Court House, marching until after dark to a point about a mile from Fairfax Station where the road intersected with the road to Alexandria. They had come a distance of 10 or 12 miles. Word of a battle taking place at Fredericksburg traveled through the ranks. It was said that Burnside had driven the Rebels from the town. There was no doubt in their minds that Fredericksburg was their destination.

The next day, December 15, they started out from Fairfax Station, early on crossing Occoquan Creek where Rebel works were still very visible. The road was very rough, and they were only able to march seven or eight miles before making camp in a pleasant wood around 4 o'clock. It began raining during the night, and the next morning the roads soon turned muddy. As a result, they marched only a short distance of fewer than four miles. At noon they halted and made camp in another stretch of woods.[7] Company F was assigned to guard the regiment's wagons, and as such they were allowed to put their knapsacks in the wagons.[8]

On December 17, they were surprised when they received orders to turn around and march back to Fairfax Station. Unbeknownst to them, Burnside had been defeated at Fredericksburg, and they were no longer needed there. The roads were still very bad and made more so as it snowed occasionally. They arrived back at Fairfax Station by 3 p.m. The newspapers revealed to them the story of Burnside's defeat the next day.[9]

Their camp was in a pine wood that had little in the way of firewood but consisted only of small trees and bushes. The weather was typical for the time of year: unseasonably warm, often rainy days that were cloudy and cheerless, and nights that were cold. Their tents were of the small shelter type with beds that consisted of pine boughs covered with a blanket. Fires were out of necessity made of green wood that required a great deal of coaxing to make it burn. The black smoke of the green wood caused the camp to become sooty. As a result, the whole camp, including their clothing, became grim and dirty. Plans to move the camp began in earnest.[10] A rumor circulated among the men was that they were changing camp because the government was seeding the area around Fairfax Station with lice, necessitating their moving every three days.[11] Four months had passed since their arrival in northern Virginia, and three months since their first and only fighting at Antietam. They had yet to receive their first pay. In a letter home, John Hill, a sergeant in Company F, wrote to his mother asking, "Are there any more regiments being raised around there?" He stated, "Tell pa if there is a chance to get me a lieutenancy by paying a hundred dollars or such a matter he had better do it as that is the way Chatfield's son got promoted. If the war is going to last three years, I might as well get big pay as anyone and ought to make some effort to get it."[12]

They remained in their camp all day Friday and Saturday. On Saturday evening, December 21, Colonel Diven and Lt. Colonel Smith traveled to Washington. The nights continued to be cold, and there was general fear that so much exposure from sleeping in the open air might start another epidemic of sickness. By Tuesday, the weather had turned more moderate. Still, they heard no news about what their next move might be. That Sunday, Pvt. Stephen Rickey of Company B died of disease at the hospital in Summit House, PA. On Wednesday the 24th, General Williams, or "Pap" as they all called him, reviewed their brigade. Some 4,000 men were in line from the five regiments of their brigade. After the review, a work crew was organized to lay out a permanent camp elsewhere.[13]

The next day was Christmas and the first one away from home for most of the men in the 107th. Instead of opening presents that morning, they moved to their new camp, a distance of about two miles. The camp was located on the Elsey farm in a pleasant wood about a mile from Fairfax Station. The dense growth of laurel and holly was cut away, and broad streets were laid out. The camp consisted of 209 huts with officers' quarters at the head of each company street. The Elsey farmhouse was near the camp and facing what was to be their parade ground. The family, although friendly, were undoubtedly Rebel sympathizers. Their farmhouse was the subject of many visits by local citizens, particularly their son-in-law Charles. He was also in the habit of visiting the camp and seemed a bright and intelligent young man. During one of his many conversations with the officers, he told of deserting from the Rebel army after the 2nd Manassas battle. All this time he was closely watched, and eventually he was arrested as a spy and lodged in Old Capital prison in Washington to await his trial.

An old brick church, a relic of bygone days, was located near the camp. The bricks were said to have been brought from Holland and that Washington had once worshiped there. The 2nd Massachusetts regiment began demolishing it for the purpose of using its bricks to build fireplaces. The other regiments in the 107th's brigade soon followed suit. Chaplain Crane of the 107th often remarked thereafter that "the bricks were still used to throw out light, or rather heat which was its twin sister." It was shortly after this that the 3rd Wisconsin and the 2nd Massachusetts moved their camp to "Wolf Run Shoals," leaving the 107th N.Y., 27th Indiana and 13th N.J. at Fairfax Station.

Two days after Christmas, Pvt. Nathaniel Finch of Company D died of disease in a hospital in Philadelphia, PA.

They rested quietly in the camp for the next three days, but during the night of the third day, December 28, they were called out to draw three days rations and told to be ready to march. Word had it that J.E.B. Stuart's cavalry had attacked Union forces at Dumfries. After drawing rations, they went to bed. Large fires were not allowed, and they spent the entire night trying to keep warm. Rising at 9 a.m. on the 29th, they were told to fall in with only their blankets and overcoats. Their knapsacks were to be left behind. Fully expecting to be heading into battle, they marched back over the same road. The weather was mild, more like fall than winter. They marched all morning, arriving at Wolf Shoals on Occoquan Creek at about 1 p.m. They moved a short way from the creek and camped by the roadside near sundown. Rumors spread about that fighting was in their front as well as at Dumfries. The next day they remained in camp until noon when word came that Stuart had attacked Fairfax Station. Then, marching all day without a halt, they arrived at Fairfax Station, their starting point, a distance of eight miles. All the while, they were fearful of Rebel cavalry that was rumored to be in the vicinity. On arriving at the station, they found it undisturbed. Stuart had instead attacked Burke's Station, which was five miles from Alexandria and Fairfax Court House. At the former, he burned bridges, and at the latter, he captured General Stoughton, whose headquarters were some distance from his detachment of troops.[14]

The end of the month meant filling out the muster rolls for November and December. By now they were due five months' pay. The weather began to turn cold again, and Colonel Diven gave the command for the men to build log huts. They rang out the old and in with the new by commencing the construction of more permanent housing. They had now spent their first Christmas and first New Year's Day away from home, but these were the least of their new experiences these past five months, and both passed with almost no notice.[15]

The end of December saw a change in the staff officers of the regiment. When Diven took over command of the regiment in October, Major Gabriel Smith had taken his position as lieutenant colonel, and Captain Newton Colby of company I was promoted to major.[16]

Construction on their new huts began on New Year's Day and continued until it was delayed by division reviews on successive days. On Saturday, January 3, General Williams reviewed their division of some ten thousand men. On Sunday, General Slocum reviewed them.[17] The review kept them in formation until two o'clock in the afternoon. Their bayonets glistened in the sun, and a long line of artillery stationed in their rear fired a salute of thirteen guns when Major General Slocum approached. The heavy booming of cannon, although from blank cartridges, sounded so much like Antietam that they felt quite at home.[18]

Construction on their log huts had progressed so that by January 6, about half of them had been completed. A typical hut had a fireplace, room for two bunks, and a stationary table built on one side with stools around it.[19]

Company H was informed that its captain, Captain E. Chalmers Clark, had been discharged from the service for disability. He had been well liked by the men in his company and the officers of the regiment as a whole. Besides being wounded at Antietam and the death of his new bride, his father had also passed away. His absence had left the company with only one officer, 1st Lieutenant Donnelly.[20]

During January, the regimental books offered up some startling figures that reflected how differently the regiment appeared after five months in the field. One thousand twenty men had left Elmira. At this time, the count stood at 527 present for duty, 300 sick in hospital, 106 deserters, 46 died of disease or killed in battle, and 19 discharged. The remainder were detailed to duty in other locations in the brigade.[21] For the next ten days, rumors concerning marching orders circulated throughout the camp. Regimental commanders were ordered to draw clothing supplies, and the ambulance and supply trains repaired their equipment. Their destination was thought to be North Carolina. They no doubt would march to Alexandria and board transports to go by sea. Surgeon Flood received orders to pack up medicines. and the Quartermaster had orders to stock up on 11 days of supplies.[22]

On January 10, Pvt. Frederick W. Wagner of Company F died of disease at Fairfax Station, VA. His father petitioned Colonel Diven to allow the body to be sent home. It was very unusual for enlisted men to be sent home for burial. As a result, many families never knew where their sons were buried. The father's request was denied.[23]

January 18 was a busy day. The sick, surrounded by their friends, were loaded into ambulances to be taken to the railroad and then on to hospitals in Washington.[24] However, Private Theophilus Krumloff of Company F would not make the trip. His death was referred to in two letters sent home by two soldiers in the regiment who might have been friends of Krumloff. One letter was written by Andrew Brockway, a private in Company C. In his letter to his sister he wrote, "Yesterday we buried one of the men of our regiment. He was a middle-aged man and leaves a wife and three children in the north. The last time that he went to the doctor the doctor told him that he was not sick that he only needed a few grains of ambition. That evening before he died the surgeon was at his captain's tent and told him that that man was not so sick as he pretended to be."[25] However, in another letter, 2nd Lt. John Hill wrote that Dr. Flood had said Krumloff suffered from diarrhea off and on for weeks until it became chronic, and he began to run down very fast. Dr. Flood remarked, "He is all used up, and his bowels are all raw and probably ulcerated in the lower parts." He died that day and was buried at Fairfax Station, VA.[26]

The next morning, they arose to a nearly clear sky with the sun shining brightly. The canvas roofing of their huts was removed, rolled up into bundles, and marked with company letters for transportation. They marched to a large field opposite the 1st Division Headquarters where all of the regiments were assembling to take their appropriate positions. Other regiments who were to remain at the station cheered them as they passed by. Units of cavalry rode to the front to take the lead, and long trains of artillery with their "Napoleons" gleaming in the sun moved into position.

It was about noon before they began their march. Each division took a different line of march although they were near enough to each other to maintain eye contact. General Geary's 2nd division took the road to the right, General Kane's 3rd division the one to the left, and the 107th regiment's 1st division took the center road. The pace was set at "route step" with "arms at will." They made little progress until almost sundown when the pace picked up. They reached Occoquan Creek about dark, crossed it on a rail bridge, and camped about two miles past it in woods where they had once before made camp.

Pickets were set out, fires kindled, and supper prepared. As the evening wore on, much camaraderie was evident, and conversation soon turned into song. Quiet soon prevailed as many turned to writing letters home or in their journals. Then sleep was enjoyed for the night.[27]

The destination of the upcoming march was Dumfries, and it provided for an amusing story about one of the characters in the regiment. John Woodruff was a company cook. He was droll and funny and never tired of telling stories. He would sit up all night to listen to the yarns of others. He was once nearly arrested for disrespect to a general. Old John, noticing the salutes being given to an approaching horseman, went to the side of the road and struck the attitude of a soldier. Then as the officer passed him, he gave him a magnificent salute with his empty frying pan. The general frowned so fiercely upon old John that he was frightened nearly out of his boots. He never tired of dropping his cooking and chasing some cavalryman, shouting and hallooing to him to hold on. When he reached the rider, he would beg his pardon for a mistake, stating that he thought it was someone else, always loudly naming "the someone else" as some ridiculous fellow or camp follower. The regiment, always attracted by the noisy maneuver, would laugh and haw-haw at the cursing of the detained horseman. Old John never tired of the joke, and the men always laughed loudly.

Woodruff was badly sold once though. It was on their march to Dumfries. The men were all hungry, had eaten nothing for a day, and had a ten-hour march before they would reach Dumfries, the only place they could get rations. So, they did as often hungry men would do. They imagined all the good eatables they could think of. They talked of dinners and bills of fare they would get at Dumfries, well knowing there was nothing there but hardtack. They discussed aloud all the most tempting meals their imaginations could suggest. But Woodruff wasn't an imaginative man, so he thought they were in earnest. They noticed his mistake and made the most of it. Quietly they all got near him as they marched and then carried their conversation on to a further extent about the prospective luxuries of Dumfries. They talked of what a splendid city it was, its miles of streets and broad avenues, and got into a heated discussion as to whether they would take street cars upon their arrival or should they all hire hacks and drive to the first-class hotels or restaurants that they had just described. They described the splendid restaurants in great detail and talked of the savory dishes they were wont to serve up to their customers. They mentioned in particular the splendid bar rooms with elegant bars, marble tops one hundred feet long, thirty bartenders with their hair parted in the middle, all sliding tumblers with lightning rapidity to the throng of drinkers. Woodruff was an attentive listener. He must have thought Dumfries to be as nice as New York City. Old Woodruff stopped, and smacking his lips loudly, stated that if he could only then and there have one whiskey straight, he would lie down in the mud and quit. Through the rest of that long and weary day, Old John talked hopefully of the city luxuries of Dumphries while continuing to plod through the mud.

What a disappointment awaited him. They reached the deserted hamlet of Dumfries. Three houses composed the whole town, and on the door of one was a placard bearing the words "Smallpox." Woodruff looked all around and wanted to know if that was all there was to this place. He then sat down on the ground, a miserable looking dejected man. When some of Company K's men attempted to joke with him about it, he turned upon them quickly, remarking, "they needn't talk, that the town looked just like Hornellsville." The Company K men retired in confusion. But old John soon recovered his spirits and went around buttonholing men, and with a serious face, asking them if this was Dumfries and if so, where he could find old Dumfry himself.[28]

They had reached Dumfries on January 20 at about 5 p.m.[29] The march had been uneventful until they reached Dumfries, where they found the encampments of several Vermont regiments, who cheered them as they came into view. The men of the 107th responded in kind. "What corps is that?" they asked. "The old Twelfth" was the response. "Bully for you! Hurrah! Hurrah! For the 12th!" and so loud and boisterous was the noise that normal conversation was impossible.

Dumfries, in addition to the three dilapidated houses, had an old, moss-covered hotel that was being used as the post commissary and a liege home with broken sashes. It alone seemed uninhabited. Nearby on a hill stood an odd, shaped edifice that served as a courthouse.

The camp of the 107th was made a half-mile beyond the village. It was in a pine thicket, which at first seemed an innocent enough location. However, as the men proceeded to set up their camp, they found many tombstones in the dense undergrowth. Their camp was situated in the center of a graveyard.[30]

They had marched fourteen miles in all and from their camp could see the Potomac River and the landing. Late in the evening around ten o'clock, a light rain began to fall. It fell steadily all during the night. Because of the rain, there was no dry wood for a fire, and their tiny shelter tents could not keep them dry. As a result, they got up the morning of the 21st both wet and cold.[31]

Breakfast that morning, due to the lack of dry wood, consisted of raw pork and hardtack, minus their usual coffee. The order to march came at 7 a.m., and by the time they started, they were completely chilled through. They marched off in the direction of Quantico Creek.[32] During that time, they received news from a Washington hospital that three of their comrades had died of disease. The deceased were Pvt. Jonathon H. Barlow of Company B, Pvt. Charles H. Luce of Company A, and Pvt. Duane Paterson of Company H.

What had been solid roads the day before had turned completely into a quagmire of mud. The mud came halfway to their knees, forcing them to march as best they could in the woods along the side of the road. The rising waters in the creek had washed the bridge away. They were forced to walk single file on a fallen tree using their rifles to balance themselves. Many of the men lost their balance and fell into the swift current that came up to their waist.[33] Not only did they get soaking wet, but many lost their guns. It took the regiment three hours to cross the creek.[34]

The regiment moved erratically along, seeking shelter wherever they could. No type of discipline was maintained, and progress was nearly impossible. Groups of them did manage to build fires. This allowed them the opportunity to drink some hot coffee and change their socks. Eventually the regiment was brought together. They attempted to march again but stopped after traveling only a mile in the rain and mud. The roads were near impassable, and the wagons could not move at all. The rain continued as they put up their tents and built fires. When they awoke the next morning, it was still raining. After breakfast, they fell in at 9 o'clock. Marching was even worse than the day before with mud now reaching all the way to their knees. On they went at an impossible pace, wading creeks and sometimes finding a solid road. They crawled along until 4 o'clock, having marched a total of only eight miles. They were now two miles from their supply base at Acquia Creek where they could replenish their completely exhausted supplies. The march had been a disaster. Equipment and supplies were thrown away in great quantities. The road was littered with mess chests, hospital fixtures, tents, and some 9,000 rounds of ammunition.

During the night there was no rain. As morning broke the clouds cleared off ,and it was very pleasant. They were still in camp when the paymaster arrived, but just as he got ready to pay them, the order to move was given. The road was still very rough and muddy. After a march of almost five miles, they passed through the village of Stafford Courthouse.[35]

As they marched through the village, a German soldier of the 11th corps called out to them, "Vot regiment is dat saay." "The 107th New York," was the response. "Ah, dat ish goot," he answered. "We ish from New York," and he turned into a sutler's tent, smoking vehemently.[36]

The 107th continued through the village to a spot a half-mile past it where they made camp in a wood near the courthouse. That evening they were paid off by Major C.W. Campbell, and they received pay up to the first of October. With money in their pockets, many of the men took the opportunity to raise their spirits further by drinking down the same, as was evident by the staggering of some through the camp.[37] The paymaster finished paying the men by 9 a.m. of the 24th.

The courthouse at Stafford was all but nonexistent. What walls that were left intact were filled with names and inscriptions from passing soldiers. Its present use was that of the post commissary. Opposite stood the jail, a building three stories high with exterior stairs leading to the upper stories. Appropriately it was being used as the guardhouse, and it housed several Rebel prisoners. There were only three houses in the village. This came as no surprise as the surrounding countryside gave no evidence of supporting any kind of agriculture or industry. Lieutenant Denniston spent his leisure time examining the land, going so far as to examine the soil. He found seashells in a hole that he dug, and the hole, several feet deep, quickly filled with water. He concluded that the area would have been better served had it remained submerged.

The largest of the three houses in the village served as the headquarters of the 11th Corps commander, General Sigel. General Slocum's commanding officer of the 12th Corps was located near the 107th's camp.[38]

The next day, a new location for the regiment's camp was laid out.[39] After resting for three days near Stafford Courthouse, they moved their camp to near Hope Landing on Acquia Creek. Once there they were given the job of building a corduroy road from the landing to the courthouse to allow for the transportation of supplies. That evening it began to rain, and then at about midnight it turned to snow. A light snow fell all of the 28th, but the mild temperature caused it to melt almost immediately. They were not so fortunate that next evening. A strong wind accompanied by a heavy snowfall covered their tiny shelter tents with eight to nine inches of snow.[40] In such weather and with only small shelter tents to protect them, they constructed beds designed not only to keep them warm but also to protect them to some extent. They laid six inches of fine brush on the ground, covered it with two rubber blankets, placed three bedticks on the blankets and their overcoats on the bed ticks. They laid on the overcoats and covered themselves with three blankets. If the weather was stormy, they placed a rubber blanket over their feet to keep dry.[41]

During the next several days, the weather cleared up. Warmer weather caused the snow to melt rapidly, and the men commenced building the corduroy road.[42] However, the melting snow turned the road to mud and made their work very difficult. A passing drove of mules was so covered with mud that the hair on their body or their ears was not visible. Several times the mule drivers fell off of their mule and completely disappeared in the mud.[43] Still they felled the trees and laid them across the road in corduroy fashion. That evening they returned muddy and tired to their neglected tents. As a result of this hard work and insufficient shelter, colds and fevers began to prevail. Likewise, the hospital filled up, and the doctors were hard pressed to keep up with the needs.

As luck would have it, two officers rode into camp and ordered an inspection. The men were called in directly from their work on the corduroy road with no opportunity to clean up. Once in formation, the inspecting officers reviewed them. One of them remarked to Major Colby, "How dirty your men look." Colby responded bluntly, "They have been engaged in dirty business." The inspecting officers seemed amazed that the men were being used so. The review was concluded, and the officers left to make their report. Over the next two days, the corduroy road was completed. During this time, it was decided that the present camp location was deemed unfit for the regiment and a new location must be sought.

The weather continued to fluctuate over the next several days, sun shining and mild one day and rain and snow the next. Regardless of the weather, disease and death began to take their toll on the men of the 107th New York. Pvt. Calvin Burlingame of Company I died at Hope Landing on February 3. On Friday morning, February 6, Private John Brewer of Company F died of typhoid fever. The rain that had started the previous day stopped in the early afternoon and allowed for his burial at 2 p.m. Lieutenant Knox of his company read a chapter from the bible and led a prayer. That same day, Pvt. Abram Denniston of Company G died of disease in a Washington hospital.

In the meantime, the regiment began moving their camp to a side hill close to Hope Landing on Acquia Creek. Some of the company streets were steep, and the log huts' foundations were dug into the hill. The huts were of the usual construction with shelter tent roofs and mud chimneys enclosed in barrels. The quarters of the company officers were at the base of the hill fronting the company streets. The field and staff officers were across the road on the bank of the creek. The quartermaster, the commissary, and the sutlers were at the entrance to the parade ground.

The new camp looked down on the landing, which jutted out into Acquia Bay. The bay was part of the creek by the same name and flowed into the Potomac River. The landing served as a receiving point for Union Army supplies. Small boats of all types brought supplies from Washington and other locations to Aquia Landing on the Potomac. In turn, these supplies were brought to Hope Landing by the little stern-wheeler steamer *Frederick Graff*. Along with supplies, the soldiers were also able to receive packages from home. Between the camp of the 107th and the landing, a beautiful, level piece of land served for drilling and parade.

It was at this time that Lieut. Colonel Smith returned to the regiment. He had been absent since they had left Fairfax Station. His resignation from the service was read at dress parade. Major Colby was promoted to fill the void. A contest for the position of major began immediately among the company officers. The primary candidates were Captain Lathrop Baldwin, Adjutant Hull Fanton, and Captain J.J. Laman. Attempts to contact Colonel Diven in Washington were made, and many letters were sent to influential people in Steuben, Chemung, and Schuyler counties. In the end it was the popularity among his fellow officers that got Captain William F. Fox of Company C the promotion to major.[44]

Several of the regiment's officers were dissatisfied with the location of their current camp. Major Colby selected a new one, and several officers went to evaluate it on Saturday. His choice was not selected in favor of another location nearby. Following the selection, they immediately began to lay out the company streets and the locations for the regiment's other requirements. The move to a new location and the construction of new shanties was evidently not enough to keep a number of the men occupied and out of trouble. Six men of different companies were tied to trees for disobedience of orders. By Tuesday the 9th, the men were busy building their shanties of log walls, a tent roof, and a fireplace with a chimney made of whatever was available. They filled in the spaces between the logs with mud, and their beds were in some cases elevated on poles to keep them from the damp ground.[45] The next day was such a very warm day that some men took baths in the creek. However, on Thursday, the weather turned cold again, and snow fell.[46] Pvt. Albert N. James of Company I died of disease that same day at Frederick, MD.

The regimental records of February 15 showed the following data: present 466, absent on detached duty 36, absent with leave 3, absent without leave 103, absent sick 286, discharged 78, died 48, total 1018.

More snow fell on the 17th. The roads continued to be very treacherous, but cavalry units were continually passing along the road near their camp. A solitary horseman could be seen going along slowly, feeling as carefully as possible for ruts. Suddenly, the horse went down into a deep hole, hiding his legs entirely. Soon he floundered out only, to slip into another one, and so on again. On one occasion a sword fell into the mud, and the cavalryman, unable to find it, remarked, "Well let it go, I don't care for one sword." Often companies of horsemen would go to the landing for forage, their horses covered with mud.[47]

By the 19th of February, the men's houses were completed, and efforts were underway to make them as habitable as possible. However, the constant rain was playing havoc with their chimneys of mud and stone. The rain contributed the uneasiness in the camp, where drinking was again a problem and led to numerous fights.[48]

The 107th had been nicely situated in its new camp for some time, and they were very lucky that they had not been required to move again. The roads, though now corduroyed, were still very difficult for travel to Stafford's Courthouse. Only cavalry units were able travel on the road. But even they continued to find it very difficult with the mud so deep. Riders were often thrown from their horses or had to dismount. On George Washington's birthday, it snowed 12 inches. Nevertheless, the day was celebrated with a series of cannon salutes.

On the 21st, Pvt. John Lalor died of disease in their camp and the letter sent by Lalor's commanding officer Captain William Morgan to Lalor's brother George read as follows:

> Camp of the 107th Regiment
> Near Hope's Landing.
> February 22, 1863
>
> George P. Lalor
> Eddy Town
> Yates County, NY
>
> Dear sir,
>
> It becomes my painful duty to inform you of the death of your brother John Lalor of my company. He was taken ill with camp fever on Tuesday February 17th and died Saturday. His remains will be placed in an old burying ground near Hope's Landing. John was a general favorite with his companions and a good soldier. I with the entire company sympathize deeply with his friends. He had two dollars and twenty-five cents in money a portrait and a wallet. The money I enclose. The others are subject to your order.
>
> Very respectfully yours,
> Wm. L. Morgan
> Capt. Co. E 107 Regmt.
> N.Y.V.[49]

Shortly after the war's end, the body of John Lalor and many, but not all, of the other 107th New York soldiers buried at Hope Landing were reinterred in the Fredericks National Cemetery.

February came to a close with two more soldiers dying of disease at Hope Landing. They were Private John R. Ackerly of Company H on February 25 and Pvt. James Fuller of Company K on February 27.

The beginning of March brought with it much milder weather. This gave the men the opportunity to construct better housing. At the same time, sickness among the men in the regiment was rising. In January, five men had died of sickness. During February another seven had died. But in the first eight days of March, seven more would die and with a total for the month of thirteen.[50]

On March 1, 1863, Pvt. James McCullough of Company G died of disease at Hope Landing, VA. On March 3, 1863, Pvt. Hiram Paddock of Company H, Pvt Silas H. Betson of Company A, and Pvt. George Compton of Company C all died of disease at Hope Landing, VA. Funerals were held on March 8. On March 7, 1863, Pvt. James W. Lovell of Company G died disease at Hope Landing, VA.

The following letter written by Daniel Scott on March 10, 1863, paints a definitive portrait of the situation in the regiment's camp.

> Hope Landing. March 10th 1863
>
> Dear Father, Mother, Sister & Brothers,
>
>     Drill hours is over, the sun is shining out clear & bright. I have nothing to busy myself so I thought I would write to pass away the time. It is nice spring weather here now & when I see a nice day like this my mind of times reverts back to the past when I was a merry laughing boy & had nothing to trouble me. I cared for nothing to trouble me. I cared for nothing only to live &

enjoy life & be happy. Oh, how little did I know of the stern realities of life & its changing and shifting scenes but this is a life of changes we must live and learn. I am well and have plenty of everything to eat and wear. But our camp is in a very unhealthy place. Sickness & death is daily doing its work in our Regt although I have been as healthy here as I ever have. The Major & doctor has gone today to look up another camp. We have a funeral every day in the Regt. Fausy is getting better. I think he will get well if he does not take cold. He had a pretty serious time of it. We have built winter quarters 4 times & I think we will move to our new camp in a few days we will not probably go more than ½ mile from our old camp. I have just received your letter and I was glad to hear from you although you say Lewis is sick and some of the family is sick all the time or nearly so. But you must not forbear to write when any of the family is sick thinking it will worry me for, I would rather know the worst you say that it is very sickly in Chemung. Well so it is in the army and every other place in the U.S. as near as I can learn by the papers. Since we came to Hopes Landing. I think we have averaged nearly a death every day. So, you may judge how healthy it is here. Our Rgmt. Is going down hill pretty fast. Some of our best and noblest boys is snatched away daily by the ruthless hand of death some of them is not sick But a day or two fever follows it is enough to melt the hardest heart to see them in their delirious moments and hear them talk of home and friends who they will never be permitted to see again on this earth you have a pretty hard row to hoe I wish I could help you in some way how willingly would I do it I know it is not convenient to go to the office very often so I will not complain if I do not get a letter every week but I would like to have you write as often as you can you speak of my getting a discharge if my health is poor if I thought there was any prospect I would get one as soon as the next man but it is a pretty hard matter to get discharged from this Regt. Leander can tell you something about it Men that have been in the General Hospital for 2 months have sent to the Capt for their descriptive list and he would not send it until he was obliged to Tell Leander that Capt. Colby has been put in Major of the Regt. and Capt. Morgan was mad be cause he was not elected and he tendered his resignation which was not excepted but he is working for his discharged now & Sam Taylor is working for the Lieutenancy Colonel Diven has been at Washington about a month we are trying to get up a Band in our Regt. & I think we will succeed Now a word to Lewis Dear Brother I am sorry to hear that you are sick but you will soon be well again and as it is getting Spring you can help Virgil & father make garden you must be a good boy Study your book and when I come home I will bring you & Mary & Virgil a nice present now I must close write when it is convenient for you to do so Give my love and best wishes to all Enquiring Friends and retain a share for yourself

From your son, Daniel Scott[51]

Captain Hector M. Slocum, captain of Company D, resigned to Colonel Diven on March 11. Colonel Diven in turn forwarded it to the Ass't Adjutant General of the 12th Corps with the following message: "Sir: I have forwarded Capt. H.M. Slocum' resignation. I recommend its acceptance. While Capt. Slocum is disposed to do his duty, he lacks the qualifications for a good officer. He has no confidence in himself, and I fear will never overcome this distrust of his own ability. As a man he is trustworthy and should in my opinion be allowed to leave his command with honor. He was most efficient in raising his company."[52]

On March 12, 1863, Pvt. Henry H. Rasco and Pvt. George S. Cone both of Compamy K died of disease at Hope Landing, VA. On March 17, 1863, Pvt. William Parks of Company C died of disease at Hope Landing, VA. On March 19, 1863, Pvt. Lewis Knickerbocker of Company K died of disease at Hope Landing, VA.

On Sunday. March 21, a directive was sent out assigning a distinctive badge to each corps. It so happened that for several months Kearny's division of the Third

Corps were wearing a distinctive diamond shaped badge of flannel on their caps. General Butterfield, Hooker's chief of staff, recognized its practical uses and advantages and conceived the idea of marking each division and each corps in a similar manner. Each division's badge was red for the first, white for the second, and blue for the third. In the case of the 12th Corps, the badge was to be a five-pointed star. Thus the 107th New York became part of the "Red Star Division." They wore this badge with honor the remainder of the war and proudly displayed it at the Grand Review in May 1865.[53]

The funeral of private Alpheus Watson of Company F was held that same Sunday, March 21. The cause of death was listed as a putrid or ulcerated sore throat. He was only nineteen and very boyish in his appearance. His younger brother George, who had enlisted with him, took his death very hard. His burial ceremony the next day was attended by nearly all of the men of the regiment. Three volleys of musketry were fired over the grave, and the men marched slowly to the beat of muffled drums and the solemn dirge of the dead march.[54]

Private David Moranville died in the camp hospital of typhoid fever a week later on March 28. He was the thirteenth man from company F to die in the short space of eight months. Just three days later, Private Daniel Cummings of the same company also died of typhoid fever.[55]

General Ruger was the commander of the brigade to which the 107th belonged. He issued orders that each company of the regiment was to have separate cooking facilities. A cookhouse was to be constructed on the crest of the hill where the camp was located. In two weeks' time, trees were cut down, dragged by mules to the tops of company streets, and the buildings constructed. Smoke curling from the chimneys and soldiers marching up and down the hill signaled completion of the order. However, the men were not happy with the situation and found it necessary to supplement their diet by acquiring additional food from the sutlers.

This situation also had its humorous side. One day an officer of the 107th had occasion to travel on the steamer *Frederick Graff* to Aquia Landing. Another passenger, Captain Steiner, assistant quartermaster of the 12th Corps, asked if the 107th was building fortifications on the hill. "Oh no," the officer replied, "those are cook houses by order of General Ruger." "My God," said the captain laughing. "I supposed they were regular forts, and so has everyone who has observed them."[56]

The weather continued to fluctuate but was of no concern to them in their comfortable little huts. On April 1, they buried Privates David P. Moranville and Daniel Cummings, both of Company F. This brought the total number of deaths during March to thirteen.[57] It was Sunday, and a service was held by Elder Crane.[58]

The regiment was now midway through their stay in their camp near Hope Landing. It was a pleasant stay for the most part, notwithstanding the large number of deaths due to sickness. They hoped for letters each day and packages from home as often as possible. Food and clothing were the most common items sent to them. The most popular clothing items included socks, suspenders, and thread, along with such delectables as pie, cakes with frosting, nuts, and candy. Stamps, envelopes, and writing paper were also favored items. All were greatly appreciated as was evidenced from this quote from a letter home: "Well I am very much obliged for everything, and you can judge from my thoughts when I look at the different packages and think of the ones that helped crack the nuts and the busy fingers that picked them out and thought of John far, far away, away down south in Dixie."[59]

Initially there had been no thought given to establishing a formal cemetery near the 107th's camp. However, the increasing number of deaths in the regiment led Colonel Diven to become dissatisfied with the present situation where the graves were being dug without any organization. Diven desired them to be placed in order at one place and requested Lieutenant H.G. Denniston to take the matter in charge. The lieutenant accordingly set about the duty and discharged it as follows. On a beautiful knoll jutting out in Acquia Bay, the dead were all placed in regular order. At the head of each grave, gravestones were erected with name, company, regiment, and epitaph appropriate to each. These headstones resembled marble and were large and well-formed, and the inscriptions were easily cut deep into them. They constructed good gravel walks, lined with holly, and a substantial, rustic fence of cedar and locust. A large block of stone stood at the front of the cemetery with the inscription "107th Regiment N.Y.V., In Peace Rest, instituted by order of Col. A.S. Diven and arranged by Lieut. H.G. Denniston." In the end, thirty-two members of the 107th New York were buried there. Officers and soldiers of different regiments visited this cemetery. Generals Slocum, Williams, and Ruger often walked through it and also the corps commander General Joseph Hooker. Capt. J.G. Lee, quartermaster of the 11th Army Corps, was so impressed with the cemetery that he asked permission to have his friend Mr. Leaman buried there and that a suitable stone be placed at the head of his grave. Leaman had died suddenly of spotted fever. Lieut. Denniston gave permission and promised to erect a marker on the grave. Captain Lee later wrote a letter of thanks to Lieut. Denniston and had a photograph taken of the grave.

This was done and the following letter from Capt. Lee expressed his acknowledgment.

Office of the 11th Army Corps, Brooks Station

Lieut. H.G. Denniston

I beg to express to you my thanks and the thanks of the young men associated with me for the very great kindness you have done us by making a stone for the grave of our departed friend Mr. Leaman. We appreciate it most warmly and can only assure you that you have won our greatest gratitude and highest esteem. I inferred from the chaplain that the stone had been placed at the grave, but one of our number was over there last evening and tells me it has not been. May I ask this further favor and though it will add another to our already great obligations, yet I trust you will cheerfully do it for me. Again, thanking you for your noble assistance in this matter and assuring you of the warm place you have won in our hearts, I am Lieutenant, most faithfully yours,

J.G.C. Lee Capt. A.Q.M.[60]

On April 8, 1863, Pvt. Andrew Dewitt died of typhoid fever at Hope Landing, VA. The following day, Commissary Sgt. Henry Inscho died at home in Lawrenceville, PA. Two days later, Teamster Pvt. William M. Cooper of Company E died at Harper's Ferry.[61]

The next day, Generals Slocum, Ruger, Knipe, Jackson, and Williams visited the camp, pronouncing it the best camp in the 12th Army Corps.[62]

The following day April 10, the 107th fell into line at 9 a.m. and marched to a large field to near Stafford Courthouse along with the remainder of the 12th Corps and the 11th Corps. There they were to be reviewed by General Hooker and President Lincoln. Twenty thousand troops representing infantry, cavalry, and artillery were gathered there. Various bands played national airs and a twenty-one-gun salute announced the arrival of the president and his party.[63] He was dressed in black with a tall stovepipe hat and riding a fine horse escorted by lancers, their red guidons fluttering in the spring breeze. The men were impressed by his horsemanship. He cantered onto the field and moved up and down the lines at a faster pace than his escort. Mrs. Lincoln was there and sat with other ladies in carriages.[64]

The president took a position next to the carriages with General Hooker and the other military dignitaries. The lancers positioned themselves on either side of them and to their rear. The 11th and 12th Corps then prepared to pass in review. The "two corps had formed in two parallel lines. Each consisted of regiments formed by division with a two-company front" and "closed in mass." At the command of a bugle, "each regiment moved at double quick, changed front." This was followed by the same formation marching at quick step around the field. The field was rolling rather than flat, and this feature caused the unusual effect of the individual regiments to disappear then reappear. When the consolidated drum corps of each brigade reached the president, they wheeled to the left and remained there, performing a musical salute every time the flag of each regiment was successively bowed in honor of the president. There were some who thought that the 107th did itself proud that day.[65]

However, there is evidence of just the opposite being true. In a letter to his parents, a bright nineteen-year-old private, Rufus Harnden, wrote that during the review, Colonel Diven gave the command to double quick too early. As a result, he was supposedly called to division headquarters and placed under arrest. Harnden at the same time also said the Surgeon Flood was under arrest for not disclosing a case of smallpox in the camp. Harnden concluded by saying that the 107th was known as the "fated regiment all over the country here." Harnden of Company A survived the war and afterwards returned to his home in Waverly, NY, where he took up the study of medicine with his father, a well-known and successful physician and surgeon. On February 25, 1873, Bellevue Hospital Medical College conferred upon him the Degree of Doctor of Medicine.[66]

Preparations began for movement of the regiment and the entire 12th Army

Corps, although a definite schedule was unknown. The men drew eight days' rations to be carried in their knapsacks and haversacks. Before this, the most they had carried was three days' rations. They packed ammunition enough for 150 rounds per man in wagons. One man from each company was assigned the responsibility for carrying wounded men from the battlefield.

# 6

# Chancellorsville

**It had been a quiet, but deadly winter at Hope Landing for the 107th New York. While Spring might bring a respite to so many deaths from disease, there was also the certainty that warm weather would bring forth a spring campaign between the forces of the Confederate General Robert E. Lee and the newly appointed Union commander Fighting Joe Hooker. While the Union forces were greatly superior in numbers, they still had to prove that their leaders were equal in battle management.**

Aside from reading about the regiment in the various weekly papers of the three counties where the regiment was raised, it was common for various dignitaries and even relatives or friends to visit the regiment at Hope Landing. During this period, among those who visited from Steuben County were the Honorable A.B. Dickinson and Charles Erwin Esq. Dickinson made a speech to the troops and "his presence was agreeable."[1]

On Tuesday, April 14, orders came to prepare to march the next day. Preparations began at five in the morning. Each man packed five days' rations in his knapsack and three days in his haversack. The feeling among the men was that they would not have to march far to engage the Rebs in a hot fight. The next day, they awoke to find it raining with the day being cold and generally disagreeable. The rain had been continuous for the last twenty-four hours, making the roads very bad.[2]

Over the next several days, the use of whiskey spread throughout the camp. There were many arrests for drunkenness including Lieutenant Harvey Denniston. There was also a general inspection of arms and equipment, and the tents were taken down and stored.[3] No orders to commence marching were received that day. On Friday, April 17, the nearby 134th New York regiment moved out, but the 107th remained in camp.[4] The next day, the *Havana Journal* in Montour Falls published the following list of promotions and resignations made in the 107th regiment by New York Governor Seymour.

Major N.T. Colby to be Lieut.-Colonel, Feb. 3, 1863, vice Gabriel A. Smith discharged.

Captain William F. Fox to be Major Feb. 3, 1863, vice N.T. Colby promoted.

1st Lieut. Samuel A. Bennett to be Captain Mar. 13, 1863, vice H.T. Slocum resigned.

2nd Lieut. O.D. Reynolds to be 1st Lieut. Mar. 13, 1863, vice S.A. Bennett promoted.

1st Sergeant Frank Frost to be 2nd Lieut. March 13, 1863, vice O.D. Reynolds promoted.

1st Lieut. John M. Losie to be Captain Jan. 26, 1863, vice M.C. Wilkinson resigned.

Edward P. Van Valkenburg to be 2nd Lieut. March 20, 1863, vice J.M. Losie promoted.

Sergeant Samuel B. Taylor to be 1st Lieut. Feb. 20, 1863, vice W.L. Morgan, Jr., resigned.

Charles J. Fox to be 1st Lieut., July 29, 1863, Co. C, original.

*Author's note: The word* vice *here refers to the previous holder of the rank.*

Sentiment in the regiment was very positive following the promotions, and even though Colonel Diven's performance was acceptable, he was still largely viewed as being incapable of commanding the 107th. One of the regiment's enlisted men made the following comment when he wrote home: "Our Colonel was offered the chance of staying and doing duty at this and other landings, but he said that if he could not have a chance to go in the field to help put down the rebellion he would resign and go home I hardly think anyone would be sorry if he should. Our captain has been promoted to major and we have got a good lieutenant colonel So if the old colonel should resign, we could get along very well the colonel reminds me of the saying that you cannot learn an old dog new tricks."[5]

On Sunday, April 19, there was a regimental inspection. The next two days found the men dealing with rain as they did guard duty and drill. On Wednesday, the regiment went toward Stafford Court House for parade drill.[6] Private Edwin W. Shaw, a musician in Company H, died of smallpox the following day.[7]

The 107th remained in camp doing guard duty and drilling until Sunday the 26th. That morning they heard Chaplain Crane "preach a very interesting war discourse." It proved to be a prelude to their movement from the landing. In the afternoon, the regiment was busy preparing for the move. Three men from each company were selected to prepare a place to encamp for the night so as to be ready to march with the remainder of the 12th Corps the next morning. They succeeded in finding a location with thick underbrush and near a flowing stream. They went about clearing the area and put everything in order for the arrival of the regiment that evening.[8]

The regiment left Hope Landing on about sundown on the 26th. Some lingered behind on the hill to take a farewell look at their camp. The moon was shining brightly, and its beams fell with a picturesque beauty on the ruins of their camp. In the distance lay the Potomac with a broad belt of silver across its surface. On their left close by were the graves of their comrades. The little graveyard lay white and still in the moonlight, and they also gave that a goodbye glance. They left it with the evening breeze sighing softly through its trees and the waters of the Acquia beating with subdued and sobbing sounds among its banks. They knew that they would never revisit the scene, and so with a fond glance toward their deserted camp and its past associations, they said goodbye and turned their faces and thoughts to meet the events of the coming week.[9]

The men marched to the Stafford Court House where they bivouacked. That evening the paymaster arrived in camp. By the morning of the 27th, he had almost completed paying the entire regiment. At eight a.m., the regiment joined its brigade, and with the remainder of the 12th Corps began its march toward the Rappahannock.[10] The 12th Corps of Maj. Gen. H.W. Slocum consisted of two divisions, the first under the command of Brig. Gen. A.S. Williams and the second under the command of Brig. Gen. J.W. Geary. Each division had three infantry brigades and one artillery brigade. The 107th New York was in the Third Brigade of the First Division.[11]

The weather was pleasant, and the roads were good. They kept up a good pace and stopped often to rest. The old 107th never looked better and apparently never felt better. They felt good about the prospect of a new campaign and the hopes of active service. The march was through a wild and desolate country that had been made so by the war. At four o'clock, they turned into a beautiful wood near Harwood Church to bivouac for the night. The hills and woodlands all around gleamed with a thousand campfires.[12] During the days' march, the 107th had been the rear guard for the brigade. They were proud that not one man had fallen out while members of the other regiments in the brigade had some straggling. All told they marched twelve miles that day, and everyone was in good spirits.

The next morning, they were up at 4 o'clock and out on the road by sunrise. That day they passed Hartwood Church. It had been a very nice building but now was torn to pieces with scrawls and drawings on the walls. The cemetery nearby had not been tended to for some time, and its shrubbery was overgrown. Sergeant Arthur S. Fitch of Company B took a piece of the church as a souvenir, and he picked violets from the cemetery.

The regiment halted for dinner at noon. While they were seated on either side of the road, General Hooker passed by and received cheers loud and long. Shortly after, the 11th Corps passed them and took the lead of the march. By half past four, they were within a half-mile of the Rappahannock River near Kelly's Ford.

When the regiment arose the morning of the 29th, it was raining, and their things were quite wet. They started at about five and soon reached Kelly's Ford on the Rappahannock. The 11th Corps had already crossed over without any opposition from the enemy. The 107th had the benefit of a pontoon bridge when they crossed over. At this point, they met the 11th Corps and the 5th Corps on either side of the road. The 12th Corps passed by both and took the advance.[13] Not long after, the countryside became wilder and more picturesque in appearance, with large hemlocks and pine lining the road. Even though there were houses along the way, not a man was to be seen. However, women came out to view the passing columns with seeming wonder and hatred. One woman exclaimed, "Good Lord! How many more is that of you?" "Oh, we reach way up north," responded a member of the 107th. "I hope you all git killed," was the reply. "Don't reckon on that, when we kill the Johnnies, we're coming back to marry you," added the soldier. "I wouldn't have the likes of you," retorted the beldame.[14] Further along the road as they were keeping step with their band by singing "John Brown's Body," they were observed by an old fellow along the road who exclaimed as he took off his old beaver hat, "Wall! You uns be right smart singers, you uns be. I never heerd such a mighty big sing in my life afore." He immediately plunked down a number twelve boot into his hat, crushing it down into the mud and leaving his foot there until they passed by.

After crossing the Rappahannock River, they were in Rebel territory, and in addition to comments from local residents, they were continually harassed with little effect by sharpshooters and small bands of Rebel militia, who had made their march more difficult by burning bridges.[15]

At about three o'clock on the 29th, they reached the Rapidan River at Germania Ford. Upon reaching the river, their line of skirmishers came upon approximately one hundred and fifty Rebels constructing a bridge. They formed a line of battle expecting more Rebels on the other side. Their cavalry rushed ahead and engaged the Rebels, who soon surrendered and were sent to the rear.[16]

On being sent to the rear, one Rebel was heard to comment, "We reckoned how you yanks want no slouches, stood water mighty waal end they war afeared thet ther boys might git a goldarned likin when we uns ketched up on to em." This conversation prompted a question from Corporal Rufus Harndon, who asked, "Say Johnnie, how far ahead are your forces?" The Rebel responded, "Well Yank, it's a mighty smart way. A stretch and a go by a level and a right smart turn, and you uns be thar." He added, "Say Yank, hev yer any tanglefoot or terbaker? I reckon as how you uns hev a right smart of both."[17]

During the brief engagement, a few of the Rebels were killed. However, one Rebel on the other side of the river attempted to escape and ran up the road on the opposite bank while a whole volley was fired at him. The dirt flew all around him, but he was unhurt. The men yelled and cheered, and some cried out not to shoot him as so brave a man deserved to escape. However, one of a party of the 3rd Wisconsin posted at a farmhouse a long way back from the river waited until the firing was through, then raised the hind sites of his rifle, rested the piece on the house porch railing, and fired. The Rebel fell dead.

The Rapidan was quite high, and there was a long discussion about the safety of fording it. The question was finally settled, and the 107th was ordered to take the lead and attempt to ford it. Captain Baldwin of Company B took the lead. He plunged into the river, and the water rose up to his waist. The regiment followed at the head of their brigade in a solid column of fours, holding their muskets and ammunition at arm's length above their heads.[18]

The cavalry was positioned down river to aid any soldiers that might lose their footing. The water was at least waist deep, but in some spots much higher and very swift, causing some to lose their footing. At least one man had a load so heavy that he was swept past the cavalry and drowned. About the time the 107th finished wading across the river, the pioneers completed a pontoon bridge, enabling the remaining troops to cross over it.[19]

After they had crossed the river, they went up the same dug road as the Rebel who had been shot while trying to escape. He was there, lying face down, stiff, and motionless. They praised his attempt to escape as they passed his body, and it was agreed that he deserved a better fate.[20]

Once across the river, they marched a short distance and bivouacked for the night. It began raining lightly, but by then they had got up their tents and made beds of cedar boughs. They had had a fatiguing and somewhat exciting day of it and were glad to finally be able to rest.

They arose the next morning, April 30, at about 4 o'clock to find it cold and raining. They got underway at 8 o'clock, and despite the rain, the roads were good. The 11th Corps was in the lead. The 107th men often passed their cavalry going to the rear with Rebel prisoners as they marched along. They marched all day through nice farming country, and they were allowed to Jayhawk (confiscate) whatever they liked, including some nice beef cattle that they enjoyed for supper. They arrived at Chancellorsville at five in the afternoon. It was a single brick house used as a tavern. They went into bivouac alongside the 5th Corps, who had arrived before them. A cheering order was read from General Hooker, stating that they had the enemy fast and prospects were fair for a glorious victory.[21] The order read, "It is with heartfelt satisfaction that the Commanding General announces to the army that the operations of the last three days have determined that our enemy must ingloriously fly or come out from behind his defenses and give us battle on our own ground where certain destruction awaits him. The operations of the Fifth, Eleventh and Twelfth Corps have been a succession of splendid achievements."[22]

The regiment awoke Saturday, May 1, to a bright clear day. The morning was spent cleaning their rifles. At about 10 a.m., they began their advance eastward on the Orange Plank Road and almost immediately the boom of artillery broke upon their ears not a mile in their front, and "we knew the ball was open." The regiment went rapidly ahead in the advance. They were soon with the artillery and formed a line in the woods 3,000 feet south of the Orange Turnpike and 3,500 feet southeast of the Furnace Road just before 1 p.m. Lee's army was directly in front of them and extended northward above the Turnpike. For the time being, the artillery did all of the fighting, and shot and shell flew over them very lively. No casualties were suffered, and after an hour or so, were ordered to retire. At about 3:30 p.m., Stonewall Jackson moved a strong force in their front. Jackson's original move had been thought to be only to determine the enemy's position. No actual fighting took place except for the 11th and the 5th Corps on their left. As they returned to the clearing from where they entered the woods and were retrieving their knapsacks, Rebel skirmishers fired on them. However, they were successful in beating back the skirmishers and retrieving their equipment. At the same time, the Rebels had moved a battery into the position they had just vacated, but the regiment had moved out of its range.

The 107th and its brigade, along with the major part of the army, moved back to its camp southwest of and near the Chancellorsville House. Their front extended in a semi-circle from the turnpike where it met Bullock Road southward and then northward until it ended near the Chancellorsville House. They were quite fatigued as it was very warm. The remainder of the day was calm until near sundown when the enemy advanced, and a fight began. Their brigade moved forward with the 2nd Massachusetts, 3rd Wisconsin, and 27th Indiana in front and the 13th New Jersey and the 107th New York in support. The front three regiments became involved, and soon the artillery made it quite a lively affair. The Rebels were beaten back and supporting action by the 13th New Jersey and the 107th New York was not necessary. However, a Rebel shell exploded over their ranks, mortally wounding Capt. N.E. Rutter of Company I. He died less than hour later. The remainder of the night was uneventful.[23]

During the night, the 12th Corps was ordered by General Slocum to erect defensive breastworks of logs and earth along their entire front. This was the first time that this corps had ever provided themselves with protection of this kind on the battlefield.

The next morning, the 12th Corps remained in its breastworks. It was during this time that Lee split his forces and began a move of General Stonewall Jackson's force in a circuitous route south of the 12th and other corps to the opposite side of what was the flank of the 11th Corps. This move by Jackson would take the better part of the day. As they passed below the 12th Corps, they were observed through an opening in the woods and thought to be in retreat. At that time, the Williams Division of the 12th Corps, which included the 107th NY and part of the 3rd Corps, moved out of their works and attacked Jackson's rear guard, shelling them and taking several hundred prisoners. During this affair, Williams' Division took no direct action and was only in support of the 3rd Corps. This attacking movement was away from the 11th Corps that was on the Orange Turnpike and to the west of the main Union body in a somewhat isolated position.

Later in the day at 6 p.m., Jackson fiercely attacked the 11th Corps and drove it westward back into the lines of the 12th Corps. When Slocum became aware of Jackson's attack, he moved Williams' division back to a position at a right angle to its previous one with its right resting on the Plank Road connected to Berry's division of the 3rd Corps and facing the retreating 11th Corps with its pursuers. He placed Geary's division in the previously constructed breast works and at a right angle to the left of Williams' division. The 12th Corps' artillery under Captain Best halted Jackson's advance for a while, but sporadic fighting broke out in the dark as both sides consolidated their positions. The 107th remained in their position, but it was a harrowing night, as the Rebels would sporadically advance with loud yells and volleys of musketry. Each attack was met with stiff resistance and resulted in no gain. The 11th Corps had moved far to the rear and above the Chancellorsville House where it was attempting to reform.

The Confederates renewed their attack Sunday, May 3, around 5 a.m., directing it mainly against the Williams and Berry divisions. Each attack was repulsed with devastating effect, as evidenced by the losses reported by the Rebel regiments involved. At 8 a.m. Slocum informed Hooker that his forces were dangerously low on ammunition. Hooker ordered Slocum to move above and to the east of the Chancellorsville House, where his men replenished their supply of ammunition. The battle continued with the other Union Corps involved. By noon the battle had quieted, and the remainder of the day remained so.[24]

After dark and at about 10 o'clock, the 107th with the remainder of the 12th Corps quietly moved out and marched to the United States Ford on the Rappahannock River in a heavily fortified position.[25] The previous three days fighting had left the regiment with five killed, 54 wounded, and 24 missing.[26] The dead included Capt. N.E. Rutter of Company I, Sgt. Horace Hotchkiss Company G, Cpl. J.E. Stratten of Company G, Pvt. Eugene E. Howe of Company K, and Pvt. Thomas F. Morris of Company K. With the exception of Captain Rutter, there is no record of burial for the enlisted men. They were evidently left on the battlefield buried or unburied. As for those listed as wounded or missing, the majority of them returned to active duty.

On Monday, May 4, the 107th remained in a strong position at the United States Ford. In their front were 26 pieces of cannon and right below them rifle pits filled with men. The Confederates were further in their front hidden by a deep ravine.

The following day, the regiment lay quietly in their entrenchments all day. Working parties were sent out and spent the day throwing up breastworks. Late in the day, a heavy thunderstorm brought a noticeable cooling of the temperature. Unfortunately, many in the regiment had no shelter in the way of blankets or tents. Many built small fires and gathered around them. After darkness fell, it was rumored that they were to retreat and cross the river. The men were greatly disappointed, and with the rain they felt even more so. Up to that point, they had supposed that they had the enemy hard pressed and would have a victorious campaign, but now it seemed to be a disastrous defeat instead. All night they remained shivering in the cold and unable to sleep. At the same time, they had visions of a bloody fight at the river crossing the next day.

On Wednesday, the regiment and its brigade began moving out at daybreak and reached the ford, where the army was quickly crossing the Rappahannock on two pontoon bridges. The 12th Corps waited until the 5th Corps was safely across. They heard cannonading down the river as they waited, but no Rebel force appeared. It was 7 o'clock by the time they were completely across the river. The rain continued, and the roads were terribly muddy. They halted an hour for dinner and kept moving steadily forward until dark, when they reached the Stafford Courthouse. They were completely exhausted, wet, and cold with no shelter readily available. Arthur Fitch and another soldier of the 107th managed to find some cavalry troopers to get dry and sleep in a tent that evening.

The following morning, the regiment laid out a camp near the courthouse, but it was not until the next day that they were issued new shelter tents and immediately put them up. In addition, they were issued new blankets, knapsacks, and other items to replace those that they lost on the Chancellorsville battlefield.[27]

Initially the new camp lay on a slight slope, and was not very appealing, but the men went to work changing all of that. They cut down cedar trees and placed them end-to-end in rows defining the streets among the neat rows of tents. The officers' tents were situated in a pleasant pine grove at the foot of the slope.

On Sunday evening of May 10, during dress parade, the resignations of Colonel Diven and Adjutant Fanton were read to the regiment along with their honorable discharge from the United States service. Colonel Diven came forward and gave a heartfelt address to the regiment. He spoke of the circumstances when he took command of the regiment, its sad condition while it was on Maryland Heights, and the duty he felt to do all he could in his power for its welfare. He had not aspired to the command of the regiment but had accepted its interests and that of the service. He bore testimony to the courage and valor the regiment had shown under trying circumstances, becoming one of the best in the field. Its health and discipline were good, and he could now leave it with honor to himself and to each soldier under him. He informed the regiment that he had written to Lieut. Colonel N.M. Crane late of the 23rd N.Y. Volunteers to become his successor and had received a favorable response. Diven described Crane as a brave and accomplished soldier, and he felt happy in having him assume the command. He assured the regiment that they would always find him their true friend, and that his home would always be open to them. He also wished them never to forget their old colonel, for forget them he never would. Adjutant Fanton also made a parting address to the Regiment.

Later in the evening, the officers of the 107th called on Diven at his quarters to bid him goodbye, and several officers made speeches expressing their own feeling and that of the command, to which the Colonel replied affectionately. The next morning Colonel Diven went through the streets of the camp bidding all goodbye and soon after left the camp for Washington along with Fanton.[28]

Chancellorsville, May 3, 1863, mortally wounded and deaths:

Captain Co. I Nat E. Rutter
Sergeant Co. G Horace Hotchkiss
Corporal C. G John E. Stratton
Private Co. F William H. Hatch
Private Co. K Eugene E. Howe
Private Co. K Theodore F. Morris
Private Co. Clark Richardson (Head wound at Aquia Bay, Va. May 8, 1863)

## Brigade Losses

| Regiment | Wounded | Killed | Missing |
|---|---|---|---|
| 27th Indiana | 20 | 126 | 4 |
| 2nd Massachusetts | 21 | 110 | 7 |
| 13th New Jersey | 17 | 100 | 24 |
| 3rd Wisconsin | 18 | 74 | 9 |
| 107th New York | 54 | 5 | 28 |

# 7

# Gettysburg

The savage fighting had gone on for two whole days in a great swirl of death around the small town of Gettysburg, PA. The dead and dying lay in long lines, in silent clusters and suffering heaps. Much more hung in the balance than the men fighting there would ever know. Now on the sultry night of July 2, 1863, the Union commander Maj. Gen. George G. Meade called together a dozen generals to his farmhouse headquarters to ponder the wisdom of staying in this position along Cemetery Ridge or maneuvering to some more tenable spot farther south. The stars fell on Mrs. Leister's small house that night. Meade himself said little in the flickering light but let his combat commanders discuss the merits and flaws of the Federal lines at Gettysburg. General Newton felt it was a bad position; the others thought a hard defeat here could very well mean the end of the United States as they knew it. Finally, General Butterfield, chief of staff, polled them. When they got to Maj. Gen. Henry W. Slocum of the Twelfth Corps, he had one reply to all questions: "Stay and fight it out!"

His reply would forever be on the lips of the men of the 107th New York Volunteer Infantry. The very last survivor of the regiment, Lt. Frank Frost had a rubber stamp made after the war. The stamp bore a star and the phrase, "Slocum's Men, Stay and Fight it out." This phrase was stamped in red ink on a great many of the pieces of the regiment's memorabilia, which Frost placed in his scrapbook. The red star was the first division insignia of the 12th and later the 20th Army Corps.[1]

With Diven gone, the command of the regiment fell on Lt. Colby. His absence from the regiment during the battle of Chancellorsville gave occasion for censure among the men. who talked openly that his presence at the battle would have given them greater confidence in him as an officer more than all the drills he inaugurated. The excuse given for his absence was illness. At about this same time, there was some difficulty between him and General Ruger, the brigade commander. Colby was placed under arrest, and while under arrest he became very sick. He was so sick that he was moved from the private home where he was staying to the military hospital where he could receive constant care. The regiment now came under the command of Capt. Losie because Lathrop Baldwin, the senior captain, was also ill.

At this same time, the pickets of all of the regiments in the brigade developed

what might have been called a "Grand Guard." It took place before the brigade headquarters. The sight of it usually attracted a great many spectators. The guard, with
officers and men included, numbered one hundred and seventy men, and the brigade
band was quite often with them. The pickets formed a chain of sentinels stretching
from the Rappahannock to the Aquia. A cavalry picket was also available in case of
a larger attack.[2]

The period from May 11 to early June saw the regiment remain in camp near the
Stafford Courthouse and participate in the normal activities of maintaining their
living facilities, the camp streets, picket duty and drilling.[3]

With Diven gone, the officers held a meeting in anticipation of Colonel Nirom
M. Crane's future arrival. A fatigue party was selected to fix up his headquarters,
etc. They erected a large wall tent near a large cedar tree on a knoll behind the line
officers' tents. The path to the tent was lined with holly and cedar. Small pine twigs
were placed on the path and the floor of the tent. At the beginning of the path, they
placed an arch of holly, pine, and laurel as well as a large red star, the insignia of the
1st Division of the 12th Army Corps.

At this time, the almost Sabbath-like quiet of their camp began to be disturbed
by rumors of intended Confederate operations. There was a great mystery in the
reported movements of General Lee, and it became evident that the regiment may
not long enjoy the pleasures of their camp life. On June 4, they received orders to
pack up and be ready to move at a moment's notice. Tents were struck and preparations made to move out. However, at 5 p.m., a countermanding order was received,
and they put their tents back up and settled back into camp. The next day, heavy firing was heard in the direction of Fredericksburg, and it caused much nervousness
and expectation among the men.

On the 6th, large groups of men were picked for an expedition from each arm of
the service including 500 from the 2nd Massachusetts and the 3rd Wisconsin. They
were sent across the Rappahannock at Beverly Ford as Lee was reported to be northward and threatening operations. They surprised Rebel cavalry there, and a sharp
fight broke out. The Rebels were reinforced but were ultimately driven from the field.

Brigadier General Thomas H. Ruger visited the camp of the 107th and rode
through its streets lined with evergreens and holly. He also visited the hospital tent
that was trimmed with evergreens and flowers. The camp was most likely the best in
his brigade. However, the camp layout must not have pleased him as he ordered the
camp to be rearranged and the officers' tents moved to the side of the hill where they
would have no shelter from the sun. His orders were promptly carried out, and the
formerly beautiful camp looked like "mischief itself." On a pine tree at the entrance
to the camp, someone nailed a board with the inscription in large capitals, "CAMP
RUGER."

The one happening of significance during this period was the regiment's meeting of the officers and enlisted men on June 8. Chaplain Crane suggested the meeting
to express the feelings of the regiment regarding the conduct of the "Copperheads"

of the North, and particularly Vallandigham of Ohio, who had just been sent within the Rebel lines where he rightly belonged. The boys turned out en masse and expressed one sentiment, that of wholly detesting all of the Rebel sympathizers in the North. Speeches were made in favor of the patriotic resolution drafted and offered by Lieut. H.G. Denniston, and it was unanimously passed as the outspoken sentiments of the soldiers who were fighting for home, country, and liberty. These resolutions were published in the Washington newspapers and the *Corning Journal*. A meeting of the officers and soldiers of the 107th New York Vols., led by Capt. J.F. Knox, Lieut. Denniston, Lieut. Van Valkenburgh, and Chaplain Crane, was held on the 8th at the camp near the Suffolk Court House, VA., at which place a series of loyal resolutions were passed unanimously.

> Resolved: That as officers and soldiers of the 107th N.Y.V., of every previous political party, we do deprecate and condemn the actions of traitors in the South, as well as their base and sneaking allies and abettors (the Copperheads) of our own North, and that we recognize in both the same principles of political degradation, and infamy, of crime and treason to our beloved country.
>
> Resolved: That above all else has experience taught us, that the course pursued by these aids and abettors of treason in the North, has tended to nerve and stimulate the rebel arms, while to our own government and army the effect has been to humiliate and dishearten. They have not only embarrassed both but have given aid and comfort to our enemies, giving them assurances of sympathy, where none exists, save in their own rotten and traitorous hearts. And while we, the 107th N.Y.V., are enduring hardships and privations, our numbers becoming decimated on battle fields in conflict for the Union, our mails are freighted with the reports of meetings held in our own State by this vile cabal, breathing a spirit of disloyalty.
>
> Resolved: That we applaud and are thankful to our Government in the sending of such rebel emissaries as Vallandigham, to the rebel lines, out of the sight and hearing of freemen, and hope that the same course may be pursued towards all like him, without an exception, that our volleys and bayonets may be directed against the enemies of our country en masse, instead of suffering by the words of treason openly preached by Copperheads and traitors in our own free North.
>
> Resolved: That the war in which our country is engaged is a most just and righteous one, and that as a loyal Regiment we will pour out our life's blood if it need be, in our country's behalf, and the principles with which the war is carried on by our government.
>
> Resolved: That if the Government will attend to Copperheads in the North, and those who sympathize with the traitors South, we will lend our every energy in putting down the rebellion, in restoring our union, and in conquering a peace. Relying always upon God and the Righteousness of our cause, for success.—That to do this we offer the record of our past history as a Regiment, for the performance of future duties on the battlefield, in behalf of the best Government the sun ever shone upon.[4]

On June 10, the expected orders came that the regiment should be ready to move at a moment's notice. This fact and the order to prepare three days cooked rations were a clear indication that they would move in the next day or two.

The following day, the regiment was visited by ex-Colonel Robert Van Valkenburgh. The former colonel of the regiment expressed his gratification at the appearance of the resolutions in the newspaper. During his visit, he attended the battalion drill, and in honor of his presence, the regiment marched in review. He left the camp as the guest of General Slocum that evening and returned to Washington the next day. That same day, Lt. Col. Colby, who was now commanding the regiment, put the regiment through a vigorous series of drills.

Finally marching orders came at 6 a.m. on the morning of June 13, and instant preparations were made to leave Stafford. The sick were placed in ambulances, and the hospitals at Hope Landing and elsewhere began the effort to move the sick and wounded to Washington. Tents were packed, knapsacks adjusted, and at 9 o'clock, the regiment left Camp Ruger and marched toward Brook's Station. The day was hot and sultry, and the road was excessively dusty. The Station was reached at 1 o'clock, and the regiment took possession of an old camp in the woods that had previously been occupied by the 36th New York, a regiment in the 11th Army Corps. The camp was shaded with maple and oak trees, and the previous regiment had left many items when it moved on.

The regiment had hardly started to clean up the camp when it was ordered back to its previous location at Stafford Court House. The return march was prompt but very fatiguing due the heat and dust. Once back at the courthouse, the regiment remained at the roadside and awaited the arrival of the other regiments of their brigade. Their mail was distributed during the time they waited, and a severe rainstorm pelted them. When the other regiments arrived, the entire brigade began a march, to where they did not know. It soon became apparent that the march was toward Dumfries.

Between the darkness and rain, it was very difficult to keep on the road, which was in horrible condition. The troops had to feel their way slowly through the mud and water. In some places along the road, there were dug ways, and owing to the darkness, some of the supply wagons were overturned. This caused delay, and it was late in the morning of the 14th before they reached Dumfries. They camped in an open field near Quantico Creek, which flowed to their left. There they awaited the arrival of the other troops from Falmouth. The arrival during the day of different corps and their supply trains presented an interesting scene when Dumfries and its surroundings were filled with armed men and their supply wagons.

On the morning of the 15th, the march commenced on the road toward the Occoquan. The day was extremely hot, and it was hard marching for the men with their heavy knapsacks and accoutrements. Many fell out by the wayside, overcome by the heat and exhaustion. The columns reached Occoquan about noon, crossed it, and bivouacked for one hour for refreshments. The march was then resumed towards Fairfax over the same road they had marched months before. But how changed was the scenery. The woodland had all been cut down, and in various places formidable entrenchments had been thrown up. These were in the charge of the Pennsylvania Reserves, who from their trim and clean appearance looked as if they had not seen much service. They lined the roads to see the dusty and tired soldiers of the "Army of the Potomac" pass.

The march took them through Fairfax Station to a hill beyond which they halted for a short time. Then they marched in the direction of the Fairfax Court House.

The men were extremely fatigued and could hardly move when General Williams ordered the brigade band to play some national airs. This infused new life into the regiments, and they all joined into a chorus of "We're Marching Along." They forgot their fatigue and stepped smartly forward with new enthusiasm. They reached the courthouse amid the cheers of the regiments who had already set up camp there. The 107th moved to the east of the regiments already in camp and pitched their tents.

The next morning, they were issued five days' rations. During the day, one of the soldiers in the regiment was diagnosed with smallpox. He was quarantined, and the remainder of the regiment was vaccinated as a precautionary measure.

The march was resumed at around 4 a.m. on the 17th, with various regiments taking different routes so as to maximize the speed of the overall troop movement toward Drainsville. However, the heat and dust again tended to counteract this effort. Reports of Rebel cavalry in the vicinity necessitated the putting out of reconnoitering parties, but it proved to be a false alarm. In addition, the heat became so unbearable that the march was halted for the remainder of the day. It was so hot that the shelter tents gave no protection from the sun's rays.

The following day the heat continued, and the march was not resumed until 10 a.m. Although a great deal of water was consumed, the men were still badly affected by both the heat and the clouds of dust that continued to choke them. Many fell out along the way but did catch up toward evening. Water was sought everywhere, and some men placed wet leaves under their caps to help reduce the effect of the heat.

At about 4 p.m., they reached a small creek and while fording it, took the opportunity to fill their canteens. Soon after a storm broke that was complete with thunder and lightning. Leesburg was reached at 9 o'clock. The men immediately began putting up their tents, and nearby fences were torn down to provide floors in the tents. They were camped near a female seminary, and the ladies serenaded them with the strains of "The Bonny Blue Flag." The regiment's drum corps returned the favor by playing "Yankee Doodle."

On Friday, June 19, three soldiers, William McKee and William Graves of the 46th Pennsylvania and Christopher Krabert of the 13th New Jersey, were to be shot for the crime of desertion. Krabert had attempted to escape but was shot in the leg and captured. Three men were selected from each regiment of the 1st division as a firing party. The officers of the 107th placed the company letters in a hat, and the first three drawn were F, H, and C. A man was then chosen from each company. At 9 a.m., the regiments formed in a line and marched to the place of execution with the drum corps playing "The Dead March." The place of execution was a large field surrounded by hills on either side. The troops formed a large square with one side open. In the center were three freshly dug graves. The guard for the execution slowly approached the center of the square of men, and an ambulance followed carrying each condemned man seated on his coffin. Once the ambulance reached the graves, the coffins were placed in front of each grave. The men, who were blindfolded and bound, were seated on their respective coffins. The provost marshall then read aloud the charges and the sentence. He was followed by a prayer given by the chaplain of the 5th Connecticut regiment. Then the guard was separated into three squads of ten men each. Once they were situated, the provost marshall gave the commands: "Ready, aim, fire." The prisoners fell back on their coffins and were immediately examined for any sign of life. Once determined to be dead, they were placed in their coffins. The band struck up a lively tune, and the assembled troops were then marched past the coffins so that each man could view the dead deserters.

It rained steadily all through that night and the next day. During the day, they heard artillery fire off in the distance, and rumor had it that it was Kilpatrick attacking Rebel cavalry at Snedeker's Gap. That same day there were command changes in the 107th. They included Lieut. Bingham of Company G being commissioned captain of Company H, and Lieut. Denniston commanding Company G in the absence of Capt. Laman.[5]

Leesburg appeared to them to be thoroughly a "Secesh" place. They thought the houses old fashioned, with roofs slanting toward the street and no awnings in any part of the town. However, there were many splendid flower gardens and vegetable gardens. They also took notice of the large Black population.[6]

Officers of the 107th took the opportunity to make friends with local people during the regiment's stay near the village. As a result, many soldiers dined at their homes and even got homemade baked goods. Lieut. John Orr of Company F made the acquaintance of the Lack family, including their daughter Mary. He had breakfast and dinner at their home and took away some biscuits for his supper. Major Colgrove of the 27th Indiana accompanied him to dinner with the Lacks.

The next day, Sunday, June 21, both Orr and Colgrove had supper with the Lacks. Captain Knox of Orr's company obtained some flour and had Orr take it to Mrs. Lack to bake bread. Lieut. Hill of the same company also visited Mary, and there appeared to be some rivalry between Hill and Colgrove.[7]

Another day passed, the weather was fair, and nothing of any major importance was going on in their camp. However, nearby, both their cavalry and artillery had engaged the Rebels and taken a number of prisoners and arms.[8]

On Tuesday the 23rd, General Williams and the 1st division of the 12th corps was in camp outside of town. At the same time, General Geary, commanding the 2nd division, was in the southern part of the town and had his men working to repair an abandon Rebel fort there. Meanwhile General Williams instructed Lieut. Denniston to take his company to ready a similar fort located on a hill near their camp. Both actions were taken in response to a rumor that the Rebel General Longstreet was said to be in the vicinity.[9]

The next day, Colonel Niron Crane finally arrived and took command of the 107th. He viewed the regiment drill and parade. He was impressed with both, and also with their general appearance. That same day, the regiment moved further to the southeast of the village and began to put up earthworks.

On Thursday orders came to strike their tents and to fall in. At the same time, seventy-five men from the 107th were assigned to continue work on the nearby breastworks. Rain commenced about noon and continued for the rest of the day.

The rain continued on Friday the 26th, when the whole of the 12th corps was awakened at 2 a.m. and ordered to pack up and be ready to march. It was about daylight when they moved toward Edward's Ferry. They were the last of the 12th corps to cross the river on a pontoon bridge. Their supply train delayed their crossing, and they were not completely across until 9 a.m. However, they were happy to be in unionist Maryland and continued marching until they passed by Poolesville, stopping at about 4 p.m. to put up their tents.[10]

It was at this time that General Hooker became at odds with the War Department over the direction of troop movements, and he turned over command of the 12th Corps to Major General George G. Meade.[11] The 107th arose at 2:30 a.m. on the 27th. It was raining and cool. They began marching at 4 a.m., crossing the Monocacy River on an aqueduct at 7 a.m. They halted for dinner at 11 a.m. and then continued marching until 11 p.m. when they bivouacked.[12]

The regiment was up the next morning and marching by 5 a.m. They marched through Petersville and then through Jefferson at 10 a.m. They halted at 11 a.m. for dinner. They continued on until they stopped and camped near Frederick at 4 p.m. Many stopped at nearby farms where they were able to purchase eggs, biscuits, and milk for supper.

It was raining when the regiment began marching at 4 a.m. on the 29th. They halted for a short while on the outskirts of Frederick. They were heartedly cheered as they marched through the city, and two-thirds of the soldiers, including some officers, were able to obtain liquor. The result was a great many drunken soldiers. However, as time passed, those soldiers sobered up, and the marching became steadier. The road was greatly obstructed by artillery and supply wagons until noon. They bivouacked at 11 p.m.[13]

The next day, they crossed the Maryland-Pennsylvania line and arrived at Littlestown around 2 p.m. As they approached Littlestown, a Rebel cavalry unit approached from the other direction. However, the cavalry retreated to the west when they realized the size of the Union forces in front of them. The residents of the town were greatly relieved and hailed the 12th Corps as it passed through the streets. When the troops were bivouacked on the other side of town, the citizens showered them with bread, cakes, and pies. In addition, there were many prayers and blessing for the men. During that same time, quartermaster stores of boots and cartridges were passed out to the men. That evening, an address by General Meade was read to the men.

Headquarters Army of the Potomac, June 30, 1863

The Commanding General requests that previous to the engagement soon expected with the enemy Corps, and all other commanding officers will address their troops explaining to them briefly the immense issues involved in the struggle. The enemy are on our soil. The whole country now looks anxiously to this army to deliver it from the presence of the foe. Our failure to do so, will leave us with no such welcome, as the swelling of millions of hearts with pride and joy at our success, would give to every soldier of this army. Houses, firesides and domestic altars are involved. The army has fought well heretofore. It is believed that it will fight more bravely than ever, if it is addressed in fitting terms. Corps and other commanders are authorized to order the instant death of any soldier who fails in his duty in this hour.

By Command Maj. Gen. MEADE[14]

On the morning of July 1, the 12th Corps began their march towards Gettysburg at 6 a.m. Arriving in the vicinity of the battle, the first division, which included the 107th—319 men strong—left the Baltimore Pike before reaching Rock Creek and moved to the right into an oak wood in front of Wolf Hill. Their officers, sighting Rebel cavalry at the top of the hill, prepared for an attack. They loaded and primed their weapons, but no sooner had they been given the order to move up the hill, they learned that Union troops had fallen back through the village of Gettysburg. The division returned to Baltimore Pike near where they had previously been and, acting as a reserve force, formed a line of battle. They remained in line until sundown when all but Company B of the 107th moved to a position behind the artillery. Company B then went out as skirmishers. At midnight the company, not having encountered the enemy, rejoined the remainder of the regiment who were already sleeping. That night the men, including those who had returned from picket duty, lay in a dreamless slumber among the rocks and woods below Wolf Hill on the extreme right of the Union lines.

The next morning, July 2, the regiment was moved to the left to a point along the southern slope of Culp's Hill. The 12th Corps did not engage the enemy and remained near Cemetery Hill that evening,[15] in front of Spangler's Spring. As they moved forward, the enemy continually harassed their skirmishers, and several men were wounded. After they reached the hill, they built log breastworks, and when they were completed, the men idly awaited events. Nothing occurred to invade the quiet until 4 p.m. At that hour, heavy artillery broke out far to the regiments' left. The regiment, although facing no immediate danger, became increasingly tense as the occasional shell from some distant Rebel battery came shrieking over their heads.

At around 6 p.m., the order came for the regiment to fall in. The 3rd Corps and other troops engaged on the left were being hard pressed, and General Slocum was ordered to send the 12th Corps to their relief. The corps moved out, leaving Green's brigade to hold their position. The regiment, along with the rest of the corps, went hurrying along lanes and by-roads and across fields in the direction of the firing. Progressing further, they frequently came under enemy fire that swept the ground with a storm of deadly missiles.

Passing near the Baltimore Pike, they looked up the road to where it passed over the crest of Cemetery Hill. There they saw a battery outlined against the sky. While at first they thought they were soon to come under the direct fire of this battery, they were heartened to discover that it was one of their own.

As they moved along, they saw numberless men, most of them wounded, struggling toward the rear and safety. They felt demoralized by the sight, but the worst was yet to come. Further on they met entire regiments, or what was left of them, that had been relieved and were passing to the rear. They moved along a lane and saw halted along its the edge the remnants of the old 86th New York that had suffered heavy casualties around Devil's Den. Many hasty greetings were exchanged as they hurried by. Among the 86th men was Captain Sam Leavitt, smoke begrimed and haggard, but smiling a welcome to his many friends in the 107th. Sergeant Arthur Fitch of the 107th thought that in his mind, Captain Leavitt must be feeling pity for them, knowing that they were about to taste the terrible experience his regiment had suffered just beyond.

At last, they arrived at their destination and went into position at the base of Little Round Top. They awaited the expected attack, but none came. The enemy had by that time exhausted his efforts and returned to his own lines. The regiment remained in the line of battle, and then cautiously withdrew to a healthier location at the base of Wolf Hill. In the process of doing so, another regiment mistakenly fired on them, and in turn the 46th Pennsylvania fired on that regiment. Fortunately, there were no injuries. Finally, they laid down in line with their arms. Their bodies were tired, and their hearts filled with doubt and anxiety for what they might face in the morning.

Early in the morning of July 3, at about 4 a.m., the 107th was moved to a position in an open field that sloped gently down to the woods around Spangler's Spring. It was here, at a distance of about 500 yards, that the enemy lay. The Baltimore Pike ran along the other edge of this field, some seventy-five yards to their rear. Still further to the rear and somewhat to their right rose the crests of McAllister's Ridge and Power's Hill.

Among those crests were posted several Union batteries, the guns commanding all the hither portion of Culp's Hill. There was no infantry in sight, either to the right or the left of the 107th. Their position was a detached one, presumably to afford support to the batteries should the enemy break through in that direction.

Shortly after daybreak, the guns on McAllister's Ridge opened fire. For two hours they maintained their fire on Culp's Hill with a tornado of shot and shell. During this time the enemy tried to drive out the Union infantry in their front, but they had no artillery to aid them. It was a musketry fight, close and deadly. From their position, the 107th men could see the clouds of white smoke rising from the frowning woods, and they knew that a fiery volcano was raging therein.

They were posted in a piece of woods to their right, just across the swail from Spangler's Spring, for an hour or so, and they were then ordered back to Culp's Hill.

Along the way back, they passed among a mass of sleeping men who had apparently came upon the ground after they had passed earlier. More than one dark form rose from his slumber and demanded to know who it was that was disturbing their sleep. It was determined that these were members of the 6th Corps, who that day had marched 32 miles from Manchester.

When they drew near their old position it was about 10 p.m. and pitch dark. Colonel Crane and Captain Brigham of Company H went ahead to reconnoiter. They did not encounter any pickets but made it all the way into their former breastworks. As they approached, some command was breaking ranks in them. The colonel said, "What command is this, sir?" The answer was, "The 2nd Louisiana, sir." Thinking quickly, Crane replied, "Oh yes sir, all right, sir," and moved with Brigham quietly back into the darkness, back toward their own regiment.

During the absence of the 12th Corps, Ewell had pushed Johnson's division forward into the entrenchments they had left. Although Green's brigade had held its ground, Johnson had successfully passed around his right and into the breastworks previously abandoned by the rest of the 12th Corps. The Rebels lay there silently, awaiting daylight to press further to the federal rear.

Posted in a piece of woods to their right, just across the swail from Spangler's Spring, were the 2nd Massachusetts and the 27th Indiana. At that time, General Williams rode up with Colonel Ruger. The general asked, "What regiment is this?" Ruger replied, "The 107th New York." "Hadn't you better send them in now?" said Williams. "Not yet, general, I have work for them here," replied Ruger. However, shortly thereafter, Lieutenant Snow of Ruger's staff delivered the order to Colonel Colegrove: "The general directs you to advance your line immediately." In his present position, Colegrove determined that it would be impossible to advance more than two regiments at a time because the open area to their front was not wide enough for all five of his regiments to advance at one time. He selected the 2nd Massachusetts and 27th Indiana to charge, one after the other. At the command, "Forward double quick," both regiments left their breastworks accompanied by deafening cheers and sprang forward. They had scarcely gained the open ground when they were met by one of the most deafening and destructive fires imaginable. Up to this time, the enemy had remained entirely concealed. It had been impossible to tell anything about its strength in their immediate front, but it was now clearly visible that the Confederates had massed a large force at that front. It was later reported that no less than three full brigades of the enemy were located behind the opposing breastworks. The 2nd Massachusetts actually made it across the meadow to the woods, but the 27th Indiana broke when they were halfway across the meadow.

The 107th watched as this little force of 559 men marched out into the open, marshy ground. They were met with a withering fire of musketry that sent them back to their position with great losses. It was a fruitless effort, and those two regiments came out of the Battle of Gettysburg with casualties of 250 men. The 2nd Massachusetts suffered 140 as killed or killed or wounded and the 27th Indiana 110.[16]

The following day, July 4, the men of the 107th viewed the bodies of over three score victims of this mad attempt laid out for burial, and in their minds, they were grateful that they had not been selected for this sacrifice. Throughout the remainder of that morning, they remained in their comparatively secure position waiting to see the results of the battle in their front.

At about 11 o'clock, there was a cessation of the firing, and then came to their ears cheers and shouts of victory. The smoke rolled away, and they saw groups of prisoners in gray moving toward the rear. Many of these men, pinned down directly in front of the breastworks and having no avenue of escape, had voluntarily come into their lines and given themselves up.

The Rebels had been driven out and away from Culp's Hill to the other side of Rock Creek, and federal forces now occupied the works. The men had a buoyant feeling in their hearts, and they thought the battle won.

And indeed, with these men on the right, it was the case. As they were congratulating each other, a group of horsemen came riding down the Baltimore Pike. Amid the dead and dying soldiers, amid the exulting cheering victors and the rusty looking downcast prisoners, the horsemen yelled out, "Here's your *New York Herald*, all the latest news."

At about 12:30 p.m., the 107th was ordered forward to occupy its old position in the breastworks. As they were moving to obey the order, having entered the woods near Spangler's Spring, a great burst of artillery fire came forth from along Lee's lines on Seminary Ridge. The regiment stopped, quickly dropping to the ground or crouching behind boulders to find shelter from the awful storm. The missiles fell everywhere, striking all around them and in the treetops above their heads.

The amount of fire was enough for the men to think that the judgment day had come, and yet throughout that cannonading of an hour's duration, not a man in the regiment was hurt. It seemed to them a miracle that they all had escaped injury. From their location, they could not see any part of the operations that followed. After a while, the artillery fire ceased and was followed by an ominous silence. Soon the silence was broken by a crash of musketry, which became a continuous roar. They heard yells and cheers but could not tell who was winning.

At last, the firing ceased and cheers, which they knew were from the throats of their own Union boys, wafted to their ears. Nearer and nearer they came, as successive parts of the long line took them up until they rolled along over the rocky brow of Culp's Hill and down the lines where they lay asking one another what had happened. They soon learned of Pickett's mighty charge and crushing defeat, and their pent-up feelings burst forth in a great ringing cheer like all the rest.

During the remainder of the day, the quiet was sparingly broken by shots between the enemy's sharpshooters and the 107th men in the breastworks. For all practical purposes, hostilities had ceased along their lines.

That evening, the 107th was sent in company with two other regiments to reinforce the Pleasanton's cavalry operating on the right flank. A rapid march of two or three miles was made, but the enemy had retreated, and the regiment laid down in a field of tall rank grass that formed a couch of down to rest their weary bodies.

Early the next morning, the regiment rejoined the brigade on Culp's Hill. There was no more fighting, and they lay quietly awaiting orders. During that time, many of the men visited the ground over which Pickett made his charge. It was one of the worst scenes of destruction that they had ever witnessed. The wounded had all been removed, but the dead lay in heaps everywhere on the field. Piles of up to ten men lay all along their front, and the woods stretching back from the breastworks were filled with their dead.

All that day, large details of men were engaged in gathering the Rebel dead for burial. Fifteen or twenty bodies were laid together in a pile, a trench was dug, the bodies laid therein and quickly covered over. Dozens of these piles could be seen all over the battlefield. The Union dead were more carefully interred, with some effort made to identify them and to mark their place of burial.

The 107th had escaped this battle with only two casualties. Private John Van Dyke, age 21 of Company K, was badly wounded by a sharpshooter's bullet as the regiment moved to reoccupy their breastworks on Culp's Hill. He was admitted to a 12th Corps field hospital where surgeon H.E. Goodman of the 28th Pennsylvania noted that he had a compound fracture of the right radius and ulna by a minié ball. The ball passed through the forearm directly over the ulna about three inches below the elbow. A resection of two and a half inches of the ulna, middle third was done by surgeon W.H. Twilford of the 27th Indiana on July 4. On July 25, he was transferred to the Letterman Hospital in Gettysburg where acting assistant surgeon Edwin Martin described his wound as a gunshot wound of the right forearm. Upon examination it was found that the ulna was fractured and the radius slightly grazed. Van Dyke was put on a medium diet; cold-water dressings were applied to the wound and quinine administered internally. He was in good condition when brought to the hospital, but in a few days, it was apparent that his strength would fail before the discharge would subside. Stimulants were given him until August 24 when it was decided to amputate his arm. A circular method was done at the middle third of his arm as the inflammation had extended to that distance. After his am was amputated, he was sent home to Hartsville, New York, where he died on September 12, 1863, of hectic fever.[17] Private Welcome Richardson of Company A was also wounded; he was discharged for disability on September 11, 1864, at Elmira.

These last three days, 107th had zealously discharged every duty assigned it, occupied several important positions, and was exposed again and again to a severe fire from the enemy. Although they had not been in the front lines and experienced many casualties, something they did not really regret, they nonetheless felt very proud of having done their duty well.

On Sunday, July 5, at 3 p.m., the regiment left their works and marched toward Littletown. They were in pursuit of Lee and his Rebel army.[18] They could see the effect of their shells as they marched through the area that had been the rebel position in their front. The Confederate losses had been dreadful. The buildings in that area had been heavily damaged, and the Rebel dead lay in heaps of eight or ten. Even the woods were filled with their dead.[19] They reached Littlestown at 4 p.m. and bivouacked there until the morning of the 7th. That day they marched through Taneytown, Woodsboro, and Walkersville to the outskirts of Frederick. The next day, they marched through Frederick, leaving on the Hagerstown Pike towards Harper's Ferry. On the way, they saw the body of a Rebel spy hanging from a tree. It was a disgusting sight as decomposition had begun.[20] They reached Crampton Gap about sundown. The regiment camped on the ridge of the mountain north of the Gap, and they could see Maryland Heights from their camp. On the 9th, they moved several miles and camped near Rohnerville. The next day, they marched to and crossed Antietam Creek near Keedysville and then camped in a battleline to the right of Sharpsburg near Bakersville.

On July 11, they moved through Bakersville and Fairplay. There was slight skirmishing in their front all day. The 107th was sent out to the front to support the pickets, and as result had to sleep in their uniforms on the ground in a cornfield. The next day, they lay in line while the remainder of the brigade and corps came up and formed a line on either end of their line. They were all ready to move forward when a heavy shower started, and their advance was postponed. Instead, they commenced building breastworks and continued through most of the night. The next day, they lay in the breastworks, and during the night they could hear the Rebel wagons crossing the Potomac River. On the 14th, they were roused early, left their breastworks, and moved past three former lines of the Rebels. When they neared the river, they saw prisoners who had been captured by their cavalry. As the prisoners passed by them, they could see that they were very tired, and their clothes were muddy. However, they were good humored as they talked with the men of the 107th. The following day, they left the area near the Potomac and marched back to near Antietam Creek. On the 15th, they moved past Maryland Heights to Pleasant Valley near Sandy Hook.[21] The next day, they moved at 7 a.m. and passed their old camp on Maryland Heights. Arthur Fitch went with Captain Knox to visit the graves of Gilbert Stickler and Amos Rogers, both of whom had died of typhoid fever when the regiment was camped there during October of 1862. While the regiment was camped near Sandy Hook, their baggage came and afforded them the ability to change into fresh clothes. They remained near Sandy Hook until the 19th, when they crossed the Potomac River on a pontoon bridge, passed through Harper's Ferry, and then crossed the Shenandoah River on a new steel bridge. They were on their way back to Virginia.

The next day they moved out at 7 a.m. Many of the men went against orders and stole chickens and pigs from local farms. However, many of them were arrested for "foraging." On the 21st, they camped near Snickersville. They remained there for several days, performing picket duty and sending out patrols into the nearby country looking for Rebel guerrillas and spies. On Friday they, along with the 2nd Massachusetts, guarded a supply train near Upperville. The next morning, they moved at 4 a.m. and halted in sight of Snickersville, where they stayed until 2 p.m. During that time, they observed large numbers of cattle being taken from the Rebs. They moved on and passed Deckerstown at 4 p.m. They finally halted for supper at 8 p.m. They continued marching until they reached near Warrenton Junction on Tuesday the 27th of July.

They made camp there, and their mail was delivered at dusk. The next day, a severe rainstorm pelted them. On Thursday, their camp was put in better order with the officers' tents placed all in line. That same day, they had a regimental inspection, and there was a dress parade. They received orders to move on the 30th. That same day, they lost the services of Captain Fox when he accidently shot himself in the leg. The following day, they left Warrenton Junction at 6 a.m. and marched to near Kelly's Ford on the Rappahannock. On the 1st of August, they crossed the river. Now that they were closer to the Rebel army, they formed battle lines and sent out skirmishers.[22]

The 12th Corps was now in a strong position of defense and would be there for several weeks. They would remain there doing picket duty until August 16, when members of their brigade, the 2nd Massachusetts, 3rd Wisconsin, and the 27th Indiana, would be transferred to New York City because of the draft riots. The 107th NY was held back purposefully because of the potential for problems should a New York state regiment participate in repressing the crowds involved in the riots. That same day, the 107th NY along with the rest of the 12th Corps would cross Kelly's Ford and march through Stevensburg to Raccoon Ford on the Rapidan River. They set up camp and began picketing along the Rapidan from Somerville Ford to Springfellow's Ford. However, the main force remained at Raccoon Ford.

Initially the opposing cavalry units spent a great deal of time shooting across the river at each other. It was not a planned initiative and was more of a nuisance for both sides. When the infantry units took over the major portion of the picket duty, they rejected the random shooting. The two sides got together and established a truce. Not only did they stop shooting, but they also began trading. The two most popular items were tobacco for the Union troops and coffee for the Confederates. However, there were still areas along the river where random firing at each other caused needless casualties. The only activity of any significance during this time was unfortunately the execution of deserters, and the troops of each of the 12th Corps divisions were ordered out to witness them. During this time, four soldiers were executed. On the bright side, there was a greater variety of food. They had soft bread three out of seven days along with pork, beef, rice, coffee, and sugar.

Overall, the picket details continued with no major engagements occurring, Because of this inactivity, Lee saw fit to move large units of his forces to Tennessee where they could be put to better use against the Union forces under Rosecrans. This caused an imbalance of forces in both Virginia and Tennessee. The war department decided to send the 11th and 12th Corps to Tennessee to bring the Union forces equal to the Confederate forces at both locations[23]

For the next 40 plus days, the 107th NY, along with the rest of regiments in the 12th Corps, spent the majority of their time in camp doing drills and reviews. They had one-hour drills twice a day: one at 7 in the morning and one in the afternoon at 6. Otherwise, they might be doing picket duty along the river. Their camp was one mile above Kelly's Ford, and it was about eight or ten rods from the river. Those men on picket duty were spread out along the riverbank.

In early September, the monotony of the camp was broken. Three Rebel cavalrymen came down the river and surrendered to their pickets. They gave up their horses, carbines, and sabers. It was interesting that their sabers were Union issue, as were their two carbines. The one rifle they had had been cut short so as to be handled more easily on horse. Two of the three horses were formerly Union cavalry. The three, all North Carolinians, had been on picket duty just across the river. It was very unusual for more than one to give themselves up at a time.[24]

On, Sept. 12 the three regiments from the brigade of the 107th NY returned from their New York City duty.[25] On Sept. 24, The 12th Corps was relieved by the 1st Corps and ordered to march to Brandy Station. The orders were received at noon to be ready to move at a moment's notice. By 2 p.m. they were underway, and by 8 p.m. they had reached Brandy Station where they bivouacked. The next day, another deserter was shot. That made five shot all together: three at Leesburg, one at Raccoon Ford and one at Brandy Station. They remained at Brandy Station for another day and then moved on to Bealton Station. That evening they were paid for two months to the beginning of September. Very few in the regiment received any pay as their clothing allotment was overdrawn. Many had been careless, actually throwing clothing away during marches or during battles. On Sunday, September 27, they bordered an Orange and Alexandria railroad train along with the 5th Connecticut, the 3rd Wisconsin, and the 2nd Massachusetts.[26] Their destination was southern Tennessee to support General Rosecrans and specifically to guard railroads in that general area. The cars that they bordered were regular boxcars used for freight and had temporary seats constructed of boards. In addition, square holes had been cut out for ventilation. Each car held approximately 40 men.[27]

### Battle of Gettysburg July 1–3, 1863
### Casualties 12th Army Corps, First Division, Third Brigade
### Brig. Gen. Thomas H. Ruger

| Regiment | Killed | Wounded | Missing* | Total |
|---|---|---|---|---|
| 27th Indiana | 23 | 86 | 1 | 110 |
| 2nd Mass. | 23 | 109 | 4 | 136 |
| 13th NJ | 1 | 20 | 0 | 21 |
| 107th NY | 0 | 2** | 0 | 2 |
| 3rd Wisc. | 2 | 8 | 0 | 10 |

*or Captured
**One died later after multiple amputations.

# 8

# Guarding Tennessee

**General Braxton Bragg's Confederate victory at Chickamauga on September 18–20, 1863, forced Union Major General Rosecrans to withdraw into the city of Chattanooga. His situation there was tenuous because his only method of supplying his army was by wagon from Nashville, and these wagons would be easy prey for guerrillas and small Confederate raiding parties. The answer to his problem was keeping open the railroad between Nashville and Chattanooga. Hence, the infusion of additional Union troops in the form of the 11th and 12th Army Corps.**

On September 23, 1863, Secretary Stanton received an urgent telegram from Assistant Secretary of War Charles A. Dana at Chattanooga. The telegram was dated September 19 and read: "No time should be lost in rushing twenty to twenty-five thousand efficient troops to Bridgeport, Alabama. If such reinforcement can be got there in season, everything is safe and this place is indispensable alike to defense of Tennessee and as a base for future operations in Georgia will remain ours."

The situation was desperate for Rosecrans and the Army of the Cumberland in the Chattanooga Valley. They had the Tennessee River behind them with Bragg and his Confederate forces commanding the heights to the east and west running a strong line across the valley from mountain to mountain.

In response to Dana's telegram, Stanton called an urgent meeting at the War Department with Halleck, Lincoln, and the secretaries of state, Seward and Chase. Stanton came right to the point, explaining Rosecrans' situation. Sherman was too far away to be of any assistance by marching to Bridgeport to relieve Rosecrans, and Burnsides had his hands full trying to hold Knoxville and control eastern Tennessee.

Then Stanton, always a railroad supporter having once been a railroad attorney, made a startling suggestion. Thirty thousand troops, he said, could be detached from the Army and sent to Chattanooga by rail to break the siege. The entire troop movement, he enthused, could be done in five days. Halleck, who had been wrong in most of his military decisions, was the first to object that it could not be done.

Even President Lincoln, an open-minded man eager for any kind of solution, had his doubts. "I will bet that if an order is given tonight," he said to Stanton, "the troops could not be gotten to Washington in five days." What Lincoln meant was that it would take that long to get them from the base in Virginia to Washington in that time, much less get them to Chattanooga.

But President Lincoln underestimated his war secretary. Adamant and unshaken in his determination to give the idea a try, certain that with good planning the task of moving two fully equipped army corps to Chattanooga, almost a thousand miles away, was possible in the given time, Stanton argued until he won his point.

When it was finally agreed, Stanton wasted no tine. For the rest of the night, he kept the wires hot, sending telegrams to railroad executives of the U.S. military railroads, the Baltimore & Ohio, and the Philadelphia, Wilmington and Baltimore railroads, and other directives to army officers in Virginia.[1]

On Sunday the 27th of September 1863, at three in the afternoon, the 107th NY and all of the 12th Corps bordered a train at Bealton Station and began a journey that ultimately would transport them to Tennessee. Their immediate destination was the capital. While they traveled through Virginia, there were many scenes of desolation. They stopped momentarily at Alexandria and at Washington, where they were fed a hot meal including meat and soft bread. They changed trains at the Washington Relay House.[2] There they boarded cars of the Baltimore and Ohio Railroad and proceeded through Harper's Ferry, Martinsburg, and Hancock to Bentwood on the Ohio River. Many of the soldiers rode on top of the cars to get a better view and enjoy the picturesque scenery of West Virginia and its mountains.

The mountains meant that there would be many tunnels, and some of them made it necessary for the men on top of the cars to "scrunch down." A serious tragedy almost befell them when the whole train (18 cars) ran off the tracks as it ran along a high embankment. It was a wonder that many were not killed, but they just went bumpity bump over the ties. Eight hours passed before they were on their way again.[3]

At Bentwood, the troops left the cars, crossed the Ohio River on pontoons, and boarded a train of the Central Ohio Railroad. This train took them through the towns of Cambridge, Zanesville, Columbus, Xenia, Dayton, Indianapolis, and Jefferson, where they crossed the river again on ferryboats to Louisville.[4]

The trip through Ohio had been an exciting one. The people turned out in crowds at each railroad station, providing an abundance of food and drink for these veterans. In addition, there were many of the fairer sex in attendance. The men, not having had much exposure to the ladies for some time, took the opportunity to throw "saucy notes" to them. It was said that many letters of correspondence were realized from these events, and in later years it transpired that many of the wives of these veterans had originally lived in Ohio.

The trip, all things considered, was a pleasant one and a chance to see more of the U.S. than 2nd Lieutenant Hadley Beal ever thought he would. At Louisville, they departed the boats and were to go by train the rest of the way. Beal got permission to be the first off of the boat. His Aunt Hannah had previously asked him to call on a friend of hers, a Mrs. Topping. Beal ran to a local hotel, the Galt House, that was run by Mr. Topping. Once at the hotel, he asked the first person he saw there where to find Mrs. Topping. The person he asked turned out to be Mr. Topping, and he gave Beal directions to his home. Beal hurried to the Topping home where he met Mrs. Topping and a young lady named Miss Amedy. They had a short conversation during which Miss Amedy gave Beal her address and wished him to write to her. Beal hurried back to the Galt House and left $50 with Mr. Topping, asking him to forward it to his parents by Adams Express. He had not expected his regiment to remain long in Louisville, only long enough to march about a mile from the ferry to the railroad depot. He took a carriage to the depot, only to learn that the regiment was not going to leave until midnight.[5]

From Louisville, they went on to Nashville. They arrived there early in the morning on October 3. They did not linger there long and went south towards Chattanooga. They passed through a delightful section of the country and finally went through the Cumberland Tunnel to Stevenson, Alabama. There they departed the train at 2 a.m. and laid down in a nearby field and slept soundly until morning. It was a great relief to get out of the dirty cars and sleep on a solid foundation. They laid there until 9 o'clock that morning, Sunday October 4, when they were ordered to go north into Tennessee for thirty miles to Decherd.[6]

On October 2, the day before the 107th New York, along with the remainder of the 12th Corps and the 11th Corps, arrived in Tennessee, Confederate General Joseph Wheeler's raiding forces entered the area just north of Chattanooga and attacked a supply wagon train between Anderson Crossroads and the village of Jasper. The train was heavily loaded with ordnance, quartermaster, and commissary stores. There were 800 six-mule wagons besides a great number of sutler's wagons. The train was guarded by a brigade of cavalry in front, a brigade of cavalry in rear, and a regiment of infantry on either flank. After a short fight, the guards were defeated and driven off, leaving the entire train in Wheeler's possession. After selecting such mules and wagons as he needed, he then destroyed the train by burning the wagons and shooting the mules. During this work he was attacked, and his pickets were driven in on both flanks and his rear. However, the Union troops were repulsed, and Wheeler's troops remained undisturbed for eight hours, during which his destruction of the wagon train was thoroughly accomplished. Just before dark, as they were retiring, a large force of Union cavalry and infantry moved upon them from Stevenson and skirmished with their rear units until dark. During the night, Wheeler moved over the Cumberland Mountains.

Early the next morning, October 4, Wheeler joined General Wharton near the foot of the mountains and went forward to attack McMinnville while the Union forces were still pressing close behind. Wheeler succeeded in capturing the Union garrison there, and an enormous supply of quartermaster and commissary stores, a total of 587 Union soldiers with arms, accouterments, and 200 horses. During that day and into the evening, Wheeler's men destroyed the stores, a locomotive, a train of railroad cars, and a bridge over Hickory Creek.

The following day, Wheeler marched to near Murfreesboro and captured a strong stockade with its garrison of 52 men that was guarding the railroad bridge over Stone's River. Afterwards they cut down the bridge and set fire to the timber. As they marched south, they destroyed the track for three miles below the bridge.

On October 6, they destroyed a train and a quantity of stores at Christiana and Fosterville and destroyed all of the railroad bridges and trestles between Murfreesboro and Wartrace, including capturing all of the guards. They also captured and destroyed a large number of stores of all kinds at Shelbyville. That night, Wheeler ordered Davidson's division to encamp on the Duck River near Warner's Bridge, Martin's division two miles farther down, and Wharton's two miles below Martin's. The next day, they headed southwest toward Framingham with the Union cavalry hot on their heels. At Framingham, they engaged the Union forces on the 7th.[7]

Following that engagement, Wheeler fled south. He escaped across the Tennessee River on October 9 at Rogersville, Alabama, but not before another 95 of his horsemen were overwhelmed by Union troops near Pulaski, Tennessee.[8]

While Wheeler was moving north towards Murfreesboro on October 5, the 107th New York moved the following morning back 30 miles to Decherd, Tennessee, and camped. At that point in time, they were moving in a direction opposite from that of Wheeler.[9] However, the regiment was now looking forward to its new duty. It, with the entire 12th and 11th Corps, were to be spread out along the railroad from Nashville to Chattanooga to prevent further Rebel forces from destroying any part of it and thereby isolating the Union forces in Chattanooga.[10] Unfortunately, these two corps had arrived in Tennessee too late to prevent Wheeler's destructive raid.

On October the 6th, the 107th New York was at Decherd. They received orders to strike their tents and move to the cars at 9 a.m. During that time, they heard rumors that the Confederate cavalry under General Wheeler had made a raid on the railroad above Tullahoma, destroying the track and burning the bridges.[11]

They did not board the train until 2 a.m. There were about 70 men to a car with as many on top that would fit there, even though the wind was blowing hard, and it was raining. They reached Tullahoma at daylight.[12] They then moved north towards Murfreesboro about 20 miles and came to a bridge that had been destroyed by Rebels. There they left the train and marched another 20 miles further, where they stopped and camped at about 4 p.m. They continued marching and reached Christiana on the 8th. During their march, they remarked how fine the country looked, with nice farms and good stands of trees. On the 10th, they moved back 23 miles by rail to Winchester.[13] From there they continued marching south on the railroad track and found it very tiresome and painful on their feet. Toward nightfall, they approached Normandy, where they supposed they would camp for the night, but General Ruger was bound to make Tullahoma, so on they went. Along the way, the railroad crossed a deep chasm that was spanned by a long bridge. The brigade

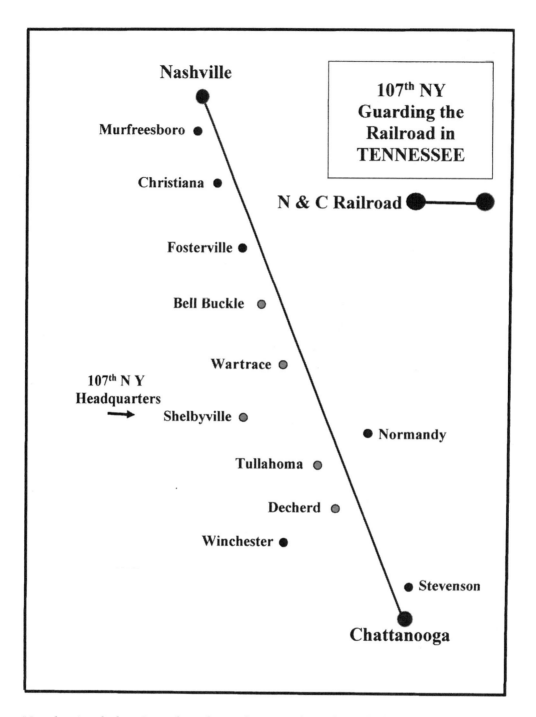

Map showing the locations where the 107th New York was located while guarding the Nashville-Chattanooga Railroad.

would have to cross this bridge in the dark in what would be a very difficult and dangerous maneuver. While they were in the process of crossing the bridge, they heard a train whistle giving notice of a train approaching from the south toward them. Company G of the 107th New York was midway across the bridge at this point. The men maintained their composure and hurried over the bridge as fast as the darkness would permit. They reached the opposite bank just seconds before the train reached the bridge. Afterwards, Colonels Crane and Colgrove went to General Ruger and requested that the men be allowed to rest for the remainder of the night. At first, he refused, but later consented. They were six miles short of Tullahoma. The men lay down in a muddy cornfield, wrapped themselves in their rubber blankets, and rested as well as they could.[14]

On the 11th, they marched through Tullahoma and on to the Elk River Bridge, reaching it at noon.[15] Along the way, they discovered that the Rebels had previously destroyed three of the railroad bridges. All three were repaired in a day and a half.[16]

At the Elk River Bridge, the 107th New York stayed on the north side of the river while the remainder of the brigade camped on the south side. The 1st Tennessee Negro regiment of the Corps d'Afrique was also stationed there, along with a portion of the 102nd Ohio Volunteers and a company of engineers. Colonel Hawley of the 3rd Wisconsin was placed in command of the post.

A Colonel Thompson commanded the 1st Tennessee Regiment of the Corps d'Afrique. They found this regiment was clean and orderly. No regiment could behave better. Several officers of the 107th watched their dress parade, and it was deemed excellent. This regiment was doing considerable picket duty, and no soldiers could be more alert. However, their one fault was being too careful, and as a result, they fired at anything out of the ordinary. But they were faithful, obeyed all orders, and did their duty. One day four of them, a corporal and three privates, were on picket duty. Guerrillas fired on them, killing one. They had difficulty loading their pieces because they were brand new to the service. The corporal and the two privates stood their ground, and while the corporal loaded their pieces, the two privates fired deliberately, each waiting his turn. The three of them remained firing until relieved by nearby soldiers who had heard their firing. The men of the 107th were greatly impressed, realizing that they had once been enslaved, and now they were men of equal stature.

The two divisions of the 12th Corps spread their regiments along the railroad from Nashville south toward Chattanooga. The 1st division, which included the 107th New York, was distributed as follows. The 123rd New York was sent to Bridgeport; the 20th Connecticut was left at Stevenson; the 3rd Maryland at Anderson; the 145th New York at Tantallon; the 5th Connecticut at Cowan; the 46th Pennsylvania with Gen. Knipe's headquarters at Decherd; the 2nd Massachusetts at Elk River Bridge; the 27th Indiana at Tullahoma; the 150th New York at Normandy; the 3rd Wisconsin at Gen. Ruger's headquarters at Wartrace; the 13th New Jersey at Bell Buckle; and the 107th New York at Fosterville. The different regiments were scattered by companies between these places, allowing for a complete line of guards along the railroad. Initially the following companies of the 107th were stationed at these locations. Company G was spread out between Fosterville and Bell Buckle. Before the remainder of the companies established themselves at various locations along the railroad, they were all ordered to Wartrace Bridge, which was now to be the headquarters of the regiment. Then two companies were sent to Shelbyville, with the balance sent to Wartrace and Wartrace Bridge, except for companies A, G and H, which were located at Bell Buckle Bridge and a nearby water tank. Two companies, A, which previously was at Bell Buckle Bridge, and C relieved the 13th New Jersey at Wartrace Bridge. All 107th New York locations immediately began to make their situations as comfortable as possible, for they believed that they would be at these locations for a considerable amount of time. It would be these regiments' responsibility to guard the railroad from the Rebel army, guerrillas, and bushwhackers. Chattanooga was the base of army supplies for all future movements, and the line of communication between it and Nashville must be maintained.

Each detachment of companies laid their camp out in regular streets and erected their shelters. Views of the railroad and surrounding country were quite extensive. The individual camps were situated so that the railroad and much of the surrounding country was easily visible, including the outlines of the Cumberland Mountains that stretched for miles until they were lost in the distance. The Bell Buckle and Wartrace creeks were near the camps and afforded the men plenty of fresh water.

The surrounding area was dotted with a number of modest farmhouses. They appeared comfortable but had no pretentions of wealth or beauty. However, the soil was rich and the climate so temperate that there were plenty of good pastures. These farms, though primitive, were prosperous and did not rely on slave labor. Most of the residents were for the Rebels as they were sympathetic to the Rebel cause, and their young men had gone off with the Rebel army. However, they had taken the oath of allegiance, and the soldiers made every effort to treat them with kindness.[17]

During the following months, various companies and entire regiments moved to different locations along the railroad, and they included for the most part campsites in the general Tullahoma, Bell Buckle, Wartrace, and Shelbyville areas. Monthly company reports tended to generalize a company's location, as did the individual soldier's journals and correspondence. These factors tended to be confusing as to when, where, and why particular events took place. Officers traveled quite often between different locations for both personal and official reasons. Ultimately, all of these units would be combined with other regiments and become part of Sherman's Georgia campaign.

The officers of the regiment quickly became familiar with the communities and the residents. They settled into commanding the pickets at each location, and when they were officer of the day, they routinely made the rounds, checking each post four times each day. Otherwise, they had free time except for writing reports, conducting inspections, and participating in various drills. If their company was located in a residential area, many of the officers boarded with local residents. Others occupied vacant buildings or constructed additions to wall tents with furniture for additional comfort. The officers enjoyed gatherings with the ladies, including those of a secessionist bent. There were informal meetings, parties, and dances. The enlisted men and officers also did a lot drinking and quite often got into trouble because of it.[18]

During this same period, Company K of the 107th New York was stationed at the Elk River Bridge. Lieutenant Russell Tuttle of that company wrote in his journal that he and Captain Sill took dinner on Monday, October 12, with a local lady. Mrs. Mason had been born in Tennessee but was for the Union. This meeting foretold that the officers of the regiment were to develop many friendships with individuals as well as families during their stay in Tennessee.

On October 14, Companies E and H arrived at Estelle Springs. Here they were accordingly detached from the remainder of the regiment. This location was so called because three springs were located there within several feet of each other. Amazingly one spring was sulphur, another was mineral, and a third was clear, soft water. The springs were located approximately one-half mile from a railroad bridge that rose sixty-five feet over the Elk River and was 17 miles from Tullahoma. The prevailing thought was that they would be moving to the front sometime soon. Having said that, they were situated in a building and hoped that they would be permitted to enjoy their good quarters for some time.[19]

A large number of the men in Company E were located in a house that had been fitted up with bunks for the enlisted men, about 25 in number; in a separate room, there were six officers and four of their servants. The servants slept under the bunks. There was plenty of food and drink. All in all, they felt it was good duty, although they were often required to do some hard marching. When they were off duty, they often played checkers and euchre. There were several buildings in the area that previously were available to the wealthy or "Nobs" that came to the springs for their health. This popularity had prompted a Dr. Estelle to lay out streets and sell quarter acre lots for a hundred dollars apiece. However, at this point in time, the buildings, long in disuse, were appropriated by the men of the 107th for use in building their shanties.[20]

In the short time there, they had constructed excellent living quarters. Once settled in their camps, they built fortifications in case they had to rebuff a large force. It rained almost every day, resulting in mud everywhere. After they were all settled in, comfortable and cozy despite the continual rain, the regiment was ordered on October 23rd to pack up and get six days rations. The pickets returned to camp, and the men began packing and swearing, while all the time the rain continued. They made Decherd that evening and camped. The next day they marched to Cowen and into and over the Cumberland Mountains for eight miles. On the 25th they continued on and reached Anderson near the Alabama state line, where they camped for the night. The next day, they resumed their march, but in the opposite direction over the same route. They marched back through Cowen, Decherd, and Tullahoma and on the 29th reached Fosterville, 12 miles south of Murfreesboro. During their return march, they passed by their old camp. A nearby Black regiment had cleaned it out. That was to be expected, but the boys said that they would skin every one of them alive if they got the chance. Fosterville was the northernmost location being guarded by their regiment. It was approximately twenty-five miles north of Tullahoma. The first night there, it rained, and in the morning, they found their camp completely surrounded by water.[21]

During the next few days, the sun came out, and both companies immediately began building their soldier houses. However, both companies received orders on November 4th to be ready to move the following morning. The next morning, the entire 107th New York moved south to new locations. Company H was then situated about eight miles further south, where they relieved one company of the 13th New Jersey at a train water tank. On arrival, they saw that the 13th New Jersey had not bothered to erect any special housing at that location. The next several days were spent cutting logs for their new houses. The remainder of the regiment was to be located between themselves and Wartrace. Fortunately, Company H was to remain at this location for the remainder of their time in Tennessee.[22]

While the various regiments were becoming more settled in their camps, their commanding officers were not so happy with the age and unworthiness of the transportation that was available, as expressed in this excerpt from General William's letter to his family. He wrote,

> I have so many posts now in the ninety miles of railroad I am guarding that my duties are greatly increased at home and away. It is no easy job to travel on this railroad, the way it is managed. The road is in a bad condition and the engines are old and worthless. It is a good day's work to get forty miles. There is a constant struggle to push forward freight cars with supplies for troops in front, but very little judgment is used in putting the road in condition to meet the demands upon it.[23]

The presence of the Union army in this area had the effect of the Black residents acting more like free people, and many were now working for their former masters. As a result, it was not uncommon for their former owners to come to the Union officers to complain about the Black residents. It was obvious they were expressing their rights. There were even occasions where the Black residents reported disloyal activities of the citizens and the presence of Confederate soldiers.[24]

By early November, Lt. Hadley Beal had set up a correspondence with the young lady, Miss Amedy, that he had met in Louisville. He included her recent letter in his letter home, admonishing his parents not to let anyone else see it because if she found out, she might be displeased.[25]

In mid–November, Company F of the 107th New York was one of five companies located near Wartrace, Tennessee. They were receiving daily newspapers and had the opportunity to see what was happening at their previous location at Kelly's Ford on the Rappahannock River in Virginia. The newspapers portrayed the elections between those who wanted to stop the war and let the South be separated and those who wanted to defeat the Rebels and save the Union. The general consensus in Tennessee was that the rebellion was in poor straits because of naval blockades and their depreciated money, which the Rebels themselves felt was entirely worthless.

Many of the officers stationed there were sending some of their pay home, although a large number did not. Additionally, the officers' much larger pay allowed them to board with the locals. Lieutenant John Hill, together with two other officers, paid $60 a month for bed and board in a private home.

Sunday the 15th was a splendid day for their regimental inspection, and it gave the officers an opportunity to wear their dress uniforms with white gloves, collars with a red sash, and their sword. Duty typically changed every four days. A different company officer would be assigned as the officer of the day, and a different group of the men were assigned picket duty. The officer of the day for each company was required to visit the lines four times during the day. One of the evening visits was usually to be made between 11 p.m. and 1 a.m. A given picket line could be two miles long and made for a somewhat difficult duty in the dark.

The Tennessee weather provided a great health benefit to the men. This was in comparison to their experiences at Hope Landing and on Maryland Heights after the battle of Antietam. It was there that upwards of one half of the men were sick with different diseases. At their present location, they had a hospital tent, but it went unoccupied.[26]

Company E was one of the other five companies located in the Wartrace area in mid–November, and second Lieutenant Hadley Beal of that company described his group's quarters as a log house built with an 8-foot ceiling, and 12 feet long with a wall tent attached. It was not unusual for the officers to hire cooks and servants. Beal had a "good natured darkie cook" nearly seven feet tall, strong as an ox and very good at foraging. Beal said he was so dark you could mark him with caulk. Beal, who had enlisted as a private, was discharged in December of 1863 for not performing his duties in an efficient manner.[27]

Prior to the arrival of the 107th New York and the other regiments, Bragg's army had overrun this area and taken away cattle, horses, mules, and grain, giving Confederate script in payment. The enslaved men from this area had left to join the Union army or work as servants for Union officers. The females were left behind and did both field and housework to survive. They drove teams, built fences, felled trees, ploughed the fields, sowed the grain, and harvested the crops. For the most part, the formerly enslaved people from this area were loyal to the Union cause.

Aside from the Confederate army itself, there was always the threat of guerrillas in the area. There was such a band under the command of a former sheriff of Bedford County named Blackwell. They operated in this general area and specifically near a place called Beach Grove that was located east of Bell Buckle. When threatened with capture, they typically retreated up into the mountains. Many were apprehended, but one of their leaders, a man called Mosley, was able to escape. However, he was later captured and imprisoned in Tullahoma.

The 107th New York men guarding the railroad were always vigilant, and bushwhackers frequently fired on them. However, the bushwhackers usually got the worst of it. No one was allowed to pass the picket lines without a special permit, and the rule was strictly enforced. It was a common occurrence for deserters of the Rebel army and natives of Tennessee to pass over the road. As they came through the lines, they were sent to Chattanooga where they received signed passes that allowed passage to their former homes.[28]

While the health of the regiment was very good, they were suffering from a lack of clothing, equipment, and other supplies. This situation might have been because the Tennessee regiments were not "fighting" regiments during this period and not deemed a priority. Below is Colonel Crane's letter seeking critically needed supplies.

Head Quarters 107 NYV
War Trace Bridge, Tenn.

Nov. 21, 1863
Capt. Wm. Ruger, A.A.G.
3rd Brigade, 1st Division
12th Army Corps, Tullahoma, Tenn.

Captain,

My men are in very bad shape as regards shoes and other clothing. I made requisitions for supplies some time since, but my Q Master says he cannot get the articles.

Many of the men are barefoot and have to borrow shoes of each other in order to go on Picket. Others are nearly destitute of pants and coats.

I cannot see any real necessity for this. Yet there may be. Ordinance cannot be obtained, and I have been trying ever since the 18th day of October. I want arms and equipment badly.

If you can do anything to hurry along those supplies you will confer a great favor.

I am nearly out of stationary, have not enough to last over three or four days.

Your Obt. Servant
N. Crane
Col. Comdg 107NY Vol[29]

An article about and letter written by Corporal James W. Pinch of the 107th New York appeared in the local Hornell newspaper in late November and early December.

Corporal James W. Pinch nephew of Samuel Pinch Esq., of this village, and belonging to the 107th N.Y. Vols. Slocum's division, started for the seat of war last Wednesday. He has been home on furlough, on account of wounds received at the battle of Chancellorsville, where he laid four days on the field before being picked up, during which time he was robbed of his watch and money by the Rebels.

Mr. Editor,

The devastating influences of war have not been so felt in this state as in Virginia. Virginia looks deserted with its once noble forest felled to make those brave boys who have gone forth to battle for their country, more comfortable, and to protect them from the chilly blasts, and disagreeable rains so frequently known and dreaded by the soldiers in the Old Dominion. The plantations of Berkeley, Prince William and other counties are in a state of ruination that will take many years to reverse. A much different state of affairs exists in Tennessee. Here we see well-cultivated farms with good fences surrounding them and neat farmhouses. The inhabitants of Tennessee are, as far as our experiences go, are genuinely loyal, despite the many privations that have been brought about by the Southern Confederacy.

The 107th NY camp is located at Wartrace Bridge, which is fifty-two miles south of Nashville and ninety miles north of Chattanooga.

Living conditions for the soldiers are very good. Good water is found in abundance. Soldier's luxuries such as butter, potatoes, and chickens are cheap and available from the farmers. The boys are ensconced in shanties that only the veterans know how to build.

There is no officer in the service better loved than Colonel Nirom M. Crane. There is not a man in the regiment who would not give his life for him. The regiment has the most perfect confidence in his ability to command.

Companies B and K are separated from the main command at Shelbyville, ten miles distant from the regiment in the interior. This place is the county seat of Bedford County and has about 5,000 inhabitants, and before the rebellion was quite a business place as it still is now. Two large Flour and one cotton mill are in continuous operation here. The Duck River offers ample facilities for waterpower. The houses are large and comfortable and built mostly of brick. Churches of many different denominations are located here, but only one offers services at present.

Recently we witnessed a scene that we hope to never witness again while we are here. It was the inhuman practice of whipping a Negro that was in vogue here before the Rebellion. The circumstances were as follows. A cavalryman being out of greenbacks and no doubt wishing some sold a horse to the Negro. The Negro suspecting nothing wrong about the horse, and there being no government brand on him, bought the horse and paid the money. A short time after he was arrested, and for two weeks lay in the guard house, a punishment sufficient in itself. After this he was taken out into the public square, his hands tied behind his back, and thirty-one lashes lay on his bare back. At the end of the punishment blood ran in streams down his back. It was too much for our Northern stomachs. We could not stand such a punishment in times like these, and there was not one among us, but that expressed his indignation at this occurrence. An innocent man, but of a different color with senses and feelings akin to us, tied and whipped in the presence of us who were fighting for his protection and freedom. It was truly shameful and a stain on those who ordered it done. If the Negro was to blame, why was he not tried by a court-martial and sent to the penitentiary at Nashville or put to work on some of the government works. We think it would have been better than to be used like a heathen. But these are curious times. J.W.P.[30]

The 145th New York was broken up December 9, 1863, with the commissioned officers discharged and the privates distributed by company to various New York regiments. Companies E and H went to the 123rd New York, Companies A, D, and F to the 150th New York, and Companies B, C, G, I, and K to the 107th New York. They were mostly foreigners and New York City roughs.[31]

The 145th New York was also referred to as the Stanton Legion. The regiment was the subject of an article in the *New York City Military Critic* following its dissolution by general order of the War Department. The article stated in part that the officers were mustered out of the army, and the men distributed into other regiments "not of this city," which makes this singular order still more harsh, as this regiment was organized in the city of New York and was presented by the city with a stand of colors in acknowledgment of its services on many hard-fought battlefields. It was the ardent wish of the officers and men to have their regimental organization restored.

In addition to the above, the *Critic* also published a short article alleging that the War Department dissolution of the 145th New York was a political move by the administration because the regiment was made up of Democrats and was part of the general plan for the re-election of Republican Abraham Lincoln.

In early December, Surgeon Flood sent a letter to the former colonel of the regiment, Alexander S. Diven, in Elmira and asked him to use his influence with the

War Department for the purpose of sending a detail home to recruit volunteers for the regiment in an effort to bring the regiment, as much as possible, to full strength. Diven's efforts in response to the letter were successful, and on December 31 a letter was written to Major General Thomas, commander of the Army of the Cumberland, ordering him to send a detail of two commissioned officers and one enlisted man from each company to Elmira for the purpose of recruiting volunteers for the regiment. The group identified for the trip to Elmira included Colonel Crane, Captain Brigham, and one enlisted man from each company. The enlisted men included Company A—Frank Bates, B—James Herrington, C—S.R. Sawyer, D—Solomon Reniff, E—Guy Adams, F—Ralph Stevens, G—David Burd, H—John Evland, I—William Wheeler, and K—John Bonney. On January 22, Colonel Crane sent a letter to Alexander Diven advising him that his group would be arriving in Elmira in six or eight days. He also told Diven that he was adding 200 men from the dissolved 145th New York to the 107th New York, bringing his total count to 820 men.

In a December 22, 1863, letter, J.J. Laman at Bell Buckle Bridge wrote to Col. Crane (although not clearly identified). He thanked him for his letter and referred to his previous letter to General Ruger sent from Raccoon Ford, VA, and dated October 4, 1863. His comment over the tardiness of the response was, "If a general can retain papers so long in his office with impunity. May God help the underlings." The content of this letter is confusing to the extent that Laman was discharged on October 25, 1863, and in this letter, he talks of still being in command of several of the regiment's companies (A and G) at this location and at Wartrace bridge three miles south.[32]

In addition to doing picket duty, small foraging groups often ventured into the countryside. These groups typically did not meet with any trouble, but that was not always the case. On the evening of December 23, an officer and four unarmed soldiers of the 27th Indiana were captured by guerrillas and taken to a place on the bank of the Elk River. Their hands were tied behind their back, and they were robbed. The men were then stood in line before their captors who, on command, fired a volley. One man was killed, three were wounded, and the officer was not hit. The officer immediately jumped into the river, removed his bonds, swam to the opposite shore, and escaped. The four soldiers were thrown into the river. Three either died of their wounds or drowned, but one made his way to safety.

General Thomas, upon hearing of this outrage, ordered that the property of all Rebel citizens living within ten miles of this incident should be assessed according to his wealth and pay toward a levy of $30,000 for a payment of $10,000 to each family of the soldiers killed. However, this measure, while successful, did not deter further bloodshed. The soldiers given the task of collecting the money had two men of those regiments killed during the collection process. The money collected amounted to more than the original levy, and the families of those two soldiers also received monies. Afterward, the 3rd Wisconsin was sent by General Slocum to Fayetteville to prevent further activities of this type. This regiment would remain there until the opening of the spring campaign into Georgia.[33]

The officers of companies A and G were in the habit of purchasing meat and vegetables from the local famers. They were planning on having a small Christmas holiday celebration. Previously a stranger had come to the camp and offered to supply such things as were needed. Many purchases were made of him. A few days before Christmas, he offered to supply the officers with turkeys for their Christmas dinner, saying that his wife was a good cook, and he would have them roasted and ready for the table. The officers took him up on his offer, and on Christmas morning, he brought two roasted turkeys to the camp. One of them was given to the noncommissioned officers' mess and the other to the officers' mess. The officers who dined on the turkey that day were Captain Lewis and Lieutenant Collson, both of Company A, and Lieutenants Denniston and Saltzman of Company G with Surgeon Flood who was visiting. With the exception of Flood, who had not eaten the turkey, the men were taken with violent pains and vomiting after dinner. Surgeon Flood examined the turkey and found it had been poisoned with arsenic. While the men affected were terribly ill, quick treatment and rest finally brought them back to good health. The man who brought the turkeys was arrested and placed in confinement. Further examination found him to be a bitter Rebel who had previously made various threats against the soldiers.[34]

It was quite normal for the families of the soldiers to inquire about what was Tennessee like, both the land and the people. The following description was taken from a letter home.

The general appearance of the country is much the same as that in the northern states. It is clear and interspersed with alternate pieces of woods, slightly rolling with not large hills until you come near to the mountains. Wartrace was about 40 miles from the mountains. The soil was a sandy loam over a clay bottom and varies in depth from six inches to three feet and, it is very rich.

The principal trees in the vicinity are hard and soft maple, white and red oak, chestnut, poplar, sweet gum, cedar, elm, hickory, ash, basswood and walnut. The principle and chief staples are corn and stock animals. They raise some wheat and oats. Cotton is not a general and common crop. The way wheat is sown is in cornfields without breaking the stalks. I have seen men sowing wheat where it appears to be in a meadow where the grass is so high and thick. I presume the reason for this is the lack of workmen. They raise both Murphy and sweet potatoes. Apples do not grow to be of a very good flavor, small and ill shaped. Peaches grow to perfection.

Their stock is generally of a good variety. Sheep are the coarse wool variety. Horses and mules are their teams. A six-mule team is used to draw about what a northern farmer would almost shoot his two-horse team if they did not draw more.

The main fault of these Tennessee farmers is that they have too much land. A farm of 200 or 300 acres is a small farm. Generally, the wealthy had slaves, but since the rebellion all the able-bodied men slaves have been sent south to some part of the Confederacy with their families as far as possible. Many have left for the north. Some, who owned as many as forty or fifty slaves at the outset of the war, now have four or five old women.

The feelings of these people near towards our cause may be illustrated by an incident that I know happened near here. A family by the name of Green who are dependent for little luxuries on the Greenbacks which Uncle Sam's boys may seem fit to exchange for milk, butter, pies etc. have openly avowed in word their feeling of friendship for the cause of the Union and were anxious to hear the news at all times. They received a letter from their son who is in the rebel service, and who recently taken prisoner. He spoke of the good treatment at the hands of the Yankees and in the best possible manner saying he would not ask better treatment and food at his father's hand. The old woman broke out in frantic raving saying that he would be killed. All this shows that although to all outward appearances they for the Union, the general opinion was that should a Rebel army come here, you would see an equally warm reception to them. That was the opinion that you could easily form were you a soldier here.

He closed the letter mentioning that Rebel deserters passed by daily. In the last three days a total of seventeen had passed through their pickets saying that the "Confederate cause is done, gone."[35]

As the year came to a close, the 107th New York was still scattered along the railroad. There were two companies at Shelbyville, five at Wartrace Bridge, two at Bellbuckle Bridge, and one at the Wartrace water tank. In addition, two officers were detached to General Williams' staff, and one officer was in charge of eighty men of the 3rd Wisconsin who did not re-enlist. It was during this time that the initial enlistment period of the veteran regiments in the 107th's brigade—the 3rd Wisconsin, 27th Indiana, and 2nd Massachusetts—had ended. The men in each of those regiments were given the opportunity to either re-enlist or go home. It was a measure of their patriotism that so many did re-enlist. In addition, a condition of re-enlistment was the granting of a twenty-day furlough.[36]

The regiment was required to report certain details regarding its service at the conclusion of each year of service. Colonel Crane wrote up the annual return for the 107th New York. The following are excerpts from the report for various occurrences during 1863: Total Deaths 41, Desertions 129, Desertions Returned 8, Officer Promotions 31, Officer Resignations 16, and Discharged for Disability 145. Of the 41 deaths reported, 29 were from disease at Hope Landing, VA.[37]

During their Tennessee service, furloughs, for the most part, were easy to come by, and they often resulted in some officers doing double and triple duty. Captain John Knox of Company F went home on furlough in January for almost a month. During that period, the company's 1st lieutenant was temporarily commanding another company. This left 2nd Lieutenant John Hill in command of the sixty-four men in the company during part of January and February. He complained that he was now forced to do the work of three men in his letter of January 28 to his sister Helen. However, he admitted he wouldn't mind if Captain Knox stayed away another month because he received an extra $10 in his pay when in command of his company.[38]

A number of the officers of the 107th New York were fortunate enough to have their wives visit them. Lieutenant Orr went by train on January 20 to Nashville to meet his wife Melissa, who had traveled all the way from Addison, NY. He arrived there the next morning to find her waiting for him in the train station. However, a man who was claiming to be a soldier was bothering her. Orr described it as a happy meeting and the beginning of their real honeymoon. They returned and reached Wartrace about dark. They spent the evening in a room in a local home. Orr described it as "rough quarters but rich in a happy reunion of wife and husband." Orr decided to find better lodgings the next day. He visited the local hotel and found the rooms there were also unacceptable. Afterwards he did find a room at the private home of a Mrs. Lloyds. The next morning, Lieutenant Hill visited him while he and Melissa were eating breakfast. Hill brought him an order to participate in a court martial in Tullahoma. Several days later, Lieutenants Hill and Whitehorne visited Orr and his wife and serenaded them. Orr commented in his journal that it was "so good to have my dear wife with me."

As time passed, the wives of lieutenants Whitehorn and Knox also joined their husbands in Tennessee. This resulted in many shared adventures for the three wives. Over the following months, there would be many walks in the evening hours, horseback riding, games of checkers, dinners, parties, church services, and cave exploring. The wives even got to ride on a railroad handcar.[39] Orr's wife Melissa would stay with her husband almost until the 107th New York left Tennessee with Sherman's Atlanta campaign. It is probable that many other officers' wives took the opportunity to visit with their husbands during their Tennessee service.

Lieutenant Hill admired Melissa greatly and commented that she didn't dip. He explained that he was referring to women who chewed snuff. These women took a small stick and splintered it by chewing on its end. Then they would dip it into snuff and then put it into their mouth. They would later spit it out just like a man chewing tobacco. It was the most disgusting thing he ever saw.[40]

Unfortunately, Melissa suffered with many complaints during her time in Tennessee. She had headaches, toothaches, and a sore arm, and just didn't feel well quite often. She was quite ill the evening she left by train to go home.[41] Quite possibly a portion of her complaints were due the fact that she became pregnant during the time that she was with her husband.[42]

In mid–November, the officers of Company F had been living in tents and boarding at a private home. Now in January, they had a large room with a fireplace in a private home and were taking their meals at an "eating house" for, as they said, a trifling 5 dollars per week.[43]

On January 27th, 2nd Lieutenant James A. Creed submitted his letter of resignation. He stated that his age of 45 rendered him unfit to perform the duties of a soldier, along with a chronic liver complaint and an ulcerated throat. Finally, there was the fact that his son had joined the service, leaving his family without anyone to provide for them or to look after their interests. Records show that he sent an identical letter on February 6th. His resignation from the regiment became official on February 16th. Prior to resigning, he told his fellow officers that he was going to attempt to obtain a position in the Invalid Corps, asking if they would sign a paper of recommendation. Instead of using the recommendation as he had told them, he went to Albany and attempted to obtain a captain's commission for the 107th New York, thereby jumping the rank of first lieutenant. He did obtain a captain's commission and returned to serve at that rank in the 107th New York. As a result, action in the form of a complaint was reported to the Assistant Adjutant General 1st 12th Army Corps by Lt. Col. Wm. Fox of the 107th. However, on March 30th, a letter from Fox removed the previous complaint about Creed's actions, approved his muster for captain, and verified his assignment as commander of Company B of the 107th New York. Regardless, the official records of the 107th New York indicate that Creed was not mustered into the regiment at the rank of captain of Company B. The record shows him the rank of Captain not mustered.[44]

At the same time, an article regarding Creed appeared in the Elmira newspaper: "The friends of Captain James A. Creed at Elmira on Tuesday evening last presented him with a splendid belt, sash and sword. Captain Creed had volunteered as a private in the 107th N.Y.V.; was at the battle of Chancellorsville, where he was promoted to a lieutenancy, and has since been made a captain."[45]

> In an April 6 letter home, Edward Kendall of Company H made a reference to Creed. He wrote: In February last James A. Creed, 2nd Lt. Co. B made application for a discharge and was discharged on a surgeon's certificate of disability. Before leaving the regiment, he circulated a paper among the officers getting their recommendation for a position in the Invalid Corps. Many signed it having the opportunity and to be glad to get rid of him. A few weeks later he appeared with a Captain's commission for Co. B, but Lieut. Col. Fox disputed his right to being mustered. He stated the facts of Creeds just resigning for disability and said that he had obtained his commission through trickery against the wishes of Colonel, Crane. The results were that Creed did not get mustered and has just left for home. To try some other dodge.

Additional references were made to Creed in Arthur Finch's journal. On Friday, March 25, Finch learned of Creed's commission. He wrote that much feeling existed among the officers and the men of Company B at this outrage on their rights. He noted that one officer would not invite Creed into his tent, and that most of the men and officers were in high spirits over his not being mustered.[46]

There had been some movement of the regiment's individual companies in the previous weeks, possibly due to a lessening of concern about danger to the railroad and a desire to better organize the regiment along the railroad. As of February 6th, Companies A, C, D, and I were now at Shelbyville, Companies K and F were at Wartrace, Companies B and E at Wartrace Bridge, and Companies H and G at their original location.

On February 12, the sixty-eight-year-old father of Thomas Putnam, a private in Company H, sent a letter to President Abraham Lincoln. Putnam was one of four brothers in Company H. The three other brothers were Elias, George, and Ebenezer. The family resided in Monterey in the town of Hornby in Steuben County. Mr. Putnam was at home with his wife and two daughters. He was not able to do much work and requested that his son be discharged so he could help his father. Additional official correspondence regarding his son appeared to indicate that the son was a deserter, had smallpox, had been taken into custody, and was in the military hospital in Elmira. An official letter written in response to the father's letter indicated that Thomas would not be discharged and would be returned to his regiment. His military record showed him to have been with the regiment at the close of the war.[47]

The regiment received two months' pay on February 12th. As was very often the case when some of the men got their greenbacks, they immediately went to a tent and begin playing cards. Others had such a great thirst for whiskey that they would take any risk and pay any price for a drink. There was still another group that wanted good things to eat. This kind would pay any price and buy everything they saw that they were not accustomed to in camp. In addition to these extravagances, everything cost three or four times more than it normally would.[48]

Quite often these soldiers were in locations where many items were not available, and they were left to their own devices. Such was the case for some of those in the 107th New York in Tennessee. Their Lieutenant Colonel William Fox sent a letter on February 24 to Captain Ruger, Assistant Adjutant General of the 3rd Brigade, 1st Division of the 12th Corps, concerning the supplying of bread to his regiment. He stated that, for the most part, the baking was done in groups of four or five men. However, in Company F, the drawing of flour and baking of bread was done for the company as a whole. He also stated that at that time, individual companies were building ovens and cookhouses in order to mess by company. At the same time, the four companies in Shelbyville under the command of Major Baldwin drew flour and had their bread baked at private homes.

While there were two sentences of death for desertion recorded in the 107th New York, such a sentence was never carried out. Private John Strait of Company I, who deserted at the battle of Antietam, and Private Sairles Simpson, also of Company I, were identified as being under a sentence of death in a letter dated February 29, 1864, from Tullahoma, TN. There is no mention in the record of each soldier pertaining to such a sentence. The letter stated that the proceedings of these cases had been forwarded to Major General Meade while the regiment had been at Kelly's Ford in Virginia on September 2, 1863, and there doesn't appear to ever have been a response concerning what action was to be taken.[49]

In mid–March at a location about 20 miles south of Wartrace, a raiding party caused a supply train to run off the track. Then they burned it, killed three Negroes, and took seven soldiers prisoner. They robbed everyone of their valuables, money, and many items of clothing. Afterwards they released the soldiers. This attack and several other instances where bushwhackers attempted to kill and or rob pickets prompted the searching for arms in local homes and their confiscation if the residents did not have permits. A small 107th New York detachment was organized and sent to search. All of the homes but one were found to have permits. That man without denied that he had any firearms in his home. When the soldiers began to search, the man admitted that he did have a pistol and a Bowie knife. The pistol that he produced was a large cavalry revolver. Further examination of house produced a government issue rifle, a sword, and a cartridge and cap box, hidden in the beds. All of the items were confiscated.[50]

A letter dated February 21, 1863, to Lt. Colonel Fox from the headquarters of the 107th New York, was responded to on the 24th. It stated that Lt. Harvey Denniston had left his post in Bell Buckle on February 6th and remained absent in Shelbyville until the 13th. During most of this time he was observed "in a helpless state of intoxication." It also mentioned that Denniston had been relieved of a General Court Martial at Tullahoma the previous December, having been sent under arrest to his regiment. Thereafter he was released by direction of Brigadier General A.S. Williams. This time he attempted to retain his position with the regiment, and a number of officers wrote letters in defense of him. These included Captain Lamans, Captain Bachman, Lt. Weller, Captain Losie, Major Baldwin, and Lt. Colonel Fox. However, he was discharged on March 31.[51]

Throughout the correspondence of the men of the 107th, there were often small references to baseball. They did not go into any detail, but just that they had played the game that day or during the time before writing the letter. It is not surprising that at any given time they would need to find something to fill up their day. If they were not on guard duty or involved in some special duty, they literally had nothing to do the whole day. As the weather became warmer, it was quite normal for them to spend the afternoon "playing ball."

The hazards of travelling by train continued during the time that the troops guarded the railroad. On April 8 a train went off the tracks and two soldiers were killed. They were brought to and buried at Wartrace.[52]

It was obvious during April that the army was preparing for the Georgia campaign. The following general order was evidence of that.

Headquarters Twelfth Army Corps
Tullahoma, Tenn., April 9, 1864
General Order No. 7

By virtue of General Orders 5 Headquarters Military Division of the Mississippi, the Eleventh and Twelfth Corps are consolidated and will hereafter compose the 20th Army Corps.

The official history of the Twelfth Army corps, from organization to the present day, and particularly its action at Antietam, Chancellorsville, Gettysburg, and its present services in the Department of the Cumberland justifies every soldier in the indulgence of a feeling of pride from his connection with it and of regret at the loss of the insignia of the Corps has been distinguished, and which has become a badge of honor. This consolidation separates me from the troops with whom I have been identified over the past eighteen months. I know however that the measure has been adopted solely with a view of promoting the interests of the service, and I would not have my personal interests or feelings, nor those of my command considered for a moment against any measure having this object in view.

The credit accorded to the soldier at the present hour is not his true reward for the privations and hardships he is enduring, nor does his reward depend upon the army or corps to which he may be attached. Let us bring this contest to a successful termination; let us peace and prosperity to this country, and to him who loves his country this consciousness of the fact that he has borne his part in the contest, and been an instrument in the accomplishment of the great work, will be the highest and best reward that can be bestowed upon him.

The cordial and earnest support afforded upon me on all occasions by the officers of my command, and the soldierly bearing and uniform good conduct of the men has rendered me deeply attached to my corps, and I leave it with feelings of profound regret.

H. W. Slocum
Major General[53]

However, General Grant countermanded this order in his letter to Halleck as follows.

> The First and Third Corps having been merged into other corps with the possibility of being filled up hereafter and restored to their corps organization, I would like to have the number of Hooker's corps changed to the Twentieth Corps. It will cause dissatisfaction to give number One to any other, but the old corps having that number. To retain either the number Eleven or Twelve will probably have the same effect with those losing their number.
>
> U.S. Grant, Lieutenant General

Now the organization of the corps was to be adjusted. The divisions of Williams and Geary would remain the same, aside from the accessions received from the Eleventh Corps. A third division was formed composed of two brigades of western troops then on duty in Tennessee and one brigade from the Eleventh Corps. This division was to be under the command of General Butterfield. There was also a fourth division, also composed of western troops under General Rousseau. This division was not to accompany the corps for the Georgia campaign but rather remain in Tennessee to guard the railroad.

In April 1864, the designation of the corps was changed to that of the XX Corps. Generals Williams and Geary still retained command of their divisions, and the men still wore their XII Corps badge. The reorganized corps adopted this badge, a five-pointed star, or pentagram. The new organization was formed by the consolidation of the XI and XII corps, to which was added some minor commands. This action of the War Department was based on the small sizes of the two corps. The XI had been extremely damaged at Gettysburg, and the XII had always been the smallest in the army. Nonetheless, the soldiers of the XII Corps were very upset at the loss of their original corps identity.

Upon the discontinuance of the XII Corps, General Slocum was assigned to the command of the District of Vicksburg but resumed the corps command of the XX Corps during the Atlanta Campaign, General Hooker having been relieved. Slocum afterwards commanded the Army of Georgia while on the March to the Sea and the Carolinas Campaign. There were several messages back and forth between Hooker, Thomas, and Sherman. In the end, the new corps' designation would remain the XX, and the star badge of the XII Corps was retained.[54]

On April 18, Colonel Crane's recruiting detachment returned from Elmira with fourteen new recruits for the 107th New York.[55]

The 107th received news of the 141st New York having been placed in the 1st brigade, 1st division, 20th Army Corps under the command of General Knipe. The 141st New York was made up of men from Chemung, Steuben, and Schuyler counties. Its initial group of enlistees were men who were actually from an overflow of those who joined the 107th New York.[56]

On April 27, citizens in Shelbyville wrote a letter to the commander of the Department of the Cumberland requesting that the 107th New York remain in the area for their protection from Confederate cavalry and guerrillas. They stated that they were loyal to the Union and would therefore be identified as such should Rebel forces make their way into the area after the majority of the Union forces moved south to Georgia.[57]

That same day, the 107th broke camp at 8 a.m., marched eight miles to Shelbyville, paraded through the main street, and bivouacked at noon. The day was very hot, and the march was very tiring. Several of the men became sick. That evening, a severe thunderstorm brought all of them welcome relief. The regiment remained in bivouac there for two days. On the 30th, they moved out at 6 a.m., providing guard for a heavily loaded supply train of the 1st Division. Their destination was Tullahoma, 18 miles away. The forward wagons of the train reached Tullahoma by dark without problem. The remainder of the train spent the rain-filled night on the road in the woods. The next day, the regiment remained in bivouac, and the remainder of the train came in at noon. The rain had made the roads very difficult and required the men to haul them for several miles using ropes. The next day, they moved south to Decherd and bivouacked. On May 3, they marched away from the railroad toward the base of the mountains, about eight miles east of Decherd. From there they marched four miles up the side of the mountain where they had dinner. Then they moved along the ridge for seven or eight miles where they bivouacked. The evening turned cold with a heavy frost. The next day they moved eight or nine miles and began to descend a slope. The slope was so steep that ropes were attached to a wagon's axle, passed around a tree, and into the hands of 15 or 20 men. The process was very difficult. After making the descent, they bivouacked for the night. Nearby was a large, free-flowing spring, the largest the men had ever seen. On May 5, they moved out at 6 a.m., marched 13 miles, and reached Bridgeport, AL, at 2 p.m. Bridgeport was nothing more than a government depot. They crossed a bridge and bivouacked on an island for the night. At that point, the 107th division headquarters was located in Ringgold, Georgia. This was direct evidence that the Georgia campaign had begun.[58]

New York Herald April 28, 1864: CHATTANOOGA 107th and 141st New York regiments

The greater part of the 20th Corps is about to make a rapid march in some direction where there will be a probability of fighting. No transportation will be allowed, but barely sufficient to carry the necessary ammunition and ten days rations of which three will be carried by the soldiers in their haversacks. Surplus Transportation, ordinance, etc., has been "turned over," and other preparations made. Scouting parties have already been sent out in the direction of Trenton. There are various surmises as to the direction to be taken, but it will be where rebels are expected to be found. No tents or baggage whatever are allowed. Officers, except those who have horses will carry their own baggage, being thus on the same footing with the soldiers. Ringgold, Trenton or Dalton is supposed to be our probable destination. Hot work ahead. The 2nd Division of the corps has just arrived. The whole three divisions are now here.[59]

Not everyone of the 107th New York would leave Tennessee in May of 1864. Private Richard Depew of Company A had deserted his regiment on July 16, 1862, the day before the battle of Antietam. However, he was subsequently returned to the regiment at Hope Landing, VA, on April 23, 1863. He was charged for desertion and sentenced to forfeit all pay due him plus $10 per month of his pay for the next six months. Then on November 23, 1863, while stationed at Bell Buckle, TN, he accidently shot off his finger. That may have been an attempt on his part to be discharged. Finally, he was arrested for desertion on August 3, 1864, in Shelbyville, TN. He had stayed behind when the regiment moved on to Georgia. During that time, he had been living with a Black woman. He was subsequently returned to duty and then captured at Goldsboro, NC, on March 24, 1865. He was later paroled and mustered out at Elmira on June 9, 1865.[60]

# 9

# Bloody Georgia

**The 107th New York was now in the First Division, Second Brigade of the new 20th Army Corps. It had retained its Red Star designation, and its brigade included all of the same regiments, including a new one: the 150th New York. After a respite of seven months in Tennessee, it was entering one of the most difficult chapters of its service. The Army of the Cumberland now included the 20th Army Corps under Major General George H. Thomas, the 4th Army Corps under Major General Oliver O. Howard, the 14th Army Corps under Major General William J. Palmer, and three Cavalry Divisions under Kilpatrick, McCook, and Garrand. Grouped with the Army of the Cumberland were two additional, but much smaller armies: the Armies of the Tennessee and Ohio.**

On May 6, the 107th New York received orders to move out. It was a very hot day, and the men put their knapsacks in the wagons. Thankfully there was a creek alongside the road. When they reached Shell Mound, five additional wagons joined their train, making a total of 140 wagons in the train. They camped at 6 p.m., having marched a total of ten miles. They were up and moving by 7 a.m. the next morning. Companies B and F were placed at the head of the train. The road was very narrow and much rougher than the day before. On the way, they passed a railroad bridge that looked to be 120 feet high. The heat had become unbearable by noon, so much so that several of the men became quite sick. They reached Lookout Valley and went into camp at 5 p.m. after having marched fourteen miles.

May 8 proved to be cool and pleasant. They began marching at 7 a.m. at the rear of the wagon train. They passed over a steep, but very good road that went around Lookout Mountain. Shortly after that, they passed through Chattanooga at 9 a.m., and moved fourteen miles further, where they stopped for dinner. At that time, the ammunition trains they were guarding were ordered on to Ringgold. After dinner, they marched ten miles and crossed the Chickamangee Creek. They marched another two miles and camped. The day's march had taken them through a very pleasant but mountainous country. On May 9, they moved at 7 a.m. and reached Ringgold at 11 a.m. They halted there and sent back surplus baggage. They moved beyond Ringgold and reached the camp of their division of the 20th Army Corps at sundown.

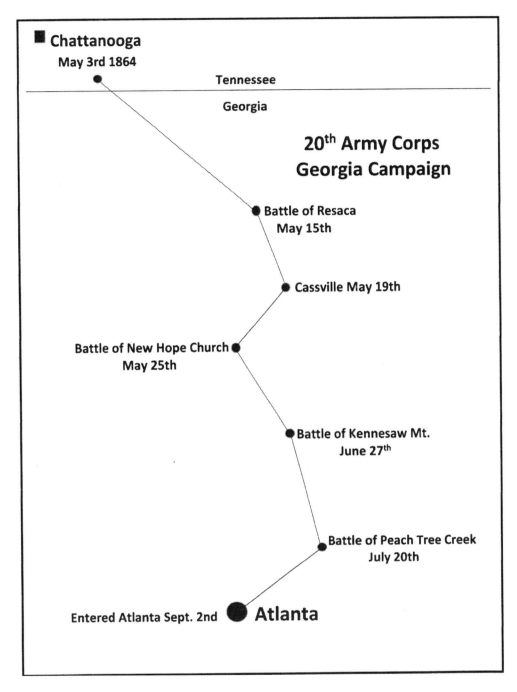

■ Chattanooga
May 3rd 1864

Tennessee

Georgia

**20th Army Corps
Georgia Campaign**

● Battle of Resaca
May 15th

● Cassville May 19th

Battle of New Hope Church ●
May 25th

● Battle of Kennesaw Mt.
June 27th

● Battle of Peach Tree Creek
July 20th

Entered Atlanta Sept. 2nd ● **Atlanta**

Map showing the battles during the campaign for Atlanta with 107th New York participation.

During the day they, received orders to march at a moment's notice. That evening they moved out at midnight. All baggage was sent to the rear except for a change of underwear. They halted at 9 a.m. on Tuesday at the mouth of Snake Creek Gap and rested there until 5 p.m. Then they moved up the Gap and went into camp at dark. It rained heavily during the night, causing the creek to overflow and the camp to flood.[1]

They broke camp at 3 p.m. on May 11 and moved from their current very muddy location up an adjacent hill and set up camp. General Hooker passed by their brigade on his way to the front and was wildly cheered by the troops. He was accompanied by General Sickles. General Butterfield's third division of the 20th Corps moved into position near them. They remained there that day and all of the next day and night. Skirmishing was quite lively some distance in their front, and there was heavy cannonading in the distance to their left. On May 13, they broke camp at 6 a.m. and moved near the front and north of Resaca. While there was skirmishing in their front all day and night, they were never engaged.

On the 14th, the 107th New York moved to the front and took a position in the skirmish line. George Carpenter of Company H was wounded in thigh. They remained in that position all morning, but otherwise were not engaged. In the afternoon, they moved around to the extreme left to reinforce regiments of the 4th Corps. During that time, they saved a 4th Corps battery from capture by the enemy. Then they moved up rapidly to the left wing and prevented a Rebel flanking attempt. Some regiments in front broke and came back through their lines. Rebel forces attempted to advance behind them, and a nearby battery opened up on them. The 3rd Brigade moved to fill the breach and opened heavy musket fire. The 1st and 2nd Brigades also advanced against the Rebels, preventing a flanking movement. The regiment slept on its arms that night.

The next day, the 107th New York charged the enemy's works, carrying them at the point of the bayonet. Their losses were not very heavy, with two killed and seven wounded. Thereafter Companies H and E were detached from the regiment to fill up a gap between the 3rd Wisconsin and 82nd Ohio of the 3rd Brigade. In an effort to stabilize their position, the regiment began building breastworks while some companies sent out skirmishers. Large numbers of captured Rebels, many of them wounded, were sent to the rear, and many of the enemy lay dead in their front. The 27th Indiana captured the colors of a Rebel regiment during the day's fighting. The enemy fell back during the night, and the 107th slept peacefully but with their arms close by.[2]

During the battle, the 141st New York of the 1st Brigade was engaged to one side of them. The 141st fought bravely, and during the battle lost one third of its men killed or wounded. When the Rebels came out to charge the 141st, they came within range on the right of the 107th, and Company B brought its guns to bear on them. The Rebs fought for 15 minutes and then returned to their entrenchments.[3]

Overall, the Confederates won the battle of Resaca, but they were forced to retreat because of a Union flanking movement that threatened to surround them. General Joseph E. Johnston retreated first to Calhoun, then to Adairsville, and finally to Cassville, where on May 19 he planned to ambush the left wing of Sherman's army as it advanced southward. However, Johnston was forced to call off the ambush when a portion of Sherman's force appeared in his rear. He then resumed his retreat and halted it on May 22 at Altoona Pass, south of the Etowah River.[4]

Cassville, Georgia May 20, 1864

My Dear Parents

This is the first good opportunity to write since the 27th of April. Since the day we left War-trace Bridge and we have been on the march until today. We have gone into camp for a day or so. Nothing of importance occurred on the march until we came to Tunnel Hill, Ga. Where we could hear the bellowing of cannon and the sharp crack of musketry which told us the Rebels were not far off. Next morning, we went into the fight and have been fighting every day for ten days and during the ten days fighting we have driven the Rebels about fifty miles toward Atlanta and they are still on the skidaddle. Our forces are following close in their rear. We captured some prisoners every day. Rebel loss is very heavy, and they are deserting very fast. I was over the battle ground at Resaca, Ga. where the heaviest part of the fighting was and the field was strewn with Rebel dead and wounded. They left the field in confusion and left their dead and wounded on the field. The prisoners all say they are tired of fighting. I read some of the rebel letters taken from the dead and they say they must hope for the best. They think this a very dark hour for the Southern Confederacy, and they fear its downfall this summer.

The 141st Regt NYV. Has been on the march with us and was with us in the fight. Their loss was very heavy. I can't tell the exact number killed & wounded. Alan Koopes one of father's Sunday School scholars was wounded. I saw David Henry, Charles Ward and David Shannon. They are well. The 107th sustained very light injuries, one killed in Co. K, one in Co. H and five wounded. Lt. Col. Fox was wounded slightly in the arm. I came out safe and well. When you write send to 107th Regt NYSV 1st Div. 2nd Brigade & 20th Army Corps.

Yours, Daniel Scott[5]

*Author's note. The term "skirmish or skirmishing" is very often misunderstood because references to it by Civil War soldiers did not explain the specific type of skirmishing being used.*

Henry Halleck's treatise titled **Elements of Military Art and Science** in 1846 and Lieutenant Colonel William J. Hardee's manual published in 1855 identified the different forms of skirmishing. Halleck's work was undoubtedly heavily influenced by his professor of tactics at West Point, Denis Mahan. The first mission for skirmishers was securing the flanks of the main body of the opposing troops. A second important use of skirmishers was to secure outposts so other troops could rest safely when the unit was not on the march. Reconnaissance was a third important task for skirmishers according to both Hardee and Halleck. Reconnaissance included finding the enemy, checking the features such as roads and bridges on the route, and securing prisoners to interrogate. Another typical mission for skirmishers was to deceive the enemy by feints or demonstrations, or bluffs and tricks. Habitual practices, for example, deploying one to two companies per regiment in the lead as skirmishers became a battlefield indicator of a regiment "just beyond the trees." A crafty use of skirmishers then was to deploy the entire regiment, thus putting eight to ten companies on the skirmish line, which would then appear to be the lead companies of four to five regiments. Another possible ploy would be troops in an open field putting forth a heavy skirmish line, which continued such a rapid fire of rifles as to keep down a corresponding hostile line behind its well-constructed trenches, while the picks and shovels behind the skirmishers fairly flew, till a good set of works was made four hundred yards distant from the enemy's and parallel to it. Halleck also emphasized the importance of skirmishers in opening the battle. In the main assault skirmishers would lead the main forces, clear the way of enemy skirmishers and fix the enemy into position for the main blow to fall upon. Halleck noted that the skirmishers should target artillerymen. Artillery fire was the greatest threat to the compact lines of battle, but relatively ineffective against the dispersed skirmish lines, furthermore, skirmishers were now armed with a rifle capable of hitting artillerymen serving their guns at distances of 400 yards or more. Skirmish doctrine as expressed in the use of open order formations, accurate fire, and the exploitation of terrain to achieve combat objectives, demonstrated the validity of Halleck's ideas.[6]

The men of the 107th New York regiment were on the skirmish line the morning of the 16th, but all was quiet. The Rebels had left the battlefield, leaving behind scores of their dead. The regiment moved at 9 a.m. south in the direction of the village of Resaca. Later they countermarched and stopped at 2 p.m. for dinner. Afterwards they marched close to the Coosawattee River. On May 17, it rained in the early morning, prompting the men to put up tents. They moved down to the river at 6 a.m. and waited for their artillery unit before crossing. Once on the other side of the river, they moved quickly and did not stop until 7 p.m. They did not rest very long that evening, getting up at 3 a.m. However, they did not move until 8 a.m. They stopped for dinner and then marched until 11 p.m. On the 19th, they moved at 1 p.m. toward Cassville.[7] They came upon the enemy's rear guard near Cassville at about 4 p.m. By the time they got into battle line, it was dark. Skirmishing began and was pretty brisk. The 107th's brigade moved in line of battle two or three miles, up and down hills, across creeks, and through the brush. At about 8 p.m., they halted the line of battle, threw out skirmishers, drew two days' rations, ate a supper of pork, hardtack, and coffee, and slept. They rose at daybreak, had breakfast, and stayed put as the Rebs had left. At about 5 a.m., the 23rd Army Corps commenced marching past their bivouac, and by noon they had moved on out of sight. The 20th Corps and the 107th remained at their location.[8]

The next day, there was no sign of the Rebels, and they entered the small village of Cassville. They found the houses deserted and sacked. A female college that bordered the village had been used as a Rebel hospital. They stayed put in the village on the 21st. That same day, orders came to draw 25 days' rations: five for each man and 20 on their wagons. In addition, they received orders to be ready to move on the 23rd. The next day, several officers of the 107th went to look at the Confederate fortifications. It looked as though they had had 35-to-40-gun emplacements, and they were in a cemetery. Orders came for them to move the next morning at daylight.

Cassville was then occupied by General Geary's 2nd Division of the 20th Corps. At the same time, the 107th's division moved on to a location one half mile north of Kingston, where they threw up breastworks and remained there until May 22.[9]

The regiment was up by 3:30 a.m. on the 23rd. They moved out of Cassville at 4:30 and marched south through Kingston. They halted near the Etowah River for dinner. Afterwards they crossed the river on a bridge constructed from canvas pontoon boats and went into camp. The next day, they passed through Stilesville and halted at 1 p.m. for dinner near Windmill Creek. After dinner, they continued on and went into camp at 6 p.m. It began raining at dusk. They had marched 14 miles that day.[10]

The 107th New York was about to experience its most devastating encounter with the Confederate army. There was nothing memorable about the tactics involved. The Rebels, both artillery and infantry, were positioned in the woods out of sight with their skirmishers well out in front of them. The brigade of the 107th charged head on toward this masked battery with accompanying infantry completely oblivious of their presence. The encounter was partially described in excruciating detail by acting Lt. Arthur Fitch of Company B.

Having been given the wrong directions, Geary's division entered the incorrect road and moved toward New Hope Church and not Dallas a few miles south. About 9 o'clock, General Hooker, reaching the top of a hill that looked down on Pumpkin Vine Creek, observed Confederate troops setting fire to the bridge over the creek. He immediately sent forth his escort, who immediately drove them away and put out the fire.

Johnson, the Confederate commander, had received information about Sherman's movement and hurried his army westward through the forests and established it on a ridge that lay across the path of Sherman's multiple corps. Hooker's divisions that were marching on three parallel roads had crossed Pumpkin Vine Creek when orders were received to march to New Hope Church. Geary's men had encountered Confederate troops in that vicinity. The church was located at a junction of roads leading to Dallas, Marietta, and Ackworth and was four miles northeast of Dallas. Because the junction of these roads would be the focal point of all of Sherman's corps, Hood had Stewart's division firmly entrenched there. The area was densely wooded and perfect for hiding a large force including artillery.[11]

William's Division including the 107th New York had stopped at noon for dinner approximately six miles from the church. After their dinner, they crossed Pumpkin Vine Creek and marched about two more miles when they about faced and crossed the creek again. They soon entered a piece of woods and formed a battle line. From that point, they marched four miles at a fast pace and then formed a skirmish line. They had unknowingly advanced to the front of a masked battery that immediately opened fire. That was followed by musketry fire. The order was given for them to lie down. However, all companies did not hear it.[12]

The 107th NY was about to experience its most devastating encounter with the Confederate army. There was nothing memorable about the tactics involved. The Rebels, both artillery and infantry, were positioned in the woods out of sight with their skirmishers well out in front of them. The brigade of the 107th charged head on toward this masked battery with accompanying infantry completely oblivious of their presence. The encounter was partially described in excruciating detail by acting Lt. Arthur Fitch of Company B.

> The advance of the 107th line had been stopped by the terrible fire of the enemy in their front. The men had closed up and began to return fire. Acting Lieutenant Arthur Fitch took his position at the rear of Company B.
> Louis Vreeland was a few paces directly in front of him and had taken the firing position when suddenly he sank down in a seating position. Fitch asked him if he was all right not realizing that anything was the matter. Vreeland made no reply. Fitch leaned over him to loosen the buckles on his knapsack. As the straps parted, he sank back upon his knapsack. His face took on a peculiar ghastly color, his jaws were relaxed and his eyes were glassy and

set. A closer inspection disclosed a sickening wound in his chest from which bright red blood was gushing. He had been shot dead within a arms length of Fitch.

Shortly there after Hay Grieves threw up his arms and fell backward to the ground. He had been struck in the head by a rifle ball and killed instantly.

As the fighting continued, the ranks became thinned by the dropping out of the wounded. The command was shouted out for the rest to take advantage of whatever protection that was available. However, not all took advantage of any available protection.

Martin McGuire stood up near Fitch to load his rifle and suddenly dropped and turned with an indescribable look of terror on his face. He crawled on his hands and knees to Fitch who bent over him. McGuire gasped in words almost intelligible, "I am hit, where can I go to get out of this." Fitch told him to crawl to the rear of the line and lie down until someone could help him to go further back out of harms way. He gave Fitch a look of despair, crawled painfully a few feet away and died. Fitch examined him and saw that he had been shot clear through the body. Martin was one of the heroic sons of Erin who gave his life for his adopted land.

There was Daniel Keener, who was called Uncle Dan for he was old and had his grown-up son Charlie in the company. He came to Fitch breathless saying that his son was wounded, and he wanted to go back to find help for him. Off he went to return a few minutes later and resumed his loading firing. Charlie would die of his wounds a few days later.

Thomas Maher a young smallish Irish teenager. A series of emphatic exclamations from nearby proved to be him standing behind a tree the rammer stuck halfway down the barrel of his gun, and he endeavoring to force it and the cartridge home by punching it against the tree, accompanying each stroke with his inimitable Irish oaths, cursing the dirty gun, the rebels and luck generally. It was ludicrous to the extreme.

Another instance of like nature was Sergeant Charles Solotski who had found refuge behind a large tree. A shell crashed into the tree bringing down a perfect avalanche of limbs and splinters upon his head. The tree was a dead one, a fact he had failed to previously notice. He speedily picked himself out of the mass of debris that covered him and sought reliable shelter. Later as they were falling back at the close of the battle, Fitch began to make fun of him with respect to his choice of a rotten tree for protection. As Fitch was speaking a grape shot came skipping along the ground, bounded up and struck his wrist a stinging blow. It glanced off, hit his leg and went on. When they emerged from the woods onto the open road, Major Baldwin came toward to them. He seized hold of Fitch exclaiming, "Oh! Arthur, thank God you are safe." Just then a missile, probably a grape shot struck the inside of his left foot and continued on down the road.

These are but a few of the incidents that occurred during this hard and difficult fight. One other was when a grape shot slammed into the brass plate of a soldier's cartridge box, penetrated to the interior of the box and lodged itself within the little tin canister that held the cartridges. This soldier was not aware of it until after the fighting was over.

One of the most miraculous escapes of the day was that of Sergeant Lauren Reader. While he was in the act of loading his gun, it was struck near the hammer by a grape or canister shot, and the entire stock was torn from the barrel, leaving him literally without lock, stock or barrel. He threw down what was left and picked up another that had been dropped by a disabled comrade. As he was ramming home a cartridge a bullet struck the hammer and bent it halfway double. Disheartened, he threw down that gun and lay down flat with his face to the ground, growling like an enraged bear. A moment later a shot of some kind passed obliquely downward through the brim of his slouched hat filling his face, mouth and eyes with loose dirt. A madder man Fitch had never seen. Reader jumped up, seized another gun and began loading and firing with infuriated energy. He escaped further accident, but later after the fighting had ceased, he discovered further damage to his person. He discovered that in addition to the brim of his hat, that no less than seven balls had struck his clothing and equipment. One shoulder strap of his knapsack was cut clean through. The buckle that fastened his haversack was shot off, his canteen was perforated by a ball, another ball had passed across his left leg and drawers without breaking the skin and an iron fry pan that was strapped on the outside of his knapsack was riddled and rendered unserviceable. However, he, himself miraculously escaped unhurt.[13]

Lt. Fitch also wrote the following historical sketch memorializing the 107th New York's experience in the Battle of New Hope Church. It was included in the "Final Report on the Battlefield of Gettysburg" published by the New York State Monuments Commission, 1900.

There were 400 of "ours" who awakened as the shrill notes of the reveille echoed among the Allatoona Hills in Georgia, at 3:30 o'clock on the morning of May 25, 1864. Four hundred seasoned veterans, young in years, but full-grown soldiers in experience. We had received our baptism of fire at bloody Antietam, faced the terror of those dark woods at Chancellorsville, and had stood "where the earth trembled" at Gettysburg. We had come with Sherman's victorious armies from Middle Tennessee well into the interior of Georgia, and thus far success had been our constant companion.

There was a buoyancy of feeling and a consciousness that we were invincible, and the sun arose that day on as confident and well-ordered an array of soldiers as anywhere marched beneath the flag. I see them now, as they stood in line on that bright May morning, the breakfast of coffee, hard tack, and meat disposed of, accoutrements slung, guns taken from the stack and carefully wiped and examined, awaiting the command for another day's advance. There is no look of care or anxiety on their faces. Theirs but to obey whatever others commanded. "Theirs, but to do." Alas! Alas! How little thought we that for more than two score of our number the "death watch" had already been set; that for many a loved comrade the last earthly bivouac had been broken, the last "harnessing up" and preparation for the day's march had been made; and that the day begun so blithely was to end in a night of death and sorrow.

At 8:30 a. m. the word "forward" is given. Our 400 quickly fall into line, the old files of four again "touch elbows," and away they go with "The loose disorder of the rout step march the song, the shout, the witticism arch," marching on to new experiences. The sun shines warm and the air is that of June. There is a look of satisfaction on the face of every soldier, and a feeling of contentment in every heart.

The "welcome noontide rest" comes. At 1:30 p. m. the column is again in motion; no enemy has appeared to dispute the advance; the roads are good, the marching easy. It is 3 o'clock in the afternoon and all is well. Suddenly a sharp "halt" passes down the line, and "the dust-brown ranks stood fast." "About face" and "March" is the command. At a quicker pace we now move back along the route just traversed; a look of eager curiosity is seen on each face; a murmur of speculation runs along the column; and as we turn from the road and cross a creek that skirts a wooded slope, and see orderlies hurrying hither and thither, cannon in position, generals in consultation, and other signs the old soldier knows so well how to interpret, there comes a seriousness of face and a silence that betokens a change in our thoughts. We press quickly on to the top of the slope, form line of battle, and stand quietly awaiting developments. The "White Star" boys of Geary's Division are there also, and the "Blue Stars" of General Butterfield's Division are ordered to join the array.

Suddenly bang, bang, bang, go the guns of a field battery, pointed into the shade of the forest that extends before us. The shriek of the flying shells and their explosions awaked with noisy echoes its gloomy recesses; but they provoke no response of hostile guns. Again, and again, they speak, but the result is the same. The day is waning. The "obstructions" must be brushed away, and Gen. Pap William's Red Stars must do it. The three brigades are drawn out in a long, straight line, stretching away to the right and left of us, aligned as if on dress parade, a living line of steel and blue. "Attention!" then a bugle note, then sharp words of command, and as one man the division moves forward. Never shall I forget that array. There was a mighty sound of tramping feet, quick cries of command: "Steady men!" "Guide on the colors!" "Steady on the right!" "Steady on the left!" "Forward there in the centre!" "Pap" Williams and his staff rode close behind us, and his bugler speaks in tones easily heard by all of us. Down the slope we go, across the narrow ravine, and up the other side.

A thinly wooded level stretches out far in front. We see our line of skirmishers pressing rapidly forward, and a moment later our peering eyes detect a skirmish line of men in gray as rapidly falling back before them. "Double-quick!" sounds the bugle. "Double-quick!" shout the officers; and with arms at a right-shoulder shift, away spring our eager men. Never shall I forget that scene. Never before nor afterwards have my eyes witnessed such a sight. As far to the left and right as the eye could see stretched that dark line undulating with the cadence of the double-quick step, crashing into the forest in all the confidence of a victory already won. But look! The skirmishers have come to a stand. They are making frantic gestures to us to stop. But the line goes on over beyond them. A little farther and the pace slackens; our straining eyes see through the trees the outlines of fortifications, while the zip, zip, whiz, whiz, of leaden missiles attracts our attention.

The line comes to a halt; from the front comes unmistakable evidence of an enemy in force awaiting us. We are fairly trapped. A frowning line of earthworks blocks the way, covering Stewart's whole division of "Joe" Johnston's army. Their fire is already getting uncomfortably hot There ensues a brief moment of preparation along our ranks, and then down came the rifles of our 400 to a "ready," and out blazes a volley that tells the waiting enemy that we are there. It was a sight thrilling beyond description, one never forgotten. I did not hear a word of command to fire. I think none was given. By a common impulse each man saw the time had come, and that first volley was as simultaneous as if they had been practicing on drill.

But a terrible response came. From the dark covert in front leaped a fiery discharge of rifle and cannon, filling the air with the rushing sound of deadly missiles. Shot and shell, canister and minie balls came tearing over us and around us and through us, ploughing great gaps in our closed ranks, sweeping away our men by files and platoons, making by that one discharge skeletons of what a moment before had been solid companies. How much the scene changed. Two hours before these boys were marching with careless glee along the sunlit road towards Dallas, in the flush of manly vigor, without a thought of the cruel fate that lay so close before them. Now they are breasting the full tide of furious battle. As if in keeping, the sky is overcast and threatening, and the growing gloom adds to the terrors of the scene. The men see their comrades falling about them, they hear the groans of the wounded, the fierce din of the conflict; they realize the hopelessness of the struggle, and that there is no chance of victory. Mutely the survivors stand with grim and resolute faces, loading and firing, keeping up the unequal contest, but with no thought of retreat.

A long, long hour of this and the remnant of our 400 are relieved; slowly they pick their way to the rear and safety. Scarcely more than half of those who answered at rollcall that morning are left. The rest are out there in the wood's dead or are lying maimed and bleeding in the hospital tents close by. Mournful was the scene. The survivors gather in little groups and relate the dreadful experiences of that fateful hour. They speak with broken voices of those who have fallen. None but has lost a friend, the companion of many a march, a comrade who had slept beneath the same blanket and shared with him his army mess.

The darkness gathers, the rain begins to fall, and far in our front we hear the exchange of picket shots. It disturbs us little more than our dead comrades. We lie down on the wet ground, with tired bodies and aching hearts, and the day and its terrors are forgotten in a merciful sleep.

Thus, ended the 25th day of May 1864. Twenty-four years have passed. There survives today a remnant of the men who shared its experiences. Is it any wonder that as they gather to pay a loving tribute to their dead comrades their faces wear a serious expression? Their thoughts are away amidst the woods of Dallas.

Oh, band in the pine woods cease,
Cease with your splendid call.
The living are brave and noble,
But the dead were bravest of all.

They throng to the martial summons,
To the loud triumphant strain,
And the dear, bright eyes of long dead friends
Appeal to the heart again.

They come to the ringing bugle,
And the deep drum's mellow roar,
Till the soul is faint with longing
For the hands we shall clasp no more."

As we follow memory's chain back to the scene I have described, how vividly appear the forms and names of those who there met a soldier's heroic death. I see Capt. John F. Knox, with drawn sword, leap to the front of Company F, and with all the emphasis that voice and action can give, urge the men a little farther forward. Then comes the fatal volley, and he is struck down with a mortal wound. Brave Knox, but a day or two before I marched by his side, and he uttered these prophetic words: "It is more than probable that we shall draw our supplies from the seacoast before Christmas." It was an inspiring thought, and some of us lived to see its realization.

The same tidal wave of death swept away his second lieutenant, John Hill,—quiet, modest, young, beloved of all. How well I remember his coming with a picket relief that first night at Gettysburg, and finding me overcome with fatigue and sound asleep (a dreadful dereliction of duty at such time), quietly awakened me and sent me with my picket guard to camp, without chiding or report to his superiors. I loved him from that hour.

From the same devoted company fell Jones, Johnson, Kelley, Miller, Mollson, Nellis, Taft and Young, all dead or mortally wounded. The only remaining commissioned officer, First Lieut. John Orr, was scarcely less fortunate, being desperately wounded, and the total of killed and disabled numbered full two-thirds of those present at rollcall that morning.

Next neighbor to them was Company B. And its ranks yielded scarcely less to the destroyer. The soldierly Hay Grieve (the best soldier in the company, so the inspection report said), the quiet Louis Vreeland, brave old Martin Maguire, the fearless Corporal Munson, of the color guard, "Charlie" Keener, Van Gelder, Cooper, Bright, and Root, all good men and true.

I recall chivalrous Sergeant. "Billy" Van Auken, of D Company, scarcely eighteen years old, twice wounded, yet insisting upon staying to "give them one more shot," and while in the act of loading his rifle struck dead by a Rebel bullet, along side of Sergeant Ford and Private Armstrong of the same company.

Company A gave up her splendid orderly sergeant, Cornelius Hammond, and duty sergeant, Charles Bolton, with Capt. John M. Losie, and a long train of wounded to swell its casualty list.

Captain, afterwards Major, Charles J. Fox, manfully held old Company C about the colors, and sees Brockway, Dressier, and Steinbeck go down to death beneath its folds.

To the Editor, Elmira Advertiser
From the 107th Regiment

107th Regiment NY Vols.
On the Battlefield near Dallas, Ga.
May 27, 1864

Dear Fairman,

On Wednesday afternoon the 25th inst, the 107th went into action with the 1st Division, 20th Army Corps, and the loss of killed and wounded was terrible.

It was the fiercest encounter our brave men ever met with, the rebels having the advantage of breastworks, and although I state with pride that we drove the rebels into their works and held the ground taken and fought until every round of ammunition was exhausted, not only in each man's cartridge box, but also, in those of our dead and wounded. It is with the greatest anguish that we look at the fearful loss of life and wounding of the brave and worn torn officers and men of our noble regiment. May the God of battles shield us from a like disaster again.

The young and noble Hill is killed and five of our efficient officers seriously wounded. Captain J.M. Losie lost his right leg above the knee. Capt. Knox received a terrible wound from a shell in his leg. Lt. Swain though wounded remains with his company and is very doing well. Lt. John Orr, Co. F, seriously wounded is reported doing well.

The 1st Div. 20th Corps was the only one fully engaged on the 25th. Skirmishing and feeling the enemy's position is still going on, and a general engagement of both armies may ensue at any moment, unless the rebels run. Col. M. N. Crane and Adjutant Benedict are well and sound as usual.

In this particular engagement 1 officer killed, 5 wounded and 22 enlisted men killed and 118 wounded.

Your, L. Baldwin
Major 107th NYV

Corrected 107th New York data for this battle is as follows. Three hundred and fifty-eight were engaged, and forty-seven of both officers and enlisted men were killed outright or died of their wounds, and one hundred forty-one of both officers and enlisted men were wounded.

On June 25, while the regiment was located at Marietta, GA, Lathrop Baldwin sent a letter of condolence to F. Munson, the father of Marcus Munson, who died of the wounds he suffered at the battle of May 25, 1864. That letter was subsequently published in the *Elmira Daily Advertiser* on July 8, 1865.

Dear sir,

You have ere this I presume heard of the death of your son Marcus at Kingston, Ga. From wounds received in battle at Dallas on the 25 of May.

I cannot let the opportunity pass to drop a line of consolation to you, and a slight tribute to the merit of Marcus as a brave young man and a true soldier who has fallen with so many others in defense of our country and our government.

From the date of his enlistment to the battle at Dallas, Marcus discharged all the duties pertaining to his position with much credit, when not disabled by sickness. At Antietam and Chancellorsville as a corporal in the color guard, a most dangerous place under fire, he exhibited to his comrades the true pluck of a brave man ready to face the enemies of his flag in deadly combat and at Dallas he received his death wounds bravely contending in the same manner under a most galling and destructive fire.

His quiet manner and unobtrusive habits were remarked by all. He sought no promotion than that of a soldier and appeared to be content and when well enjoyed himself in his daily camp duties.

Allow me to drop a tear with you in the irreparable loss of you son- a loss which I fully comprehend, I cannot fully realize.

Sergeant Arthur Fitch has, I believe, has enclosed a letter to you from a comrade of Marcus, giving you the particulars of his death at Kingston. I am very respectfully,

Your obedient servant,
L. Baldwin

On May 26, the 4th Corps was engaged from the morning all through the day with infantry and artillery. The 107th was not involved and remained bivouacked. That same day, they secured the bodies of Sgt. Force and Pvt. Couch and buried them. They were unable to locate the body of Pvt. Margeson. The next morning, the artillery opened up on the enemy at 5 a.m. There was no infantry engagement except for sharpshooters. Later there was engagement on their left, but the 107th remained in the same location that day and through the night. Lt. Weller was placed in command of Company F because of the loss of its officers during the battle fought the day before.

The next day, there was skirmishing in their front during the morning and into the night. They moved the camp behind a hill and remained bivouacked there until June 1. During that period, they were not engaged, but skirmishing and heavy artillery action occurred in their general vicinity. On the 1st, they broke camp at 10:30 in the morning, and the 15th Army Corps moved into the space as they left. They moved on to a new location where at 4 a.m., their brigade relieved Hovey's brigade of 23rd Corps in a breastwork. They remained there all day and experienced heavy skirmishing. The nearby battery of the 1st New York artillery began firing late in the day.

On June 3, the weather was cloudy and raining, and the regiment remained in works but did send out a skirmish party that captured a Rebel captain. The next day, the rain continued as did the skirmishing. However, they moved their camp about a half mile to the left and bivouacked for the night. The rain continued through the night with fog the next morning. They broke camp at 9:30 a.m. and marched to the left three more miles as the Rebels had withdrawn from the area. They bivouacked for the night.

They came up on the enemy on June 6. They broke camp at 5 a.m. and marched about three miles when they came up on the enemy. Company F was sent out for skirmish at 8:30 a.m. They were on the line all day but never engaged the enemy as none were seen on their front. They were relieved at 8 p.m. During that day, the regiment built a line of heavy works near Lost Mountain. They remained there all night.[14]

On June 7, they were lying in temporary breastworks in line of battle on a ridge fronting a high mountain called Lost Mountain. Their skirmish line was some 30 yards in their front. The opposing armies were alternately talking and shooting at each other. They eventually tried to strike up a trade. The Rebels wanted to trade tobacco for coffee. The trade would have been made except for the fact that Rebel replacement pickets came up to the line, and they wanted to fire on the 107th men. This was somewhat of a common occurrence and typically little harm was done.[15]

The weather improved the next day, and it was warm and pleasant. It was made more beautiful as there was not any skirmishing. The regiment remained there for the next two days and nights. On June 10, they broke camp 8:30 a.m. but did not move. The 23rd Army Corp advanced ahead, formed line, and experienced some skirmishing.[16]

The 107th had been on this campaign for a little more than a month when Edward Kendall wrote home on June 11 and expressed some of his feelings concerning the campaign up to that point. He wrote,

> Since leaving Tennessee we have constantly been on the march, resting only a day or two now and then. The country here is splendid and every spot of ground is planted. There is much corn, wheat, rye, oats. Cotton fields are far and few between. The land appears to be very plentiful, including many farm animals. However, the majority of the homes are now empty with only the poor, who had nothing to risk, remaining. These conditions are beneficial to the troops, but it is inevitable that at this relatively quiet time the men's thoughts return to the events at New Hope Church. We were on the field for only one hour and in that time, we lost 149 killed and wounded. One officer was killed and six wounded. Twenty-six enlisted men were killed and 116 wounded. Of the wounded one officer died and one had a leg taken off. Four of the wounded enlisted men later died and a large number had limbs taken off. The wounded were mostly severe. There were nineteen others only slightly wounded and they were not counted in the report. Sgt. Benjamin Force was killed by a musket ball to the head. It seems hard that he should fall a sacrifice to his country. I cannot describe my feelings at his death. He has been my mess mate and tent mate for a long time, and we shared the duties of a soldier's life together until a short time before leaving Wartrace when I was situated so that it was impossible to mess with him. Still, I had ever cherished feelings of the deepest friendship for him and to see him whose place in his company will ever be missed to see him die was the most trying part of my soldier's life. Yet such is war. We have saved his watch, diary, photograph album and a lock of his hair which will be sent to his friends as soon as opportunity presents.[17]

On June 11, it was raining and foggy. They broke camp at 1:30 p.m. and marched until they bivouacked for the night. The next day, it rained while they worked to strengthen their works. There was heavy artillery fire at 6 p.m., but after that it was quiet all evening. It rained again the 13th and there was slight skirmishing with the Rebs on Lost Mountain (also known as Pine Hill). The next day, they were still at Lost Mountain; however the Rebs had retreated during the night.[18]

The regiment moved to Lost Mountain on the 14th. It was during that day that a group of high-ranking Rebel officers were observed out in the open taking stock of the action below them. A Union battery was ordered to concentrate fire on them. Confederate General Leonidas Polk was struck dead by a shell.[19] The 107th broke camp at 1:30 and moved about two miles to the right to the rear of the 2nd Division, where they formed a line of battle. The division advanced another mile and engaged the enemy for about two hours. After that they built breastworks. The loss to the 2nd Division was slight.

The next day, Rebel artillery fired on their works but did not cause any damage. After the Union batteries shelled them, no more was heard from them. One of the Rebel sharpshooters did wound George Stickler of Company F. He was transported to a hospital in Indianapolis, IN. He was still there when the 107th was mustered out at the end of the war. Over the next several days, there was skirmishing and minor artillery battles but no pitched battles with the Confederates, who were continually retreating. The 107th Brigade moved on after them, often taking time to build breastworks. At the same time, they would continually advance past Rebel fortifications that had been evacuated.[20]

The regiment left their camp the afternoon of the 15th and moved about two and a half miles in line of battle to the left of the 2nd division of their corps. They threw up breastworks that night. The next day, they were subjected to very severe cannonading for a short time, but their own batteries soon silenced them. Four men were wounded, but none were severe. On the 17th, they saw that the Rebels had left what had been a very strong position during the previous night. The 107th followed them closely for some three miles when they came to another line of works that Rebels had also vacated. On the 19th, they followed them to another line of works on Kennesaw Mountain. There the skirmish line engaged them. After a short while, when the current skirmish line was about to be relieved, Pvt. Daniel Simmonson of Company F, who had come from the 145th New York, was fatally shot in the head. On the 20th, they moved to the left about four or five miles and rested. Rain, which had continued all the past week, resulted in very high streams and full swamps, but the men were still in good spirits, asking only for plenty of hardtack, pork, and coffee. During this period, the Rebs were steadily falling back. The 107th's division held the heights of Marietta, and they had good communications with the Atlantic and Western Railroad. The Rebs had a large force but were very afraid of the Union artillery. Their breastworks were deep ditches as they did not trust those above ground.[21]

On the 21st, the 20th Corps established itself on a hill near what was called the Kolb house. The 107th, along with the rest of Williams' 1st Division, was massed by brigades in the woods on the Kolb's farm. Ruger's brigade, which included the 107th New York, was on the right, Knipe in the center, and Robinson on the left. The 23rd Corps continued the line on the right with Strickland's brigade next to Rugers. Geary's division was on Williams' left, and Butterfield was held in reserve. Artillery commanded all of the ground in front of Williams. At 4 p.m. Stevenson's division of Hood's Corps attacked. They were immediately driven into confusion by the artillery and volleys from Ruger's regiments. A second charge by the Confederates had the same result, and they retreated from the field to their works.[22] During the fight, the 107th had sent companies A, C, E, G, K, and I as skirmishers in support of the 3rd Wisconsin, and they drove the Rebel skirmishers beyond an open field.

The next day was pleasant and warm. The same companies were still on the skirmish line. That morning, the left of their line advanced, and the Rebel artillery began firing. However, it caused no damage. Their section moved forward, driving Rebs before them. Then they took a position on a ridge. The Rebs charged them, but they were repulsed. Anthony Boyce of Company H was killed during the Rebel charge. Later they constructed works, and all was quiet during the night.

The following morning, some of the men ventured out in front of their works and counted twenty Rebs dead. Later the regiment advanced a quarter mile and commenced building new works. Their immediate area remained quiet, but there was heavy artillery firing on their left near Kennesaw Mountain and skirmishing some distance in their front. The next two days were more of the same. On the 26th, they broke camp at 3 a.m., moved in order to fill a gap in the lines, and began to build another works.[23] The next day, their brigade relieved the 2nd division of the 20th Corps. The 107th was placed on a crest behind excellent breastworks in support of some batteries. Five or six batteries were located close by them. At 8 o'clock in the morning, the batteries opened fire on the Reb pickets, causing them to skedaddle. The Rebel artillery returned fire, but all of their shells either went over their breastworks or fell short. However, two horses that were part of the batteries near them were killed.[24]

The 4th and 14th Corps, who were well in the 107th front, charged and carried the enemy's works. The entire 20th Army Corps had been held in reserve and did not participate in the June 27 battle of Kennesaw Mountain. The units involved were the IV, XIV, XV, and XVI corps. Later in the day, the 107th's brigade moved forward a short distance. The 107th remained inactive on the 28th, with minor skirmishing forward of them as well as some artillery action. The next four days were more of the same. There had been no casualties in the regiment since the 22nd.[25]

In the general forward movement of the Sherman's armies following evacuation of Kennesaw Mountain, the 20th Corps marched several miles in the direction of the Chattahoochee River. On July 5, they went into position on a high ridge overlooking the Confederate lines on the other side of the river. From that position they also had their first glimpse of Atlanta, "The Gate City of the South." On the next day, they crossed the Nickajack Creek, and three days later on July 9, they advanced to the banks of the Chattahoochee River. The corps would remain there quietly until the 17th, although other parts of Sherman's army would be engaged in active movements. Immediately the troops on both sides entered into an agreement that there would be no unnecessary firing from either side of the river. It is related that one day, while the pickets were idly standing on each side of the river in their respective places, a Confederate officer rode up and ordered his men to fire on the Yanks across the river. However, they refused to violate their agreement. It was further understood that when hostilities were resumed by either side that the first volley would be fired into the air. If it were not for the sound of distant cannon, there was nothing to remind the soldiers that they were in the midst of an active campaign.[26]

The current position of the 107th also allowed them a perfect view of the defenses of Atlanta. They could see sturdy earthworks, and they had also placed sharpened stakes at 45-degree angles forty feet in the front of their works, forming a regular fence. They were covered with brush to further impede any charge. They had taken many prisoners on this march, and many had given up voluntarily.[27]

The 107th, along with the rest of the 20th Corps, broke camp in the afternoon of the 17th of July and crossed the Chattahoochee River at dusk and bivouacked. The next day, they remained in camp until dark, when they moved about a mile to the right toward the railroad. They moved again the next day. On the 20th, the corps crossed Nancy's Creek, during which they were subjected to artillery fire that resulted in wounding two or three men. They moved approximately a mile further and formed a line. They remained inactive there until near 3 p.m.

The Confederates attacked the strongly entrenched 4th Corps first. Then they struck the 2nd and 3rd division of the 20th Corps, who were also strongly entrenched. In the 1st division, only the 1st and 3rd brigades were involved. The 2nd brigade, of whom the 107th was a member, was not involved. However, Major Lathrop Baldwin, who was commanding the brigade's skirmish line, was severely wounded in the head. The ball entered the left temple and came out over his left eye. After being wounded, he fell and lay if as if dead. His boots were taken from him. Soon thereafter, the Rebels were driven back by a flanking movement by portions of the 14th corps. Then Baldwin was rescued. The 107th only suffered one other casualty when Pvt. Bonny of Company K was wounded in the arm. The 27th Indiana of their brigade did relieve another regiment when it ran out of ammunition. Colonel Colegrove of that regiment was severely wounded from a shell grazing his side and breaking his arm. The 1st division lost heavily, but the Rebels were driven off. The sister regiment of the 107th, the 141st New York, lost 49 killed or wounded out of 150 involved. Its colonel was killed; the lieutenant colonel lost his arm, the major's hip was severely wounded, and both of the adjutant's legs were severely wounded.

The following day, the regiment was occupied with burying the dead and caring for the wounded. However, they did suffer two more losses: Privates Isaac Middleton of Company H and Henry Holland of Company B. The Rebels fell back to their strong fortifications about a mile from Atlanta.[28]

# 10

# Siege and Occupation of Atlanta

**The Siege of Atlanta commenced after the Battle of Peach Tree Creek on July 20, 1864, and what was referred to as the Battle of Atlanta two days later on July 22, 1864. The Battle of Atlanta was fought southeast of the city and was the second straight battle for the newly appointed head of the Confederate army, General John Bell Hood. Union Major General McPhearson, commander of the Army of Tennessee, was killed while reconnoitering the enemy's front, but the Union forces prevailed despite being in a disadvantageous position. Hood's forces, broken and defeated, retreated behind the defenses of the city of Atlanta. The city would not fall until September the 2nd.**

When General McPherson, commander of the Army of Tennessee, was killed, the popular thought was that General Hooker would replace him as commander of the three corps that had been under McPherson. However, General Howard was given command of the three corps. General Hooker, by right of seniority, would typically have been given the command. He was upset over not receiving the command and asked to be relieved of command of the 20th Corps. He was then ordered to Washington. General Alpheus Williams was placed in temporary command of the 20th Corps. The general feeling among the men was that General Slocum would eventually be given command of their corps.[1] In two weeks' time, there was good news for the men. On August 7, Major General Henry Warner Slocum was named commander of the 20th Corps. The men of the107th New York regiment were extremely pleased.[2]

The city of Atlanta was too large to be completely surrounded by Union troops, so Sherman instructed that troops were to be placed along the northern and western borders. The plan was that the troops would build a continuous line of strong earthworks even while under fire. These fortifications would be close to and parallel with the fortifications of the enemy, and the Union lines were to cover a front of over five miles. Each brigade would be situated with each regiment of that brigade side by side along the line.[3]

The 107th New York had broken camp on the morning of the 22nd and marched to near the Rebel works located on a ridge. The Rebels opened up with shot and shell and made two charges on the regiment's skirmishers. During the first action,

Isaac Middleton of Company H was killed, and Henry Howland of Company B was wounded. Howland would die the following day. The second charge did not result in any casualties.

The 107th advanced closer to Atlanta on July 23, and their bivouac was situated near a battery of 20 lb. parrot rifles. The battery shelled Atlanta all during the night, and fire was visible in the city.[4]

The regiment's work continued to be unceasing both day and night over the next several days. During the day, the men kept close to the works to avoid stray bullets from the Reb pickets. At night their sleep was frequently broken by an advance on their pickets. Up to that time, the Rebs had not made a full night attack where the 107th had been brought into action, although there had been times when they were close. The Rebs had attacked the line of troops in their front and also against either flank. In those instances, they were repulsed without need for the 107th's assistance.[5]

On July 27, the 13th New Jersey of their brigade distinguished itself in an attack on the enemy's line. On a knoll in front of this regiment stood three buildings that were occupied by Rebel sharpshooters. Twenty volunteers were ordered to burn these buildings. The regiment formed a line with the volunteers in its rear, moved forward, and captured a large number of Rebels. They held that advanced position while the volunteers burned the houses. Once that was accomplished, they retreated to their works amid the cheers of their admiring spectators.[6]

At that time, the regiment's right flank was adjacent to the railroad that ran from Marietta to Atlanta. The regiment had been on the front line since July 26, where they were strongly entrenched and ready for any attack. The nearby parrot rifles continued their barrage of Atlanta. Their missiles fell on the forts surrounding Atlanta, and some even landed in the city itself. At the same time, pieces of shell landed in the regiment's works, but fortunately no soldiers there had been hurt. However, when the soldiers heard incoming shells, some movement toward shelter was made, and that continued over and over until the shelling declined.[7]

As long as the current strategy was in place, there would continue to be situations that would result in the unforeseen wounding and deaths of soldiers on both sides. The following letter illustrates one such circumstance.

August 1, 1864
Near Atlanta

Mr. Scott,

I have to announce to you the sad intelligence that your son Daniel B. Scott is dead. 30 of the 107th and 13 of a Jersey regiment were detailed as skirmishers to penetrate the Rebel lines, as soon as it was dark enough, at a distance of three hundred yards. On the morning of the 31st myself, Daniel and four others, when the proper signal was given, mounted the pits. Daniel being in the advance demanded a surrender when one of the Rebs rose up and surrendered. Daniel bringing at the same time his piece down as an acknowledgment of the same. But no sooner had he done this than the cowardly Reb shot him in the region of the stomach. He fell and was carried to the hospital where he died this morning Aug. 1st.

We not only regret that we have lost a good and efficient soldier, but a praying Christian man, and while we mourn his loss and deeply sympathize with his affiliated friends we are proud to know that he fell a noble sacrifice for his country.[8]

Captain Martin V.B. Bachman
107th NY Vols Co. E

There was sad news all around as the regiment received the news that Major Baldwin, who was badly wounded at the Battle of Peach Tree Creek, had died of his head wound on July 30 at a hospital in Chattanooga.

August 1 saw a resumption of skirmishing and artillery fire. This activity continued through the week to varying degrees with a number of men either wounded or killed. Corporal Byron Guiwitte was wounded on August 2. On the 3rd, Sergeant Guy Adams of Company E was shot in the head and killed by a sharpshooter. When Adams was shot, his tent mate Private Stephen Corwin attempted to get him to safety and was also shot and killed. Two days later, Private John Dougherty of Company I was shot and killed while on picket. Sunday was quiet, as was typically the case. The artillery barrage continued all the next week until Sunday the 13th, when it was quiet again. During the previous week, Private Patrick Dore of Company C was killed. On the 17th, the Rebs burned a house in their front, and that same day Sgt. Samuel Kinney of Company G was wounded. He would die the next day. Private Eleazer Mowers of the same company was also killed. During the evening of the 18th, a shell exploded between the different picket lines and illuminated the entire area, creating quite a display.[9]

After a time, the men were not actively constructing breastworks, but the long hours and dangers of picket duty were wearing on them. At one point, Colonel Crane of the 107th became very concerned about the negative effect that the situation along the front was having on his men. However, he was confident that his men were up to the task. His letter of August 12 to his brigade illustrated his thoughts.

August 12, 1864

Dear sir,

My command has suffered terribly. I commenced with the advance of this army last April, with six hundred muskets, and now I have just three hundred and seven fit for duty. I have lost over two hundred and fifty in battle, and am losing more almost every day. I have also lost some of my best and bravest officers, among others Major Baldwin. Just now we are within 300 yards of the enemy's lines and are compelled to burrow like rabbits to escape the bullets and shells which are aimed at us from every available point and at all hours of the day and night. We have lain in the trenches nearly three weeks, and I can assure you that this sort of work is wearing us out very fast however, we can and do stand it with a good heart. Our army line is about twelve miles long and I think we are good for the work before us. Hood's army has been very recently strongly reinforced; and how soon we shall take Atlanta I can not tell but hope quite strongly.

Camp of the 107th NY near Atlanta
Commander of the 107th NY Vols.
Colonel Nirom M. Crane

The regiment continued to remain in the same position. Their proximity to the Rebels again resulted in several casualties. Pvt. William Edgerton was slightly wounded in the shoulder. Pvt. John Bolton was severely wounded in the leg. Pvt. Patrick Dore was killed while on picket duty, and Pvt. William Walton sustained a slight leg wound.

Rebel shells continued to fall near their works, and some of the damage they did was quite interesting. One shell struck the nearby railroad track. It cut a piece of the track out and sent it airborne; it landed close to a nearby battery. When the battery crew picked up the piece of track, they thought it had been fired from a Rebel battery. In addition, that same battery crew had two of their guns explode at nearly the same time. Thankfully, no one in the crew was hurt.

While the regiment was in their current position, they and nearby regiments were able to forage for food back from their line some five or six miles. While this wasn't a daily occurrence, they found the opportunity to do it every so often.[10]

The following week, the regiment's duty and location remained the same, and shelling by both sides continued on a regular basis. Their duty there continued to be calm most of the time, but death was always lurking. Sgt. Samuel Kinney died after being shot in the right breast, and Pvt. Eleazar Mowers was also hit and killed by a minié ball. One was standing near his tent while the other was walking leisurely along when he was hit.[11]

Finally, the Rebel pickets agreed to a cease fire. As a result, the men on both sides were able to walk around and show their heads. Still the men had to deal with the artillery fire day and night. While the noise of the battery close by made sleeping very difficult, most of them "managed to do so after a fashion."[12]

Toward the end of August, Sherman decided to raise the siege at that area and move the 20th Corps back to the Chattahoochee River to guard the bridges and railroad. He also determined that there would have to be another flanking movement. His plan was to move the main army to south and east of Atlanta and destroy railroad track there. This action caused Hood to twice engage the Union forces. Hood's troops were defeated both times. The result would ultimately lead to the evacuation of Hood's army from Atlanta.[13]

The 107th and the entire 20th Corps left their works the evening of August 25 and relocated to the banks of the Chattahoochee River. There they were nicely located on the heights on the south side of the river, overlooking it and the valley through which it flowed. They were guarding a large railroad bridge and a ford across the river as well as their lines of communications. The men of the 107th and entire 20th Corps were glad to leave their previous location because of the continuous cannon fire and the potential for infantry action.[14]

On September 1, General Ruger, commander of the 1st Division of the 20th Corps, ordered members of his 2nd brigade to go out on reconnaissance toward Atlanta the following morning.

Below is the order directing members of the 107th NY along with squads from the other regiments in its brigade to investigate the status of the Confederate army in Atlanta. It was led by Capt. H.G. Bringham of the 107th New York.

*Author's note: My review of other descriptions of the initial entry of Union troops into Atlanta show them to be both incorrect and incomplete.*

Headquarters 2nd Brig. 1st Div. 20 A.C.
September 1st 1864
Circular
Detail for Fatigue Sept. 2nd, 1864

|  | C.O. | NCO | Privates |
|---|---|---|---|
| 2nd Mass Vols | 1 Lieut. | 2 | 15 |
| 13th NJ Vols | 1 Lieut. | 2 | 15 |
| 107th NY Vols | 1 Capt. | 2 | 15 |
| 3rd Wisc Vol | 1 Capt. | 2 | 15 |
| 150th NY Vols | 1 Lieut. | 2 | 20 |

The details from 2nd Mass, 13th NJ, 107th NY, 150th NY Vols will assemble in rear of the 13th NJ at seven (7) o'clock a.m.

The detail from 3rd Wis Vols will also assemble At seven (7 ) o'clock and will receive instructions From Col. Hawley.

Capt H.G. Brigham 107th NY Vols will be detached as the Officer from that Regt and will Report to these Hdqtrs for instructions at seven (7) o'clock a.m.

By Comd of
Brig Gen TH Ruger Comdg[15]

The reconnaissance group left their camp at 4 a.m., found the Rebel works empty, and marched on into Atlanta. They found that the city had been badly damaged by the constant shelling. There was scarcely a home or commercial building that had escaped damage. Some families had dug a cave in their garden. They had laid a floor with carpet and furnished it for living to escape the constant shelling. Some soldiers would visit these caves during the occupation, and they saw how comfortable they were.

When the detail marched into the city, the residents, mostly fine-looking young ladies, came out to see them and waved their hankies. One officer made a mental note to make their acquaintance as soon as possible. Some of the residents held the stars and stripes, which brought cheers from the soldiers. Many in the regiment felt a great deal of pride that they had succeeded in forcing Hood to evacuate the city.

On September 2, the remainder of the 20th Corps moved into the city, while the remainder of the army stayed outside. Several hundred Rebel troops were found hidden in different parts of the city. They doubtless planned to change into civilian clothes and remain as citizens of the city. They, including a Rebel captain, were immediately placed in confinement while still in their uniforms.

The regiment set up their camp on a green near the Macon railroad depot. Many of the 107th officers quickly furnished their quarters with sofas, chairs, bookcases, writing tables, and large dining tables that were taken from nearby homes. They planned on finding mattresses to finish their new homes. As if their new abodes weren't enough, food in the city was plenty. They dined on roast pig, potatoes, bread, pickled onions, coffee, and apple dumplings for dessert.[16]

Back home in Elmira, it was reported in the *Elmira Star-Gazette* that Atlanta had been taken. The residents celebrated by hanging a large banner across Water Street between Baldwin and Lake Street that read, "Atlanta is Ours."[17]

When the 107th New York regiment got within sight of Atlanta, they saw the stars and stripes floating over the town, and cheers went up. They saw firsthand that their shells had damaged almost every house. There was desolation everywhere. Many a poor woman waved her handkerchief and cried, "God bless you boys." There were also some poor men who had hidden themselves for months waiting for them.[18]

Atlanta was a strategic place from a military point of view, and the Rebels had fortified it with all the skill that their engineers possessed. It was situated on a system of railroads extending throughout Georgia. It was the junction for communication throughout the Confederate states and served as the source of troops and munitions that could easily be sent to Virginia, Alabama, and the Carolinas. This would account for the extensive effort made to prevent Sherman's army from capturing the city. When the army came close to the city, the Confederate General Hood attempted to draw Sherman away from Atlanta by moving a portion of his army north and behind Sherman. Because Sherman's army was significantly larger than Hood's, he was able to send General Thomas after Hood and still maintain a significant presence in front of Atlanta. At that time, Sherman advised President Lincoln of his plan to take Atlanta, move south through Georgia to Savannah, and finally north through the Carolinas.[19]

On September 5, the 107th moved their camp to near the Atlanta railroad depot where they reported to Colonel A. Beckwith, the chief commissary of substance and quartermaster supplies. They would guard these supplies until November 15 when they were ordered to join their brigade in preparation for the march to Savannah.[20] Colonel Crane was placed in command of three regiments. They included in addition to the 107th New York, the 66th Ohio and the 19th Michigan. Initially the duties of these regiments required more than the usual hours on duty. After a few days, things were sorted out, and duty hours became more regular. Large quantities of supplies were being received daily, and there were many large buildings available for the storage of military supplies. The 107th camp was about 1,300 feet to the left of the main depot of the Macon railroad terminal.

As the troops were able move around the city, they saw evidence of the shelling everywhere. The people of Atlanta, a city of about 25,000, had mostly left town as the result of the following notice that was published at the direction of General Sherman. At that point in time, he wanted to use Atlanta wholly for military purposes.[21]

NOTICE, ATLANTA, GA., September 8, 1864.

To the Citizens of Atlanta:

Major-General Sherman instructs me to say to you that you must all leave Atlanta; that as many of you as want to go North can do so, and that as many as want to go South can do so, and that all can take with them their movable property, servants included, if they want to go, but that no force is to be used, and that he will furnish transportation for persons and property as far as Rough and Ready, from whence it is expected General Hood will assist in carrying it on. Like transportation will be furnished for people and property going North, and it is required that all things contemplated by this notice will be carried into execution as soon as possible.

All persons are requested to leave their names and number in their families with the undersigned as early as possible, that estimates may be made of the quantity of transportation required.

JAMES M. CALHOUN Mayor[22]

The residents of Atlanta were given their choice of leaving the city travelling either north or south, and for the most part they chose the former.[23]

On September 8, Lieutenant Weller was placed in charge of a unit of 58 men who were to guard the large quantities of commissary supplies that were being received.[24]

Capt. John Orr arrived in Atlanta at 11 a.m. on September 13. He had recovered from the injury that he received at the battle of New Hope Church. He made the following note in his journal that day: "The 20th Corps 1st to occupy Atlanta under Gen Slocum Sept 2, 1864."

The next morning, he, along with Lt. Whitehorne, called on Col. Crane. Afterwards he went to the mustering officer to get mustered back into the 107th. However, the officer was out of the required forms. Later he was able obtain the forms from the regiment's adjutant and was then mustered in. On the 15th, he had dinner with Captains Brigham and Bachman along with Col. Crane and the adjutant. The following day, he took command of Company F, replacing Lt. Weller who had filled in after Knox's death during the battle of New Hope Church. Orr would spend the next several days working with Weller to bring the company's records up to date.[25]

The next day, Lt. Weller was put in command of a mounted city patrol. He had great difficulty keeping the streets clear due to the large number of supply wagons that were also generating a great deal of dust.[26]

During the occupation of Atlanta, the army opened a hospital in the Atlanta Female Institute, a school for women that had opened in 1859. One day an enlisted man brought a bible found there in one of the rooms to his company captain Paul Collison. There was an inscription inside the bible reading, "Presented to the Atlanta Female Institute by the Sophomore Class of 1860." Collison, wanting to preserve the bible, sent it to Elmira in the care of Dr. Tracy Beadle. At some point during the occupation, the Institute was torn down to allow the soldiers remaining in the city to build shanties. All of its contents were thought lost. Years later, an article in the *Elmira Star-Gazette* about the bible found its way to Atlanta. That article caused a great deal of correspondence between the *Atlanta Constitution* newspaper, the *Star-Gazette* and Collison. As a result, the bible was sent to the *Atlanta Constitution*. It was then passed along to veterans of the 42nd Georgia regiment, who in turn presented it to Miss Amanda Mason, a surviving member of the 1860 sophomore class, on July 10, 1910.[27]

While the institute was used as a hospital, the following 107th New York soldiers died of disease there. In mid–September, David LaTourette of Company F died of chronic diarrhea. He and his brother William had been transferred from the 145th New York. They had both been wounded at the battle of New Hope Church. William would go on to serve until the end of the war. LaTourette, along with the other six listed below, would ultimately be buried in the Marietta National Cemetery.[28]

| | |
|---|---|
| Pvt. David LaTourette Co. F | B-1113 |
| Pvt. Henry Stevens Co. A | B-1172 |
| Sgt Wm Personius Co. D | B-1158 |
| Pvt. Henry Mellen Co. F | B-1100 |
| Pvt. John McCarrick Co. C | B-1096 |
| Pvt. Wm Graves Co. A | B-1159 |
| Pvt. Archilest Campbell Co. C | B-1127 |

On September 19, there was a large prisoner exchange when a thousand Rebel prisoners were marched out of the city, and a thousand Union men were brought into the city. Before the end of the month, 446 Rebel prisoners were exchanged for a like number of Union soldiers. Lt. Weller continued to patrol the streets and found everything in good order through to the 23rd when he was re-assigned as an assistant quartermaster.[29]

On September 22, Private John McCanna, age 17, was mustered into the regiment's Company C. He was assigned to a tent with his father, Private Henry McCanna. They were tentmates for the remainder of the war.[30]

Although the presidential election was not until November 8, each company was preparing for it. There was a general consensus that Lincoln would win over George B. McClellan, his former top Civil War general.

By October 1, the 107th's sister regiment, the 141st New York, had been placed under the command of Colonel Crane. It moved its camp nearer to that of the 107th and was assigned to guard duty. By the 4th, all but the 20th Corps had moved north of Atlanta to prevent additional problems by Hood.

By this time, things were settling down for the regiment. They were constructing residences using whatever materials were available, and there were many. They were even attending church, and the brigade band was giving concerts. Unfortunately, some of their activities included too much drinking, and there was at least one instance when a soldier was made to stand at attention for an hour for failure to attend morning roll call.[31] There were also penalties for officers. Capt. Bachman, Lt. Colson, and Lt. Saultsman were all placed in the brig for drunkenness. On the bright side, the soldiers were entertained to a minstrel show put on by a Michigan engineers' unit.[32]

The 20th Corps continued to be the only contingent of troops inside the city, and Colonel Crane was commanding the 141st New York, the 19th Michigan, and the 66th Ohio regiments, in addition to the 107th.[33]

There had been no mail until the 15th on account of the railroad destruction by the Rebs between Nashville and Atlanta. The 107th was doing mounted patrols throughout the city. Lt. Weller of Company H was the head of these patrols, but Col. Crane re-assigned him to the position of Acting Regimental Quartermaster. In his new position, he had charge of drawing and issuing all clothing rations and other stores required by the regiment. He had his own horse, equipment, two assistants, a commissary, and a quartermaster sergeant. They did all the heavy work while he supervised. He was to be exempt from fighting and remained in the rear with the supply trains. In addition, he had his own wagon to carry his things. Along with his new duties, Weller was provided with an office in a little white house on Mitchell Street in the central part of the city. Weller, in a letter to his future wife Nettie, stated, "The nicest of the whole thing is there is a fine-looking young lady living next door to my office. She plays the piano and sings beautifully. My ears are greeted with sweet music for my evenings." This same house was used by Col. Crane and his staff. At this time, all the army, with the exception of the 20th Corps, had left their area to prevent the Rebels from severing their communications. The officers of the 107th felt that they would remain in Atlanta throughout the winter."[34]

The presidential election was less than a month away when Captain John Orr of Company F wrote to his friend back home in Steuben County.

Camp 107th Regt NY Vols
Atlanta Oct, 18th 1864
Friend Johnson,

The communication I promised you for various reasons has been delayed until the present time. The Army in this Department has changed front to the rear, not merely as a military maneuver, but as a matter of necessity. The rebels have made a bold movement to destroy our communications with the rear. Thus far they have met with poor success. The troops in and around Atlanta (belonging mostly to the 20 AC) are suffering more perhaps from this Rebel raid than any other portion of this army. Our rations are limited in variety, yet none of our men (I am well) are suffering for want of food as much as the entire "rebel army." The most that disturbs us now is fear that we cannot get our votes home. We care more about this than being deprived of rations. There seems to be but one opinion here as to the result of the coming election; those who vote for McClellan acknowledge his case to be a hopeless one. The 107th will give Lincoln a large majority. Company F has as many McClellan men as any other in the regiment and will give Lincoln nearly a two thirds majority. As soon as Sherman occupied Atlanta, he commenced encircling it with a line of forts and formidable breast works that are now nearly finished rendering the place almost impregnable, and only requiring a very small force to defend it. We are now in the very heart of the so called "Southern Confederacy" and we find many public documents and literary works that show the principles that actuate the leaders of this cursed, yes I may say this doomed rebellion. Below I give you some extracts taken verbatim from a geography compiled and printed expressly for Jeff and his philanthropic brethren. The author says in the preface of his geography that his is the only work that in existence that approximates doing justice to the country now composing the Confederate States of America, its actual condition and resources having been studiously concealed by every "Yankee work." The following questions and remarks explain what has heretofore been concealed from the public view. "Question: Best example of a Republican form of government in the world? Answer: Confederate States of America." Under the influence of slavery, which is the cornerstone of her government fabric and which is expressly recognized in the Constitution as it is in the word of God. The independence of man is being asserted and the Christian religion has full sway. This is the most desirable country in North America. The people are the finest, most prosperous and enlightened in the world. Its constitution expressly acknowledges the existence of a god. Speaking of the United States; it is remarked that infidelity and reckless puritanical fanaticism is fast robbing the people of all ennobling traits of character. What think you patriots of Steuben, can we compromise or treat for peace with a class of people who are teaching their children that we are infidels and heathens, that our form of government is tyrannical and unjust because it has not slavery for its cornerstone to rest on. No sir, we can never obtain permanent peace only by crushing out these absurd and traitorous principles which actuate those now in arms against us.

Very Respectfully, J. Orr (New York State Historical Association, Cooperstown, NY)

The soldiers were impressed by the size of the railroad repair shops and especially the very large roundhouse that was capable of handling from 40 to 50 units. They also saw several foundries where Confederate munitions were manufactured. Many homes in the city were uninhabitable, and many other buildings were so damaged that they were torn down and housing for the soldiers was being constructed. Some buildings were transformed into hospitals, and prior stores were being used for storing military goods. The city was quickly being transformed into a military depot.[35]

Memories of the battle at New Hope Church still lingered as Captain Orr mailed Hill's diary to his father. The regiment received their first pay in eight months.[36] Privates received as much as $108,[37] and because of the large amounts, many of the men sent a large portion of their pay home. This particular time, they decided to place the individual amounts together in one package in order to save money.

Colonel Crane and a number of officers and enlisted men were given furloughs. Colonel Crane, who had been having problems with his eyes, left for home the morning of the 27th to see a doctor. One of the officers going home was Captain Lamon of Company G, and he took Hill's belt and sword with him to present them to Hill's father. At the same time, a promotion came through for Allen Sill to lieutenant colonel. On October 28, there was a thunderstorm, and lightning struck a munitions dump, setting it on fire. The next day, the regiment received orders to prepare for a fifty-day campaign. There was no mention of where or when in the order.[38]

By the end of October, orders came to send all surplus supplies to the rear and to requisition enough clothing for fifty days. There were rumors that they soon would be leaving the city. They had much enjoyed their stay in Atlanta and were very disappointed that it was coming to an end. At the same time, large quantities of supplies and the last of the civilians were leaving the city by train[39]

As November began, it became apparent to the men in the 107th that preparations were being made for a new campaign. All equipment was either being repaired or replaced. All extra baggage and machinery were being sent back to Chattanooga.

November 8th was election day, and a dress parade was held. In addition, instructions for food and ammunition supplies were identified. Each soldier was to receive two days of hard bread, salt, and meat; five days of sugar; and ten days of coffee to be carried in haversack and 60 rounds cartridges on the person of each man.

Special squads' personnel were removing all citizens and military goods. The 17th corps moved into the city to relieve the 20th corps.

The next day, a small Rebel force attacked a city outpost but were easily driven off. The regiment received word that Lincoln had been re-elected president.

Over the next several days, the trains were busy moving citizens out of the city. Most of the old buildings in the city including the smaller round house were destroyed by fire. Sections of the railroad were destroyed, and the large roundhouse was torn down. The city was now empty except for soldiers. All of the public buildings had been torn down, and the Chattahoochee bridge was destroyed. On the 14th, General Sherman and General Howard came into town.[40]

Before starting on the march, two engineering regiments assisted by the 2nd Massachusetts and the 107th New York blew up buildings at the railway station, including the machine shops of the Georgia Railroad, and set fire to the wreckage. Other shops and foundries that had been used to manufacture war material for the Confederacy were burned. The fire spread to adjoining buildings in the business sector, and soon the greater part of the city was in flames. As the soldiers of the departing army reached the hills on the eastern side of Atlanta and turned to look at the doomed city, it was hidden beneath a dense cloud of smoke through which great tongues of flame shot upward, making an appalling sight that nothing but the exigencies of war could justify.[41]

# 11

# March to the Sea

**Sherman decided to divide his army into right and left wings for the upcoming march. The right wing was to be commanded by General Howard and made up of the 15th and 17th Corps and designated as the Army of Georgia. The left wing was to be commanded by General Slocum and made up of the 14th and 20th Corps and was designated by its former name, the Army of Tennessee. In addition, there was a division of cavalry under General Kilpatrick. These combined forces consisted of 55,329 infantry, 5,063 cavalry, and 1,812 artillery. There were 65 pieces of artillery with each gun, caisson, and forge drawn by eight horses. In the trains were 2,500 wagons and 600 ambulances. Each wagon train when on the road was five miles long. A pontoon train of canvas boats accompanied each train. Each bridge train had a capacity of 900 feet. The two armies would march to Savannah by two different but parallel routes to discourage attacks by the Rebels, and they were to maintain their food supplies by foraging.**

On November 12th, Sherman's army began detaching itself from all communications with the rear. Atlanta was set to be destroyed, with the exception of its homes, churches, and a few businesses. The initial destination of the march was Milledgeville.[1]

The 107th was up at 4 a.m. on November 15th. They moved at 6 a.m. to the outer breastworks and joined the remainder of their brigade. During their march, they passed a number of rifle pits and other fortifications. Some of the road was very rough. They reached Decatur at 12 noon and stopped for dinner. At that time, they were ordered to do guard duty with the wagon train. They continued on until dusk, when they went into camp, and some of the men were detailed for picket duty. They had marched fifteen miles that first day and were bivouacked near Stone Mountain. Sleeping was difficult because of the constant movement of wagons in their immediate area.[2]

The 107th and the rest of Sherman's army had left Atlanta entirely deserted by human beings except for a few soldiers here and there. The houses were vacant. There was no traffic or trade of any kind, and the streets were empty. Beautiful roses were blooming in the gardens of fine houses, but a terrible stillness and solitude covered all. In the North, there could be no understanding of how these people were suffering for the crimes of their leaders.

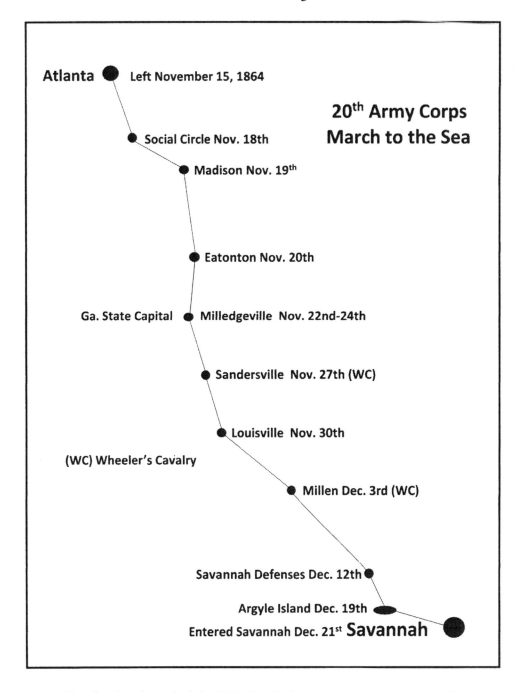

Atlanta ● Left November 15, 1864

20th Army Corps
March to the Sea

● Social Circle Nov. 18th

● Madison Nov. 19th

● Eatonton Nov. 20th

Ga. State Capital ● Milledgeville Nov. 22nd-24th

● Sandersville Nov. 27th (WC)

● Louisville Nov. 30th

(WC) Wheeler's Cavalry

● Millen Dec. 3rd (WC)

Savannah Defenses Dec. 12th ●

Argyle Island Dec. 19th ●

Entered Savannah Dec. 21st Savannah ●

Map showing the path of the 107th New York during its march to Savannah.

Atlanta was in flames. A grand and awful spectacle was there to be viewed in that beautiful city. By order, the chief engineer had destroyed by powder and fire all the storehouses, train depots, and manufacturing facilities. The heaven was one expanse of flying burning cinders. Every instant there were the sharp detonation or the smothered booming sound of exploding shells and powder stored in the buildings. Next to Richmond, this city had furnished more material for continuing the war than any other in the South.[3]

The next day, the 107th was up at 5 a.m. but did not move out until 2 p.m. because their division was now at the rear of the train, which they continued to guard. The march was again very hard and made more so by the constant stopping of the train. At dusk they were ordered to move forward and prepare supper. The regiment and the brigade got confused during the move and in the process lost Colonel Sill who had taken Colonel Crane's place while he was north in Hornell. They finally halted and had supper at 7 p.m. without their colonel. Once again on the march, they crossed the Yellowstone River. They finally were able to find their colonel. During marches there were always stragglers. This day was no exception, but they complicated matters by setting a church on fire. They finally went into camp near Sheffield at midnight, having marched ten miles that day.

On the 17th, they were up at sunrise but did not move until 10 a.m. They were positioned on either side of the wagon train as they marched. They marched until 1 p.m., when they halted for dinner. They had a very successful day foraging, bringing in a number or hogs and a quantity of sweet potatoes. After dinner, they marched at a slower pace than usual, stopping quite often. They halted at 10 p.m. but not long enough to have supper. They marched on, with many men dropping off to the side of the road and building campfires. They finally stopped near Covington at 1 a.m. on the 18th, had supper, and were off to sleep by 2 a.m. Their sleep only lasted until 5 a.m. when they were up again. However, they did not move until 9 a.m. The road at this point was very good, and they were moving along quickly.[4]

Reveille was sounded at daybreak on the 18th, and the train moved at 10 a.m. They stopped for dinner at Social Circle and later passed through Rutledge. During the day, they spent some time tearing up railroad tracks, and men were sent out foraging. Brigade headquarters directed the 107th New York to send out men from Companies D and K to forage and to round up any stragglers that they might come across. A total of 44 men commanded by Captain George W. Reid and Lt. George Humphrey were in the group. Reid was a peculiar addition to the 107th New York because he was the only officer from the former 145th New York who was allowed to remain on active duty after the 145th New York was broken up and the enlisted men of that regiment added to other regiments. This group went off on its mission with instructions not to venture too far from the route of the march.[5]

At that time, a Rebel unit known as Shannon's Scouts, an offshoot of the 8th Texas Cavalry, was in the general area looking to create trouble. They came across a pen of hogs that had been collected by foragers. When the Rebels located nine stragglers along the road, they killed three and wounded four. The other two escaped into the woods. This Rebel group left the road but kept close to the route that the Union troops were taking. They then came across two more Union soldiers, probably more stragglers, and killed them. Moving along with the woods between them and the train's rear guard, they became aware of the 107th foraging group that was even further in the woods and unknowingly separated from their regiment by the Rebels. The Rebels moved to surround them and took them all prisoner without any shots fired. They stole all their possessions and turned them over to some local citizens. The prisoners were later transported to a prison in Florence, SC. At the time, it was not known what had happened to them. All of the men survived this experience and would return home by the end of the war.[6]

*Author's note: The specific details of this event are in question. However, Capt. Reid with sixteen men from Company D and twenty-seven men from Company K had been detailed for foraging. They were ultimately captured, robbed, and imprisoned. This can be verified. However, a small group of Company D men were foraging separate from the main foraging party and were not seen by the Rebels. They were able to escape capture and rejoin the regiment during the march. It appears that the majority, if not all, of the captured survived and were eventually paroled.[7]*

The muster roll of December 31, 1864, for Company K of the 107th New York revealed that the number of men left in the company after the episode near Social Circle was two sergeants and four privates.[8] During this same period of time, two others of the 107th New York regiment were captured. They were undoubtedly stragglers. This was not unusual occurrence on long marches. These two were Pvt. Peter Howe of Company F and Pvt. John Hughes of Company C.[9]

The 107th marched 22 miles on the 18th and camped near Madison that evening. They had no idea what had happened to their foragers. It rained most of the evening. The next day, they moved at 8 a.m. The roads were very muddy, making it difficult for both men and the heavily laden wagons. They reached Madison, the Moran County seat, and bivouacked six miles beyond it at 4 p.m. It rained again that evening. On the 20th, the roads were still very bad, and the continuing rain made them worse. They bivouacked at 9 p.m. north of Eatonton. Thus far, their attempts at foraging were very successful, and despite the rain they had managed to march 18 miles. The rain continued on the 21st as they drew closer to the state capitol of Milledgeville. Colonel Sill, who had taken command of the 107th during Colonel Crane's absence, was arrested, and Captain Fox was placed in command of the regiment. They had marched a total of 12 miles.

The weather was very cold. The ground was frozen, and a strong wind was blowing the morning of November 22nd. The train to which the 107th New York regiment belonged was up at 4 a.m. and moved out two hours later. They crossed the Little River at 10 a.m. and approached the outskirts of Milledgeville.[10] At this time, General Slocum ordered the 107th New York and the 3rd Wisconsin to move forward, occupy the city, and act as provost guards. Slocum's orders were to enter the city with music playing and colors flying and take formal military possession of the city. Major Fox assembled the brigade band, which included members from each of the brigade's regiments. They entered the city at 3 p.m. to the wild acclaim of the local Black population, who looked upon the Yankees as their deliverers from bondage.[11]

They had entered with no opposition and found that the legislature and most of the citizens had left town. However, a number of Rebel sick and wounded soldiers had been left behind. The 107th marched to the square that stretched about the capitol and set up camp along with the 3rd Wisconsin. Guards were put in place at various locations including the arsenal, the armory, and the public works. The entire contingent of troops was to be under the command of Colonel Hawley of the 3rd Wisconsin.[12]

The only persons who were left in the town were enslaved people. Sherman saw that provisions were distributed to them, and they were told not to be afraid. However, one old man responded, "I spose dat you'se true, but massa, youse go away tomorrow and anudder white man'll come." He had never known anything but persecution and injury from the white man and had been kept in such ignorance of the northern army that he did not have any faith in any white man.

This terrorism was a striking feature of slavery. The former slaves had been told that as soon as the Union soldiers got them into their clutches, they would be put in front of them in battle and killed if they did not fight. They were also told that their women and children would be thrown into the Chattahoochee River, and that when the buildings were burned in Atlanta, they had been filled with Black people.[13]

Shortly after their arrival, Sgt. Ebenezer Helmes of Company K of the 107th

Sgt. Helmes of the 107th New York raising the American flag on the Georgia State House in Milledgeville, Georgia (*Harper's Weekly*, January 7, 1865).

made his way to the roof of the state house where he held the American flag for all to see. He had been accompanied to the roof by an artist of *Harper's Weekly*, Alexander Davis. As a result, the image of Helmes appeared on the cover of the January 7, 1865, issue of *Harper's Weekly*.

Companies from both regiments were immediately sent to the nearby Rebel arsenal, which contained a large quantity of Confederate arms and ammunition. They threw all of the ammunition into the river and burned all of the arms and other equipment. In addition to these arms, there was also a large quantity of old-fashioned rifles and shotguns, as well as thousands of pikes and bowie knives that had been manufactured by the state for the militia. Once all the equipment was removed, the arsenal was burned.[14]

Several 107th officers had an opportunity to visit the local mental institution. The director gave them a tour of the establishment. There were approximately fifty women and one hundred men confined there. The officers saw that there were several attractive women in the group. One in particular seemed rather normal to them. The director told them that she was from the state of New York and had been engaged to a Confederate officer. He had broken off the engagement, and as a result, she had a mental collapse. The director told them that she was getting better. In fact, she sat down to a piano and played and sang for them.[15]

Colonel Hawley provided a detailed list of property seized and destroyed. Over the period of two days, many items were seized and destroyed. The following items were burned: 2,300 muskets, smooth-bore, caliber .69; 10,000 rounds cartridges, caliber .69; 300 sets accouterments; 5,000 lances; 1,500 cutlasses; and 15 boxes U.S. standard weights and measures. Items thrown into the river included 170 boxes fixed artillery ammunition; 200 kegs powder; and 16 hogsheads salt. Approximately 1,800 bales of cotton were disposed of by General Sherman, but the manner of disposition was not reported to Hawley. Finally, about 1,500 pounds tobacco was taken and distributed among the troops generally. Besides the property enumerated by Hawley, miscellaneous articles, such as harnesses, saddles, canteens, tools for repairing war materials, caps, etc., were burned in a building located in the square near the State House.[16]

Many of the officers situated themselves in the local Episcopal Church. The enlisted men confiscated a large number of chickens and pigs. These were to be made available to the regiment. Some officers, as was the usual case, took advantage of the fact that some citizens had remained in the city and tried to have a friendly conversation with them. Captain John Orr took the opportunity to clean up, shave, and put on his good uniform. He met and then had dinner with a family named Calloway. That same day he was made aware of a Mrs. Cook, who had been mistreated by several soldiers. After reviewing the situation, he assigned a guard at her home to prevent any further such occurrences. Mrs. Cook was not the only resident in the city whose property was provided a guard.[17]

Lt. Edwin Weller of Company H was one of a number of officers from both regiments who entered and toured the State House. There they found millions of dollars in Georgia state money in bills of all denominations. The bills lacked the signature of the governor, but that didn't make any difference to them. The men of both regiments helped themselves to the money. Lt. Weller either carried or mailed a page of the uncut bills back to his home near Montour Falls, NY, where they are displayed in the Montour Falls Public Library.[18]

Another action by the 107th and 3rd Wisconsin regiments included going about the city searching for cotton. They burned all that they found, provided that that action would not unnecessarily cause any damage to nearby buildings. Any cotton stored in the city was "bonded" so that it would not be turned over to the Confederate government or used for its benefit. The 107th sent out a detachment to search for tobacco. They found enough to fill two wagons, and that quantity was enough to keep the army supplied until they reached Savannah.[19]

On Wednesday, November 23, the main body of Sherman's left wing assembled in Milledgeville, which soon resembled a vast army camp even though the principal bivouac was on the McKinley plantation outside of town. Since the weather was unusually cold, picket fences and outhouses became the principal supply of firewood for 30,000 soldiers. Thus, gardens and private enclosures were turned into open thoroughfares for horses and men. Church buildings provided greater protection from the cold than army tents, and church pews made excellent fuel. All church buildings and their contents suffered some damage. The organ of the Episcopal Church was ruined when sorghum was poured into the pipes. Army officers, from provost guards to General Sherman himself, were besieged with petitions from citizens who sought protection from seizures and vandalism. In truth, overt destruction of factories, residences, and warehouses was rare. Only three or four private residences in the vicinity of the town were burned. These included the home of the state treasurer John Jones and the country homes of Judge Iverson Harris and Dr. William A. Jarrett. Harris had attracted Sherman's attention by urging planters along the path of the march to destroy everything upon which the invaders might subsist. At Jarrett's plantation, the overseer Patrick Kane had too zealously defended his employer's property. He was shot to death, and the property was burned. Kane was the only known fatality during the army's presence in the area.

The train depot and the bridge spanning the Oconee were burned by military order. The arsenal that stood on the east side of the statehouse was blown up after all of its contents were removed. On the opposite side of the square, the fireproof magazine was blown up. Although some cotton was destroyed as the result of miscarried orders, the bulk of it was left untouched in the warehouses. The Oconee Mill, the textile factory, and the foundry all escaped destruction. This was probably because their owners were northerners or men of foreign birth. Sherman honored almost every excuse for not applying the torch.[20]

While it is not known if Sherman ever ordered the destruction of the penitentiary, he might have justly done so since it functioned as an armament factory.

Prior to the Union troops' arrival, the governor of Georgia had paroled most of the prisoners from the prison. Those that he paroled agreed to join a unit that was organized to oppose the advancing Union troops. The prisoners who did not join the unit then celebrated their newfound freedom by setting fire to the prison.[21] However, the fire only partly destroyed its buildings. There is no record of what happened to those prisoners who set the fire, but one of them was a woman who was serving a life sentence for killing her husband. Dressed in a federal uniform and plying an ancient trade, she found hospitality and refuge with the 33rd Indiana Regiment.

While the Statehouse was not burned, it was the object of extensive vandalism. Some of the younger officers of the 3rd Wisconsin and the 107th New York regiments staged a mock session of the legislature there during which there was much horseplay. The horseplay included a parody on the ordinance of secession. Although a teetotaler, Judson Kilpatrick reportedly took the speaker's stand and regaled the assembly with tales of the cavalry's gallant campaigns against enemy wine cellars and whiskey storerooms. After a round of speechmaking, the congressmen drew up a series of resolutions, including one declaring the Georgia Ordinance of Secession a damned farce.[22]

The affair attracted a large number of soldiers who later ransacked the building, breaking windows, chairs, and desks, and writing obscenities on the walls. Many of the library books on the shelves in the basement were thrown out of the windows, where they were trampled on by horses. Other books were carried off by both officers and soldiers.[23]

On November 24, the men were up at 4 a.m. and moved at daybreak. They crossed the Oconee River, marched 8 miles, and stopped for dinner. They marched until dusk and camped. The next day, their route took them over Buffalo Creek five times. The bridges over each of the creeks had been burned by the Rebels and required their engineers to construct new ones. In addition, the roads were very bad, and the area was largely uninhabited, making foraging very poor. On the 26th, they marched toward Sandersville where their brigade encountered and skirmished with Wheeler's cavalry. The Rebels retreated back through the village. The 107th formed a line of battle but were not engaged.

In Sandersville, they were able locate a large number of chickens and hogs. At the same time, they took notice of some pretty girls in the village. They took time out to destroy a length of railroad tracks and burn the railroad station. The next day, they moved to the head of the brigade when they left the village. Once outside of Sandersville, the area became very thinly settled. They marched steadily all afternoon and went into camp near Davisboro. On the 28th, they marched along the railroad, destroying it as they went along. They observed several large swamps in that same area. They went into camp at 8 p.m. near Millerstown. The next day, they continued along the railroad and sent out Company F to forage. They returned with seven hogs and a quantity of potatoes, all of which was divided up among the regiment for dinner. Afterwards they tore up more railroad and burned two bridges along with a quantity of lumber. On the 30th, the landscape changed dramatically as the countryside became heavily wooded with the exception of the presence of many large swamps. That afternoon, they crossed a narrow but deep stream called the Oguache River. Later, when they were near Louisville, they made camp.[24]

On December 1, the 107th moved at 9 a.m. with their division in the lead of the 20th Corps. They crossed a large, dismal, and foreboding swamp that left their clothes covered with mud. They bivouacked at 10 p.m. on the other side of the swamp. The next morning, they crossed another large swamp, but once past the swamp, the roads were good, and the weather improved. Their foraging group brought in forty hogs. They crossed the Augusta railroad and went through their usual process, tearing up the rails and burning the ties. Later in the day, they crossed a branch of the Savannah River. On December 3, they crossed a creek near Millen, GA, and dealt with a swamp flooded by a Rebel-built dam. They passed a large plantation that appeared to have a large stockade that they presumed may have been built to house Union prisoners.

The next morning, they moved out at 7 a.m. with their brigade leading the march. During the march, they crossed Black Creek. Their column was harassed by Joe Wheeler's cavalry during the day. They made camp at 4:30 p.m. On the 5th, they did not move until dark. Again, they were faced with marching through a swampy area. They marched all night but made only two miles. The marching continued through swamp lands for the next two days. It was made worse by the continual rain. They bivouacked near Springfield on the 7th. They were now only 28 miles from their destination. The next day, they moved 12 miles beyond Springfield. All of the 107th was on picket. The roads and the weather had greatly improved. On the 9th, they moved at 8:30 a.m. and had gone five miles when the Rebels opened up with cannon fire in their front. The regiment was deployed on the right side of the road in knee deep water in a rice field. They advanced against the Rebels, who immediately fled. The 107th, 3rd Wisconsin, and 2nd Massachusetts followed them for two miles with no further contact.[25]

The Rebs moved the Union prisoners who were confined at Andersonville to Millen, a low marshy country. The yard confining the enlisted men was built over a small creek where the water came from a swamp that was green with filth. There were 650 Union men buried in trenches, with no pains or care taken with their bodies, instead simply placed in two or three deep and covered with dirt. As the Union troops approached Millen, the Confederates sent them to Columbia, SC. [26]

The men met their first sign of resistance on December 9 at Monteith Swamp at a station of the Charleston and Savannah Railroad. The First Division was in the advance. Its pioneers were, as usual, removing the trees that had been felled to slow their advance when a Rebel battery began dropping shells among them. A brigade was sent off to the right in a flanking movement while the troops in their front kept their attention. The 3rd Wisconsin captured several of them, but the main body got away.

The next day, December 10, they reached the Charleston and Savannah Railroad just in time to drive back a Charleston train and occupy the riverbank. There they were able to capture two river boats, the *Ida* and the *Resolute*. In addition, their artillery drove back two Rebel gun boats, the *Macon* and the *Sampson*.

The line of Rebel defenses for Savannah was reached on December 12. Their troops were placed in front of the city from the Savannah River around to the Ogeechee. The 20th Corps was on the extreme left with the 1st Division near the main road leading up from the city.

On the 16th, Carmen's brigade was sent across the Savannah River to occupy Argyle Island and the South Carolina shoreline. After locating there, they were attacked by Wheeler's cavalry. The 107th had two men wounded during the fight. The 107th and its brigade remained in that position until the Rebels evacuated the city. When that happened, their entire force came near the 107th's location during its retreat into South Carolina. The brigade moved to the Georgia side of the river during the night of the 21st. At the same time, the remainder of the army had captured Fort McAllister and entered the city.[27]

December 16 also brought the welcome announcement that personal mail service was now available. This was wonderful news to the men because that service had not been available since they left Atlanta. Lt. Russell Tuttle had the opportunity to bring his father up to date regarding himself and the regiment. He let his father know that in general, he and the regiment were all well. The march to Savannah had been an easy one, and they had lived very well off the land during the march. He also told his father the line of the march for the 20th Corps. He listed Atlanta, Decatur, Stone Mountain, Sheffield, Social Circle, Rutledge, Madison, Eatonton, Milledgeville, Louisville, Davisboro, Millen, Springfield, Cherokee Hill, and their present location about four miles from Savannah and one mile from the Savannah River. Their brigade's specific location at that time was Argyle Island, where they were protecting the rice mills and actually running them.

Communications with the fleet had also been made, and they were able to get copies of the *New York Tribune* for the dates of December 8 and 10. In addition, they saw in the December 8 edition that a large amount of mail for Sherman's army had left the north on the steamer *Fulton* that same day. That news created a great deal of excitement for all of the men to stand down and not to engage in any show of force with respect to the Rebel army because of the great quantity of mail on the way to them. At that time, there was no idea of what Sherman's plans were for advancing on Savannah. 1st Lt. Russell Tuttle's expectations were that they might spend a large amount of time in Savannah once they were in the city, and he contemplated having his civilian clothes expressed to Savannah.[28]

On the 19th, the 107th went to work loading rice from the mill on Argyle Island until noon. Early that morning, the other regiments in their brigade had crossed the river into South Carolina. They encountered some Rebel forces and asked the 107th to cross over and help them. It was about 2 p.m. when the 107th crossed over and advanced in a line of battle. Companies B and C were deployed as skirmishers along a dike and skirmished with a Rebel cavalry unit until dark. Companies F, G, H, I, E, and A of the 107th were engaged heavily with the Rebels but had only two wounded. The entire 2nd brigade made it safely across to the Georgia shore while they held the line against the Rebs. During the evening, they heard what sounded like the Confederate army leaving the city. The regiment remained bivouacked until the next day. The next day, their pickets were continually harassed by Reb cavalry that they saw in the distance throughout the day. A Rebel gunboat came up in the afternoon and fired on them. On the 21st, the city surrendered to General Geary, and their brigade began recrossing the river to Argyle Island. During that maneuver, the Reb cavalry harassed the 150th New York, wounding their colonel and others in that regiment. The entire brigade got over to the island by nightfall. Before they had left the island, Arthur Fitch was wounded in the left leg and evacuated to a hospital in Savannah on the 23rd. He would remain in Savannah until January 15, during which time he was promoted to the rank of 1st Lieutenant. He was then discharged from the army and returned home to Elmira.[29]

The 107th entered Savannah on December 21. The march from Atlanta to Savannah had been an almost bloodless one. It was fortunate for everyone that they did not have to fight their way into town. They had made all the necessary preparations to storm the town. They had moved their artillery into position and were ready to move the following morning. However, that night the Rebel army "got out of the way."

Their first impression as they marched into Savannah was that it was a beautiful city, very tastefully laid out with pleasant streets and parks. There were very elegant private residences everywhere and very fine public buildings. There was no question in their minds that there must have been a great deal of wealth there before the war. While the city was spectacular, there were many instances of it that appeared to be abandoned.

The 107th entered the city several days before Christmas day and set up their camp. There were a number of reviews of troops prior to that of the 20th Corps, which was reviewed on the morning of December 30. The review consisted of 20,000 men.

Lt. Edwin Weller of Company H, as was his custom, made notice of pretty young women wherever he was. His attendance and observations the previous day at the review of the 14th Corps proved that point. He wrote to his future wife Nettie, stating, "There was a quantity of ladies to witness the review, and there were plenty of pretty girls. I saw some splendid looking ladies out to the review the other day. All those I have seen are very dressy indeed and always appear on the streets in their fine silks and satins." Weller was an assistant to Colonel Crane, and they shared an office in a house. He remarked that it was furnished in good army style consisting of one table, one stand, a washbowl and pitcher, two chairs and one camp stool, and his office desk and table. The brigade moved their camp to the western suburbs after the first of the year. Weller again was in a house where he had an office in the parlor and an adjoining room for storage.[30]

During his time in the city, 1st Lt. Russell Tuttle took the opportunity to not only purchase some books but to also search through these abandoned houses for additional volumes. He was then able to express them home to his father for a nominal sum. Finally reaching Savannah meant that the 107th men could write home again.

The men observed that the port was hardly open because of the many obstructions still remaining in the river. However, they saw boats coming up by the way of Warsaw Sound. There was no question that this was an important seaport. Further evidence of that was the great number of foreign flags flying from the residences of the consuls of other countries.[31]

However, as time went on, the men of the 107th found Savannah very monotonous and lonesome. This was the farthest they had ever been from home. There was scarcely any mail, and they had no newspapers from the north. They commented that the local little "one horse" newspaper was quickly read and then thrown aside.

*Author's Note: It is amazing to see such a familiar term used in this time period.*

The soldiers moved about the city but saw little of real interest to purchase. The articles of food were expensive, and there was confusion because the citizens were used to pricing everything based on Confederate money. The high prices precluded the men from buying enough food necessary for single meal. Initially potatoes sold at wholesale for up to $50 per barrel and retail for 20 cents per pound. Apples were two for a quarter. Butter was $1.50 per pound and cheese $1.00. However, prices became more reasonable because of the realization that regular U.S. currency was better than Confederate money. The retail prices for everything dropped to half of the previous sale price.

During the time the army was located in and around the city, it was obvious that they were preparing for another campaign. Each regiment was drawing new clothing and replacing the equipment that had seen better days. They knew that South Carolina would be their next objective and "would soon feel the dread realities of war."

Colonel Crane finally returned to the regiment and received a cordial welcome from everyone. In addition, several officers were promoted. Lt. Robert Gansevoort of Company I was promoted to Captain of Company G, 2nd Lt. Jacob Saltzman to 1st. Lt. of Company G, and 1st Sgt. Arthur Fitch to 1st Lt. Company B.[32]

While the 107th was located near Savannah, the regiment still had to forage for supplies. On one such occasion, Lt. Edwin Weller happened by a large plantation where he met a young lady who was living there with her aunt. She asked Weller if she might have transportation into the city. He kindly offered to do so if she would walk the mile and a half to where he had an ambulance in which she might ride. However, as she did not feel disposed to walk to the main body of his foragers, he felt that she really wasn't that intent on going into the city.

During its march to the sea, the 107th had marched 255 miles in 25 days, alternately skirmishing, bridge building, clearing away obstructions, and destroying railroad track and other public property. Its casualties were three killed, 21 wounded, and 94 missing including Captain Reid's captured foraging group. The regiment captured three officers, 34 enlisted men, and a large number of enslaved men who insisted on, "Gwine along with you alls." They confiscated 1800 bales of cotton at Milledgeville, which was passed over to General Sherman Two steamers were captured: the *Ida,* which was burned, and the Resolute, which contained a large quantity of arms and ammunition.

In addition, there was a large quantity of items that were appropriated for use by the brigade. They included seven horses, 58 mules, 177,118 lbs. of corn, 205,500 lbs. of fodder, 95,000 lbs. of sweet potatoes, 95,000 lbs. of fresh meat, 20,000 lbs. of rice unthreshed, 500 bushels threshed, 13 barrels of syrup, 1,000 lbs. of sugar, six barrels of salt, 1,000 lbs. of bacon, 1,500 lbs. of meal and flour, and 1,500 lbs. of tobacco. It captured the following military stores in Milledgeville: 2,300 muskets, 10,000 rounds of ammunition, 300 sets of infantry accoutrements, 500 pikes, 1,200 cutlasses, 200 kegs of powder, and 170 cases of artillery ammunition.

The brigade destroyed 14 miles of railway track, four railway bridges, five cotton gins, and 400 bales of cotton. Considering that this was the work of but one brigade in the whole army. Imagine how much total property was used or destroyed and how greatly the resources of the enemy were crippled by "Sherman's March."[33]

Privates Rodney E. Harris and Lucius T. Stanley of the 107th New York made various maps for the 12th and 20th Corps during the war. On the march from Atlanta to Savannah, Harris was detailed to the map-making section of the 20th Corps, where he made a series of maps that portrayed the corps' path taken during the "Great March."[34]

General Sherman wrote the following to President Lincoln in his official report:

> As to the rank and file, they seemed so full of confidence in themselves that I doubt that they want a compliment from me, but I must do them the justice to say that whether called on to fight, to march, to wade streams, to make roads, clear out obstructions, build bridges, make corduroy or tear up railroads they have done it with alacrity and a degree of cheerfulness unsurpassed. The behavior of our troops in Savannah has been so manly, so quiet, so perfect, that I take it as the best evidence of discipline and true courage.[35]

Of all such praises, the 107th was entitled to its due share.

The regiment remained in Savannah only a few days. During that time, Sherman held a series of reviews of the different corps that composed his army. The last review was of the 20th Corps, and as usual, it eclipsed all the others. The 107th had taken special pains as to its appearance and appeared to the very best advantage. The review was held December 30. On the 31st, the 3rd Division of the 20th Corps was ordered across the river.

During this period, the men of the regiment were collecting lumber and bricks and trying to improve their housing. However, they otherwise had heavy duty working on fortifications of the city. They also took the opportunity to venture around the city. They were thankful for the quiet time, but there were always rumors of moving north to the Carolinas.

On January 6, Colonel Crane returned to the regiment. Many of the men went to the headquarters and welcomed him back. The regiment returned to its normal camp duties. What available clothes that were in supply were handed out, as were accoutrements.

It was seldom that the men refused an order or acted up in some sort of manner. When Private John Lewis of Company F, who had previously been in the 145th New York, refused to obey an order, he was tied by his wrists to a tree. He finally agreed to comply at 11 p.m. that evening and was released.

On January 12, Kilpatrick's cavalry was reviewed in the city. They were a very rough looking group. Secretary of War Stanton, who was visiting, attended the review.[36]

January 17, 1865, was the regiment's last day in Savannah. The stay of the soldiers had been a pleasant one. Little duty had been required of them. They had been given opportunity to rest and prepare for the longer and arduous campaign which was to follow. The 20th Corps was reviewed by Generals Sherman and Slocum. They marched into the city and passed the reviewing stand. While Geary's division had been camped inside the city, the other divisions were camped outside. They were granted passes to go into the city. where they enjoyed themselves strolling about the wide streets and conversing with the citizens, who as a general rule were pleasant and courteous to the soldiers. The General Casimir Pulaski monument erected to this hero of the American Revolution was of great interest to the soldiers.[37]

# 12

# The Carolinas

**The last leg of Sherman's campaign began when his armies started leaving Savannah on January 18, 1865, crossed into South Carolina, and headed north. While Sherman was traveling north, Confederate General Robert E. Lee would surrender his army to General Ulysses S. Grant at Appomattox, Virginia, and President Abraham Lincoln would be assassinated by John Wilkes Booth in Washington, D.C. The Confederate forces facing Sherman during the Carolinas Campaign were again led by Joseph E. Johnston, who replaced John Bell Hood after Hood's series of defeats near Atlanta, Georgia.**

Historians have not accorded the space to Sherman's operations in the Carolinas that the campaign would warrant. The march to the sea has been celebrated in story and song until it has diverted attention from the greater strategic movements and successful fighting in this final epoch of the war. Sherman said that in relative importance, the campaign in the Carolinas was to the march through Georgia as ten to one.

The large amount of rainfall during the initial weeks of the Carolina campaign, resulting in the high water in the Savannah River and the surrounding lowlands, would be a major factor in the progress of the campaign. The general plan was to have Slocum march to the left and west in the general direction of Augusta, while the right wing moved by an easterly route in the direction of Charleston. However, Sherman's intentions did not include either city in his line of march. This was merely his effort to make the Rebels divide their forces in order to guard each city. When the real objective of his army was realized, it would be too late for the much smaller armies of the Rebels to manage an effective defense. The relative size of Sherman's forces was 60, 079 compared to the Rebels with less than half that number. The 20th Corps at that time reported 13,434 present for duty.[1]

The movement began in the second week in January. The 3rd division, already on South Carolina soil, pushed forward to Hardeeville along the Charleston and Savannah R.R., and the 1st Division including the 107th New York followed it. The rest of the army was sent forward to the right to Pocatalico by water.[2]

On the morning of Wednesday, January the 18th, the 107th moved out at 8 a.m. at the head of their brigade with the 1st division of the 20th Army Corps. The 107th was now under the command of Colonel Hawley of the 3rd Wisconsin as Colonel Crane had gone home on leave. They marched through the city of Savannah and then across a pontoon bridge to Hutchinson Island and then to the South Carolina shore. They camped on grounds that were previously the camp of the 3rd Division. When the 3rd Division left, they foolishly burned the quarters they had constructed. Thus, the division to which the 107th belonged had to deal with the burned out remains.[3]

Continued heavy rains interfered greatly with their movements, and for a few days the high water actually had them surrounded. On the 19th they marched to Purrysburg on the Savannah River, which was four miles below Hardeeville. The rain had made the march most uncomfortable, and shortly after they went into camp near Purrysburg, the water rose so high in the river that all the country around them was under water. Their trains were unable to reach them, and some wagons were swept away by the rising water.

They were confined to their camp near Purrysburg for a week until the rains ceased, and the waters abated. Two days' march brought them to Robertsville, where they were to be joined by the rest of the Left Wing. However, instead of friendly blue coats, they found a respectable force of grey coats awaiting them and a lively fight ensued. The Rebs speedily retired after shelling from the batteries of 107th's division. Thereafter 107th went into camp and engaged in building a corduroy road down to the ferry.[4]

On the 19th, they didn't move until 2 p.m. The road was excellent, and they made good time. They camped at sundown near the town of Hardeeville. They moved at 9 a.m. in the pouring rain the next day and reached Hardeeville at 11 a.m. They moved on slowly as the road was flooded. They camped at 3 p.m. next to one of the channels of the Savannah River. The area was very muddy as it had continued to rain all day, and there was scarcely any dry wood for a fire. A transport loaded with supplies came up the river at dusk. It closely followed a U.S. navy gunboat. The transport was unloaded in the rain on the 21st and immediately returned to Savannah.

By noon time, it was again raining very hard, causing some of the men in the 107th to move their tents to higher ground. When it continued raining hard the next day, the 107th moved its entire camp. They heard that the Confederate Fort Fisher had been defeated on January 15, resulting in the capture of 1,700 prisoners, 70 cannons, and a large amount of munitions. On the 23rd it was still raining, and another transport came up with supplies. It continued raining all day, and there was water everywhere.

The rain finally stopped the next morning at 9 a.m. However, sickness was beginning to appear, with the cold and wind making things worse. On the 26th, the weather was very cold, and the men of the 107th and others in their brigade began building fireplaces to improve their situation. Corporal Guy Rathbone of Company B died of spotted fever (typhus) and was buried next to their camp.

The next day, orders came at 12 p.m. to pack up and move out. They marched until dusk. Where they finally made their camp, it was higher and dryer, but the weather remained very cold. On the 28th, the 107th New York moved ahead as an advanced guard. Company F was sent out on picket and did some foraging at the same time, returning with a quantity of potatoes and chickens. The regiment went into camp near a very fine residence just past 2:30 p.m. They received mail while there in camp. The weather had become mild, but it turned very cold that night. That morning wagons were again sent out for forage.

On the 30th, they moved at 8 a.m. and then halted at 10:30 when they heard skirmishing up ahead. They formed a battle line and moved on into Robertsville, but the Rebels had been driven out of the town and now were situated close by just beyond a swamp.

On Wednesday February 1, it was clear and warm as the regiment was busy that morning laying out a regular camp. They had a dress parade in the afternoon. That same day, the 14th Corps began its move into South Carolina when it crossed the Savannah River on a pontoon bridge three miles below Sister's Ferry. Company B of the 107th was detailed to forage the next day. On the 2nd, their brigade had a parade drill at 1 p.m., and Company B was successful at foraging and brought in hams and miscellaneous items on a wagon. The regiment received orders to move at 9 a.m. the next morning.

On February 3, they moved at 10 a.m. and marched only three miles before halting as the 3rd division was directly ahead of them. The combination of several swamps and the Rebels blocking the road with fallen trees made their progress very slow. The land in that area was mostly covered with pine trees that were often on fire for the purpose of obtaining turpentine. They marched at a slow pace after it became dark and didn't stop until 9 p.m. when they camped in a low wet place.

The next day, they moved at 6:30 a.m. and placed Companies F and B ahead as skirmishers, but Rebels were never sighted. They went into camp at 3 p.m. and shortly after that their forage unit returned with hogs and sweet potatoes. On February 5, they were assigned to guarding the wagon train. Their march took them along a stretch of bad roads and swamps. They were very surprised to pass a splendid house with a fine lawn just before dark. Shortly thereafter they reached the Bainville Pike, which turned out to be a much better road, and they were able to march at a faster pace. They went into camp at 8 p.m.

The next morning, they moved at 7 a.m. with the 1st division leading and their brigade in the rear. They halted often to let the wagon train catch up. They stopped at 4 p.m. and went into camp at a large and dry location. On the 7th, they moved at 7 a.m. and immediately had to cross a large swamp for a mile. On the other side, they found excellent Rebel fortifications but no Rebels. The weather turned as night fell with wind and rain. It rained all night and the next morning. They began marching that day without having had breakfast as it was impossible to start a fire. However, they had marched only one mile before stopping and preparing breakfast. They continued on and reached the Carolina and Atlanta Railroad, where their brigade went into camp.

Later that day, the 107th was sent up the road to a small village called Grahamsville where Companies B and F were detailed to guard private property for the remainder of the day. Such action typically meant that the property owner was a northerner. Guards placed at a nearby store found 50 pounds of plug tobacco. The tobacco was handed out to each man as they passed in the line of march. While they were marching through that town, someone set fire to a large quantity of bailed cotton. The fire put the town in danger, and it was necessary for the march to halt while they put out the fire.

On February 10, they moved at 8:30 a.m. toward Blackville, and they had a hard time getting through a swamp with the headquarters' wagons. They went into camp at 8 p.m. The next day was spent tearing up rails, piling them on top of ties, and setting the ties on fire. When rails were hot enough, they bent them until the ends crossed.

The Edisto River was reached by a different road on the 12th, and thereafter they crossed a small stream while moving through a swamp. They were held up several times waiting for the troops in their front to get out of the way. The next day, they were assigned to guarding the train, and their division was placed at the rear. Their camp that evening was located near the Edisto River. On the 14th they had to wait for the entire train to cross the river as they were still positioned at its rear. The next day, the 107th's brigade was positioned at a crossroad to guard against the possibility of an attack from either side of the line of march. They camped at the end of that day at a very poor location that was made worse by the rain. In addition, there was neither any quantity of wood nor water available. To make a bad situation even worse, they were placed on quarter rations of hard bread, sugar, and coffee.

They were assigned to guarding the train on the 16th, and their brigade was located at the rear of the train. Their route that day took them through a large swamp that slowed down their progress considerably. During the course of the entire day, they saw no sign of human life even though they were nearing Columbia, the capitol of South Carolina. The 20th Corps, being in the left wing of the campaign, would pass the capital on the opposite side of the river. However, the men were each issued 60 rounds at ammunition as a precaution. They did hear cannonading as they neared the city. The regiment sent out members of Company F for forage along with other brigade teams. However, they only succeeded in bringing back a few potatoes. It was evident that the 14th Corps, who was in their advance, had cleaned out any forage that had been in the area.

On the 18th they sent out another regimental forage group while they were halted as the 14th Corps crossed the river. They crossed the river the next day and camped just beyond it. Their foragers were successful this day, bringing home two beef cattle. They moved at 3p.m., with their division in the rear of the 3rd Division. They continued marching in the rear of the 3rd Division, and during that day, they heard that the right wing had left Columbia in ashes.

Their foragers continued to be very successful, and on the 20th, they brought in a wagon load of meal and flour. They remained in place that day while the 3rd division crossed the river. The next day, they moved to cross the river. The cavalry went first and the infantry second with the 107th in the lead. The river at this point was 230 yards wide and after crossing it, they were eight miles from Winnsboro. On the 22nd, the 2nd Division was placed in the lead with 107th guarding the train. As they neared Winnsboro, the land became more cleared and populated with nice houses. They reached Winnsboro at noon and went into camp. While they were getting situated, the men of Company I captured a Rebel lieutenant who was found close to their camp, and they put him in the brig. Forage details from 150th New York, 3rd Wisconsin, and the 13th New Jersey were ahead of the advance guard. Consequently, they were disciplined, and the forage taken from them.

The 107th was detailed on Feb 23rd to guard 50 wagons of the train. They were still passing through a populated area, and while their foragers were getting substantial amounts of meat, potatoes, and flour, it was not enough to satisfy the needs of the regiment. They camped at 7pm ¾ mile from the Wateree River. They had marched twenty miles that day and were very tired. The next day was spent crossing the river on a pontoon bridge.

February 25th turned out to be a disaster of sorts. It rained very hard all day. They moved out before having breakfast, and their forage detail came back completely empty handed. Later that same day, their corps took the wrong road and met head on with the 17th Corps. The rain continued all night and didn't stop until nine the next morning. Conditions were so bad because of the rain that they did not move that day. However, their foragers were finally successful and brought in considerable meal and meat, which they needed very badly. It began raining again at dark and it continued all night.

On the 27th, the rain slowed, and they moved in the afternoon after the road had been corduroyed. The next morning, they were detailed to guard the train's 1st Division, which passed the 2nd and 3rd Divisions. They crossed Hanging Rock Creek at 10 a.m. and camped at a nice location just two miles beyond the creek. That evening men from their regiment who had escaped from the Rebs found their way into their camp. These men had been able to escape while they were being transferred from one location to another.[5]

On March 12, Edward Kendall wrote home and recounted his own story of the 107th New York's travels during February. He wrote:

> We have lived wholly off the land since the 10th of February, drawing no rations whatever save a little coffee and sugar. We have had plenty of everything needful. The country through which we have passed has been stripped clean of corn, meat, potatoes, cattle and horses of which the latter with mules we have captured a large number. Our regiment forage detail on one day captured over forty good horses and mules and the 150th NY of our brigade captured over seventy.
>
> Our corps left Robertsville and moved rapidly striking the Augusta & Charleston RR about dusk on the 7th of February one mile east of Graham Turnout. Our regiment was ordered on to the station and camped there for the night. Found plenty of forage and food along with 4 or

500 bales of cotton which was destroyed. We moved along the railroad tearing up the track, twisting the rails to until we reached Williston. On the 11th we left the railroad crossing the south Edisto River at Duncan's Bridge. On the 13th we crossed the north Edisto. On the 17th we crossed the Saluda River 12 miles above Columbia. On the 20th crossed the Broad River. On the 20th passed through Winnsboro a very pretty little town. On the 23rd crossed the Catawba.[6]

For a long time during this march, there was a great rivalry among the "Darkies" as to who among them were the best dancers, singers, and even wrestlers. They came from Georgia, South Carolina, and Virginia. There was no question that they were far more talented than the white entertainers in blackface who performed in minstrel shows. These men from the piney lands of South Carolina, where the stage and auditorium were mother earth and the footlights were pitch pine knots or fence rails, had no rivals. During the halts of the wagon train at night, they would form a circle and while one of them did a song and dance, the others would clap time and join in the chorus. One of their songs went like this: "My old missus promised me, when she died, she'd set me free, Now the old girl is dead and gone. And left old Sambo hilling up corn, then my high bold hoss running around, Walk Jawbone, Jennie come along. All in all, they furnished a world of amusement and helped to while away many tedious hours."[7]

It was raining on March 1st, the 107th was guarding the wagon train, and the road was being corduroyed most of the way. The area was sparsely settled, but foragers were successful and came in with hams, flour, and dried apples. The next day, the 107th was in the advance of the 20th Corps and crossed the great Pee Dee River at Cheraw, SC.[8]

Each day, foragers were sent out, and March 2 was no exception. That day Private William R. Hammond of Company A, along with three comrades, started out on a foraging expedition. They did not return that night but stayed at a nearby plantation. The next afternoon, they ran across another forager from the 107th and sent him back to the regiment with a horse well loaded with ham, sweet potatoes, dried peaches, etc. That night, they stayed at a plantation not very far from Rockingham, NC. They started out after breakfast, and after going a mile or so, rode up a lane to a house and to talk to two ladies in their yard. Looking down the road in the direction they were headed, they saw a squad of soldiers coming in their direction. The ladies asked them if they were their men, remarking that Confederate soldiers had been there yesterday. Hammond and his comrades responded that Union troops had camped just back up the road a little way and were confident the men were Kilpatrick's Cavalry because of their uniforms. The troopers continued up the lane toward Hammond and the others. When they reached the four men, the troopers all drew their revolvers and ordered them to surrender. The Rebs made them dismount their horses and took their arms. The prisoners were then made to mount two mules, two of them to each mule. Then they marched them to the Rebel Joe Wheeler's headquarters.

On the way they stopped for breakfast. The leader of the squad of eleven Rebels was a sergeant. The sergeant noticed Hammond's boots and said, "That's a good pair of boots, Yank. I think that they will fit me. Take them off and let me try them on." Hammond replied, "No, I don't want to part with them. Father sent them to me from home, and I want to keep them." The sergeant kept repeating his order for Hammond to take them off, and Hammond kept telling him that his Pa sent them to him, and he wanted to keep them. Finally, the sergeant drew his revolver, cocked it, swore at Hammond, saying, "Yank, if you don't pull those boots off, I'll put a hole through you." Hammond decided he had better take the boots off. In return for the $15.00 pair of boots, the sergeant gave Hammond an old pair of woman's shoes that were rundown at the heel and nearly worn out. With the trade completed, the Rebs remounted their prisoners again two to a mule, and with two guards, sent them off to General Wheeler's headquarters, which was not far away.

When nearly there, they dismounted, and their guards said to them, "Well boys, we will have to prowl you." Hammond and the others didn't know what "prowl" meant, but they soon found out. The Rebs commenced going through their pockets. They all had some money, and each had a watch. The Rebs took all that they could find. Hammond lost a good jackknife and a fine felt hat that he had received with the boots. However, they didn't get Hammond's money. When they went to search him, he pulled his pants pockets wrong side out to show them he didn't have any money. His money was in a thin pair of pants under his army pants.

Later they were interviewed by General Wheeler, and after he was done with them, he sent them with two guards to Wade Hampton's headquarters. The two guards were mounted while the prisoners had to walk. They traveled all day in a light rain and were unable to find Hampton or his headquarters. Just as it was getting dark, they ran into Wheeler's Cavalry and were put under his provost guard with thirteen other prisoners. They were put into an unfinished slave shanty that had no doors or windows. None of the four 107th men had blankets, but they were able to stand around the fire to dry out and get warm. Then they lay on the floor of the shanty for as long as they could stand it. The next morning, they had quite an appetite, not having had a mouthful to eat in twenty-four hours. However, the Rebs gave them nothing to eat. They picked up some corn that the horses and mules had left. Then they got a tin from one of the other prisoners, roasted the corn, and ate it.

They marched all that day and into the night. It drizzled all the next day, but they got even wetter when they had to wade two creeks up to their waists. They were still marching near midnight when they heard a wagon train off through the woods to the right and going in the same direction that they were. They thought that it might be one of their trains, as they supposed that Wheeler would have his trains in their front.

Soon they heard firing up ahead. Their guards cocked their guns and ordered them off to the left into the woods. In the darkness, Hammond laid down beside a log and soon was asleep. He woke up shivering with the cold and could neither see nor hear anyone except the train that he had heard before. He looked around in the dark, listened, and crept across the road and through the woods until he came to the train. At first, he could not tell if it was a Union train or Confederate. After walking along the edge of the woods for some distance, he asked a driver what train it was. The driver replied, "First Division cavalry train, sah." Hammond said, "Whose trains?" The driver said, "Massa Kilpatricks, sah." Hammond felt very much relieved and happy.

A wagon master came along, and Hammond told him who he was. The wagon master got off his horse and told Hammond to get on. He got in a wagon and offered Hammond enough hardtack to keep him eating until daylight. For once the hardtack tasted very good to Hammond. As he sat there, he thought to himself that he had been a prisoner for nearly two days without anything to eat but some parched corn and one half of a small tea biscuit.

It was now March 7. Soon after daylight, the train stopped for breakfast. Hammond took breakfast with some of the train guards, one of whom had an extra horse that he let him ride. He rode along until about noon, when he met one of the three with whom he had been captured. They immediately started out for their regiment. They found the 107th the next morning at about nine o'clock. The other two boys made it back to the regiment two days later, and they were all right.[9]

While Hammond and his fellow foragers were away from the 107th, the regiment had a brief encounter with the Rebels. On March 3, the brigade approached the Chesterfield courthouse and had a brisk but brief skirmish with a Rebel cavalry unit under General Butler. They continued to move forward beyond the courthouse. As they approached a bridge over a small stream, they came face to face with a force of infantry and artillery. At that point the brigade of the 107th was ordered to advance against the Rebel force. A dashing charge and a sharp fight of a few minutes sufficed to drive the Rebels back, and they took possession of the bridge or what was left of it. The Rebels had set fire to it as the 107th with its brigade approached. Their opponents at the bridge proved to be an advance unit for a larger force at Cheraw under Johnston, Hardee, and Hampton. However, they were put to the test the following day by the 17th Corps. The Rebels lost the fight, along with 25 cannon and a large number of military stores, arms, etc.

They marched to Sneedsboro on the 4th. It was just over the border into North Carolina and near the Great Pee Dee River. They laid there for a day of rest and then marched six miles along the river to near Cheraw. There a pontoon bridge was constructed, and they crossed the river. They were now in the pine woods district that bordered the coastline of the Carolinas. Their day long march continued through a magnificent forest of pines. The trees rose, naked of branches, for eighty or ninety feet and then were crowned with a tuft of pure green. They were wide apart, and frequently two columns of troops or wagons could be seen marching side by side. The ground was clear of underbrush and covered with the needles that had fallen from the trees for many years. At night when all were still in the camp, the wind through the treetops made magnificent music. Their next destination was Fayetteville on the Cape Fear River. The roads would have been excellent except for the rain that began to fall. The sandy roads now resembled quicksand. Foraging also became difficult as this area was very sparsely settled. There was little farming as this area relied mostly on tar, pitch, and turpentine for income. This area was also more dangerous because the enemy's cavalry was bolder and more numerous.[10]

On Wednesday, March 8, a group of twenty soldiers from the 107th New York regiment moved out at 8 a.m. on a foraging mission. Rations were dangerously low, and foragers under the command of Lieut. Abram Whitehorn were sent out. In addition to the enlisted men, the group included Captain Fox, Adjutant Benedict, and Sergeant Wells of Company K. Foraging would be difficult as they were in the midst of pine trees being gouged for turpentine. Many of the trees were on fire, creating a nasty atmosphere along with the rain that fell all the previous day and into the evening.

The foragers made their way north from the main line of march in the direction of Rockingham. They had gone a great distance from the main body of troops when they entered a fenced field. Moving across the field, they looked for an opening in the fence on the other side. They had almost crossed the field when they spotted a large cavalry unit in Federal blue uniforms. However, as the group came closer, it became apparent that they were Rebels. The Rebels had evidently spotted them first and were moving to cut off any escape. Some of the Rebel cavalrymen dismounted and stationed themselves where the foragers had entered the field. They opened fire, hitting several of the men who were attempting to escape. However, Major Charles Fox, 1st Lieutenant/Adjutant Samuel Benedict, and Sergeant David Wells turned quickly and beat a hasty retreat. Their horses proved much faster than those of the Rebels, and they escaped. The three men who had been shot from their horses included Pvt. William Williams of Company C, Cpl. William Dickerson of Company E. and Private Charles Cole of Company E. Williams and Dickerson were killed, while Cole was severely wounded.

Those captured included:

| | |
|---|---|
| Pvt. William Gossler Co. A | 2nd Lt. Abram Whitehorn Co. H |
| Pvt. Peter Weed Co. A | Pvt. Robert Akin Co. H |
| Pvt. Joseph McKay Co. B | Pvt. John Eveland Co. H |
| Pvt. Thomas Ford Co. C | Pvt. Augustus Foster Co. H |
| Pvt. Stephen Huber Co. D | Pvt. Joseph Darrin Co. I |
| Pvt. Henry Seibert Co. G | Pvt. James Turrell Co. I |
| Pvt. John Stamp Co. G | Pvt. Edward Wheeler Co. I |

Private Charles Cole had been shot from his horse by a Rebel who had jumped up from behind a bush and shot him point blank in the right side as he rode by. He was knocked from his horse and fell unconscious. The Rebels, thinking him dead, removed his shoes and clothing and left him lying in the field. Those that had escaped saw Cole fall from his horse, and they too assumed that he had been killed. Fortunately, the minié ball had passed through his body without hitting any vital organs.

Shortly after the Confederates left the field with their captives, two barefoot women and a Black man from a nearby farm found Cole. They were preparing to bury him when they noticed a spark of life. The man picked up Cole and carried him back to their farm, placing him in a rude hut with a dirt floor. The hut was behind the barn and in a place where few would venture.

While the remainder of the 107th continued its march through North Carolina, the story of Private Charles Cole would continue out of their sight. Back in the town of Catlin in Chemung County, NY, Cole's blind mother began to have visions about her son. The family had received notification from Charles' commanding officer that he had been killed. While the family grieved, his mother, Nancy Bailey Cole, assured them that there had been a mistake. She told the family she had seen in a vision that Charles had been shot, but that two barefoot women and a Black man had found him and were taking care of him. The family reconfirmed his death with the army but could not get his mother to accept his death.

As time went on, Nancy kept on giving progress reports about Charles, and she would not allow any talk of his death in her presence. When she indignantly refused to consent to memorial services, the family humored her and secretly had a service performed. She kept on with almost daily reports about her son. The family was very gentle with her even though it was disconcerting to them while they mourned the loss of Charles. She was consistent in her descriptions and very specific about the details of her visions. The rest of the family could hardly ignore her, as she was active with household chores despite her blindness. She described the rude hut with the dirt floor and how Charles was feeling better and sitting up.

One morning she announced at breakfast, "Charles has started home now," and that a Black man helped him and cooked warm food for him at night. Nancy Bailey Cole had never seen a Black man even when she had sight. This new detail made her visions seem even more bizarre to the family. To make matters even worse, she began leaving a sandwich and burning a candle in the kitchen window. The family worried that the candle was a fire hazard and that the sandwich would draw mice. She would become furious if she found the candle blown out or the sandwich taken. The family ultimately decided to let her do what she wanted. It was easier to do that than face her wrath. She was aware that they did not believe her visions, but they did not shake her faith.

In the meantime, Charles had slowly improved in health with the aid of herbal medicines and nourishment. Eventually, he set out with the aid of the Black man for Wilmington, NC. The man helped him get there, often getting food from the Black communities on the way. Once in Wilmington, Charles was given some clothes and shoes that were too small, requiring him to cut out the toes. Here the man turned back, leaving Charles to go on alone. While in Wilmington, Charles took the opportunity to write home, telling his family that he was all right and on his way home. On he walked to Washington, where he found the city in chaos with all variety of soldiers and civilians wandering about.

He reported to the army, hoping to get enough money for transportation home, but the army red tape stymied his efforts. In frustration, he began walking and working his way home. Before he left, he again wrote to his family. However, his family had not received any of his letters, and to all except his mother he was gone, a victim of the war.

One morning in June when the family came to breakfast, Nancy hushed everyone saying, "Charles is home." They all exchanged knowing looks, fearing that she was getting worse. To humor her, they all went to the spare room. There on the floor, dirty and unkempt, lay Charles sound asleep. In their great excitement, they all fell upon him. His mother had one terrible moment as she felt his face. She had only known his face as clean-shaven as it was when he went off to war, and now it was covered with a full beard. Otherwise, her visions had been totally correct, even down to his open-toed shoes.[11]

*Author's Note: All those captured, with the exception of Private Akin, survived their captivity. Their service records for the most part are incomplete and do not document their return to the regiment. Private Akin's record states that he died on the date of the event.*[12]

On March 9, Adjutant Benedict reported the capture of Lieutenant Whitehorn and the other foragers. It rained all the next day, and the 107th and its brigade, while in the rear of the 20th Corps, crossed the head waters of Great Pee Dee River. They were greatly hampered by the roads and made only six miles that day. They went into camp at 10 p.m., and all were wet and worn out. On the 11th, they moved out at 5 a.m. and had to wade through a swamp before crossing the Lumber River. They found the road almost impassable and were forced to corduroy most of it. However, later they did find a nice place to camp. The weather cleared the next day, and they moved quickly toward Fayetteville.[13]

In a letter written on March 12 to his future wife Nettie, Edwin Weller of the 107th asked her to tell Daniel Tracy that Charley Cole was wounded and taken prisoner by the enemy on March 8 while out foraging. Tracy ran a dry goods store in Havana (now Montour Falls) and was married to Nettie's sister Louise. Weller sent this word so that Tracy might inform Cole's father, who was one of his customers.[14]

On Sunday, March 13, the 107th had inspection, and afterwards Colonel Crane went into Fayetteville. He remarked on his return that it was as large as Atlanta. A steam tug arrived that same day, thus opening communications with Wilmington and allowing mail to be sent out. The next day, General Sherman arrived and established his headquarters in an arsenal just outside of town. The town had only one principal street and the buildings were old and dingy. Later in the day, the 107th New York along with the 1st Division passed in review for Sherman and then marched out of the town. They crossed the river four miles up the road to Raleigh and camped. They remained in camp on the 15th. Nothing of any consequence occurred that day except a minor skirmish with some Rebels by a foraging group. The next day proved to be reminiscent of their earlier marches. They moved out at 8 a.m., and it began raining at noon, when they stopped for dinner. Afterwards they moved on and camped near the Cape Fear River. At 7 p.m., they were ordered to move up the road and waded through mud and knee-deep water for five miles. They finally camped behind a series of breastworks that had been put up by Kilpatrick's cavalry because of a large force of Rebels in their front. Their brigade then relieved the cavalry.[15]

On March 15, Captain Robert McDowell of the 141st New York and a member of the map-making staff of the 20th Army Corps was stopped at about noon along with the entire train in order to allow Kilpatrick's cavalry to move to the head of the train. Soon thereafter, rain set in, and his group sought shelter in an old cooper shop (barrel shop). There they found a Rebel note addressed to General Sherman that was written on a barrel stave and asked for "Mr. Corporal Kilpatricko." It stated that they were not regularly armed with the Spencer repeating rifle, and they needed rubber blankets, etc., for the summer campaign. They urged General Sherman to trot out Mr. Corporal Kilpatricko in order that they might procure these articles. The writer of the note signed himself, "A Rebel." It was duly forwarded to General Sherman. McDowell further noted in his journal that Kilpatrick was regarded with contempt by the Union as well as the enemy.[16]

The battle of Averasboro was fought on March 16, 1865, four miles south of a little hamlet of the same name at a point on the Cape Fear River Road that went from Fayetteville to Raleigh at a crossroads that moved off towards Goldsboro. The 107th had been marching three days towards Raleigh with the cavalry in the advance and the 1st and 3rd divisions of the 20th Corps following. On the afternoon of the 15th, the cavalry ran into a strong body of Rebel infantry. On the morning of March 16, the 1st Division hurried forward to their assistance, and the 3rd Division with their artillery was soon brought into the battle. The enemy was in a strong position and held it for almost three hours until the Union "Buffalo Battery" of Newkirk and Winegar that was formerly commanded by Cothran began shelling them. At that point, Case's brigade of the 3rd Division moved to the left and charged the Rebels' right flank, driving their whole line back in confusion. The result was the capture of three pieces of artillery and 200 prisoners.

The Rebels fell back a half a mile. They were joined by additional troops and occupied a strong line of entrenchments. The battle reached new heights when McLaw's division, assisted by Wheeler's and Hampton's cavalry, made a fierce charge on the right flank of the 107th's division and contacted Kilpatrick's cavalry, forcing it back. As a result, they gained a position that enabled them to enfilade the Union line. The 107th's brigade suffered severely from this crossfire but maintained its position until Kilpatrick rallied his men and regained his position.

Portions of the 14th Corps came up during the afternoon, and a general advance of the Union line ensued. The enemy was forced into its works, and darkness concluded the day's conflict. When the morning dawned, the enemy had vanished. The 3rd Division followed their path as far as Averasboro and found much evidence of the Rebels' hasty retreat. There were large numbers of dead and wounded along the road and in houses.

One hundred and twenty-eight of their dead were buried by the 107th and other units, and 78 of their wounded were left in the Union field hospital with enough supplies to keep them comfortable until locals came to their aid. The loss on the Union side was 77 killed and 477 wounded. Of this number, more than half were from the 1st Division, and the 107th's brigade and regiment suffered proportionately. Among the killed were Captain Grafton and Lieutenant Starrow of the 2nd Massachusetts. Colonel Morse of that regiment was wounded, as were Captain Woodford and Lieutenant Wattles of the brigade's staff. In the 107th, the casualties were as listed below.

Pvt. John Morgan Co. G          Pvt. Elias Rinker Co. E
Cpl. William R. Christler Co. C    Pvt. Gottfried Oelschlaeger Co. E

The 107th New York crossed the Lumber River on March 9, and it was an experience that would never be forgotten. The men approached the river through a swamp that was under water. Owing to the heavy rains, it was impossible to tell where the river began or where it ended. As a result, the men thought before they reached the other side that they had struck it lengthwise rather than crosswise. They entered Fayetteville two days later. They found and destroyed numerous stores of military munitions and facilities there. Shortly thereafter, a federal boat arrived from Wilmington with the first news they had heard from the outside world since leaving Savannah. In addition, they were able to send letters north.

They left Fayetteville and marched three days straight towards Raleigh with their cavalry in the advance and the first and third divisions of the 20th Corps following. They were four miles south of the village of Averasboro at a crossroads on the Cape Fear River Road that led to Goldsboro. On the afternoon of March 15, their cavalry ran into a strong body of Rebel infantry. The next morning, the first division with the 107th moved quickly ahead to aid the cavalry along with the third division and their artillery. The enemy was in a strong position and held the Union forces in check for almost three hours. During that time, the Rebel batteries were silenced. Finally, the Union forces executed a flanking movement on the Rebel right, and they were driven back in confusion, losing three pieces of artillery and had two hundred men taken prisoner.

The Rebels fell back a half mile into a strong set of entrenchments with additional troops and the cavalry units of Wheeler and Hampton. During the action, the Rebels succeeded in flanking the Union line and causing considerable damage to the brigade of the 107th. Kilpatrick's cavalry initiated a strong repulse, and the Rebels retreated to their entrenchments.

During the afternoon, the 14th corps moved into the Union lines, and the

Rebels were neutralized as darkness fell on the 16th. There was no further activity during the night, and when morning of the 17th came, the enemy had disappeared. The 3rd division of the 20th Corps followed the Rebel route of retreat as far as Averasboro and along the way found many dead and wounded on the road and in the houses. The Union forces buried 128 of the Rebel dead on the battlefield, while 78 Rebel wounded were left in the Union field hospital with enough supplies to last them until their friends could reach them.

The Union 20th Corps' loss was 77 killed and 477 wounded. Of that number, more than half were of the division of the 107th. Their brigade and regiment suffered the same number in proportion. The killed and wounded in the 107th numbered between 20 and 30.

The following is a list of the 107th NY casualties by company:

**Company A**: Cpls. Charles Hemingway, leg, severe; Bartholomew Sullivan, hip, severe; John Hall, leg, severe; Pvts. Martin Glynn, leg, since amputated; John Ilitz, arm, severe; Nelson Downy, thigh, severe.

**Company B**: Cpl. Cornelius Murray, hip severe. **Company C**: Cpls. Charles F. Abbey, leg amputated; Wm. R. Christer, leg, since died; Pvts. Martin Byrns, shoulder and chest; Lewis Mathias, thigh, severe; Giles McMillen, leg, severe.

**Company E**: Pvts. Elias Rinker, neck, since died, Alfred C. Hawkins, leg, since died; Harland E. Hasiland, head, slight; Thomas Heckner, leg, slight.

**Company F**: 1st Sgt. Jefferson Young, thigh and arm, severe. Pvt. John W. Corson, leg, slight.

**Company G**: 1st Lt. Jacob Saltsman, head severe; 1st Sgt Jefferson Young, thigh and arm severe; 1st Sgt. Geo. Browning, wrist severe. Cpl. John Greene, head, severe. Pvts. A.B. Morgan, both legs, severe; John Morgan, bowels, since died.

**Company H**: Thomas Putnam, thigh, since died.

**Company I**: Cpls. Geo. Wescott, side, slight; Charles Wright, side, slight. Pvt. Henry Johnson, shoulder, severe. (Havana Journal, May 13, 1865)

During the Carolinas campaign, a number of 107th New York men were captured. On February 23, Company B, Pvt. Patrick Tranor; Company D, Pvt. Wm. Lorell; and Comoany F, Pvt. Wm. De Waters. On March 8, Company H, Lt. Abram Whitehorn and Cpl. Augustus C. Foster."

Following the battle of Averasboro, Johnston assembled a force of 25,000 at Smithfield on the flank of the path the Union forces, where he was hoping to flank them and destroy the left wing of Sherman's army. On the morning of March 19, he attacked Morgan's division of the 14th Corps. That corps lost three pieces of artillery, and many of its men were taken prisoner. Carlin's division of the 14th Corps, and Ward's division of the 20th Corps, and the division of the 107th moved to support the Union line. The situation when the 107th arrived was extremely critical. However, when they moved into the line, they were able to check the Rebel advance. What appeared initially to be a disaster was slowed, but a tense situation continued. The 107th and all of the other Union regiments slept on their arms that night. During the night, the 15th Corps came up. When the morning of the 20th came, the 17th Corps arrived, and the entire strength of Sherman's army was ready for a fight. A battle ensued, but early in the afternoon, the greater size of the Union forces allowed for the beginning of a flanking movement, and the Rebels withdrew from the battlefield towards Smithfield that night. The 107th New York had survived with none killed in their last action of the American Civil War, which occurred on Monday, March 19, 1865, at the battle of Bentonville.

The 107th New York entered Goldsboro on March 21, leaving the enemy to fall back to the Raleigh area. They needed rest and repairs, and the few days that they would remain there were none too long for that purpose. In addition to the 20th Corps, Terry's 10th Corps had arrived from Wilmington as well as the 23rd Corps under Schofield, who had been with them in Atlanta. It was an opportunity for the soldiers of the 107th to visit with friends in these other commands.

The 107th spent March 22 cutting down trees and placing them in the front of their works, afterward throwing up dirt to further strengthen them. Later in the morning, the Rebels charged their line, attempting to force them out of their works, but were unable to do so. It was quiet the remainder of the day, and they received an order to be ready to move at 5 a.m. the next morning. However, their supply train and wounded would be leaving that night to travel to Goldsboro. The next day, it was raining hard, causing the 107th, along with the other troops, not to move until 10 a.m. It wasn't long before the Rebels drove in their videttes. This caused some excitement, but soon all was quiet. Captain Bachman, who had been in their skirmish line, came back to the main group feeling quite ill.

It began to rain hard again during the afternoon. The Rebels made another attack at dusk. While the attack did not amount to anything, the men were instructed to sleep with their arms, regardless. The constant rain caused the men to refer to it as "acorn rain battlefield" because the 14th Army Corps' badge was an acorn. It had been a trying day for the 107th, and all were worn out. They again received orders to move out at 5 a.m.

On the 23rd, their pack animals were sent off first. Their pickets came in, and they were replaced by cavalry. The regiment did not move until 7 a.m. They crossed the Goldsboro Road and passed the hospital that now only contained Rebel wounded who were being moved out.

They crossed the main road and stopped for dinner at 12 p.m. After dinner they had to wait for the wagons train to get out of the way before they could resume marching. The road was very rough and had to be corduroyed nearly all the way. The regiment was detailed for picket and marched ahead of the brigade. The remainder of the day passed without incident.

The next day they moved at 8 a.m. and soon crossed a swamp. They marched at a fast pace in order to keep ahead of the 15th Corps. They passed the advance of the 17th Army Corps and halted in a large field at noon for dinner. The wind began to blow, filling the air with sand. After dinner, they moved toward the river. They halted after crossing and then moved along with the 150th New York to the rear of the train.

On the 25th, they were awakened at 1 a.m. and ordered to pack their animals. This action led to their complaints that being on a campaign gets worse every day. They finally moved at 7 a.m. and reached Goldsboro at 11 a.m. They found it surrounded by large fortifications, and they set up a temporary camp. Their rations were very low, and meals consisted of just small portions of raw corn and meal. The next day, they went about laying out a permanent camp, and Sherman issued orders stating that they were to remain at their current location indefinitely.[17]

Also, on March 25, Lt. Edwin Weller wrote to his fiancée from Goldsboro, NC:

> We are in camp, arrived here yesterday around noon and occupy this city now. Since we left Fayetteville, we have had two hard fights, but we whipped the enemy badly. In the last fight we captured all of the enemy's hospitals with a large number of sick and wounded along with several pieces of artillery and horses. We have heard nothing of Lt. Whitehorn who was captured. I shall send you a list of casualties including prisoners from our last campaign to the Havana Journal for relatives. Our loss in our entire army in these last two engagements will probably reach one thousand killed and wounded and missing with another thousand taken prisoner by rebel cavalry, mostly when foraging. I estimate that they took between 1 and 2,000 prisoners during the campaign. Many federal prisoners of the Rebels escaped when they were being moved from prison to prison.[18]

A train went to Kingston for supplies on March 26 because their rations were very low. They were living on only corn and meal. The 27th was spent making their camp more habitable and to be uniform and conform to certain measurements. The tents were to be 8ft × 10ft with 3ft sides. Later in the day, supplies were delivered to the camp by boat from Wilmington and distributed to the men. In addition, there was a large delivery of mail. The next day, the men of the brigade were still hard at work getting their tents ship shape. They now had daily mail delivery at 4 p.m. When the camp was finally finished, it was clean and in a pleasant location on high ground out of the mud.

The 107th New York and the 150th New York, a Duchess County regiment, shared picket duty on the 29th. There was a minor event with Rebels at the outer perimeter of the camp where the Federal troops were herding cattle. Otherwise, it was quiet, and thoughts were turning to home and family.

On April 1, the regiment remained in camp, but the general feeling among them was that they would be moving soon. The men were very much surprised when it was announced that General Joseph A. Mower was taking command of 20th Corps from General Alpheus Williams. Williams then returned to command the 1st or Red Star Division of the 20th Corps. There was little activity over the next three days except for a corps review held on the 5th.

The next day, a rumor spread that Richmond, the capital of the Confederacy, and another Confederate stronghold, Petersburg, had fallen to Grant. The camp was the scene of a tumultuous amount of celebrating and nearly everyone was drunk. The general celebration included the firing of salutes, muskets, and rockets that out did any Fourth of July they ever experienced. Their enthusiasm knew no bounds, and they were eager to go for Johnston forthwith and finish up the war.[19] Things in the camp returned to normal the next several days, and on the 9th, they understood that Sherman had received an order from Grant to push Johnston just as he, Grant, was pushing Lee to surrender.

On April 10th, the 2nd brigade of the 107th moved at daylight in rear of the 1st Brigade, leading the 20th Corps through Goldsboro back toward Fayetteville by way of the road to Smithville. The heat of the day had the effect of the road being strewn with blankets and overcoats that were shed by the soldiers in blue. They camped at dusk in sight of Smithville. The next day, they were detailed to guard the wagon train. They passed through Smithville and crossed the Neuse River at 4 p.m. and went into camp. That same day, they had heard that Lee had surrendered to Grant, and the men went wild with joy. The next day they moved at 8 a.m. and were still detailed to guard the wagon train. They also participated in building some sections of corduroy road.

They reached Raleigh on the 14th at 11 a.m. and camped one mile south of the city. Over the next several weeks, they heard all sorts of rumors as well real news. First, they heard that Johnston had surrendered. Loud cheering broke among the 107th boys, but that news proved inaccurate. Then on April 17th, they heard the sad news about the assassination of President Lincoln and the attempt on the life Secretary Seward. Many in the 107th vowed vengeance on the South. The next day, they heard that the surrender agreement between Sherman and Johnston had not been approved by the president. On the 22nd, the 107th and the rest of the 20th Corps assembled in Raleigh for a review by General Sherman. The surrender agreement for Johnston was approved on the 26th. A general order to proceed to Washington was announced four days later, along with an order to behave themselves on the march.[20]

# 13

# The Last March,
# the Grand Review, and Home

**The 10th and 23rd Corps were to remain in North Carolina for garrison duty, and the remaining corps that were part of the Armies of Tennessee and Georgia, 65,000 strong, were to march north through Virginia and on to Washington, D.C., where they would participate in the Grand Review. The Army of the Potomac, 80,000 strong, marched in the Grand Review parade on May 23, and the armies of Tennessee and Georgia marched down Pennsylvania Avenue on the 24th. After the review, the 107th NY would arrive home in about two weeks' time.**

The 107th New York and the remainder of the armies of Tennessee and Georgia broke camp at 5 a.m. on Sunday April 30 and marched thirteen miles to the Neuse River. They crossed the river, marched an additional fifteen miles, and made camp at 4:30 p.m. Later they mustered for two months' pay. The following day, they broke camp at 7 a.m. and marched fifteen miles to the Tar River and bivouacked at 6 p.m. They were issued two days' rations of oats. On May 2, they broke camp at 6 a.m., crossed the Tar River on a pontoon bridge, and marched twenty miles. They bivouacked at 6 p.m. on the Hamsun's plantation and mail was distributed. They broke camp at 5:30 a.m. on May 3 and marched eighteen miles, passing through Williamsboro. They crossed over the majestic Roanoke River and camped on the Virginia side at 7 p.m.[1] On the state line was a board nailed to a tree upon which someone had written, "Carry me back to old Virginny." As the boys of the 107th passed by it, they took up the refrain and seemed scarcely less pleased to enter the state than they were a year or two before.[2]

On the May 4, they broke camp at 6 a.m. and crossed both Allen's Creek and the Meherrin River at Stafford's Bridge. They marched a total of twenty-two miles that day. The next day, it was cloudy and hazy with a little rain. They broke camp at 8 a.m., and their march of nineteen miles took them to the banks of the Nottaway River, where they camped for the night. The weather improved the next day; it was sunny and warm. They crossed both the big and little Nottaway Rivers, passed through a village, and were watched by many residents. They marched a total of fourteen miles and camped at Wellsville Station.[3] During that day, the word was passed around that John Wilkes Booth, the man who had killed the president, had been shot. They were

224

amazed at the amount of damage that had been caused by the Army of the Potomac.[4] On Sunday, May 7, they went out foraging in the early morning and obtained two loads of corn fodder for brigade headquarters. Edwin Weller took dinner at a Mrs. Fisk's. All told, they marched twenty miles and crossed the Appomattox River. They camped at Clover Hill for the night.[5] The pace had been very fast and brutal on the men, but most of the officers were mounted. That day, they heard that several of the men in the 14th Corps had died.[6]

Lt. Edwin Weller was assigned to lead an ongoing foraging detail that primarily traveled along a parallel road to the main column. Whenever they found grain that they could purchase, they sent one of their men to the main column so that wagons could be brought to their location and loaded with the grain. Weller enjoyed the duty because their smaller unit could take its time and stop at the plantations along the way. They could also take meals at any plantation they were near during mealtime. They generally hit upon a plantation for dinner where there were some "good looking damsels."[7] As might be the case when the men of the 107th New York were left to their own devices, they found entertainment in "drink," so much so that the officers were very concerned.

Crossing the Meherrin, Nottoway, and Appomattox rivers, they reached Richmond on May 11. They had made tremendously long marches averaging over twenty miles per day. But, although all were eager to reach home, none could see the necessity of "forced marches" now that the war was ended.

They marched through Richmond at noon. Their line of march took them past Libby Prison, Castle Thunder, and the State House, as well as the commercial district that had been set fire by Confederate soldiers on April 3, 1865, when they left the city in the face of the Union advance. During their march through the city, they preserved the strictest discipline, and their step was timed to the music being played, "Yankee Doodle." The bearing of every soldier on the 107th evidenced the esprit of men who had marched victoriously thousands of miles through the Rebel states. The people who lined the streets and watched the passage of their troops saw and felt the moral force of discipline.

They camped near Brook Church in a violent thunderstorm. Consequently, the roads were muddy the following day, which slowed the pace of their march. Regardless they made it to the banks of the South Anna River. They crossed the tracks of the Virginia Central Railroad, the New and Little Rivers, and rested near the North Anna River. The next day, they reached the Spotsylvania Court House, and on the 15th, they passed over the former battlefield where scores of Union soldiers still remained unburied.[8]

The men of the 107th brigade strolled around the battlefield, and a party of them discovered the bodies of two Union soldiers of the old 1st Corps lying on the ground unburied. They went further on and entering the woods, they saw the bones of a large number of men belonging to the 2nd Corps who fell during Hancock's charge on the Confederate works. Their bodies lay where they fell a year before, unburied.

Nothing but their bones remained, the flesh having been absorbed by long exposure or eaten by animals. Skulls and bones lay scattered about. There were over two hundred bodies at this one spot, and further to the left, another similar spectacle was found.

After resting for hour, they resumed their march. After a march of about nine miles, they reached the former battleground of Chancellorsville. The ruins of the Chancellor house appeared the same as it had two years before on May 3, 1863. Their brigade marched down and drew up in line at the exact spot where the regiment engaged the enemy that memorable Sunday. Their dead lay where they had fallen. A man in the 13th New Jersey picked up a skull and exclaimed that belonged to his brother who was killed at that area. Some pretenses of burial had been made by the Confederates, dirt having been thrown over the bodies where they lay, and the bones of many of the dead were now lying on the surface. Rain had washed a good deal of it away. In the woods, there were hundreds of Confederate graves giving evidence of their great losses.[9]

The men remained on the battlefield for two hours. Later they camped near the United States Ford. Their conversations that evening were of the past ... of the deadly struggles, of their slain comrades, and their long and arduous efforts in different campaigns. They had been on many battlefields, many had been captured and were in prison suffering, the deprivations of Rebel cruelty and barbarism. Here they had conquered and had returned and encamped on the identical spot where in 1863, they rested before crossing the swollen waters of the Rappahannock River. The remainder of the march northward lay through familiar places and past old campgrounds that revived memories of the Virginia campaign, nearly every mile recalling incidents of former service on these famous plains.

On May 16, they crossed the river at the United States Ford and marched past the Gold Mines toward Catlett's Station and encamped near Mill Creek. The next day they rested near Brentville. The 18th found them marching over old and familiar ground to Fairfax Station, and on May 19, they reached Clouds Mills near Alexandria. The long march of 1,200 miles from Chattanooga with all its dangers and hardships was ended.[10]

They remained in camp until May 24, when they left at 5 a.m. and went into Washington where they marched in the Grand Review.[11] Two days after the Grand Review, three members of the 107th New York, Lt. George B. Humphrey with Sergts Hubbard and Hall, obtained a pass to visit the Capitol from a former officer of their regiment, Lt. Colonel Newton T. Colby of the 19th VRC who then was the superintendent of Old Capitol Prison. Colby had previously been a Lt. Colonel of the 107th New York.[12]

After the Grand Review, the regiment moved four miles out of the city towards Bladensburg, MD, where they camped. The regiment remained in camp for the most part after May 25. On June 3, their final muster rolls were approved, and the next day the regiment made an application to be relieved from duty and mustered out.

While waiting to be mustered out of the military service, the soldiers of the 107th were free to venture wherever they wished in the immediate area. On May 29, Nathan Dykeman, who had taken the bible from Dunker Church, decided to go with his brother James and another soldier to the nearby Bladensburg railroad station after the noon roll call. They were walking on the railroad tracks near a curve when they saw a train ahead of them. Dykeman stepped off the track and onto a parallel track. His companions stepped completely off both sets of tracks. As they were watching the train ahead of them, another train came around the curve behind Dykeman. It was traveling on the same tracks where he stood. The sound of the train ahead of him blocked out that of the train coming behind him. That train's engine struck him and threw him several feet in the air, killing him instantly,. He was the last fatality of the 107th New York.[13]

Dykeman's body was sent to Washington on May 30, where it was embalmed and then sent home.[14]

**Headquarters Military Division of the Mississippi,
in the Field, Washington, D.C., May 30,1865**

The general commanding announces to the Armies of the Tennessee and Georgia that the time has come for us to part. Our work is done, and armed enemies no longer defy us. Some of you will go to your homes, and others will be retained in military service till further orders.

And now that we are all about to separate, to mingle with the civil world, it becomes a pleasing duty to recall minding the situation of national affairs when, but little more than a year ago, we gathered about the cliffs of Lookout Mountain, and all the future was wrapped in doubt and uncertainty.

Three armies had come together from distant fields, with separate histories, yet bound by one common cause; the union of our country, and the perpetuation of the Government of our inheritance. There is no need to recall to your memories Tunnel Hill, with Rocky-Face Mountain and Buzzard-Roost Gap, and the ugly forts of Dalton Island.

We were in earnest, and paused not for danger and difficulty, but dashed through Snake-Creek Gap and fell on Resaca; then on to the Etowah, to Dallas, Kennesaw; and the heats of summer found us on the banks of the Chattahoochee, far from home, and dependent on a single road for supplies. Again we were not to be held back by any obstacle, and crossed over and fought four hard battles for the possession of the citadel of Atlanta. That was the crisis of our history. A doubt still clouded our future, but we solved the problems, destroyed Atlanta, struck boldly across the state of Georgia, severed all the main arteries of life to our enemy, and Christmas found us in Savannah.

Waiting there only long enough to fill our wagons, we, we again began a march which, for peril, labor, and results, will compare with any ever made by an organized army. The floods of the Savannah, the swamps of the Combahee and Edisto, the "high hills" and rocks of the Santee, the flat quagmires of the Pedee and Cape Fear Rivers were all passed in mid-winter, with its floods and rains, in the face of an accumulating enemy; and after the battles of Averasboro and Bentonville, we once more came out of the wilderness, to meet our friends at Goldsboro. Even then we paused only long enough to get new clothing, to reload our wagons, again pushed on to Raleigh and beyond, until we met our enemy suing for peace, instead of war, and offering to submit to the injured laws of his and our country. As long as that enemy was defiant, nor mountains, nor rivers, nor swamps, nor hunger, nor cold, had checked us; but he, who had fought us hard and persistently, offered submission, your general thought it wrong to pursue him further, and negotiations followed, which resulted, as you well know, in his surrender.

How far the operations of this army contributed to the overthrow of the Confederacy and the peace which now dawns upon us, must be judged by others, not by us; but that you have done all that men could do has been admitted by men in authority, and we have a right to join in the universal joy that fills our land because the war is over, and our government stands vindicated before the world by the joint action of the volunteer armies and navy of the United States.

To such as remain in the service, your general need only to remind you that success in the past is due to hard work and discipline, and that the same work and discipline are equally important in the future. To such as go home, he will only say that our favored country is so grand, so extensive, so diversified in climate, soil, and productions, that every man may find a home and occupation suited to his taste; none should yield to the natural impatience sure to result from our past life of excitement and adventure. You will be invited to seek new adventures abroad; do not yield to the temptation, for it will lead only to death and disappointment.

Your general bids you farewell, with the full belief that, as in war you have been good soldiers, so in peace you will make good citizens; and if, unfortunately, a new war should arise in our country, "Shermans army" will be the first to buckle on its old armor, and come forth to defend and maintain the Government of our inheritance.

By order of Major-General W.T. Sherman,
L. M. Dayton Assistant Adjutant General.

The next days were spent doing the necessary paperwork. The muster-out rolls were approved on June 3 along with an application to be relieved from duty, and they were mustered out of the army on June 5. On June 6 they broke camp at 4 p.m. They left Washington at 9 p.m. for Baltimore, where they slept on a hard pavement from midnight until morning in a hard rain. They left Baltimore at 10 a.m. and reached Elmira at 9 a.m. on June 8.[15]

The first of the war-torn regiments of brave, 107th Volunteers reached home on June 8 at the early hour of 8 a.m., contrary to the intelligence received the previous evening that they would not arrive until 2 p.m. Consequently, preparations for their reception were not in so advanced a stage of forwardness as they otherwise would have been had the early hour of their arrival been fully understood. But the ringing of the First Baptist Church bell quickly gave the glad warning, and people eagerly rushed to the depot to catch a sight of the noble and battle-stained veterans.

After a little waiting, the 19th Rest. V.R.C. arrived from Camp Chemung with their band and drum corps under the command of Colonel Lewis to form an escort on the march through the city and to Barracks 1. The route was quickly taken down Main Street to Church to Lake and then on to the Barracks. Crowds of people thronged the streets, cheers and loud acclimations greeting every step of the march. Flowers and bouquets were showered upon the brave fellows. Ladies vied in showing their regard for the defenders of the country. The boys appreciated the favors shown and felt that the welcome compensated in some measure for the trials, the losses, and hardships of battles and campaigning. Bells rang out their stirring peals, cannons sent forth their thunder tones, and inspiring music of bands enlivened the march from the depot to the barracks.

Immediately after reaching the barracks, details were made to turn in the regimental property. As soon as the men were ready, a light breakfast was served of cold meat, bread, and warm coffee in anticipation of the full dinner to be laid out for their enjoyment at 3 p.m. in the public park.

In view of the very large number of returning soldiers seeking accommodations at Barracks No. 1, permission was granted by Major Wilson, the commandant, to pitch their tents in the open field opposite the enclosure where the men would remain until paid off and discharged. This arrangement probably was no inconvenience at the warm season of the year and greatly preferable to crowded barrack bunks.

A little before two p.m., a company of the 1st Regiment Veteran Reserves with the celebrated band of the same regiment under the command of Captain M. Elbert marched from Camp Chemung to Barracks No. 1 to escort the 107th to the dinner tables prepared by the ladies in the public park. The route was down Lake to Water, along Water to Main, and up Main to the park.

The 107th marched splendidly with the unwavering step of old veterans. Its banners battered and torn in shreds showed the hard fights through which they had been triumphantly borne. Not one had been soiled by a Rebel hand. Upon these were inscribed the names of battlefields which would be ever held sacred and venerated for the security they brought to imperiled liberty.

A greater crowd than in the morning everywhere thronged the lines of march. Bells sent out even merrier peals and the booming of cannon again intoned the measured tread of marching veterans. Gladness and rejoicing reigned supreme.

The ladies of Elmira, under the leadership of Mrs. A.S. Diven, vied in preparing a feast fit for the returning heroes. The tables were loaded with the food and made to groan under the delicacies of the season. Fairy hands and beautiful housewifery had evoked the most appetizing productions of cakes, sweetmeats, and fresh fruits. Bread, biscuits, pies, and cakes were present in unending variety. Vases and holders of beautiful and exquisite flowers set off the attractive array and adorned the display. Fruits from the tropics—oranges, lemons, pineapples—and confectionary added additional flavor and zest to the prospective meal.

The tables had been placed in long rows beneath the trees at the southern side of the park, which afforded the thickest foliage and shade. Adjoining booths were set up; one festooned with flags and mottoes was fitted with tables for the officers. Other booths offered ice water and lemonade as well as the huge cauldron for boiling coffee.

A picture of Abraham Lincoln draped in mourning was in front of the officers' booth. The trees were decorated with flags and banners inscribed with the following mottoes:

Grant, Sherman, Sheridan, Slocum
Baldwin Fallen but Not Forgotten
Sweet Sleep the Brave who rest, With all their honors countless Blest
Cheers for Our Returning Heroes, Tears for their Fallen Comrades
Welcome Home Brave Boys
We Honor the Brave

A Hearty welcome to the boys who fought beneath Old Glory's folds
Our Martyred Heroes
Their shrine will be the nation's heart, Their monument the People's Love
Hurrah they come with fife and drum; those noble hearts true with lofty
    cheer we welcome here, our gallant boys in blue!
The saviors of our country, let us wear them in our heart of hearts

Following dinner, Tracy Beadle gave a speech of welcome. He commenced by referring to the dark overshadowing of the outset of the rebellion, the gloomy years of
1860 and 1861, and when the national cause grew darker, the call for 300,000 more
men. The 107th Regiment New York Volunteers was the very first to obey the summons. Within a few short days from the hills and valleys of Chemung, Steuben, and
Schuyler, a regiment of one thousand men sprang to arms, fully equipped to beat
back the boastful foe. As a reward for its alacrity and eager patriotism, the state
awarded the prize banner. Thus recognized, it went forth to fight its country's battles. Hardly had it reached the field, ere the fray and battle array were ready for its
untried bravery. Antietam baptized it with virgin glory. Chancellorsville, Gettysburg, the campaigns of Georgia, South and North Carolina completed the glorious
record of brave deeds and achievements. For such gallantry and bravery, the people gave them this free hearted and outspoken welcome. He also spoke in the most
touching and feeling language of the dead who sleep the sleep that knows no waking,
pillowed upon the memories of friends and countrymen left behind. He hoped that
at last the heavenly gate would be open to one and all of the brave soldiers who had
risked their lives and periled their all in their country's defense.

Colonel Crane briefly and modestly replied in word of thanks for the generous reception his regiment had received. General A.S. Diven alluded to his connection with the regiment, first as lieutenant colonel and afterwards as its commanding
officer. He had been with it in the thickest of battles at Antietam and Chancellorsville. Its bravery had been tested to the utmost and never found wanting in his own
experience. It was a most gratifying reflection that he had ever belonged to the regiment. It would be one of the happiest memories of his whole life. He continues that
since his fortunes had been cast away from it, he had followed its course through
battles and campaigns with an eager, watchful eye. He had been proud of its accomplishments, of the name it had earned in the army for its order, discipline, and obsti-
nacy on the field of battle. In closing, he referred to the distinguished praise paid the
army in the farewell orders of Generals Sherman and Slocum for their conduct as
good and obedient soldiers. It would not appear wrong in him perhaps, to hope that
they would disperse to their homes and again settle down as good and upright citizens, tilling the soil, plying the mechanical arts, and engaging in all the avocations
of peaceful industry. Their history, he had no doubt, would show to the world how
brave soldiers could become good and reliable citizens and prove the bone and sinew
of the country in every time of national need.

This text was printed in the *Daily Advertiser.*

And so, we have delighted to honor those who have stood next to the cannon's mouth, those who have given their lives for ours. Yes, the memory of these latter should be cherished fresh and green in all coming years until we ourselves are laid beneath the green grassy sod. There was happiness and rejoicing yesterday over the safe return of loved ones, of fathers, brothers, lovers, but alas too, there were pallid lips, tear filled eyes as they wandered here and there over the battle heroes, discerning no cherished form, no stay of life's hope and happiness. To many such, the future seemed blank and cheerless for the dread sacrifice that had been made on the common altar of the nation's preservation, but no nobler death can there be than, "to die for one's country." We will sympathize then with the friends of the lost. We will mourn with them, and we will be encouraged ever to bless the providence that has caused heroes to give up their lives so nobly and unselfishly. Soon their homes will receive these surviving men of war, no men of peace. Another more cherished welcome will greet them there. The heart will well forth its best affections, and the events of the three years past will be told with a thrilling import. Such happiness and joy will be worth all losses incurred, all the sufferings of long absence from that dearest spot on earth, "Home Sweet Home."

In that same edition of the *Daily Advertiser* was the following short article about Private Francis Finley of Company B, of the 107th NY Volunteers, formerly of the 145th NYV, stating that he was severely cut and stabbed the previous evening somewhere in the vicinity of Barracks No. 1.[16] Those who were previously members of the 145th New York still had to be transported to their home base in New York City.

Company H of the 107th New York Volunteers was the only unit raised in Schuyler County. On the evening of June 9, the members of that company were greeted by Hull Fanton, former adjutant of the regiment. A generous outpouring of local citizens was assembled at the depot to welcome the returning heroes. They were escorted by the Havana Brass Band and marched around the square to the north entrance of the Montour House where they heard the music of the "Red, White and Blue" as sung from the balcony by a party of young girls. Never was the heart of the masses more deeply interested in a ceremony, and every eye seemed to glimmer with delight over the return of those battle-worn soldiers whose diminished ranks told a sad tale of the Rebel missiles of death. Only 34 of 100 who left Havana three years ago had returned to receive the blessings and a tribute of gratitude for the many deeds of valor by the good old 107th. Her history was an untarnished one, and her name would ever be held in sacred remembrance.

The men of the company sat down around a table that was beautifully decorated with nature's choicest flowers, and the bountiful repast was just what could be expected from the worthy landlord and hostess of this popular hotel. They enjoyed a rich choice beverage of everything that pertains to the first tables and such as would bring from the heart of the soldier an ungovernable gush of gratitude, both to the donor and to those who are his instruments in pleasing the weary travelers who fought to defend their neighbors' rights and had now returned from their labors with their mission fully performed. Heartfelt thanks and cheering countenances told well of the result of Adjutant Fanton's endeavors to entertain and please this honorable assemblage. To the ladies, they offered words of thanksgiving as beautiful bouquets were strewn before the rank and file of Company H. One soldier exclaimed, "Heaven bless you!" After supper was over, Adjutant Fanton gave a brief history of the regiment.[17]

The preliminary work of enrolling your heroic Company, of the now famous and battle-stained 107th Regiment was commenced on the 17th day of July 1862. The following day the active co-operation of H. Delos Donnelly and Lewis O. Sayler, of the town of Hector, was secured, and during the entire work the generous assistance of Hon. Charles Cook, who advanced the money to pay the bounties, and that of Peter Tracy, Wm. Skellenger, Adam G. Campbell, John Campbell, Henry C. Winton and E. Chapman Clark, who contributed towards the funds to pay the expenses incurred. Messrs. A.V. Mekell, N.M. Mathews, Madison Treman and E.C. Spaulding of Hector; Hon. Samuel Lawrence and Abraham Lawrence, of Catharine; Isaac H. Hill, A.M. Williams, JOHN Morrow, Stephen F. Griffith, of Tyrone; Lorenzo Webber, of Orange; and many others, whose names do not occur to me, rendered great assistance in the several towns in forwarding enlistments, literally using, not only their time, but giving freely of their means.

On Monday evening, July 21st, a staff was raised in front of the Bank of Havana, under which was my office at the time, and flag was run up which had been furnished by Gen. Van Valkenburg, the universally designated leader of the new Regiment. Thereafter the spot became the company headquarters, and there the members of the company were sworn into the service, being afterwards mustered at Elmira by Major A.T. Lee, of the Regular Army. Thursday, July 24th, Special Orders No. 487, from the General Headquarters, State of New York, Adjutant General's office, authorized me now formally to enroll; and the next day 64 recruits went to Elmira for examination and muster. The 26th, Frank M. Cronkrite commenced work in the town of Tyrone; the 29th, the second squad of recruits went forward; the 31st, the third and last; the 30th, commenced paying the bounties from moneys advanced by Mr. Cook. The first days of August were busy ones, getting the enlistment papers in proper shape, and in preparations for mustering into the United States Service. In this work of detail Edwin Weller was efficient, while George W. Jackson was quite indispensable. The morning of the 7th, the election for officers was held by order of Col. Van Valkenburg, resulting in the election of Clark, Donnelly and Sayler, for the respective positions of Captain, First and Second Lieutenants. In thus relinquishing my charge, I took, as I then supposed, final leave of the Company and its destinies, most strangely though, and unexpectedly, I became connected more intimately with the Regiment, and Providentially have I trust, a small portion of the honor and glory which you and other brave men have won.

Then came the sad leave takings, the parting good-bye, and the start for Washington, by the way of Harrisburg and Baltimore, in the early morning of Thursday the 14th of August, arriving at Washington during the forenoon of the 15th. From thenceforth, the history and recollections of Company H is that of the 107th. After an informal review by President Lincoln, accompanied by Secretary Seward, the first march was made down Pennsylvania Avenue and 14th Street to, and across the Long-Bridge, now on to the "sacred soil," continuing until late in the evening, and then conducted by one of Gen. Casey's Aids upon field our first bivouac, three or four miles from the South end of Long Bridge, on heights of Arlington, Southwest of Arlington House, and near Fort Albany. The discomforts, as was thought then of that first night in the open air, and the touching thoughts brought up as the next morning was ushered by that now, never to be forgotten first.—Quickly after this, succeeded marching and counter-marching, the camp was changed every few days, and no effort was spared to place matters in shape for that memorable campaign which so soon was heralded by the booming of Rebel guns within hearing the Capitol.—When can we forget "tedious," "awful" "hard," march to Alexandria? And then up the hill to the south of Fort Lyon, and your dreams of "Heavy Artillery drill" therein, or its companion march back to the vicinity Fort Albany, and thunder of the Second Bull Run, as we eagerly watched and listened to the battle roar afar off, which was the next day brought still nearer home, as we mutely, thoughtfully stood by road side gazed at long line of ambulances carrying their precious loads of wounded to Washington hospitals.

Then that toughening experience, that actual hard march to Maryland the evening September 6th by the way of Georgetown aqueduct, and thence to Rockville 10 miles the same night, bivouacking about halfway only to be routed out with eyes half open an hour afterwards. Comrades, would it require much fancy to catch the echoes of the songs sung to beguile the time that night.—"John Brown's body lies moldering in the ground," "Six hundred thousand more," and others of a like character, and then that one of Sergeant Whitehorn's that reminded us of home and dear friends there. But follow me still. You were all there, that weary Sabbath day's rest in the beautiful fair grounds at Rockville, and the tiresome week's progress towards Frederick, and that Tuesday morning's triumphal march through city, and the afternoon and night's march "strategically," in a half circle, and the final bivouac on right of the South Mountain battle field, thence a straight line over the hills next day through the "Gap" near where Gen. Reno fell, and our comrades of the gallant 89th under Capt. Coryell, fought past the line of dead rebels by the road side, continuing on during the same afternoon through Boonsboro. Can you ever forget the lying of our Brigade cloud in mass the meadow near Keedysville, under the hills, when cannon so grandly thundered, the day before "Antietam?" and when for first time that heart stilling command was given by Gen. Gordon, "load at will!" And then that night's march, crossing the Antietam, and going so silently into the night's bivouac in rear General Hooker's position, and not far from house which next day was used by our Corps as a hospital, and to which, the ambulances were so constantly moving even then with the wounded from the picket line on left. Moving at daylight in column by division, through fields and up to the extreme front. I shall never forget how your Company looked as I took Orderly Weller's report, a minute or so before our introduction to the first shell, which fortunately did not explode. Deploying on the first division into line of battle, again as we reached the west of the cornfield, which at night, was so completely covered with our own and the rebel dead. It was just then that Gen. Mansfield fell, who but a few minutes before had passed us, when ordered forward from there by Gen. Gordon, who rode up and announced that we were driving the enemy. The 107th advanced through the ploughed field, and into edge of the woods beyond, when the first man fell in Regiment. Cyrus I. Covill of Co. H, being instantly killed, while near him, shortly after, Matthew S. Dawson, Charles Mathews and Ethan Worden, mortally wounded, and Josiah S. Gregory, Stephen Edwards, and I think, James Wilson dangerously, and who after- wards honorably discharged; Edward's re-enlisted into your Company, and died at Savannah last winter, I am informed. You can never forget that day, nor those scenes. Early in afternoon, Capt. Clark, your first commander, was wounded, falling heroically for himself and for you. Though it was not yours to fire a gun, still the duty done by the Regiment was most important, supporting Cothran's 1st N.Y. Artillery. In front of the guns, when battle ceased, I counted afterwards near 200 rebels, dead and dying, and score of our own men, all so sadly telling fearful obstinate fighting, and the terrible effects of the battle strife. Then our Banner, which you have in keeping to-night, received its badge of honor, having been rent by shell, and there, or near there, fell the eighty dead wounded of our first fight. From daylight till dark, the conflict raged in fury. The ground trembled beneath us, bullets and shells were not scarce. From raw recruits you were transformed with those brave leaders Van Valkenburg, Diven and Smith into veterans, and carries away from that field the pledge seal upon your colors. That 17th day of September was one of the battle days of the century.

Then came those autumn days at Maryland Heights. Our camp had hardly pitched tents, before Joseph Couse died. Company H not only lost first man battle, but the first to fall a victim to disease was Corporal Couse.—Ah! that never to be forgotten burial; the muffled drums, the funeral march, the sad and mourning company, as his remains were conveyed to their resting place in the little garden in the rear of old Mr. Wessell's. The desolation of fever, the sick in the open air and the old log barn, the long line of graves above Harper's Ferry on the heights of Bolivar. My old comrades, these things you cannot forget, for you were there and saw them as I did. Then, there in the midst of our utter despair, and heart sickening surroundings Heaven sent us the welcome sight of a pitying woman's face in the brave hearted Mrs. Diven, our Colonel's wife, who faced, as we can truthfully say the pestilence without flinching and proved herself worthy to be a brave soldier's wife.

Late in October when the frosts had tipped the mountain heights and the Virginia landscape with their varied colors, we made the march back to, and encamped near Antietam Ford, the "Iron Works," or the "Forge," as it was called, that pleasant camp, and the bluffs upon the Potomac was a pleasant spot, how bravely we set to work at our "Winter Quarters," and resumed work on the "Colonel's oven; only joyful recollections cluster there, for on that spot we left no grave yard."

On the 10th of December the line of march was taken up, and we passed again into Virginia, round the base of the Shenandoah and into Louden Valley, and into a succession of winter bivouacs, keeping steadily on through Leesburg, passing Hillsborough and Fairfax Court House, until we halted again in the "Pines" at Fairfax Station. The subsequent reconnaissance to Wolf-Run Shoals and beyond, and back again to the Station to find our baggage and camp equipage all piled ready for burning, for fear of the "raiders." Those were the days that the "stray chickens" in that vicinity yielded up their innocent lives for refusing to take the oath and "akin" mouths, and the Colonel, and sometimes the Adjutant had something better for dinner than "hard tack." As a matter of course the men of Co. H knew nothing of these proceedings, for were not the "details" always strictly made, and "all men present or accounted for?" while the Virginian farmer sought for his poultry, hogs and so forth, and swore because he found them not. The middle of January saw us again moving. Passing by Dumfries thence by Acquia to Stafford Court House and Hope Landing. When gazing at the broad Potomac, making ourselves comfortable in the mud, and building "corduroy roads" was the order. Sacred to the memory is the little spot at Hope Landing, where the dead of the 107th lie buried, then by the lone graves, then unknown. You buried Ackley and Shaw. From there you sent home all that remained of the true soldier George W. Cutler. Towards that lovely spot adorned and beautified by the Regiment went the line of strollers after the Dress Parade.—Around it still clusters a world of memories.

"Chancellorsville" not only broke up the home like camp at the Landing but made busy work with the ranks of the Regiment. Company H there had wounded Johnson, Orr and John Van Loon, while Albert Swallow and John I. Griffeth, who was afterwards killed in front of Atlanta, were returned among the missing. Many other battle-fields speak of your valor, endurance and courage; but it is hardly fair for me to recount those. Shortly after this time my connection with the Regiment ceased, and others present will speak of them.

You were at Gettysburg, and a part of the never-to-be-forgotten campaign west, and in the matchless march of Sherman from Atlanta "down to the sea." I was rejoiced when a letter from one of your officers announced to me that the flag of the 107th was the first to wave over the Georgia State House, at Milledgeville. Let us hear from Capt. Brigham about these things, who, though a Steuben man, we claim to be one of us by the battles in which he has reclined with you; and to Orderly Weller, Sergeants Cronkrite and Kendall, who return Lieutenants, promotions worthily and justly merited and earned. A word from Lieut. Whitehorn, the faithful. It would have been a joy for him to have been with you here to-night, but sudden illness prevents. He sends word by Sergeant Potter to make his regretful acknowledgements.

It is a great pleasure, woven in as it is with sad reminders, old soldier friends and companions, that as many of you come back to us, to be here on this occasion as I see before me. It is a peculiar gratification personally, that your Colonel, the accomplished officer and fearless commander, feels you to be so worthy as to trust to your guardianship and keeping the colors of the Regiment—the battle-flags of the 107th—to display them to us, with your treasured arms, and right welcome faces. This is a day and an occasion in your Company's history not soon to be erased from memory. Allow me now to call the original Roster of the Company, which has been kindly furnished me from Washington, and let us see how many are present to say "here." When I have finished, our old Chaplain, who always brought us the news, who so frequently executed our commissions in the city, and gave us heedful counsel, will address you. We shall all remember Chaplain Crane. Alas! of the 98 on the list, only 29 to answer to the roll call. With a heart full of regard for all of you, I bid you welcome here. The great gathering of citizens to night on your arrival, the enthusiasm of their greeting, the shower of flowers from fair hands, and the welcome of song by the little ones, attest that the greeting is alike shared by us all. It was then proposed (Mr. Fanton having the original roster of the Company), that the name of each man be called, and if present, he should answer. Dear reader, occasionally a man would make manifest his presence, but blank indeed was that original Roster. By far too many of those noble boy's sleep beneath the fold of their country s emblem, and the vacant seats around the family altar tell too strong of the devastations of war. "God gave, and God taketh away." Chaplain Crane, known as the "fighting Parson," was then called upon, and gave a brief history of the Regiment, taking it from the time Adjutant Fanton left off in his remarks, down to a still later day. We had hoped to have been able to give his remarks, but they are not at hand. His associations with the boys, he said, were the happiest days of his life, and his many anecdotes or matter-of-fact stories that occurred during camp-life, were interesting to all, and seemed to recall to the memory of the boys many pleasing reflections, as cheer after cheer would greet him as he spoke.

Our citizens can never forget the battle-scarred banners of the Regiment, which were permitted to accompany this little band to our village. Their tattered shreds and still defiant stripes added a solemnity to the occasion. Would they find words to tell their own story? Color-bearers have fallen beneath their folds not to an unlimited number. One shattered staff spoke in itself of its usage, and those brave boys who have fallen while bearing them onward to victory, are not to be forgotten. Their memory is engraved on the record of our free Republic. The hour having arrived for the parting, a cordial shake of the hand was given to all; not such a one as was given three years ago, but one of reward for services rendered—Never can the boys forget the reception given them by Adjutant Fanton, and the citizens of this village. The demonstration was gotten up on short notice, and the boys seemed highly entertained, and well repaid for their visit. They went back to Elmira to be mustered out of the service, on the same evening. "HULL," we are aware, is not the man to speak for himself; but we can say without any hesitation, that the boys of Co. H. 107th, express many thanks for his kind reception, and we bear witness that the citizens of Havana are indebted to him, in a great measure, for the complete success of the entertainment.[18]

The men of the 107th New York remained in Elmira or at least in the general area of Corning and Havana until June 19, when they were paid in full and discharged from the army.[19]

# 14

# The 107th New York Volunteer
# Infantry Association Reunions

**In 1867, the veterans of the 107th New York decided to organize a regimental association for the members of their regiment. However, over the years and especially when the number of living members dwindled, they decided to vote in members of other regiments, honorary members, and wives. The meetings were held annually on September 17, the anniversary of their first engagement at the battle of Antietam near Sharpsburg, MD. The meetings lasted until 1931 and typically consisted of a sit-down dinner and speeches. Following those, members got together in conversation to recall their experiences during the war. Occasionally, they made special trips to battlefields or such places as Grant's Tomb. The reunions of special significance are presented here.**

Special recognition must be given to Arthur S. Fitch, whose letters, journal, and articles written after the war provided exceptional material for this effort, and to Frank Frost, the last living member of the regiment, who collected numerous items of interest related to the regiment, all of which are in the vaults of the Chemung County Historical Society.

The organizational meeting for the establishment of the 107th New York's veterans' association and annual reunions was held December 20, 1867, at the Hathaway House in Elmira. The following rules were adopted.

I. The organization is to be called the "107th New York Volunteer Regimental Association."

II. All officers and men who were members of the 107th N.Y. Vols. And have been honorably discharged shall be by virtue of that connection, shall be members of this association.

III. The officers of the association shall consist of a president, three vice presidents, recording secretary, corresponding secretary, and regimental committee of nine.

IV. These officers shall be elected at the annual reunion and shall hold their office for one year or until their successors are designated.

V. Before each annual reunion the president of the association shall designate some member of the association as "Officer of the day," who shall in conjunction with the regimental committee have charge of the proceedings for the reunion.

    VI. The duties of the foregoing officers be as their respective titles indicate.

    VII. At every reunion of the association there shall be some member designated to deliver at the succeeding meeting an address upon some topic of regimental interest.

    Officers were then named for the following year. President: General A.S. Diven; 1st Vice President: Colonel N.M. Crane; 2nd Vice President: Major C.J. Fox; 3rd Vice President; Lieutenant Colonel A.N. Sill; Recording Secretary: Lieutenant R.M. Tuttle; Corresponding Secretary: Adjutant Hull Fanton; Captain J. Miles. Following the assignment of officers of the association, various other matters were discussed and resolved. At 3 p.m., all were seated for a dinner, and afterward a number of sentiments were voiced and toasts made to many.

    That day, General Diven had been away in New York City, but he arrived on the evening train, and he and others were able to join the group at the Hathaway House for dinner. Afterwards the festivities of the evening were greatly prolonged with many reminiscences and stories of army life and experiences.[1]

    The first reunion was a very simple affair and was held on September 17, 1868, at the Montour House in Havana (now Montour Falls). Approximately forty-five veterans of the regiment were in attendance. Following their meeting, they all adjourned outside of the Montour House to where a "Liberty Pole" had been erected by some of the members of the regiment who resided in that village. From the top of the pole there floated one of the old camp flags of the regiment. They gathered around the flag and sang "Rally Round the Flag Boys" while accompanied by Compton's Coronet Band.[2]

    In 1869, the reunion banquet was held at the Rathbun House in Elmira. At precisely half past two, the veterans of the 107th New York and veterans of other regiments raised in the same congressional district, along with their lady friends, wives, and invited guests numbering in all about eighty persons, sat down to an "elegant and bountiful meal." After dinner, tributes were paid to the very first regiment to be raised from this congressional district, the 23rd NY Volunteer Infantry, as well as other regiments including the 86th New York, the 141st New York, and the 179th New York, all from the 23rd congressional district. All in all, there were fifteen sentiments expressed and responded to. Then a letter from General Slocum was read expressing his thanks for an invitation to the occasion and regretting his inability to attend. Finally, a toast was made in silence to the memory of President Lincoln, upon which the occasion was adjourned.[3]

    The 1870 reunion was held at the Rathbun House again. The local Elmira newspaper saw fit to print the entire dinner offerings in the newspaper, and indeed it appeared to be a sumptuous meal. The association's members were so impressed with the meal that they voted to make their host an honorary member and quarter-master of their association. The newspaper article referenced several speeches covering the regiment's experiences during the war, but no details were included in the article.[4]

The reunion in 1872 was notable due to the lengthy presentation by Arthur Fitch. It appeared afterwards in the *Elmira Advertiser,* and it presented the regiment's quiet times away from the struggles of the war. His full and complete talk follows.

Among the pleasant memories of our regimental life, those connected with the winter quarters of '62 and '63 occupy a prominent place. At this time of reunion, we can do no better than to invoke for our pleasure the aid of that greatest of magicians, our memory. Let him take us ten years backward and then by his mystic light we will once again visit former scenes and gather around campfires of the past.

The battle of Antietam had been fought. We had buried our dead, our wounded comrades were cared for, and once again we gathered around the campfires that warmed and cheered us upon the bleak hillsides of Maryland Heights.

You all will remember that spot. We had not then acquired that wonder proficiency of making ourselves comfortable which in later campaigns formed so prominent a feature of our regimental character. Besides everything was unsettled, war, the country and its future, and our own immediate prospects were shrouded by more than the usual darkness that hides the coming days. Our men, however, took a cheerful view of things, and made the best of our uncomfortable quarters. We had company drills to occupy our time, and as the whole army was encamped near us, we could easily pass away the idle hours amidst the surrounding bustle which always attends the camps of a grand army.

The balloon "Atlantic" with its daily ascensions produced a prolific source of amusement for our boys. While at night we would sit and watch the many thousand tent lights that gleamed so brightly from the opposite hills.

It was here that sickness struck down our men. The epidemic raged fearfully. Every day there was a funeral. Still Surgeon Flood and his assistants. Overcame the disease and brought it to a complete end.

They were dark days though and the men will never forget the friendship of Colonel Diven's wife. For long and weary days her kind voice and gentle hand were ever at the bedside of the sick and dying. Her aid raised many a quiet one to life and her woman's gentleness softened the hard lot of many a dying soldier. No one here will ever forget her and her devotion at that time will always stand prominent among the reminiscences of our regimental life.

It was while we were camped there that Colonel Van Valkenburg left us. He went away with the good wishes of all and we remember him today as a brave soldier, a gentleman, a generous and gentle man.

From Maryland Heights we moved on to Antietam Ford. Here we built snug winter quarters and the men began to show a capability of adapting themselves to circumstances of all kinds. We had some little picket duty to perform along the banks of the canal, but it was light duty and was more form than anything else. Many will remember the deep gorge where the picket reserves had their fires and the house of the old widow where the officers and men occasionally got a meal. While in the camp there was heavy fall of snow and then the snow-balling fun evolved.

The regiment was well fed here, and everything was faithfully provided by the quarter-master Ed. Graves. We had jolly times here. At night the sounds from the tents told of music, songs, laughter and fun of all kinds, and today all will say that the camp at Antietam Ford as among the good times. But our feelings of quiet contentment were broken one day when Colonel Smith's orderly came tapping at the door of our shanty with marching orders. All were surprised, although there was a story afloat afterwards that good Chaplain Crane had learned the whole thing before even Colonel Smith had heard of it. The story is that our worthy Chaplain and his friend Simon van Etten were in a séance during which the spirits imparted the information that we would move on a certain day. Curious enough by virtue of a coincidence the spiritual information proved correct as Chaplain Crane could have wished even had he been a devout spiritualist instead of a skeptic on such matters.

So, when one afternoon when the sun with red slanting beams was shining low in the north, we broke camp. With a kindly feeling for our old quarters, we bid adieu to its dismantled cabins and deserted streets.

Across the Shenandoah, down through the Loudon Valley, all through the chill December nights with nothing but a blanket between us and the frost and snow our division pushed on until with one night at a late hour we bivouacked at Fairfax. Here we made another camp even better and neater than the one at Antietam Ford. Battalion drills were resumed here with Colonel Diven taking personal charge. The regiment gave evidence daily of marked improvement and all seemed contented with a soldier's life. While encamped here we were ordered out once for active duty to intercept some raiders. We marched as far as Wolf Run Shoals and then returned without having seen a rebel. This little march was noticeable for some very fast marching on our way home with the seven miles made in a little less than two hours.

We were in hopes that our Fairfax camp would have been a more permanent one, and so our disappointment was great when we learned one day from Adjutant Fanton that we were under marching orders. It was the time of Burnsides mud march. The rain fell heavily making the march very muddy, tiresome and tedious. At Occoquan Creek we found the stream swollen and turbid and the bridge gone. A log was the only means of crossing. The passage on the log furnished an amount of fun that went far to enliven the weariness and discomfort felt during the march as many fell off of the log. It was a continuous roar of laughter from both sides of the stream.

Two more days of hard marching and we find ourselves at Stafford Court House. A few days spent there in shelter tents and then we are ordered to Hope Landing. So, on we go over the muddiest of roads, and on a cold bleak day in January 1863 in what is often alluded to by our men as the Valley Forge of the 107th. Our first night was passed without tents. Many of the men sat up all night about the fires to keep warm. Others slept soundly beneath their blankets and let the falling snow pile up upon their sleeping bodies. The men all took their situation good naturedly and sat around their fires many singing songs to cheer the hours of that long winter's night.

We all remember Frank Cronkrite's cheerful songs in that camp. He would often sing "Happy are we tonight boys," and we all wondered why he would sing such words at that time. Perhaps like Frank Tapley, he thought it was a virtue to be jolly under such circumstances, and certainly Mark Tapley with all his troubles was never jolly under more disheartening circumstances than those that surrounded our little isolated camp at Valley Forge. While here our men were detailed for building corduroy roads. It was hard, wet, dirty work and the exposure cost the regiment many lives. At that time an inspection was ordered. Under the present circumstances the regiment was in no condition to make a favorable impression. The inspecting officer criticized the condition of the regiment in harsh terms. When he came to Captain Miles' company and growled about the soiled condition of the muskets, the captain smiled broadly and invited him to look at our spades and shovels claiming that they at least were bright and that those were the tools which the government now kept our men at work. Our inspection report was unfavorable, and we felt that an injustice had been done to us. But Colonel Diven, who had been away, soon returned to our camp and he moved our camp to a new and better location. We moved a short distance to New Hope landing and there we built permanent winter quarters. The camp was beautifully located on a side hill overlooking Acquia Creek and the Potomac. Shortly after the 13th NJ of our brigade made a camp on an adjoining hill. At evening their bugles sounding sweetly in the distance added a new charm to our camp in the way of neighborly companionship.

The 13th NJ was well disciplined and often drilled with us on the sandy plain between the two camps. We all lived well at Hope Landing as General Hooker provided a generous commissary. In addition, there were scores of sutler shops anchored in the stream and plenty of fish and oysters in the bay. While we were here Colonel Smith left us being obliged to do so on account of his health. The parted with him with regret as the colonel had always proved himself a gentleman and a very "prince of good fellows."

Our camp life moved smoothly along, and the regiment attained a marked proficiency in drill. But the exposure and hard work at Valley Forge took a toll on the men and we buried twenty-two in a short space of time. The funeral scenes of Maryland Heights were reenacted. Every day the three volleys rang out over the waters of the bay and again the fifers played the plaintive air of "Roslyn Castle" so often that the soldiers unconsciously fell into the habit of whistling the tune as they went about their daily duties.

Chaplain Crane always took charge of the funerals, and the boys of the 13th NJ were wont to remark that our chaplain was heavy on funerals. He knew just how to do it and all will recall to mind his solemn and accurate tread as he marched along at the head of the funeral procession. There was a good choir in the regiment supplied with books furnished by the Young Men's Christian Association of Elmira, and there was always good singing at the grave. We used to sit in our camp and watch the little procession as it passed by. We would listen to the muffled drumbeats and wailing fifes as the train moved on across the plain. Then the sound of the drums would cease and across the distance would come the tones of the chaplain's prayer. Then sweetly on the soft Spring air came the sound of the choir singing some old familiar hymn. Then a pause broken by the sharp volleys of the firing party playing their last tribute of respect to their buried comrade and the funeral was over.

The graveyard of the regiment was in a beautiful spot. It was on a knoll next to the riverbank and was shaded by two great trees. A neat stone bearing a suitable inscription marked each soldier's resting place. The graves were all in exact rows and in the center of the ground was an extra stone on which Lt. Denniston had with exquisite taste had placed simply the words, "107 NY In Place Rest." You will remember that our tactics described the order "In Place Rest" as being one in which the men were tired and weary with their drill, they could rest themselves in any position merely keeping in line so that when they heard the bugle call "Attention" they might spring promptly to their places. So, we laid in ranks in lines, our comrades tired and weary with life's battles inscribed above them the order "In Place Rest," and left them waiting for the one great bugle note which in some coming time shall sound through the all the world.

And here we must not pass without recalling to memory our chaplain and the active part he took during our camp life at Hope Landing. We remember his evening meetings around a great blazing bonfire. The great man had a peculiar way of getting up a meeting. He would build a great fire at night under the trees in the main street. Then standing by it all alone he would sing so loud that the men in the neighboring camps would stop and listen. Then one by one the men would leave their tents and gathering around the chaplain would soon have a meeting in full blast. The scene often was one fit for a painter. Overhead the dark branches of the trees rendered still blacker the darkness of the night as their branches reflected the firelight from below. The burly form of the chaplain stood with uncovered head an earnest face stood by the fire. Every part of his body was replete with earnestness and the deep strong lines of his face showed stronger in the fitful shadows of the firelight. Around him are the men who constitute his regimental church, a church that knows no narrow creed, but one in which all can join. There is a strange, but earnest look on their faces as they pray and sing, and one could easily imagine as he gazed upon those rough bearded men gathered there that as he heard them sing and listened to their prayers that the days of Cromwell and Miles Standish were upon us or that their spirits were hovering over this strange scene.

Then there was that Sunday before Chancellorsville. We broke camp that evening, but the chaplain announced services in the afternoon. In view of the battle before them the men all attended. Under the trees out in the air of that beautiful April day, the chaplain made himself a pulpit of drums and laid his bible on it. Then he preached and it was an impressive sermon. He told them what they all knew to be true, that a battle was close at hand, and that hence many of them were listening to his warnings for the last time, that before another Sabbath that many of them would be beyond the reach of religion and his offices. The men felt that his words were true and granted him the attention that such an occasion demanded.

The chaplain was good at other things besides preaching and funerals. He was a jovial comrade and companion, and in many ways, he made himself a useful man for the regiment. He was a pious hardworking bluff and hearty man. The men all liked him, believing in his piety and never held it inconsistent with his well-known temperance views if at the end of a hard day's march, he consented to share with a comrade the contents of his bottle of Plantation Bitters. **Note:** Bitters was an herb-infused alcoholic mixture. Named for its bitter taste. In fact, he was a model of an army chaplain, and with him for their spiritual wants and Surgeon Flood for bodily ailments the regiment was well provided.

It was April 25th, when we broke camp and started for Stafford to be in readiness to move with our division on the following day. It was dark before all had left and some of us lingered behind on the hill to take a farewell look at our camp. The moon was shining brightly, and its beams fell with a picturesque beauty on the ruins of our camp. In the distance lay the Potomac with a broad belt of silver across its surface. On our left close by were the graves of our comrades. The little graveyard lay white and still in the moonlight and we also gave that a goodbye glance. We left it with the evening wind sighing softly through its trees and waters of Acquia beating with subdued and sobbing sounds upon its banks. We knew that we should never re-visit the scene and so with a fond glance toward our deserted camp and its pleasant associations, we said goodbye and turned our faces and our thoughts to meet the events of the coming week.

We bivouacked that night at Stafford and were paid off there the next day. Then when the brigade band played the old quick step of, "Marching Along," the different regiments filed into the road and away we went to Chancellorsville. It was beautiful Spring weather, and the peach trees were blooming on every side, while the air rang with the sounds of the marching army. Wednesday evening found us at the Germanna Ford of the Rapidan. A party of rebel troops were building a bridge. They were surprised and captured. One rebel attempted to escape and ran up the dug way road of the opposite bank while a whole volley was fired at him. The dirt flew all around him, but he was unhurt. Our men yelled and cheered, and some cried out not to shoot him as so brave a man deserved to escape. However, one of a party of the 3rd Wisconsin posted at a farmhouse a long way back from the river waited till the firing was through then raised the hind sights of his rifle, rested the piece on the railing of the piazza and fired. The rebel fell dead. Afterwards when we crossed the river, we went up the same dug road. The man was there lying face down, stiff and motionless. Our men as they passed his body, praised his daring attempt to run the gauntlet and it was agreed he deserved a better fate.

The Rapidan was high when we reached it and a long discussion ensued among the generals about the safety of fording it. The question was finally settled and the 107th was ordered to take the lead and ford. Colonel Baldwin then captain of Company B, was the first man in. Here goes he said and plunged in up to his arms. The regiment followed in a solid column of fours, holding their muskets and ammunition at arm's length above their heads. So solid a mass did our men make that the water damned up and was a foot higher on the other side. The men were accordingly ordered to thin out the column as a matter of safety. Some men belonging to other regiments were drowned in crossing. Thursday night we reached the Chancellor House.

On Friday we fell in line to await orders. A long stream of men was marching by and taking positions farther up the road, and still no sign of the enemy nor a shot heard. Suddenly a cry arose, "See there! See there!" All looked towards the woods beyond us. Over them was a white cotton ball of smoke denoting a bursting shell. Then came the dull boom of the gun that fired it. Captain Bachman took out his watch and said, "Twenty minutes past twelve, the first gun of the battle of Chancellorsville." That afternoon was spent reconnoitering during which occurred the skirmish for our knapsacks which at one time we had left outside our picket line. Friday night found us in line in a dense piece of woods while a sharp musketry fire was going on in our immediate front. The firing ceased and at dusk there was a lull along the whole line. Then three shells in quick succession were thrown at our line and the third and last one killing Captain Rutter. His loss was deeply felt by all and in later campaigns we missed him greatly in the social circle of the regiment. He was a gentleman and a soldier, and there was not one of all our number whose loss would have occasioned more regret. Green be the turf above him for all loved him that knew him, and all praised him that named him. That night we slept on our arms with the rebel lines directly in our front. Saturday was passed building breastworks until four o'clock in the afternoon when we were ordered to advance. We moved out slowly with Colonel Diven riding at our head smoking a cigar and taking things cool. We moved on about two miles and then heard the roar of a battle in our rear. The order to counter march at a double quick was given, and we returned to our breastworks to cover the disastrous retreat of the 11th Corps. During the night the position was changed, heavy volleys and artillery duels were kept up nearly the whole night. The battle opened fiercely on Sunday morning, but a new line was formed, and new dispositions of the regiment were made. The right and left wings were in separate detachments with both holding their own but suffering heavy losses. By noon the whole army was in retreat. Then came the return to United States Ford and the massing of the army on the riverbank. There was great anxiety because of a severe rainstorm, but the army recrossed the river. The 107th was the first to cross the Rapidan even though the pontoon bridge was breaking up. Continuing on the 107th was the last to cross the Rappahannock. The regiment returned to Stafford and went into camp. They had lost one third of their number in killed and wounded and added fresh laurels pleasant quarters and none to the record of the regiment.[5]

The association formally celebrated Independence Day at least once during its existence. The following notice appeared in the Elmira newspapers before the fourth of July in 1873.

FOURTH OF JULY
1776—Independence Day—1873

The 97th anniversary of our National Independence will be observed by the 107th Regimental Association by a Basket Picnic at the Havana Glen to which all soldiers, sailors and the citizens throughout the counties of Chemung, Steuben, Schuyler, Tompkins, Yates and Seneca are respectfully invited. No formal table will be spread, but everybody attending are expected to bring provisions for their own and friends' picnic repast.

Gen. Alex. S. Diven of Chemung will make an address and other exercises appropriate to the day will be had which will be announced by a future programme. Good music in attendance. The members of Montour Post No. 22 G.A.R. of Havana and Baldwin Post No. 6 of Elmira have signified their intention to attend the picnic in a body, and other posts of the G.A.R. are expected to be present. A general rally of all of the veterans of the counties named is urged.

THE VETERAN'S FOURTH AT HAVANA GLEN
Picnic of the One Hundred and Seventh Regiment Association
ORATION OF GENERAL A.S. DIVEN

The Fourth of July was suitably observed by veterans of this and adjoining counties by a "basket picnic" under the auspices of the 107th Regimental Association at Havana Glen. At 9:30 a.m., Post Baldwin No. 6, G.A.R. left their headquarters on Lake Street accompanied by delegations of veterans of the 107th and other regiments and, under the escort of LaFrance's band, marched through Water, Main and Third streets to the Depot. Asa's fine music and the soldierly bearing of the procession made the parade quite an attractive one and called out a throng of admiring spectators.

At the Depot, the veterans were joined by a large multitude of citizens who embarked on the Northern Central excursion train at 10:30 a.m. for Havana (Montour Falls). The train was a large one, comprising of eleven heavily laden coaches. On arriving at Havana, the veterans and their friends were met by Montour Post No. 22, G.A.R. and under the marshalship of Lt. Edwin Weller, officer of the day, the line was formed and marched through the village to the Glen. The arrangements by the comrades of Montour Post to complete the comfort of their visiting comrades were ample. Carriages were at the Depot to transport the baskets of provisions and the disabled soldiers and sailors in attendance. At the Glen they had provided wall tents and established a fine little encampment with a row of stacked muskets to add to the military aspect of the scene. It was lunch time when the party reached the Glen, so baskets were speedily emptied of their contents by the nimble hands of the ladies, and the grounds soon presented a most inviting appearance. The reposts were opened in true army style on the grass covered ground under the shade of the trees, and all seemed to partake with full grown army appetites.

The wants of the inner man having been satisfied, the picnickers began to assemble around the speakers' stand. At two p.m., officers of the 107th association were seated on the stand. In front of the stand was a large throng of people made up of old and young of both sexes with a liberal number of soldiers in uniform. All were seated under the beautiful canopy of the overhanging trees with the interest they felt in the occasion plainly marked on their upturned faces.

Chaplain Crane opened with a prayer, followed by Hull Fanton reading the Declaration of Independence. Following him, the association president Dr. Flood introduced General Diven. Diven's talk was well received with strong applause at times and with tear filled eyes when he described the wounding and deaths of the heroes of the regiment. He began by commenting that their memories of the events of the war were still clear in their minds. He continued:

Comrades, ten years of peaceful pursuits have not effaced the recollections of the war. Nothing binds men together like mutual suffering and danger. How little we remember of our light pleasures and our companions in amusements. How Indelibly is fixed in our memories our sufferings and our companions in sufferings, our danger and our companions in danger, our griefs and our companions in grief. How hearts Mutually oppressed cling to each other. And where are these affinities more than in the dreaded realities of war?

Remember our first battle at Antietam, "It was the last time that we were ever spoiling for a fight." No stirring, thrilling excitement came with the morning's dawn. The sun came up resplendent as any summer sun, but we looked not on its splendor. We looked, Alas! Upon the most ghastly scene that had ever sickened our hearts. Fields that the day before waving in ripening grain were this morning covered with festering dead. And all day we gathered not sheaves to the garner, but corpses to the grave. Great heaven what a harvest. At the approach of evening, we left the field tainted with decomposing bodies of horses and men fearfully commingled. The heart sickened with the dreaded realities of war.

To the inexperienced the most dreadful part of a soldier's life is considered the strife of battle. Not so, remember the camps on Maryland Heights, Stafford Court House or Hope Landing. If there is one recollection more than another that we would be glad to obliterate it is surely of those pestilential camps. That dreadful pneumonia cough, that fever that crazed the brain, the sure precursor of death. Those solemn funerals, the tunes of which we conveyed our comrades to their graves still haunt me in my dreams.

We must remember as we pass that horrid march towards Fredericksburg and all the discomforts of that winter. How gladly we hailed the order of march for the Spring campaign of '63. Never a prisoner left a dungeon more eagerly than our camp, when we marched toward Chancellorsville under the proud banner of the 12th Army Corps. There we met the flying columns of the 11th Corps driven back by the fierce onset of Stonewall Jackson like chaff before the wind. How at early morning we just as we were about to eat the scant supply of provisions sent to us, the battle opened. We struggled with foe until the last round of ammunition was exhausted, and then we stood with fixed bayonets waiting for reinforcements. They replaced us, but almost immediately they fell back into and through our line. We countermarched and formed a new line near the Chancellorsville house only to be driven back by Rebel artillery.

It was a bloody day for the 107th. Many a brave comrade went to the rear in the arms of his companions. Many were left on the field in cold death, and there was little burying of the dead of that day's fight. A forest fire left little but charred bones to tell where the brave had fallen.

There was one particular incident that I should tell. As we had returned from a short but sharp skirmish. I stepped out to speak to General Ruger who was passing by. As I did a bursting shell covered, he and myself with mud. At the same time Captain Ruger who was at my side was mortally wounded.

The weather turned dark, and we were exposed to rain and the Rapidan rose to flood stage endangering our retreat and a confident enemy on our front challenging our advance. We waited for the order of our commander. And it is due to our courage to say that we waited with the hope that the order would be to advance rather than to acknowledge defeat and turn our backs to the foe. We would have gladly seen our pontoons swept from our moorings leaving us to victory, death or capture. For myself I can only say, and I believe I can say it for the regiment, that no order was so unwillingly obeyed as that of retreat from Chancellorsville. 1873[6]

The reunions continued to be held every year on September 17. The 1878 annual reunion was held at the Odd Fellows Hall on Lake Street in Elmira. The first mention of the subject of raising a monument to the memory of the men of the regiment who died during the war was introduced. After remarks by General Diven, Colonel G.I. Smith, Dr. P.H. Flood and others, it was thought advisable to appoint a committee to aid in the raising of the necessary funds. Over four hundred dollars were thereupon raised for the statue. A monument committee held a meeting and was organized as follows: Gen. Diven as chairman, P.H. Flood as treasurer, and A.S. Fitch as secretary. The committee would visit local citizens for subscriptions to which it was hoped that they will liberally respond A circular was ordered to be prepared and sent to each member of the regiment soliciting contributions for the monument.[7]

On Friday September 22, 1882, 107th NY Regimental association unveiled their granite and bronze memorial statue. The statue is an exact copy of the one on the Boston Common. The whole monument stands seventeen feet seven inches high with a base six by eight feet and the statue itself is seven feet three and one fourth inches in height. The monument base which was manufactured by A.W. Ayres of Elmira is of granite. On the front of its base are the raised dates "1861–1865." The lower base is polished on all four sides and on three of the sides there are cut in sunken letters the names of the battles in which the regiment participated. On the front or west side are "Antietam, Chancellorsville, Gettysburg, Resaca and New Hope Church." On the right side, "Pine Knob, Culps Farm, Kennesaw Mountain, Peach Tree Creek, Siege of Atlanta"; on the left side, "Sherman's March, Siege of Savannah, Carolinas, Averasboro, Bentonville." The upper section is ornamental with the number of the regiment "107" in a laurel wreath beneath a star and above the large, raised letters and polished letters "N.Y. Vols."

The monument is one of which Elmira and her veterans may well be proud and no more commanding and central location for it than that named above could be selected. The bronze statue which alone cost $1,600 in duplicate of its Boston original came from the bronze foundries of Bureau Brothers and Heaton, Philadelphia. The granite base is excellently wrought and its cost in addition to that of the statue was $900 making the entire cost, independent of the donated site, $2,500.

Application was made to the Board of Supervisors of Chemung County for the site on courthouse square for the monument. The board granted permission and then an appeal was made to the citizens of Elmira for aid to the fund. The money subscribed by the surviving comrades of the regiment covered nearly half of the cost of the monument. The contributions from all three counties quickly

107th New York memorial statue souvenir given out by the *Elmira Sunday Telegram* (John Trice).

107th New York Memorial Statue erected on Lake Street in Elmira, New York, in 1888 on the anniversary of the battle of Antietam (John Trice, author's collection).

succeeded in reaching the required goal so that this monument would forever be a remembrance of their more than 200 comrades who did not return from the war but will always be a part of their reunions.[8]

Several years after the 107th New York memorial statue had been erected, the following story was published about a happening that occurred as Arthur Fitch and Frank Frost were walking near the memorial statue. The story was subsequently printed in a small booklet that was made available to the veterans of the regiment and their friends. The booklet was titled "The Bronze Soldier," and credit for the story was given to Arthur S. Fitch, Brevet Captain Retired, 107th NYV Infantry. The following narrative was taken from the author's personal copy:

There had been a meeting of the post to discuss arrangements for Memorial Day. At a late hour Comrade Frank Frost and I walked leisurely down Lake Street. Our minds ran back to the old war days. Our talk was reminiscent. As we drew near the Court House park, the soldier's monument attracted our attention, and we halted. The grassy terrace about the monument looked inviting and we entered the grounds and seated ourselves thereon. The street was deserted and an unusual quiet prevailed. Our talk reverted to the battles inscribed upon the granite pedestal above us. They were battles that we had each participated in. Some of them were historic, 'Antietam, Chancellorsville, Gettysburg, Atlanta, Sherman's March to the Sea, Savannah, Carolinas—names that thrill every patriotic heart. We had "fought over" two or three of these, unmindful of the passing time, and were about taking up the Atlanta campaign, when the city clock clanged out the hour of 12—mid-night. Aroused from our meditation, we began to "limber up" for the homeward march.

A noise over our head attracted our attention. We gazed upward to the bronze figure that crowns the monument and were amazed to see in the dim light a movement of the hitherto rigid form. As we gazed there came a distinct command, "Attention." The figure relaxed from the long "parade rest," and stood at "attention." Then came "Shoulder Arms." Up swung the old Springfield to a shoulder. "Arms Port" followed, then "Break Ranks," as the hand of the bronze soldier rattled against the rifle stock, the figure leaped down from the pedestal and stood beside us. Too much surprised to speak, we stood fast and stared. "How are you, comrades of the 107th?" spoke the figure. "Glad to see you. Fortunate that you happened here at this time—the time of my annual rest. It's mighty hard work to stand up there for a whole year—that is—it would be were I flesh like you. What do you think about it, eh?" and the figure actually poked his thumb against Comrade Frost's ribs and grinned.

Comrade Frost loves an old soldier so well that the supernatural character of the Comrade who thus addressed him had no chilling effect upon him, and he said, "I never tried it for more than five minutes at a time, but I stood on a barrel once for four hours for some trifling neglect of duty. That was before I became such a fighter, when I was a sergeant. I was promoted afterward." The bronze figure laughed and said: "Sit down, boys; let's talk," and he proceeded to talk. He did all the talking. Neither Frost nor myself are shorthand writers, so could save but a portion of the utterances of our strange visitor.

"You fellows don't remember me. I was killed at Averasboro, North Carolina, in 1865, after passing safely through all the great battles that preceded it. Yes, the name is on the monument, next to the last battle Sherman's army fought. There were several of us mustered out at that time. But say, those were great days. I just stand up there thinking about them, having nothing else to do. You who continue to live are too busy to remember as I do. You forget more than you remember. It's all as real and vivid to me as if it were happening now."

How grandly patriotic everybody was in 1862, when President Lincoln called for 300,000 men, that is when you and I enlisted. Why, in one month more than 1,000 men were enrolled here in Elmira and were organized into a regiment and were on their way to the seat of war.

What a lot of young fellows we were; how little we knew what a soldier's life was. Do you remember that first march of our campaign? We were so green that we could hardly turn around without falling over one another, but we could carry a gun, and when the orders came to march into Maryland there were 1,000 of us in line, and we marched as bravely as those old "vets" of the Second Massachusetts and Third Wisconsin and 'Twenty-seventh Indiana, with whom we were brigaded.

That first march to battle—can you fellows ever forget it? How we sang "Old John Brown" as we crossed over the Potomac into Maryland that warm September night. How the bright gun barrels glistened in the moonlight. What a lot of us there were? Never afterward did the 107th muster as many men in line. How strange it all was—that first march. Do you remember how the first night's bivouac was disturbed by that bloodcurdling sound of "long roll?" The nerviest man among us shivered as he heard it. Do you remember how awkwardly we proceeded as we tried to prepare our first morning meal? Most of us compromised on a cup of half-cooked coffee and a hard tack. How we straggled after forage until the provost guard materialized into a thing to fear, and army orders crystallized into "obey or suffer the consequences." Oh, we had lots of things to learn before we ceased to be "green 'uns"—small wonder though— for three weeks before this first campaign began, we were at our peaceful homes in York state. Nevertheless, we were thought good soldiers enough to become targets for rebel shooters, and all this "freshness" ended, when, a week later, we came to the field whose name heads the battle list up there on the worst front of the monument. I should like to talk to you until daylight about Antietam, but you know all about it. There was never after that battle any question as to the soldierly qualities of "Ours."

Well, boys, don't forget in these days of comfort, the awful hardships of that first winter at Maryland Heights, Fairfax and Stafford. You cannot remember as well as I that there were more than 200 of the boys in the hospitals at Harper's Ferry, and that funerals were of daily occurrence. More than one poor boy died in his own bleak quarters. Do you remember the boys of company F working all night to make a coffin in which to bury poor Barnes, and how they, sometimes traveled to the other side of the mountain in search of boards enough to frame a rude box for some dead comrade?

Rations were poor—and clothing and camp equipage were hard to get. And the first marches we made southward in December, when the weather was so cold that the water froze in our canteens. There were days and nights of cold rain and sleet, and marches through mud almost impassable. How it tried souls and bodies, too. What a lot of the boys gave out under it. Do you remember the little cemetery at Hope Landing with the two dozen or more graves of our dead boys? And then the spring came, bringing us to that second battle named, "Chancellorsville," and more tough times, from which, with scarce a rest, we come to No. 3, up there, "Gettysburg." How the earth shook there during that tremendous cannonade. That's where there was glory enough to go all around. Are you tired, boys? If you are not let me talk a little longer. I don't get a chance very often. We dead comrades don't forget, and we don't want you living ones to forget.

After Gettysburg, you know, we were sent to the west and became a part of the grand old army of Sherman. And there began a series of operations that added fresh laurels to our flag, and a long addition to the list of our dead. Look at the battle-roll up there, "Resaca," "New Hope Church," "Pine Knob," "Culp's Farm," "Kennesaw," "Peach Tree Creek." It was at "Resaca" we saw the gallant advance of our sister regiment, the 141st. Archie Baxter can tell you about it.

It was glorious, and then a week later the 107th caught it at New Hope Church, or Dallas. They nearly wiped us out there. Then it came the turn of the 141st at "Peach Tree"—a gloriously deadly fight for them; and so, for four full months there was scarcely a day without the sounds of a conflict—soldiers' graves all along the battle road for 150 miles. But Atlanta was ours at last, and "'fairly won."

Then came that famous "March to the Sea" and the siege and capture of Savannah, followed by a longer march and more trying times through the Carolinas. You know the rest. The end of the war and your peaceful march northward to Washington. What a circuit you had made, when you came back after three years to your camp, and what a change in the appearance of the regiment. Instead of the 1,000 less than 300; the bright new flags faded and tattered. The fresh young boys transformed into bronzed and manly veterans. Nearly as many sleeping in soldiers' graves as marched in the grand review.

Do you think of those boys? You will on Memorial Day. They are a part of your glorious history. They camped with you, stood picket with you, marched with you, fought with you, endured with you, and died by your side. In the consideration of your glorious army record they should be accorded a part no less prominent than the living ones. They are in bivouac in the beyond waiting to welcome you to a grand reunion. Don't forget them. My time is up. Good-bye, boys, hope I haven't tired you; the relief guard is coming. There are enough of us to stand guard here, a year at a time, as long as this monument shall need a guard." At this the bronze figure saluted and sprang back to his position, there was a distinct murmur of voices, a rattling of arms, and as we turned away the dawning light fell upon the again immovable figure, and as we gazed into each other's faces, each beheld an expression, no less thoughtful than that upon the bronze face above us.

∗ ∗ ∗

In 1885, the 19th annual reunion of the 107th Regiment N.Y. Volunteers was held on the battlefield of Antietam on the 23rd anniversary of the regiment's first engagement. The comrades assembled at Erie Depot on September 16, where they boarded the train. There were approximately 70 men, mostly from the 107th New York and a number of men from other regiments. A delightful ride of 11 hours brought the excursionists to the Sharpsburg railroad station. Here they were met by the mayor, a multitude of local citizens, and comrades from the local G.A.R. post. A reception followed that pleasantly finished the days experiences.

The morning of the 17th dawned warm and cloudless like that other morning twenty-three years ago. They proceeded to the national cemetery where they were greeted by Captain W.A. Donaldson, the cemetery director. The cemetery is located on the ground that was held by Lee's army during the battle. There is a tower from which every part of the battlefield can be seen. The comrades separated into small groups and went off to visit the field in detail. The old Dunker church was the objective of many. There they reach the lane where the right wing advanced on the morning of the battle. The lane immediately took on a familiar look, and they soon found the spot where they had lain. Colonel Diven found the stump of a tree and exclaimed, "It is the very spot where I stood when the regiment advanced to this place." It was while lying here that they encountered a perfect storm of the enemy's missiles. Here their beautiful blue banner was torn to pieces by an enemy shell.

The next thing was to locate the place where the regiment lay when ordered to support the batteries in a cleared field in front of the woods. This was the spot where Theodore Smith of Company F was struck by a shell and lost his leg. While in this spot, they discovered a bullet, half embedded in a stump. Frank Frost found a rusted canteen that had lain undisturbed since the battle. Pieces of bone and part of a skull were also found.

From this point, they moved to the rear to the stone house where the spring was and many of the wounded were carried. This house was where Theodore Smith had his leg amputated. He visited the house and found the very room where his leg was amputated; the same family was still occupying the house. A portion of the group then went back to the Line farm where the regiment bivouacked the night of the 16th. The course of their advance the following morning was easily followed. At a point where the regiment formed a line of battle, a rest was taken. Here it was that General Mansfield rode out and spoke these words, "Ah boys! We shall do a fine thing today. We have got them where we want them, they cannot escape with the skin of their teeth." He then rode forward, and within minutes was shot and mortally wounded. His body was placed on a blanket and carried from the field by the men, passing directly through the line as they stood waiting the order to go forward. This incident made a lasting impression on everyone.

Having traversed the battlefield pretty completelym the men returned to the town and rested. A few of them visited "Bloody Lane" where it is said that blood actually filled the ditches. Some visited Burnsides Bridge, and some strolled back to the cemetery and rested, recounting their experiences during the battle. The day passed in like manner, and by 9:15p.m., they were gathered at the train station ready to proceed to Gettysburg.

Once the group was in the cars, a business meeting was held. Officers were chosen for the next year and resolutions adopted. The 18th of September was spent at the Gettysburg battlefield, but a description was not included in the newspaper. Instead, there were accounts about the following three nights: September 6, 1862, September 16, 1862, and September 16, 1885.

The First Night: the night of September 6, 1862, the beginning of the first march, the first campaign of the 107th regiment. What survivor of the regiment can forget it?

The welcome marching orders, the hurried preparations, the filling of the haversacks and canteens, the rolling and slinging of blankets, (haversacks and tents were left behind) the falling in, the standing in line ready for the "forward that came just as night fell, off at last, one thousand men, boys we call them now, fresh from home, marching in columns of four, guns at right shoulder, the long column winding out and away up hill and down dale, with a steady tramp, tramp, the cadence broken only by the laugh, the shout."

The night air grows cool and crisp, the pace quickens, the moon shines down among the dark mass of men, horses, wagons and artillery. It glistens upon the bayonets and gun barrels, and the line becomes a rippling, tossing stream of shimmering steel. Ah, who can forget it. As they cross the Potomac along the old aqueduct bridge someone begins to chant the "Battle hymn of the Republic." More and more began singing until all sang the chorus, "Glory, glory Hallelujah." Alas, that night's march would be the only march the 107th regiment made with full ranks. Never again was there such an unbroken line of its members and so the memory of that first march will be best remembered by all of the surviving members.

The Second Night: September 16, 1862, a dark night chilly and foreboding, there in a clover field wet with dew, facing a grim wood where in lie the enemy. The men are bivouacking the, "the night before the battle." No shouts or songs now. The stillness of the night is broken by hostile picket shots close in front. What are the thoughts that fill the minds of the men as they lie there anxiously awaiting the morning?

The Third Night: September 16, 1885, A handful of veteran survivors are again approaching that historic field. The scene is changed, the youthful faces, the elastic step, the flush of youth no longer appear. They are men, bearded and thoughtful, gray haired and grizzly many of them. They come in luxurious cars through the thriving and picturesque valleys of the Susquehanna and the Cumberland whereas throughout the land blessed peace reigns unchallenged and no dread of the morrow disturbs them.

*The Elmira Daily Advertiser* printed an article on September 29, 1885, that told a story about Theodore G. Smith, who was wounded at the battle of Antietam.

An Advertiser reporter, on his rounds after news, stopped in at the office of the county clerk the other afternoon. Deputy Theodore G. Smith was just wrapping up a little box and the curiosity of the reporter of course prompted an inquiry. The box was reopened to allow an inspection of its contents, which were curious indeed. There was a grape shot, Minnie ball from an Enfield rifle, several round rebel bullets with one or two flattened pieces of lead that were once bullets and had struck stones when fired from a rifle. A small piece of bone was among the collection, and an inquiry was made as to the object of its preservation.

"I keep that," said Mr. Smith, to mark a coincidence that has but few parallels. Now that bone, a doctor tells me, is from the right leg of a human skeleton. It is a fragment of the lower joint fitting in the ankle. When I was at the old battlefield of Antietam Captain Ezra Gleason and I by the courtesy of a very kind old resident Sharpsburg, Henry Neikirk made a tour of the places along Antietam Creek that had been most eventful to us during the war. Our regiment was in what was regarded, and especially by those in the immediate vicinity, as the thickest of the Antietam fight. That was where I had my leg shot off. I was seventeen years old, and the events of the battle stay by me better than any other, you may be sure. When we were down last week Mr. Neikirk drove us over north of Sharpsburg about a mile to the old Dunkard church. It was just beyond this that we were located, a little to the northeast, not many rods. I located by means of a lane the spot that I thought was the place of our sharpest battle. We were all lying down shooting over a knoll. I found the same large pile of stones that was on my left hand and a large stump, now considerably rooted away, that was on my right. There were certain fences that I remembered seeing. I was lying on my face when a solid shot from a rebel battery came over and struck me just above the ankle, tearing away my ankle and foot. I lay there some time before being carried to a hospital, and the picture of the surroundings became firmly fixed in my memory. I was able on our return visit to locate my position within, I am sure, a very few feet. That piece of bone was picked up by Arthur Fitch the other day within a very short distance of where I was shot, and I preserve it, not claiming it was part of me when I was a soldier boy but look upon the finding of it as a remarkable coincidence. It is not unreasonable to suppose that this piece of bone was shot away from my right leg twenty-four years ago."

The reporter's interest in Mr. Smith's first visit to the Antietam battlefield since the day it was irrigated with human blood having been aroused, many questions followed. Mr. Smith said that after locating the spot upon which he was wounded he followed the course over which he was carried to the hospital. He was first taken to the house of Samuel Poffenburger. The floor was covered with the wounded and there was no place for him, so the stove was dumped out of doors, and he was given a bed on the brick floor in front of the old-fashioned fireplace. He was next taken to the barn of B.H. Hoffman where three days after the wounding his limb was amputated. On his recent visit Mr. Smith went to these places and found the same families living there, and very interesting people they were.[9]

### Gettysburg Battlefield September 17, 1888
#### The 107th NY Monument on Culps Hill
#### Address by General Alexander S. Diven

Comrades and Citizens:

Perhaps the period of greatest despondency in the struggle for the preservation of the Union was in the last days of June and on the 1st of July 1862. On the 3d day of April 1862, the Government was so sure of its strength as to order recruiting for the army to cease. This order must have been given either in ignorance of the strength of the enemy or without calculating the waste of the army from sickness, desertion and the casualties of battle. While other fields of contest were not overlooked, the great expectation of the Nation was centered on the occupation of Richmond and the capture of Lee's army as the ending of the struggle. Early in the winter of 1862 an army considered by all, including its gallant commander, equal to the achievement, was in the field. A campaign was commenced that was confidently believed would meet this expectation. Why it then was not realized I do not consider, further than to say that it was not from want of courage, bravery, or skill on the part of the grand old Army of the Potomac, or the generalship of its com-mander. After the most heroic contest in a battle lasting from the 25th of June to the 2d of July, against unequaled numbers, instead of entering Richmond, all that was achieved was a base on the James River, from which Richmond might be besieged. However insignificant this advan-tage may have been regarded at that time, it took an equally protracted campaign and equally sanguinary series of battles to obtain the same base at a later date. Critics of the conduct of the war are, and perhaps always will be, divided as to the wisdom of abandoning this base of oper-ations in 1862, to be obtained at a later day by a greater expenditure of time, money and life. I allude to these events only to show the state of feeling throughout the country, from the fact that a campaign that was confidently expected to end the Rebellion had only obtained a base from which Richmond might be besieged. The whole country seemed paralyzed, if not in despair, by this dis appointment. At this juncture the Governors of most of the loyal States, at the sug-gestion of Governor Morgan of our own State, tendered to the President their aid to increase the army. Answering the address of these governors, the President issued a proclamation call-ing for volunteers to the number of 300,000 and indicating the proportion of each State. On the night of the 6th of July, sharing in common with almost everybody the gloom that seemed to envelop the Nation, at a late hour, sitting on the doorstep of my lodgings, a boy came to me, say-ing the President wanted to see me at Mr. Seward's house. Never before having received so dis-tinguished a summons, I followed the messenger at once. Arriving at the Secretary's house, I found there none but the Secretary, Mr. Van Valkenburgh and Theodore Pomeroy. On enter-ing the room, Mr. Seward, without the customary greeting, in what was for him a most abrupt manner, said: "Diven, can't you go home and raise a regiment?" To make my answer a little more curt than the question, I said "Yes." He then rose hastily and greeted me with more warmth than he had ever shown towards me before, and then told me that the President had been with him until a late hour; that he had sent for a number of the New York members of Congress, whom the President had asked to raise regiments; that they had not met with much encouragement, more than a promise to think of it; that Pomeroy and Van Valkenburgh had agreed to go home and try, and they at a late hour suggested that he send for me; that the President and all had left, as it was past 12, and that Van Valkenburgh and Pomeroy had waited to see what I would say. He then said: "Your promptness was somewhat a surprise, but nothing could gratify me more. Be off to-morrow."

By this time, I began to consider the undertaking I had assumed so promptly. I asked him to give me a letter to Charles Cook, the value of whose influence I well understood. He at once sat down and wrote probably the most laconic letter of his life. It simply said, "Help Diven." I have alluded to the events leading up to this interview at the Secretary's house, because it was then and there the One hundred and seventh Regiment had its inception. Van Valkenburgh, Pome-roy, and myself, late as it was, went to Pomeroy's rooms and arranged that they should leave in the morning, and that I should remain until the session of the House, and ask leave of absence for each one. I desired to stay because a few days before I had prepared a bill for the enlistment of colored troops, giving notice of its introduction, and was waiting until, in the order of busi-ness, I could introduce it. The bill was in my desk in the House, and I wanted to commit it to some member friendly to its passage. In asking leave of absence, I obtained leave for remarks, and used the privilege to allude to this bill, and to make an argument in its favor. I gave it to the care of Thaddeus Stevens, who greatly improved its provisions before its passage. I allude to this as a good excuse for disobeying Seward's order to leave in the morning. As it was, I reached home on the evening of the 8th, in time to forward my letter to Cook, with a letter of my own about as remark able for brevity as the one forwarded, and, coming from me, not at all remark able for some bad grammar. I had the satisfaction the next day but one to receive a printed hand-bill containing a copy of Seward's letter and mine and calling a war meeting at the courthouse in Havana. And that meeting opened the ball for recruiting the One hundred and seventh. In the meantime, General Van Valkenburgh had convened what was called the senatorial commit-tee for volunteer recruiting for the Twenty-seventh Senatorial District, and arranged for enlist-ing and officering a regiment, with Van Valkenburgh as colonel, myself as lieutenant colonel, and Colonel Smith as major. A series of meetings was arranged for Corning, Bath and Addison, which were attended and addressed by Van Valkenburgh, Smith, and others. There was no occa-sion for a meeting in Elmira. Every man, woman and child seemed to be a recruiting agent, and so rapid were the enlistments, that after the meetings alluded to, Van Valkenburgh had all he could do in attending to the mustering in and organizing the recruits, an office for which he New York at Gettysburg. was thoroughly qualified, having discharged this duty in organizing the first volunteers for the service. On this occasion he was assisted by Colonel Smith. Meantime a series of war meetings for different places in the counties of Schuyler, Chemung, Steuben, and Allegany were advertised. The late Dr. Tracy Beadle, Rev. Thomas K. Beecher and I addressed these meetings, Dr. Beadle furnishing his carriage for our conveyance. I had more than once attended public meetings on political and other occasions when excitement ran high, but I never witnessed anything to com pare with the enthusiasm attending these gatherings. There were no divisions, no politics, nothing but a united zeal to sustain the Government. These meetings were arranged for two each day, one by day and one by night. Most of our night meetings were out-door by torchlight, for want of halls large enough to contain the crowd. Appeals at these meetings were for enlistments for those willing to enlist, and for money from those that did not enlist, to be given as bounty to those that did. Our appeals in either case never went unan-swered. We had gone through the program for Schuyler, Chemung, and Steuben, and were at our third meeting in Allegany, when I was telegraphed by Van Valkenburgh that the regiment was full, organization complete, and ordered at once to Washington. I left in the middle of a grand meeting at Friendship to join the regiment, and I always consider the service I rendered the country in raising the regiment much greater than commanding it. We had at these meetings not only recruited the quota for this regiment, but a surplus of 400 to be organized in another regiment. In about four weeks from the time General Van Valkenburgh and myself left Wash-ington, we were back with as fine a regiment as was ever mustered into service. On leaving the cars at Washington Station we were formed in line and reviewed by the President and Secretary Seward, who were there awaiting our arrival. This distinction was awarded us in consideration of our being the first to respond to the call for 300,000. In addition to this honor the Governor of our State presented us a banner. We, however, had little precedence in this exhibition of loyalty from our own and other States. New regiments from all parts of the country arrived faster than they could be assigned to brigades and divisions. Our own regiment was not assigned to a bri-gade until on the march to meet the enemy at Antietam, and when the order came assigning us to General Gordon's brigade, I spent half a day among a confused mass of moving troops trying to find him. I have no occasion to detail events known to you as well as to myself, between our arrival at Washington and our first battle at Antietam; but I am proud to say that at that first baptism of war the regiment acquitted itself, not as a regiment of raw recruits, but as tried veter-ans. And we were so reported by our commanding general. It was by accident that we were placed in a position that is most trying to real courage. We had been ordered by General Gordon to change our position, and while executing that order were stopped by General French and ordered to support a battery whose support had just retreated. And there for weary hours under fire from the enemy, without emptying a musket, we kept our position until the suspension of the fight. I need not remind you of the weary life of the regiment from its participation in this, its first great battle, to that of its next at Chancellorsville, in which it lost nothing of the

**Veterans of the 107th New York at their Gettysburg battlefield memorial on Culps Hill. Colonel Nirom Crane in the top hat (courtesy John Trice).**

reputation gained at Antietam, other than to allude to our losses from sickness. Soon after Antietam, while encamped at Maryland Heights, we were first deprived of our honored, revered, and loved Colonel Van Valkenburgh, from a disease caused by exposure, from which he never fully recovered, resulting in his death a few months ago. Added to this was a prevailing disease, designated by the doctors as pneumonia, that continued with the regiment through the winter, and to which more than 100 of our comrades succumbed. At Fairfax Station, on a forced march to participate in the battle of Fredericksburg, we were ordered to send all unable to endure a forced march to Washington. Lieutenant Colonel Smith, being at that time on the sick list, was detailed with about thirty disabled men in accordance with this order, and the regiment was thereafter deprived of his valuable services. It should be mentioned that on the resignation of Van Valkenburgh I was advanced to the Colonelcy, and Major Smith to the lieutenant colonelcy, and on Smith's resignation, Captain Colby was advanced to lieutenant colonel, and Capt. William F. Fox to the rank of major. These were the only changes in the field and staff of the regiment during my command. The battle of Chancellorsville, it seems to me, was the saddest event of the war. Our defeat arose from no want of bravery on the part of our troops, and few regiments exhibited more courage than the One hundred and seventh. There may have been a Providence in that defeat. It emboldened the enemy to take the offensive in leading to his overthrow on this battlefield. Soon after Chancellorsville I left the regiment, and its course after that can be better related by the officer succeeding me. I knew enough of it, however, to state that it lost none of its reputation, and that its service clearly entitled it to the recognition given it on this occasion. The field of no battle in the world is marked by mementos of events as this. Statues to mark the places where heroes fell, and monuments to tell where regiments fought and bled. Comrades, we that still survive may justly take pride in that our regiment is not left out in these testimonials of a Nation's gratitude.[10]

Address by Gen. N.M. Crane.

Comrades of the One hundred and seventh New York:

After over a quarter of a century we are again assembled upon this immortal battlefield, a small number of those who stood with us on that day. The circumstances by which we are surrounded are very different from those of July 2 and 3, 1863. We are assembled here to-day for the purpose of dedicating this beautiful monument, presented to us by the great and noble State of New York, to commemorate the bravery, valor and self-sacrifice made by you on that day on behalf of our State and Nation. It was upon this line that the glorious old Twelfth Corps stood, firm as the rocks by which we are surrounded, for long hours resisting the assaults of our enemies directed upon this point for the purpose of turning this flank of our army. After twenty-six years I again see, in imagination, the long lines of gray rushing upon us with savage energy. Amid flame and smoke, amid the roar of musketry and storm of deadly missiles, with the dead and wounded falling around us, the gallant One hundred and seventh stood like a wall, firm and unfaltering, determined that no power should move us from our position. On our right and left the gallant men of other regiments resented the furious attack for hours, until the enemy was hurled back, shattered and bleeding from our determined front. At this point, on that memorable day, you assisted to repulse one of the famous fighting corps of Lee's army, Jackson's old corps, and sent them to the rear defeated, shattered, and demoralized. On this line was made one of the most ferocious assaults, with long and stubborn determination, that was made on this field, not excepting the famous charge of Pickett's Division at a later hour of the same day on another part of our lines, the defeat of which foreshadowed the result of this great battle. This monument will be a lasting record of your devotion and bravery as long as granite will endure. Future generations will visit this famous field, and gaze with wonder and admiration upon this spot, made sacred by your blood and devotion. Many comrades who stood side by side with us on that day have found a bloody grave, from the Tennessee to Atlanta, from Atlanta to the Sea, and at Bentonville and Averasboro. Time has silvered the hair of all of us, and in a few more years all who are now present will have passed away. But you leave to your children a lasting legacy more valuable than all else on earth—the record of a faithful, brave devotion to your country, and the knowledge that by your deeds and suffering this grand and glorious Nation was preserved, and the liberties handed down to us by our forefathers were preserved and maintained ; that the curse of slavery was forever wiped out from this continent, and millions of human beings forever made free ; that the great principle was carried out that all men were born free and equal and shall have equal rights under the constitution and laws ; and that you demonstrated to the world that the government made by the people and for the people will be forever maintained Mr. Krauth, as the representative of the One hundred and seventh New York Volunteers, I hand over the custody of this monument to the Gettysburg Battlefield Association, which you represent, knowing it will be in safe keeping, and forever preserved for the purposes intended.[11]

Twenty-Fourth Annual Reunion
*107th N.Y. Vols.*
Elmira, N.Y. Sept. 1, 1890

COMRADE,

The twenty-fourth annual reunion of the 107th Regiment, N.Y. Vols. will be held at Elmira September 17th 1890.

Headquarters will be at the rooms of Baldwin Post No. 6, in the State Armory on East Church Street.

Business meeting at 12:30 p.m. Reunion dinner at 2 p.m.

It is hoped that every comrade who cannot be present will send a word of Greeting.

Please acknowledge on within postal card the receipt of this notice, correcting errors if any, in name or Postoffice address, in order that everyone maybe marked "Present" or "Accounted For" at roll call.

ARTHUR S. FITCH EDWARD KENDALL
Secretary President[12]

The twenty-fourth Reunion was held on September 17, 1890, at the New York State Armory on Church Street in Elmira. It was held there by invitation of Post Baldwin No. 6, Grand Army of the Republic at the rooms of the post in the armory.

Edward Kendall was the association's president for this reunion and was also the primary speaker. He opened the meeting with the following presentation.

Comrades it gives me great pleasure to greet so many of you on this twenty-fourth annual reunion of the 107th New York Volunteers. As the years go by I look forward to these meetings with comrades as the event of the year which must be kept, and at each reunion I promise myself that if my life should be spared to be present, to grasp your hands in friendship. Let us cherish these reunions, the memories that they bring and as the roll is called, we find that some comrade has fallen out. We are reminded that it is to take rest from which no bugle nor roll of drum shall call again

Twenty-eight years ago, on the 25th of July at the age of nineteen, I with about twenty-five others, attended the office of Dr. Flood and was examined and I was passed as one suitable recruit. I did not enlist until August 6, 1862, when I enlisted in company H and left Elmira with the regiment August 13th. After reaching Washington and having been reviewed by the president we crossed the Long Bridge into Virginia. Here on the left of the road near Fort Albany we passed our first night in a field. I lost my pillow on that night. That included my knapsack and all its contents, which I found it quite a task to replace. We received our Springfield rifles on August 19. From this time on we were kept busy perfecting ourselves in the duties of a soldier.

On the night of September 6, we commenced our first campaign, the all-night march. During the halts in the morning, we made our first attempts to make coffee by cooking it in our drinking cups we had stopped on Sunday morning at the Rockville, Md fair grounds. We were brigaded here with the Third Wisconsin, Twenty Seventh Indiana, Second Massachusetts and the Thirteenth New Jersey, which organization was kept until the close of the war. *Author's note: The 150th NY was later added to their brigade.*

While the battle of South Mountain was in progress, we were sent up the valley for several miles; our forces having gained the battle we were ordered back. On the morning of September 17th, we entered the battlefield and almost immediately a shell struck our regiment near our colors and killing and wounding several just as we were entering the woods in front of Dunker Church. The next shell struck Cyrus Covill the second man from my left and killed him instantly. It exploded as it passed Stephen Edwards severely injuring his neck and head so it was thought that he could not possibly survive. He did survive and was discharged. However, he re-enlisted and joined the regiment just before the Atlanta Campaign. He died soon after reaching Savannah. *Author's note: He died of chronic diarrhea February 15, 1865, in Savannah, GA.*

After we came out of the woods in front of Dunker Church we were halted, ordered to counter march and move to the left and rear while Company H was standing waiting its turn, Company A being a head of us was moving off when an aide rode up and said, "For God's sake save this battery!" Our captain E.C. Clark, now of Dubuque, Iowa, who on that day was wounded by a minnie ball through the lung, which ball still remains under his shoulder blade, drew his sword and called Company H to attention, and then forward file right march, and we were placed in the rear of Battery M. First New York. Standing there in line while the rest of our regiment was forming on our right except for Company E which was on our left, and here from early morning until after 3 o'clock in the afternoon we received our first lessons in battle.

That this position was one of peril is attested to by our long list of killed and wounded and by our colors riddled with shot and shell. During the lulls in the firing the orderly would call the company rolls, and I not answering one of those calls, was awakened having been trying to sleep. When the rebels made their charges moving from the woods steadily, several lines deep, our shells met them. As they came farther canister would strike the ground in their front spread out like a fan and whole companies would apparently be taken out at a time. On and still on, until at last forced to retreat they moved off as steadily as they advanced leaving almost wide rows of their dead. During one of these charges a private of Company C got upon a rock where he could view the entire scene unmindful of bullets, swinging his hat cried, "Bullie, set them up on the other alley." In the New York Tribune of 1889 one John B. Kittle of Deckerstown, NJ claimed this from a member of Company C, 89th New York under his own supervision. After being relieved and making our coffee, we again were formed on the edge of the woods. While lying down in line a solid shot came bounding through the woods and passed over our company. A comrade who had joined us there lying near said to me, "Ed, I have such a cold." He had not been in the battle, and he served his full term in the Invalid Corps.

After Antietam our camp at Maryland Heights during the hot Autumn days and chilly nights, the strain and exposure of the late campaign and the extra fatigue work cutting timber on the mountain side caused our having nearly 300 sick. The first death from sickness was Cpl. Joseph Couse of Company H. I was in charge of the firing squad and his burial in the rear of the old house on the mountain was the most solemn funeral service I ever attended. These burials were frequent during the fall and winter Ethan Worden of Company H died October 22, 1862. I was detailed to procure boards for the purpose of making a coffin. We procured them about three miles from camp, taking the base boards from a door yard fence. In a letter home October 28, 1862, I made mention, Company H has a very large sick list. The prevailing diseases are diarrhea, rheumatism and fevers. This morning as corporal, I had charge of the men who were to see the doctor. There were 36 who came to get quinine tablets. Our sick list had been increasing for a week and taking out those who are in hospital, detailed on special duty and our sick in camp, there are not 40 men to do duty in our company. Leaving this camp on October 29, 1862, for Antietam Ford where we remained until December 10, 1862, when we moved and finally camped for a short time at Fairfax Station. Here F.M. Cronkrite, Ben Force, Elijah Putnam, George Carpenter and I were tenting together. On the morning of January 19, 1863, each was determined that the other should build a fire, and while we were trying to decide that matter, orders came to pack up and fall. We ceased our quarreling and finally got our coffee. On January 23rd we reached Stafford Court House, tired and hungry. Five hard tack per man had been issued that morning, nothing else. My men had a small quantity of coffee and a small piece of pork which Cronkrite put into a pan and said we could have a smell if we could not have a bite. About midnight rations were issued. Our march finally ended the night of 27th of January 1863 in the rain at Hope Landing. It both rained and snowed during the night and snowed all the next day. On the morning of the 29th some 8 or 10 inches had fallen. Here we built corduroy roads, were inspected, performed the many duties of camp life with a large sick list and many deaths until the 27th of April when we left our camp and entered upon the Chancellorsville campaign.

I found among my papers a table of the condition of the regiment on August 15, 1862. Commissioned officers: 38, Enlisted men: 980 Total: 1,018. On February 15, 1863 six months afterwards here were: Dead and Discharged: 9 officers and 117 enlisted men, Sick: 3 officers and 286 enlisted men, On Leave: officers 3 and enlisted men 103, Absent Detailed 2 officers and 31 enlisted men, Present 26 officers, 440 enlisted men.

The roll call by Secretary Fitch showed the total number of survivors on the roll to be 333. Of these, 84 answered present and 110 answered by mail; many of those were read. The roster shows the membership scattered in nearly every state in the nation. There were six on the membership roll that had died since the last reunion.

Next, the *Elmira Sunday Telegram* presented each man in attendance a souvenir copy of a photograph of the tattered battle flag of the 107th from Antietam.

The group was then photographed by Larkin in front of the Armory. After the taking of the photograph, the men went back into the Armory and sat down for dinner. Following dinner were a series of remarks by various attendees, and the meeting was adjourned at 5:30 p.m.

The 25th Annual Reunion of the 107th New York Volunteers took place in 1891 and featured the following presentation.

THE CAMPAIGNS OF THE 107th NY Volunteers,
By Capt. H.G. Brigham.
AUTUMN-LEAVED COMRADES OF THE OLD ONE HUNDRED AND SEVENTH:

What a change has been wrought since last I met you in your spring leaves of years ago. Many an autumn has passed since then, and leaf after leaf has fallen from the grand old tree, also many of the greener foliage was cut down then, so full of nourishment like the cedar and pines we felled at Fairfax and Stafford to corduroy our way. They too of the old regiment have gone to pave the way for us, and soon we must follow.

Comrades, it has not been my pleasure to meet with you in all this time, and you cannot tell how strongly my heart has yearned to be with you. It has seemed to me as though I had been on detached service; and if I were to live this life over, I would say to the commander, "Please excuse me; I would prefer to stay with the boys; detail someone else."

We then thought it pretty hard times. It was fearful hard, still among the happiest days of my life were spent in the army. It hard its dark days and glorious jolly ones! Jay Gould's money could not buy the panorama for us. Those who did not go or stay with us, do not know what the grandeur of life is. I have been compelled to live at hotel tables of all grades, the best to the poorest on this continent, still there never one to equal the table de hotel Poncho, going through Georgia which fairly groaned with those elegant hams, sweet potatoes and honey. And for the next course came the "Goober nuts and the canteen had its grand round." From thence we withdrew to our spacious drawing room and there lit the pipe loaded with the elegant aromatic of the James and the next moment it was "Fall in Johnny, get your gun, your sword and your pistol and go out and argue with the boys in gray the constitutionality of the, right of way." Do you recall when we left the old Elmira barracks and the green squash on the plates that they gave us? It was then pretty hard to get down. It was soon harder to get. That beautiful bread that we threw in the air. Had it been electrified with the electric lights of today it would have been a far greater electrical display than our electric fountain at Lincoln Park in Chicago. When we got to the front, we did not throw it away because it was worth more than our 2:40 gold. We could give the gold up, but never the bread. We soon became speculators because we were short on money and long on whisky before we arrived at Harrisburg. By the time we arrived at Camp Seward we were short on both. From this Company G and one other of the regiments were detached and assigned to Fort Lyon. This was the first business that I had as I had invested about $50 as my share in some furniture for my location in the fort, assuming that I would be there three years if not killed sooner. This was the last furniture that I bought. Right of possession gave us more furniture later on. You will recall the German officer who was to drill us. I did not know if he owned the German army or if we were in the German army. He drilled us so much that I dreamed nights of a walk along the Rhine and took kindly to lager beer for a while.

Our next experience was on picket duty at Second Bull Run. (Lt.) Colonel Diven was then the officer of the day of our brigade; General French came along with his division, and I thought he was going to swallow Colonel Diven whole. He wanted to know whether or not he was in the enemy's country, or what those things were meaning the boys who had their coats unbuttoned, and were lying on the grass with their cartridge boxes beside them. I happened to be present and heard the conversation, whereupon I made the best time I knew over the hill to where I was doing my first duty as a lieutenant of the picket, hustled the boys up, told them to button up and get in shape. I said I guessed King Charles or General Jackson was coming, and as his august body came within saluting distance, we gave it to him. Then he raised his hat and said: "Now I know we are protected by soldiers. Who commands that line, sir?" "Colonel Diven, sir," I replied.

We claim no action in this battle of Bull Run, other than the action on the drum of the ear. What green soldiers we were then. We could scarcely turn around without stepping on ourselves! September 5th finds us at Fort Albany; on the 6th we marched to join McClellan's army; on the 8th we were attached to Gordon's Brigade, Williams' Division; arrived at Frederick, Md., on the 13th and on the 14th we waded the Monocacy Creek, and soon after saw the shells bursting over South Mountain. After this came the memorable Antietam, September 17th, this was in reality our opening chorus. Here, in my old company, G, eleven fell killed and wounded by one shell, among them was poor little Willie Everts, merely a child of sixteen, with both legs shot away. He soon died. His agonizing cries in the din of the battle I shall hear to my grave. Here we found war a reality. It was here that the noble General Mansfield was shot from his horse and soon died. I can see his gray beard now, as he reeled and fell from his horse into the hands of one of his aids. Proud are we of him. Our corps commander then!

From September 22nd to December 10th, we were encamped on Maryland Heights, and at Antietam Ford, where we listened to the daily sad dirge of the drum which answered to the havoc created in our ranks by typhoid fever. December 10th we again broke camp, marched through the Loudoun Valley, and thence for the battle of Fredericksburg December 12 via Wolf Run Shoals, where we received the compliments of a few of their stray shells that to us was trivial. Thence in the 15th to near Dumphries and the 17th back Fairfax Station, thence to Occoquan River and back to Fairfax Station on December the 29th. January 29, 1863, we broke camp at Fairfax Station in a fearful storm, and again we marched, yes, our mud march. Think of mud in a brickyard before it goes to press, and you get some idea of it. We arrived at Stafford Court House on the 23d, left there on the 27th, and marched through streams, rain, and sleet until we arrived at Hope Landing, on Aquia Bay, where we encamped. The sleet turned to snow, and we awoke in the morning with at least six inches of snow over us. Here we encamped for the winter, and again the sad funeral dirge was heard, as we buried seventeen comrades who died of fever. We laid them in a neat little regimental graveyard, each with a headstone erected by his comrades. April 26th, we struck tents and marched via Stafford Court House to Kelly's Ford, on the Rappahannock, and on the 30th arrived at Germania Ford on the Rapidan. Here we captured a lot of Confederates building a bridge, and drove their lines over the river. We crossed in water up to our necks and advanced the line beyond a mile. On May 1st we reached the Chancellorsville House. In the afternoon we made a reconnaissance and found the enemy in full force. We returned to our camp overnight, built elegant breastworks, and on Saturday afternoon got ourselves in light marching order to go after and capture Lee's wagon train. While we were on a quick march after it, an orderly came riding up with orders for us to return at once, as the Eleventh Corps had broken, and the enemy had the works. Back we marched; and there we found them. Those works we built, and we wanted them. Stone wall Jackson's command was in them. Was there ever such lurid works of hell? Hand to hand, our shell into us, and then into them, their shells into them, and then into us. We each had many cannons back of us, and we each became the objective of concentrated fires. Here was where the great Stonewall Jackson fell. Finally, the darkness brought a lull. Here we lay, face to face, with videttes firing, until the light of day, when we again commenced that desperate fight which continued until nearly noon. We were then relieved by a Zouave command, but we had no sooner got twenty rods to the rear than they broke like a western cyclone, and again we had to face and hold our line with fixed bayonets until relieved by more reliable troops. This was an awful struggle for existence. How fortunate we were to have for our brigade commander Gen. Thomas A. Ruger, who fought so heroically against the stone wall of Jackson's Brigade, and who found the red stars invincible. And how sad the ending! Many of our killed and wounded were burned in the woods. It was here that poor Capt. Nat. Rutter was mangled by a shell, and soon died. Here many joined the silent camp. Of Company G, to which I then belonged, was killed poor Sergeant Hotchkiss, Corporal

Stratton, and seven others wounded, one of whom was then little Jimmie Voorhees, and who has since carried a wooden leg. To this we gave on May 1st, 2d, and 3d, our especial attention, with about two days' grace before we crossed that pontoon at United States Ford. Thence that awful mud march to Stafford Court House. Here the Johnnies were very kind to have built houses and evergreen parks for us; all we had to do was to finish the roofs. Still, after one- or two-days' rest there, we became very active; but salt and soap put a quietus to it. On June 13th, we headed for the Pennsylvania campaign. We marched to Dumfries, thence to Fair-fax Court House, and thence on the Pike to Leesburg, where Colonel Crane joined and com-manded us from June 24, 1863. Thence on to Ball's Bluff, where we again put up rifle pits. On the 26th, we crossed the Potomac at Edwards Ferry, on pontoons. Then we went on to Pool-esville, Maryland, Frederick City, Middletown, and Littlestown. Now came the great vibra-tion of aerial notes at Gettysburg; and proud are we, the One hundred and seventh, to have been in it. It was America's great battle. While we were fortunate in it, we grandly did our duty, and faced hell. We were fortunate, far more so than those who faced us. Here I received the compliments of some jolly Confederates on my knee; but was hurt only temporarily. The One hundred and seventh was engaged as follows: July 1st we had a light skirmish and sup-ported battery all night; on the 2d were building breast works all day under a galling shell fire; at evening we left the works and went to support the Third Corps, which was hard pressed, and as they were holding their own, we were ordered back to our works. Here our brigade halted in double columns of divisions, and ready for moving about forty rods in the rear of our works. Colonel Crane said to me, "I guess we had better go down and see what is there before we advance the men." I told him I thought it would be well. It was too dark to distin-guish troops, and as we got to our works, some command was just breaking ranks in them. The colonel said: "What command is this, Sir?" I think the answer was, "The Second Louisi-ana, sir." Colonel Crane said: "Oh, yes, sir; all right, sir." As we did not care to associate with them then and there, we changed direction to the rear and got back to our command. Where-upon the colonel ordered a deployment of the regiment, and I think it was the One hundred and forty-seventh Pennsylvania that fired on us, and the Forty-sixth Pennsylvania, Colo-nel Selfridge, fired on them, all mistaking each other. Here we arranged to retake the works on the morning of the 3d, which was done at such a fearful loss to the Second Massachusetts and Twenty-seventh Indiana regiments of our brigade. In the morning, the 4th, it rained, and we made a reconnaissance in support of Pleasanton's Cavalry to the enemy's left, return-ing to the works that day. Sunday, the 5th, at 3 p. m., we left the works and marched through Littlestown, Frederick City, Crampton's Gap, crossed Antietam Bridge, and on the 10th encamped on the old Antietam battlefield. On the 11th formed line of battle at Fair Play and lay till noon, when the One hundred and seventh and the Third Wisconsin made a reconnais-sance of two miles and found the enemy in force. July 12th, it threw up works in front of them; on the 14th, chased them to Williamsport and to the river at Falling Waters; and you all rec-ollect the competitive drill, the heavens, the Johnnies, and us. First the clouds would burst with hail upon us, and we with hail on the Johnnies, and they on us. It was "Hail Columbia." And this was done with us and the Johnnies practically to keep our powder dry, and as we lay in that conflict it would seem as if an avalanche of mud would deluge us. Thunder, lightning, hail, mud, bullets! It was a grand spectacular scene. And all this time the brave little General Kilpatrick getting in his work.

From here we wound our way back over the Antietam grounds to Maryland Heights, crossed the Potomac at Harper's Ferry thence the Blue Ridge near Snickersville, Ashley's, Manassas to Warrenton Junction where we subsisted on green corn and blackberries until we went to Kelly's Ford where we arrived August 1, and remained there drilling and swap-ping coffee for tobacco with the Johnnies. Do you not recollect the old gray horse of the Con-federate grand rounds which we used to watch daily with our glasses. Again, on September 16, we strike tent and General Kilpatrick crosses at our Kelley's Ford and General Beaufort at Rappahannock Ford. The old white horse with his rider must have been surprised for he rides round and round in a circle until he is taken in. We now march to Raccoon Ford. Here the Confederate sharpshooters make it lively for us as we lay in the mud. On the 18th we witnessed a deserter shot. On the 24th we went o Brandy Station, thence to Bealton, passing over the Manassas battle ground, thence to Alexandria, Washington, and on to the Relay House. Here we received Horace Greeley's favorite order, "Go west young man." From this time on we are under the command of General Hooker of whose name every man of the 20th Corps was proud, and he in turn was proud of his fighting star corps.

At Baltimore we took the Baltimore and Ohio Railroad through Maryland, West Virginia, Ohio, Indiana, and into Kentucky and Tennessee where we encamped on the Nashville Road. At each station in Ohio and Indiana it seemed as though the people could not do enough for us. These were the first real victuals we had seen since we had left home and we nearly foundered. Here many a pretty girl would catch it on the cheek as our train would depart from the various depots, all good naturally of course, for the love of country. Many a correspondent then by our brief depot flirtations. Poor chaplain Crane! How many letters we signed his name to, and address, enclosing a photo purporting to be his with a request to be answered. These letters were loaded with honey. He couldn't understand these epistles for a while, but he eventually, "caught on." God bless the old chaplain.

Arriving at Nashville October 3rd, we go down through Murfreesboro to Dechard where first guard railroad in the west. Thence to Tullahoma, Wartrace and Fosterville where companies H and I were detached and garrisoned one mile from there. From here the regiments and headquarters were as follows: Brigade headquarters at Tullahoma with headquarters of the regiment at Shelbyville. Some of the regiment at Wartrace under the command of Lt. Colonel William F. Fox, a detachment at Bellbuckle und the command of Captain John J. Lamon and my command at Bragg's Bridge where put in as good a time as we could possibly desire. No neater, happier better soldiers existed than here. The weather was as such as to make us enjoy the drill, and if there was a game that the boys were not into, then I do not know it. Baseball, hunting quail and turkey, playing cards, fighting dogs and chickens and courting Confederate girls. All had its many grand rounds. If you question the latter, Major "Charlie" Fox or Captain Bachman. Do you remember Colonel William F. Fox's artillery practice with a bursted piece, shelling the cavalry in the woods from Shelbyville? What a commotion it caused! How the orderlies flew from Tullahoma for each commandant to be on the alert as it was supposed that the Johnnies had shelled our cavalry.

While here we received the broken remnants of the 145th NY to swell our shrunken columns. And a good acquisition they were to us, as they proved themselves good soldiers and soon became a part and parcel of us. April 27, 1864, we broke camp and assemble on our colors at Shelbyville preparatory to Sherman's Atlanta campaign. How proud our colonel must have been to be the commander of such healthy, well drilled, disciplined soldiers as were assembled there again. And no regiment could have been prouder of their commander than we of the 107th NY of our loved, brave colonel, Nirom M. Crane. April 30th, we are on our way again.

We now, May 14th, first crossed arms with Johnston's army at Snake Creek Gap, Ga. A division of the 4th Corps here had been flanked from their works, and left to the enemy two field pieces whereupon our brigade (Ruger's) was ordered to the conflict. We went in, advanced over a high hill, charged down through a valley on the double quick and recaptured the pieces. And then went up three time three a tiger. You know what that means. Yes, the "stars" own the work. Right after this came our first recognition from the western army which came in the form of, "Bully for the paper collars, boys," an article which they really believed we always wore in the eastern army, but which in reality was an unknown quantity. We were no feather beds, but drilled, disciplined, fighting soldiers of the Potomac, and ever after passing them, we could hear them say, "Oh say, those are Hooker's men!" The next day, May 15th the battle of Resaca occurred. Here we double quicked by the right flank for quite a distance and for a while the Johnnies were all "pitchers" and no "catchers." This was where our lieutenant colonel, William F. Fox was wounded by the explosion of a shell. We passed in the rear of

Harrison's brigade, going on the right by file into line and then moved solidly and steadily on the enemy like an endless chain carrying logs to a mill. Again, it is three times three is a tiger! We had their works.

On May 16th, we followed the enemy across the Oostanaula River to Pine Chapel and on May 19th found them entrenched at Cassville. We drove them from their entrenchments and as they were retreating in the dark, their firing looked like fireflies on the hillside. On the 2nd we crossed the Etowah River and then came the sad May 25th at Dallas, Ga. Here we lost nearly half of the regiment present killed or wounded. Among the dead lay the noble Capt. John F. Knox, Lieutenant Hill and scores of brave fellows. Here Captain Losie lost a leg, and here I lost Sgt. Bennie Force, Cpl. Van Vleet, Myron Couch and John Morgenson all killed, also Orderly Charles H. Duryea badly wounded. Out of 44 present for duty of my loved Company H, 18 were either killed or wounded. From May 26th through the 28th we were constantly under fire while supporting a battery. On the 29th the enemy made four distinct attacks upon our works and each time was repulsed. On the 30th and 31st we were under heavy artillery fire. On June 1st we moved three miles to the left and took a position under the hill near Dallas Gap. On June 2nd we were again supporting the "Buckskin" battery which we did by skirmishing, getting under the enemy's works and holding their guns still thereby giving Buckskin good leeway at them. However, they cut loose with one piece and hit one of Buckskin's guns in the nozzle, removing it from its trunnions. This was considered an insult by its commander, and they had to take a lively three-gun volley. He was known as Buckskin and his four-gun volley throughout our army. His real name was Captain Hubert Dilger, Battery I, 1st Ohio Light Artillery and he was formerly in the Prussian army.

We were constantly moving and building breastworks under fire until the 14th when we moved to near Pine Mountain and lay in support of Knapp's Battery. You recollect that here were Generals Sherman, Hooker and Williams. Hooker remarked to General Sherman, "I guess we had better try a shell up to those quarters," and Sherman said, "All right." Hooker ordered the gunner to place his piece on it, looked over it and said, "Let her go!" That was the shell that killed the rebel General Polk. We watched with our glasses and saw the men run when the shell burst but rally a moment later around the body. Prisoners taken by us a few minutes later said it was General Polk. On the 19th the enemy fell back again to Kennesaw Mountain and on the 22nd to Kolb's farm. This was in the way of a surprise party. We were marching by the right flank with our ordinance wagons immediately on our right on the road, and our left protecting that of the skirmish line also marching by the right flank. The first we were aware of, "zip, bing, bang" is the music on our skirmish line and something has broken loose. Pell-mell come our skirmishers, followed closely by a line of Hood's men. We halt, front, as we are in the woods at the edge of a sloping field and begin to play our hose on them. For a while there was music in the air. Shortly after they were reinforced by two more lines of battle, whereupon batteries M and I, First New York that were on our flank and a twelve-pound smooth bore forms on the other flank. On came the Johnnies and when within twenty rods they gave us their stuff and then they lay down and took our fire until under the cover of dark they withdrew. This was the greatest punishment I think I ever saw Inflicted. Our batteries enfiladed them and our infantry poured in a direct fire. Why they should have taken it, I am at a loss to know. For having three lines to our one they should have done better or retubed to the rear. It was useless on their part to lose so many men. Their agonizing cries and moaning of the wounded were saddening to hear. You all recollect the general officer on the cream horse urging them on. Here Company H had among the killed Anthony Boyce, a brave soldier. Here Sgt. Elias Putnam stepped out about two rods ahead of the line and was giving them their death shots. I told him to come back as he would be killed there. He looked at me with tears running down his cheeks and said, "Captain, I can't. I will have revenge for Bennie." He was referring to Sgt. Force who was killed at Dallas, Ga. On the 27th we moved up and supported artillery on Kennesaw Mountain. On July 1st Hiram R. Hawley, a conscript who was sent to my company on the 30th was found dead in the morning. The surgeon pronounced that his death was from fear. He ought to have lived to see a battle.

On the 10th the enemy fell back across the Chattahoochee. We followed them up to their works at Peach Tree Creek. This where our brave Major Baldwin was killed while he was commanding the skirmish line. His command was driven back and he remained, firing at the enemy. He was shot in the head. Soon the line rallied and recaptured his body which had been robbed of his coat, boots and watch. He shortly was relieved of his misery by death. In this fight our brigade was in the second line of battle. The first line was suffering greatly as could be seen by the wounded men coming out. As we were at the edge of a field and the men engaged in our immediate front were in the woods.

It made our men nervous thinking there would be nothing left in front but dead. Of course, they soon built works in our front. Here the men got more nervous and began to get their guns in position to resist. General Hooker was there and said, "Keep cool boys, keep cool. Don't you see that little rise there?" I think that it was Martin Ryan, a noble soldier of the regiment, who said, "Yes sir." Hooker replied and said, "Just wait until you see the whites of their eyes. It's a damn good place to bury them." It was here the captain Bennett of our regiment, then on William's staff, was sitting on his horse when a ball struck the ground, glanced up and hit his forehead. While it did not prove serious, it made him rather sea sick for an hour or so. July 22nd was the battle of Atlanta. Here the Rebels charged our lines and were repulsed. This is where McPherson fell. He was to us what Stonewall Jackson was to the Rebels.

Here we lay besieging the city, getting more and more affectionate, and nearer and dearer to them until we are in their works under the mammoth forts. Here we go on and off picket in the still night as it is not healthy to move around too much in the daytime. Inconsequence we lay there in the trenches on our side during rain, mud and shine not allowing our heads higher than our works, the tops of which are made of empty cartridge boxes filled with sand and placed so as to permit a port view. We arranged them so as to prevent the enemy from running their guns out of their embrasures on us, and from this position we made I unhealthy for their cannoneers. Here in our works, we had a grand show every evening. Every five minutes we would give them a shell from our siege pieces. Then our band played our national airs, and alternately they played theirs. The works of each army were close together. This was a play to which none had tickets except the soldiers, and they all had front row seats.

September 2nd, Atlanta was evacuated, and the 107th NY were the among the first to enter for which they were given a position of honor in the city, that of guard duty, which to us was our first soft snap. It was here that we had our club rooms containing two billiard tables with about half a yard of cloth gone from each. The balls were three quarters chipped. We used rake handles for cues with leather nailed on the ends. Before we left the club at night, we were generally left-handed, near sighted and cross eyed. Before leaving Atlanta, we leveled the rounded, freight depot and tore up all the track in the city as a military necessity. On November 16th at 6am we were up in line and commenced, "The March to the Sea." At our last view of the city its flames soaring into the air, an act that I shall consider radically wrong and that it was not by order of General Sherman. We first marched through Decatur and then to Milledgeville, Ga. Where the flag of the 107th NY flag flew over the state house and was held there by Sgt. Ebenezer Helms. They found a great library, ordinance stores and the state's treasury. Each soldier became a statesman, and many obtained Confederate money and made it useable by signing the name of the governor of Georgia to it. They organized a mock Georgia legislature and elected General Kilpatrick as Speaker of the House. Each member was seated with special equipment. Each had a flint-lock horse pistol, a sabre made from a scythe and a jug of whiskey. Had the Confederates known our condition that night they could have easily taken us as we were too tired when through to offer resistance.

We left Milledgeville on the 24th and started on a "tear up" of the railroads. We cross piled, set fire to and heated the rails and gave each a "gain twist." Many a tree there, if not cut down, is in the embrace of an iron rail which we entwined when hot. We followed that avocation for quite a distance at intervals. From there they marched to Sandersville where we had a brush. You recall the Confederate who stood on the church steps firing on our skirmishers until he was killed, no doubt he thought he had done his conscientious duty.

Again, we marched on tearing up railroads and cross the Ogeechee River. On December 3rd we arrived at Millen Prison. From here I had two companies and some wagons with which I started north six miles for forage. Arriving at a plantation, I asked the lady of the house if she would be kind enough to get dinner for myself and three or four other officers. Her reply was that she would see us dead first. I told her that we were not fit subjects to die as we were not prepared, and that I was prepared to pay her for it. It mattered not to her as her happiness would be our death. A little later she learned that we were New York troops, and as she was born and raised in our vicinity, she sent for us and said we could have dinner. She wanted to know something about her northern friends. The dinner was fairly good, and it was gotten up by Calico. After the dinner the wagons were loaded up with hams and sweet potatoes. Then we started back to the main column.

While we were returning, we were attacked by Confederate cavalry, but our group was too large for them and they backed off. Shortly after, an old man with a shot gun met us. He claimed he was out hunting squirrels, but I presumed that he was a guerilla. It was lucky for him that we were not dead sure of it.

On December 4th we crossed the Little Ogeechee River and marched to Savannah on December 10th. There we found the city fortified. On Sunday December 11th the 107th NY and the 2nd Massachusetts made a reconnaissance across the swamp and found the enemy in force. We received orders to proceed six miles north to Argyle Island Which we did on December 6th. We crossed over to the island and took possession of a rice mill which we worked with our Georgia contrabands (Former slaves ]. While there some of the skirmishers of the 150th NY with Battery M, 1st NY captured the Confederate steamer Ida and the 3rd Wisconsin infantry captured the Confederate steamer Resolute, each of which were tenders for Confederate ironclads. While here Major Fox and I thought it would be fun to go fishing. So, we got a yawl boat and went to the southside of the island where we anchored to a torpedo timber that stuck out of the water. We thought it was the bow of some sunken craft. Then we saw a boat coming up the river from Savanah. We thought it was a merchant vessel. We noticed it broad side about 11am when she opened with a goose egg and sent it over us and into the rice mill. What could of the black birds got out of there and then. Major and I did not stay in the yawl much longer.

After this our brigade crossed over to the South Carolina shore where we had frequent skirmishes. We formed a crescent with our right and left resting on the shore and each day at high tide their gunboats would come up and shell us. On the 20th we could hear the Rebels retreating at evening over their pontoons and we reported same to headquarters, but in the morning, we found them encircling friends. In the afternoon they afforded us one of the most beautiful and exciting skirmishes we had had. They advanced on our right with cavalry. We held fire until they were in good range and then dropped them most effectively from their saddles. We made it most hot for them that they had to dismount and march to the rear. Then their infantry tried it, but the dikes were to our advantage and their disadvantage, and they were glad to quit. When their gunboats would shell us, the shells would go over us and into them and the Johnnies would holler over us, "Lay down Yanks, those darn fools of ours will kill the whole of us yet. Get down, get down, there comes another bucket of swill."

Our 2nd Division, 20th Army Corps took possession of Savannah as it was the first to enter and orders were issued for us to return. We withdrew our forces from South Carolina to Argyle Island in the evening and brought in the skirmish line next. Captain Arthur S. Fitch was wounded during this move. We spent Christmas in Savannah. From this point we made a faint on Augusta but go to Robertsville. And Blackburn Turnout where our pickets had a small brush with Rebel cavalry and then we traveled north-easterly feeling that we owned the country.

Here Lt. Whitehorn joined us one day, he being in command of the forage detail that was captured when it was some 25 miles from the main column when his orders were not to stray more than five miles or the Johnnies would take him. He said there were no Johnnies who could take him. This I think was March 8th. His detail consisted of 22 men. Major Fox and Adjutant Benedict thought it would be fun to accompany them for the day. So, they started off and got to a place called Solomon's Grove. Lt. Whitehorn met a body of men dressed in blue, naturally thought they were Kilpatrick's. After passing flanks, the Rebs halted, fronted, drew sabre and ordered Whitehorn to surrender. He thinking that he could whip the whole Confederacy, refused to surrender. Many of his men had their guns strapped to their saddles, and the Rebs had the woods full back of them. Whitehorn was struck over the head with a sabre and shot through the arm. One man was killed and three wounded. Among the wounded was Cole of Company E shot through the lungs, and in his condition, he made his way a distance of sixty miles into our lines again. I hope he is living yet. Silas Grey of Company H was cut over the head with a sabre and fell from his horse. He played possum on the Johnnies and got into our lines. A truer, better soldier was never enlisted. After this conflict the Rebs sighted Major Fox and Adjutant Benedict and they immediately started a race for our lines. The Johnnies were unable to catch them, and they made it safely back to their lines. Except for Gray and Cole all of the others went to some Confederate prison.

Company E gave one of its excellent sergeants, Peter Compton; while from Company G fell Corporal Tomes, Privates Alderman, Jackson, Long, Sanford, and Smith, heroes all. Company H mourns her noble sergeant, Benjamin Force, and the names of Couch, Youmans, and Van Vleet, are still cherished among the hills of Schuyler. None are more deserving in this brief mention than Orderly Sergeant Marcy and Sergeant Eugene Thatcher who, with Alden and Horton, represent the sacrifice made by Company K. The same may be said of Corporal Newberry, and Privates Carpenter and Decker, of Company I. These all died a voluntary offering on the altar of their country. It seems fitting on this occasion that this rollcall should be made. In the homes throughout Chemung, Steuben, and Schuyler, these names will invoke feelings mingled with pride and regret, as their heroism and tragic fate are recalled.

> What is there to be said or done?
> They are departed, we remain.
> Their race is run, their crowns are won.
> They will not come to us again.
>
> Cut off by fate before their prime.
> Could harvest half the golden years,
> All they could leave, they left us—time.
> All we give, we gave them ... tears[13]

*Author's note: Brigham's narrative appeared in print twice, first in the* Elmira Sunday Telegram *of September 27, 1891, and later as an edited version in the three-volume work* New York at Gettysburg. *The version here is the edited version. Captain Brigham of Company H felt a particular closeness to the men of the 107th New York who had sacrificed their lives in the service of their country. When he died, he was laid to rest in the National Cemetery in Marietta, Georgia, where thirty-two other members of the 107th New York who died in Georgia are buried.*

The 1898, 32nd reunion of the 107th New York regiment was held at the invitation of Charles H. Duryea of New York City around the tomb of General Grant at Riverside in that city. It was an appropriate place for such a gathering, and a deeper interest was given to the occasion by the memories it evoked of scenes in which the great commander played such an important part.

A day of visiting and sightseeing preceded the regular reunion day. The survivors of the regiment to the number of about half a hundred, many accompanied by their wives and their invited guests, made a tour of Manhattan Island, visited the parks and places of public interest, crossed the great bridge to Brooklyn and inspected the navy yard and the battleships fresh from the conflicts of our latest war. At the invitation of Col. James E. Jones, a well-known son of Steuben, they visited the Aquarium at Battery Park, having added to their reminiscence the story of their triumphant march down Broadway.

Friday evening, they were given a special reception and entertainment at a hall on 125th Street. By the thoughtful care of Sergeant Duryea, a unique program had been arranged which was thoroughly enjoyed by all present. It included a welcome address by Capt. H.G. Donnelly of Company H now a successful lawyer of York, recitations by Mrs. Folsom, Miss Andrews, "Little Maude," musical selections by a quartet of male voices and an orchestra. All were heartily encored. Professor Bamber delighted the audience with a violin solo and was twice recalled. Col. Jones and A.B. Vorhis were present to greet their friends from old Steuben, the former making some exceedingly happy remarks in his original and witty style.

The reunion exercises were held Saturday afternoon following an extensive carriage ride through Central and Morningside parks. There were present Col. G.L. Smith, Col. N.T. Colby, Adj. Hull Fanton and about fifty officers and men from the different companies. A stirring and eloquent address was made by Dr. Ezra Squier Tipple of New York. Standing in the shadow of the magnificent monument where the regiment was gathered, he drew anew the lesson of patriotism that was taught alike by great generals and the most obscure soldier in command in their struggle to save the Union and to perpetuate American institutions. Remarks were also made by the president of the association Col. Smith, by Capt. H.G. Brigham of Chicago and by Lieut. R.M. Tuttle of Hornellsville.

The business of the association followed. Letters of remembrance were read by many in attendance. The officers of the previous year were re-elected. A resolution was adopted admitting to membership the wives and descendants of the soldiers of the regiment.[14]

The reunion in 1908 was, if anything, a sad one. During the time from the reunion in 1907 to this reunion, 18 veterans of the 107th NY had died. Among those who had died were Lt. Colonel Allen Sill, 1st. Lieutenant Edwin Weller and 1st. Lieutenant Russell Tuttle all of whom played important roles during the war.

The Rev. B.J. Tracey, president of the association, presided over the event. Secretary Frank Frost and Treasurer Theodore Smith, both of whom have held their position for 37 years, were re-elected to their positions. It was evident that women were now involved in managing the association reunions when Mary Manning was elected to the position of assistant secretary.[15]

Many letters of greeting were read, and they illustrated that many of the veterans had left the area and were now living as far away as Washington state.

The reunion held on September 17, 1912, celebrated the 50th anniversary of the formation of the 107th New York regiment. Fifty-nine of the survivors of the regiment marched from the gates of their former camp at Hoffman St. and Water St. to the 107th NY monument on Lake St. and then to the Lake St. Presbyterian Church for lunch. Afterwards they proceeded to the Armory on Church St. for a social gathering.[16]

In 1917, the regiment celebrated its 50th anniversary, and action was taken concerning the beautiful and embroidered regimental banner that had been presented to the regiment by President Lincoln when it was the very first to arrive in Washington on August 14, 1862, in answer to his call for 300,000 more troops.

The regiment did not take the banner with them to war. Instead, it had been stored at Seward's home in Washington. After the war ended, A.S. Diven had possession of the flag until his death, when it was turned over to former Colonel G.L. Smith, then to L.W. Babcock, and then to Frank Frost, who currently had it. At the reunion, the membership voted to place the banner in some public building in Elmira, there to remain as a memorial of the grand 107th New York. This action was taken because the members realized that in a short time, none of them would be present to see that the banner was in proper hands.

The banner story would hardly be complete without a reference to Lafayette Brown. He was a member of the 107th and an excellent cabinet maker who worked in the Pullman palace car shops in Elmira. These shops adjoined the Erie shops and extended to East Fifth Street, one large building being yet in use for storage and other purposes. The banner was elegantly framed by Mr. Brown as a favor to the boys of the 107th, and it was an expert piece of work.[17]

In 1931, there were only seven members of the regiment still living, and only three were able to attend the association's last dinner meeting. Four of the survivors lived in Elmira. On Thursday September 24, Frank Frost, Frank Brown of Elmira, and Frank Burgess of Olean were the honored guests at a dinner held at the Federation Building in Elmira. The other surviving members who were unable to attend were Josiah Gregory and William R. Hammond, both of Elmira, and S.B. Enscho and Silas Kimble, both of Bath.

When it appeared that the old soldiers intended to pass up their 65th annual reunion because they were so few and unable to attend, Judson T. Cole of Elmira Heights immediately made plans for the event honoring them.

Thus came to a close the annual September reunions of the 107th New York veterans of the Civil War. Captain Frank Frost was the last of that group of gallant men to pass. He had kept a scrapbook containing many of the newspaper accounts of the regiment's reunions, as well as other related material. The scrapbook and other 107th materials are now in the possession of the Chemung County Historical Society located in Elmira, NY.[18]

The monument in front of the courthouse on Lake Street in Elmira was dedicated to the men in the 107th New York regiment who died in order to preserve the Union and will forever be visible to future generations as a reminder of their sacrifice.

# Appendix:
# Regimental Roster

This roster was produced by scanning the 1903 New York State Adjutant-General Report and converting the scanned document to Microsoft Word. Every attempt has been made to edit and correct the resulting data. All data shown in brackets are taken from other sources.

ABBEY, CHARLES—Age, 18 years. Enlisted at Elmira, to serve three years, and mustered in as private, Co. C, July 30, 1862; promoted corporal, May 1, 1863; sergeant April 1, 1865; absent, wounded and in hospital at Elmira, N.Y., at muster out of company. [Gunshot wound, 1/3 lower left leg amputated by surgeon P. Flood, 107th NY, on March 16, 1865; discharged August 13, 1865.]

ABBEY, WILLIAM H.—Age, 34 years. Enlisted, July 23, 1862, at Elmira, to serve three years; mustered in as private, Co. C, July 24, 1862; promoted corporal, January 1, 1863; mustered out, June 10, 1865, at Brown Hospital, Louisville, Ky.

ABBOTT, CHARLES W.—Age, 19 years. Enlisted, July 18, 1862, at Elmira, to serve three years; mustered in as private, Co. B, July 23, 1862; discharged for disability, March 30, 1863, at Convalescent Camp, Va.

ABBOTT, FRANKLIN J.—Age, 21 years, Enlisted, July 19, 1862, at Elmira to serve three years; mustered in as corporal, Co. B, July 22, 1862; returned to ranks, no date; transferred to Veteran Reserve Corps, September 7, 1863, as Franklin G.

ABEL, DAVID—Age, 44 years. Enlisted at Elmira, to serve three years, and mustered in as private, Co. C, August 4, 1862; died of typhoid fever, October 29, 1862, at hospital, Harper's Ferry, Va., as Able.

ABRAMS, ALMON J.—Age, 38 years. Enlisted at Wayland, to serve three years, and mustered in as private, Co. I, August 1, 1862; deserted, September 7, 1862, at Rockville, Md., as Almond J.

ACKERLEY, JOHN R.—Age, 18 years. Enlisted, July 25, 1862, at Montour, to serve three years; mustered in as private, Co. H, August 1, 1862; died of typhoid fever, February 25, 1863, at Hope Landing, Va.; also borne as Akerley.

ACKLEY, GILBERT—Age, 39 years. Enlisted, July 23, 1862, at Cameron, to serve three years; mustered in as private, Co. F, July 29, 1862; mustered out, July 28, 1865, at Louisville, Ky.

ACKLEY, SAMUEL—Age, 21 years. Enlisted at Elmira, to serve three years, and mustered in as private, Co. D, August 5, 1862; deserted, July 1, 1863, near Gettysburg, Pa.

ADAMS, GUY C.—Age, 18 years. Enlisted, July 7, 1862, at Elmira, to serve three years; mustered in as private, Co. E, July 18, 1862; promoted sergeant, March 1, 1863; killed, August 3, 1864, near Atlanta, Ga. [Gunshot to head]

ADAMS, WILLIA.—Age, 18 years. Enlisted at Elmira, to serve three years, and mustered in as private; Co. C, July 9, 1862; deserted, November 5, 1862, at Antietam, Md.

AKERLEY, see Ackerley.

AKIN, ROBERT—Age, 24 years. Enlisted, July 25, 1862, at Hector, to serve three years; mustered in as private, Co. H, July 30, 1862; captured, no date; died, March 8, 1865.

ALBIN, JAMES M.—Corporal, Co. G, One Hundred and Forty-fifth Infantry;

transferred to Co. A, this regiment, January 12, 1864; wounded in action, May 25, 1864, at Dallas, Ga.; mustered out with company, June 5, 1865, near Washington, D.C.

ALDEN, CHARLES—Age, 24 years. Enlisted, August 9, 1862, at Howard, to serve three years; mustered in as private, Co. K, August 12, 1862; killed in action, May 25, 1864, near Dallas, Ga.

ALDERMAN, THERON—Age, 26 years. Enlisted at Elmira, to serve three years, and mustered in as private, Co. G, August 2, 1862; killed in action, May 25, 1864, at Dallas, Ga.

ALDRICH, HENRY B.—Age, 19 years. Enlisted, July 23, 1862, at Addison, to serve three years; mustered in as private, Co. F, July 25, 1862; died of camp fever, November 16, 1862.

ALEXANDER, GEORGE H.—Private, Co. C, One Hundred and Forty-fifth Infantry; transferred to Co. A, this regiment, January 12, 1864; absent, sick in hospital, since April 1864, and at muster out of company.

ALLEN, GEORGE W.—Age, 35 years. Enlisted at Elmira, to serve three years, and mustered in as private, Co. A, June 16, 1862; mustered out, May 29, 1865, at McDougall Hospital, New York harbor.

ALLEN, JOHN S.—Age, 21 years. Enlisted, July 21, 1862, at Elmira, to serve three years; mustered in as private, Co. B, July 23, 1862; transferred to Veteran Reserve Corps, August 11, 1863. (Deserted at Frederick hospital, Feb. 20, 1863)

AMAN, JOSEPH—Age, 39 years. Enlisted, July 21, 1862, at Elmira, to serve three years; mustered in as private, Co. E, July 23, 1862; discharged for disability, February 3, 1863, at Washington, D.C.

AMES, STEPHENS W.—Age, 18 years. Enlisted, December 10, 1863, at Addison, to serve three years; mustered in as private, Co. B, December 29, 1863; transferred to Co. A, Sixtieth Infantry, June 5, 1865.

AMEY, CHARLES H—Age, 23 years. Enlisted, August 11, 1862, at Hornellsville, to serve three years; mustered in as private, Co. K, August 19, 1862; transferred to Co. A, Eighteenth Regiment, Veteran Reserve Corps, August 1, 1863; mustered out with detachment, June 28, 1865, at Washington, D.C.

ANDERSON, JOHN—Private, Co. B, One Hundred and Forty-fifth Infantry; transferred to Co. D, this regiment, no date,

and deserted, December 31, 1863, while on detached service, at New York City.

ARMSTRONG, HENRY—Age, 35 years. Enlisted at Elmira, to serve three years, and mustered in as private, Co. D, August 4, 1862; wounded in action, May 25, 1864, at Dallas, Ga.; died of his wounds June 1, 1864, at Kingston, Ga.

ARNOLD, ABRAM—Age, 21 years. Enlisted at Elmira, to serve three years, and mustered in as private, Co. E, August 12, 1862; mustered out with company, June 5, 1865, near Washington, D.C.

ARNOLD, JAMES H.—Age, 23 years. Enlisted at Elmira, to serve three years, and mustered in as musician, Co. H, August 11, 1862; transferred to Co. I, Ninth Regiment, Veteran Reserve Corps, March 16, 1864; mustered out, August 11, 1865, at Washington, D.C.

ARNOLD, STEPHEN—Age, 40 years. Enlisted at Plattsburg, to serve three years, and mustered in as private, Co. K, March 9, 1864; captured, November 18, 1864, while on Sherman's march to the sea; paroled, no date; transferred to Co. B, Sixtieth Infantry, June 5, 1865; prior service in Co. G, Twenty-third Infantry.

ARNOT, JOHN B.—Age, 18 years. Enlisted at Elmira, to serve three years and mustered in as private, Co. A, June 23, 1862; died of typhoid fever, October 23, 1862, at Bolivar Heights, Va.

ARNOT, WILLIAM—Age, 18 years. Enlisted at Elmira, to serve three years, and mustered in as private, Co. A, June 24, 1862; promoted corporal, prior to October 1863; returned to ranks, April 1, 1864; wounded in action, May 25, 1864, near Dallas, Ga.; mustered out with company, June 5, 1865, near Washington, D.C.; also borne as Wm. H.

ASHLAND, PETER—Private, Co. I, One Hundred and Forty-fifth Infantry; transferred to Co. K, this regiment, January 12, 1864; absent, sick, since July 18, 1868, and at muster out of company.

ATWATER, URIAH E.—Age, 18 years. Enlisted at Elmira, to serve three years, and mustered in as private, Co. E, July 17, 1862; discharged for disability January 9, 1863, at Fairfax Seminary, Va.

ATWOOD, JR., HARLOW—Age, 33 years. Enrolled at Elmira, to serve three years, and mustered in as private, Co. E, July 19, 1862; as second lieutenant, August 18, 1862; discharged, December 10, 1862. Commissioned second lieutenant, September 6, 1862, with rank from July 28, 1862, original.

AUSTIN, LOCKWOOD—Age, 23 years. Enlisted at Prattsburg to serve three years, and mustered in as private, Co. K, February 15, 1864; died of disease, August 5, 1864, at hospital, Nashville, Tenn.

AUSTIN, PETER—Age, 43 years. Enlisted, July 23, 1862, at Elmira, to serve three years, and mustered in as private, Co. O, July 24, 1862; discharged for disability, February 19, 1868, at Elmira, N.Y.

AVERILL, SELDON M.—Age, 19 years. Enlisted, July 15, 1862, at Elmira, to serve three years; mustered in as private, Co. B, July 16, 1862; transferred to U.S. Engineer Corps, October 24, 1862.

BABCOCK, ENOCH H.—Age, 29 years. Enlisted, August 8, 1862, at Hornellsville, to serve three years; mustered in as private, Co. K, August 9, 1862; transferred to Veteran Reserve Corps, January 29, 1864.

BABCOCK, LAYMAN W.—Age, 22 years. Enlisted at Elmira, to serve three years, and mustered in as private Co. A, July 17, 1862; promoted corporal, prior to October 1863; sergeant, July 1, 1864; mustered out with company, June 5, 1865, near Washington, D.C.

BABCOCK, WILSON U.—Age, 21 years. Enlisted, July 16, 1862, at Elmira, to serve three years; mustered in as private, Co. A, July 17, 1862; mustered out with company, June 5, 1865, near Washington, D.C., as Wilson W.

BACHMAN, GOTTFRIED—Age, 23 years. Enlisted at Elmira, to serve three years, and mustered in as private, Co. E, August 9, 1862; absent, sick in hospital, at muster out of company; also borne as Buchmann.

BACHMAN, MARTIN V. B.—Age, 24 years. Enrolled at Elmira to serve three years, and mustered in as first lieutenant, Co. B, July 24, 1862; as captain, Co. E, March 21, 1863; mustered out with company, June 5, 1865, near Washington, D.C. Commissioned first lieutenant, September 6, 1862, with rank from July 24, 1862, original; captain, May 11, 1863, with rank from March 20, 1863, vice W.L. Morgan, resigned. [Provost Marshal, Wartrace, Tennessee Dec. 1863 to Apr. 27, 1864]

BACKMAN, CHARLES M.—Age, 19 years. Enlisted, June 6, 1862, at Elmira, to serve three years; mustered in as sergeant, Co. E, June 9, 1862; mustered out to date June

5, 1865, at Nashville, Tenn.; also borne as Bachman.

BAGLEY, ABEL D.—Age, 43 years. Enlisted at Elmira, to serve three years, and mustered in as private, Co. C, July 31, 1862; discharged for disability, February 19, 1863, at hospital, Harper's Ferry, Va.

BAGLEY, WILLIAM A.—Age, 34 years. Enlisted at Elmira, to serve three years, and mustered in as sergeant, Co. A, July 17, 1862; captured, October 21, 1864, near Atlanta, Ga.; paroled, no date; mustered out, June 22, 1865, at hospital, York, Pa.

BAILEY, SYLVESTER C.—Age, 21 years. Enlisted, July 21, 1862, at Elmira, to serve three years; mustered in as private Co. C, July 22, 1862; deserted, October 24, 1862, at Aquia Bay, Va.; returned under President's proclamation, March 27 1863, again deserted, April 21, 1863, at Aquia Bay, Va.

BAKER, CHARLES E.—Age, 33 years. Enlisted, July 30, 1862, at Canisteo, to serve three years; mustered in as private, Co. K, July 31, 1862; wounded in action, May 25, 1864, near Dallas, Ga.; mustered out, May 18, 1865, at Hospital No. 14, Nashville, Tenn.

BAKER, THOMAS—Private, Co. C, One Hundred and Forty-fifth Infantry; transferred to Co. A, this regiment, January 12, 1864; to Veteran Reserve Corps, January 15, 1864.

BALDWIN, LATHROP—Age, 32 years. Enrolled at Elmira, to serve three years, and mustered in as captain, Co. B, July 24, 1862; as major, November 1, 1863; as lieutenant-colonel, July 9, 1864; wounded in action, July 20, and died of his wounds, July 30, 1864, at Peach Tree Creek, Ga. Commissioned captain, September 6, 1862, with rank from July 24, 1862, original; major, October 15, 1863, with rank from September 5, 1863, vice W.F. Fox, promoted; lieutenant-colonel, July 20, 1864, with rank from July 8, 1864, vice W.F. Fox, discharged for disability.

BALLARD, HIRAM R.—Age, 21 years. Enlisted, August 1, 1862, at Elmira, to serve three years; mustered in as private, Co. H, August 4, 1862; transferred to Second Company, Second Battalion, Veteran Reserve Corps, July 1, 1865; mustered out, July 15, 1865, at Elmira, N.Y.

BALLOU, WILLIAM H.—Age, 22 years. Enlisted, July 22, 1862, at Hornellsville, to serve three years; mustered in as musician, Co. K, July 6, 1862; promoted corporal, prior to April 10, 1863; wounded in action, May 25,

1864, near Dallas, Ga.; mustered out with company, June 5, 1865, near Washington, D.C.

BARBER, WASHINGTON—Age, 22 years. Enlisted, July 26, 1862, at Addison, to serve three years; mustered in as private, Co. F, July 29, 1862; mustered out, June 10, 1865, at Chattanooga, Tenn.; also borne as George W.

BARDON, JACOB—Age, 39 years. Enlisted, July 21, 1862, at Elmira, to serve three years; mustered in as private, Co. D, July 24, 1862; discharged, March 28, 1863, at Philadelphia, Pa., as Bardow.

BARLOW, JONATHAN H.—Age, 39 years. Enlisted at Elmira, to serve three years, and mustered in as private, Co. B, July 19, 1862; died of typhoid fever, January 20, 1863, at Eckington Hospital, Washington, D.C., as Jonathan W.

BARNES, ENOS P.—Age, 27 years. Enlisted, July 28, 1862, at Addison, to serve three years; mustered in as private, Co. F, July 29, 1862; died of camp fever, October 25, 1862.

BARNUM, HENRY—Age, 25 years. Enlisted at Wayland, to serve three years, and mustered in as private, Co. I, July 31, 1862; deserted, October 16, 1862, at Maryland Heights, Md.

BARR, JOHN—Private, Co. G, One Hundred and Forty-fifth Infantry; transferred to Co. E, this regiment, January 12, 1864; mustered out with company, June 5, 1865, near Washington, D.C.

BARRETT, GEORGE—Age, 18 years. Enlisted at Elmira, to serve three years, and mustered in as private, Co. G, August 4, 1862; discharged for disability, March 20, 1863, at Fairfax Seminary, Va.

BARRY, WICKHAM J.—Age, 18 years. Enlisted, July 28, 1862, at Addison, to serve three years; mustered in as corporal, Co. F, July 29, 1862; returned to ranks, October 30, 1863; mustered out with company, June 5, 1865, near Washington, D.C. Commissioned, not mustered, second lieutenant, December 7, 1864, with rank from August 27, 1864, vice J.H. Saltsman, promoted.

BARTO, WILLIAM H.—Age, 23 years. Enlisted, July 21, 1862, at Elmira, to serve three years; mustered in as private, Co. D, July 24, 1862; wounded in action, May 25, 1864, at Dallas, Ga.; absent, sick in hospital, Nashville, Tenn., at muster out of company. [gunshot wound, excision middle left ulna by surgeon L.W. Kennedy 123rd NY on May 26, 1864]

BASKINS, ERASTUS M.—Age, 28 years. Enlisted, July 15, 1862, at Elmira, to serve three years; mustered in as private, Co. E, July 18, 1862; died of fever, November 3, 1862, at Harper's Ferry, Va.

BATES, FRANK—Age, 21 years. Enlisted, July 21, 1862, at Elmira, to serve three years; mustered in as musician, Co. A, July 22, 1862; mustered out with company, June 5, 1865, near Washington, D.C.

BATHRICK, CHARLES—Age, 31 years. Enlisted, August 8, 1862, at Hornellsville, to serve three years; mustered in as private, Co. K, August 9, 1862; mustered out with company, June 5, 1865, near Washington, D.C.

BAUER, FREDERICK—Age, 19 years. Enlisted at Elmira, to serve three years, and mustered in as private, Co. E, August 12, 1862; deserted and captured, September 17, 1862, at Maryland Heights, Md., during battle of Antietam; paroled, no date; no further record.

BEACH, VICTOR L.—Age, 22 years. Enlisted, July 14, 1862, at Elmira, to serve three years; mustered in as private, Co. B. July 16, 1862; deserted, March 27, 1863, from hospital, at Washington, D.C.

BEAL, C. HADLEY—Private, Co. H, Eighty-fourth Infantry; mustered in as second lieutenant, Co. E, this regiment, May 13, 1863; discharged, December 20, 1863, as Caleb H. Commissioned second lieutenant, December 29, 1862, with rank from December 25, 1862, vice H. Atwood, Jr., resigned.

BEARD, STEPHEN A.—Age, 25 years. Enlisted, July 14, 1862, at Elmira, to serve three years; mustered in as private, Co. B, July 16, 1862; transferred to Veteran Reserve Corps, November 15, 1863.

BEARDSLEY, BEACH—Age, 22 years. Enlisted, July 23, 1862, at Elmira, to serve three years; mustered in as corporal, Co. D, July 24, 1862; returned to ranks prior to April 10, 1863; again promoted corporal, no date; died of typhoid fever, August 11, 1863, at Fairfax Seminary, Va.

BECK, JOHN G.—Age, 22 years. Enlisted at Wayland, to serve three years, and mustered in as corporal, Co. I, July 30, 1862; returned to ranks prior to April 10, 1863; discharged for disability, April 20, 1863, at General Hospital, Baltimore, Md.; also borne as Buck.

BECKHORN, FREDERICK—Age, 19 years. Enlisted, July 25, 1862, at Elmira, to serve three years; mustered in as wagoner, Co. B, July 26,1862; discharged for disability, October 31, 1862.

BECKWITH, ALEXANDER D.—Age, 18 years. Enlisted, July 29, 1862, at Elmira, to serve three years; mustered in as private, Co. A, July 30, 1862; mustered out with company, June 5, 1865, near Washington, D.C.

BEEMAN, GIDEON M.—Age, 38 years. Enlisted at Wayland, to serve three years, and mustered in as wagoner, Co. I, August 6, 1862; died of typhoid fever, October 22, 1862, at Harper's Ferry, Va.; also borne as Beman.

BEERS, GEORGE A.—Age, 22 years. Enlisted at Elmira, to serve three years, and mustered in as private, Co. B, July 12, 1862; promoted corporal, May 28, 1863; returned to ranks, July 1, 1863; wounded in action, July 3, 1863, at Gettysburg, Pa.; absent, sick in hospital, at muster out of company.

BEESLEY, JOHN—Age, 43 years. Enlisted at Elmira, to serve three years, and mustered in as private, Co. E, July 30, 1862; mustered out with company, June 5, 1865, near Washington, D.C.

BELCHER, NELSON—Age, 25 years. Enlisted at Addison, to serve three years, and mustered in as private, Co. F, August 5, 1862; deserted, March 8, 1863, at Hope Landing, Va.

BELL, JACOB—Private, Co. I, One Hundred and Forty-fifth Infantry; transferred to Co. C, this regiment, January 11, 1864; mustered out, June 20, 1865, at Slough Hospital, Alexandria, Va.

BELL, JOHN—Age, 37 years. Enlisted at Elmira, to serve three years, and mustered in as private, Co. C, July 17, 1862; deserted, August 13, 1862, at Elmira, N.Y.

BELL, SIMEON D.—Age, 31 years. Enlisted at Havana, to serve three years, and mustered in as private, Co. H, July 25, 1862; promoted corporal, prior to April 10, 1863; mustered out, July 24, 1865, at hospital, Washington, D.C. as Simon L.

BEMAN, see BEEMAN.

BEMIS, GEORGE A.—Age, 18 years. Enlisted, August 5, 1862, at Campbell, to serve three years; mustered in as private, Co. F, August 6, 1862; promoted corporal, June 8, 1863; sergeant, April 16, 1864; wounded in action, May 25, 1864, at Dallas, Ga.; returned to ranks, January 16, 1865; again promoted corporal, April 9, 1865; mustered out with company, June 5, 1865, near Washington, D.C.

BENEDICT, SAMUEL N.—Age, 30 years. Enrolled, July 17, 1863, at Fosterville, Tenn., to serve three years; mustered in as first lieutenant and adjutant, September 7, 1863;

mustered out with regiment, June 5, 1865, near Washington, D.C.; prior service as first lieutenant, Co. F, Twenty-third Infantry. Commissioned first lieutenant and adjutant, July 28, 1863, with rank from July 17, 1863, vice H. Fanton, discharged for promotion.

BENEDICT, VOLKERT—Age, 21 years. Enlisted, July 25, 1862, at Elmira, to serve three years; mustered in as private, Co. G, August 2, 1862; absent, sick in hospital, at Elmira, N.Y., since October 29, 1862, and at muster out of company.

BENEDICT, WILLIAM A.—Age, 23 years. Enlisted, July 23, 1862, at Addison, to serve three years; mustered in as private, Co. F, July 29, 1862; discharged for disability, February 23: 1863; again enlisted, January 5, 1864, at Homer and mustered in as private, Co. B, January 8, 1864; wounded in action, May 15, 1864, at Resaca, Ga.; mustered out, June 6, 1865, at hospital, Camp Dennison, Ohio.

BENJAMIN, WILLIAM H.—Age, 30 years. Enlisted at Corning, to serve three years, and mustered in as private, Co. I, August 11, 1862; absent, sick in hospital, at York, Pa., since December 10, 1862, and at muster out of company.

BENNETT, BARTLET—Age, 25 years. Enlisted, July 8, 1862, at Elmira, to serve three years; mustered in as private, Co. E, July 22, 1862; promoted sergeant, prior to April 10, 1863; first sergeant, July 1, 1864; mustered out with company, June 5, 1865, near Washington, D.C.

BENNETT, GEORGE W.—Age, 25 years. Enlisted, July 15, 1862, at Elmira, to serve three years; mustered in as corporal, Co. E, July 18, 1862; returned to ranks prior to April 10, 1863; wounded in action, May 25, 1864, at Dallas, Ga.; mustered out with company, June 5, 1865, near Washington, D.C.

BENNETT, GEORGE W.—Private, Co. C, One Hundred and Forty-fifth Infantry; transferred to Co. K, this regiment, January 12, 1864; captured in action, November 18, 1864, near Social Circle, Ga.; paroled, February 28, 1865; mustered out with detachment, June 29, 1865, at hospital, York, Pa.

BENNETT, SAMUEL A.—Age, 29 years. Enrolled at Elmira. to serve three years, and mustered in as first lieutenant, Co. D, August 4, 1862; as captain, March 14, 1863; mustered out with company, June 5, 1865, near Washington, D.C. Commissioned first lieutenant, September 6, 1862, with rank from August 4, 1862, original; captain, March 27, 1863, with rank from March 13, 1863, vice H.M. Stocum, resigned.

BENNETT, SYLVESTER—Age, 24 years. Enlisted at Elmira, to serve three years, and mustered in as private, Co. E, July 22, 1862; wounded in action, September 17, 1862, at Antietam, Md.; discharged for wounds, March 6, 1863.

BENSON, JOSEPH—Age, 24 years. Enlisted at Elmira, to serve three years, and mustered in as private, Co. B, July 26, 1862; mustered out with company, June 5, 1865, near Washington, D.C.

BERGER, JEDIAH—Age, 21 years. Enlisted at West Union, to serve three years, and mustered in as private, Co. I, July 31, 1862; mustered out with company, June 5, 1865, near Washington, D.C.

BERNHARD, GEORGE N.—Private, Co. I, One Hundred and Forty-fifth Infantry; transferred to Co. C, this regiment, January 11, 1864; absent, detailed as orderly at Headquarters, Military Division of the Mississippi, New Bern, N.C., since April 26, 1865, and at muster out of company; also borne as George M.

BERRY, ALBERT R.—Age, 18 years. Enlisted, July 27, 1862, at Elmira, to serve three years; mustered in as musician, Co. B, July 28, 1862; transferred to Co. A, Fifth Regiment, Veteran Reserve Corps, no date; mustered out, July 5, 1865, at Burnside Barracks, Indianapolis, Ind.

BERRY, DEXTER—Age, 30 years. Enlisted at Corning, to serve three years, and mustered in as private, Co. I, August 11, 1862; became deaf and dumb by shell explosion, May 3, 1863, at Chancellorsville, Va.; discharged for disability, July 1, 1863, at Convalescent Camp, Alexandria, Va.

BESLEY, JOHN—Age, 25 years. Enlisted, July 22, 1862, at Elmira, to serve three years; mustered in as private, Co. B, July 23, 1862; discharged for disability, December 10, 1862; subsequent service, in Twenty-fourth Cavalry.

BETSON, SILAS H.—Age, 18 years. Enlisted, July 16, 1862, at Elmira, to serve three years; mustered in as private, Co. A, July 17, 1862; died of typhoid pneumonia, March 3, 1863, at camp, Hope Landing, Va.

BIRCHELL, THOMAS B.—Corporal, Co. K, One Hundred and Forty-fifth Infantry; transferred to Co. F, this regiment, as private, January 12, 1864; absent, in hospital, Washington, D.C., since October 5, 1868, and at muster out of company.

BIRD, DAVID—Age, 25 years. Enlisted at Elmira, to serve three years, and mustered in as corporal, Co. G, July 16, 1862; promoted sergeant, January 1, 1863; mustered out, May 12, 1865, at Elmira, N.Y.; also borne as Burd

BIRMINGHAM, MICHAEL—Age, 25 years. Enlisted at Elmira, to serve three years, and mustered in as private, Co. D, July 31, 1862; discharged November 20, 1862.

BISHOP, AMANY R—Age, 23 years. Enlisted at Elmira, to serve three years, and mustered in as private, Co. A, July 8, 1862; deserted, February 19, 1863, from hospital, Camp A, Frederick, Md., as Amorry R.

BLAKESLEY, CHAUNCEY—Age, 30 years. Enlisted at Elmira, to serve three years, and mustered in as private, Co. G, July 24, 1862; deserted, January 18, 1863, at Fairfax Station, Va.

BLOOMENTHAL, FREDERICK—Private, Co. C, One Hundred and Forty-fifth Infantry; transferred to Co. H, this regiment, January 12, 1864; mustered out with company, June 5, 1865, near Washington, D.C.

BLOS, MARTIN—Age, 35 years. Enlisted at Elmira, to serve three years, and mustered in as private, Co. E, July 28, 1862; promoted corporal, prior to April 10, 1863; captured in action, May 3, 1863, at Chancellorsville, Va.; paroled, October 1863; wounded in action, June 16, 1864, near Pine Knob, Ga.; died, December 16, 1864, at Louisville, Ky., of injuries received on railroad; also borne as Bloss. [Injured when regiment transferred to Tennessee]

BLOSSOM, EUGENE F.—Age, 18 years. Enlisted at Elmira, to serve three years, and mustered in as private, Co. D, July 23, 1862; wounded in action, May 25, 1864, at Dallas, Ga.; mustered out, June 28, 1865, at Elmira, N.Y.

BLOSSOM, JASON B.—Age, 38 years. Enlisted, July 21, 1862, at Elmira, to serve three years; mustered in as musician [drummer], Co. D, July 23, 1865, transferred to Veteran Reserve Corps, January 1, 1865. [Taken prisoner at Chancellorsville]

BOARDMAN, JOSEPH—Private, Co. C, One Hundred and Forty-fifth Infantry; transferred to Co. A, this regiment, January 12, 1864; wounded in action, May 25, 1864, near Dallas, Ga.; mustered out with company, June 5, 1865, near Washington, D.C.

BOARDMAN, WILLIAM H.—Age, 23 years.

Enlisted at Wayland, to serve three years, and mustered in as private, Co. I, August 1, 18623 deserted, November 16, 1862, at Antietam Ford, Md.

BOLT, HENRY D.—Age, 19 years. Enlisted at Elmira, to serve three years, and mustered in as sergeant, Co. D, July 17, 1862; returned to ranks, no date; deserted, December 10, 1862, at Antietam Ford, Md.

BOLTON, CHARLES—Age, 23 years. Enlisted at Elmira to serve three years, and mustered in as corporal, Co. A, July 16, 1862; promoted sergeant, prior to October 1863; wounded in action, May 25, 1864, near Dallas, Ga.; died of his wounds, June 20, 1864, at Chattanooga, Tenn.

BOLTON, JOHN—Private, Co. B, One Hundred and Forty-fifth Infantry; transferred to Co. D, this regiment, January 12, 1864; wounded in action, August 10, 1864, at Atlanta, Ga.; mustered out, May 20, 1865, at Hospital No. 3, Nashville, Tenn.

BONHAM, ROBERT T.—Age, 20 years. Enlisted, August 5, 1862, at Campbell, to serve three years; mustered in as private, Co. F, August 6, 1862; wounded in action, May 3, 1863, at Chancellorsville, Va.; transferred to Twenty-second Company, Second Battalion, Veteran Reserve Corps, March 23, 1864; mustered out, August 5, 1865, at Douglass Hospital, Washington, D.C.

BONNEY, JOHN N.—Age, 19 years. Enlisted, August 9, 1862, at Plattsburg, to serve three years; mustered in as private, Co. K, August 12, 1862; wounded [arm] in action, July 20, 1864, at Peach Tree Creek, Ga.; mustered out with company, June 5,1865, near Washington, D.C.

BONNEY, WILLIAM L—Age, 21 years. Enlisted, August 9, 1862, at Plattsburg, to serve three years; mustered in as corporal, Co. K, August 12, 1862; promoted sergeant, prior to April 10, 1863; first sergeant, September 1, 1864; captured in action, November 18, 1864, near Social Circle, Ga.; exchanged, February 28, 1865; mustered out with detachment, June 22, 1865, at hospital, York, Pa.

BOOTH, ELISHA—Age, 38 years. Enlisted at Elmira, to serve three years, and mustered in as private, Co. G, August 6, 1862; discharged for disability, December 26, 1862, at Philadelphia, Pa.

BORDEN, ALBERT V.—Age, 30 years. Enlisted at Elmira, to serve three years, and mustered in as corporal, Co. G, August 4, 1862; died of typhoid fever, October 25, 1862, in hospital at Harper's Ferry, Va.

BORDEN, WARUM—Age, 19 years. Enlisted, July 9, 1862, at Elmira, to serve three years; mustered in as private, Co. G, July 10, 1862; discharged for disability, February 14, 1863, at Fairfax Seminary, Va., as Warren.

BORST, IRA A.—Age, 40 years. Enlisted, July 11, 1862, at Elmira, to serve three years; mustered in as private, Co. C, July 12, 1862; captured in action, December 15, 1864, near Savannah, Ga.; paroled, no date; mustered out, June 2, 1865, at Elmira, N.Y.

BORST, PHILO—Age, 21 years. Enlisted at Elmira, to serve three years, and mustered in as corporal, Co. C, July 9, 1862; discharged for disability, February 4, 1863, at hospital, Philadelphia, Pa.

BOWERS, WILLIAM—Age, 32 years. Enlisted at Campbell, to serve three years, and mustered in as private, Co. F, August 6, 1862; promoted corporal, November 1, 1863; wounded in action, May 25, 1864, at Dallas, Ga.; returned to ranks, April 9, 1865; mustered out, July 5, 1865, at Sickles Hospital, Washington, D.C.

BOYCE, ANTHONY—Age, 19 years. Enlisted, August 9, 1862, at Montour, to serve three years; mustered in as private, Co. H, August 4, 1862; killed in action, June 22, 1864, at Culp's Farm, Ga.

BRACE, see Brale.

BRADLEY, ELIJAH B.—Age, 26 years. Enlisted, July 14, 1862, at Elmira, to serve three years; mustered in as private, Co. C, July 16, 1862; wounded in action, May 25, 1864, at Dallas, Ga.; mustered out, May 26, 1865, at hospital, Chattanooga, Tenn.

BRADLEY, OSCAR F.—Age, 31 years. Enlisted at Addison, to serve three years, and mustered in as private, Co. F, August 5, 1862; discharged for disability, April 20, 1863.

BRADLEY, OSCAR F.—Age, 33 years. Enlisted at Westfield, to serve three years, and mustered in as private, Co. C, February 29, 1864; died of cholera morbus, September 17, 1864, at No. 2 hospital, Nashville, Tenn. [Same man as above.]

BRADY, DENNIS—Private, Co. I, One Hundred and Forty-fifth Infantry; transferred to Co. H, this regiment, January 12, 1864; absent., a paroled prisoner, at Camp Parole, Annapolis, Md., at muster out of company. [Captured at Chancellorsville while with the 145th NYV and at Camp Parole at the time of transfer to 107th NYV]

BRAGG, GEORGE—Age, 19 years. Enlisted, July 23, 1865, at Corning, to serve three years; mustered in as corporal, Co. I, July 24, 1862; promoted sergeant, October 1863; killed in action, July 26, 1864, near Atlanta, Ga.; also borne as George W.

BRALE, DANIE—Age, 25 years. Enlisted at Corning, to serve three years, and mustered in as corporal, Co. I, August 7, 1862; discharged for disability, April 28, 1864, as Brace.

BRANNAN, PATRICK—Private, Co. C, One Hundred and Forty-fifth Infantry; transferred to Co. K, this regiment, January 12, 1864; drowned, December 9, 1864, near Nashville. [Was patient at Dennison General Hospital]

BRAY, FRANK—Age, 23 years. Enlisted at New York city, to serve three years, and mustered in as private, Co. G, March 23. 1864; wounded in action, May 25, 1864, at Dallas, Ga.; transferred to Co. B, Sixtieth Infantry, June 5, 1865.

BRAYTON, SWEET—Age, 26 years. Enlisted, August 14, 1862, at Hornellsville, to serve three years; mustered in as private, Co. K, August 13, 1862; promoted corporal, October 1, 1863; captured in action, November 18, 1864, near Social Circle, Ga.; paroled, no date; mustered out with detachment, June 19, 1865, at Elmira, N.Y.

BRAZEE, ABRAM—Age, 22 years. Enlisted at Elmira, to serve three years, and mustered in as private, Co. C, July 22, 1862; deserted, September 18, 1862, at Antietam, Md., as Branzee.

BRENNAN, HUGH—Age, 18 years. Enlisted at Elmira, to serve three years, and mustered in as private, Co. G, August 6, 1862; mustered out with company, June 5, 1865, near Washington, D.C.

BRENNING, FREDERICK—Private, Co. I, One Hundred and Forty-fifth Infantry; transferred to Co. C, this regiment, January 11, 1864; promoted corporal, August 1, 1864; mustered out with company, June 5, 1865, near Washington, D.C., as Breining.

BREW, MARTIN—Age, 21 years. Enlisted at Elmira, to serve three years, and mustered in as private, Co. B, July 27, 1862; transferred to U.S. Engineer Corps, April 16, 1863; also borne as Bren.

BREWER, HENRY—Age, 23 years. Enlisted, August 11, 1862, at Wheeler to serve three years; mustered in as private, Co. I, August 13, 1862; died, October 16, 1862, at Harper's Ferry, Va.

BREWER, JAMES N.—Age, 21 years. Enlisted at Elmira, to serve three years, and mustered in as private, Co. G, July 31, 1862; mustered out with company, June 5, 1865, near Washington, D.C.

BREWER, JOHN—Age, 18 years. Enlisted, July 29, 1862, at Campbell, to serve three years; mustered in as private, Co. F, August 11, 1862; died of brain fever [at Hope Landing], February 6, 1863.

BREWER, THOMAS J.—Age, 24 years. Enlisted, July 31, 1862, at Elmira, to serve three years; mustered in as corporal, Co. G, August 4, 1862; promoted sergeant, November 1, 1863; mustered out with company, June 5, 1865, near Washington, D.C.

BRICKWEDDE, JOSEPH—Age, 21 years. Enlisted, July 8, 1862, at Elmira, to serve three years; mustered in as private, Co. A, July 18, 1862; deserted, September 17, 1862, at Antietam, Md., as Briekwede.

BRIGGS, Jr., HENRY—Age, 44 years. Enlisted at Elmira, to serve three years, and mustered in as private, Co. B, July 18, 1862; transferred to Co. I, Twenty-first Regiment, Veteran Reserve Corps, April 6, 1864; discharged, July 25, 1865, at barracks, Trenton, N. J.

BRIGGS, JONATHAN—Age, 44 years. Enlisted at Elmira, to serve three years, and mustered in as private, Co. C, August 2, 1862; transferred to Veteran Reserve Corps, September 1, 1863.

BRIGHAM, H. GUSTAVUS—Age, 26 years. Enrolled at Elmira, to serve three years, and mustered in as first lieutenant, Co. G, August 6, 1862; as captain, Co. H, May 24, 1863; mustered out with company, June 5, 1865, near Washington, D.C. Commissioned first lieutenant, September 6, 1862, with rank from August 6, 1862, original; captain, June 8, 1863, with rank from May 23, 1863, vice H.D. Donnelly, resigned.

BRIGHT, JOHN—Age, 21 years. Enlisted, July 21, 1862, at Elmira, to serve three years; mustered in as private, Co. B, July 23, 1862; wounded in action, May 25, 1864, at Dallas, Ga.; died of chronic diarrhea, June 27, 1864, at Cumberland Hospital, Nashville, Tenn.

BROAS, WILLIAM H.—Age, 21 years. Enlisted, July 21, 1862, at Elmira, to serve three years; mustered in as private, Co. A, July 22, 1862; wounded in action, September 17, 1862, at Antietam, Md.; discharged for disability, December 4, 1862, at Elmira, N.Y.

BROCKWAY, ANDREW—Age, 21 years. Enlisted at Elmira, to serve three years, and mustered in as private, Co. C, July 25, 1862; killed in action, May 25, 1864, near Dallas, Ga.

BRONELL, see Brownell.

BRONSON, IRVING—Age, 19 years. Enrolled at Canisteo, to serve three years; mustered in as second lieutenant, Co. C, July 29, 1862; as first lieutenant, February 4, 1863; mustered out with company, June 5, 1865, near Washington, D.C. Commissioned second lieutenant, September 6, 1862, with rank from July 29, 1862, original; first lieutenant, May 4, 1863, with rank from February 3, 1863, vice O.J. Fox, promoted; captain, not mustered, January 18, 1865, with rank from September 27, 1864, vice C.J. Fox, promoted.

BROWN, ALONZO P.—Private, Co. G, One Hundred and Forty-fifth Infantry; transferred to Co. E, this regiment, January 12, 1864; mustered out with company, June 5, 1865, near Washington, D.C.

BROWN, ANDREW J.—Age, 18 years. Enlisted at Elmira, to serve three years, and mustered in as private, Co. B, July 19, 1862; mustered out with company, June 5, 1865, near Washington, D.C.

BROWN, CHARLES—Private, Co. G, One Hundred and Forty-fifth Infantry; transferred to Co. E, this regiment, January 12, 1864; mustered out with company, June 5, 1865, near Washington, D.C.

BROWN, DANIEL—Age, 39 years. Enlisted, July 16, 1862, at Elmira, to serve three years; mustered in as private, Co. E, July 17, 1862; discharged for disability, April 2, 1863.

BROWN, EDWARD P.—Age, 18 years. Enlisted, July 21, 1862, at Elmira, to serve three years; mustered in as private, Co. E, July 24, 1862; discharged for disability, June 3, 1863, at Philadelphia, Pa.

BROWN, FRANCIS M.—Age, 18 years. Enlisted, July 21, 1862, at Elmira, to serve three years; mustered in as private, Co. A, July 22, 1862; wounded in action, September 17, 1862, at Antietam, Md.; discharged for disability, November 17, 1862, at Elmira, N.Y.

BROWN, JOHN K.—Age, 20 years. Enlisted, July 23, 1862, at Wayland, to serve three years; mustered in as sergeant, Co. I, July 24, 1862; wounded in action, September 17, 1862, at Antietam, Md.; discharged for wounds April 3, 1863, at Convalescent Camp, Alexandria, Va.

BROWN, JOHN W.—Age, 29 years. Enlisted at Elmira, to serve three years, and mustered in as private, Co. G, August 6, 1862; discharged for disability, July 3, 1863, at Elmira, N.Y.

BROWN, SAMUEL W.—Age, 34 years. Enlisted at Elmira, to serve three years, and mustered in as private, Co. C, August 7, 1862'; mustered out with company, June 5, 1865, near Washington, D.C.

BROWN, THEODORE S.—Age, 22 years. Enlisted, July 16, 1862, at Elmira, to serve three years; mustered in as private, Co. C, July 13, 1862; transferred to Veteran Reserve Corps, September 1, 1863.

BROWNELL, ASA—Age, 29 years. Enlisted, July 28, 1862, at Addison, to serve three years; mustered in as corporal, Co. F, July 29, 1862; wounded in action, September 17, 1862, at Antietam, Md.; returned to ranks, March 2, 1864; promoted corporal, no date; again returned to ranks, April 9, 1865; mustered out as corporal, July 27, 1865, at Elmira, N.Y.

BROWNELL, DAVID S.—Age, 18 years. Enlisted at Hornellsville, to serve three years, and mustered in as private, Co. K, January 13, 1864; captured in action, November 18, 1864, near Social Circle, Ga.; paroled, no date; transferred to Co. B, Sixtieth Infantry, June 5, 1565; also borne as Bronell.

BROWNELL, DELOS H.—Age, 18 years. Enlisted, July 24, 1862, at Hornellsville, to serve three years; mustered in as private, Co. K, August 5, 1862, captured in action, November 18, 1864, near Social Circle, Ga.; paroled, no date; mustered out with company, June 5, 1865, near Washington, D.C.

BROWNELL, JOHN A.—Age, 24 years. Enlisted, July 22, 1862, at Hornellsville, to serve three years; mustered in as private, Co. K, July 26, 1862; captured in action, November 18, 1864, near Social Circle, Ga.; paroled, no date [3/6/65]; mustered out with company, June 5, 1865, near Washington, D.C. [Paroled at Wilmington, S.C., in prison at Florence, S.C. ]

BROWNRIGG, GEORGE—Age, 25 years. Enlisted, July 23, 1862, at Elmira, to serve three years; mustered in as sergeant, Co. G, August 6, 1862; promoted first sergeant, September 1, 1864; wounded in action, March 11, 1865, at Averasborough, N.C.; returned to sergeant, no date; mustered out, May 20, 1865, at Elmira, N.Y.

BRUNER, GEORGE—Age, 34 years. Enlisted at West Union, to serve three years, and mustered in as private, Co. I, August 3, 1862; mustered out with company, June 5, 1865, near Washington, D.C.

BUCHMANN, see Bachman.

BUCK, see Beck.

BUCK, ALIC—Age, 21 years. Enrolled at Wayland, to serve three years, and mustered in as private, Co. I, August 2, 1862; deserted, November 16, 1862, at Antietam Ford, Md.

BUCKHOUT, Jr., JACOB G.—Age, 20 years. Enlisted at Elmira, to serve three years, and mustered in as corporal, Co. D, July 18, 1862; returned to ranks, no date; deserted, October 25, 1862, from camp, at Maryland Heights, Md., as Buckout.

BUNDY, CHARLES O.—Age, 23 years. Enlisted, July 16, 1862, at Elmira, to serve three years; mustered in as corporal, Co. A, July 17, 1862; returned to ranks prior to April 10, 1863; mustered out with company, June 5, 1865, near Washington, D.C.

BURD, see Bird.

BURGESS, BENJAMIN F.—Age, 18 years. Enlisted, August 7, 1862, at Elmira, to serve three years; mustered in as [priv]ate, Co. D, August 8, 1862; promoted corporal, March 9, 1864; wounded [hand] in action, May 25, 1864, at Dallas, Ga.; captured in action, November 18, 1864, near Social Circle, Ga.; paroled, no date; mustered out with company, June 5, 1865, near Washington, D.C.

BURGET, WILLIAM M. J.—Age, 42 years. Enlisted at Elmira, to serve three years, and mustered in as private, Co. G, August 6, 1862; transferred to Veteran Reserve Corps, October 5, 1863.

BURKE, WILLIAM—Age, 21 years. Enlisted at Elmira, to serve three years, and mustered in as private, Co. C, August 6, 1862; transferred to Co. H, Third Regiment, Veteran Reserve Corps, no date; transferred to this regiment, March 11, 1864; mustered out with company, June 5, 1865, near Washington, D.C.

BURLINGHAM, CALVIN L—Age, 19 years. Enlisted at Wayland, to serve three years, and mustered in as private, Co. I, July 31, 1862, died of typhoid pneumonia, February 3, 1863, near Hope Landing, Va.

BURNETT, JOHN—Age, 21 years. Enlisted at Elmira, to serve three years, and mustered in as private, Co. D, August 6, 1862; discharged for disability, August 25, 1863. [May 3, 1863, amputated upper 1/3 left leg, right circular, for gunshot wound]

BURNS, FRANCIS—Private, Co. 0, One Hundred and Forty-fifth Infantry; transferred to Co. I, this regiment, January 12, 1864; wounded in action, May 25, 1864, near Dallas, Ga.; mustered out, May 9, 1865, at Cincinnati, Ohio.

BURNS, JAMES—Age, 27 years. Enlisted, June 8, 1862, at Elmira, to serve three years; mustered in as private, Co. E, June 9, 1862; deserted, June 25, 1863, at [hospital] Jefferson, Ind.

BURRELL, ALMON W.—Age, 27 years. Enlisted, July 30: 1862, at Canisteo, to serve three years; mustered in as sergeant, Co. K, Jiffy 31, 1862; died, January 6, 1863, at Philadelphia,

BURRIS, GEORGE—Age, 21 years. Enlisted at Elmira, .to serve three years, and mustered in as private, Co. D, August 9, 1862; wounded in action, May 25, 1864, near Dallas, Ga.; mustered out with company, June 5, 1865, near Washington, D.C.

BURT, CHARLES—Age, place, date of enlistment, and muster in as private, Co. F, not stated; mustered out with company, June 5, 1865, near Washington, D.C.

BYRNE, MARTIN—Private, Co. I, One Hundred and Forty-fifth Infantry; transferred to Co. C, this regiment, January 11, 1864; wounded, no date; mustered out, May 28, 1865, at McDougall Hospital, New York harbor.

CALKINS, JOHN M.—Age, 30 years. Enlisted at Elmira, to serve three years, and mustered in as sergeant, Co. C, July 9, 1862; mustered out with company, June 5, 1865, near Washington, D.C. Commissioned, not mustered, second lieutenant, January 18, 1865, with rank from October 26, 1864, vice J.J. Shepherd, promoted.

CALKINS, RUFUS—Age, 40 years. Enlisted, July 22, 1862, at Elmira, to serve three years; mustered in as private, Co. D, July 24, 1862; transferred to Veteran Reserve Corps, July 1, 1863; also borne as Caulkins.

CALLAGHAN, PATRICK—Age, 21 years. Enlisted at Elmira, to serve three years, and mustered in as private, Co. D, August 7, 1862; wounded in action, September 17, 1862, at Antietam, Md.; died of his wounds, no date; also borne as Calligham, and Callahan.

CAMFIELD, WILLIAM—Age, 27 years. Enlisted, July 21, 1862, at Elmira, to serve three years, and mustered in as private, Co. A, July 29, 1862; deserted, October 12, 1862, at Maryland Heights, Md., as Canfield.

CAMPBELL, ARCHELIST—Age, 18 years. Enlisted, July 17, 1862, at Elmira, to serve three years; mustered in as private, Co. Q, July 24, 1862; died of chronic diarrhea, October 25, 1864, at hospital, Atlanta, Ga.

CAMPBELL, GEORGE W.—Age, 32 years. Enlisted, June 10, 1862, at Elmira, to serve three years; mustered in as private, Co. A, June 18, 1862; mustered out with company, June 5, 1865, near Washington, D.C.

CAMPBELL, NATHANIEL W.—Age, 21 years. Enlisted July 15, 1862, at Elmira, to serve three years; mustered in as private, Co. C, July 22, 1862; mustered out June 2, 1865, at Elmira, N.Y.

CAMPBELL, THEODORE—Age, 18 years. Enlisted, June 9, 1862, at Elmira, to serve three years; mustered in as private, Co. A, June 10, 1862; mustered out with company, June 5, 1865, near Washington, D.C.

CANFIELD, see Camfield.

CANNON, JOHN—Private, Co. K, One Hundred and Forty-fifth Infantry; transferred to Co. 17, this regiment, January 12, 1864; mustered out with company, June 5, 1865, near Washington, D.C.

CAREY, BENJAMIN—Age, 18 years. Enlisted at Elmira, to serve three years, and mustered in as private, Co. B, July 24, 1862; mustered out with company, June 5, 1865, near Washington, D.C.

CAREY, PETER—Sergeant, Co. I, One Hundred and Forty-fifth Infantry; transferred to Co. F, this regiment, as private, January 12, 1864; absent, sick at hospital, Washington, D.C., at muster out of company.

CARL, EDWARD A.—Age, 25 years. Enlisted at Elmira, to serve three years, and mustered in as private, Co. B, July 16, 1862; discharged, December 11, 1862, at hospital, Philadelphia, Pa., as Edwin A.

CARMODY, THOMAS—Age, 20 years. Enlisted at Corning, to serve three years, and mustered in as corporal, Co. I, August 5, 1862; promoted sergeant, prior to October 1863; first sergeant, June 30, 1864; mustered out with company, June 5, 1865, near Washington, D.C.

CARPENTER, CASSIUS—Age, 18 years. Enlisted at Elmira, serve three years, and mustered in as private, Co. C, July 16, 1862; mustered out with company, June 5, 1865, near Washington, D.C.

CARPENTER, GEORGE—Age, 18 years. Enlisted at Elmira to serve three years, and mustered in as private, Co. H, July 25, 1862; promoted corporal, prior to December 1863; wounded in action, May 13, 1864, at Resaca, Ga.; mustered out with company, June 5, 1865, near Washington, D.C.

CARPENTER, HENRY—Age, 26 years. En-

listed at Elmira, to serve three years, and mustered in as private, Co. D, August 6, 1862; wounded in action, May 25, 1864, at Dallas, Ga.; transferred to Co. D, Sixth Regiment Veteran Reserve Corps, no date; mustered out with detachment, July 10, 1865, at Cincinnati, Ohio.

CARPENTER, LEVI—Age, 44 years. Enlisted, July 25, 1862, at West Union, to serve three years; mustered in as private, Co. I, July 26, 1862; killed in action, May 25, 1864, at New Hope Church, Ga.

CARR, WILLIAM H.—Age, 24 years. Enlisted at Elmira, to serve three years, and mustered in as private, Co. G, July 31, 1862; mustered out with company, June 5, 1865, near Washington, D.C.

CARR, WILLIAM P.—Age, 30 years. Enlisted, July 28, 1862, at Addison, to serve three years; mustered in as private, Co. 17, August 5, 1862; transferred to Veteran Reserve Corps, September 30, 1863.

CARTON, JOHN—Age, 29 years. Enlisted at Elmira, to serve three years, and mustered in as private, Co. C, July 9, 1862; discharged for disability, May 25, 1863, at hospital, David's Island, New York harbor.

CASH, JOHN—Private, Co. G, One Hundred and Forty-fifth Infantry; transferred to Co. E, this regiment, January 12, 1864; mustered out with company, June 5, 1865, near Washington, D.C.

CASTER, ALBERT—Age, 21 years. Enlisted, August 4, 1862, at Canisteo, to serve three years; mustered in as private, Co. K, August 8, 1862; captured, November 18, 1864, near Social Circle, Ga.; paroled, no date; mustered out with detachment, June 19, 1865, at Elmira, N.Y.

CASTER, CHARLES—Age, 24 years. Enlisted, August 11, 1862, at Elmira, to serve three years; mustered in as private, Co. K, August 13, 1862; wounded in action, May 25, 1864, near Dallas, Ga.; mustered out, May 29, 1865, at McDougall Hospital, New York harbor.

CASTLE, WILLIAM H.—Age, 25 years. Enlisted at West Union, to serve three years, and mustered in as private, Co. I, July 28, 1862; deserted, October 1, 1862, at Maryland Heights, Md.

CASTOR, HOWARD—Age, 18 years. Enlisted at Elmira; to serve three years, and mustered in as private, Co. I, August 8, 1862; wounded in action, September 17, 1862, at Antietam, Md.; discharged for wounds, no date.

CAULKINS, see Calkins.

CAVANAUGH, MICHAEL— Private, Co. C, One Hundred and Forty-fifth Infantry; transferred to Co. H, this regiment, January 12, 1864; mustered out with company, June 5, 1865, near Washington, D.C.

CHAPLAIN, WILLIAM H.—Age, 33 years. Enlisted, July 19, 1862, at Elmira, to serve three years; mustered in as private, Co. A, July 22, 1862; deserted, July 8, 1863, at Crampton Gap, Md., as Chaplin.

CHATMAN, ALONZO—Age, 30 years. Enlisted at Elmira, to serve three years, and mustered in as private, Co. G, August 8, 1862; wounded in action, September 17, 1864, at Antietam, Md.; mustered out with company, June 5, 1865, near Washington, D.C.; also borne as Chapman.

CHERRY, JAMES B.—Age, 18 years. Enlisted, July 25, 1862, at Addison, to serve three years; mustered in as private, Co. F, July 29, 1862; mustered out with company, June 5, 1865, near Washington, D.C. Commissioned, not mustered, first lieutenant, November 18, 1864, with rank from October 5, 1864, vice R. H. Gansevoort, promoted.

CHIDSEY, LUCIEN B.—Age, 32 years. Enlisted at Elmira, to serve three years, and mustered in as private, Co. K, August 11, 1862; promoted quartermaster sergeant, August 13, 1862; discharged for disability, no date.

CHRISTLER, HELMUS—Age, 26 years. Enlisted at Elmira to serve three years, and mustered in as private, Co. C, August 9, 1862; transferred to Fifty-first Company, Second Battalion, Veteran Reserve Corps, November 15, 1863; mustered out, August 8, 1865, at Philadelphia, Pa.; also borne as Crisler.

CHRISTLER, WILLIAM—Age, 34 years. Enlisted, July 15, 1862, at Elmira, to serve three years; mustered in as private, Co. C, July 22, 1862; wounded in action, May 25, 1864, at Dallas, Ga.; mustered out with company, June 5, 1865, near Washington, D.C.

CHRISTLER, WILLIAM R.—Age, 24 years. Enlisted at Elmira, to serve three years, and mustered in as private, Co. C, August 9, 1862; promoted corporal, August 1, 1864; killed in action, March 17, 1865, near Averasborough, N.C. [March 16, 1865, lower left leg amputated by Surgeon Chapman 123rd NY]

CHURCH, DAVID—Age, 44 years. Enlisted, July 21, 1862, at Elmira, to serve three years; mustered in as private, Co. E, July 24, 1862; discharged for disability, May 25, 1863, at David's Island, New York harbor.

CHURCH, WILLIAM—Age, 18 years. Enlisted, June 8, 1862, at Elmira, to serve three years; mustered in as private, Co. E, June 9, 1862; died of fever, August 2, 1864, at Hospital No. 2, Chattanooga, Tenn.; also borne as William L.

CHURCHILL, JACKSON V.—Age, 32 years. Enlisted at Elmira, to serve three years, mustered in as corporal, Co. D, July 29, 1862; returned to ranks, no date; mustered out with company, June 5, 1865, near Washington, D.C.

CLAIR, WILLIAM—Private, Co. C, One Hundred and Forty-fifth Infantry; transferred to Co. H, this regiment, January 12, 1864; wounded in action, May 25, 1864, at Dallas, Ga.; mustered out with company, June 5, 1865, near Washington, D.C.; also borne as Clare.

CLARK, ALVA—Age, 31 years. Enlisted, July 18, 1862, at Elmira, to serve three years; mustered in as private, Co. E, July 22, 1862; mustered out with company, June 5, 1865, near Washington, D.C.; also borne as Alvah.

CLARK, ASA M.—Age, 36 years. Enlisted, July 30, 1862, at Canisteo, to serve three years; mustered in as private, Co. K, July 31, 1862; mustered out with company, June 5, 1865, near Washington, D.C.

CLARK, DANIEL C.—Age, 31 years. Enlisted, July 18, 1862, at Elmira, to serve three years; mustered in as private, Co. E, July 22, 1862; deserted, October 2, 1862, at Maryland Heights, Md.

CLARK, ERASTUS C.—Age, 25 years. Enrolled at Elmira, to serve three years, and mustered in as captain, Co. H, August 10, 1862; wounded in action, September 17, 1862, at Antietam, Md.; discharged for disability, December 24, 1862. Commissioned captain, September 6, 1862, with rank from August 7, 1862, original.

CLARK, FRANCIS—Age, 27 years. Enlisted, July 25, 1862, at Corning, to serve three years; mustered in as private, Co. I, July 26, 1862; deserted, October 1, 1862, at Maryland Heights, Md.

CLARK, JAMES M.—Age, 21 years. Enlisted, July 30, 1862, at Elmira, to serve three years; mustered in as private, unassigned, August 1, 1862; discharged, August 1862.

CLARK, JOHN C.—Age, 44 years. Enlisted at Havana, to serve three years, and mustered in as private, Co. H, July 25, 1862; wounded in action, July 22, 1864, at Atlanta, Ga.; absent, wounded, and in hospital at Elmira, N.Y., at muster out of company.

CLARK, NATHANIEL L.—Age, 35 years. Enlisted at Thurston, to serve one year, and mustered in as private, Co. I, September 28, 1864; absent, assigned to company, May 1, 1865; never reported to company.

CLARK, WILLIAM—Age, 23 years. Enlisted at Elmira, to serve three years, and mustered in as private, Co. C, July 19, 1862; discharged for disability, January 20, 1863, at Emory Hospital, Washington, D.C.

CLAWSON, JOHN M.—Age 31 years. Enrolled at Campbell to serve three years, and mustered in as private Co. F, August 6, 1862; promoted corporal November 16, 1862; sergeant October 1, 1863; mustered in as second lieutenant January 11, 1865; mustered out with company June 5, 1865, near Washington, D.C. Commissioned second lieutenant July 12, 1864, with rank from May 25, 1864, vice J.D. Hill, killed in action.

CLEARWATER, GARRY—Age 34 years. Enlisted at Elmira to serve three years and mustered in as private, Co. I, August 1, 1862; discharged for disability February 14, 1863, at Convalescent Camp, Alexandria, Va.

CLEARWATER, GARRY—Age 34 years. Enlisted at Elmira to serve three years, and mustered in as private, Co. B, July 23, 1862; discharged January 5, 1863, at hospital in Philadelphia, Pa.

CLEAVER, WILLIAM—Age 32 years. Enlisted August 2, 1862, at Corning to serve three years; mustered in as corporal, Co. I, August 7, 1862; mustered out with company June 5, 1865, near Washington, D.C., as William H.

CLINTON, CHARLES—Age, 33 years. Enlisted, July 26, 1862, at Addison, to serve three years; mustered in as private, Co. F, July 29, 1862; promoted corporal, November 13, 1862; sergeant, June 8, 1863; mustered out with company, June 5, 1865, near Washington, D.C.

CLINTON, Jr., HARMON—Age, 25 years. Enlisted, July 26, 1862, at Addison, to serve three years; mustered in as private, unassigned, August 2, 1862; no further record.

CLOSE, RUSSELL G.—Age, 28 years. Enlisted at Elmira, to serve three years, and mustered in as private, Co. C, July 23, 1862; mustered out with company, June 5, 1865, near Washington, D.C.

COATS, CHARLES M.—Age, 19 years. En-

listed, June 16, 1862, at Elmira, to serve three years; mustered in as private, Co. G, July 16, 1862; transferred to Veteran Reserve Corps, no date; discharged with detachment, June 29, 1865, as of Co. G, Twelfth Regiment, Veteran Reserve Corps, at Washington, D.C.

COE, EPHRAIM—Age, 43 years. Enlisted, August 8, 1862, at Hornellsville, to serve three years; mustered in as private, Co. K, August 9, 1862; transferred to One Hundredth Company, Second Battalion, Veteran Reserve Corps, no date; mustered out with detachment, July 15, 1865, at Augur Hospital, Washington, D.C.

COGANS, CHARLES W.—Age, 18 years. Enlisted at Elmira, to serve three years, and mustered in as private, Co. D, July 28, 1862; wounded in action, May 25, 1864, at Dallas, Ga.; mustered out with company, June 5, 1865, near Washington, D.C.

COGSWELL, GEORGE—Age, 18 years. Enlisted at Elmira, to serve three years, and mustered in as private, Co. E, July 26, 1862; promoted corporal, December 1, 1863; sergeant, April 9, 1865; mustered out with company, June 5, 1865, near Washington, D.C.

COLBY, NEWTON T.—Age, 30 years. Enrolled at Corning, to serve three years, and mustered in as captain, Co. I, August 11, 1862; as major, December 31, 1862; as lieutenant-colonel, February 4, 1863; discharged for disability, September 5, 1863. Commissioned captain, September 6, 1862, with rank from August 9, 1862, original; major, December 30, 1862, with rank from October 21, 1862, vice G.L. Smith, promoted; lieutenant-colonel, March 27, 1863, with rank from February 3, 1863, vice G.L. Smith, discharged.

COLE, CHARLES L.—Age, 20 years. Enlisted, July 21, 1862, at Elmira, to serve three years; mustered in as private, Co. E, July 26, 1862; wounded and captured, March 8, 1865, at Rockingham, N.C.; escaped, April 28, 1865; mustered out, June 19, 1865, at Elmira, N.Y.

COLE, ELIJAH—Age, 30 years. Enlisted, July 21, 1862, at; Elmira, to serve three years; mustered in as private, Co. B, July 22, 1862; transferred to Co. F, Sixteenth Regiment, Veteran Reserve Corps, November 15, 1863; mustered out, July 29, 1865, at Harrisburg, Pa.

COLE, SYLVESTER—Age, 30 years. Enlisted, July 30, 1862, at Canisteo, to serve three years; mustered in as private, Co. K, July 31, 1862; discharged, March 6, 1863, at Washington, D.C.

COLE, WILLIAM A.—Age, 18 years. Enlisted at Rathbone, to serve three years, and mustered in as private, Co. A, December 31, 1863; transferred to Co. A, Sixtieth Infantry, June 5, 1865.

COLEMAN, EDWARD J.—Age, 18 years. Enlisted, August 11, 1862, at Elmira, to serve three years; mustered in as private, Co. K, August 13, 1862; wounded in action, May 25, 1864, at Dallas, Ga.; captured in action, November 18, 1864, near Social Circle, Ga.; died, March 30, 1865, at Wilmington, N.C.

COLLAINS, SAMUEL—Age, 43 years. Enlisted at Elmira, to serve three years, and mustered in as private, Co. D, August 4, 1862; discharged, April 10, 1863, as Collins.

COLLINS, ELIJAH—Age, 20 years. Enlisted at Elmira, to serve three years, and mustered in as private, Co. E, July 22, 1862; mustered out with company, June 5, 1865, near Washington, D.C.

COLLINS, JOHN—Private, Co. I, One Hundred and Forty-fifth Infantry; transferred to Co. C, this regiment, January 12, 1864; wounded in action, May 25, 1864, at Dallas, Ga.; promoted corporal, October 1, 1864; mustered out with company, June 5, 1865, near Washington, D.C.

COLLSON, JONATHAN—Age, 22 years. Enlisted, August 6, 1862, at Elmira, to serve three years; mustered in as private, Co. A, August 8, 1862; discharged for disability, December 9, 1862, at Elmira, N.Y.

COLLSON, PAUL—Age, 29 years. Enrolled, July 21, 1862, at Elmira, to serve three years; mustered in as sergeant, Co. A, July 22, 1862; promoted first sergeant, no date; mustered in as second lieutenant, December 25, 1862; mustered out with company, June 5, 1865, near Washington, D.C. Commissioned second lieutenant, March 23, 1863, with rank from December 24, 1862, vice T.K. Middleton, promoted.

COLLSON, PHILANDER—Age, 18 years. Enlisted, July 24, 1862, at Elmira, to serve three years; mustered in as private, Co. A, July 30, 1862; discharged for disability, February 10, 1863, at Elmira, N.Y.; subsequent service as private, Co. G, Eighth Artillery.

COLLWELL, GEORGE—Age, 18 years. Enlisted at Elmira, to serve three years, and mustered in as private, Co. D, July 31, 1862; deserted, September 6, 1862, at Georgetown, D.C.

COMPTON, GEORGE—Age, 19 years. Enlisted, July 21, 1862, at Elmira, to serve three years; mustered in as private, Co. C, July 22, 1862; died of typhoid fever, March 3, 1863, at camp, Aquia Bay, Va.

COMPTON, LEWIS P.—Age, 21 years. Enlisted, August 7, 1862, at Hammondsport, to serve three years; mustered in as private, Co. K, August 8, 1862; mustered out, July 6, 1865, at Elmira, N.Y.

COMPTON, PETER C.—Age, 30 years. Enlisted, July 15, 1862, at Elmira, to serve three years; mustered in as corporal, Co. E, July 18, 1862; promoted sergeant, March 1, 1863; wounded in action, May 25, 1864, near Dallas, Ga.; died of his wounds, June 30, 1864, at Chattanooga, Tenn.

COMPTON, ZERA—Age, 22 years. Enlisted at Elmira, to serve three years, and mustered in as musician, Co. A, August 5, 1862; mustered out with company, June 5, 1865, Washington, D.C.

CONE, GEORGE S.—Age, 19 years. Enlisted, July 15, 1862, at Hornellsville, to serve three years; mustered in as private, Co. K, August 5, 1862; died, March 12, 1863, at Aquia Bay, Va.

CONKLIN, ALBERT—Age, 21 years. Enlisted, August 4, 1862, at Addison, to serve three years; mustered in as private, Co. F, August 5, 1862; deserted, November 22, 1862, at Antietam Ford, Md., as Albert A.

CONNER, THEODORE W.—Age, 18 years. Enlisted at Elmira, to serve three years, and mustered in as private, Co. C, July 9, 1862; promoted corporal, July 1, 1863; mustered out with company, June 5, 1865, near Washington, D.C.

COOK, JUSTUS A.—Age, 19 years. Enlisted at Westfield, to serve three years, and mustered in as private, Co. C, February 29, 1864; transferred to Co. A, Sixtieth Infantry, June 5, 1865.

COOK, SETH D.—Age, 34 years. Enlisted at Elmira, to serve three years, and mustered in as first sergeant, Co. O, July 9, 1862; discharged for disability, February 5, 1863, at hospital, Frederick, Md.

COOKE, WILLIAM N.—Age, 21 years. Enlisted at Prattsburg, to serve three years, and mustered in as private, Co. K, February 15, 1864; wounded in action, May 25, 1864, at Dallas, Ga.; captured, November 18, 1864, near Social Circle, Ga.; paroled, no date; transferred to Co. B, Sixtieth Infantry, June 5, 1865.

COON, MATTHEW M.—Age, 35 years. Enlisted at Corning, to serve three years, and mustered in as private, Co. I, August 7, 1862; discharged for disability, April 24, 1864.

COOPER, FREDERICK D.—Age, 18 years. Enlisted at Campbell, to serve three years, and mustered in as private, Co. B, January 5, 1864; wounded in action, May 25, 1864, at Dallas, Ga.; mustered out to date, May 16, 1865, at Hospital No. 14, Nashville, Tenn.

COOPER, HARRISON D.—Age, 18 years. Enlisted at Campbell, to serve three years, and mustered in as private, Co. B, January 5, 1864; died of chronic diarrhea, July 7, 1864, at hospital, Nashville, Tenn.; also borne as Devalso H.

COOPER, HENRY—Age, 40 years. Enlisted at Elmira, to serve three years, and mustered in as private, Co. C, August 5, 1862; deserted, February 10, 1863, at [Hospital] Frederick City, Md.

COOPER, JOHN L.—Age, 31 years. Enlisted, August 8, 1862, at Elmira, to serve three years; mustered in as private, Co. A, August 11, 1862; mustered out with company, June 5, 1865, near Washington, D.C.

COOPER, WILLIAM L—Age, 34: years. Enlisted, July 21, 1862, at Elmira, to serve three years; mustered in as wagoner, Co. E, July 22, 1862; died of fever, April 11, 1863, at Hopes Landing, Va.

CORNELL, SAMUEL J.—Age, 23 years. Enlisted at Campbell, to serve three years, and mustered in as private, Co. F, August 6, 1862; promoted corporal, prior to April 10, 1863; transferred to Veteran Reserve Corps, September 30, 1863, as Johnson Cornell; also borne as Cornwell.

CORNER, GEORGE—Age, 26 years. Enlisted at Elmira, to serve three years, and mustered in as private, Co. B, July 23, 1862; transferred to Co. I, Ninth Regiment, Veteran Reserve Corps, March 10, 1864; mustered out, with detachment, June 27, 1865, at Washington, D.C.

CORNER, JACOB—Age, 21 years. Enlisted, July 21, 1862, at Elmira, to serve three years; mustered in as private, Co. B, July 23, 1862; mustered out with company, June 5, 1865, near Washington, D.C.

CORSON, JOHN—Private, Co. K, One Hundred and Forty-fifth Infantry; transferred to Co. F, this regiment, January 12, 1864; mustered out with company, June 5, 1865, near Washington, D.C., as John N.

CORTRIGHT, MARCUS—Age, 24 years. Enlisted at Elmira, to serve three years, and mustered in as private, Co. A, August 7, 1862; discharged for disability, January 18, 1863, at Alexandria, Va., as Corthight; also borne as Marcus P. Courtright; subsequent service as private, Co. I, One Hundred and Forty-seventh Infantry.

CORWIN, DANIEL—Age, 36 years. Enlisted, July 9, 1862, at West Union, to serve three years; mustered in as private, Co. I, July 24, 1862; killed in action, September 17, 1862, at Antietam, Md., as Daniel F.

CORWIN, STEPHEN—Age, 40 years. Enlisted at Elmira, to serve three years, and mustered in as private, Co. E, July 26, 1862; killed, August 3, 1864, near Atlanta, Ga.

CORWIN, THEOPHILUS—Age, 32 years. Enlisted at Corning, to serve three years, and mustered in as private, Co. I, August 3, 1862; mustered out with company, June 5, 1865, near Washington, D.C.

COSS, GEORGE—Age, 26 years. Enlisted at Elmira, to serve three years, and mustered in as private, Co. G, August 5, 1862; discharged for disability, March 14, 1864, at Wartrace, Tenn.

COSTELLO, MICHAEL—Age, 43 years. Enlisted, July 17, 1862, at Corning, to serve three years; mustered in as private, Co. I, July 21, 1862; transferred to Veteran Reserve Corps, March 12, 1864.

COUCH, MYRON G.—Age, 20 years. Enlisted, July 29, 1862, at Havana, to serve three years; mustered in as corporal, Co. H, July 30, 1862; returned to ranks prior to April 10, 1863; killed in action, May 25, 1864, at Dallas, Ga.

COULTER, WILLIAM—Age, 30 years. Enlisted, July 17, 1862, at Elmira, to serve three years; mustered in as private, Co. D, July 24, 1862; mustered out with company, June 5, 1865, near Washington, D.C.

COURTNEY, OWEN—Private, Co. I, One Hundred and Forty-fifth Infantry; transferred to Co. O, this regiment, January 12, 1864; mustered out with company, June 5, 1865, near Washington, D.C.

COURTRIGHT, see Cortright.

COURTRIGHT, JOHN—Age, 27 years. Enlisted at Erwin, to serve three years, and mustered in as private, unassigned, December 28, 1863; no further record.

COUSE, JOSEPH—Age, 19 years. Enlisted at Burdett, to serve three years, and mustered in as corporal, Co. H, July 25, 1862; died of congestion of brain, October 1, 1862, at Maryland Heights, Md.

COVELL, JR., JAMES—Age, 44 years. Enlisted, July 26, 1862, at Addison, to serve three years; mustered in as private, Co. F, July 29, 1862; deserted, November 15, 1863, at hospital, York, Pa., as Covill.

COVILL, CYRUS J.—Age, 23 years. Enlisted, July 28, 1862, at Elmira, to serve three years; mustered in as private, Co. H, August 4, 1862; killed in action, September 17, 1862, at Antietam, Md.

COVILL, WILLIAM H.—Age, 21 years. Enlisted, July 28, 1862, at Elmira, to serve three years; mustered in as private, Co. H, August 4, 1862; promoted corporal, May 1, 1864; wounded in action, June 1, 1864, near Kennesaw Mountain, Ga.; mustered out with company, June 5, 1865, near Washington, D.C.

COWLEY, MICHAEL—Age, 21 years. Enlisted at Elmira, to serve three years, and mustered in as sergeant, Co. O, July 9, 1862; promoted first sergeant, January 1, 1863; mustered out with company, June 5, 1865, near Washington, D.C.

COX, WILLIAM E.—Age, 21 years. Enlisted, July 17, 1862, at Elmira, to serve three years; mustered in as private, Co. D, July 28, 1862; mustered out with company, June 5, 1865, near Washington, D.C.

COYKENDALL, CHARLES—Age, 18 years. Enlisted at Elmira, to serve three years, and mustered in as private, Co. H, July 25, 1862; discharged for disability, June 30, 1863, as Charles H.

CRAFORD, see Crawford;

CRANDALL, WALTER—Age, 18 years. Enlisted at Addison, to serve three years, and mustered in as private, Co. F, July 29, 1862; absent, detached to Veteran Reserve Corps, since May 7, 1863, and at muster out of company.

CRANE, EMMET—Age, 23 years. Enlisted, July 28, 1862, at Addison, to serve three years; mustered in as private, Co. F, July 29, 1862; discharged for disability, October 18, 1862.

CRANE, EZRA F.—Age, 52 years. Enrolled at Elmira, to serve three years, and mustered in as captain, Co. A, July 28, 1862; discharged, August 9, 1862, and mustered in as chaplain, August 13, 1862; discharged, September 17, 1863; prior service as chaplain, Twenty-third Infantry. Commissioned captain, September 6, 1862, with rank from July 23, 1862, original; chaplain, September 6, 1862, with rank from August 9, 1862, original.

CRANE, MANLEY D.—Age, 21 years. Enlisted, July 23, 1862, at Addison, to serve three years; mustered in as private, Co. F, July 29, 1862; promoted corporal, January 16, 1865; mustered out with company, June 5, 1865, near Washington, D.C.

CRANE, NIROM M.—Age, 35 years. Enrolled, May 19, 1863, at Hornellsville, to serve three years, and mustered in as colonel, June 24, 1863; mustered out with regiment, June 5, 1865, near Washington, D.C.; prior service as lieutenant-colonel, Twenty-third Infantry. Commissioned colonel, May 21, 1863, with rank from May 19, 1863, vice A.S. Diven, resigned.

CRANE, PETER—Private, Co. I, One Hundred and Forty-fifth Infantry; transferred to Co. C, this regiment, January 19, 1864; to Veteran Reserve Corps, January 16, 1865, as Crann.

CRANE, WILLIAM B.—Age, 18 years. Enlisted at Elmira, to serve three years, and mustered in as private, Co. G, August 4, 1862; mustered out with company, June 5, 1865, near Washington, D.C.

CRANMER, HIRAM M.—Age, 39 years. Enlisted at Corning, to serve three years, and mustered in as private, Co. C, December 29, 1863; wounded in action, May 25, 1864, at Dallas, Ga.; transferred to Co. A, Sixtieth Infantry, June 5, 1865, as Hiram N.; also borne as Crammer.

CRANS, JOHN H.—Age, 21 years. Enlisted at Addison, to serve three years, and mustered in as private, Co. F, July 29, 1862; promoted corporal, January 1863; wounded, May 3, 1863, Atlanta campaign, Ga.; discharged for disability, November 29, 1863, at Central Park Hospital, New York City.

CRANSTON, MICHAEL—Private, Co. I, One Hundred and Forty-fifth Infantry; transferred to Co. C, this regiment, January 19, 1864; died of typhoid fever, March 19, 1864, at his home in New York City.

CRANTS, MOSES M.—Age, 18 years. Enlisted at Elmira, to serve three years, and mustered in as private, Co. G, July 31, 1862; mustered out with company, June 5, 1865, near Washington, D.C.

CRAWFORD, LEWIS W.—Age, 29 years. Enlisted, February 24, 1864, at Rathbone, to serve three years; mustered in as private, unassigned, February 25, 1864; dishonorably discharged, July 24, 1865, at Elmira, N.Y., as Craford; prior service in Co. D, Twenty-third Infantry.

CRAWFORD, ROBERT—Private, Co. K, One Hundred and Forty-fifth Infantry; transferred to Co. F, this regiment, January 12, 1864; mustered out with company, June 5, 1865, near Washington, D.C.

CREDEN, JEREMIAH—Private, Co. B, One Hundred and Forty-fifth Infantry; transferred to Co. D, this regiment, January 12, 1864; absent, sick in hospital, at Chattanooga, Tenn., at muster out of company.

CREDNER, CARL—Private, Co. B, One Hundred and Forty-fifth Infantry; transferred to Co. D, this regiment, January 12, 1864; absent, sick in hospital, at Wilmington, N.C., and at muster out of company.

CREED, CLARENCE A.—Age, 19 years. Enlisted at Elmira, to serve three years, and mustered in as private, Co. B, December 15, 1863; transferred to Co. A, Sixtieth Infantry, June 5, 1865, as Clarence E.

CREED, JAMES A.—Age, 45 years. Enrolled, July 29, 1862, at Elmira, to serve three years; mustered in as first sergeant, Co. B, July 23, 1862; as second lieutenant, March 21, 1863; discharged for disability, February 16, 1864. Commissioned second lieutenant, May 11, 1863, with rank from March 20, 1863, vice G. Swain, promoted; captain, not mustered, March 23, 1864, with rank from March 16, 1864, vice L. Baldwin promoted.

CRISLER, see Christier.

CRONKRITE, FRANK M.—Age, 29 years. Enrolled at Tyrone, to serve three years, and mustered in as sergeant, Co. H, July 25, 1862; promoted sergeant-major, June 23, 1863; mustered in as second lieutenant, Co. E, March 25, 1864; mustered out with company, June 5, 1865, near Washington, D.C. Commissioned second lieutenant, February 9, 1864, with rank from December 20, 1863, vice C.H. Beal, resigned.

CROOK, BURR—Age, 18 years. Enlisted, July 22, 1862, at Elmira, to serve three years; mustered in as private, Co. D: July 23, 1862; discharged, February 25, 1863.

CROW, DAVID—Age, 21 years. Enlisted, July 25, 1862, at Elmira, to serve three years; mustered in as private, Co. E, July 26, 1862; wounded in action, September 17, 1862, at Antietam, Md.; discharged for wounds, May 15, 1863, at hospital, Antietam, Md. [middle 1/3 right leg amputated on September 17, 1862, ]

CROWLEY, DAVID—Age, 22 years. Enlisted at Elmira, to serve three years, and mustered in as private, Co. C, July 24, 1862; wounded in action, May 3, 1863, at Chancellorsville, Va.; discharged for wounds, August 29, 1864, at hospital, West Philadelphia, Pa.

CRUM, CLARK—Age, 21 years. Enlisted July 21, 1862, at Elmira, to serve three years; mustered in as private, Co. E, July 24, 1862; wounded and captured in action, September 17, 1862; reported deserted, September 18, 1862, at Antietam, Md.; no further record.

CULLY, JOHN—Private, Co. C, One Hundred and Forty-fifth Infantry; transferred to Co. H this regiment, January 12, 1864; mustered out, May 30, 1865, at New York City.

CUMMINGS, DANIEL—Age, 22 years. Enlisted at Addison, to serve three years, and mustered in as private, Co. F, July 29, 1862; died of brain fever, March 31, 1863

CUMMINGS, JOHN—Age 23 years. Enlisted at Elmira, to serve three years, and mustered in as private, Co. D, July 24, 1862; mustered out with company, June 5, 1865, near Washington, D.C.

CUMMINGS, JOHN—Age, 43 years. Enlisted at Elmira, to serve three years, and mustered in as private, Co. G, August 4, 1862; discharged for disability; no date.

CURRAN, BERNARD—Age, 26 years. Enlisted July 22, 1862, at Bath, to serve three years, and mustered in as sergeant, Co. G, July 25, 1862; dishonorably discharged and drummed out of camp for stealing, November 9, 1862, at Antietam Ford, Md.

CURRAN, RICHARD C.—Private, Co. B, One Hundred and Forty-fifth Infantry; transferred to Co. G, this regiment, January 12, 1864; wounded in action, May 25, 1864, at Dallas, Ga.; mustered out with company, June 5, 1865, near Washington, D.C.

CURRY, WILLIAM—Private, Co. I, One Hundred and Forty-fifth Infantry; transferred to Co. C, this regiment, January 12, 1861; mustered out with company, June 5, 1865, near Washington D.C., as Currey.

CUTTER, GEORGE W.—Age, 19 years. Enlisted, July 29, 1862, at Havana, to serve three years; mustered in as private, Co. H, July 30, 1862; died of typhoid fever, March 5, 1863, at Hope Landing, Va.

DAILY, DENNIS—Private, Co. H, One Hundred and Forty-fifth Infantry; transferred to One Hundred and Fifty-first Co., Second Battalion, Veteran Reserve Corps, no date; to Co. H, this regiment, February 14, 1865; mustered out with company, June 5, 1865, near Washington, D.C.

DANIEL, JOHN O.—Age, 21 years. Enlisted,

at Elmira, to serve three years, and mustered in as private, Co. B, July 9,2, 1862; mustered out with company, June 5, 1865, near Washington, D.C., as Daniels.

DANIELS, AUGUSTUS—Age, 19 years. Enlisted at Elmira, to serve three years, and mustered in as private, Co. A, July 16, 1862; died of consumption, October 1, 1862, at Fairfax Court House, Va.

DANNELL, JOHN O.—Age, 18 years. Enlisted at Elmira, to serve three years, and mustered in as private, Co. A, July 17, 1862; mustered out with company June 5, 1865, near Washington, D.C., as Donnell.

DARBY, PHILIP—Private, Co. K, One Hundred and Forty-fifth Infantry; transferred to Co. F, this regiment, January 12, 1864; mustered out with company June 5, 1865, near Washington, D.C.

DARRIN, JOSEPH H.—Age, 21 years. Enlisted at Troopsburg to serve three years, and mustered in as private, Co. I, August 7, 1862; captured in action, March 8, 1865, near Fayetteville, N.C.; paroled, no date; mustered out with detachment, May 31, 1865, at Elmira, N.Y., as Derring; also borne as Derrin.

DAVIS, FRANKLIN G.—Age, 18 years. Enlisted, July 18, 1862, at Elmira, to serve three years; mustered in as private, Co. B, July 19, 1862; mustered out with company, June 5, 1865, near Washington, D.C.

DAVIS, GEORGE W.—Age, 18 years. Enlisted, July 19, 1862, at Elmira, to serve three years; mustered in as private, Co. B, July 22, 1862; wounded in action, September 17, 1862, at Antietam, Md.; discharged for wounds, January 11, 1863, at hospital, Frederick City, Md.

DAVIS, JOHN—Private, Co. K, One Hundred and Forty-fifth Infantry; transferred to Co. F, this regiment, January 12, 1864; mustered out with company, June 5, 1865, near Washington, D.C.

DAVIS, WILLIAM H.—Age, 18 years. Enlisted July 14, 1862, at Elmira, to serve three years; mustered in as corporal, Co. B, July 16, 1862: returned to ranks, June 30, 1863; wounded in action May 15, Resaca, Ga.; absent in hospital since, and at muster out of company.

DAVIS, WILLIAM R.—Age, 44 years. Enlisted at Elmira, to serve three years, and mustered in as sergeant, Co. B, July 23, 1862; returned to ranks, no date; transferred to Twentieth Regiment, Veteran Reserve Corps, December 15, 1863; died, July 25, 1864, in hospital, at Point Lookout, Md.

DAWLEY, PHILANDER—Age, 18 years. Enlisted July 29, 1862, at Canisteo, to serve three years; mustered in as private, Co. K, July 31, 1862; died of fever, May 14, 1864, in hospital, at Murfreesboro, Tenn.

DAWSON, MATTHEW S.—Age, 21 years. Enlisted at Havana, to serve three years, and mustered in as private Co. H, July 25, 1862; wounded in action, September 17, 1862, at Antietam, Md.; died of his wounds, October 1, 1862, at Frederick, Md.

DAY, ORLEANS N.—Age, 23 years. Enlisted at Wayland, to serve three years, and mustered in as private, Co. I, August 5, 1862; deserted, November 16, 1862, at Antietam Ford, Md.; also borne as Orleans M.

DAYTON, MARCUS—Age, 18 years. Enlisted, July 23, 1862, at Elmira, to serve three years; mustered in as private Co. D, July 24, 1862; died of typhoid fever, October 28, 1862, at Harper's Ferry, Va.

DECATOR, ABRAM—Age, 39 years. Enlisted at Elmira, to serve three years, and mustered in as private, Co. A, July 22, 1862; died of typhoid fever, October 13, 1862, at Bolivar Heights, Va., as Abraham; also borne as Deentun.

DECKER, AMOS—Age, 18 years. Enlisted, July 21, 1862, at Elmira, to serve three years; mustered in as private, Co. B, July 23, 1862; deserted, December 9,1862, at Antietam Ford, Md.; apprehended, October 23, 1863; absent in arrest [Fort Columbus, Ky.] since, and at muster out of company, at Fort Columbus, New York harbor.

DECKER, JOHN J.—Private, Co. K, One Hundred and Forty-fifth Infantry; transferred to Co. I, this regiment, January 12, 1864; killed in action, May 25, 1864, at New Hope Church, Ga.

DECKER, PETER—Age, 44 years. Enlisted, July 21, 1862, at Elmira, to serve three years; mustered in as private, Co. D, July 22, 1862; discharged, April 2, 1863, as Peter I.

De GRAW, JOHN—Age, 24 years. Enlisted at Elmira, to serve three years, and mustered in as private, Co. B, July 22, 1862; discharged for disability, August 13, 1863, at hospital, Philadelphia, Pa.

De GROAT, JOHN—Age, 43 years. Enlisted at Corning, to serve three years, and mustered in as musician, Co. I, August 11, 1862; discharged for disability, August 20, 1863, at hospital, Baltimore, Md., as De Groat.

De GROAT, VINSON—Age, 22 years. Enlisted at Rathbone, to serve three years, and mustered in as private, Co. I3, December 31, 1863; transferred to Co. A, Sixtieth Infantry, June 5, 1865; prior service in Co. C, Twenty-third Infantry; also borne as Vincent.

De GRUSHE, JOHN B.—Private, Co. I, One Hundred and Forty-fifth Infantry; transferred to Co. H, this regiment, January 12, 1864; to Veteran Reserve Corps, February 11, 1864, as John D. De Gushe.

DELANO, GEORGE F.—Age, 24 years. Enlisted, July 15, 1862, at Elmira, to serve three years; mustered in as private, Co. E, July 18, 1862; deserted, September 18, 1862; at Antietam, Md.; also borne as G. T.

DELANY, WILLIAM—Private, Co. I, One Hundred and Forty-fifth Infantry; transferred to Co. C, this regiment, January 11, 1864; wounded in action, May 25, 1864, at Dallas, Ga.; mustered out with company, June 5, 1865, near Washington, D.C., as Delaney.

DELAP, EPHRAIM—Age 29 years. Enlisted at Elmira, to serve three years, and mustered in as private, Co. B, July 23, 1862; mustered out with company, June 5, 1865, near Washington, D.C.

DELAP, LEWIS H.—Age, 18 years. Enlisted at Elmira, to serve three years, and mustered in as private, Co. E, June 9, 1862; mustered out with company, June 5, 1865, near Washington, D.C.

DENHOLM, DAVID—Private, Co. I, One Hundred and Forty-fifth Infantry; transferred to Co. C, this regiment, January 11, 1864; mustered out with company, June 5, 1865, near Washington, D.C., as Dunholm.

DENNIN, JOHN—Age, 20 years. Enlisted at Auburn, to serve one year, and mustered in as private, unassigned, April 6, 1865; mustered out with detachment, May 15, 1865, at Harts Island, New York harbor.

DENNISTON, ABRAHAM—Age, 35 years. Enlisted at Elmira, to serve three years, and mustered in as private, Co. G, August 6, 1862; died, February 6, 1863, in hospital at Washington, D.C.

DENNISTON, HARVEY G.—Age, 32 years. Enrolled at Elmira, to serve three years, and mustered in as corporal, Co. G, August 6, 1862; as second lieutenant, November 3, 1862; as first lieutenant, May 24, 1863; discharged, to date March 31, 1864; subsequent service as captain, One Hundred and Eighty-eighth Infantry. Commissioned second lieutenant, November 24, 1862, with

rank from October 27, 1863, vice E. Gleason, resigned; first lieutenant, August 13, 1863, with rank from May 23, 1863, vice H.G. Brigham, promoted.

DENSMORE, ORRIN S.—Age, 20 years. Enlisted, July 24, 1862, at Addison, to serve three years; mustered in as private, Co. I, July 31, 1862; discharged for disability, March 20, 1863, at Convalescent Camp, Alexandria, Va.

DEPEW, RICHARD—Age, 18 years. Enlisted at Elmira, to serve three years, and mustered in as private, Co. A, July 17, 1862, captured and paroled subsequent to December 1864; mustered out, June 9, 1865, at Elmira, N.Y.

DERR, HENRY C.—Age, 21 years. Enlisted, July 17, 1862, at Elmira, to serve three years; mustered in as private, Co. C, July 18, 1862; discharged for disability, August 26, 1863, at hospital, Convalescent Camp, Alexandria, Va.

DERRING and DERRIN, see Darrin

DEUEL, JOHN—Age, 35 years. Enlisted, August 4, 1862, at Addison, to serve three years; mustered in as corporal, Co. F, August 5, 1862; returned to ranks, no date; discharged for disability, March 19, 1863, as Duel.

DEVINE, MICHAEL—Private, Co. G, One Hundred and Forty-fifth Infantry; transferred to Co. E, this regiment, January 12, 1864; mustered out with company, June 5, 1865, near Washington, D.C.; also borne as Divine.

DEVOE, RUSSELL R.—Age, 18 years. Enlisted, July 21, 1862, at Elmira, to serve three years; mustered in as musician, Co. D, July 22, 1862; grade changed to private, no date; captured in action, November 18, 1864, near Social Circle, Ga.; paroled, no date; mustered out with company, June 5, 1865, near Washington, D.C.

DEVORE, JAMES—Age, 26 years. Enlisted at Elmira, to serve three years, and mustered in as private, Co. B, July 26, 1862; discharged for disability, January 1, 1863, at hospital, Elmira, N.Y.

DEWAINE, JOHN T., see John Duwaine.

De WATERS, PHILIP—Private, Co. K, One Hundred and Forty-fifth Infantry; transferred to Co. F, this regiment, January 19, 1864; mustered out with company, June 5, 1865, near Washington, D.C.

De WATERS, WILLIAM—Private, Co. K, One Hundred and Forty-fifth Infantry; transferred to Co. F, this regiment, January

12, 1864; mustered out, June 13, 1865, at Annapolis, Md.

DEWITT, ANDREW—Age, 23 years. Enlisted, July 29, 1862, at Havana, to serve three years; mustered in as private, Co. H, July 30, 1862; died of typhoid fever, April 8, 1863, at Hope Landing, Va., as Devitt.

DICKENS, JAMES L.—Age, 21 years. Enlisted, July 29, 1862, at Montour, to serve three years; mustered in as private, Co. H, July 30, 1862; mustered out with company, June 5, 1865, near Washington, D.C.; also borne as Dickins.

DICKERSON, MARK—Age, 28 years. Enlisted, August 4, 1862, at Addison, to serve three years; mustered in as private, Co. F, August 5, 1862; discharged for disability, February 14, 1863, as Dickinson.

DICKERSON, WILLIAM—Private, Co. G, One Hundred and Forty-fifth Infantry; transferred to Co. E, this regiment, January 12, 1864; promoted corporal, July 1, 1864; killed in skirmish, March 8, 1865, in South Carolina as Dickinson.

DICKINS, ROBERT B.—Age, 21 years. Enlisted, July 25, 1862, at Havana, to serve three years; mustered in as private, Co. H, July 29, 1862; wounded in action, May 25, 1864, at Dallas, Ga.; transferred to Veteran Reserve Corps, January 16, 1865, as Albert B.

DICKINSON, EDWARD—Age, 35 years. Enlisted at Elmira, to serve three years, and mustered in as private, Co. G, December 7, 1863; died of chronic diarrhea, July 20, 1864, in hospital at Nashville, Tenn.

DICKINSON, HIRAM L.—Age, 21 years. Enlisted at Elmira, to serve three years, and mustered in as private, Co. G, August 6, 1862; absent in hospital at Jeffersonville, Ind., since August 1864, and at muster out of company.

DININNY, THEODORE W.—Age, 26 years. Enlisted at Campbell, to serve three years, and mustered in as private, Co. F, August 6, 1862; discharged for disability, June 3, 1863.

DIVEN, ALEXANDER S.—Age, 52 years. Enrolled at Elmira, to serve three years, and mustered in as lieutenant-colonel, August 13, 1862; as colonel, October 21, 1862; discharged, May 11, 1863. Commissioned Lieutenant-colonel, September 6, 1862, with rank from July 29, 1862, original; colonel, October 21, 1862, with rank from same date, vice R.B. Van Valkenburgh, resigned.

DIVINE, see Devine.

DIXON, WILLIAM H.—Age, 26 years.

Enlisted at Elmira, to serve three years, and mustered in as private, Co. A, July 17,1864; killed August 11, 1864, while on picket near Atlanta, Ga.

DOBBELBEISS, see Dubblebeiss.

DONLON, WILLIAM—Age, 18 years. Enlisted, July 30, 1862, at Hornellsville, to serve three years; mustered in as private, Co. K, July 31, 1862; captured in action, November 18, 1864, near Social Circle, Ga.; exchanged, February 28, 1865; mustered out with detachment, June 22, 1865, at General Hospital, York, Pa.; also borne as Donalon.

DONNELL, see Dannell.

DONNELL, WILLIAM B.—Age, 36 years. Enlisted, July 29, 1862, at Elmira, to serve three years; mustered in as private, Co. A, July 23, 1862; promoted corporal, prior to April 10, 1863; discharged for disability, January 12, 1864, at Tullahoma, Tenn., as William P.

DONNELLY, HENRY D.—Age, 22 years. Enrolled at Elmira, to serve three years, and mustered in as first lieutenant, Co. H, August 10, 1862; as captain, December 25, 1862; discharged, May 23, 1863. Commissioned first lieutenant, September 6, 1862, with rank from August 7, 1862, origins; captain, February 23, 1863, with rank from December 24, 1862, vice E.C. Clark, discharged.

DONNELLY, JOHN—Private, Co. O, One Hundred and Forty-fifth Infantry; transferred to Co. H, this regiment, January 12, 1864; mustered out with company, June 5, 1865, near Washington, D.C.

DONOHUE, DANIEL—Private, Co. K, One Hundred and Forty-fifth Infantry; transferred to Co. F, this regiment, January 12, 1864; wounded in action, May 25, 1864, at Dallas, Ga.; mustered out with company, June 5, 1865, near Washington, D.C.; also borne as Donahue.

DONOHUE, PATRICK—Private, Co. G, One Hundred and Forty-fifth Infantry; transferred to Co. E, this regiment, January 12, 1864; absent in hospital at Murfreesboro, Tenn., since April 27, 1864, and at muster out of company.

DOOLITTLE, SAMUEL—Age, 19 years. Enlisted, July 10, 1862, at Corning, to serve three years; mustered in as private, Co. I, July 24, 1862; promoted corporal, no date; deserted, December 9, 1862, at Antietam Ford, Md.

DORE, PATRICK—Private, Co. I, One Hundred and Forty-fifth Infantry; transferred to Co. C, this regiment, January 12, 1864; killed, August 11, 1864, while on picket near Atlanta, Ga.

DOUGHERTY, JOHN—Private, Co. K, One Hundred and Forty-fifth Infantry; transferred to Co. I, this regiment, January 12, 1864; killed in action, August 5, 1864, in front of Atlanta, Ga.

DOUGLAS, JAMES—Private, Co. K, One Hundred and Forty-fifth Infantry; transferred to Co. F, this regiment, January 12, 1864; promoted corporal, June 1864; mustered out with company, June 5, 1865, near Washington, D.C.

DOWNEY, TIMOTHY—Private, Co. B, One Hundred and Forty-fifth Infantry; transferred to Co. G, this regiment, January 19, 1864; wounded in action, May 25, 1864, at Dallas, Ga.; mustered out with company, June 5, 1865, near Washington, D.C.; also borne as Downing.

DOWNING, NELSON—Age, 18 years. Enlisted at Elmira, to serve three years, and mustered in as private, Co. A, July 18, 1862; wounded in action, March 16, 1865, at Averasborough, N.C.; mustered out, May 20, 1865, at Elmira N.Y., as Downer.

DOYLE, JAMES—Age, 35 years. Enlisted August 6, 1862, at Hornellsville, to serve three years; mustered in as private, Co. K, August 8, 1862; captured in action, November 18, 1864, near Social Circle, Ga.; paroled, no date; mustered out with detachment, June 19, 1865, at Elmira, N.Y.

DRAKE, GEORGE W.—Age, 22 years. Enlisted, July 21, 1862, at Elmira, to serve three years; mustered in as private, Co. B, July 22, 1862; mustered out with company, June 5, 1865, near Washington, D.C.

DRAKE, GEORGE W.—Age, 34 years. Enlisted, August 4, 1862, at Cameron, to serve three years; mustered in as private, Co. F, August 5, 1862; mustered out, July 3, 1865, at Elmira, N.Y.

DRAKE, THEODORE—Age, 24 years. Enlisted at Elmira, to serve three years, and mustered in as corporal, Co. A, July 22, 1862; discharged for disability, December 18, 1862, at Philadelphia, Pa.

DREHER, CLEMENCE—Private, Co. I, One Hundred and Forty-fifth Infantry; transferred to Co. C, this regiment January 12, 1864; killed in action, May 25, 1864, near Dallas, Ga., as Clement; also borne as Dreehen.

DRUMMOND, HENRY—Age, 40 years. Enlisted at Corning, to serve three years; mustered in as musician, Co. I, August 11, 1862; promoted principal musician, November 1, 1863; mustered out with regiment June 5, 1865, near Washington, D.C.

DUBBLEBEISS, HENRY—Private, Co. B, One Hundred and Forty-fifth Infantry; transferred to Co. D, this regiment, no date; discharged, January 2, 1864; borne as Dobbelbeiss.

DUBOIS, JOHN H.—Age, 18 years. Enlisted at Elmira, to serve three years, and mustered in as private, Co. B, July 18, 1862; mustered out, June 8, 1865, at Field Hospital, Nashville, Tenn., as Du Bois.

DUEL, see Deuel.

DUNHAM, ALEXANDER—Age, 20 years. Enlisted, July 25, 1862, at Havana, to serve three years; mustered in as private, Co. H, July 29, 1862; wounded in action, July 25, 1864, at Dallas, Ga.; mustered out with company, June 5, 1865, near Washington, D.C.

DUNHAM, SYLVESTER—Age, 38 years. Enlisted at Elmira, to serve three years, and mustered in as private, Co. H, August 4, 1862; mustered out with company, June 5, 1865, near Washington, D.C.

DUNHOLM, see Denholm.

DUNN, ISRAEL—Age, 18 years. Enlisted at Elmira, to serve three years, and mustered in as private, Co. G, August 4, 1862; mustered out with company, June 5, 1865, near Washington, D.C.

DUNN, LUKE—Private, Co. I, One Hundred and Forty-fifth Infantry; transferred to Co. H, this regiment, January 12, 1864; to Veteran Reserve Corps, no date.

DURFEE, BURLINGTON—Age, 35 years. Enlisted at Havana, to serve three years, and mustered in as private, Co. H, July 25, 1862; wounded in action, May 25, 1864, at Dallas, Ga.; deserted, August 15, 1864, from hospital at Nashville, Tenn.

DURFEE, STEPHEN B.—Age, 22 years. Enlisted at Havana, to serve three years, and mustered in as private Co. H, July 25, 1862; deserted, September 17, 1862, at Antietam, Md.

DURYEA, CHARLES H.—Age, 21 years. Enlisted, August 4, 1862, at Elmira, to serve three years; mustered in as corporal, Co. H, August 5, 1862; promoted sergeant, prior to April 10, 1863; first sergeant, December 1, 1863; wounded in action, May 25, 1864, at Dallas, Ga.; mustered out May 11, 1865, Elmira, N.Y.

DUWAINE, JOHN—Age, 18 years. Enlisted at Elmira, to serve three years, and mustered in as private, Co. G, March 31, 1864; transferred to Co. B, Sixtieth Infantry, June 5, 1865; also borne as John T. Dewaine.

DYKEMAN, JAMES F.—Age, 22 years. Enlisted, July 25, 1862, at Havana, to serve three years; mustered in as private, Co. H, July 29, 1862; wounded in action, May 25, 1864, at Dallas, Ga.; mustered out, May 13, 1865, at Elmira, N.Y.

DYKEMAN, NATHAN F.—Age, 24 years. Enlisted, July 25, 1862, at Havana, to serve three years; mustered in as corporal, Co. H, July 29, 1862; promoted sergeant, December 1, 1863; killed by the cars, May 29, 1865, [Hit by railroad train].

EAPLEY, PATRICK—Private, Co. I, One Hundred and Forty-fifth Infantry; transferred to Co. C, this regiment January 12, 1864; mustered out with company, June 5, 1865, near Washington, D.C., as Eaphy.

EARLY, JOHN F.—Age, 20 years. Enlisted at Elmira, to serve three years, and mustered in as private, Co. K, February 15, 1864; captured in action, November 18, 1864, near Social Circle, Ga.; paroled, no date; transferred to Co. B, Sixtieth Infantry, June 5, 1865.

EATON, NATHANIEL—Age, 43 years Enlisted, July 22, 1862, at Elmira, to serve three years; mustered in as private, Co. C, July 23, 1862; discharged for disability, August 27, 1863, at Jarvis Hospital, Baltimore, Md.

EDGERTON, WILLIAM W.—Age, 18 years. Enlisted, July 7, 1862, at Elmira. to serve three years; mustered in as private, Co. A, July 21, 1862; mustered out with company, June 5, 1865, near Washington, D.C.

EDWARDS, STEPHENS—Age, 20 years. Enlisted, July 28, 1862, at Montour, to serve three years; mustered in as private, Co. H, August 2, 1862; discharged for disability, January 13, 1863, at Washington, D.C.

EDWARDS, STEPHEN—Age, 20 years. Enlisted, February 11, 1864, at Wayne, to serve three years; mustered in as private, Co. H, February 15, 1864; died of chronic diarrhea, February 15, 1865, at Savannah, Ga.

EDWARDS, WILLIAM S.—Private, Co. G, One Hundred and Forty-fifth Infantry; transferred to Co. E, this regiment, January 12, 1864; wounded in action, May 25, 1864, at Dallas, Ga.; mustered out with company, June 5, 1865, near Washington, D.C.

EGBERT, JOHN D.—Age, 19 years. Enlisted, July 21, 1862¢ at Elmira, to serve three years; mustered in as private, Co. A, July 22, 1862; wounded in action, September 17, 1862, at Antietam, Md.; discharged for disability, January 6, 1863, at Philadelphia Pa.

EGGINTON, WILLIAM—Corpora], Co. I, One Hundred and Forty-fifth Infantry; transferred to Co. C, this regiment, as private, January 12, 1864; mustered out with company, June 5, 1865, near Washington, D.C.

ELDRED, JOSEPH S.—Age, 19 years. Enlisted, July 25, 1862, at Havana, to serve three years; mustered in as private, Co. H, July 29, 1862; discharged, April 13, 1864, at New York City.

ELLIS, GUY.—Age, 21 years. Enlisted at Elmira, to serve three years, and mustered in as private Co. D, July 28, 1862; transferred to One Hundred and Eighth Company, Second Battalion, Veteran Reserve Corps, October 22, 1864; mustered out, July 27, 1865, at Harrisburg, Pa.

ELLIS, MYRON—Age, 29 years. Enlisted at Allen, to serve three years, and mustered in as private, Co. B, February 1, 1865; transferred to Co. A, Sixtieth Infantry, June 5, 1865.

ELLSWORTH, JOHN H.—Age, 24 years. Enlisted at Elmira, to serve three years, and mustered in as private, Co. D, July 19, 1862; discharged for disability, June 2, 1863, at hospital, Frederick City, Md.

ELY, W. MARTIN—Age, 23 years. Enlisted at Corning, to serve three years, and mustered in as private, Co. I, August 7, 1862; discharged for disability May 6, 1863.

EMER, MARK—Age 27 years. Enlisted at Elmira, to serve three years, and mustered in as private, Co. C, July 16, 1862; absent in hospital, at Washington, D.C., since October 1803, and at muster out of company.

ENSECO, JAMES—musician, Co. C, One Hundred and Forty-fifth Infantry; transferred to Co. H, this regiment, January 12, 1864; mustered out with company, June 5, 1865, near Washington, D.C., as Enscho; also borne as Enscoe, Ensico.

EUMANS, JASON J.—Age, 18 years. Enlisted, July 29, 1862, at Montour, to serve three years; mustered in as private, Co. H, July 30, 1862; wounded in action, May 25, 1864, at Dallas, Ga.; died of wounds, August 8, 1864, at Sherman Hospital, Nashville, Tenn., as Youmans.

EVANS, CHARLES E.—Age, 25 years. Enlisted at Corning, to serve three years, and mustered in as private, Co. C, December 29, 1863; transferred to Co. A, Sixtieth Infantry, June 5, 1865.

EVELAND, JOHN—Age, 19 years. Enlisted, July 25, 1862, at Havana, to serve three years; mustered in as private, Co. H, July 29, 1862; captured and paroled, no date; mustered out with detachment, June 9, 1865, at Elmira, N.Y.

EVERETS, CHARLES F.—Age, 43 years. Enlisted, July 21, 1862, at Elmira, to serve three years; mustered in as corporal, Co. E, July 24, 1862; returned to ranks, no date; mustered out, with detachment, August 2, 1865, at Sickles Hospital, Washington, D.C.

EVERETT, JOHN—Age, 18 years. Enlisted, July 7, 1862, at Corning, to serve three years; mustered in as private, Co. I, July 24, 1862; transferred to Co. B, Fifth Regiment, Veteran Reserve Corps, January 2, 1865; mustered out, July 24, 1865, at Burnside Barracks, Indianapolis, Ind.

EVERETT, WILLIAM L—Age, 19 years. Enlisted at Elmira, to serve three years, and mustered in as private, Co. G, July 6, 1862; killed in action, September 17, 1862, at Antietam, Md.

FANCHER, WILLIAM—Age, 18 years. Enlisted at Rathboneville, to serve three years and mustered in **as** private, Co. A, January 1, 1864; transferred to Co. A, Sixtieth Infantry, June 5, 1865.

FANSCEY, JAMES S.—Age, 26 years. Enlisted at Elmira, to serve three years, and mustered in as private, Co. A, July 23, 1862; promoted corporal, prior to April 10, 1863; returned to ranks, no date; discharged for disability, September 14, 1863, at Washington, D.C., as Fansey.

FANTON, HULL—Age, 29 years. Enrolled at Elmira, to serve three years, and mustered in as first lieutenant and adjutant, August 13, 1862; discharged for promotion to organization, not stated, May 10, 1863. Commissioned first lieutenant and adjutant, November 28, 1862, with rank from August 8, 1862, original.

FARRELL, WILLIAM—Private, Co. I, One Hundred and Forty-fifth Infantry; transferred to Co. I, this regiment, January 12, 1864; mustered out, with company, June 5, 1865, near Washington, D.C., as William J.

FAULKNER, JOSEPH P.—Age, 21 years. Enlisted at Elmira, to serve three years;

mustered in as corporal, Co. D, July 25, 1862; wounded in action, May 25, 1864, at Dallas, Ga.; promoted sergeant, August 1, 1864; mustered out., with company, June 5, 1865, near Washington, D.C.

FAY, EDWIN G.—Age, 21 years. Enrolled, July 14, 1860, at Elmira, to serve three years; mustered in as sergeant, Co. C, July 16, 1862; promoted sergeant-major, January 1, 1863; mustered in as second lieutenant, Co. C, May 3, 1863; mustered out, to date June 5, 1865. Commissioned second lieutenant, May 4, 1863, with rank from February 3, 1863, vice I. Bronson, promoted.

FAY, FRANCIS C.—Age, 18 years. Enlisted at Elmira, to serve three years, and mustered in as private, Co. C, July 19, 1862; mustered out with company, June 5, 1865, near Washington, D.C.

FELL, JAMES A.—Private, Co. I, One Hundred and Forty-fifth Infantry; transferred to Co. B, this regiment, January 12, 1864; to Veteran Reserve Corps, March 29, 1864.

FELL, WILLIAM—Age, 20 years. Enlisted at Elmira, to serve three years, and mustered in as private, Co. A, July 16, 1863; died of inflammation of the lungs, December 2, 1864, at Jeffersonville, Ind.

FENNO, GEORGE J.—Age, 24 years. Enlisted, August 5, 1862, at Elmira, to serve three years; mustered in as private, Co. H, August 7, 1862; discharged for disability, February 10, 1863, at Philadelphia, Pa.

FERGUSON, see Furgerson.

FINCH, NATHANIEL—Age, 19 years. Enlisted, July 21, 1862, at Elmira, to serve three years; mustered in as private Co. D, July 9,4, 1862; died of typhoid fever, December 27, 1862, at Philadelphia, Pa.

FINLEY, FRANCIS—Private, Co. I, One Hundred and Forty-fifth Infantry; transferred to Co. B, this regiment, January 12, 1864; mustered out with company, June 5, 1865, near Washington, D.C.

FINNEGAN, SAMUEL—Private, Co. K, One Hundred and Forty-fifth Infantry; transferred to Co. F, this regiment, January 12, 1864; mustered out with company, June 5, 1865, near Washington, D.C., as Finegan.

FINNEGHAN, JOHN—Private, Co. B, One Hundred and Forty-fifth Infantry; appointed musician, no date; transferred to Co. D, this regiment, January 12, 1864; mustered out with company, June 5, 1865, near Washington, D.C., as Finnegan.

FISK, AMOS—Age, 22 years. Enlisted at

Elmira, to serve three years, and mustered in as private, Co. G, August 6, 1862; wounded in action, September 17, 1862, at Antietam, Md.; discharged for disability, December 17, 1862, at Frederick, Md.

FISK, PHINEAS—Age, 27 years. Enlisted, July 27, 1862, at Elmira, to serve three years; mustered in as private, Co. G, August 6, 1862; transferred to Veteran Reserve Corps, July. 23, 1863.

FITCH, ARTHUR S.—Age, 18 years. Enrolled, July 14, 1862, at Elmira, to serve three years; mustered in as corporal, Co. B, July 16, 1862; promoted sergeant, November 1, 1862; first sergeant, June 8, 1863; mustered in as first lieutenant, August 27, 1864; mustered out with company, June 5, 1865, near Washington, D.C. Commissioned first lieutenant, December 7, 1864, with rank from August 27, 1864, vice J. Orr, promoted.

FLANAGAN, PATRICK—Age, 37 years. Enlisted at Elmira, to serve three years, and mustered in as private, Co. B, July 26, 1862; promoted corporal, June 30, 1863; returned to ranks, December 1863; absent, sick in hospital, Nashville, Tenn., since July 2, 1864, and at muster out of company.

FLOOD, JOHN—Age, 20 years. Enrolled at Elmira, to serve three years, and mustered in as private, Co. D, August 4, 1862; promoted hospital steward, March 1, 1863; mustered in as assistant surgeon, May 5, 1863; discharged, September 17, 1863. Commissioned assistant surgeon, May 4, 1863, with rank from April 20, 1863, vice J.D. Hewitt, promoted.

FLOOD, PATRICK H.—Age, 50 years. Enrolled at Elmira, to serve three years, and mustered in as surgeon, July 22, 1862; mustered out with regiment, June 5, 1865, near Washington, D.C. Commissioned surgeon September 6, 1862, with rank from July 19, 1862, original.

FLORENCE, HIRAM—Age, 28 years. Enlisted at Corning, to serve three years, and mustered in as private, Co. I, July 25, 1862; discharged for disability, January. 28, 1863.

FLYNN, JAMES—Corporal Co. I, One Hundred and Forty-fifth Infantry transferred to Co. H, this regiment January 12, 1864, mustered out with company, June 5, 1865, near Washington, D.C.

FLYNN, JEROME—Age, 18 years. Enlisted, July 21, 1862, at Elmira, to serve three years; mustered in as private, Co. A, July 22, 1862; deserted, September 17, 1862, at Antietam, Md.

FOOT, RICHARD—Age, 34 years. Enlisted at Elmira, to serve three years, and mustered in as private, Co. E, July 22, 1862; discharged for disability, December 4, 1863, at Central Park Hospital, New York city.

FORCE, BENJAMIN—Age, 19 years. Enlisted at Elmira, to serve three years, and mustered in as private, Co. H, August 4, 1862; promoted corporal, prior to April 10, 1863; sergeant, prior to October 1863; killed in action, May 25, 1864, at Dallas, Ga.

FORD, LINUS S.—Corporal, Co. B, One Hundred and Forty-fifth Infantry; transferred to Co. D, this regiment, January 12, 1864; promoted sergeant, March 5, 1864; wounded in action, May 25, 1864, and died of his wounds, June 3, 1864, at Dallas, Ga.

FORD, THOMAS—Private, Co. I, One Hundred and Forty-fifth Infantry; transferred to Co. C, this regiment, January 12, 1864; mustered out with company, June 5, 1865, near Washington, D.C.

FORRESTER, DAVID—Age, 44 years. Enlisted at Wayland, to serve three years, and mustered in as private, Co. I, August 1, 1862; deserted, September 7, 1862, at Rockville, Md.

FOSTENSEN, FREDERICK—Age, 33 years. Enlisted at Elmira, to serve three years, and mustered in as private, Co. B, July 23, 1862; died of wound received accidentally, June 28, 1864, at Nashville, Tenn.

FOSTER, AUGUSTUS C.—Age, 21 years. Enlisted, July 25, 1862. at Havana, to serve three years; mustered in as private, Co. H, July 29, 1862; promoted corporal, prior to April 10, 1863; captured and paroled, no date; mustered out with detachment June 9, 1865, at Elmira, N.Y.

FOX, CHARLES B. S.—Age, 21 years. Enlisted at Elmira, to serve three years, and mustered in as private, Co. D, August 4, 1862; mustered out with company, June 5, 1865, near Washington, D.C., as Charles F.

FOX, CHARLES J.—Age, 20 years. Enrolled, July 18, 1862, at Elmira, to serve three years; mustered in as first lieutenant, Co. C, July 29, 1862; as captain, February 4, 1863; mustered out with company, June 5, 1865, near Washington, D.C. Commissioned first lieutenant, March 23, 1863, with rank from July 29, 1862, Co. O, original; captain, May 4, 1863, with rank from February 3, 1863, vice W.F. Fox, promoted; major, not mustered, October 17, 1864, with rank from September 27, 1864, vice A.N. Sill, promoted.

FOX, LAWRENCE—Corporal, Co. B, One Hundred and Forty-fifth Infantry; transferred to Co. D, this regiment, January 12, 1864; captured, November 18, 1864, [at Social Circle, Ga.], on Sherman's march to the sea; paroled, no date; transferred to Co. A, Sixtieth Infantry, June 5, 1865.

FOX, WILLIAM F. Age, 22 years. Enrolled, July 29, 1862, at Elmira, to serve three years; mustered in as captain, Co. Q, July 30, 1862; injured in action by the explosion of a shell, September 17, 1862, at Antietam, Md.; mustered in as major, February 4, 1863; wounded in action, May 3, 1863, at Chancellorsville, Va.; mustered in as lieutenant-colonel, October 15, 1863; wounded in action, May 15, 1864, at Resaca, Ga.; discharged for disability, July 8, 1864. Commissioned captain, September 6, 1862, with rank from July 29, 1862, original; major, March 27, 1863, with rank from February 3, 1863, vice N.T. Colby, promoted; lieutenant-colonel, October 15, 1863, with rank from September 5, 1863, vice N.T. Colby, discharged.

FRANCIS, JOHN M.—Age, 18 years. Enlisted at Elmira, to serve three years, and mustered in as private, Co. D, July 23, 1862; mustered out with company, June 5, 1865, near Washington, D.C.

FRENCH, JOHN H.—Age, 18 years. Enlisted, July 18, 1862, at Elmira, to serve three years; mustered in as private, Co. A, July 23, 1862; wounded in action, September 17, 1862, and died of his wounds, September 19, 1862, at Antietam, Md.

FRENCH, JOSEPH—Age, 23 years. Enlisted, July 21, 1862, at Elmira, to serve three years; mustered in as private, Co. B, July 23, 1862; mustered out with company, June 5, 1865, near Washington, D.C.

FRENCH, Jr., PHILIP—Age, 28 years. Enlisted, August 7, 1862, at Elmira, to serve three years; mustered in as private, Co. A, August 9, 1862; mustered out with company, June 5, 1865, near Washington, D.C.

FROST, FRANK—Age, 21 years. Enrolled, July 17, 1862, at Elmira, to serve three years; mustered in as first sergeant, Co. D, July 24, 1862; as second lieutenant, March 14, 1863; as first lieutenant, July 10, 1863; mustered out with company, June 5, 1865, near Washington, D.C. Commissioned second lieutenant, March 27, 1863, with rank from March 13, 1863, vice O.D. Reynolds, promoted; first lieutenant, October 15, 1863, with rank from July 9, 1863, vice Odell D. Reynolds, resigned.

FROST, MADISON—Age, 29 years. Enlisted at Havana, to serve three years, and mustered in as private, Co. H, July 25, 1862; discharged for disability, April 27, 1863, at Convalescent Camp, Alexandria, Va.

FULLER, FRANK G.—Age, 25 years. Enlisted, July 28, 1862, at Addison, to serve three years; mustered in as corporal, Co. F, July 29, 1862; promoted sergeant, prior to April 10, 1863, and first sergeant, no date; returned to ranks, October 1, 1868; discharged, to date June 18, 1864.

FULLER, GEORGE—Age, 30 years. Enlisted at Elmira, to serve one year, and mustered in as private, unassigned, September 6, 1864; no further record.

FULLER, GEORGE W.—Age, 22 years. Enlisted, July 19, 1862, at Elmira, to serve three years; mustered in as private, Co. A, July 23, 1862; mustered out with company, June 5, 1865, near Washington, D.C.

FULLER, JAMES—Age, 26 years. Enlisted, August 5, 1862, at Canisteo, to serve three years; mustered in as private, Co. K, August 8, 1862; died, February 27, 1863, at Aquia Bay, Va.

FULLER, RICHARD—Age, 26 years. Enlisted at Wayland, to serve three years, and mustered in as private, Co. I, August 1, 1862; wounded in action, May 25, 1864, at Dallas, Ga; promoted corporal, January 15, 1865; mustered out with company, June 5, 1865, near Washington, D.C.

FURGERSON, PATRICK—Private, Co. G, One Hundred and Forty-fifth Infantry; transferred to Co. E, this regiment, January 12, 1864; mustered out with company, June 5, 1865, near Washington, D.C.; also borne as Ferguson.

GAFFNEY, PATRICK—Private, Co. B, One Hundred and Forty-fifth Infantry; transferred to Co. D, this regiment, January 12, 1864; mustered out with company, June 5, 1865, near Washington, D.C.

GAGE, BYRON—Age, 21 years. Enlisted, July 21, 1862, at Elmira, to serve three years; mustered in as corporal, Co. B, July 22, 1862; returned to ranks, November 1, 1862; wounded in action, May 25, 1864, at Dallas, Ga.; mustered out with company, June 5, 1865, near Washington, D.C., as Byron H.

GANONG, ROBERT S.—Age, 19 years. Enlisted at Elmira, to be three years, and mustered in as private, Co. E, July 22, 1862; captured, July 1, 1863; paroled, November 12, 1863; mustered out with company, June 5, 1865, near Washington, D.C., as Ganoung.

GANSEVOORT, ROBERT H.—Age, 26 years. Enrolled at Elmira, to serve three years, and mustered in as private, Co. I, August 11, 1862; promoted sergeant, prior to April 1863; mustered in as first lieutenant, September 4, 1863; as captain, Co. G, October 26, 1864; mustered out with company, June 5, 1865, near Washington, D.C.; prior service as second lieutenant, Battery E, First Artillery. Commissioned, not mustered, second lieutenant, August 13, 1863, with rank from May 23, 1863, vice H.G. Denniston, promoted; first lieutenant, August 8, 1863, with rank from May 24, 1863, vice J.R. Lindsay, promoted; captain, November 18, 1864, with rank from October 25, 1864, vice J.J. Lamon, resigned.

GARDNER, CALEB L.—Age, 34 years. Enlisted at Corning, to serve three years, and mustered in as private, Co. I, August 7, 1862, deserted, December 10, 1862, at Antietam Ford, Md., as Gardiner.

GARDNER, OWEN O.—Age, 21 years. Enlisted at Havana, to serve three years; mustered in as private, Co. H, July 25, 1862; mustered out with company, June 5, 1865, near Washington, D.C.

GARLOCK, EDWIN M.—Age, 32 years. Enlisted, July 23, 1862, at Elmira, to serve three years; mustered in as private, Co. A, July 25, 1862; transferred to Co. C, Twelfth Regiment, Veteran Reserve Corps, September 14, 1863; transferred to this regiment, March 23, 1864; absent, detached as telegraph operator, since April 25, 1864, and at muster out of company, as Edwin W.

GARRISON, ABRAM N.—Age, 18 years. Enlisted, July 31, 1862, at Montour, to serve three years; mustered in as private, Co. H, August 4, 1862; mustered out with company, June 5, 1865, near Washington, D.C.

GARRITT, JACOB—Age, 21 years. Enlisted at Elmira, to serve three years, and mustered in as private, Co. A, July 16, 1862; discharged for disability, December 19, 1863, at Elmira, N.Y.

GAY, EDWARD R.—Age, 20 years. Enlisted, August 11, 1862, at Canisteo, to serve three years; mustered in as private, Co. K, August 13, 1862; mustered out with company, June 5, 1865, near Washington, D.C.

GEICKLER, ADOLPH—Private, Co. I, One Hundred and Forty-fifth Infantry; transferred to Co. C, this regiment, January 19, 1864; mustered out with company, June 5, 1865, near Washington, D.C., as Geocklin.

GERE, WILLIAM W.—Age, 36 years. Enlisted, August 4, 1862, at Cameron, to serve three years; mustered in as private, Co. F, August 5, 1862; discharged for disability, January 27, 1863.

GIBBS, JOHN—Private, Co. K, One Hundred and Forty-fifth Infantry; transferred to Co. F, this regiment, January 12, 1864; mustered out with company, June 5, 1865, near Washington, D.C., as John W.

GILLETT, AUGUSTUS—Age, 21 years. Enlisted, July 21, 1862, at Elmira, to serve three years; mustered in as private, Co. E, July 24, 1862; deserted, September 7, 1862, between Camp Seward and Rockville, Md.

GILMORE, PETER—Private, Co. G, One Hundred and Forty-fifth Infantry; transferred to Co. E, this regiment, January 19, 1864; discharged for disability, April 1, 1864, at Indianapolis, Ind.

GILMORE, THOMAS—Age, 19 years. Enlisted at Corning, to serve three years, and mustered in as private, Co. I, August 1, 1862; wounded in action, May 25, 1864, at Dallas, Ga.; discharged for wounds, July 20, 1865, at Central Park Hospital, New York, city. [amputated middle 1/3 left leg on May 25, 1864]

GLEASON, DAVID—Age, 27 years. Enlisted at Elmira, to serve three years, and mustered in as private, Co. G, August 6, 1862; discharged for disability, February 6, 1863, at Philadelphia, Pa.

GLEASON, EZRA—Age,—years. Enrolled at Elmira, to serve three years, and mustered in as second lieutenant, Co. G, August 10, 1862; discharged, October 27, 1862. Commissioned second lieutenant, September 6, 1862, with rank from August 6, 1862, original.

GLYNN, MARTIN—Private, Co. C, One Hundred and Forty-fifth Infantry; transferred to Co. A, this regiment, January 12, 1864; wounded in action, May 25, 1864, at Dallas, Ga., and March 16, 1865, at Averasboro, N.C.; absent, wounded, at muster out of company. [amputated middle 1/3 right leg on March 16, 1865]

GOFF, HIRAM S.—Age, 21 years. Enlisted, August 2, 1862, at Howard, to serve three years; mustered in as private, Co. K, August 5; 1862; mustered out with company, June 5, 1865, near Washington, D.C.

GOFF, SIMEON M.—Age, 25 years. Enlisted, August 6, 1862, at Elmira, to serve three years; mustered in as private, Co. K, August

8, 1862; died of disease, September 27, 1864, at hospital, Chattanooga, Tenn.

GOLDEN, CHARLES—Age, 27 years. Enlisted at Elmira to serve three years, and mustered in as private, Co. C, July 9, 1862; promoted corporal, November 1, 1862; sergeant, July 27, 1863; returned to ranks, April 1, 1865; again promoted corporal, May 1, 1865; mustered out with company, June 5, 1865, near Washington, D.C.

GOLDER, WILLIAM—Private, Co. K, One Hundred and Forty-fifth Infantry; transferred to Co. I, this regiment, January 12, 1864; captured, February 11, 1865, near Blackville, S. C.; paroled, May 8, 1865; mustered out, July 1, 1865, at New York city.

GOLDSMITH, GEORGE H.—Age, 21 years. Enlisted, June 9, 1862; at Elmira, to serve three years; mustered in as private, Co. A, June 10, 1862; promoted corporal, prior to April 10, 1863; sergeant, prior to October 1863; first sergeant, July 1, 1864; mustered out with company, June 5, 1865, near Washington, D.C.

GOLDSMITH, ROBERT—Age, 23 years. Enlisted at Elmira to serve three years, and mustered in as private, Co. A, June 25, 1862; wounded in action, September 17, 1862, at Antietam, Md.; discharged for disability, January 5, 1863, at Philadelphia, Pa.

GOODELL, HARMON—Age, 22 years. Enlisted, July 17, 1862, at Elmira, to serve three years; mustered in as private, Co. C, July 18, 1862; deserted, November 19, 1862, at Antietam Ford, Md., as Harrison.

GOODRICH, JOHN M.—Enrolled at Elmira, to serve three years; mustered in as first lieutenant, Co. K, August 13, 1862; discharged, January 13, 1863. Commissioned first lieutenant, September 6, 1862, with rank from August 9, 1862, original.

GOODRICH, SAMUEL—Age, 45 years. Enlisted at Havana, to serve three years, and mustered in as private, Co. H, July 25, 1862; transferred to Co. F, Fourteenth Regiment, Veteran Reserve Corps, August 31, 1863; mustered out with detachment June 26, 1865, at Washington, D.C., as Samuel W.

GOSSLER, WILLIAM M.—Age, 20 years. Enlisted at Elmira, to serve three years, and mustered in as private, Co. A, July 19, 1862; promoted corporal, April 1, 1864; returned to ranks, September 1, 1864; wounded and captured in action, March. 8, 1865, at Rockingham, N.C. paroled, no date; mustered out with company, June 5, 1865, near Washington, D.C.

GRAHAM, WILLIAM—Age, 26 years. Enlisted at Elmira, to serve three years, and mustered in as private, Co. B, July 18, 1862; promoted corporal, November 1, 1862; sergeant, April 1, 1865; mustered out with company, June 5, 1865, near Washington, D.C.

GRANGER, GIDEON S.—Age, 37 years. Enlisted at Wayland, to serve three years, and mustered in as private, Co. I, August 1, 1862; deserted, September 1, 1862, at Camp Seward, near Fort Craig, Va.

GRANT, CHARLES L.—Age, 24 years. Enlisted at Corning, to serve three years, and mustered in as private, Co. I, February 15, 1864; transferred to Co. B, Sixtieth Infantry, June 5, 1865.

GRANT, JOHN F.—Age, 30 years. Enlisted at Corning, to serve three years, and mustered in as private, Co. I, August 8, 1862; mustered out with company, June 5, 1865, near Washington, D.C.

GRANT, LANSING L.—Age, 18 years. Enlisted at Corning, to serve three years, and mustered in as private, Co. I, February 15, 1864; transferred to Co. B, Sixtieth Infantry, June 5, 1865.

GRAVES, EDWARD PAYSON—Age, 22 years. Enrolled at Elmira, to serve three years, and mustered in as first lieutenant and quartermaster, July 22, 1862; discharged, to date June 13, 1864, for promotion to captain and assistant quartermaster. Commissioned first lieutenant and quartermaster September 6, 1862, with rank from July 18, 1862, original.

GRAVES, JOHN W.—Age, 21 years. Enlisted at Elmira, to serve three years, and mustered in as private, Co. A, August 4, 1862; discharged for disability, February 7, 1863, at Philadelphia, Pa.

GRAVES, WASHINGTON—Age, 39 years. Enlisted at Elmira, to serve three years and mustered in as private, Co. H, July 25, 1862; mustered out with company, June 5, 1865, near Washington, D.C.

GRAVES, WILLIAM L.—Age, 22 years. Enlisted at Elmira, to serve three years, and mustered in as private, Co. A, August 4, 1862; died of chronic diarrhea, October 24, 1864, at Division Field Hospital, Atlanta, Ga.; also borne as William J.

GRAY, SILAS D.—Age, 27 years. Enlisted, July 25, 1862, at Havana, to serve three years; mustered in as private, Co. H, July 29, 1862; promoted corporal, no date; wounded in action, March 8, 1865, at Rockingham, N.C.;

mustered out with company, June 5, 1865, near Washington D.C.

GREEK, JOSEPH H.—Age, 20 years. Enlisted at Elmira, to serve three years, and mustered in as private, Co. G, August 5, 1862; promoted corporal, November 15, 1862; died February 17, 1865, at hospital, Nashville, Tenn.

GREEK, JR., WILLIAM—Age, 27 years. Enlisted at Campbell, to serve three years; mustered in as private, Co. F, August 6, 1862; mustered out, June 23, 1865, at Louisville, Ky.

GREEN, CHARLES D.—Age, 37 years. Enlisted at Elmira, to serve three years, and mustered in as private, Co. A, August 7, 1862; discharged for disability, February 28, 1863, at Alexandria, Va.

GREEN, JOHN—Age, 19 years. Enlisted at Elmira, to serve three years, and mustered in as private, Co. G, August 6, 1862; promoted corporal, December 31, 1864; wounded in action, March 16, 1865, at Averasboro, N.C.; mustered out, July 19, 1865, at Elmira, N.Y.

GREEN JR., JASON—Age, 19 years. Enlisted at Hornellsville, to serve three years, and mustered in as private, Co. E, January 4, 1864; transferred to Co. K, August 9, 1864; captured in action, November 18, 1864, near Social Circle, Ga.; paroled, no date; transferred to Co. B, Sixtieth Infantry, June 5, 1865.

GREEN, ORLANDO—Age, 25 years. Enlisted, July 21, 1862, at Elmira, to serve three years; mustered in as private, Co. B, July 22, 1862; wounded in action, May 25, 1864, at Dallas, Ga.; died of his wounds, April 27, 1865, at hospital, Elmira, N.Y.

GREEN, SAMUEL—Age, 18 years. Enlisted, July 25, 1862, at Elmira, to serve three years; mustered in as private, Co. B, July 26, 1862; discharged for disability, December 31, 1862, at hospital, Philadelphia, Pa.

GREGORY, GEORGE—Private, Co. G, One Hundred and Forty-fifth Infantry; transferred to Co. E, this regiment, January 12, 1864; to One Hundred and Fourth Company, Second Battalion, Veteran Reserve Corps, August 29, 1864; mustered out, July 8, 1865, at Washington, D.C.

GREGORY, JOSIAH S.—Age, 18 years. Enlisted, July 29, 1862, at Elmira, to serve three years; mustered in as private, Co. E, August 4, 1862; discharged for disability November 30, 1862, at Philadelphia, Pa.

GREGORY, MARSHALL S.—Age, 21 years.

Enlisted at Elmira, to serve three years, and mustered in as private, Co. D, August 5, 1862; deserted, September 6, 1862, at Georgetown, D.C.

GREGORY, WARREN S.—Age, 27 years. Enlisted at Corning, to serve three years, and mustered in as corporal, Co. I, August 7, 1862; promoted sergeant, January 15, 1865; mustered out with company, June 5, 1865, near Washington, D.C.

GRELL, MARTIN—Private, Co. B, One Hundred and Forty-fifth Infantry; transferred to Co. D, this regiment, January 12, 1864; promoted corporal, March 9, 1864; captured in action, November 19, 1864, at Rutledge, Ga.; paroled, March .10, 1865; mustered out with detachment, June 13, 1865, at Annapolis, Md.

GRIEVES, HAY.—Private, Co. I, One Hundred and Forty-fifth Infantry; transferred to Co. B, this regiment, January 12, 1864; killed in action, May 25, 1864, at Dallas, Ga.

GRIFFEN, PATRICK—Private, Co. B, One Hundred and Forty-fifth Infantry; transferred to Co. B, this regiment, January 12, 1864; wounded in action, May 25, 1864, at Dallas, Ga.; mustered out with company, June 5, 1865, near Washington, D.C., as Griffin.

GRIFFIN, THOMAS—Age, 18 years. Enlisted at Elmira, to serve three years, and mustered in as private, Co. A, July 16, 1862; transferred to Co. E, Twentieth Regiment Veteran Reserve Corps, November 16, 1863; mustered out, July 1, 1865, at Camp Cadwalader, Philadelphia, Pa.

GRIFFITH, JOHN J.—Age, 22 years. Enlisted at Elmira, to serve three years, and mustered in as private, Co. H, July 25, 1862; wounded in action, May 25, 1864, at Dallas, Ga.; died of his wounds, August 21, 1864, at hospital, Chattanooga, Tenn.

GUERNSEY, GEORGE R.—Age, 21 years. Enlisted at Corning, to serve three years, and mustered in as private, Co. I, August 8, 1862; wounded, no date; mustered out, June 12, 1865, at Louisville, Ky.

GUERNSEY, JAMES—Age, 38 years. Enlisted at Elmira, to serve three years, and mustered in as private, Co. C, July 22, 1862; discharged for disability, October 20, 1862, at hospital, Washington, D.C., as Gurnsey; also borne as Gurnzy; again enlisted and mustered in as private, December 15, 1863; mustered out, June 19, 1865, at hospital, Buffalo, N.Y.

GUIWITS, BYRON—Age, 18 years. Enlisted at Elmira, to serve three years, and mustered in as private, Co. G, July 31, 1862; promoted corporal, January 1, 1864; wounded in action, May 3, 1863, at Chancellorsville, Va.; mustered out with company, June 5, 1865, near Washington D.C.; also borne as Guitvits.

GUNN, WYRAM—Age, 44 years. Enlisted, August 8, 1862, at Hornellsville, to serve three years; mustered in as musician, Co. K, August 9, 1862; mustered out, August 2, 1865, at Elmira, N.Y.

GUYON, JOHN W.—Private, Co. C, One Hundred and Forty-fifth Infantry; transferred to Co. G, this regiment, January 12, 1864; mustered out with company, June 5, 1865, near Washington, D.C.

HAARSTRICH, JOSEPH—Private, Co. I, One Hundred and Forty-fifth Infantry; transferred to Co. C, this regiment, January 12, 1864; wounded in action, May 25, 1864, at Dallas, Ga.; mustered out with company, June 5, 1865, near Washington, D.C.

HACKLEY, JEREMIAH H.—Age, 18 years. Enlisted at Elmira, to serve three years, and mustered in as private, Co. A, July 22, 1862; mustered out with company, June 5, 1865, near Washington, D.C.

HADLEY, JENNISON B.—Age, 24 years. Enlisted, August 8, 1862, at Hornellsville, to serve three years; mustered in as private, Co. K, August 9, 1862; promoted corporal, October 1, 1863; captured, November 18, 1864, near Social Circle, Ga.; paroled, no date; mustered out with company, June 5, 1865, near Washington, D.C.

HADLEY, JUDSON A.—Age, 18 years. Enlisted, June 7, 1862, at Elmira, to serve three years; mustered in as private, Co. E, June 9, 1862; deserted, May 1, 1863, at Chancellorsville, Va.

HADLOCK MOSES L—Age, 25 years. Enlisted, July 28, 1862, at Addison, to serve three years; mustered in as corporal, Co. E, July 29, 1862; returned to ranks, February 28, 1863; mustered out with company, June 5, 1865, near Washington, D.C.

HAGER, PETER—Age, 19 years. Enlisted, July 21, 1862, at Elmira, to serve three years; mustered in as private, Co. E, July 24, 1862; promoted corporal, prior to April 10, 1863; wounded in action, May 25, 1864, at Dallas, Ga.; promoted sergeant, October 14, 1864; transferred to Veteran Reserve, no date.

HAGGERSTON, HENRY—Age, 18 years. Enlisted at Dix, to serve one year, and mustered in as private, Co. C, September 3, 1864;

mustered out with company, June 5, 1865, near Washington, D.C.

HAIGHT, EDWARD ROWE—Private, Co. B, One Hundred and Forty-fifth Infantry; transferred to Co. D, this regiment, January 12, 1864; mustered in as first lieutenant, Co. F, December 26, 1864; mustered out with company, June 5, 1865, near Washington, D.C.; also borne as Edward Rowe Hayt. Commissioned first lieutenant, August 22, 1864, with rank from August 20, 1864, vice Harvey G. Denniston, discharged.

HAIGHT, NATHANIEL—Age, 42 years. Enlisted at Elmira, to serve three years, and mustered in as wagoner, Co. C, July 29, 1862; discharged for chronic rheumatism and old age, May 11, 1863, at hospital, Philadelphia, Pa.

HALL, BRAY D.—Age, 18 years. Enrolled at Elmira, to serve three years, and mustered in as private, Co. A, July 16, 1862; promoted corporal, July 18, 1862; commissary sergeant, November 1, 1862; mustered out with regiment, June 5, 1865, near Washington, D.C.

HALL, CHARLES A.—Age, 20 years. Enlisted at Elmira, to serve three years, and mustered in as sergeant, Co. E, June 24, 1862; retrained to ranks prior to April 10, 1863; deserted, April 15, 1864, at hospital, Philadelphia, Pa.; prior service in Co. D, One Hundred and Fourth Infantry.

HALL, JEREMIAH—Age, 20 years. Enlisted, August 5, 1862, at Elmira, to serve three years; mustered in as private, Co. G, August 6, 1862; promoted corporal, November 1, 1863; mustered out with company, June 5, 1865, near Washington, D.C.

HALL, JOHN—Age, 26 years. Enlisted at Elmira, to serve three years, and mustered in as private, Co. A, July 17, 1862; promoted corporal, prior to October 1863; wounded in action, March 16, 1865, at Averasborough, N.C.; absent since and at muster out of company. [portion of left fibula excised on March 19, 1865]

HALL, SCHUYLER—Age, 31 years. Enlisted at Elmira, to serve three years, and mustered in as private, Co. D, August 1, 1862; discharged for disability, August 23, 1863, at New York city.

HALL, WILLIAM H.—Age, 22 years. Enlisted at Elmira, to serve three years, and mustered in as private, Co. H, July 25, 1862; mustered out with company, June 5, 1865, near Washington, D.C.

HALLETT, BARTLETT—Private, Co. C, One Hundred and Forty-fifth Infantry; transferred to Co. H, this regiment, January 12, 1864; mustered out, to date June 30, 1865, at Hospital No. 1, Murfreesboro, Tenn.

HALLOWICK, JOHN—Age, 37 years. Enlisted, July 29, 1862, at Elmira, to serve three years; mustered in as private, Co. D, July 24, 1862; captured, November 18, 1864, on march to the sea; paroled, no date; mustered out with company, June 5, 1865, near Washington, D.C., as Holwick; also borne as Halwick.

HAM, ALBERT—Age, 18 years. Enlisted., August 4, 1862, at Elmira, to serve three years; mustered in as private, Co. H, August 5, 1862; discharged for disability, February 25, 1863, at Washington, D.C.

HAMILL, GEORGE W.—Age, 43 years. Enlisted, July 21, 1862, at Hornellsville, to serve three years; mustered in as private, Co. K, July 26, 1862; mustered out, June 9, 1865, at Nashville, Tenn.

HAMILTON, STEWART—Age, 42 years. Enlisted, July 24, 1862, at Elmira, to serve three years; mustered in as private, Co. D, July 26, 1862; discharged, March 6, 1863, at Harper's Ferry, Va.

HAMMOND, CORNELIUS—Age, 23 years. Enlisted, July 19, 1862, at Elmira, to serve three years; mustered in as sergeant, Co. A, July 29, 1862; promoted first sergeant, prior to October 1863; killed in action, May 25, 1864, at Dallas, Ga.

HAMMOND, MILES—Age, 23 years. Enlisted, June 24, 1862, at Elmira, to serve three years; mustered in as private, Co. E, June 26, 1862; discharged for disability, October 14, 1862, at Meridian Hill, D.C.

HAMMOND, URIAH S.—Age, 27 years. Enlisted, July 21, 1862, at Elmira, to serve three years; mustered in as private, Co. A, July 22, 1862; mustered out with company, June 5, 1865, near Washington, D.C.

HAMMOND, WILLIAM H.—Age, 24 years. Enlisted, August 11, 1862, at Elmira, to serve three years; mustered in as private, Co. K, August 13, 1862; wounded in action May 3, 1863, at Chancellorsville, Va.; discharged for disability, February 9, 1864.

HAMMOND, WILLIAM R.—Age, 17 years. Enlisted, July 19, 1862, at Elmira, to serve three years; mustered in as private, Co. A, July 22, 1862; mustered out with company, June 5, 1865, near Washington, D.C.

HAND, JOSIAH—Age, 34 years. Enlisted at Elmira, to serve three years, and mustered in as private, Co. E, June 7, 1862; died of disease, November 7, 1862, at Wilmington, Del.

HARDENBURG, MOSES—Age, 28 years. Enlisted at Corning, to serve three years, and mustered in as private, Co. I, August 11, 1862; promoted corporal, prior to April 10, 1863; transferred to Co. D, Seventh Regiment, Veteran Reserve Corps, no date; mustered out with detachment, June 30, 1865, at Washington, D.C.; also borne as Moses D.

HARDENBURGH, LYMAN M.—Age, 31 years. Enlisted at Corning, to serve three years, and mustered in as sergeant, Co. I, August 7, 1862; returned to ranks, June 30, 1864; mustered out, June 13, 1865, at White Hall Hospital, Philadelphia, Pa.

HARNDEN, RUFUS S.—Age, 18 years. Enlisted at Elmira, to serve three years, and mustered in as corporal, Co. A, June 18, 1862; wounded in action, May 3, 1863, at Chancellorsville, Va.; returned to ranks, no date; mustered out, June 5, 1865, at Chattanooga, Tenn.

HARRINGTON, see Herrington.

HARRINGTON, AVERY P.—Age, 43 years. Enlisted at Elmira, to serve three years, and mustered in as private, Co. D, July 30, 1862; discharged, April 20, 1863.

HARRINGTON, HARVEY—Age, 26 years. Enlisted, July 21, 1862, at Elmira, to serve three years; mustered in as private, Co. B, July 23, 1862; wounded in action, September 17, 1862, and died of his wounds, September 18, 1862, at Antietam, Md.

HARRIS, ANDREW J.—Age, 34 years. Enlisted at Elmira, to serve three years, and mustered in as private, Co. G, August 4, 1862; mustered out, May 29, 1865, at McDougall Hospital, New York, harbor.

HARRIS, EDWIN P.—Age, 26 years. Enlisted at Elmira, to serve three years, and mustered in as private, Co. G, July 31, 1862; mustered out with company, June 5, 1865, near Washington, D.C.

HARRIS, RODNEY E.—Age, 18 years. Enlisted at Elmira, to serve three years, and mustered in as private, Co. A, August 7, 1862; mustered out with company, June 5, 1865, near Washington, D.C.

HARRISON, WILLIAM—Age, 18 years. Enlisted July 23, 1862, at Corning, to serve three years; mustered in as private, Co. I, July 31, 1862; deserted September 17. 1862, at Antietam, Md.

HARRISON, WILLIAM—Age, 18 years.

Enlisted, July 30, 1862, at Hornellsville, to serve three years; mustered in as private, Co. K, July 31, 1862; died, February 18, 1865, at Dalton, Ga.

HARTT, SMITH—Age, 44 years. Enlisted at Elmira, to serve three years, and mustered in as private, Co. D, July 28, 1862; absent, sick in hospital at Philadelphia, Pa., since June 14, 1863, and at muster out of company.

HASKELL, HENRY T.—Age, 35 years. Enlisted, July 12, 1862, at Elmira, to serve three years; mustered in as private, Co. E, July 22, 1862; promoted corporal, prior to April 10, 1863; returned to ranks, no date; deserted, April 15, 1864.

HATCH, WILLIAM H.—Age, 37 years. Enlisted, July 26, 1862, at Addison, to serve three years; mustered in as private, Co. F, July 29, 1862; killed in action, May 3, 1863, at Chancellorsville, Va.

HATHAWAY, DANIEL F.—Age, 19 years. Enlisted, August 4, 1862, at Campbell, to serve three years; mustered in as corporal, Co. F, August 6, 186.2; died of typhoid fever, November 3, 1862.

HATHORN, JR., JOHN—Age, 18 years. Enlisted at Elmira, to serve three years, and mustered in as private, Co. A, July 22, 1862; promoted corporal, no date; mustered out with company, June 5, 1865, near Washington, D.C.

HAUBER, WILLIAM H.—Age, 22 years. Enlisted, July 23, 1862, at Corning, to serve three years; mustered in as private, Co. I, July 24, 1862; promoted corporal, prior to October 1863; returned to ranks, prior to April 1864; wounded in action, May 25, 1864, at Dallas, Ga.; promoted corporal, January 15, 1865; mustered out with company June 5, 1865, near Washington, D.C.

HAVENS, ROBERT C.—Age, 26 years. Enlisted, July 21, 1862, at Elmira, to serve three years; mustered in as private, Co. A, July 9, 1862; captured and paroled, no dates; mustered out, June 12, 1865, at Elmira N.Y.

HAVILAND, GEORGE L—Age, 27 years. Enlisted at Elmira, to serve three years, and mustered in as private, Co. A, July 18, 1862; deserted, April 18, 1863, at Hope Landing, Va.

HAVILAND, HARLAND E.—Age, 19 years. Enlisted, July 20, 1862, at Elmira, to serve three years; mustered in as private, Co. E, July 22, 1862; wounded in action, March 16, 1865, at Averasboro, N.C.; mustered out, June 29, 1865, at Elmira, N.Y.; also borne as Haveland.

HAWKINS, ALFRED C.—Private, Co. G, One Hundred and Forty-fifth Infantry; transferred to Co. E, this regiment, January 12, 1864; wounded in action, March 16, 1865, at Averasboro, N.C.; mustered out, July 5, 1865, at Davids Island, New York harbor.

HAWLEY, HIRAM R.—Age, 20 years. Enlisted at Cameron, to serve three years; mustered in as private, Co. H, February 24, 1864; died of heart disease, July 1, 1864, in camp, near Kenesaw Mountain, Ga.

HECKNER, THOMAS—Private, Co. G, One Hundred and Forty-fifth Infantry; transferred to Co. E, this regiment, January 12, 1864; mustered out with company, June 5, 1865, near Washington, D.C.; also borne as Hicknor.

HEDGE, see Hodge.

HELMER, WILLIAM—Age, 45 years. Enlisted, July 23, 1862, at Corning, to serve three years; mustered in as private, Co. I, July 24, 1862; discharged for disability, October 5, 1863, at Washington, D.C., as Hermann.

HELMES, EBENEZER W.—Age, 34 years. Enlisted, July 30, 1862, at Canisteo, to serve three years; mustered in as private, Co. K, July 31, 1862; promoted sergeant, prior to October 1863; mustered out with company, June 5, 1865, near Washington, D.C.

HEMMINWAY, CHARLES R.—Age, 18 years. Enlisted at Elmira, to serve three years, and mustered in as private, Co. A, July 16, 1862; promoted corporal, prior to October 1863; wounded in action, March 16, 1865, at Averasborough, N.C.; absent since and at muster out of company; also borne as Hemmingway.

HENDAL, FRANCIS—Age, 39 years. Enlisted, June 12, 1862, at Elmira, to serve three years; mustered in as Sergeant, Co. E, June 16, 1862; promoted first Sergeant, March 1, 1863; discharged, June 29. 1864. by promotion to second lieutenant One Hundred and Ninth Regiment U.S. Cavalry.

HENDERSON, RUFUS J.—Age, 18 years. Enlisted at Elmira, to serve three years, and mustered in as private, Co. G, August 5, 1862; wounded in action, September 17, 1862, at Antietam, Md.; discharged for disability, October 24, 1864, at Elmira, N.Y.

HEINDRICKS, WILLIAM—Age, 31 years. Enlisted, July 23, 1862, at Corning, to serve three years; mustered in as private, Co. I, July 24, 1862; discharged for disability, January 7, 1864, at York, Pa.

HENDRICKSON, ZACHARIAH—Sergeant, Co. K, One Hundred and Forty-fifth Infantry; transferred to Co. F, this regiment, as private, January 12, 1864; absent, sick at muster out of company.

HENNESSY, MICHAEL—Private, Co. C, One Hundred and Forty-fifth Infantry; transferred to Co. H, this regiment, January 12, 1864; mustered out with company, June 5, 1865, near Washington, D.C.; also borne as Hennessee.

HENYON, HIRAM—Private, Co. I, One Hundred and Forty-fifth Infantry; transferred to Co. C, this regiment, January 12, 1864; deserted, August 9, 1864, from St. Elizabeth Hospital, Washington Heights, D.C.; also borne as Henion.

HENYON, JAMES H.—Private, Co. I, One Hundred and Forty-fifth Infantry; transferred to Co. C, this regiment, January 12, 1864; captured September 17, 1864; paroled, no date; mustered out, August 14, 1865, at New York city, as James A. Henion.

HERMANN, see Helmer.

HERRICK, JOSEPH—Age, 22 years. Enlisted at Elmira, to serve three years, and mustered in as private, Co. C, August 5, 1862; deserted, September 17, 1862, at Antietam Ford, Md.

HERRINGTON, ANDRUS—Age, 18 years. Enlisted at Elmira to serve three years, and mustered in as private, Co. D, August 6, 1862; transferred to Veteran Reserve Corps, July 1, 1863; also borne as Harrington.

HERRINGTON, CORNELIUS W.—Age, 27 years. Enlisted, July 30, 1862, at Addison, to serve three years; mustered in as private, Co. F, August 2, 1862; discharged for disability, February 10, 1863.

HERRINGTON, JAMES—Age, 21 years. Enlisted at Elmira, to serve three years, and mustered in as corporal, Co. B, July 23, 1862; promoted sergeant, prior to October 1863; wounded, July 30, 1864 near Atlanta, Ga.; transferred to Co. H, Fifth Regiment, Veteran Reserve Corps, no date; mustered out, July 19, 1865, at Burnside Barracks, Indianapolis, Ind.

HERRINGTON, JAMES—Age, 18 years. Enlisted at Elmira, to serve three years, and mustered in as private, Co. G, July 31, 1862; wounded in action, May 25, 1864, at Dallas, Ga.; discharged for disability, April 12, 1865, at Madison, Ind. [Kennedy of 123rd NY amputated upper 1/3 left humerus]

HERRINGTON, JOHN—Age, 22 years. Enlisted, July 21, 1862, at Elmira, to serve three years; mustered in as private, Co. B, July 23, 1862; mustered out with company, June 5, 1865, near Washington, D.C., as Harrington.

HERRINGTON, MILES S.—Age, 24 years. Enlisted at Elmira, to serve three years, and mustered in as private, Co. D, August 6, 1862; captured, November 18, 1864, on march to the sea; paroled, no date; mustered out with company, June 5, 1865, near Washington, D.C.; also borne as Harrington.

HERRINGTON, SEVILIAN—Age, 21 years. Enlisted at Elmira, to serve three years, and mustered in as private, Co. B, July 22, 1862; wounded in action, May 25, 1864, at Dallas, Ga.; promoted corporal, April 1, 1865; mustered out with company, June 5, 1865, near Washington, D.C.

HESS, ALFRED I.—Age, 26 years. Enlisted at Wayland, to serve three years; mustered in as sergeant, Co. I, August 5, 1862; deserted, as private, at Elmira, N.Y.; never reported since muster in.

HETTIS, CHESTER H.—Age, 33 years. Enlisted at Wayland, to serve three years, and mustered in as private, Co. I, August 1, 1862; mustered out with company, June 5, 1865, near Washington, D.C.

HEWITT, JAMES D.—Age, 29 years. Enrolled at Elmira, to serve three years, and mustered in as assistant surgeon, August 8, 1862; dismissed, May 1, 1863; prior service in Sixty-sixth Infantry; subsequent service as surgeon, One hundred and Nineteenth Infantry. Commissioned assistant surgeon, September 6, 1862: with rank from August 7, 1862, original.

HIBLER, JOHN H.—Age, 23 years. Enlisted, July 18, 1862, at Elmira, to serve three years; mustered in as private, Co. E, July 22, 1862; discharged for disability, September 11, 1863, at Washington, D.C.

HICKNOR, see Heckner.

HILL, EUGENE—Age, 18 years. Enlisted at Tyrone, to servo three years; mustered in as sergeant, Co. H, July 25, 1862; discharged for disability, March 6, 1863, at Frederick, Md.

HILL, JOHN D.—Age, 19 years. Enrolled, July 26, 1862, at Addison, to serve three years; mustered in as sergeant, Co. F, August 5, 1862; promoted first sergeant, prior to April 1863; mustered in as second lieutenant, June 8, 1863; killed in action, May 25, 1864, at Dallas, Ga. Commissioned second lieutenant, May 11, 1863, with rank from March 23, 1863, vice J. Orr, promoted.

HILLERY, see Tobias.

HILLICK, PATRICK—Private, Co. O, One Hundred and Forty-fifth Infantry; transferred to Co. H, this regiment, January 12, 1864; wounded in action, May 25, 1864, at Dallas, Ga.; mustered out with company, June 5, 1865, near Washington, D.C.; also borne as Hillock.

HIMROD, DAVID G.—Age, 24 years. Enrolled and appointed assistant surgeon, at Elmira, to serve three years, August 20, 1862; discharged, May 13, 1863. Commissioned assistant surgeon, September 6, 1862, with rank from August 16, 1862, original.

HINMAN, THOMAS Y.—Private, Co. B, One Hundred and Forty-fifth Infantry; transferred to Co. G, this regiment, January 12, 1864; wounded in action, May 25, 1864, at Dallas, Ga., and August 15, 1864, near Atlanta, Ga.; mustered out with company, June 5, 1865, near Washington, D.C.; also borne as Thomas G.

HINTZ, JOHN—Private, Co. C, One Hundred and Forty-fifth Infantry; transferred to Co. A, this regiment, January 12, 1864; to Veteran Reserve Corps, July 1, 1864; retransferred to this regiment, September 18, 1864; wounded in action, March 16, 1865, at Averasborough, N.C.; mustered out, July 19, 1865, at Albany, N.Y., while in hospital, Troy, N.Y.

HOAG, ELISHA—Age, 23 years. Enlisted at Wayland, to serve three years, and mustered in as private, Co. I, August 5, 1862; wounded in action, May 25, 1864, at Dallas, Ga.; mustered out with company, June 5, 1865, near Washington, D.C.

HOAG, JOHN E.—Age, 25 years. Enlisted, July 29, 1862, at Cameron, to serve three years; mustered in as private, Co. F, July 29, 1862; discharged for disability, March 27, 1863.

HODGE, EDGAR—Age, 24 years. Enlisted at Elmira, to serve three years, and mustered in as private, Co. H, August 4, 1862; wounded in action, May 25, 1864, at Dallas, Ga.; mustered out, December 5, 1865, at Elmira, N.Y., as Hedge.

HOGANCAMP, see Hovencamp.

HOGANCAMP, LEZRA—Age, 18 years. Enlisted, December 25, 1863, at Big Flats, to serve three years; mustered in as private, Co. I, December 26, 1863; transferred to Co. B, Sixtieth Infantry, June 5, 1865, as Lezar Hovencamp.

HOGG, THOMAS L.—Age, 18 years. Enlisted, June 27, 1862, at Elmira, to serve three years; mustered in as private, Co. E, June 30, 1862; mustered out with company, June 5, 1865, near Washington, D.C.

HOLMES, GEORGE H.—Age, 28 years. Enlisted at Tarrytown, to serve three years; mustered in as private, unassigned, January 11, 1865; mustered out, May 9, 1865, at Harts Island, New York harbor.

HOLOHAN, MICHAEL—Private, Co. G, One Hundred and Forty-fifth Infantry; transferred to Co. E, this regiment, January 12, 1864; wounded in action, May 25, 1864, at Dallas, Ga.; discharged for disability, May 19, 1865, at Ladies Home Hospital, New York city, as Holihan; also borne as Hoolohan.

HOLWICK, see Hallowick.

HOMMER, see Hummer.

HOPKINS, THOMAS—Age, 20 years. Enlisted, June 14, 1862, at Elmira, to serve three years; mustered in as private, Co. E, June 16, 1862; promoted corporal, prior to April 10, 1863; sergeant, July 1, 1864; mustered out with company, June 5, 1865, near Washington, D.C.

HORNER, THOMAS—Age, 21 years. Enlisted at Elmira, to serve three years; mustered in as corporal, Co. O, July 9, 1862; promoted sergeant, November 1, 1862; mustered out with company, June 5, 1865, near Washington, D.C.

HORTON, WILLIAM N.—Age, 21 years. Enlisted, August 11, 1862, at Elmira, to serve three years; mustered in as private, Co. K, August 13, 1862; promoted corporal, October 1, 1863; killed in action, May 25, 1864, near Dallas, Ga.

HOTCHKISS, HORACE—Age, 21 years. Enlisted, July 22, 1862, at Avoca, to serve three years; mustered in as sergeant, Co. G, July 23, 1862; killed in action, May 3, 1863, at Chancellorsville, Va.

HOUSE, MENZO—Age, 28 years. Enlisted, August 11, 1862, at Wheeler, to serve three years; mustered in as private, Co. K, August 13, 1862; captured, November 18, 1864, near Social Circle, Ga.; exchanged, February 28, 1865; mustered out with detachment, June 22, 1865, at hospital, York, Pa.

HOUSE, PETER A.—Age, 25 years. Enlisted, August 11, 1862, at Wheeler, to serve three years; mustered in as private, Co. K, August 18, 1862; captured, November 18, 1864, near Social Circle, Ga.; exchanged, February 28, 1865; mustered out with detachment, June 22, 1865, at hospital, York, Pa.

HOVENCAMP, GEORGE H.—Age, 18 years. Enlisted, August 8, 1862, at Elmira, to serve three years; mustered in as private, Co. I, August 11, 1862; promoted quartermaster-sergeant, August 13, 1862; returned to ranks, no date; mustered out with company, June 5, 1865, near Washington, D.C.; also borne as Hogancamp.

HOWARD, ALONZO B.—Age, 23 years. Enrolled at Hornellsville, to serve three years, and mustered in as second lieutenant, Co. K, August 13, 1862; as first lieutenant, January 14, 1863; as quartermaster, June 1, 1864; mustered out with regiment, June 5, 1865, near Washington, D.C. Commissioned second lieutenant, September 6, 1862, with rank from August 9, 1862, original; first lieutenant, February 23, 1863, with rank from January 13, 1863, vice J.M. Goodrich, resigned; quartermaster, July 12, 1864, with rank from June 1, 1864, vice E.P. Graves, promoted captain and assistant quartermaster.

HOWARD, GILBERT—Age, 29 years. Enlisted at Elmira, to serve three years, and mustered in as private, Co. E, August 19, 1862; mustered out with company June 5, 1865, near Washington, D.C.

HOWE, EUGENE E.—Age, 18 years. Enlisted, August 5, 1862, at Hornellsville, to serve three years; mustered in as private, Co. K, August 8, 1862; killed in action, May 8, 1863, at Chancellorsville, Va.

HOWE, PETER R.—Age, 33 years. Enlisted, July 26, 1862, at Addison, to serve three years; mustered in as private, Co. F, July 29, 1862; captured and paroled, no dates; mustered out with detachment, June, 1865, at Hicks Hospital, Baltimore, Md.

HOWLAND, HENRY C.—Age, 18 years. Enlisted at Elmira, to serve three years, and mustered in as private, Co. B, July 24, 1862; wounded in action, July 23, 1864, and died of his, July 23, 1864, near Atlanta, Ga.

HOYT, JOSEPH V.—Age, 18 years. Enlisted at Elmira, to serve three years, and mustered in as private, Co. E, July 5, 1862; wounded in action, July 30, 1864, and died of his wounds, August 18, 1864, near Atlanta, Ga.

HUBBARD, CLARENCE—Age, 18 years. Enlisted at Campbell, to serve three years, and mustered in as musician, Co. F, August 6, 1862; promoted principal musician, September 1, 1864; mustered out with regiment, June 5, 1865, near Washington, D.C.

HUBBS, FRANKLIN—Private, Co. K, One Hundred and Forty-fifth Infantry; transferred to Co. F, this regiment, January 19, 1864; mustered out with company, June 5, 1865, near Washington, D.C.

HUBER, CHARLES—Age, 22 years. Enlisted at Elmira, to serve three years, and mustered in as private, Co. G, August 8, 1862; wounded in action, May 25, 1864, at Dallas, Ga.; mustered out with company, June 5, 1865, near Washington, D.C.

HUBER, JOHN—Age, 23 years. Enlisted, July 29, 1862, at Bath, to serve three years; mustered in as musician, Co. G, August 6, 1862; discharged for disability, no date, at Convalescent Camp, Va.

HUBER, STEPHEN—Private, Co. B, One Hundred and Forty-fifth Infantry; transferred to Co. D, this regiment, January 12, 1864; wounded in action, May 25, 1864, at Dallas, Ga.; captured, March 8, 1865, at Solemn Grove, N.C.; paroled, March 30, 1865, at Aikens Landing, Va.; mustered out with detachment, June 13, 1865, at Annapolis, Md.

HUDERHILL, see Underhill.

HUGHES, GEORGE—Age, 30 years. Enlisted at Elmira, to serve three years, and mustered in as private, Co. E, July 22, 1862; deserted, February 18, 1863, at Hope Landing, Va.

HUGHS, JOHN—Private, Co. C, One Hundred and Forty-fifth Infantry; transferred as a musician to Co. G, this regiment, January 12, 1864; captured, during Savannah campaign and paroled, no date; mustered out, June 14, 1865, at Camp Parole, Annapolis, Md., as Hughes.

HULBERT, JAMES—Age, 19 years. Enlisted, July 23, 1862, at Hornellsville, to serve three years, as private, Co. K; deserted before muster in.

HULL, FRANK—Age, 18 years. Enlisted at Elmira, to serve three years, and mustered in as private, Co. C, July 24, 1862; mustered out with company, June 5, 1865, near Washington, D.C.

HULLETT, SAMUEL—Age, 25 years. Enlisted, July 20, 1862, at Elmira, to serve three years; mustered in as private, Co. E, July 22, 1862; promoted corporal, no date; returned to ranks, December 1, 1863; mustered out with company, June 5, 1865, near Washington, D.C., as Hulet; also borne as Samuel S.

HULSE, ALBERT—Private, Co. G, One Hundred and Forty-fifth Infantry; transferred to Co. E, this regiment, January 12, 1864; mustered out with company, June 5, 1865, near Washington, D.C.

HUMMER, GEORGE W—Age, 42 years. Enlisted at Elmira, to serve three years, and mustered in as private, Co. D, July 25, 1862; discharged for disability, June 29, 1863, as Hemmer.

HUMPHREY, GEORGE W.—Age, 19 years. Enrolled at Elmira, to serve three years; mustered in as sergeant, Co. D, July 17, 1862; promoted first sergeant, March 13, 1863; mustered in as second lieutenant, January 16, 1864; wounded in action, May 25, 1864, at Dallas, Ga.; mustered out with company, June 5, 1865, near Washington, D.C. Commissioned second lieutenant, February 9, 1864, with rank from July 19, 1863, vice F. Frost, promoted.

HURD, WILLIAM M.—Age, 29 years. Enlisted at Elmira, to serve three years, and mustered in as corporal, Co. B, July 22, 1862; discharged, November 22, 1862, at hospital, Frederick City, Md., for wounds received in action.

HURLBURT, WILLIAM—Age, 37 years. Enlisted, July 28, 1862, at Addison, to serve three years; mustered in as musician, Co. F, July 29, 1862; discharged for disability, April 21, 1863, at hospital, Frederick, Md.

HUSH, WILLIAM—Age, 42 years. Enlisted, July 30, 1862, at Hornellsville, to serve three years; mustered in as private, Co. K, July 31, 1862; mustered out with company, June 5, 1865, near Washington, D.C.

HUSTED, GEORGE O.—Age, 22 years. Enlisted, July 28, 1862, at Woodhull, to serve three years; mustered in as sergeant, Co. F, July 29, 1862; discharged for disability, January 27, 1863.

HUTCHINSON, HORATIO ROSS—Age, 18 years. Enlisted, July 26, 1862, at Addison, to serve, three years; mustered in as private, Co. F, July 29, 1862; mustered out with company, June 5, 1865, near Washington, D.C.

HUTCHINSON, RUSSELL J.—Age, 18 years. Enlisted at Elmira, to serve three years, and mustered in as private, Co. A, July 17, 1862; wounded in action, May 27, 1864, at New Hope Church, Ga.; promoted sergeant, January 1, 1865; mustered out with company, June 5, 1865, near Washington, D.C.

HUTCHINSON, WILLIAM—Age, 30 years. Enlisted, July 25, 1862, at Addison, to serve three years; mustered in as private, Co. F, July 29, 1862; wounded in action, May 3, 1863, at Chancellorsville, Va.; discharged for disability, May 12, 1864, at New York City

HYATT, LA FAYETTE—Age, 19 years. Enlisted at Burdett, to serve three years, and mustered in as private, Co. H, July 25, 1862; deserted, September 22, 1862, at Maryland Heights, Md.

HYLAND, THOMAS—Private, Co. I, One Hundred and Forty-fifth Infantry; transferred to Co. C, this regiment, January 12, 1864; mustered out with company, June 5, 1865, near Washington, D.C.

INSCHO, HENRY—Age, 22 years. Enlisted at Elmira, to serve three years, and mustered in as private, Co. I, August 11, 1862; promoted commissary sergeant, August 13, 1862; died April 9, 1863.

JACKSON, GEORGE M.—Age, 24 years. Enlisted at Elmira, to serve three years, and mustered in as sergeant, Co. H, August 7, 1862; discharged, May 19, 1863, at Elmira, N.Y.

JACKSON, JACOB W.—Age, 39 years. Enlisted, July 21, 1862, at Elmira, to serve three years; mustered in as private, Co. B, July 22, 1862; died of consumption, October 28, 1862, at hospital, Philadelphia, Pa.

JACKSON, JOHN T.—Age, 30 years. Enlisted, July 28, 1862, at Addison, to serve three years; mustered in as sergeant, Co. F, July 29, 1862; discharged for disability, January 28, 1863, at hospital, Germantown, Pa.

JACKSON, WILLIAM—Private, Co. B, Ono Hundred and Forty-fifth Infantry; transferred to Co. G, this regiment, January 12, 1864; wounded in action, May 25, 1864, at Dallas, Ga.; died of his wounds, June 4, 1864, at hospital, Chattanooga Tenn. [May 25, 1864, amputated lower 1/3 right femur]

JACOBS, RICHARD—Age, 43 years. Enlisted, August 8, 1862, at Corning, to serve three years; mustered in as private, Co. I, August 11, 1862; mustered out, June 9, 1865, at Sickles Hospital, Alexandria, Va.

JAMES, ALBERT N.—Age, 21 years. Enlisted at Corning, to serve three years, and mustered in as private, Co. I, August 8, 1862; died, February 11, 1863, at hospital, Frederick, Md., as Janes.

JAMES, OSCAR F.—Age, 18 years. Enlisted, August 5, 1862, at Elmira, to serve three years; mustered in as private, Co. D August 7, 1862; captured, November 18, 1864, while on Sherman's campaign [Savannah, Ga.]; paroled, no date; mustered out with company, June 5, 1865, near Washington, D.C., as Janes.

JAPHET, JAMES A.—Age, 25 years. Enlisted, August 7, 1862, at Canisteo, to serve three years; mustered in as private, Co. K, August 8, 1862; discharged, April 10, 1863, at Baltimore, Md.

JEMERICK, GOTLEIB—Private, Co. B, One Hundred and Forty-fifth Infantry; transferred to Co. D, this regiment, January 12, 1864; discharged, April 1, 1864, to accept commission as first lieutenant, Fifty-fifth Kentucky Infantry; also borne as Jennerick.

JESSOP, DANIEL—Age, 38 years. Enlisted, July 31, 1862, at Montour, to serve three years; mustered in as private, Co. H, August 1, 1862; transferred to Co. I, Twelfth Regiment, Veteran Reserve Corps, April 14, 1864; mustered out, July 6, 1865, at Elmira, N.Y.

JOHNSON, ALBERT A.—Private, Co. F, One Hundred and forty-fifth Infantry; transferred to Co. F, this regiment, January 12, 1864; wounded in action, May 25, 1864, and died of his wounds, June 1, 1864, at Dallas, Ga. [P. Flood of 107th NY amputated lower 1/3 right femur]

JOHNSON, ALLEN—Age, 21 years. Enlisted, July 14, 1862, at Elmira, to serve three years; mustered in as private, Co. B, July 16, 1862; deserted, September 1864.

JOHNSON, ALONZO—Age, 22 years. Enlisted, August 6, 1862, at Elmira, to serve three years; mustered in as private, Co. G, August 8, 1862; killed in action, September 17, 1862, at Antietam, Md.

JOHNSON, BENJAMIN—Age, 35 years. Enlisted, July 21, 1862, at Elmira, to serve three years; mustered in as private, Co. B, July 22, 1862; promoted corporal, June 30, 1863; sergeant, January 1, 1865; mustered out with company, June 5, 1865, near Washington, D.C.

JOHNSON, CHARLES L.—Age, 21 years. Enlisted, July 14, 1862, at Hornellsville, to serve three years; mustered in as private, Co. K, July 26, 1862; promoted corporal, prior to April 10, 1863; captured, November 18, 1864, near Social Circle, Ga.; paroled, no date; died, March 12, 1865, at Annapolis, Md.

JOHNSON, CHAUNCEY—Age, 19 years. Enlisted, July 17, 1862, at Elmira, to serve three years; mustered in as private, Co. D, July 24, 1862; mustered out with company, June 5, 1865, near Washington, D.C.

JOHNSON, EMERY C.—Age, 23 years. Enlisted, July 19, 1862, at Elmira, to serve three years; mustered in as sergeant, Co. D, July 24, 1862; promoted first sergeant, March 5, 1864; wounded in action, May 25,

1864, at Dallas, Ga.; captured, November 18, 1864, while on Sherman's Savannah campaign; paroled, no date; mustered out with detachment, May 31, 1865, at Elmira, N.Y., as Emory.

JOHNSON, HENRY.—Age, 18 years. Enlisted at Bradford, to serve three years, and mustered m as private, Co. E, March 2, 1864; transferred to Co. I, no date; wounded in action, March 16, 1865, at Averasboro, N.C.; mustered out, June 5, 1865, at Elmira, N.Y.

JOHNSON, SAMUEL—Age, 21 years. Enlisted, August 4, 1862, at Wayland, to serve three years; mustered in as private, Co. I, August 5, 1862; died of typhoid fever, October 30, 1862, Harper's Ferry, Va.

JOHNSON, WILLIAM—Age, 81 years. Enlisted at Wayland, to serve three years, and mustered in as private, Co. I, August 2, 1862; discharged for disability, no date.

JOHNSON, WILLIAM H.—Age, 21 years. Enlisted at Havana to serve three years; mustered in as private, Co. H, July 25, 1862; wounded in action, May 3, 1863, at Chancellorsville, Va.; transferred to Co. B, Twenty-fourth Regiment, Veteran Reserve Corps, February 15, 1864; mustered out with detachment, June 26, 1865, at Washington, D.C.

JOHNSON, WILLIAM H—Age, 26 years. Enlisted, August 2, 1862, at Elmira, to serve three years; mustered in as private, Co. A, August 4, 1862; promoted corporal, prior to April 10, 1863; deserted, May 15, 1863, at Stafford Court House, Va.

JOLINE, PHILIP A.—Corporal, Co. K, One Hundred and Forty-fifth Infantry; transferred to Co. F, this regiment, January 12, 1864; wounded in action, May 25, 1864, at Dallas, Ga.; mustered out, May 29, 1865, at Louisville, Ky.

JONES, ALBERT E.—Age, 24 years. Enlisted, August 9, 1862, at Prattsburg, to serve three years; mustered in as private, Co. K, August 13, 1862; captured, November 18, 1864, near Social Circle, Ga.; mustered out with detachment, June at Elmira, N.Y., as Albert F.

JONES, JAMES B.—Age, 22 years. Enlisted, July 28, 1862, at Addison, to serve three years; mustered in as private, Co. F, July 29, 1862; wounded in action, May 25, 1864, at Dallas, Ga.; died of his wounds, June 5, 1864, at New Hope Church, Ga.

JONES, LEROY M.—Age, 18 years. Enlisted, July 18, 1862, at Elmira, to serve three years;

mustered in as private, Co. B, July 23, 1862; deserted, August 13, 1862, from barracks, at Elmira, N.Y.

KALAHAR, JOHN—Age, 30 years. Enlisted at Elmira, to serve three years, and mustered in as private, Co. G, August 6, 1862; killed in action, September 17, 1862, at Antietam, Md.

KANALA and KANALY, see Kennaly.

KANE, MOR.RIS—Age, 21 years. Enlisted at Elmira, to serve three years, and mustered in as private, Co. B, July 22, 1862; wounded in action, May 25, 1864, at Dallas, Ga.; mustered out, July 20, 1865, at Louisville, Ky.

KEAFEIR JOH—Private, Co. B, One Hundred and Forty-fifth Infantry; transferred to Co. G, this regiment, January 12, 1864; wounded in action, August 9, 1864, near Atlanta, Ga.; mustered out with company, June 5, 1865, near Washington, D.C.; also borne as Keefer.

KEARNS, JOHN—Private, Co. B, One Hundred and Forty-fifth Infantry; transferred to Co. D, this regiment, January 12, 1864; absent, sick in hospital at Washington, D.C., since April 1864, and at muster out of company.

KEENER, CHARLES S.—Age, 21 years. Enlisted, July 21, 1862, at Elmira, to serve three years; mustered in as private, Co. B, July 23, 1862; wounded in action, May 25, 1864, at Dallas, Ga.; died of his wounds, July 30, 1864, at Kingston, Ga.

KEENER, DANIEL—Age, 44 years. Enlisted at Elmira, to serve three years, and mustered in as private, Co. B, July 18, 1862; promoted corporal, June 30, 1863; mustered out with company, June 5, 1865, near Washington, D.C.

KELLEY, WILLIAM—Age, 22 years. Enlisted at Vernon, to serve three years, and mustered in as private, Co. I, January 11, 1865; transferred to Co. B, Sixtieth Infantry, June 5, 1865.

KELLISON, SAMUEL O.—Age, 18 years. Enlisted, July 29, 1862, at Hornellsville, to serve three years; mustered in as sergeant, Co. K, July 31, 1862; discharged, December 31, 1862, at Philadelphia, Pa.; subsequent service in company, unassigned, Sixth Cavalry.

KELLY, EDWIN—Age, 41 years. Enlisted at Elmira, to serve three years, and mustered in as private, Co. G, July 31, 1862; mustered out with company, June 5, 1865, near Washington, D.C.; also borne as Edwin P.

KELLY, GEORGE N.—Age, 38 years. Enlisted at Elmira, to serve three years, and mustered in as private, Co. K, August 9, 1862; mustered out, May 22, 1865, at Louisville, Ky.

KELLY, JAMES—Age, 37 years. Enlisted at Campbell, to serve three years, and mustered in as private, Co. F, August 6, 1862; mustered out with company, June 5, 1865, near Washington, D.C., as Kelley.

KELLY, JAMES—Private, Co. G, One Hundred and Forty-fifth Infantry; transferred to Co. E, this regiment, January 12, 1864; captured, December 15, 1864, near Savannah, Ga.; paroled, no date; mustered out with company, June 5, 1865, near Washington, D.C.

KELLY, 2nd, JAMES—Private, Co. K, One Hundred and Forty-fifth Infantry; transferred to Co. F, this regiment, January 12, 1864; killed in action, May 25, 1864, at Dallas, Ga.

KELLY, WILLIAM R.—Age, 28 years. Enlisted, August 11, 1862, at Greenwood, to serve three years; mustered in as private, Co. K, August 13, 1862; died, October 9, 1862, at Harper's Ferry, Va.

KENDALL, EDWARD—Age, 19 years. Enlisted at Elmira, to serve three years; mustered in as corporal, Co. K, August 6, 1862; promoted sergeant, October 1863; sergeant-major March 5, 1864; mustered out with regiment, June 5, 1865, near Washington, D.C. Commissioned, not mustered, second lieutenant, January 18, 1865, with rank from October 26, 1864, vice R.M. Tuttle, promoted.

KENNALY, JAMES—Age, 38 years. Enlisted, July 15, 1862, at Corning, to serve three years; mustered in as private, Co. I, July 26, 1862; wounded in action, May 3, 1863, at Chancellorsville, Va.; discharged for disability, October 5, 1863, at Washington, D.C., as Kanala; also borne Kanaly.

KENNEDY, JAMES—Private, Co. I, One Hundred and Forty-fifth Infantry; transferred to Co. B, this regiment, January 19, 1864; deserted, October 1864.

KENNEDY, JOHN—Age, 21 years. Enlisted at Auburn, to serve one year, and mustered in as private, unassigned, April 6, 1865; mustered out with detachment, May 15, 1865, at Hart Island, New York harbor.

KENNEDY, JOHN R.—Age, 21 years. Enlisted at Elmira, to serve three years, and mustered in as private, Co. C, August 7, 1862; deserted, August 13, 1862, at Elmira, N.Y.

KERR, JOHN—Private, Co. C, One Hundred and Forty-fifth Infantry; transferred to Co.

H, this regiment, January 17, 1864; mustered out with company, June 5, 1865, near Washington, D.C.

KESTER, TUNIS—Age, 31 years. Enlisted at Corning, to serve three years, and mustered in as sergeant, Co. I, August 2, 1862; promoted first sergeant, prior to October 1863; returned to ranks, June 30, 1864; mustered out with company June 5, 1865, near Washington, D.C.

KETCHUM, AMOS—Age, 19 years. Enlisted, July 21, 1862, at Hornellsville, to serve three years; mustered in as corporal, Co. K, August 11, 1862; wounded in action, May 25, 1864, near Dallas, Ga.; mustered out, June 30, 1865, at Elmira, N.Y.

KIES, LYMAN—Age, 27 years. Enlisted, July 28, 1862, at Elmira, to serve three years; mustered in as private, Co. C, August 1, 1862; deserted, October 2, 1862, at Maryland Heights, Md.; also borne as Kyes.

KILLFOIL, JAMES—Private, Co. C, One Hundred and Forty-fifth Infantry; transferred to Co. A, this regiment, January 12, 1864; to Co. A, Sixtieth Infantry, June 5, 1865.

KILMER, GEORGE—Age, 21 years. Enlisted, July 21, 1862, at Elmira, to serve three years; mustered in as private, Co. B, July 23, 1862; wounded in action, May 25, 1864, near Dallas, Ga.; mustered out with company, June 5, 1865, near Washington, D.C.; also borne as Killinor.

KIMBALL, DAVID F.—Age, 23 years. Enlisted, August 4, 1862, at Campbell, to serve three years; mustered in as private, Co. F, August 5, 1862; wounded in action, May 3, 1863, at Chancellorsville, Va.; transferred to Co. F, Nineteenth Regiment, Veteran Reserve Corps, January 15, 1864; mustered out with detachment, July 13, 1865, at Elmira, N.Y.; also borne as Kimble.

KIMBLE, BENJAMIN—Age, 44 years. Enlisted, July 28, 1862, at Addison, to serve three years; mustered in as private, Co. F, July 29, 1862; mustered out with company, June 5, 1865, near Washington, D.C.

KIMBLE, JAMES S.—Age, 21 years. Enlisted at Elmira, to serve three years, and mustered in as private, Co. C, July 12, 1862; deserted, September 18, 1862, at Antietam, Md., as Kimball.

KIMBLE, SILAS—Age, 18 years. Enlisted, February 8, 1864, at Addison, to serve three years; mustered in as private, Co. E, February 15, 1864; transferred to Co. A, Sixtieth Infantry, June 5, 1865, as Kimball.

KINNER, FREDERICK B.—Age, 30 years. Enlisted, August 6, 1862, at Canisteo, to serve three years; mustered in as private, Co. F, August 7, 1862; wounded in action, May 25, 1864, at Dallas, Ga.; mustered out with company, June 5, 1865, near Washington, D.C.

KINNEY, SAMUEL—Age, 22 years. Enlisted, July 17, 1862, at Bath, to serve three years; mustered in as corporal, Co. G, July 24, 1862; promoted sergeant, prior to April 10, 1863; first sergeant, prior to April 1864; wounded in action, August 17, 1864, and died of his wounds, August 18, 1864, at Atlanta, Ga.

KNAPP, ALLEN C.—Age, 18 years. Enlisted, August 6, 1862, at Elmira, to serve three years; mustered in as private, Co. G, August 11, 1862; discharged for disability, no date, at Washington, D.C.

KNAPP, IRA C.—Age, 23 years. Enlisted, August 9, 1862, at Montour, to serve three years; mustered in as private, Co. H, August 4, 1862; absent, sick at hospital, Baltimore, Md., since June 13, 1863, and at muster out of company.

KNAPP, JOHN B.—Age, 21 years. Enlisted, August 11, 1862, at Elmira, to serve three years; mustered in as corporal, Co. K, August 12, 1862; deserted, May. 24, 1864, at Cassville, Ga.

NAPP, JOHN M.—Age, 42 years. Enlisted, July 19, 1862, at Elmira, to serve three years; mustered in as private, Co. A, July 28, 1862; mustered out with company, June 5, 1865, near Washington, D.C.

KNICKERBOCKER, LEWIS—Age, 21 years. Enlisted, August 11, 1862, at Elmira, to serve three years; mustered in as private, Co. K, August 13, 1862; died, March 19, 1863, at Aquia Bay, Va.

KNICKERBOCKER, MARTIN—Age, 22 years. Enlisted, August 11, 1862, at Elmira, to serve three years; mustered in as private, Co. K, August 13, 1862; mustered out, June 13, 1865, at Louisville, Ky.

KNIFFIN, GEORGE—Age, 21 years. Enlisted, July 25, 1862, at Elmira, to serve three years; mustered in as private, Co. H, July 25, 1862; discharged for disability April 3, 1863, at Baltimore, Md.

KNIGHT, OSCAR H.—Age, 18 years. Enlisted at Elmira, to serve three years, and mustered in as private, Co. K, August 11, 1862; wounded in action, May 25, 1864, at Dallas, Ga.; captured, November 18, 1864, near Social Circle, Ga.; paroled, no date;

mustered out with detachment, June 22, 1865, at Hicks Hospital, Baltimore, Md.

KNOWLTON, WILLIAM H.—Age, 18 years. Enlisted at Campbell, to serve three years, and mustered in as private, Co. C, January 4, 1864; transferred to Co. A, Sixtieth Infantry, June 5, 1865.

KNOX, JOHN F.—Age, 25 years. Enrolled, August 4, 1862, at Campbell, to serve three years; mustered in as second lieutenant, Co. F, August 10, 1862; as first lieutenant, November 1, 1862; as captain, March 23, 1863; wounded in action, May 25, 1864, and died of his wounds, May 29, 1864, at Dallas, Ga. Commissioned second lieutenant, September 6, 1862; with rank from August 12, 1862, original; first lieutenant, February 23, 1863, with rank from November 1, 1862, vice J.M. Roe, resigned; captain, May 11, 1863, with rank from March 23, 1863, vice J.H. Miles, resigned.

KOHLMAN, CHRISTIAN—Private, Co. I, One Hundred and Forty-fifth Infantry; transferred to Co. C, this regiment, January 12, 1864; mustered out with company, June 5, 1865, near Washington, D.C.

KRUMLOFF, THEOPHILUS—Age, 44 years. Enlisted, July 26, 1862, at Addison, to serve three years; mustered in as private Co. F, July 29, 1862; died of camp fever, January 18, 1863.

KYES, see Kies.

KYSOR, ASA W.—Age, 24 years. Enlisted, August 2, 1862, at Howard, to serve three years; mustered in as private, Co. K, August 5, 1862; absent, sick in hospital, at muster out of company.

KYSOR, WARREN P.—Age, 21 years. Enlisted, August 2, 1862, at Howard, to serve three years; mustered in as private, Co. K, August 5, 1862; wounded in action, May 25, 1864, near Dallas, Ga.; discharged, May 3, 1865, at Elmira, N.Y.

LADOW, WILLIAM W.—Age, 18 years. Enlisted at Westfield, to serve three years, and mustered ill as private, Co. E, February 27, 1864; died of fever, June 11, 1864, at Chattanooga, Tenn.

LA DUE, EDMUND K.—Age, 26 years. Enrolled, January 18, 1864, at Shelbyville, Tenn., to serve three years; mustered in as assistant surgeon, February 11, 1864; mustered out with regiment, June 5, 1865, near Washington, D.C. Commissioned assistant surgeon, January 29, 1864, with rank from January 18, 1864, vice J.M. Flood, resigned.

LALOR, JOHN—Age, 18 years. Enlisted, July 21, 1862, at Elmira, to serve three years; mustered in as private, Co. E, July 22, 1862; died of fever, February 21, 1863, Hopes Landing, Va.

LAMON, JOHN J.—Age, 32 years. Enrolled at Elmira, to serve three years; mustered in as captain, Co. G, August 10, 1862; discharged for disability, October 25, 1864, as Laman. Commissioned captain, September 6, 1862, with rank from August 6, 1862, original.

LAMPHEAR, WILLIAM H.—Age, 22 years. Enlisted, July 21, 1862, at Hornellsville, to serve three years; mustered in as private, Co. K, July 26, 1862; captured, November 18, 1864, near Social Circle, Ga.; paroled, no date; absent, in hospital, at muster out of company.

LANDEN, LEONARD—Age, 18 years. Enlisted, July 21, 1862, at Elmira, to serve three years; mustered in as private, Co. E, July 24, 1862; promoted corporal and returned to ranks, no dates; again promoted corporal, July 1, 1864; mustered out with company, June 5, 1865, near Washington, D.C.; also borne as Landon.

LANE, ABRAHAM—Private, Co. G, One Hundred and Forty-fifth Infantry; transferred to Co. E, this regiment, January 12, 1864; mustered out with company, June 5, 1865, near Washington, D.C.; also borne as Abram.

LANE, CHARLES—Age, 40 years. Enlisted, July 17, 1862, at Corning, to serve three years; mustered in as private, Co. I, July 24, 1862; discharged for disability, January 26, 1864, at York, Pa.

LANE, JOHN—Age, 21 years. Enlisted, August 2, 1862, at Montour, to serve three years; mustered in as private, Co. H, August 4, 1862; wounded in action, May 25, 1864, at Dallas, Ga.; mustered out with company, June 5, 1865, near Washington, D.C.

LAPPAN, JAMES—Private, Co. C, One Hundred and Forty-fifth Infantry; transferred to Co. H, this regiment, January 12, 1864; mustered out, June 3, 1865, at Louisville, Ky.

LATTOURETTE, DAVID—Corporal, Co. K, One Hundred and Forty-fifth Infantry; transferred to Co. F, this regiment, January 12, 1864; wounded in action, May 25, 1864, at Dallas, Ga.; died of chronic diarrhea, September 18, 1864, in First Division Field Hospital, Atlanta, Ga.

LATTOURETTE, WILLIAM M.—Corporal, Co. F, One Hundred and Forty-fifth

Infantry; transferred to Co. F, this regiment, January 12, 1864; wounded in action, May 25, 1864, at Dallas, Ga.; mustered out with company, June 5, 1865, near Washington, D.C., at William W.

LAWSEN, FREDERICK—Private, Co. B, One Hundred and Forty-fifth Infantry; transferred to Co. G, this regiment, January 12, 1864; wounded in action, May 25, 1864, at Dallas, Ga.; absent, in hospital at New York city, at muster out of company.

LAYTON, PHILIP—Age, 21 years. Enlisted at Elmira, to serve three years, and mustered in as private, Co. G, August 5, 1862; wounded in action, May 25, 1864, at Dallas, Ga.; mustered out with company, June 5, 1865, near Washington, D.C.

LEACH, EUGENE—Age, 19 years. Enlisted, July 16, 1862, at Elmira, to serve three years; mustered in as private, Co. C, July 18, 1862; mustered out with company, June 5, 1865, near Washington, D.C.

LEACH, GEORGE—Age, 21 years. Enlisted, July 18, 1862, at Elmira, to serve three years; mustered in as private, Co. B, July 19, 1862; wounded in action, May 25, 1864, at Dallas, Ga.; mustered out, May 23, 1865, at Fortress Division Hospital, Murfreesboro, Tenn., as George K.

LEAVENWORTH, D. D.—Age, 21 years. Enlisted at Elmira, to serve three years, and mustered in as corporal, Co. C, July 9, 1862; wounded in action, September 17, 1862, at Antietam, Md.; discharged for disability, February 5, 1863, at hospital, Philadelphia, Pa., as David D.

LEAVENWORTH, JOHN R.—Age, 25 years. Enlisted at Elmira, to serve three years, and mustered in as private, Co. K, August 11, 1862; mustered out with company, June 5, 1865, near Washington, D.C.

LEBECK; EMIL—Private, Co. I, One Hundred and Forty-fifth Infantry; transferred to Co. C, this regiment, January 19, 1864; wounded in action, May 25, 1864, at Dallas, Ga.; mustered out with company, June 5, 1865, near Washington, D.C., as Liebeck; also borne as Leibeck.

LE GRO, SAMUEL D.—Age, 27 years. Enlisted at Elmira, to serve three years, and mustered in as private, Co. G, August 6, 1862; promoted corporal, January 1, 1863; sergeant, September 1, 1864; mustered out with company, June 5; 1865, near Washington, D.C.

LENHOFF, JOHN A.—Corporal, Co. I, One Hundred and Forty-fifth Infantry; transferred to Co. K, this regiment, January 12, 1864; to Co. H, no date; mustered out with Company, June 5, 1865, near Washington, D.C.

LEONARD, GEORGE—Age, 21 years. Enlisted at Elmira, to serve three years, and mustered in as private, Co. B, July 16, 1862; wounded in action, May 25, 1864, at Dallas, Ga.; mustered out with company, June 5, 1865, near Washington, D.C.

LEONARD, LYMAN—Age, 35 years. Enlisted at Elmira, to serve three years, and mustered in as private, Co. B, July 16, 1862; deserted, October 4, 1862, from camp, at Maryland Heights, Md.

LE ROY, NICHOLAS—Age, 26 years. Enlisted, July 17, 1862; at Elmira, to serve three years; mustered in as sergeant, Co. G, July 23, 1862; mustered out with company, June 5, 1865, near Washington, D.C.

LEWIS, ALONZO D.—Age, 28 years. Enlisted at Elmira, to serve three years; mustered in as corporal, Co. C, July 9, 1862; returned to ranks, no date; deserted, March 8, 1863, at Convalescent Camp, Va.

LEWIS, EDMOND—Private, Co. B, One Hundred and Forty-fifth Infantry; transferred to Co. G, this regiment, January 12, 1864; died of hydrocele, April 24, 1864, at hospital, Tullahoma, Tenn.; also borne as Edward.

LEWIS, JESSE B.—Age, 26 years. Enlisted at Elmira, to serve three years, and mustered in as sergeant, Co. C, July 9, 1862; discharged for disability, February 10, 1863, at Convalescent Camp, Alexandria, Va.

LEWIS, JOHN—Private, Co. K, One Hundred and Forty-fifth Infantry; transferred to Co. F, this regiment, January 12, 1864; mustered out with company, June 5, 1865, near Washington, D.C.

LEWIS, SAMUEL—Age, 43 years. Enlisted at Elmira, to serve three years, and mustered in as private, Co. C, August 5, 1862; discharged for disability, March 7, 1863, at Elmira, N.Y.

LIBOLT, JAMES—Age, 18 years. Enlisted, July 18, 1862, at Elmira, to serve three years; mustered in as private, Co. E, July 26, 1862; promoted corporal, July 1, 1864; mustered out with company, June 5, 1865, near Washington, D.C.

LIEBECK, see Lebeck.

LINDSAY, GEORGE W.—Age, 24 years. Enlisted, August 6, 1862, at Elmira, to serve three years; mustered in as private, Co. D, August 7, 1862; captured, November 18, 1864, while on Sherman's Savannah campaign; paroled, no date; absent, at Camp Parole, Annapolis, Md., at muster out of company; also borne as Lindslay.

LINDSAY, JOHN R.—Age, 22 years. Enrolled at Canisteo, to serve three years; mustered in as private, Co. K, August 11, 1862; promoted sergeant-major, August 13, 1862; second lieutenant, Co. I, January 1, 1863; mustered in as first lieutenant, June 2, 1863; as captain, November 1, 1863; mustered out with company, June 5, 1865, near Washington, D.C. Commissioned second lieutenant, December 30, 1862, with rank from October 21, 1862, vice N.E. Rutter, promoted; first lieutenant, May 11, 1863, with rank from December 8, 1862, vice B.C. Wilson, resigned; captain, August 18, 1863, with rank from May 1, 1863, vice N.E. Rutter, killed in action.

LINSED, MATHEW—Age, 32 years. Enlisted, July 21, 1862, at Elmira, to serve three years; mustered in as private, Co. B, July 22, 1862; transferred to Twentieth Regiment, Veteran Reserve Corps, December 15, 1863, as Lindsed; mustered out with detachment, July 10, 1865, at Frederick City, Md.; also borne as Lindsey.

LINZA, AARON—Age, 35 years. Enlisted, July 10, 1862, at West Union, to serve three years; mustered in as private, Co. I, July 24, 1862; discharged for disability, January 7, 1864, at York: Pa.

LITTLEFIELD, CHARLES W.—Age, 28 years. Enlisted at West Union, to serve three years, and mustered in as private, Co. I, August 8, 1862; promoted corporal, prior to April 1863; sergeant, prior to October 1863; mustered out with company, June 5, 1865, near Washington, D.C.

LOBDELL, ISAAC N.—Age, 18 years. Enlisted, September 8, 1864, at Elmira, to serve one year; mustered in as private, Co. D, September 14, 1864; died of chronic diarrhea, April 25, 1865, at David's Island, New York, harbor,

LOBDELL, PHILIP F.—Age, 21 years. Enlisted at Elmira, to serve three years, and mustered in as private, Co. D, August 7, 1862; promoted corporal, March 13, 1863; mustered out with company, June 5, 1865, near Washington, D.C.

LOCKE HIRAM L—Age, 18 years. Enlisted, July 23, 1862, at Elmira, to serve three years;

mustered in as private, Co. D, July 24, 1862; captured, November 18, 1864, while on Sherman's Savannah campaign; paroled, no date; mustered out with detachment, June 14, 1865, at Elmira, N.Y.

LOCKWOOD, DUNNING—Age, 19 years. Enlisted, July 19, 1862, at Elmira, to serve three years; mustered in as private, Co. B, July 22, 1862; wounded in action, May 3, 1863, at Chancellorsville, Va.; promoted corporal, February 16, 1864; mustered out with company, June 5, 1865, near Washington, as Dunning. K.

LONG, WALTER B.—Private, Co. O, One Hundred and Forty-fifth Infantry; transferred to Co. G, this regiment, January 12, 1864; Killed in action, May 25, 1864, at Dallas, Ga.

LONGCOY, WILLIAM H.—Age, 19 years. Enlisted at Elmira, to serve three years, and mustered in as private, Co. A, August 11, 1862; wounded in action, May 3, 1863, at Chancellorsville, Va.; promoted corporal, January 1, 1865; mustered out with company, June 5, 1865, near Washington, D.C.

LONGWORTHY, R. SHERMAN—Age, place, date of enlistment, and muster in as private, Co. B, not stated; transferred to Thirty-eighth Company, Second Battalion, Veteran Reserve Corps, no date; discharged for disability, July 19, 1865, at Finlay Hospital, Washington, D.C.

LOOP, JOHN B.—Age, 32 years. Enlisted at Elmira, to serve three years, and mustered in as private, Co. A, July 18, 1862; wounded in action, May 3, 1863, at Chancellorsville, Va.; mustered out, July 17, 1865, at Elmira, N.Y.

LORDEN, MICHAEL—Age, 20 years. Enlisted, July 9, 1862, at Elmira, to serve three years; mustered in as private, Co. E, July 9, 1862; promoted corporal, prior to April 10, 1863; returned to ranks, March 1864; mustered out with company, June 5, 1865, near Washington, D.C.; also borne as Lordon.

LOSIE, JOHN M.—Enrolled at Elmira, to serve three years, and mustered in as second lieutenant, Co. A, July 28, 1862; promoted first lieutenant, August 9, 1862; mustered in as captain, January 27, 1863; wounded in action, May 25, 1864, near Dallas, Ga.; discharged for wounds, January 21, 1865. Commissioned second lieutenant, September 6, 1862, with rank from July 23, 1862, original; first lieutenant,—, with rank from August 9,

1862, vice C. Wilkinson, promoted; captain, March 23, 1863, with rank from January 26, 1863, vice M.O. Wilkinson, resigned.

LOVELL, ELIJAH G.—Age, 19 years. Enlisted at Elmira, to serve three years, and mustered in as private, Co. D, July 28, 1862; mustered out with company, June 5, 1865, near Washington, D.C.

LOVELL, JAMES W.—Age, 26 years. Enlisted at Elmira, to serve three years, and mustered in as private, Co. G, August 6, 1862; died of fever, March 7, 1863, at Hope Landing, Va.

LOVELL, JOHN—Age, 34 years. Enlisted at Dix, to serve one year, and mustered in as private, Co. D, September 5, 1864; mustered out with company, June 5, 1865, near Washington, D.C.

LOVELL, MYRON F.—Age, 25 years. Enlisted at Elmira, to serve three years, and mustered in as private, Co. D, July 28, 1862; mustered out with detachment, June 14, 1865, at Elmira, N.Y.

LOVELL, WILLIAM E.—Age, 18 years. Enlisted, July 21, 1862, at Elmira, to serve three years; mustered in as private, Co. D, July 22, 1862; captured and paroled, no dates; mustered out with detachment, May 31, 1865, at Elmira, N.Y.

LOVERHOUSE, ANTONIO—Private, Co. I, One Hundred and Forty-fifth Infantry; transferred to Co. C, this regiment, January 12, 1864; wounded in action, June 16, 1864, at Golgotha, Ga.; deserted, November 15, 1864, at Atlanta, Ga., as Loverhaus.

LOWE, JOHN G.—Age, 27 years. Enlisted, July 15, 1862, at Elmira, to serve three years; mustered in as musician, Co. E, July 18, 1862; grade changed to private, no date; deserted, October 23, 1862, at Harper's Ferry, Va.

LUCE, CHARLES H.—Age, 27 years. Enlisted at Elmira, to serve three years, and mustered in as private, Co. A, July 19, 1862; died of disease, January 21, 1863, at Washington, D.C.

LUNGER, WILLIAM H.—Age, 21 years. Enlisted, August 11, 1862, at Howard, to serve three years; mustered in as private, Co. K, August 13, 1862; mustered out with company, June 5, 1865, near Washington, D.C.

LYNCH, JAMES—Private, Co. C, One Hundred and Forty-fifth Infantry; transferred to Co. H, this regiment, January 12, 1864; mustered out with company, June 5, 1865, near Washington, D.C.

LYNCH, MELVIN J.—Age, 21 years. Enlisted at Addison, to serve three years, and mustered in as private, Co. F, July 29, 1862; wounded in action, May 25, 1864, at Dallas, Ga.; absent, wounded, at muster out of company.

LYON, HENRY—Age, 18 years. Enlisted, July 29, 1862, at Havana, to serve three years; mustered in as corporal Co. H July 30, 1862; returned to ranks, no date; discharged, June 22, 1863, at Baltimore, Md.

LYONS, THOMAS—Corporal, Co. I, One Hundred and Forty-fifth Infantry; transferred to Co. C, this regiment, January 12, 1864; mustered out with company, June 5, 1865, near Washington, D.C.

MACK, ENOCH—Age, 21 years. Enlisted at Elmira, to serve three years, and mustered in as corporal, Co. O, July 9, 1862; discharged for disability, February 4, 1863, at hospital, Philadelphia, Pa.

MADDEN, MICHAEL—Age, 26 years. Enlisted at Addison, to serve three years, and mustered in as private, Co. F, August 5, 1862; promoted corporal, November 13, 1862; sergeant, February 28, 1863; returned to ranks, April 16, 1864; wounded in action, May 25, 1864, at Dallas, Ga.; promoted corporal, October 1, 1864; sergeant, January 16, 1865; mustered out with company, June 5, 1865, near Washington, D.C.

MAHAN, MICHAEL—Age, 29 years. Enlisted, August 6, 1862, at Elmira, to serve three years; mustered in as private, Co. A, August 7, 1862; mustered out with company, June 5, 1865, near Washington, D.C., as Meehan.

MAHER, THOMAS—Age, 21 years. Enlisted at Elmira, to serve three years; mustered in as private, Co. B, July 26, 1862; mustered out with company, June 5, 1865, near Washington, D.C.

MALLETT, EPHRAIM N.—Age, 21 years. Enlisted, July 21, 1862, at Elmira, to serve three years; mustered in as corporal, Co. D, July 24, 1862; returned to ranks, no date; discharged, October 12, 1864, at Philadelphia, Pa.

MALLETT, NICHOLAS—Age, 20 years. Enlisted at Poughkeepsie, to serve three years, and mustered in as private, Co. D, November 23, 1864; transferred to Co. A, Sixtieth Infantry, June 5, 1865; also borne as Mollet.

MALLON, PATRICK—Private, Co. C, One Hundred and Forty-fifth Infantry; transferred to Co. A, this regiment, January 12, 1864; wounded in action, May 15, 1864, at Resaca, Ga.; mustered out with company, June 5, 1865, near Washington, D.C.

MAPES, HENRY—Age, 21 years. Enlisted at Elmira, to serve three years, and mustered in as private, Co. H, July 25, 1862; appointed wagoner, no date; discharged for disability, March 9, 1863, at Frederick, Md.

MARA, BRYAN—Age, 18 years. Enlisted, July 22, 1862, at Elmira, to serve three years; mustered in as private, Co. C, July 23, 1862; wounded in action, May 25, 1864, at Dallas, Ga.; mustered out, November 18, 1865, at Elmira, N.Y.

MARANVILLE, DAVID D.—Age, 18 years. Enlisted, July 26, 1862, at Woodhull, to serve three years; mustered in as private, Co. F, August 5, 1862; died of camp fever, March 28, 1863; also borne as Moranville.

MARBLE, CHARLES J.—Age, 18 years. Enlisted, July 25, 1862, at Addison, to serve three years; mustered in as private, Co. F, July 29, 1862; promoted corporal, November 1, 1803; mustered out with company, June 5, 1865, near Washington, D.C.

MARCY, OSCAR W.—Age, 27 years. Enlisted, August 7, 1862, at Avoca, to serve three years; mustered in as corporal, Co. K, August 8, 1862; promoted sergeant, prior to April 10, 1863; first sergeant, prior to October 1863; killed in action, May 25, 1864, at Dallas, Ga.

MARGESON, JOHNSON B.—Age, 18 years. Enlisted, July 28, 1862, at Montour, to serve three years; mustered in as private, Co. H, August 9, 1862; killed in action, May 25, 1864, at Dallas, Ga.

MARSHALL, HARVEY S.—Age, 18 years. Enlisted, August 4, 1862, at Cameron, to serve three years; mustered in as private, Co. F, August 5, 1862; wounded in action, May 25, 1864, at Dallas, Ga.; mustered out with company, June 5, 1865, near Washington, D.C.

MARSHALL, ISAIAH R.—Age, 21 years. Enlisted, July 30, 1862, at Hornellsville, to serve three years; mustered in as private, Co. K, July 31, 1862; deserted, November 13, 1862, at Sharpsburg, Md.

MARSHALL, SOLOMON—Age, 43 years. Enlisted, August 4, 1862, at Addison, to serve three years; mustered in as private, Co. F, August 5, 1862; discharged for disability, April 22, 1863.

MARTIN, JOHN—Age, 21 years. Enlisted, July 20, 1862, at Corning, to serve three years; mustered in as private, Co. I, July 26, 1862; deserted, September 10, 1862, near South Mountain, Md.; arrested, claimed, and returned to Seventy-eighth Infantry.

MARTIN, JOHN P.—Age, 18 years. Enlisted, July 20, 1862, at Elmira, to serve three years; mustered in as private, Co. E, July 22, 1862; left sick in hospital at Frederick City, Md., September 1862; deserted, no date, and enlisted in Co. C, Eighth Artillery, February 1864.

MARTIN, NEWIEL—Age, 42 years. Enlisted at Wayland, to serve three years, and mustered in as private, Co. I, August 9, 1862; absent, in hospital at New Albany, Md., at muster out of company; also borne as Newell.

MARTIN, PATRICK—Private, Co. C, One Hundred and Forty-fifth Infantry; transferred to Co. G, this regiment, January 12, 1864; to Veteran Reserve Corps, January 16, 1864.

MASHENKARP, GEORGE—Private, Co. 13, One Hundred and Forty-fifth Infantry; transferred to Co. G, this regiment, January 12, 1864; mustered out with company, June 5, 1865, near Washington, D.C., as Mashenkarb.

MASIER, AMBROSE—Age, 44 years. Enlisted at Elmira, to serve three years, and mustered in as musician, Co. G, August 6, 1862; wounded in action, September 17, 1862, at Antietam, Md.; discharged for disability, April 29, 1863, at Convalescent Camp, Alexandria, Va., as Moshier.

MATHER, WILLIAM L.—Age, 42 years. Enlisted at Elmira, to serve three years, and mustered in as private, Co. H, August 4, 1862; discharged for disability, February 11, 1863, at Convalescent Camp, Alexandria, Va., as Wm. B. Matthews.

MATHIAS, FRANCIS—Age, 41 years. Enlisted at Elmira, to serve three years, and mustered in as private, Co. C, July 29, 1862; wounded in action, May 25, 1864, at New Hope Church, Ga.; discharged for wounds, January 27, 1865, at hospital, Columbus, Ohio.

MATHIAS, LOUIS—Age, 35 years. Enlisted at Erwin, to serve three years, and mustered in as private, Co. C, December 28, 1863; died of gunshot wound, May 6, 1865, at New Bern, N.C.

MATTHEWS, CHARLES—Age, 21 years. Enlisted at Hector, to serve three years, and mustered in as musician, Co. H, August 12, 1862; died of typhoid fever, October 13, 1862, at Harper's Ferry, Va.

MATTHEWS, MORGAN B.—Age, 35 years. Enlisted at Elmira, to serve three years, and mustered in as private, Co. D, July 25, 1862; mustered out with company, June 5, 1865, near Washington, D.C.

MAXWELL, JAMES—Age, 21 years. Enlisted at Elmira, to serve three years, and mustered in as private, Co. D, August 2, 1862; deserted, August 7, 1862, at Elmira, N.Y.

MAYNARD, SAMUEL—Age, 39 years. Enlisted, September 3, 1864, at Rathbone, to serve one year; mustered in as private, Co. D, September 12, 1864; captured, November 18, 1864, on march to the sea; paroled, no date; absent, at Camp Parole, Annapolis, Md., at muster out of company.

McCANNO, JOHN—age, 17 years. Enlisted, September 12, 1864, at Southport, to serve one year; mustered in as private, Co. C, September 22, 1864; mustered out with company, June 5, 1865, near Washington, D.C.

McCARRICK, JOHN—Age, 38 years. Enlisted, July 14, 1862, at Elmira, to serve three years; mustered in as musician, Co. C, July 16, 1862; died of typhoid fever, October 11, 1864, in hospital, Atlanta, Ga.

McCARTHY, DANIEL—Private, Co. B, One Hundred and Forty-fifth Infantry; transferred to Co. D, this regiment, January 12, 1864; to Veteran Reserve Corps, January 16, 1864.

McCARTY, FAYETTE—Age, 18 years. Enlisted, July 25, 1862, at Elmira, to serve three years; mustered in as private, Co. G, July 26, 1862; died of measles, April 18, 1864, at Bell Buckle, Tenn.

McCARTY, FRAZIER—Age, 18 years. Enlisted at Elmira, to serve three years, and mustered in as private, Co. G, July 9, 1862; mustered out with company, June 5, 1865, near Washington, D.C.

McCASLIN, GEORGE—Age, 18 years. Enlisted at Elmira, to serve three years, and mustered in a private, Co. G, August 4, 1862; transferred to Veteran Reserve Corps, October 3, 1863.

McCASLIN, JOHN—Age, 22 years. Enlisted at Elmira, to serve three years, and mustered in as private, Co. G, August 4, 1862; promoted corporal, April 1, 1863; mustered out with company, June 5, 1865, near Washington, D.C.

McCLINTEK, JAMES—Age, 18 years. Enlisted, July 20, 1862, at Elmira, to serve three years; mustered in as private, Co. E, July 22, 1862; missing in action, November 20, 1864; no further record; also borne as McClintick.

McCOY, CHARLES —Age, 18 years. Enlisted, July 25, 1862, at Elmira, to serve three years; mustered in as private, Co. B, July 26, 1862; mustered out with company, June 5, 1865, near Washington, D.C.

McCULLOUGH, JAMES—Age, 23 years. Enlisted at Elmira, to serve three years, and mustered in as private, Co. G, August 6, 1862; died, March 1, 1863, at Hope Landing, Va.

McCULLOUGH, THOMAS—Age, 32 years. Enlisted, August 6, 1862, at Hornellsville, to serve three years; mustered in as private, Co. K, August 8, 1862; discharged, January 15, 1863, at Washington, D.C.

McGANIGAL, CORNELIUS—Private, Co. B, One Hundred and Forty-fifth Infantry; transferred to Co. D, this regiment January 12, 1864; captured, October 17, 1864, in Georgia; released, November 16, 1864, at Ailkens Landing, Va.; mustered out, June 8, 1865, at Annapolis, Md., as McGunnigle.

McGINITY, PATRICK—Private, Co. C, One Hundred and Forty-fifth Infantry; transferred to Co. H, this regiment, January 12, 1864; mustered out with company, June 5, 1865, near Washington, D.C.

McGOVERN, JAMES D.—Age, 44 years. Enlisted at Elmira, to serve three years, and mustered in as private, Co. A, July 30, 1862; discharged for disability, March 16, 1863, at Stafford Court House, Va., as McGorven.

McGRATH, THOMAS—Private, Co. I, One Hundred and Forty-fifth Infantry; transferred to Co. B, this regiment, January 12, 1864; mustered out with company, June 5, 1865, near Washington, D.C.

McGREGOR, CORNELIUS.—Age, 23 years. Enlisted, July 26, 1862, at Addison, to serve three years; mustered in as private, Co. F, July 29, 1862; wounded in action, June 16, 1864, at Golgotha, Ga.; captured in action, July 19, 1864, at Noses Creek, Ga.; exchanged, March 1, 1865; mustered out, June 19, 1865, at Elmira, N.Y., as McGregor.

McGUCIN, WILLIAM L.—Age, 25 years. Enlisted at Elmira, to serve three years, and mustered in as private, Co. D, July 17, 1862; deserted, December 13, 1862, near Leesburg, Va.

McGUIRE, FRANK—Private, Co. I, One Hundred and Forty-fifth Infantry; transferred to Co. B, this regiment, January 19, 1864; mustered out with company, June 5, 1865, near Washington, D.C.

McGUIRE, MARTIN—Private, Co. I, One

Hundred and Forty-fifth Infantry; transferred to Co. B, this regiment, January 12, 1864; killed in action, May 25, 1864, at Dallas, Ga.

McGUNNIGLE, see McGanigal.

McKAY, JOSEPH—Age, 23 years. Enlisted at Albany, to serve one year, and mustered in as private, Co. B, December 7, 1864; captured and paroled, no dates; mustered out, May 29, 1865, at Elmira, N.Y., as McCay.

McKEE, WILLIAM—Corporal, Co. C, One Hundred and Forty-fifth Infantry; transferred to Co. F, this regiment, as private, January 12, 1864; absent, sick in New York city, at muster out of company.

McKEE, WILLIAM H.—Age, 41 years. Enlisted, July 8, 1862, at Elmira, to serve three years; mustered in as private, Co. E, July 19, 1862; discharged, January 21, 1863, at Washington, D.C.

McKINNEY, HENRY—Age, 42 years. Enlisted at Erwin, to serve three years, and mustered in as private, Co. C, January 5, 1864; transferred to Co. A, Sixtieth Infantry, June 5, 1865; prior service in Co. D, Twenty-third Infantry, as McCenna.

McLAUGHLIN, DANIEL—Private, Co. K, One Hundred and Forty-fifth Infantry; transferred to Co. I, this regiment, January 12, 1864; wounded in action, May 25, 1864, at Dallas, Ga.; mustered out with company, June 5, 1865, near Washington, D.C.

McLAUGIILIN, WILLIAM—Private, Co. C, One Hundred and Forty-fifth Infantry; transferred to Co. H, this regiment, January 1, 1864; mustered out with company, June 5, 1865, near Washington, D.C.

McMILLEN, GILES—Age, 38 years. Enlisted at Elmira, to serve three years, and mustered in as private, Co. C, July 29, 1862; wounded in action, May 25, 1864, at Dallas, Ga.; absent, wounded and in hospital, at Elmira, N.Y., at muster out of company.

McNULTY, EDWARD—Private, Co. I, One Hundred and Forty-fifth Infantry; transferred to Co. 13, this regiment, January 19, 1864; wounded in action, May 25, 1864, at Dallas, Ga.; discharged for wounds May 8, 1865, at hospital, Madison, Ind.

McPHERSON, GEORGE—Age, 30 years. Enlisted at Rathboneville, to serve one year, and mustered in as private, Co. A, August 27, 1864; died of chronic diarrhea, April 5, 1865, at David's Island, New York harbor.

McTIGHE, MICHAEL—Corporal, Co. B, One Hundred and Forty-fifth Infantry;

transferred to Co. D, this regiment, January 12, 1864; mustered out with company, June 5, 1865, near Washington, D.C.

McWILLIAMS, JOSEPH E.—Age, 18 years. Enlisted, July 25, 1862, at Elmira, to serve three years; mustered in as private, Co. A, July 26, 1862; mustered out with company, June 5, 1865, near Washington, D.C.

MEAD, JOHN—Age, 18 years. Enlisted at Elmira, to serve three years, and mustered in as private, Co. A, July 17, 1862; mustered out with company, June 5, 1865, near Washington, D.C.

MEEHAN, see Mahan.

MEEKER, GEORGE—Private, Co. K, One Hundred and Forty-fifth Infantry; transferred to Co. F, this regiment, January 12, 1864; mustered out with company, June 5, 1865, near Washington, D.C.

MELKER, ISAAC—Private, Co. I, One Hundred and Forty-fifth Infantry; transferred to Co. B, this regiment, January 12, 1864; mustered out with company, June 5, 1865, near Washington, D.C.

MELLON, FREDERICK—Private, Co. K, One Hundred and Forty-fifth Infantry; transferred to Co. F, this regiment, January 12, 1864; died of disease, October 7, 1864, at First Division Field Hospital, Twentieth Army Corps, Atlanta, Ga.

MENGES, JOSEPH—Private, Co. B, One Hundred and Forty-fifth Infantry; transferred to Co. D, this regiment, January 12, 1864; mustered out with company June 5, 1865, at Washington, D.C.

MEREY, see Morey.

METZER, JOSEPH—Age, 21 years. Enlisted at Elmira, to serve three years, and mustered in as private, Co. E, August 12, 1862. deserted April 15, 1864; also borne as Mitzger.

MICHALY, DOMINIQUE—Age, 20 years. Enlisted, July 15, 1862, at Elmira, to serve three years; mustered in as private, Co. E, July 17, 1862; captured in action, May 3, 1863, at Chancellorsville, Va.; paroled, no date; deserted, December 1863, from Camp Parole, Annapolis, Md.

MIDDLETON, ISAAC—Private, Co. C, One Hundred and Forty-fifth Infantry; transferred to Co. H, this regiment, January 12, 1864; killed on skirmish line, July 22, 1864, near Atlanta, Ga.

MIDDLETON, THOMAS K.—Age, 24 years. Enrolled at Elmira, to serve three years, and mustered in as first sergeant, Co. A, July 17, 1862; as second lieutenant, November 1,

1862; as first lieutenant, Co. H, April 5, 1863; discharged, September 14, 1863. Commissioned second lieutenant, May 9, 1863, with rank from August 9, 1862, vice J.M. Lode, promoted; first lieutenant, March 23, 1863, with rank from December 24, 1862, vice H.D. Donnelly, promoted.

MILES, AARON K.—Age, 22 years. Enlisted at Elmira, to serve three years, and mustered in as private, Co. D, August 2, 1862; wounded, June 14, 1863; transferred to Veteran Reserve Corps, September 7, 1863; discharged with detachment, June 28, 1865, as of Twelfth Regiment, Veteran Reserve Corps, at Washington, D.C.

MILES, JAMES H.—Enrolled at Elmira, to serve three years; mustered in as captain, Co. F, August 10, 1862; discharged, March 23, 1863. Commissioned captain, September 6, 1862, with rank from August 6, 1862, original.

MILLAGE, LEWIS L.—Age, 21 years. Enlisted, July 25, 1862, at Montour, to serve three years; mustered in as private, Co. H, July 30, 1862; mustered out with company, June 5, 1865, near Washington, D.C.

MILLER, ABRAHAM—Age, 20 years. Enlisted at Elmira, to serve three years, and mustered in as private, Co. A, July 19, 1862; mustered out with company, June 5, 1865, near Washington, D.C.

MILLER, ABRAHAM—Age, 18 years. Enlisted, July 26, 1862, at Addison, to serve three years; mustered in as private, Co. F, July 29, 1862; died of camp fever, October 16, 1862.

MILLER, CHARLES—Private, Co. K One Hundred and Forty-fifth Infantry; transferred to Co. F, this regiment, January 12, 1864; mustered out with company, June 5, 1865, near Washington, D.C.

MILLER, ENOCH L.—Age, 23 years. Enlisted at Elmira, to serve three years, and mustered in as private, Co. G, August 4, 1862; promoted corporal and sergeant, prior to April 10, 1863; returned to ranks, November 1, 1863; mustered out with company, June 5, 1865, near Washington, D.C.

MILLER, FREEMAN—Age, 24 years. Enlisted, August 4, 1862, at Elmira, to serve three years; mustered in as private, Co. H, August 5, 1862; mustered out with company, June 5, 1865, near Washington, D.C.

MILLER, GEORGE—Age, 21 years. Enlisted at Elmira, to serve three years, and mustered in as private, Co. D, August 4, 1862;

promoted corporal, December 1, 1863; sergeant, March 1, 1865; mustered out with company, June 5, 1865, near Washington, D.C.

MILLER, SAMUEL—Age, 22 years. Enlisted, July 28, 1862, at Addison, to serve three years; mustered in as private, Co. F, July 29, 1862; killed in action, May 25, 1864, at Dallas, Ga.

MILLS, FRANCIS M. Age, 21 years. Enlisted, August 5, 1862, at Campbell, to serve three years; mustered in as private, Co. F, August 6, 1862; mustered out with company, June 5, 1865, near Washington, D.C.

MINNEMEYER, EDWIN G.—Corporal, Co. I, One Hundred Forty-fifth Infantry; transferred to Co. C, this regiment, January 12, 1864; returned to ranks, August 1, 1864; mustered out with company, June 2, 1865, at Nashville, Tenn., as Edward G.

MISNER, ELSON M.—Late second lieutenant, One Hundred and Forty-fifth Infantry. Commissioned, not mustered, second lieutenant, this regiment, March 30, 1864, with rank from March 23, 1864, vice J.A. Creed, resigned; subsequent service as captain, Eightieth Infantry.

MITCHELL, CHARLES—Age, 21 years. Enlisted, July 17, 1862, at Elmira, to serve three years; mustered in as private, Co. D, July 18, 1862; wounded in action, May 3, 1863, at Chancellorsville, Va.; discharged, October 15, 1864.

MITCHELL, HARMON O.—Age, 21 years. Enlisted, August 6, 1862, at Elmira, to serve three years; mustered in as corporal, Co. H, August 7, 1862; deserted, December 10, 1862, at Antietam Ford, Md., as Harrison O.

MITCHELL, JAMES P.—Age, 21 years. Enlisted, July 21, 1862, at Elmira, to serve three years; mustered in as private, Co. B, July 23, 1862; discharged for disability, December 23, 1862, at hospital, Frederick City, Md.

MITCHELL, LAFAYETTE—Age, 18 years. Enlisted, August 2, 1862, at Howard, to serve three years; mustered in as private, Co. K, August 5, 1862; deserted, May 1, 1864, at Shelbyville, Tenn.

MITZGER, see Metzer.

MOFFIT, FRANK—Private, Co. I, One Hundred and Forty-fifth Infantry; transferred to Co. C, this regiment, January 12, 1864; deserted June 2, 1863, at hospital, Washington, D.C.

MOLLET, see Mallett.

MOLSON, JAMES S.—Age, 19 years. Enlisted, July 26, 1862, at Addison, to serve three years; mustered in as private, Co. F, July 29, 1862; wounded in action, May 25, 1864, and died of his wounds, May 26, 1864, at Dallas, Ga.

MONDAY, JOHN—Private, Co. K, One Hundred and Forty-fifth Infantry; transferred to Co. F, this regiment, January 12, 1864; mustered out with company, June 5, 1865, near Washington, D.C., as Mundy.

MOON, WILLIAM T.—Age, 34 years. Enlisted at Hornellsville, to serve three years, and mustered in as private, Co. K, November 27, 1863; captured: November 18, 1864, near Social Circle, Ga.; paroled, no date; transferred to Co. B, Sixtieth Infantry, June 5, 1865; prior service in Co. G, Twenty-third Infantry, as Wm. F.

MOORE, JAMES M.—Private, Co. K, One Hundred and Forty-fifth Infantry; transferred to Co. F, this regiment, January 12, 1864; mustered out with company, June 5, 1865, near Washington, D.C.

MOORE, PATRICK—Private, Co. B, One Hundred and Forty-fifth Infantry; transferred to Co. D, this regiment, January 12, 1864; wounded in action, May 25, 1864, at Dallas, Ga.; mustered out with company, June 5, 1865, near Washington, D.C.

MOORE, WILLIAM H.—Age, 20 years. Enlisted at Elmira, to serve three years, and mustered in as private, Co. A, July 17, 1862; deserted, November 28, 1862, at Antietam Ford, Md.

MORANVILLE, see Maranville.

MOREHOUSE, FRANCIS M.—Age, 21 years. Enlisted, July 21, 1862, at Elmira, to serve three years; mustered in as corporal, Co. D, July 26, 1862; no further record.

MOREY, CHARLES E.—Age, 19 years Enlisted August 7, 1862, at Canesteo, to serve three years; mustered in as private, Co. K, August 8, 1862; wounded in action, May 25, 1864, near Dallas, Ga.; mustered out with company, June 5, 1865, near Washington, D.C., as Morrey; also borne as Merey.

MOREY, CHESTER—Age, 24 years. Enlisted, July 18, 1862, at Elmira, to serve three years; mustered in as private, Co. B, July 19, 1862; mustered out with company, June 5, 1865, near Washington, D.C.; also borne as Morrey.

MORGAN, AMBROSE—Age, 33 years. Enlisted at Elmira, to serve three years, and mustered in as private, Co. G, August 6, 1862; wounded in action, March 16, 1865, near Averasboro, N.C.; mustered out with company, June 5, 1865, near Washington, D.C.; also borne as Ambrose B.

MORGAN, JAMES—Private, Co. K, One Hundred and Forty-fifth Infantry; transferred to Co. I, this regiment, January 12, 1864; discharged, February 27, 1864, at New York city, for disability, from wounds received while foraging.

MORGAN, JOHN. Private, Co. B, One Hundred and Forty-fifth Infantry; transferred to Co. G, this regiment, January 12, 1864; wounded in action, May 25, 1864, at Dallas, Ga.; died, no date, of wounds received in action, March 16, 1865, at Averasborough, N.C.

MORGAN, JOHN—Age, 20 years. Enlisted, July 14, 1862, at Elmira, to serve three years; mustered in as corporal, Co. B, July 16, 1862; returned to ranks and promoted corporal, no dates; returned to ranks, June 30, 1863; mustered out with company, June 5, 1865, near Washington, D.C.

MORGAN, PETER—Private, Co. B, One Hundred and Forty-fifth Infantry; transferred to Co. G, this regiment, January 12, 1864; to Veteran Reserve Corps, no date.

MORGAN, WILLIAM L.—Age, 45 years. Enrolled, June 11, 1862, at Elmira, to serve three years; mustered in as captain, Co. E, July 28, 1862; discharged, March 20, 1863; prior service as second lieutenant, Fiftieth Engineers; subsequent service as captain, First Veteran Cavalry. Commissioned captain, September 6, 1862, with rank from July 28, 1862, original.

MORGAN, JR., WILLIAM L.—Age, 21 years. Enrolled, July 15, 1862, at Elmira, to serve three years; mustered in as first lieutenant, Co. E, August 13, 1862; discharged, February 29, 1863; prior service as second lieutenant, Fiftieth Engineers. Commissioned first lieutenant, September 6, 1862, with rank from July 28, 1862, original.

MORREY, see Morey.

MORRIS, HIRAM C.—Age, 25 years. Enlisted, July 29, 1862, at Havana, to serve three years; mustered in as private, Co. H, July 30, 1862; promoted corporal, May 1, 1864; wounded in action, May 25, 1864, at Dallas, Ga.; mustered out with company, June 5, 1865, near Washington, D.C.

MORRIS, THEODORE F.—Age, 18 years. Enlisted, August 4, 1862, at Hornellsville, to serve three years; mustered in as private,

Co. K, August 5, 1862; killed in action, May 3, 1863, at Chancellorsville, Va.

MORSE, EDWARD—Age, 21 years. Enlisted, July 14, 1862, Elmira, to serve three years; mustered in as sergeant, Co. July 16, 1862; promoted first sergeant, January 1, 1865; mustered out with company, June 5, 1865, near Washington, D.C.

MORSE, JAMES H.—Age, 22 years. Enlisted, July 20, 1862, at Corning, to serve three years; mustered in as private, Co. I, July 26, 1862; mustered out with company, June 5, 1865, near Washington, D.C.

MORSE, MOSES H—Age, 42 years. Enlisted, July 23, 1862, at Addison, to serve three years; mustered in as private, Co. F, July 29, 1862; discharged for disability, July 21, 1863; discharged for disability, July 21, 1863.

MORSE, THOMAS E.—Age, 30 years. Enlisted, August 5, 1862, at Elmira, to serve three years; mustered in as private, Co. H, August 7, 1862; promoted corporal, October 1, 1862; discharged for disability, February 3, 1863, at Washington, D.C.

MOSHIER, see Masier.

MOSS, WILLIAM F.—Age, 18 years. Enlisted at Havana, to serve three years, and mustered in as private, Co. H, July 25, 1862; mustered out with company, June 5, 1865, near Washington, D.C.

MOTT, SAMUEL—Age 22 years. Enlisted, July 24, 1862, at Corning, to serve three years; mustered in as private, Co. I, August 7, 1862; transferred to Co. B, Sixtieth Infantry, June 5, 1865; also borne as Samuel H.

MOWERS, ELEAZER J.—Age, 30 years. Enlisted at Elmira, to serve three years, and mustered in as private, Co. G, August 2, 1862; killed in action, August 17, 1864, near Atlanta, Ga.

MULFORD, LEE—Age, 18 years. Enlisted, July 25, 1862, at Addison, to serve three years; mustered in as private, Co. F, July 29, 1862; promoted corporal, February 28, 1863; sergeant, November 1, 1863; mustered out with company, June 5, 1865, near Washington, D.C.

MULLENBROOK, JOSEPH—Private, Co. I, One Hundred and Forty-fifth Infantry; transferred to Co. B, this regiment, January 12, 1864; mustered out with company, June 5, 1865, near Washington, D.C., as Mullenbook.

MUNDAY, WILLIAM—Private, Co. K, One Hundred and Forty-fifth Infantry; transferred to Co. I, this regiment, January 12, 1864; wounded in action, June 22, 1864, at Culp's Farm Ga.; mustered out with company, June 5, 1865, near Washington, D.C.

MUNDY, see Monday.

MUNSON, MARCUS M.—Age, 19 years. Enlisted, July 19, 1862, at Elmira, to serve three years; mustered in as private, Co. 13, July 22, 1862; promoted corporal, prior to April 10, 1863; wounded in action, May 25, 1864, at Dallas, Ga.; died of his wounds, June 4, 1864, at hospital, Kingston, Ga.

MURPHY, EUGENE—Private, Co. C, One Hundred and Forty-fifth Infantry; transferred to Co. H, this regiment, January 19, 1864; mustered out with company, June 5, 1865, near Washington, D.C.

MURPHY, JOHN H.—Private, Co. C, One Hundred and Forty-fifth Infantry; transferred to Co. H, this regiment, January 12, 1864; to Co. D, Fifth Regiment, Veteran Reserve Corps, no date; mustered out, July. 10, 1865, at Indianapolis, Ind.

MURPHY, MARTIN—Private, Co. I, One Hundred and Forty-fifth Infantry; transferred to Co. C, this regiment, January 12, 1864; mustered out with company, June 5, 1865, near Washington, D.C.

MURPHY, WILLIAM—Private, Co. K, One Hundred and Forty-fifth Infantry; transferred to Co. I, this regiment, January 12, 1864, mustered out with company, June 5, 1865, near Washington, D.C.

MURRAY, CORNELIUS—Age, 21 years. Enlisted, July 21, 1862, at Elmira, to serve three years; mustered in as private, Co. B, July 23, 1862; wounded in action, May 25, 1864, at Dallas, Ga.; promoted corporal, January 1, 1865; absent, wounded and in hospital, at muster out of company.

MYERS, JOHN—Private, Co. C, One Hundred and Forty-fifth Infantry; transferred to Co. A, this regiment, January 12, 1864: mustered out with company, June 5, 1865, near Washington, D.C.

NELLIS, JAMES B.—Age, 18 years. Enlisted at Campbell, to serve three years, and mustered in as private, Co. F, January 4, 1864; wounded in action, May 25, 1864, at Dallas, Ga.; died of his wounds, September 7, 1864, at Joe Holt Hospital, Jeffersonville, Ind.

NEWBARY, CHARLES—Private, Co. K, One Hundred and Forty-fifth Infantry; transferred to Co. I, this regiment, January 12, 1864; killed in action, May 25, 1864, at New Hope Church, Ga., as Newbury; also borne as Newberry.

NEWBARY, DAVID—Private, Co. K, One Hundred and Forty-fifth Infantry; transferred to Co. I, this regiment, January 12, 1864; mustered out with company, June 5, 1865, near Washington, D.C., as Newbery; also borne as Newbury.

NEWCOMBE, HARLIN G.—Private, Co. K, One Hundred and Forty-fifth Infantry; transferred to Co. I, this regiment, January 12, 1864; mustered out with company, June 5, 1865, near Washington, D.C.; also borne as Hurlin G.

NEWTON, JEROME B.—Age, 42 years. Enlisted, August 11, 1862, at Avoca, to serve three years; mustered in as private, Co. K, August 13, 1862; on detached service in Co. F, Fourth U.S. Artillery, from March 20, 1863, to March 1864; killed in action, May 15, 1864, at. Resaca, Ga.

NICHOLS, JAMES—Age, 21 years. Enlisted, July 7, 1862, at Elmira, to serve three years; mustered in as private, Co. E, July 9, 1862; deserted, April 28, 1863, at Ely's Ford, Va.

NICHOLSON, JOHN A—Age, 24 years. Enlisted, August 11, 1862, at Elmira, to serve three years; mustered in as private, Co. K, August 13, 1862; wounded in action, May 25, 1864, at Dallas, Ga.; captured, November 18, l864, near Social Circle, Ga.; exchanged, February 28, 1865; mustered out with detachment, June 22, 1865, at hospital, York, Pa.

NICHOLSON, PERRY—Age, 34 years. Enlisted, July 29, 1862, at Canesteo, to serve three years; mustered in as private, Co. K, July 31, 1862; discharged for disability, September 8, 1863, at Alexandria, Va.

NICHOLSON, WILLIAM J.—Age, 18 years. Enlisted at Rathbone, to serve three years, and mustered in as private, Co. A, January 1, 1864; transferred to Co. A, Sixtieth Infantry, June 5, 1865.

NILES, HARRISON—Age, 21 years. Enlisted, August 4, 1862, at Elmira, to serve three years; mustered in as private, Co. G, August 6, 1862; promoted corporal, January 1, 1863; mustered out with company, June 5, 1865, near Washington, D.C.

NIVER, CHARLES—Age, 27 years. Enlisted at Elmira, to serve three years, and mustered in as private, Co. A, July 30, 1862; mustered out, July 1, 1865, at Elmira, N.Y., as Nivers.

NOLAN, MICHAEL—Private, Co. K, One Hundred and Forty-fifth Infantry; transferred to Co. I, this regiment, January 12, 1864; captured, November 18, 1864, near Social Circle, Ga.; paroled, April 28, 1865; mustered out, June 30, 1865, at New York city

NOLAN, THOMAS—Private, Co. C, One Hundred and Forty-fifth Infantry; transferred to Co. A, this regiment, January 12, 1864; to Co. A, Sixtieth Infantry, June 5, 1865.

NOLES, ANDREW—Age, 37 years. Enlisted at Elmira, to serve three years, and mustered in as private, Co. G, August 6, 1862; transferred to One Hundred and Sixty-sixth Company, Second Battalion, Veteran Reserve Corps, May 31, 1864; mustered out with detachment, June 27, 1865, at Point Lookout, Md.

NOLES, JOHN—Private, Co. W, One Hundred and Forty-fifth Infantry; transferred to Co. I, this regiment, January 12, 1864; mustered out with company, June 5, 1865, near Washington, D.C.

NORTHRUP, EVERET P.—Age, 18 years. Enlisted at Elmira, to serve three years, and mustered in as corporal, Co. E, June 16, 1862; deserted, September 7, 1862, between Camp Seward and Rockville, Md.

NORTON, CHARLES H.—Age, 18 years. Enlisted, July 29, 1862, at Hornellsville, to serve three years; mustered in as private, Co. K, July 31, 1862; wounded in action, May 3, 1863, at Chancellorsville, Va.; mustered out with company, June 5, 1865, near Washington D.C.

NORTON, GEORGE R.—Age, 32 years. Enlisted, August 11, 1862, at Greenwood, to serve three years; mustered in as private, Co. K, August 13, 1862; wounded in action, May 3, 1863, at Chancellorsville, Va.; mustered out with company, June 5, 1865, near Washington, D.C.

O'BRIEN, MICHAEL—Age, 28 years. Enlisted, July 28, 1862, at Addison, to serve three years; mustered in as private, Co. E, July 29, 1862; deserted, August 1, 1862, at Elmira, N.Y.

ODELL, JAMES—Age, 19 years. Enlisted, June 15, 1862, at Elmira, to serve three years; mustered in as private, Co. A, June 16, 1862; transferred to Fiftieth N.Y. Engineers, October 24, 1862, as O'Dell.

OELSCHLAEGER, GOTTFRIED—Age, 41 years. Enlisted, July 21, 1862, at Elmira, to serve three years; mustered in as private, Co. E, July 24, 1862; missing in action, March 22, 1865, near Bentonville, N.C.; no further record.

OEST, HENRY R.—Age, 39 years. Enlisted,

July 25, 1862, at Elmira, to serve three years; mustered in as private, Co. B, July 26, 1862; wounded in action, May 15, 1864, at Resaca, Ga.; absent in hospital, wounded, at muster out of company.

OGDEN, HENRY J.— Age, 21 years. Enlisted, July 29, 1862, at Havana, to serve three years; mustered in as private, Co. H, July 30, 1862; mustered out with company, June 5, 1865, near Washington, D.C.

O'HERN, MICHAEL—Age, 19 years. Enlisted at Elmira, to serve three years, and mustered in as private, Co. A, July 16, 1862; mustered out with company, June 5, 1865, near Washington, D.C.

OLMSTEAD, ALEXANDER—Age, 33 years. Enlisted, July 23, 1862, at West Union, to serve three years; mustered in as private, Co. I, July 24, 1862; discharged for disability, October 8, 1863, at Chestnut Hill Hospital, Philadelphia, Pa.

ONDERDONK, JAMES—Private, Co. C, One Hundred anti Forty-fifth Infantry; transferred to Co. A, this regiment, January 12, 1864; mustered out with company, June 5, 1865, near Washington, D.C., as James D.

O'NEIL, WILLIAM—Private, Co. I, One Hundred and Forty-fifth Infantry; transferred to Co. B, this regiment, January 12, 1864; to Veteran Reserve Corps, June 30, 1864, as O'Niel.

O'RILEY, JAMES—Private, Co. C, One Hundred and Forty-fifth Infantry; transferred to Co. A, this regiment, January 12, 1864; promoted corporal, January 1, 1865; mustered out with company, June 5, 1865; near Washington, D.C., as O'Reilly.

ORMSBY, ADIN—Age, 21 years. Enlisted, August 6, 1862, at Howard, to serve three years; mustered in as private, Co. K, August 8, 1862; died, May 18, 1864, at hospital, Covington, Ky.

ORMSBY, EDWARD—Private, Co. I, One Hundred and Forty-fifth Infantry; transferred to Co. B, this regiment, January 12, 1864; mustered out, July 5, 1865, at New York City.

ORR, GEORGE H.—Age, 21 years. Enlisted, July 28, 1862, at Addison, to serve three years; mustered in as private, Co. F, July 29, 1862; discharged for disability, November 1, 1862.

ORR, JOHN—Age, 26 years. Enrolled, July 28, 1862, at Addison, to serve three years; mustered in as first sergeant, Co. F, July 29, 1862; as second lieutenant, November 1, 1862; as first lieutenant, March 24, 1863;

wounded in action, May 25, 1864, at Dallas, Ga.; mustered in as captain, May 31, 1864, mustered out with company, June 5, 1865, near Washington, D.C. Commissioned second lieutenant, February 23, 1863, with rank from November 1, 1862, vice John E. Knox, promoted; first lieutenant, May 11, 1863, with rank from March 23, 1863, vice J.F. Knox, promoted; captain, July 12, 1864, with rank from May 25, 1864, vice J.F. Knox, died of wounds received in action.

ORR, ROBERT—Age, 30 years. Enlisted at Havana, to serve three years, and mustered in as private, Co. H, July 25, 1862; wounded in action, May 3, 1863, at Chancellorsville, Va.; transferred to Co. E, Seventh Regiment, Veteran Reserve Corps, April 16, 1864; mustered out with detachment, June 29, 1865, at Washington, D.C.

OSBORN, LAWRENCE W.—Age, 28 years. Enlisted, July 9, 1862, at Elmira, to serve three years; mustered in as corporal, Co. C, July 19, 1862; deserted, December 12, 1862, at Leesburg, Va.

OSBORNE, THEODORE—Age, 25 years. Enlisted at Corning, to serve three years, and mustered in as private, Co. I, August 7, 1862; wounded in action, May 25, 1864, at New Hope, Ga.; absent, in hospital at New Albany, Ind., and at muster out of company; also borne as Osbourn.

OSBURN, THOMAS R.—Age, 20 years. Enlisted, July 21, 1862, at Elmira, to serve three years; mustered in as private, Co. A, July 22, 1862; mustered out with company, June 5, 1865, near Washington, D.C.; also borne as Osborn.

OSTERHOUT, JAMES F.—Age, 25 years. Enlisted at Elmira, to serve three years, and mustered in as private, Co. O, July 29, 1862; wounded in action, May 3, 1863, at Chancellorsville, Va.; discharged for wounds, October 13, 1863, at hospital, Philadelphia, Pa.

OSTRANDER, WILLIAM H.—Age, 23 years. Enlisted at Elmira, to serve three years, and mustered in as private, Co. C, July 12, 1862; mustered out with company, June 5, 1865, near Washington, D.C.

OVERHISER, LEVI B.—Age, 22 years. Enlisted, August 11, 1862, at Canisteo, to serve three years; mustered in as private, Co. K, August 13, 1862; promoted corporal, March 1, 1864; captured in action, November 18, 1864, near Social Circle, Ga.; paroled, no date; mustered out with company, June 5, 1865, near Washington, D.C.

OVERTON, JOSIAH—Sergeant One Hundred and Forty-fifth Infantry, Co. G, One Hundred Forty-Fifth Infantry; transferred to Co. F, this regiment, as private, January 12, 1864; absent, wounded, since July 3, 1863, at Gettysburg, Pa., and at muster out of company.

OWEN, HENRY—Age, 30 years. Enlisted, August 1, 1862, at Montour, to serve three years; mustered in as private, Co. H, August 4, 1862; discharged for disability, February 4, 1863, at Philadelphia, Pa.

OWEN, JAMES—Private, Co. B, One Hundred and Forty-fifth Infantry; transferred to Co. G, this regiment, January 12, 1864; wounded in action, May 25, 1864, at Dallas; Ga.; mustered out with company, June 5, 1865, near Washington, D.C.

PADDOCK, H. IRA—Age, 28 years. Enlisted at Elmira, to serve three years, and mustered in as private, Co. H, August 4, 1862; died of typhoid fever, March 2, 1863, at Hope Landing, Va.

PADDOCK, JOHN N.—Age, 18 years. Enlisted at Elmira, to serve three years, and mustered in as private, Co. G, August; 5, 1862; promoted corporal, September 1, 1863; mustered out with company, June 5, 1865, near Washington, D.C.

PAINE, JOHN—Age, 23 years. Enlisted, July 16, 1862, at Elmira, to serve three years; mustered in as private, Co. C, July 18, 1862; discharged for disability, February 4, 1863, at; hospital, Philadelphia, Pa., as Payne.

PALMER, ELIAS—Age, 34 years. Enlisted at Elmira, to serve three years, and mustered in as private, Co. G, August 4, i862; mustered out with company, June 5, 1865, near Washington, D.C.

PALMER, HENRY—Age, 23 years. Enlisted at Elmira, to serve three years, and mustered in as private, Co. C, July 19, 1862; mustered out, May. 31, 1865, at Island Hospital, Harper's Ferry, Va.

PALMER, JOHN—Age, 23 years. Enlisted at Stamford, to serve one year, and mustered in as private, Co. E, January 4, 1865; transferred to Co. A, Sixtieth Infantry, June 5, 1865.

PARIS, TYLER—Age, 21 years. Enlisted, July 22, 1862, at Avoca, to serve three years; mustered in as private, Co. G, July 23, 1862; wounded in action, September 17, 1862, at Antietam, Md.; mustered out with company, June 5, 1865, near Washington, D.C.

PARKER, JOHN S.—Age, 34 years. Enlisted, August 2, 1862, at Elmira, to serve three years; mustered in as private, Co. G, August 6, 1862; discharged for disability, as musician, December 19, 1862, at Philadelphia, Pa.

PARKS, WILLIAM—Age, 21 years. Enlisted at Elmira, to serve three years, and mustered in as private, Co. Q, July 18, 1862; died of typhoid fever, March 7, 1863, in camp at Aquia Bay, Va.

PARSELS, DAVID B.—Age, 18 years. Enlisted, July 26, 1862, at Addison, to serve three years; mustered in as private, Co. F, July 29, 1862; wounded in action, May 25, 1864, at Dallas, Ga.; mustered out with company, June 5, 1865, near Washington, D.C.; also borne as Parsolls.

PARSELS, VALENTINE J.—Age, 18 years. Enlisted at Addison, to serve three years, and mustered in as private, Co. F, December 10, 1863; wounded in action, May 25, 1864, at Dallas, Ga.; transferred to Co. B, Sixtieth Infantry, June 5, 1865; also borne as Parsolls.

PATERSON, DUANE—Age, 18 years. Enlisted, July 29, 1862, at Montour, to serve three years; mustered in as private, Co. H July 30, 1862; died of typhoid fever, January 23, 1863, at Washington, D.C., as Dewayne Patterson.

PATTERSON, GEORGE W.—Age, 25 years. Enlisted at Elmira, to serve three years, and mustered in as private, Co. D, July 23, 1862; discharged, June 30, 1863.

PAUL, HIRAM—Age, 33 years. Enlisted at Lindley, to serve three years, and mustered in as private, Co. C, January 4, 1864; wounded in action, May 25, 1864, at Dallas, Ga.; transferred to Co. A Sixtieth on June 5, 1865.

PAYNE, see Paine.

PEN, REUBEN R.—Age, 43 years. Enlisted, July 24, 1862, at Elmira, to serve three years; mustered in as private, Co. E, July 22, 1862; discharged for disability, February 4, 1863.

PENDERGAST, PATRICK—Enrolled, June 23, 1863, at Fosterville, Tenn., to serve three years; mustered in as assistant surgeon, June 24, 1863; mustered out with regiment, June 5, 1865, near Washington, D.C. Commissioned assistant surgeon, June 13, 1863, with rank from same date, vice D.G. Himrod, resigned.

PERRY, THOMAS—Age, 27 years. Enlisted at Elmira, to serve three years, and mustered in as private, Co. E, August 4, 1862; deserted, September 7, 1862, between Camp Seward and Rockville, Md.

PERSONIUS, WILLIAM J.—Age, 21 years Enlisted, July 18, 1862, at Elmira, to serve three years; mustered in as private, Co. D, July 24, 1862; promoted corporal, prior to April 10, 1863; sergeant, December 1, 1863; died, October 5, 1864, at First Division, Twentieth Army Corps, Hospital, Atlanta, Ga.

PETERS, ELEAZER C.—Age, 22 years. Enlisted, July 15, 1862, at Elmira, to serve three years; mustered in as private, Co. B, July 16, 1862; promoted commissary sergeant, April 9, 1863; mustered out with regiment, June 5, 1865, near Washington, D.C.

PHELPS, JOSEPH J.—Age, 20 years. Enlisted, July 17, 1862, at Elmira, to serve three years; mustered in as private, Co. D, July 24, 1862; promoted corporal, prior to April 10, 1863; sergeant, June 1, 1864; captured, November 18, 1864, while on Sherman's Savannah campaign; paroled, no date; mustered out, May 31, 1865, at Elmira, N.Y.

PHOENIX, SAMUEL J.—Age, 29 years. Enlisted, July 26, 1862, at Addison, to serve three years; mustered in as private, Co. F, July 29, 1862; promoted corporal, February 28, 1863; sergeant, January 11, 1865; mustered out with company, June 5, 1865, near Washington, D.C.

PINCH, JAMES W.—Age, 23 years. Enlisted, July 4, 1862, at Hornellsville, to serve three years; mustered in as private, Co. K, July 31, 1862; promoted corporal, prior to April 10, 1863; wounded in action, May 3, 1863, at Chancellorsville, Va., returned to ranks, April 1864; captured, November 18, 1864, near Social Circle, Ga.; exchanged, February 28, 1865; mustered out, July 13, 1865, at Buffalo, N.Y.

PLATT, DAVID—Age, 44 years. Enlisted at Elmira, to serve three years, and mustered in as private, Co. D, August 4, 1862; deserted, September 17, 1862, at Antietam, Md.

PLIMPTON, ALBERT M.—Age, 27 years. Enlisted, August 5, 1862, at Hornellsville, to serve three years; mustered in as sergeant, Co. K, August 8, 1862; discharged, April 7, 1863, at Baltimore, Md.

PLOSS, PHILIP H.—Private, Co. K, One Hundred and Forty-fifth Infantry; transferred to Co. F, this regiment, January 12, 1864; mustered out with company, June 5, 1865, near Washington, D.C.

POLLARD, WILLIAM—Private, Co. G, One Hundred and Forty-fifth Infantry;

transferred to Co. E, this regiment, January 12, 1864; mustered out with company, June 5, 1865, near Washington, D.C.; also borne as Pollock.

POND, LEANDER—Age, 19 years. Enlisted, August 10, 1862, at Corning, to serve three years; mustered in as private, Co. I, August 11, 1862; absent, in hospital at Washington, D.C., at muster out of company.

POOLEY, FIELD—Age, 21 years. Enlisted at Bath, to serve three years, and mustered in as corporal, Co. G, August 5, 1862; promoted sergeant, January 1, 1864; mustered out with company, June 5, 1865, near Washington, D.C.

POTTER, CHARLES E.—Age, 29 years. Enlisted, July 25, 1862, at Montour, to serve three years; mustered in as private, Co. H, August 7, 1862; promoted corporal, prior to April 10, 1863; sergeant, May 1, 1864; mustered out with company, June 5, 1865, near Washington, D.C.

POTTER, DAVID—Age, 20 years. Enlisted, July 16, 1862, at Elmira, to serve three years; mustered in as private, Co. E, July 22, 1862; deserted, September 29, 1862, at Maryland Heights, Md.

POWELL, ANDREW—Corporal, Co. K, One Hundred and Forty-fifth Infantry; transferred to Co. I, this regiment, January 12, 1864; mustered out with company, June 5, 1865, near Washington, D.C.

POWELL, JOHN—Private, Co. K, One Hundred and Forty-fifth Infantry; transferred to Co. I, this regiment, January 12, 1864; died of chronic diarrhea, August 31, 1864, at hospital, New Albany, Ind.

POWELL, JOHN W.—Age, 27 years. Enlisted, July 22, 1862, at Elmira, to serve three years; mustered in as private, Co. O, July 23, 1862; mustered out with company, June 5, 1865, near Washington, D.C.

POWELL, VERNON—Age, 21 years. Enlisted at Corning, to serve three years, and mustered in as private, Co. I, August 8, 1862; deserted, October 19, 1862, at Maryland Heights, Md.

PRATT, EZRA—Age, 24 years. Enlisted at Elmira, to serve three years, and mustered in as private, Co. D, July 17, 1862; deserted, December 10, 1862, at Antietam Ford, Md.

PRESTON, CLARK—Age, 25 years. Enlisted, August 4, 1862, at Tremont, to serve three years; mustered in as private, Co. K, August 5, 1862; captured, November 18, 1864, near Social Circle, Ga.; paroled, no date;

mustered out with detachment, June 19, 1865, at Elmira, N.Y.

PUTMAN, GEORGE M.—Age, 18 years. Enlisted at Elmira, to serve three years, and mustered in as corporal, Co. H, August 4, 1862; returned to ranks, prior to April 10, 1863; mustered out with company, June 5, 1865, near Washington, D.C.; also borne as Putnam.

PUTNAM, EBENEZER—Age, 24 years. Enlisted, August 4, 1862, at Elmira, to serve three years; mustered in as private, Co. H, August 5, 1862; deserted, December 23, 1862, at Smoketown, Md., as Putman.

PUTNAM, ELIAS—Age, 21 years. Enlisted at Elmira, to serve three years, and mustered in as private, Co. H, July 25, 1862; promoted corporal, prior to April 10, 1863; sergeant, prior to October 1863; mustered out with company, June 5, 1865, near Washington, D.C., as Elias G.

PUTNAM, LEONARD—Private, Co. G, One Hundred and Forty-fifth Infantry; transferred to Co. E, this regiment, January 12, 1864; mustered out with company, June 5, 1865, near Washington, D.C.

PUTNAM, THOMAS—Age, 26 years. Enlisted, August 4, 1862, at Elmira, to serve three years; mustered in as private, Co. H, August 5, 1862; wounded in action, March 16, 1865, at Averasboro, N.C.; mustered out, to date June 5, 1865, at Elmira, N.Y.

QUICK, FRANCIS—Age, 21 years. Enlisted, July 26, 1862, at Addison, to serve three years; mustered in as private, Co. F, July 29, 1862; sentenced by general court-martial, September 15, 1863, to be dishonorably discharged; August 25, 1865, expiration of term.

QUIGLEY, MICHAEL—Age, 33 years. Enlisted, July 17, 1862, at West Union, to serve three years; mustered in as private, Co. I, July 24, 1862; captured, November 18, 1864, near Social Circle, Ga.; no further record.

QUIMBY, EPHRAIM—Age, 26 years. Enlisted, July 16, 1862, at Elmira, to serve three years; mustered in as private, Co. A, July 17, 1862; discharged for disability, February 4, 1863, at Philadelphia, Pa.

RAGAN, Jr., PATRICK—Age, 29 years. Enlisted at Elmira, to serve three years, and mustered in as private, Co. D, July 25, 1862; mustered out with company, June 5, 1865, near Washington, D.C.

RANDALL, PORTER—Age, 32 years.

Enlisted at Elmira, to serve three years, and mustered in as private, Co. C, July 17, 1862; promoted corporal, January 1, 1863; sergeant, October 1, 1864; mustered out with company, June 5, 1865, near Washington, D.C.

RANDOLPH, SAMUEL F.—Enlisted at Elmira, to serve three years, and mustered in as private, Co. E, June 9, 1862; deserted, no date, at Elmira, N.Y., as Rundolph.

RASCO, HENRY H.—Age, 19 years. Enlisted, July 29, 1862, at Hornellsville, to serve three years; mustered in as private, Co. K, July 31, 1862; died, March 12, 1863, at Hope Landing, Va.

RATHBONE, CHARLES—Age, 20 years. Enlisted at Corning, to serve three years, and mustered in as corporal, Co. I, July 28, 1862; returned to ranks, no date; deserted, August 23, 1863, while attached to Battery F, Fourth U.S. Artillery, at Kelly's Ford, Va.

RATHBONE, GUY.—Age, 18 years. Enlisted, July 21, 1862, at Elmira, to serve three years; mustered in as private, Co. B, July 23, 1862; promoted corporal, prior to October 1863; died, January 25, 1865, of spotted fever, at hospital, First Division, Twentieth Army Corps, S. C.

READING, JR., PIERSON B.—Age, 29 years. Enlisted, July 26, 1862, at Addison, to serve three years; mustered in as private, Co. F, July 29, 1862; mustered out with company, June 5, 1865, near Washington, D.C.

REAMER, WILLIAM—Age, 42 years. Enlisted at Elmira, to serve three years, and mustered in as private, Co. G, August 1, 1862; discharged for disability, May 30, 1863, at Washington, D.C.

REARDON, WASHINGTON O.—Private, Co. K, One Hundred and Forty-fifth Infantry; transferred to Co. I, this regiment, January 12, 1864; mustered out with company, June 5, 1865, near Washington, D.C., as Washington A.

REASE, see Rees.

RECE, EDWARD—Age, 41 years. Enlisted, July 23, 1862, at Elmira, to serve three years; mustered in as private, Co. G, July 24, 1862; discharged for disability, February 9, 1863, at hospital, Washington, D.C., as Rice.

REED, GEORGE W.—Age, 43 years. Enlisted at Wayne, to serve three years, and mustered in as private, Co. G, August 6, 1862; transferred to Co. F, Nineteenth Regiment, Veteran Reserve Corps, December 31, 1863; re-enlisted as a veteran, August 11, 1864;

mustered out with detachment, November 15, 1865, at Elmira, N.Y.

REED, JAMES—Private, Co. I, One Hundred and Forty-fifth Infantry; transferred to Co. O, this regiment, January 12, 1864; to Veteran Reserve Corps, March 15, 1864.

REED, SAMUEL H.—Age, 32 years. Enlisted at Corning, to serve three years, and mustered in as private, Co. I, August 8, 1862; promoted corporal, prior to April 10, 1863; wounded in action, May 25, 1864, at Dallas, Ga.; mustered out with company, June 5, 1865, near Washington, D.C.

REEDER, JACKSON B. F.—Age, 25 years. Enlisted at Elmira, to serve three years, and mustered in as private, Co. D; August 2, 1862; deserted, September 7, 1862. near Rockville, Md.

REEDER, LAUREN T.—Age, 19 years. Enlisted, July 19, 1862, at Elmira, to serve three years; mustered in as private, Co. B, July 22, 1862; promoted corporal, January 1, 1863; sergeant, June 30, 1863; mustered out with company, June 5, 1865, near Washington, D.C.; also borne as Loren T.

REES, THOMAS D.—Age, 23 years. Enlisted, July 30, 1862, at Montour, to serve three years; mustered in as private, Co. H, August 4, 1862; discharged for disability, June 8, 1863, at York, Pa., as Rease; also borne as Reese.

REEVE, THOMAS H.—Private, Co. G, One Hundred and Forty-fifth Infantry; transferred to Co. K, this regiment, January 12, 1864; to navy, April 14, 1864, as Thomas R.

REID, GEORGE W.—Age, 33 years. Enrolled near Atlanta, Ga., to serve three years, and mustered in as captain, Co. K, August 22, 1864; captured in action, November 18, 1864, near Social Circle, Ga.; paroled, February 1865; discharged, May 15, 1865; prior service as captain, One Hundred and Forty-fifth Infantry. Commissioned captain, July 27, 1864, with rank from same date, vice J.A. Creed, not mustered.

RENIFF, SOLOMON R.—Age, 18 years. Enlisted at Elmira, to serve three years, and mustered in as private, Co. D, August 4, 1862; wounded in action, May 25, 1864, at Dallas, Ga.; absent, detached as orderly to Captain Blair, since September 5, 1864, and at muster out of company.

REYNOLDS, CHARLES H.—Age, 39 years. Enlisted, August 4, 1862, at Rathbone, to serve three years; mustered in as corporal, Co. F, August 5, 1862; returned to ranks, no

date; discharged for disability, January 28, 1863.

REYNOLDS, EDWIN M.—Age, 27 years. Enlisted, July 26, 1862, at Addison, to serve three years; mustered in as private, Co. F, July 29, 1862; died of camp fever, November 21, 1862.

REYNOLDS, ODELL D.—Age, 41 years. Enrolled, August 4, 1862, at Elmira, to serve three years; mustered in as second lieutenant, Co. D, August 9, 1862; promoted first lieutenant, April 5, 1863; discharged for disability, July 9, 1863. Commissioned second lieutenant, September 6, 1862, with rank from August 4, 1862, original; first lieutenant, March 27, 1863, with rank from March 13, 1863, vice S.A. Bennett, promoted.

RHOADES, JOSEPH C.—Age, 32 years. Enlisted at Elmira, to serve three years, and mustered in as wagoner, Co. D, August 4, 1862; discharged for disability, March 5, 1864, at Washington, D.C., as Rhodes.

RHODES, ALMON G.—Age, 20 years. Enlisted, June 6, 1862, at Elmira, to serve three years; mustered in as private, Co. E, June 9, 1862; deserted, April 15, 1864.

RHODES, WILLIAM—Private, Co. K, One Hundred and Forty-fifth Infantry; transferred to Co. I, this regiment, January 12, 1864; to One Hundred and Fifty-first Company, Second Battalion, Veteran Reserve Corps, no date; deserted, March 8, 1865; returned to this regiment, no date; transferred to Co. B, Sixtieth Infantry, June 5, 1865.

RHYMELS, JOHN—Age, 44 years. Enlisted at Elmira, to serve three years, and mustered in as private, Co. C, July 9, 1862; discharged for disability, July 10, 1863, at hospital, Convalescent Camp, Alexandria, Va., as Rhynols.

RICE, see Rece.

RICE, JOHN—Age, 24 years. Enlisted at Corning, to serve three years, and mustered in as private, Co. E, January 5, 1864; transferred to Co. I, February 5, 1864; to Co. B, Sixtieth Infantry, June 5, 1865; prior service, Co. D, Twenty-third Infantry.

RICHARDSON, CLARK—Age, 27 years. Enlisted, July 23, 1862, at Elmira, to serve three years; mustered in as private, Co. C, July 24, 1862; wounded in action, May 3, 1863, at Chancellorsville, Va.; died of his wounds, May 8, 1863, at Aquia Bay, Va.

RICHARDSON, WELCOME E.—Age, 20 years. Enlisted, August 8, 1862, at Elmira, to serve three years; mustered in as private, Co. A, August 9, 1862; wounded in action, July 3, 1863, at Gettysburg, Pa.; discharged for disability, September 11, 1864, at Elmira, N.Y.

RICKEY, JOHN—Age, 18 years. Enlisted at Elmira, to serve three years, and mustered in as private, Co. H, July 25, 1862; mustered out with company, June 5, 1865, near Washington, D.C.

RICKEY, STEPHEN—Age, 39 years. Enlisted, July 15, 1862, at Elmira, to serve three years; mustered in as private, Co. B, July 16, 1862; died of consumption, December 22, 1862, at hospital, Summit House, Pa.

RIGGS, EDWARD H.—Age, 18 years. Enlisted, July 16, 1862, at Elmira, to serve three years; mustered in as private, Co. A, July 18, 1862; transferred to Veteran Reserve Corps, July 1, 1863.

RINKER, ELIAS—Age, 38 years. Enlisted, July 19, 1862, at Elmira, to serve three years; mustered in as private, Co. E, July 22, 1862; wounded in action, March 16, 1865, and died of his wounds, March 19, 1865, at Averasborough, N.C.

RIORDAN, THOMAS—Age, 42 years. Enlisted at Elmira, to serve three years, and mustered in as private, Co. C, July 18, 1862; transferred to Veteran Reserve Corps, July 1, 1863.

RITCHIE, GILBERT—Private, Co. K, One Hundred and Forty-fifth Infantry; transferred to Co. I, this regiment, January 12, 1864; mustered out with detachment, August 2, 1865, at Sickles Hospital, Washington, D.C.

ROBBINS, EPHRAIM—Age, 40 years. Enlisted at Elmira, to serve three years, and mustered in as private, Co. B, July 23, 1862; discharged for disability, November 23, 1862.

ROBERTS, WILLIAM H.—Age, 21 years. Enlisted at Elmira, N.Y. to serve three years; mustered in as wagoner, Co. A, July 22, 1862; mustered out with company, June 5, 1865, near Washington, D.C.

ROBINSON, LEWIS B.—Age, 33 years. Enlisted at Campbell, to serve three years, and mustered in as private, Co. F, August 6, 1862; discharged for disability, January 24, 1863.

ROBINSON, NELSON A.—Age, 21 years. Enlisted, June 27, 1862, at Bath, to serve three years; mustered in as private, Co. G, July 9, 1862; died, December 18, 1862, at hospital, Smoketown, Va.

ROE, J. MILTON—Enrolled at Elmira, to serve three years, and mustered in as first lieutenant, Co. F, August 10, 1862; discharged for disability, November 1, 1862. Commissioned first lieutenant September 6, 1862, rank from August 6, 1862, original.

ROGERS, AMOS S.—Age 21years. Enlisted, July 28, 1862, at Addison, to serve three years; mustered in as sergeant, Co. F, July 29, 1862; died of typhoid fever, October 7, 1862.

ROGERS, BENJAMIN F.—Age, 32 years. Enlisted, July 30, 1862, at Elmira, to serve three years; mustered in as private, Co. D, August 8, 1862; wounded in action, May 25, 1864, at Dallas, Ga.; mustered out with company, June 5, 1865, near Washington, D.C.

ROGERS, NELSON B.—Age, 20 years. Enlisted, July 17, 1862, at Elmira, to serve three years; mustered in as corporal, Co. D, July 24, 1862; promoted sergeant, March 13, 1863; returned to ranks, December 13, 1863; mustered out with company, June 5, 1865, near Washington, D.C.

ROGERS, RICHARD A.—Age, 21 years. Enlisted at Corning, to serve three years, and mustered in as private, Co. I, August 9, 1862; deserted, October 20, 1862, at Maryland Heights, Md.

ROLLS, CHARLES—Age, 18 years. Enlisted at Rathbone, to serve three years, and mustered in as private, Co. A, December 10, 1863; transferred to Co. A, Sixtieth Infantry, June 5, 1865.

ROOD, BENJAMIN F.—Age, 18 years. Enlisted at Westfield, to serve three years, and mustered in as private, Co. E, February 27, 1864; transferred to Co. A, Sixtieth Infantry, June 5, 1865.

ROOT, AUSTIN—Age, 21 years. Enlisted, July 26, 1862, at Addison, to serve three years; mustered in as private, Co. F, July 29, 1862; appointed musician and returned to grade of private, no dates; mustered out with company, June 5, 1865, near Washington, D.C.

ROOT, OSCAR M.—Age, 26 years. Enlisted at Rathbone, to serve three years, and mustered in as private, Co. B, December 31, 1863; wounded in action, May 25, 1864, at Dallas, Ga.; died of chronic diarrhea, August 24, 1864, at Brown Hospital, Louisville, Ky.

RORICK, JOHN W.—Age, 20 years. Enlisted at Elmira, to serve three years, and mustered in as private, Co. C, July 29, 1862; deserted, August 13, 1862, at Elmira, N.Y.

RORICK, SYLVANIUS R.—Age, 28 years. Enlisted at Elmira, to serve three years, and mustered in as private, Co. C, July 29, 1862; deserted, September 18, 1862, at Antietam, Md.

ROSENCRANS, DANIEL—Age, 23 years. Enlisted, July 28, 1862, at Addison, to serve three years; mustered in as private, Co. F, July 29, 1862; mustered out with company, June 5, 1865, near Washington, D.C.

ROWLEE, ELIJAH C.—Age, 40 years. Enlisted at Corning, to serve three years, and mustered in as private, Co. I, August 4, 1862; promoted corporal, prior to April 10, 1863; mustered out with company, June 5, 1865, near Washington, D.C.

ROWLEY, CICERO—Age, 22 years. Enlisted at Elmira, to serve three years, and mustered in as private, Co. C, July 26, 1862; deserted, November 19, 1862, at Antietam Ford, Md.

RUMSEY, GEORGE—Age, 18 years. Enlisted, July 21, 1862, at Elmira, to serve three years, and mustered in as private, Co. A, July 22, 1862; died of variola, July 25, 1863, at Washington, D.C.

RUMSEY, JEREMIAH—Age, 27 years. Enlisted at Elmira, to serve three years, and mustered in as private, Co. G, August 6, 1862; deserted, August 14, 1863, at Fort Schuyler, New York harbor.

RUNDOLPH, see Randolph.

RUSSELL, DAVID—Age, 32 years. Enlisted, July 17, 1862, at Elmira, to serve three years; mustered in as private, Co. E, July 19, 1862; discharged for disability, February 9, 1863, at Washington, D.C.

RUSSELL, HARRISON—Age, 23 years. Enlisted, August 11, 1862, at Tremont, to serve three years; mustered in as private, Co. K, August 13, 1862; discharged, February 6, 1863, at Convalescent Camp, Va.

RUTTER, NATHANIEL E. Enrolled at Elmira, to serve three years, and mustered in as second lieutenant, Co. I, August 11, 1862; as captain, December 31, 1862; killed in action, May 1, 1863, at Chancellorsville, Va. Commissioned second lieutenant, September 6, 1862, with rank from August 9, 1862, original; captain, December 30, 1862, with rank from October 21, 1862, vice N.T. Colby, promoted.

RYAN, JOHN—Private, Co. G, One Hundred and Forty-fifth Infantry; transferred to Co. K, this regiment, January 12, 1864; deserted, April 7, 1864, when ordered to his regiment from hospital; apprehended, prior to June 1864; transferred to Veteran Reserve Corps, no date.

RYAN, JOHN—Age, 27 years. Enlisted, July 21, 1862, at Hornellsville, to serve three years; mustered in as private, Co. K, July 24, 1862; died, October 21, 1862, at Harper's Ferry, Va.

RYAN, MARTN—Age, 22 years. Enlisted at Elmira, to serve three years, and mustered in as private, Co. G, August 5, 1862; transferred to navy, April 20, 1864.

RYDER, see Smith.

SABINE, RANSOM—Age, 41 years. Enlisted, July 22, 1862, at Addison, to serve three years; mustered in as private, Co. F, July 29, 1862; detached to Veteran Reserve Corps, May 6, 1863; returned to company, April 8, 1864; wounded in action, May 25, 1864, at Dallas, Ga.; discharged for disability, September 11, 1864, as Ransom H. Sabine.

SAGE, MARTIN—Age, 24 years. Enlisted, August 11, 1862, at Canisteo, to serve three years; mustered in as private, Co. K, August 13, 1862; died, October 4, 1862, at Maryland Heights, Md.

SAGER, WILLIAM L.—Age, 24 years. Enlisted at Elmira, to serve three years, and mustered in as private, Co. G, August 6, 1862; mustered out with company, June 5, 1865, near Washington, D.C.; also borne as Seaget and Sewzer.

SALTZMAN, JACOB H.—Age, 23 years. Enrolled at Kanona, to serve three years, and mustered in as first sergeant, Co. G, July 16, 1862; promoted second lieutenant, May 27, 1863; mustered in as first lieutenant, January 3, 1865; mustered out with company, June 5, 1865, near Washington, D.C.; also borne as Sattsman. Commissioned second lieutenant, August 18, 1863, with rank from May 24, 1863, vice R.H. Gansevoort, promoted; first lieutenant, December 7, 1864, with rank from July 8, 1864, vice G. Swain, promoted.

SAMUEL, SALOMON—Age, 37 years. Enlisted, July 23, 1862, at Elmira, to serve three years; mustered in as private, Co. E, July 25, 1862; deserted, April 15, 1864.

SANDFORD, DAVID—Age, 21 years. Enlisted, July 23, 1862, at Bath, to serve three years; mustered in as private, Co. G, July 25, 1862; killed in action, May 25, 1864, at Dallas, Ga.; also borne as David B.

SANDS, WILLIAM D.—Age, 18 years. Enlisted at Elmira, to serve three years, and mustered in as private, Co. C, July 26, 1862; wounded in action, June 22, 1864, at Culp's Farm, Ga.; promoted corporal, May 1, 1865;

mustered out with company, June 5, 1865, near Washington, D.C.

SANFORD, DAVID D.—Age, 35 years. Enlisted, August 6, 1862, at Elmira to serve three years; mustered in as private, Co. D, August 7, 1862; promoted sergeant, prior to April 10, 1863, and returned to ranks, no date; transferred to Co. G, March 18, 1864; absent, in hospital at Buffalo, at muster out of company.

SAPPLE, see Yaple.

SATERLY, JOHN H—Age, 30 years. Enlisted at Elmira, to serve three years, and mustered in as corporal, Co. B, July 22, 1862; discharged for disability, March 6, 1863, at hospital, Washington, D.C., as Satreply.

SAVORY, FRANKLIN—Age, 21 years. Enlisted at Corning, to serve three years, and mustered in as private, Co. I, August 1, 1862; promoted corporal, June 30, 1864; mustered out with company, June 5, 1865, near Washington, D.C.

SAWNEY, JAMES—Sergeant, Co. C, One Hundred and Forty-fifth Infantry; transferred to Co. F, this regiment, as private, January 12, 1864; absent, at New York city for conscripts, since July 26, 1863, and at muster out of company.

SAWYER, JOHN—Age, 31 years. Enlisted at New York city, to serve three years, and mustered in as private, Co. F, January 14, 1864; promoted corporal, January 16, 1865; transferred to Co. B, Sixtieth Infantry, June 5, 1865, as John G.

SAWYER, SYLVESTER—Age, 23 years. Enlisted at Elmira, to serve three years, and mustered in as private, Co. C, August 9, 1862; wounded in action, May 25, 1864, at Dallas, Ga.; mustered out with company, June 5, 1865, near Washington, D.C., as Sylvester R.

SAXTON, LEVI H.—Age, 23 years. Enlisted at Elmira, to serve three years, and mustered in as private, Co. C, July 22, 1862; mustered out with company, June 5, 1865, near Washington, D.C.

SAYLER, LEWIS O.—Age, 21 years. Enrolled at Elmira, to serve three years, and mustered in as second lieutenant, Co. H, August 10, 1862; dismissed, November 22, 1862, as Saylor. Commissioned second lieutenant, September 6, 1862, with rank from August 7, 1862: original.

SCARVILL, THOMAS—Age, 30 years. Enlisted at Elmira, to serve three years, and mustered in as private, Co. G, August 4, 1862; mustered out with company, June 5, 1865, near Washington, D.C., as Searvill.

SCHOFF, CHRISTIAN F. L.—Private, Co. I, One Hundred and Forty-fifth Infantry; transferred to Co. C, this regiment, January 12, 1864; wounded in action, May 25, 1864, at Dallas, Ga.; mustered out with company, June 5, 1865, near Washington, D.C.; also borne as Shoff.

SCHUSZLER, WILLIAM J.—Age, 29 years. Enlisted, July 21, 1862, at Elmira, to serve three years; mustered in as corporal, Co. A, July 22, 1862; promoted sergeant, prior to October 1863; mustered out with company, June 5, 1865, near Washington, D.C.

SCOTT, DANIEL B.—Age, 20 years. Enlisted at Elmira, to serve three years, and mustered in as private, Co. E, August 12, 1862; promoted corporal, July 1, 1864; wounded in action, July 30, 1864, and died of his wounds, August 1, 1864, near Atlanta, Ga.

SCOTT, LEANDER—Age, 27 years. Enlisted, June 13, 1862, at Elmira, to serve three years; mustered in as corporal, Co. E, June 21, 1862; discharged, May 6, 1863, at Elmira, N.Y.; subsequent service in Sixteenth Artillery.

SEAGER and SEWZER, see Sager.

SEARLES, EDWARD—Age, 34 years. Enlisted at Elmira, to serve three years, and mustered in as private, Co. A, August 7, 1862; wounded in action, May 25, 1864, at Dallas, Ga.; mustered out with company, June 5, 1865, near Washington, D.C.

SEARS, WALLACE W.—Age, 18 years. Enlisted at Ulysses, to serve three years, and mustered in as private, Co. H, December 31, 1863; wounded in action, May 25, 1864, at Dallas, Ga.; transferred to Co. B, Sixtieth Infantry, June 5, 1865.

SEARVILL, see Scarvill.

SEIBELT, HENRY—Musician, Co. B, One Hundred and Forty-fifth Infantry; transferred to Co. G, this regiment, January 12, 1864; captured in action, March 8, 1865, at Salem Grove, N.C.; released, March 30, 1865, at Aikens Landing, Va.; mustered out, June 19, 1865, at hospital, Annapolis, Md., as Seybelt; also borne as Sibelt.

SELATSKI, see Solarskil.

SHAFFNER, HENRY—Private, Co. I, One Hundred and Forty-fifth Infantry; transferred to Co. C, this regiment, January 12, 1864; mustered out, June 19, 1865, at Slough Hospital, Alexandria, Va., as Sehoffner; also borne as Shoffner.

SHAUGER, JACOB—Age, 22 years. Enlisted

at Elmira, to serve three years, and mustered in as private, Co. B, July 16. 1862; deserted, August 12, 1862, from barracks at Elmira, N.Y.

SHAVER, JOHN L.—Age, 28 years. Enlisted, August 11, 1862, at Avoca, to serve three years; mustered in as private, Co. K, August 13, 1862; deserted, October 29, 1862, on the march in Va.

SHAW, EDWIN W.—Age, 18 years. Enlisted, July 30, 1862, at Montour, to serve three years; mustered in as private, Co. H, August 1, 1862; appointed musician, no date; died of small-pox, April 23, 1863, at Hope Landing, Va.

SHEARS, DANIEL—Age, 18 years. Enlisted, July 18, 1862, at Elmira, to serve three years; mustered in as private, Co. B, July 22, 1862; transferred to Co. A, Ninth Regiment, Veteran Reserve Corps, July 1, 1863; mustered out with detachment, June 24, 1865, at Washington, D.C.

SHEPARD, JOHN J.—Age, 29 years. Enrolled, July 22, 1862, at Corning, to serve three years; mustered in as first sergeant, Co. I, July 24, 1862; as second lieutenant, June 8, 1863; as first lieutenant, February 10, 1865; mustered out with company, June 5, 1865, near Washington, D.C. Commissioned second lieutenant, May 11, 1863, with rank from December 8, 1862, vice J.R. Lindsay, promoted; first lieutenant, January 18, 1865, with rank from October 26, 1864, vice J. Bronson, promoted.

SHERMAN, CHARLES—Age, 19 years. Enlisted at Elmira, to serve three years, and mustered in as private, Co. B, July 18, 1862; mustered out with company, June 5, 1865, near Washington, D.C.

SHERMAN, EDWARD—Age, 22 years Enlisted, August 9, 1862, at Elmira, to serve three years; mustered in as private, Co. E, August 12, 1862; died of fever, November 8, 1862, at Harper's Ferry, Va.

SHERMAN, EDWIN P.—Age, 18 years. Enlisted, July 25, 1862, at Elmira, to serve three years; mustered in as private, Co. A, July 28, 1862; discharged for disability, August 9, 1862, at Elmira, N.Y.

SHERMAN, SAMUEL L.—Age, 28 years. Enlisted at Elmira, to serve three years, and mustered in as private, Co. D, July 17, 1862; mustered out with company, June 5, 1865, near Washington, D.C.

SHERNER, MICHAEL—Age, 29 years. Enlisted, July 30, 1862, at Hornellsville, to serve three years; mustered in as private, Co.

K, July 31, 1862; wounded in action, May 25, 1864, at Dallas, Ga.; mustered out with company, June 5, 1865, near Washington, D.C.

SHERON, FRANK—Private, Co. B, One Hundred and Forty-fifth Infantry; transferred to Co. G, this regiment, January 12, 1864; deserted, prior to June 1864.

SHERWOOD, HARRY—Age, 22 years. Enlisted at Elmira, to serve three years, and mustered in as private, Co. D, July 17, 1862; promoted corporal, no date; deserted, December 12, 1862, at Leesburg, Va.

SHERWOOD, LEWIS—Age, 34 years. Enlisted, July 22, !862, at Elmira, to serve three years; mustered in as private, Co. D, July 24, 1862; mustered out with company, June 5, 1865, near Washington, D.C.

SHOFF, see Schoff.

SHOFFNER, see Shaffner.

SHORT, ROBERT—Age, 33 years. Enlisted, August 4, 1862, at Addison, to serve three years; mustered in as private, Co. F, August 5, 1862; absent, detached to First Division Ordnance, Train, Twentieth Army Corps, at muster out of company.

SIBELT, see Seibelt.

SICKLES, DANIEL D.—Age, 40 years. Enlisted at Elmira, to serve three years, and mustered in as private, Co. D, July 17, 1862; promoted corporal, prior to April 10, 1863; returned to ranks, December 1863; mustered out with company, June 5, 1865, near Washington, D.C.

SILL, ALLEN N.—Age, 34 years. Enrolled at Elmira, to serve three years, and mustered in as captain, Co. K, August 11, 1862; as major, July 31, 1864; as lieutenant-colonel, September 27, 1864; mustered out with regiment, June 5, 1865, near Washington, D.C. Commissioned captain, September 6, 1862, with rank from August 9, 1862, original; major, July 20, 1864, with rank from July 8, 1864, vice L. Baldwin, promoted; lieutenant-colonel, October 17, 1864, with rank from September 27, 1864, vice L. Baldwin, deceased.

SIMMER, JACOB—Age, 21 years. Enlisted, July 14, 1862, at Elmira, to serve three years; mustered in as private, Co. B, July 16, 1862; mustered out with company, June 5, 1865, near Washington, D.C.

SIMMONS, SIMEON S.—Age, 25 years. Enlisted at Havana, to serve three years, and mustered in as private, Co. H, July 25, 1862; mustered out with company, June 5, 1865, near Washington, D.C.

SIMMONSON, DANIEL—Private, Co. K, One Hundred and Forty-fifth Infantry; transferred to Co. F, this regiment, January 12, 1864; killed in skirmish, June 19, 1864, near Marietta, Ga.

SIMPSON, SAIRLES—Age, 34 years. Enlisted at West Union, to serve three years, and mustered in as private, Co. I, August 5, 1862; transferred to Co. B, Sixtieth Infantry, June 5, 1865.

SINCLAIR, HENRY—Private, Co. G, One Hundred and Forty-fifth Infantry; transferred to Co. I, this regiment, January 12, 1864; absent, sick in hospital, since June 1, 1863, and at muster out of company.

SLAVIN, JOHN—Age, 25 years. Enlisted, August 4, 1862, at Hornellsville, to serve three years; mustered in as private, Co. K, August 8, 1862; mustered out with company, June 5, 1865, near Washington, D.C.

SLAWSON, ISAAC—Age, 24 years. Enlisted at Elmira, to serve three years, and mustered in as private, Co. D, August 4, 1862; captured, no date; died, February 18, 1863, at Richmond, Va., as Slauson.

SLAWSON, MOSES—Age, 21 years. Enlisted at Elmira, to serve three years, and mustered in as private, Co. D, July 30, 1862; discharged for disability, July 8, 1863, as Slauson.

SMALLEY, see Smolley.

SMEAD, JAMES B.—Age, 18 years. Enlisted at Elmira, to serve three years, and mustered in as private, Co. D, August 7, 1862; discharged, May 13, 1865, at National Hospital, Baltimore, Md., as Sineed.

SMITH, DAVID—Age, 40 years. Enlisted, July 21, 1862, at Elmira, to serve three years; mustered in as private, Co. D, July 31, 1862; captured, November 18, 1864, while on Sherman's Savannah campaign; paroled, no date; absent, at Camp Parole, Annapolis, Md., at muster out of company.

SMITH, EDWARD—Age, 20 years. Enlisted at Elmira, to serve three years, and mustered in as private, Co. G, August 4, 1862; wounded in action, May 25, 1864, at Dallas, Ga.; mustered out with company, June 5, 1865, near Washington, D.C.

SMITH, EZEKIEL—Age, 18 years. Enlisted, June 9, 1862, at Elmira, to serve three years; mustered in as private, Co. E, June 9, 1862; discharged, February 11, 1864.

SMITH, GABRIEL L.—Age, 38 years. Enrolled at Elmira, to serve three years, and mustered in as first lieutenant and adjutant, July 24, 1862; as major, August 13, 1862; as

lieutenant-colonel, October 21, 1862; discharged for disability, February 3, 1863; not commissioned first lieutenant and adjutant. Commissioned major, September 6, 1862, with rank from August 9, 1862, original; lieutenant-colonel, October 18, 1862, with rank from October 21, 1862, vice A.S. Diven, promoted.

SMITH, HENRY P.—Age, 19 years. Enlisted at Elmira, to serve three years, and mustered in as private, Co. A, July 19, 1862; died of typhoid fever, October 13, 1862, at Bolivar Heights, Va.

SMITH, IRA—Age, 19 years. Enlisted, July 21, 1862, at Hornellsville, to serve three years; mustered in as private, Co. K, July 31, 1862; discharged, February 17, 1863, at Convalescent Camp, Va.

SMITH, IRA E.—Age, 22 years. Enlisted at Elmira, to serve three years, and mustered in as private, Co. G, August 2, 1862; no further record.

SMITH, IRA L.—Age, 35 years. Enlisted at Bath, to serve three years, and mustered in as corporal, Co. G, July 25, 1862; discharged for disability, December 29, 1862, at Washington, D.C.

SMITH, IRA R.—Age, 25 years. Enlisted, August 6, 1862, at Cameron, to serve three years; mustered in as private, Co. F, August 7, 1862; mustered out with company, June 5, 1865, near Washington, D.C.

SMITH, JAMES H.—Age, 18 years. Enlisted at Elmira, to serve three years, and mustered in as private, Co. E, August 12, 1862; promoted corporal, December 1, 1863; sergeant, October 14, 1864; mustered out with company, June 5, 1865, near Washington, D.C.

SMITH, JOHN—Age, 24 years. Enlisted at Elmira, to serve three years, and mustered in as private, Co. B, July 18, 1862; deserted, September 17, 1862, at Antietam, Md.

SMITH, JOHN A.—Age, 23 years. Enlisted, July 30, 1862, at Hornellsville, to serve three years; mustered in as private, Co. K, July 31, 1862; discharged, March 26, 1863, at New York city.

SMITH, JONATHAN E.—Enlisted, July 31, 1862, at Elmira, to serve three years; mustered in as private, Co. G, August 2, 1862; died, November 18, 1864, at hospital, Chattanooga, Tenn.

SMITH, MELVIN V.—Age, 23 years. Enlisted at Wayland, to serve three years, and mustered in as private, Co. I, July 31, 1862;

absent, detached in Exchange Barracks, Louisville, Ky., at muster out of company.

SMITH, MERRITT F.—Age, 21 years. Enlisted, August 11, 1862, at Canisteo, to serve three years; mustered in as wagoner, Co. K, August 12, 1862; discharged, February 17, 1863, at Convalescent Camp, Va.

SMITH, MONTGOMERY—Age, 25 years. Enlisted at West Union, to serve three years, and mustered in as private, Co. I, August 1, 1862; mustered out, May 31, 1865, at Elmira, N.Y.

SMITH, ROBERT—Age, 24 years. Enlisted at Elmira, to serve three years, and mustered in as private, Co. D, July 17, 1862; wounded in action, May 3, 1863, at Chancellorsville, Va.; transferred to Veteran Reserve Corps, September 26, 1863.

SMITH, RYDER—Private, Co. G, One Hundred and Forty-fifth Infantry; transferred to Co. K, this regiment, January 12, 1864; absent, sick, since June 1, 1863, and at muster out of company; also borne as Smith Ryder.

SMITH, THEODORE—Private, Co. K, One Hundred and Forty-fifth Infantry; transferred to Co. I, this regiment, January 12, 1864; wounded, no date; mustered out, May 16, 1865, at Louisville, Ky.

SMITH, THEODORE G.—Age, 17 years. Enlisted, July 28, 1862, at Addison, to serve three years; mustered in as private, Co. F, August 5, 1862; wounded in action, September 17, 1862, at Antietam, Md.; discharged for disability, December 6, 1862.

SMITH, WILLIAM—Age, 40 years. Enlisted, July 20, 1862, at West Union, to serve three years; mustered in as private, Co. I, July 24, 1862; mustered out with company, June 5, 1865, near Washington, D.C.

SMITH, WILLIAM R.—Private, Co. B, One Hundred and Forty-fifth Infantry; transferred to Co. D, this regiment, January 12, 1864; mustered out with company, June 5, 1865, near Washington, D.C.; also borne as William H.

SMOLLEY, JOSEPH—Age, 23 years Enlisted at Corning, to serve three years, and mustered in as private, Co. I, August 7, 1862; wounded in action, May 25, 1864, at Dallas, Ga.; mustered out with company, June 5, 1865, near Washington, D.C.

SNOW, GEORGE—Age, 44 years. Enlisted at Danville, to serve one year, and mustered in as private, Co. F, September 9, 1864; deserted, November 10, 1864, at Atlanta, Ga.

SNYDER, JEREMIAH—Age, 18 years.

Enlisted, July 31, 1862, at Montour, to serve three years; mustered in as private, Co. H, August 2, 1862; discharged for disability, March 23, 1863, at Harper's Ferry, Va.

SOLATSKI, CHARLES—Age, 30 years. Enlisted, July 14, 1862, at Elmira, to serve three years; mustered in as sergeant, Co. B, July 19, 1862; mustered out with company, June 5, 1865, near Washington, D.C.; also borne as Solatski and Selatski.

SPENCER, ANDREW J.—Age, 21 years. Enlisted, July 21, 1862, at Elmira, to serve three years; mustered in as private, Co. E, July 22, 1862; transferred to Veteran Reserve Corps, July 1, 1863.

SPENCER, ARCHIBALD—Age, 18 years. Enlisted at Elmira, to serve three years, and mustered in as private, Co. E, August 12, 1862; mustered out with company, June 5, 1865, near Washington, D.C., as Archibald G.

SPENCER, CUMMING—Age, 27 years. Enlisted at Elmira, to serve three years, and mustered in as private, Co. E, July 26, 1862; deserted, August 12, 1862, at Elmira, N.Y.

STAGE, VAN BUREN—Age, 22 years. Enlisted, July 25, 1862, at Elmira, to serve three years; mustered in as musician, Co. B, July 26, 1862; died of typhoid fever, October 13, 1862, at Harper's Ferry, Va.

STAMP, JOHN A.—Age, 21 years. Enlisted at Elmira, to serve three years; mustered in as private, Co. G, August 6, 1862; captured, no date, during Goldsboro campaign; paroled, no date; mustered out, May 31, 1865, at Elmira, N.Y.

STANLEY, LUCIUS T.—Age, 18 years. Enlisted, July 17, at Elmira, to serve three years; mustered in as corporal A, July 28, 1862; mustered out with company, June 5, 1865, near Washington, D.C. see Sixty-fifth Infantry.

STANTON, SIMON—Age, 21 years. Enlisted at Elmira, to serve three years, and mustered in as private, Co. D, July 18, 1862; mustered out with company, June 5, 1865, near Washington, D.C.

STEILER, JOHN T.—Age, 39 years. Enlisted, June 12, 1862, at Elmira, to serve three years; mustered in as corporal, Co. E, June 16, 1862; returned to ranks, December 1, 1862; deserted, May 22, 1863, at hospital, Baltimore, Md.

STENBECK, AXEL F.—Age, 22 years. Enlisted, July 10, 1862, at Elmira, to serve three years; mustered in as private, Co. C, July 12, 1862, promoted corporal, prior to October 1863;

wounded in action, May 25, 1864, at Dallas, Ga.; returned to ranks, May 1, 1865; mustered out with company, June 5, 1865, near Washington, D.C., as Alex F. Steinbeck.

STENBECK, FRANS T.—Age, 24 years. Enlisted, July 15, 1862, at Elmira, to serve three years; mustered in as private, Co. C, July 16, 1862; killed in action, May 25, 1864, near [New Hope Church ] Dallas, Ga.; also borne as Francis I. Steinbeck.

STEPENFIELD, CHARLES—Age, 19 years. Enlisted at Elmira, to serve three years, and mustered in as private, Co. C, July 18, 1862; deserted, November 5, 1862, at Antietam Ford, Md.

STEPENFIELD, GEORGE—Age, 21 years. Enlisted, July 16, 1862, at Elmira, to serve three years; mustered in as private, Co. C, July 17, 1862; mustered out with company, June 5, 1865, near Washington, D.C.

STEPENFIELD, JOHN—Age, 29 years. Enlisted, July 17, 1862, at Elmira, to serve three years; mustered in as private, Co. C, July 18, 1862; deserted, November 5, 1862, at Antietam Ford, Md.

STEPENFIELD, WILLIAM H.—Age, 23 years. Enlisted at Elmira, to serve three years, and mustered in as private, Co. C, July 29, 1862; deserted, November 5, 1862, at Antietam Ford, Md.

STEVENS, HARMON—Age, 28 years. Enlisted, August 3, 1862, at Elmira, to serve three years, and mustered in as private, Co. G, August 6, 1862; mustered out, with company, June 5, 1865, near Washington, D.C.

STEVENS, HENRY—Private, Co. C, One Hundred and Forty-fifth Infantry; transferred to Co. A, this regiment, January 12, 1864; died of scrofula, September 29, 1864, at Division Field Hospital, Atlanta, Ga.

STEVENS, HOMER—Age, 23 years. Enlisted at Rathboneville, to serve three years, and mustered in as private, Co. A, December 30, 1863; wounded in action, May 25, 1864, at Dallas, Ga.; transferred to Co. A, Sixtieth Infantry, June 5, 1865, as Stephens.

STEVENS, JESSE E.—Age, 19 years. Enlisted at Elmira, to serve three years, and mustered in as private, Co. G, August 6, 1862; killed in action, September 17, 1862, at Antietam, Md.

STEVENS, RALPH—Age, 23 years. Enlisted, August 5, 1862, at Campbell, to serve three years; mustered in as private, Co. F, August 6, 1862; wounded in action, May 25, 1864, at Dallas, Ga.; discharged for disability, March 4, 1865.

STEWART, DANIEL A.—Age, 22 years. Enlisted at Elmira, to serve three years, and mustered in as private, Co. H, August 4, 1862; died of typhoid fever, September 18, 1863, at hospital, Newton University, Baltimore, Md.

STEWART, OLIVER D.—Age, 18 years. Enlisted at Addison, to serve three years, and mustered in as private, Co. B, December 10, 1863; promoted corporal, April 1, 1865; transferred to Co. A, Sixtieth Infantry, June 5, 1865.

STEWART, ROBERT—Private, Co. B, One Hundred and Forty-fifth Infantry; transferred to Co. D, this regiment, January 12, 1864; mustered out with company, June 5, 1865, near Washington, D.C.

STICKLER, GEORGE W.—Age, 18 years. Enlisted, August 5, 1862, at Campbell, to serve three years; mustered in as private, Co. F, August 6, 1862; wounded in action, June 19, 1864, at Noses Creek, Ga.; absent, in hospital at Indianapolis, Ind., at muster out of company.

STICKLER, GILBERT C.—Age, 21 years. Enlisted, August 5, 1862, at Campbell, to serve three years; mustered in as private, Co. F, August 6, 1862; died of camp fever, October 1, 1862.

STILLSON, LYMAN—Age, 23 years. Enlisted, August 9, 1862, at Corning, to serve three years; mustered in as private, Co. I, August 11, 1862; mustered out with company, June 5, 1865, near Washington, D.C.

STILLWELL, STEPHEN—Private, Co. G, One Hundred and Forty-fifth Infantry; transferred to Co. F, this regiment, January 12, 1864; absent, in hospital, since October 5, 1863, and at muster out of company.

STOBO, JOHN—Age, 18 years. Enlisted at Elmira, to serve three years, and mustered in as private, Co. D, August 7, 1862; promoted corporal, November 1, 1862; returned to ranks, no date; mustered out with company, June 5, 1865, near Washington, D.C., as Stobe.

STOCKING, HENRY—Age, 37 years. Enlisted at Elmira, to serve three years; mustered in as private, Co. G, July 31, 1862; wounded in action, May 25, 1864, at Dallas, Ga.; mustered out with company, June 5, 1865, near Washington, D.C.

STOCUM, HECTOR—Age, 26 years. Enrolled, August 4, 1862, at Elmira, to serve three years; mustered in as captain, Co. D, August 9, 1862; discharged, March 13, 1863, as Hecker M. Slocurn. Commissioned captain, September 6, 1862, with rank from August 4, 1862, original.

STODDARD, ALANSON—Age, 18 years. Enlisted, July 26, 1862, at Addison, to serve three years; mustered in as private, Co. F, July 29, 1862; wounded in action, May 25, 1864, at Dallas, Ga.; discharged for wounds, August 13, 1864.

STOKES, THOMAS J.—Age, 29 years. Enlisted at Elmira, to serve three years; mustered in as private, Co. K, August 9, 1862; transferred to Veteran Reserve Corps, September 30, 1863, as Steaks.

STORMS, CHARLES H.—Age, 21 years. Enlisted, August 11, 1862, at Elmira, to serve three years; mustered in as private, Co. K, August 13, 1862; died, June 19, 1864, at hospital, Chattanooga, Tenn.

STRAIT, JOHN—Age, 25 years. Enlisted at Rexville, to serve three years, and mustered in as private, Co. I, July 30, 1862; deserted, September 18, 1862, at Antietam, Md.

STRATTON, JOHN E.—Age, 38 years. Enlisted at Elmira, to serve three years, and mustered in as private, Co. G, August 6, 1862; promoted corporal, November 10, 1862; killed in action, May 3, 1863, at Chancellorsville, Va.

STRIKER, FREDERICK W.—Corporal, Co. I, One Hundred and Forty-fifth Infantry; transferred to Co. F, this regiment, as private, January 19, 1864; absent, sick in hospital, since May 1, 1863, and at muster out of company.

STRYKER, FRANK—Age, 19 years. Enlisted at Wheeler, to serve three years, and mustered in as private, Co. G, July 31, 1862; deserted, October 29, 1862, at Maryland Heights, Md.

STRYKER, FRANK W.—Corporal, Co. I, One Hundred and Forty-fifth Infantry; transferred to Co. H, this regiment, as private, January 12, 1864; wounded in action, May 3, 1863, at Chancellorsville, Va.; absent, in hospital at Philadelphia, Pa., at muster out of company.

SULLIVAN, BARTHOLOMEW—Age, 18 years. Enlisted, July 21, 1862, at Elmira, to serve three years; mustered in as private, Co. A, July 22, 1862; promoted corporal prior to April 10, 1863; wounded in action, May 16, 1865, at Averasborough, N.C.; mustered out, June 7, 1865, at Albany, N.Y.

SUTHERLAND, JOHN—Age, 21 years. Enlisted at Elmira, to serve three years, and mustered in as private, Co. D, August 6, 1862; promoted hospital steward, August 7, 1862; mustered out with regiment, June 5, 1865, near Washington, D.C.

SUTTEN, AMERY N.—Age, 44 years. Enlisted, September 17, 1864, at Elmira, to serve one year; mustered in as private, Co. B, September 19, 1864; mustered out with company, June 5, 1865, near Washington, D.C.

SWAIN, GEORGE—Age, 42 years. Enrolled, July 24, 1862, at Elmira, to serve three years; mustered in as second lieutenant, Co. B, July 26, 1862; as first lieutenant, June 2, 1863; wounded in action, May 25, 1864, at Dallas, Ga.; mustered in as captain, September 25, 1864; mustered out with company, June 5, 1865, near Washington, D.C. Commissioned second lieutenant, September 6, 1862, with rank from July 24, 1862, original; first lieutenant, May 11, 1863, with rank from March 20, 1863, vice M.V.B. Bachman, promoted; captain, September 19, 1864, with rank from July 8, 1864, vice A.N. Sill, promoted.

SWALLOW, ALBERT—Age, 18 years. Enlisted at Elmira, to serve three years, and mustered in as private, Co. H, July 25, 1862; captured in action, May 3, 1863, at Chancellorsville, Va.; paroled, no date; transferred to Veteran Reserve Corps, January 16, 1864.

SWEET, JERRY J.—Age, 36 years. Enlisted, July 29, 1862, at Hornellsville, to serve three years; mustered in as private, Co. K, July 31, 1862; mustered out with company, June 5, 1865, near Washington, D.C.

SWEITZER, WILLIAM S.—Age, 32 years. Enlisted at Elmira, to serve three years, and mustered in as sergeant, Co. E, July 22, 1862; discharged for disability, March 25, 1863, at Georgetown, D.C.; also borne as Switzer.

SWEZEY, STEPHEN J.—Private, Co. G, One Hundred and Forty-fifth Infantry; transferred to Co. E, this regiment, January 1864; discharged for disability, January 6, 1864, at Central Park Hospital, New York city, as Sweozey.

TAFT, JAMES BENEDICT—Age, 22 years. Enlisted at Addison, to serve three years, and mustered in as private, Co. F, August 11, 1862; wounded in action, May 25, 1864, at Dallas, Ga.; died of his wounds, June 9, 1864, at New Hope Church, Ga.

TAFT, JOHN G.—Age, 19 years. Enlisted, July 28, 1862, at Addison, to serve three years; mustered in as private, Co. F, July 29, 1862; appointed wagoner, prior to October 1863; mustered out with company, June 5, 1865, near Washington, D.C.

TAFT, STEPHEN A.—Age, 21 years. Enlisted, July 22, 1862, at Elmira, to serve three years; mustered in as private, Co. C, July 23, 1862; deserted, February 4, 1863, at Aquia Bay, Va.

TAYLOR, EMANUEL—Age, 29 years. Enlisted, July 30, 1862, at Elmira, to serve three years; mustered in as private, Co. G, August 6, 1862; promoted corporal, prior to October 1863; returned to ranks, no date; died of chronic diarrhea, August 10, 1864, at Nashville, Tenn.

TAYLOR, SAMUEL B.—Age, 31 years. Enrolled, June 15, 1862, at Elmira, to serve three years; mustered in as first sergeant, Co. E, June 21, 1862; as first lieutenant, February 21, 1863; mustered out with company, June 5, 1865, near Washington, D.C. Commissioned first lieutenant, March 28, 1863, with rank from February 20, 1863, vice W.L. Morgan, Jr., resigned.

TAYLOR, SHELDON G.—Age, 35 years. Enlisted, August 7, 1862, at Canisteo, to serve three years; mustered in as private, Co. K, August 8, 1862; discharged, March 20, 1863, at Convalescent Camp, Va.

TEAL, JACOB—Age, 42 years. Enlisted at Elmira, to serve three years, and mustered in as private, Co. B, July 22, 1862; mustered out with company, June 5, 1865, near Washington, D.C.

TEETER, SMITH—Age, 27 years. Enlisted, August 17, 1864, at Elmira, to serve three years; mustered in as private, Co. B, August 18, 1864; transferred to Co. A, Sixtieth Infantry, June 5, 1865.

TEN BROECK, JOHN—Age, 31 years. Enlisted, July 18, 1862, at Elmira, to serve three years; mustered in as private, Co. B, July 19, 1862; mustered out with company, June 5, 1865, near Washington, D.C.

TENBROOK, WILLIAM G.—Age, 18 years. Enlisted at Elmira, to serve three years, and mustered in as corporal, Co. A, June 21, 1862; returned to ranks prior to October 1863; mustered out with company, June 5, 1865, near Washington, D.C.

TEILRELL, see Turrell.

TERRELL, CHARLES S.—Private, Co. G, One Hundred and Forty-fifth Infantry; transferred to Co. E, this regiment, January 12, 1864; wounded in action, May 25, 1864, at Dallas, Ga.; mustered out with company, June 5, 1865, near Washington, D.C.

TERWILLIGER, CHARLES G.—Age, 37 years. Enlisted at Elmira, to serve three years, and mustered in as private, Co. B, July 22, 1862; died of typhoid fever, October 15, 1862, at Harper's Ferry, Va.

THACHER, EUGENE—Age, 18 years. Enlisted, July 21, 1862, at Hornellsville, to serve three years; mustered in as corporal, Co. K, August 11, 1862; promoted sergeant, September 1, 1863; killed in action, May 25, 1864, near Dallas, Ga., as Eugene Q.

THEURRER, FREDERICK—Private, Co. I, One Hundred and Forty-fifth Infantry; transferred to Co. C, this regiment, January 12, 1864; to Veteran Reserve Corps, January 15, 1864, as Thuerer.

THOMPSON, CHARLES W.—Age, 18 years. Enlisted, July 24, 1862, at Hector, to serve three years; mustered in as private, Co. H, July 25, 1862; deserted, September 22, 1862, at Maryland Heights, Md.

THORNTON, GEORGE W.—Age, 18 years. Enlisted, July 17, 1862, at Elmira, to serve three years; mustered in as private, Co. D, July 22, 1862; deserted, September 18, 1862, at Antietam, Md.

THORP, CHARLES—Age, 21 years. Enlisted at Elmira, to serve three years, and mustered in as private, Co. C, August 2, 1862; mustered out with company, June 5, 1865, near Washington, D.C.

THRALL, FAYETTE—Age, 21 years. Enlisted at Corning, to serve three years, and mustered in as private, Co. I, August 11, 1862; mustered out with company, June 5, 1865, near Washington, D.C.

THRALL, SIMEON J.—Age, 19 years. Enlisted at Corning, to serve three years, and mustered in as private, Co. I, July 29, 1862; promoted corporal, prior to October 1863; sergeant, January 15, 1865; mustered out with company June 5, 1865, near Washington, D.C.

THUERER, see Theurrer.

TILFORD, LEWIS C.—Age, 18 years. Enlisted, July 25, 1862, at Elmira, to serve three years; mustered in as private, Co. E, July 26, 1862; mustered out with company, June 5, 1865, near Washington, D.C.

TILLMAN, JAMES—Age, 21 years. Enlisted at Elmira, to serve three years; mustered in as musician, Co. C, July 18, 1862; mustered out with company, June 5, 1865, near Washington, D.C.

TITUS, CHARLES W.—Age, 22 years. Enlisted, July 26, 1862, at Addison, to serve three years; mustered in as private, Co. F, July 29, 1862; mustered out with company, June 5, 1865, near Washington, D.C.

TITUS, GEORGE R.—Age, 19 years. Enlisted, July 28, 1862, at Elmira, to serve three years; mustered in as private, Co. C, August 1, 1862; absent, in hospital at Philadelphia, Pa., since April 10, 1863, and at muster out of company.

TOBIAS, HILLORY H.—Age, 21 years. Enlisted, August 2, 1862, at Howard, to serve three years; mustered in as private, Co. K, August 13, 1862; captured, November 18, 1864, near Social Circle, Ga.; exchanged, February 28, 1865; mustered out with detachment, June 29, 1865, at hospital, York, Pa., as Tobias H. Hillery.

TOBIAS, WRIGHT—Age, 27 years. Enlisted at West Union, to serve three years, and mustered in as private, Co. I, July 28, 1862; deserted, October 8, 1862, at Maryland Heights, Md.

TOLES, JAMES J.—Age, 18 years. Enlisted, July 17, 1862, at Elmira, to serve three years; mustered in as private, Co. D, July 22, 1862; captured, November 18, 1864, near Social Circle, Ga.; paroled, no date; mustered out with company, June 5, 1865, near Washington, D.C.

TOMER, ADAM—Age, 22 years. Enlisted at Elmira, to serve three years, and mustered in as private, Co. G, August 5, 1862; promoted corporal, May 15, 1863; killed in action, May 25, 1864, at Dallas, Ga [New Hope Church].

TONGUE, ELI—Age, 21 years. Enlisted, July 15, 1862, at Elmira, to serve three years; mustered in as private, Co. E, July 16, 1862; wounded in action, September 17, 1862, at Antietam, Md.; promoted corporal, October 14, 1864; mustered out, October 3, 1865, at New York city.

TONGUE, HIRAM—Age, 34 years. Enlisted, July 26, 1862, at Addison, to serve three years; mustered in as private, Co. F, July 29, 1862; discharged for disability, December 6, 1862.

TONGUE, WILLIAM—Age, 19 years. Enlisted, July 23, 1862, at Elmira, to serve three years; mustered in as private, Co. E, July 26, 1862; wounded in action September 17, 1862, at Antietam, Md.; deserted, April 15, 1864; subsequent service in One Hundred and Sixty-first infantry.

TOTTEN, CYRUS L.—Age, 25 years. Enlisted, July 21, 1862, at Hornellsville, to serve three years; mustered in as corporal, Co. K, July 26, 1862; promoted sergeant, June 1, 1864; absent, sick in hospital, at muster out of company.

TOWNSEND, HORACE—Age, 37 years.

Enlisted, July 31, 1862, at Montour, to serve three years; mustered in as private, Co. H, August 4, 1862; mustered out with company, June 5, 1865, near Washington, D.C.

TRACY, BENJAMIN J.—Age, 22 years. Enlisted, July 15, 1862, at Elmira, to serve three years; mustered in as private, Co. E, July 18, 1862; promoted corporal, October 14, 1864; mustered out with company, June 5, 1865, near Washington, D.C.

TRACY, JAMES M.—Age, 32 years. Enlisted, July 15, 1862, at Elmira, to serve three years; mustered in as private, Co. E, July 18, 1862; mustered out with company, June 5, 1865, near Washington, D.C.

TRAINOR, JOHN—Age, 18 years. Enlisted at Elmira to serve three years, and mustered in as private, Co. A, July 19, 1862; wounded in action, May 3, 1863, at Chancellorsville, Va.; transferred to Co. H, Twelfth Regiment, Veteran Reserve Corps, October 9, 1863; transferred to this company, April 5, 1864; mustered out with company, June 5, 1865, near Washington, D.C.; also borne as Trainer

TRAVER, JOHN—Age, 19 years. Enlisted, June 17, 1862, at Elmira, to serve three years; mustered in as private, Co. A, June 18, 1862; captured, April 12, 1865, on campaign of the Carolinas; paroled, May 1, 1865; mustered out, June 30, 1865, at New York city; also borne as Travor.

TRAYNOR, PATRICK—Age, 21 years. Enlisted at Elmira, to serve three years, and mustered in as private, Co. B, July 24, 1862; mustered out with company, June 5, 1865, near Washington, D.C.

TROBRIDGE, HENRY—Age, 19 years. Enlisted, June 10, 1862, at serve three years, Co. E, June 26, 1862; deserted, August 12, 1862, at Elmira, N.Y., as Trowbridge.

TRUMBLE, JOHN—Age, 21 years. Enlisted at Elmira, to serve three years, and mustered in as private, Co. D, July 28, 1862; captured, November 18, 1864, near Social Circle, Ga.; paroled, no date; mustered out, June 22, 1865, at Elmira, N.Y., as Trumbell; also borne as Trumbull.

TUNIS, WILLIAM J. H.—Age, 16 years. Enlisted at Elmira, to serve three years, and mustered in as private, Co. A, June 23, 1862; discharged for disability, April 3, 1863, at Smoketown, Md.

TURRELL, JAMES—Age, 21 years. Enlisted, July 7, 1862, at Corning, to serve three years; mustered in as private, Co. I, July 24, 1862;

captured, March 8, 1865, near Fayetteville, N.C.; paroled, no date; mustered out with detachment, May 31, 1865, at Elmira, N.Y., as Tyrel; also borne as Terrell.

TUTTLE, RUSSELL M.—Age, 22 years. Enrolled at Hornellsville, to serve three years, and mustered in as first sergeant, Co. K, August 12, 1862; as second lieutenant, January 14, 1863; as first lieutenant, June 1, 1864; mustered out with company, June 5, 1865, near Washington, D.C. Commissioned second lieutenant, February 23, 1863, with rank from January 13, 1863, vice A.B. Howard, promoted; first lieutenant, July 12, 1864, with rank from June 1, 1864, vice A.B. Howard, appointed quartermaster.

TYLER, EMERY O.—Age, 18 years. Enlisted, July 22, 1862, at Elmira, to serve three years; mustered in as private, Co. B, July 23, 1862; mustered out with company, June 5, 1865, near Washington, D.C.

TYLER, THEODORE—Enlisted, July 22, 1862, at Elmira, to serve three years; mustered in as private, Co. G, and deserted July 24, 1862, at Elmira, N.Y.

TYRRELL, IRA M.—Age, 44 years. Enlisted, July 21, 1862, at Elmira, to serve three years; mustered in as private, Co. E, July 24, 1862; discharged, January 15, 1863, at Washington, D.C.

USHER, JEREMIAH—Private, Co. B, One Hundred and Forty-fifth Infantry; transferred to Co. D, this regiment, January 12, 1864; wounded in action, May 25, 1864, at Dallas, Ga.; transferred to Co. A, Sixtieth Infantry, June 5, 1865.

VANAUKEN, WILLIAM E.—Age, 21 years. Enlisted at Elmira, to serve three years, and mustered in as private, Co. D, August 7, 1862; promoted corporal, promoted April 10, 1863; sergeant, March 5, 1864; killed in action, May 25, 1864, at Dallas.

VAN CAMP, ANDREW J.—Age, 18 years. Enlisted, July 21, 1862, at Elmira, to serve three years; mustered in as private, Co. E, July 24, 1862; died of fever, November 3, 1862, at Harper's Ferry, Va.

VAN DEVERE, LEWIS—Private, Co. I, One Hundred and Forty-fifth Infantry; transferred to Co. I, this regiment, January 12, 1864; mustered out with company, June 5, 1865, near Washington, D.C., as Vandervere.

VAN DYCK, JOHN—Age, 23 years. Enlisted, August 6, 1862, at Canisteo, to serve three years; mustered in as private, Co. K, August 8, 1862; wounded in action, July 3, 1863, at Gettysburg, Pa.; died of his wounds, September 10, 1863, at Hartsville, N.Y.

VAN DYKE, TIMOTHY—Private, Co. B, One Hundred and Forty-fifth Infantry; transferred to Co. G, this regiment, January 12, 1864; to Veteran Reserve Corps, February 10, 1864.

VAN ETTEN, HARLAN—Age, 20 years. Enlisted at Corning, to serve three years, and mustered in as private, Co. I, August 11, 1862; mustered out with company, June 5, 1865, near Washington, D.C.

VAN GELDER, ELI B.—Age, 18 years. Enlisted, July 21, 1862, at Elmira, to serve three years; mustered in as private, Co. B, July 24, 1862; discharged for disability, January 30, 1863, at hospital, Washington, D.C.

VAN GELDER, LEVI B.—Age, 18 years. Enlisted, July 21, 1862, at Elmira, to serve three years; mustered in as private, Co. B, July 24, 1862; wounded in action, May 25, 1864, at Dallas, Ga.; died of his wounds, July 29, 1864, at Nashville, Tenn.

VAN GORDER, WILLIAM—Age, 41 years. Enlisted, July 21, 1862, at Elmira, to serve three years; mustered in as private, Co. B, July 23, 1862; transferred to Veteran Reserve Corps, November 4, 1863.

VAN GUILDER, ROBERT J.—Age, 24 years. Enlisted, July 18, 1862, at Elmira, to serve three years; mustered in as private, Co. B, July 18, 1862; discharged for disability, December 10, 1862, at hospital, Washington, D.C.

VAN LOON, CHRISTOPHER—Age, 44 years. Enlisted, August 4, 1862, at Elmira, to serve three years; mustered in as private, Co. H, August 5, 1862; mustered out with company, June 5, 1865, near Washington, D.C.; also borne as Van Loon.

VAN LOON, FREDERICK—Age, 21 years. Enlisted, August 4, 1862, at Elmira, to serve three years; mustered in as private, Co. H, August 5, 1862; mustered out with company, June 5, 1865, near Washington, D.C.

VAN LOON, JOHN—Age, 42 years. Enlisted, August 4, 1862, at Elmira, to serve three years; mustered in as private, Co. H, August 5, 1862; wounded in action, May 3, 1863, at Chancellorsville, Va.; discharged for disability, October 28, 1863, at Washington, D.C.; also borne as Van Loon.

VAN NESS, FOSTER—Age, 21 years. Enlisted, July 14, 1862, at Elmira, to serve three years; mustered in as private, Co. B, July 16, 1862; transferred to U.S. Engineer Corps, April 16, 1863.

VAN VALKENBURGH, EDWARD P.—Age, 24 years. Enrolled at Hope Landing, Va., to serve three years, and mustered in as first lieutenant, Co. A, March 20, 1863; as captain, January 21, 1865; mustered out with company, June 5, 1865, near Washington, D.C.; prior service as private, Co. I, First Mich. Engineers. Commissioned first lieutenant, March 23, 1863, with rank from March 20, 1863, vice J.M. Losie, promoted; captain, July 31, 1865, with rank from January. 21; 1865, vice J. M. Losie, discharged.

VAN VALKENBURGH, ROBERT B.—Age, 40 years. Enrolled at Elmira, to serve three years, and mustered in as colonel, August 13, 1862; discharged, October 9, 1862. Commissioned colonel, September 6, 1862, with rank from August 9, 1862, original.

VAN VLEET, JAMES F.—Age, 24 years. Enlisted, August 4, 1862, at Elmira, to serve three years; mustered in as private, Co. H, August 5, 1862; promoted corporal, prior to April 10, 1863; sergeant, June 1, 1864; mustered out with company, June 5, 1865, near Washington, D.C.

VAN VLEET, JOHN D. M.—Age, 19 years. Enlisted, July 27, 1862, at Montour, to serve three years; mustered in as private, Co. H, July 30, 1862; wounded in action, May 25, 1864, at Dallas, Ga.; died of his wounds, June 24, 1864, at hospital, Chattanooga, Tenn.

VAUGHN, JOSEPH—Corporal, Co. F, One Hundred and Forty-fifth Infantry; transferred to Co. F, this regiment, as private, January 12, 1864; absent, sick at New York city, at muster out of company.

VEAZIE, ARTHUR—Age, 18 years. Enlisted at Corning, to serve three years, and mustered in as private, Co. I, August 7, 1862; wounded in action, May 15, 1864, at Resaca, Ga., and May 25, 1864, at Dallas, Ga.; mustered out with company, June 5, 1865, near Washington, D.C.

VELIE, FRANKLIN—Age, 23 years. Enlisted at Elmira, to serve three years, and mustered in as private, Co. C, August 4, 1862; wounded in action, May 25, 1864, at Dallas, Ga.; mustered out with company, June 5, 1865, near Washington, D.C.

VELIE, WILLIAM—Age, 27 years. Enlisted at Elmira, to serve three years, and mustered in as private, Co. C, July 22, 1862; discharged for disability, February 28, 1863, at hospital, Philadelphia, Pa.

VINCENT, RICHARD—Age, 21 years. Enlisted at Elmira, to serve three years, and mustered in as private, Co. D, July 19, 1862; mustered out with company, June 5, 1865, near Washington, D.C.

VOSBURGH, DAVID D.—Age, 24 years. Enlisted at Elmira, to serve three years, and mustered in as private, Co. D, July 25, 1862; discharged, December 24, 1862.

VREDENBURGH, FRANCIS D.—Age, 21 years. Enlisted at Elmira, to serve three years, and mustered in as private, Co. D, August 8, 1862; deserted, no date, from hospital.

VREELAND, LOUIS W.—Private, Co. I, One Hundred and Forty-fifth Infantry; transferred to Co. B, this regiment, January 12, 1864; killed in action, May 25, 1864, at Dallas, Ga.

VROMAN, JAMES—Age, 19 years. Enlisted at Elmira, to serve three years, and mustered in as private, Co. G, August 4, 1862; transferred to Veteran Reserve Corps, January 15, 1864, as Vrooman.

WAGER, ANDREW H.—Age, 18 years. Enlisted at Elmira to serve three years, and mustered in as private, Co. H, July 25, 1862; wounded in action, May 25, 1864, at Dallas, Ga.; discharged for disability, March 21, 1865, at hospital, Louisville, Ky.

WAGNER, FREDERICK W.—Age, 20 years. Enlisted, July 30, 1862, at Addison, to serve three years; mustered in as private, Co. F, August 5, 1862; died of camp fever, January 10, 1863.

WAGNER, PETER—Age, 21 years. Enlisted, July 18, 1862, at Elmira, to serve three years; mustered in as private, Co. B, July 19, 1862; promoted corporal, January 1, 1863; wounded no date; mustered out, June 19, 1865, at David's Island, New York, harbor; also borne as Peter Wagner, Jr.

WAIT, WILLIAM H.—Age, 18 years. Enlisted, July 7, 1862, at Elmira, to serve three years; mustered in as private, Co. E, July 18, 1862; mustered out with company, June 5, 1865, near Washington, D.C.

WALKER, FRANCIS M.—Age, 22 years. Enlisted, July 21, 1862, at Elmira, to serve three years; mustered in as sergeant, Co. D, July 23, 1862; mustered out with company, June 5, 1865, near Washington, D.C.

WALKER, WASHINGTON—Age, 19 years. Enlisted at Corning, to serve three years, and mustered in as private, Co. I, July 29, 1862; deserted, December 9, 1862, at Antietam Ford, Md.

WALKER, WILLIAM F.—Private, Co. K, One

Hundred and Forty-fifth Infantry; transferred to Co. I, this regiment, January 12, 1864; mustered out, May 20, 1865, at Foster Hospital, New Berne, N.C.

WALLACE, SYLVANUS—Enlisted, July 22, 1862, at Elmira to serve three years; mustered in as private, Co. G, July 25, 1862; discharged for disability, March 20, 1863, at Fairfax Seminary, Va.

WALLACE, WILLIAM H.—Age, 34 years. Enlisted at Elmira, to serve three years, and mustered in as corporal, Co. E, July 26, 1862; mustered out, June 17, 1865, at Elmira, N.Y.

WALTERS, ALFRED—Private, Co. K, One Hundred and Forty-fifth Infantry; transferred to Co. I, this regiment, January 12, 1864; died of chronic diarrhea, January 29, 1865, at Nashville, Tenn., as Alfred S.

WALTERS, CORNELIUS—Private, Co. K, One Hundred and Forty-fifth Infantry; transferred to Co. I, this regiment, January 12, 1864; wounded in action, May 25, 1864, at Dallas, Ga.; mustered out with company, June 5, 1865, near Washington, D.C.

WALTON, WILLIAM—Corporal, Co. B, One Hundred and Forty-fifth Infantry; transferred to Co. E, this regiment, January 12, 1864; returned to ranks, March 26, 1864; mustered out with company, June 5, 1865, near Washington, D.C.

WAMBOUGH, GEORGE W.—Age, 27 years. Enlisted, July 26, 1862, at Addison, to serve three years; mustered in as wagoner, Co. F, July 29, 1862; discharged for disability, June 3, 1863, as Wornbough.

WANSER, see Wauser.

WARD, ALBERT—Age, 21 years. Enlisted, July 15, 1862, at Elmira, to serve three years; mustered in as corporal, Co. C, July 22, 1862; wounded in action, May 3, 1863, at Chancellorsville, Va.; promoted sergeant, no date; discharged for wounds, July 27, 1863, at hospital, Washington, D.C.

WARNER, JOHN H.—Age, 18 years. Enlisted at Rathboneville, to serve three years, and mustered in as private, Co. A, December 31, 1863; transferred to Co. A, Sixtieth Infantry, June 5, 1865.

WARNER, WILLIAM F.—Age, 18 years. Enlisted at Elmira, to serve three years, and mustered in as private, Co. G, August 6, 1862; mustered out with company, June 5, 1865, near Washington, D.C.

WATSON, ALPHEUS D.—Age, 19 years. Enlisted, August 4, 1862, at Addison, to serve three years; mustered in as private, Co.

F, August 5, 1862; died of putrid sore throat, March 21, 1863.

WATSON, GEORGE D.—Age, 18 years. Enlisted, August 2, 1862, at Addison, to serve three years; mustered in as private, Co. F, August 5, 1862; wounded in action, June 21, 1864, at Noses Creek, Ga.; mustered out with company, June 5, 1865, near Washington, D.C.

WAUSER, ABRAHAM E.—Age, 28 years. Enlisted at Elmira, to serve three years, and mustered in as private, Co. D, August 1, 1862; absent, in hospital at Nashville, Tenn., at muster out of company; also borne as Wenser and Wanser.

WEED, PETER—Age, 19 years. Enlisted at Elmira, to serve three years, and mustered in as private, Co. A, July 17, 1862; captured and paroled, no dates; promoted corporal, March 1, 1865; mustered out, June 6, 1865, at Elmira, N.Y.

WEEKS, GEORGE—Age, 18 years. Enlisted at Corning, to serve three years, and mustered in as private, Co. I, August 6, 1862; mustered out with company, June 5, 1865, near Washington, D.C., as Wicks.

WEEKS, JAMES—Age, 18 years. Enlisted, August 4, 1862, at Addison, to serve three years; mustered in as private, Co. F, August 5, 1862; transferred to Co. B, Sixtieth Infantry, June 5, 1865.

WEIDNER, JOHN—Private, Co. G, One Hundred and Forty-fifth Infantry; transferred to Co. E, this regiment, January 12, 1864; promoted corporal, October 14, 1864; mustered out with company, June 5, 1865, near Washington, D.C.

WELLER, EDWIN—Age, 22 years. Enrolled, July 25, 1862, at Havana, to serve three years; mustered in as first sergeant, Co. H, July 30, 1862; as first lieutenant, November 2, 1863; mustered out with company, June 5, 1865, near Washington, D.C.; also borne as Weller. Commissioned first lieutenant, October 22, 1863, with rank from September 14, 1863, vice T.K. Middleton, resigned. as Wellar.

WELLS, A. HENRY—Age, 23 years. Enlisted at Elmira, to serve three years, and mustered in as corporal, Co. D, July 31, 1862; no further record.

WELLS, DAVID C.—Age, 22 years. Enlisted, August 6, 1862, at Howard, to serve three years; mustered in as sergeant, Co. K, August 8, 1862; returned to ranks prior to October 1863; promoted sergeant,

September 1, 1864; mustered out with company, June 5, 1865, near Washington, D.C.

WELTY, WILLIAM—Age, 21 years. Enlisted at Elmira, to serve three years, and mustered in as private, Co. C, July 23, 1862; mustered out with company, June 5, 1865, near Washington, D.C.

WEMPLE, EPHRAIM V.—Age, 26 years. Enlisted at Elmira, to serve three years, and mustered in as corporal, Co. G, August 2, 1862; discharged for disability, no date, at Convalescent Camp, Va., as Wimple, Ephraim N.

WEMPLE, JOHN H.—Age, 28 years. Enlisted at Elmira, to serve three years, and mustered in as private, Co. G, August 4, 1862; wounded in action, May 25, 1864, at Dallas, Ga.; mustered out with company, June 5, 1865, near Washington, D.C., as Wimple.

WERDEIN, ADOLF—Age, 31 years. Enlisted at Wayland, to serve three years, and mustered in as private, Co. I, August 4, 1862; promoted corporal, prior to October 1863; sergeant, June 30, 1864; mustered out with company, June 5, 1865, near Washington, D.C., as Worden, Adolphus.

WESCOTT, GEORGE—Age, 23 years. Enlisted, August 7, 1862, at Corning, to serve three years; mustered in as private, Co. I, August 12, 1862; promoted corporal, January 15, 1865; mustered out with company, June 5, 1865, near Washington, D.C.

WEST, DEAN—Age, 22 years. Enlisted at Elmira, to serve three years, and mustered in as private, Co. D, July 30, 1862; mustered out with company, June 5, 1865, near Washington, D.C.

WETMORE, DIX—Age, 44 years. Enlisted at Wayland, to serve three years, and mustered in as private, Co. I, August 4, 1862; transferred to Veteran Reserve Corps, no date.

WHEAT, GEORGE W.—Age, 37 years. Enlisted at Elmira, to serve three years, and mustered in as private, Co. B, July 2, 1862; discharged for disability, February 29, 1864, at hospital, Camp Dennison, Ohio.

WHEATON, FRANCIS—Age, 18 years. Enlisted, July 31, 1862, at Elmira, to serve three years; mustered in as private, Co. G, August 6, 1862; died, October 10, 1862, at hospital, Harper's Ferry, Va.

WHEELER, EDWARD—Age, 19 years. Enlisted at Corning, to serve three years, and mustered in as private, Co. I, August 4, 1862; Captured in action, March 8, 1865, near Fayetteville, N.C.; paroled, no date;

mustered out with detachment, May 31, 1865, at Elmira, N.Y.

WHEELER, NELSON—Age, 21 years. Enlisted at Corning, to serve three years, and mustered in as private, Co. I, August 5, 1862; mustered out with company, June 5, 1865, near Washington, D.C.

WHEELER, WILLIAM—Age, 21 years. Enlisted, June 9, 1862, at Elmira, to serve three years; mustered in as private, Co. A, June 10, 1862; mustered out with company, June 5, 1865, near Washington, D.C.

WHEELER, WILLIAM—Age, 27 years. Enlisted at Corning, to serve three years, and mustered in as private, Co. I, August 8, 1862; mustered out with company, June 5, 1865, near Washington, D.C.

WHEELER, WILLIAM B.—Age, 22 years. Enlisted, July 29, 1862, at Montour, to serve three years; mustered in as private, Co. H, July 30, 1862; mustered out, June 12, 1865, at Crittenden Hospital, Louisville, Ky.

WHITE, CHARLES—Private, Co. G, One Hundred and Forty-fifth Infantry; transferred to Co. E, this regiment, January 12, 1864; mustered out with company, June 5, 1865, near Washington, D.C.

WHITE, FRANCIS L.—Age, 30 years. Enlisted, August 11, 1862, at Greenwood, to serve three years; mustered in as private, Co. K, August 13, 1862; wounded in action, May 25, 1864, near Dallas, Ga.; discharged, February 9, 1865.

WHITE, HENRY F.—Age, 28 years. Enlisted at Elmira, to serve three years, and mustered in as private, Co. A, July 16, 1862; wounded in action, September 17, 1862, at Antietam, Md.; discharged for disability, January 1.2, 1863, at Philadelphia, Pa.

WHITE, JAMES—Age, 28 years. Enlisted, July 7, 1862, at Elmira, to serve three years; mustered in as private, Co. E, July 18, 1862; wounded in action, May 25, 1864, at Dallas, Ga.; mustered out with company, June 5, 1865, near Washington.

WHITE, LEONARD—Age, 31 years. Enlisted at Elmira, to serve three years, and mustered in as private, Co. H, July 25, 1862; transferred to Co. I, Ninth Regiment, Veteran Reserve Corps, March 16, 1864; mustered out, June 22, 1865, at Washington, D.C.

WHITE, MILLANKTON—Age, 44 years. Enlisted, July 21, 1862, at Elmira, to serve three years; mustered in as private, Co. E, July 24, 1862; discharged for disability, February 14, 1863, at Fairfax Seminary, Va.

WHITE, PARLEY S.—Age, 27 years. Enlisted at Campbell, to serve three years, and mustered in as private, Co. F, August 6, 1862; died of camp fever, November 2, 1862.

WHITEHEAD, AARON—Age, 42 years. Enlisted at Elmira, to serve three years, and mustered in as wagoner, Co. G, August 6, 1862; discharged for disability, as private, January 9, 1863, at Philadelphia, Pa.

WHITEHEAD, HORACE—Corporal, Co. I, One Hundred and Forty-fifth Infantry; transferred to Co. O, this regiment, January 12, 1864; returned to ranks, August 1, 1864; mustered out with company June 5, 1865, near Washington, D.C.

WHITEHORN, ABRAM—Age, 32 years. Enrolled, July 25, 1862, at Havana, to serve three years; mustered in as sergeant, Co. H, August 2, 1862; as second lieutenant, June 9, 1863; captured, no date; paroled, February 1865; discharged, to date May 15, 1865. Commissioned second lieutenant, May 11, 1863, with rank from February 25, 1863, vice L.O. Sayler, dismissed.

WHITFORD, AUGUSTUS L—Age, 34 years. Enlisted at Elmira, to serve three years, and mustered in as private, Co. G, July 31, 1862; transferred to Co. B, Sixtieth Infantry, June 5, 1865.

WICKS, see Weeks.

WIGGINS, JOHN B.—Age, 24 years. Enlisted, July 5, 1862, at Elmira, to serve three years; mustered in as private, Co. A, July 21, 1862; mustered out with company, June 5, 1865, near Washington, D.C.

WILCOX, JAMES—Age, 25 years. Enlisted at Elmira, to serve three years, and mustered in as private, Co. G, August 8, 1862; died of typhoid fever, June 30, 1864, at hospital, Chattanooga, Tenn.

WILKINSON, ALBERT—Sergeant, Co. G, One Hundred and Forty-fifth Infantry; transferred to Co. F, this regiment, as private, January 12, 1864; absent, in hospital at Louisville, Ky., since October 18, 1863, and at muster out of company.

WILKINSON, GEORGE—Age, 26 years. Enlisted, July 30, 1862, at Elmira, to serve three years; mustered in as private, Co. C, August 1, 1862; deserted, August 31, 1862, at Arlington Heights, Va.

WILKINSON, MELVILLE C.—Age, 26 years. Enrolled at Elmira, to serve three years, and mustered in as first lieutenant, Co. A, July 23, 1862; promoted captain, August 9, 1862; discharged, January 26,

1863. Commissioned first lieutenant, September 6, 1862, with rank from July 23, 1862, original; captain, September 6, 1862, with rank from August 9, 1862, vice E.E. Crane, appointed chaplain.

WILLIAMS, CHARLES—Private, Co. K, One Hundred and Forty-fifth Infantry; transferred to Co. I, this regiment, January 12, 1864; to Co. I, Sixtieth Infantry, June 5, 1865.

WILLIAMS, HENRY—Private, Co. K, One Hundred and Forty-fifth Infantry; transferred to Co. I, this regiment, January 12, 1864; mustered out, June 20, 1865, at Harts Island, New York, harbor.

WILLIAMS, JAMES W.—Age, 40 years. Enlisted at Elmira, to serve three years, and mustered in as private, Co. B, July 22, 1862; promoted corporal, prior to April 10, 1863; wounded in action, May 3, 1863, at Chancellorsville, Va.; transferred to Fourteenth Regiment, Veteran Reserve Corps, no date; mustered out, July 22, 1865, at Elmira, N.Y.

WILLIAMS, JOHN P.—Age, 27 years. Enlisted at Elmira, to serve three years, and mustered in as private, Co. D, August 1, 1862; deserted, no date, at Elmira, N.Y.

WILLIAMS, WILLIAM—Age, 21 years. Enlisted, July 14, 1862, at Elmira, to serve three years; mustered in as private, Co. C, July 16, 1862; wounded in action, May 25, 1864, near Dallas, Ga.; killed in a skirmish, March 8, 1865, near Rockingham, N.C.

WILLOUR, ALONZO—Age, 37 years. Enlisted at Bath, to serve three years, and mustered in as private, Co. G, August 4, 1862; mustered out with company, June 5, 1865, near Washington, D.C.; also borne as Willow.

WILLOVER, CHARLES P.—Age, 21 years. Enlisted, July 15, 1862, at Elmira, to serve three years; mustered in as private, Co. E, July 18, 1862; promoted corporal, no date; died of fever, October 26, 1862, at Harper's Ferry, Va.

WILLSON, A. D.—Private, Co. G, One Hundred and Forty-fifth Infantry; transferred to Co. K, this regiment, January 12, 1864; to Veteran Reserve Corps, January 16, 1864.

WILSON, ALBERT D.—Private, Co. G, One Hundred and Forty-fifth Infantry; transferred to Co. E, this regiment, January 12, 1864; deserted, February 28, 1865; see A.D. Willson, Co. K.

WILSON, BENJAMIN C.—Age, 31 years. Enrolled at Elmira, to serve three years; mustered in as first lieutenant, Co. I, August

11, 1862; discharged, December 21, 1862. Commissioned first lieutenant, September 6, 1862, with rank from August 9, 1862, original.

WILSON, JAMES—Age, 33 years. Enlisted, August 1, 1862, at Montour, to serve three years; mustered in as private, Co. H, August 2, 1862; discharged for disability, November 12, 1862, at Convalescent Camp, Alexandria, Va.

WIMPLE, see Wemple.

WINTERS, MARTIN—Private, Co. B, One Hundred and Forty-fifth Infantry; transferred to Co. G, this regiment, January 19, 1864; mustered out with company, June 5, 1865, near Washington, D.C.

WISNER, JEFFERY A.—Age, 18 years. Enlisted at Elmira, to serve three years, and mustered in as sergeant, Co. A, July 17, 1862; returned to ranks prior to October 1863; discharged, May 17, 1864, for promotion to second lieutenant, One Hundred and Seventy-ninth Infantry.

WITT, HENRY—Age, 28 years. Enlisted at Corning, to serve three years, and mustered in as private, Co. I, February 24, 1864; transferred to Co. B, Sixtieth Infantry, June 5, 1865; prior service in Co. D, Twenty-third Infantry.

WOMBOUGH, see Warnbough.

WONSER, see Wauser.

WONSER, JOHN H.—Age, 32 years. Enlisted at Elmira, to serve three years, and mustered in as private, Co. D, August 1, 1862; deserted, September 7, 1862; returned, April 15, 1863; again deserted, April 29, 1863, at Kelly's Ford, Va.; also borne as Wouser.

WOOD, JAMES C.—Age, 21 years. Enlisted at Elmira, to serve three years, and mustered in as private, Co. H, July 25, 1862; discharged for disability, August 14, 1863, at Convalescent Camp, Alexandria, Va.

WOOD, JEREMIAH V.—Age, 32 years. Enlisted at Elmira, to serve three years; mustered in as corporal, Co. O, July 9, 1862; promoted sergeant, prior to April 10, 1863; died of typhoid fever, May 30, 1864, at Fourth Army Corps Field Hospital, near Dallas, Ga.

WOOD, LEWIS—Age, 44 years. Enlisted, August 4, 1862, at Elmira, to serve three years; mustered in as private, Co. K, August 11, 1862; mustered out, May 29, 1865, at Mc Dougall Hospital, New York harbor.

WOOD, WALTER—Age, 22 years. Enlisted, July 14, 1862, at Elmira, to serve three years;

mustered in as sergeant, Co. B, July 16, 1862; transferred, as private, to Sixth Regiment, Veteran Reserve Corps, September 30, 1863; mustered out as quartermaster-sergeant, with detachment, July 5, 1865, at Cincinnati, O., as Walter H.

WOOD, WILLIAM W.—Corporal, Co. K, One Hundred and Forty-fifth Infantry; transferred to Co. F, this regiment, January 12, 1864; mustered out with company, June 5, 1865, near Washington, D.C.

WOODRUFF, LEWELLYN—Age, 18 years. Enlisted, July 21, 1862, at Elmira, to serve three years; mustered in as private, Co. E, July 24, 1862; wounded in action, May 3, 1863, at Chancellorsville, Va.; discharged for disability, September 25, 1863, at Convalescent Camp, Va.

WOODRUFF, WILSON—Age, 23 years. Enlisted, July 9, 1862, at Elmira, to serve three years; mustered in as private, Co. C, July 12, 1862; transferred to Veteran Reserve Corps, February 15, 1864.

WORDEN, ADOLPHUS, see Adolf Werdein.

WORDEN, ETHAN—Age, 20 years. Enlisted at Elmira, to serve three years, and mustered in as private, Co. H, July 25, 1862; died of typhoid fever, October 22, 1862, at Harper's Ferry, Va.

WORRELL, JOHN—Age, 35 years. Enlisted at Addison, to serve three years, and mustered in as private, Co. G, December 10, 1863; died of chronic diarrhea, August 19, 1864, in field hospital, near Atlanta, Ga.

WOUSER, see Wonser.

WRIGHT, CHARLES—Private, Co. K, One Hundred and Forty-fifth Infantry; transferred to Co. I, this regiment, January 12, 1864; promoted corporal, January 15, 1865; mustered out with company, June 5, 1865, near Washington, D.C.

WRIGHT, FREDERICK A.—Age, 23 years. Enlisted at Elmira, to serve three years, and mustered in as private, Co. C, July 9, 1862; discharged for disability, February 4, 1863, at hospital, Philadelphia, Pa.

WRIGHT, Jr., GILBERT—Age, 24 years. Enlisted, July 28, 1862, at Hornellsville, to serve three years; mustered in as corporal, Co. K, July 31, 1862; promoted sergeant, prior to October 1863; wounded in action, May 25, 1864, near Dallas, Ga.; mustered out, July 12, 1865, at Elmira, N.Y.

WYNNE, PATRICK—Private, Co. C, One Hundred and Forty-fifth Infantry; transferred to Co. H, this regiment, January 12,

1864; mustered out with company, June 5, 1865, near Washington, D.C.

YAPLE, CHANCY C.—Age, 45 years. Enlisted, June 11, 1862, at Elmira, to serve three years; mustered in as musician, Co. E, June 16, 1862; mustered out September 19, 1865, as of Co. F, at Elmira, N.Y., as Sapple.

YEOMANS, JAMES A.—Age, 21 years. Enlisted, July 29, 1862, at Havana, to serve three years; mustered in as wagoner. Co. I, July 30, 1862; wounded in action, May 25, 1864, at Dallas, Ga.; mustered out with company, June 5, 1865, near Washington, D.C.; also borne as Youmans.

YOUMANS, see Eumans.

YOUMANS, OLIVER—Age, 30 years. Enlisted at Elmira, to serve three years, and mustered in as private, Co. C, July 9, 1862; mustered out with company, June 5, 1865, near Washington, D.C.

YOUNG, CHARLES H.—Age, 23 years. Enlisted at Rathboneville to serve three years, and mustered in as private, Co. F, March 30, 1864; transferred to Co. B, Sixtieth Infantry, June 5, 1865.

YOUNG, CURTIS S.—Age, 32 years. Enlisted at Rathboneville, to serve three years, and mustered in as private, Co. F, December 31, 1863; transferred to Co. B, Sixtieth Infantry, June 5, 1865.

YOUNG, FREDERICK W.—Age 21 years, at Addison, to serve three years; mustered in as private, Co. F, July 29, 1862; promoted corporal, April 16, 1864; wounded in action, May 25, 1864, at Dallas, Ga.; mustered out with company, June 5, 1865, near Washington, D.C.

YOUNG, Jr., JAMES B.—Age, 25 years. Enlisted, July 28, 1862, at Addison, to serve three years; mustered in as corporal, Co. F, July 29, 1862; transferred to Sixteenth Company, Second Battalion, Veteran Reserve Corps, September 1, 1863; mustered out with detachment, June 29, 1865, at Washington, D.C.; also borne as Youngs.

YOUNG, WILLIAM H—Age, 22 years. Enlisted at Rathboneville, to serve three years, and mustered in as private, Co. F, March 30, 1864; killed in action, May 25, 1864, at Dallas, Ga.

YOUNGS, THOMAS JEFFERSON—Age, 25 years. Enlisted, July 28, 1862, at Addison, to serve three years; mustered in as private, Co. F, July 29, 1862; promoted sergeant, March 9, 1863; first sergeant, January 19, 1865; mustered out, July 5, 1865, at Elmira, N.Y., as Young.

ZEIGLER, FREDERICK—Private, Co. G, One Hundred and Forty-fifth Infantry; transferred to Co. K, this regiment, January 12, 1864; absent, sick, since October 5, 1863, and at muster out of company.

ZIMMERMAN, REUBEN—Age, 19 years. Enlisted, July 24, 1862, at Hornellsville, to serve three years; mustered in as corporal, Co. K, July 31, 1862; discharged March 20, 1863, at Baltimore, Md.

# Chapter Notes

## *Chapter 1*

1. *Elmira Advertiser*, July 7, 1862
2. *Elmira Advertiser*, June 7, 1862
3. Adjutant Hull Fanton speech 17th reunion 107th Reg't Assoc. Sept. 17, 1883
4. *Havana Journal*, July 12, 1862
5. *Elmira Advertiser*, May 30, 1862
6. *Elmira Advertiser*, May 31, 1862
7. *Elmira Advertiser*, June 3, 1862
8. *Elmira Advertiser*, June 4, 1862
9. *Elmira Advertiser*, June 18, 1862
10. *Elmira Weekly Gazette*, June 19, 1862
11. Memoirs of Col. Silas W. Burt, Former AIG, NY Nat'l Guard. Edited by the NY State Historian and issued as *War of the Rebellion Series—Bulletin, No. 1*
12. *Addison Advertiser*, July 2, 1862
13. *History of Chemung County*, Ausborn Towner
14. *Elmira Advertiser*, July 12, 1862
15. *Elmira Advertiser*, July 19, 1862
16. A.S. Diven speech, 5th 107th Regimental Reunion, Sept. 17, 1871
17. *Elmira Advertiser & Republican*, July 19, 1862
18. *Havana Journal*, July 12, 1862
19. *Addison Advertiser*, July 16, 1862
20. *Havana Journal*, July 19, 1862
21. *Elmira Advertiser*, May 7, 1862
22. *Elmira Advertiser*, May 27, 1862
23. *Havana Journal*, July 19, 1862
24. Original handbill is on display in the Montour Falls Library
25. *Havana Journal*, July 19, 1862
26. *Elmira Advertiser*, July 12, 1862
27. *Elmira Advertiser*, July 19, 1862
28. *Addison Advertiser*, July 16, 1862
29. *Elmira Advertiser*, July 19, 1862
30. Hull Fanton speech 17th reunion 107th Reg't Assoc. Sept. 17, 1883
31. *Elmira Gazette*, July 17, 1862
32. *Elmira Advertiser*, July 26, 1862
33. *Elmira Advertiser*, July 19, 1862.
34. *Havana Journal*, June 14, 1862
35. Report of the New York State Asst. Adjutant General on raising troops for the Civil War.
36. *Elmira Advertiser*, July 19, 1862
37. Arthur S Fitch's Journal, Chemung County Historical Society
38. Elmira Depot, General Order No. 4, May 25, 1861
39. Arthur S. Fitch's Journal
40. *Steuben Courier*, July 23, 1862
41. *Hornellsville Tribune*
42. *Elmira Advertiser*, July 26, 1862
43. *Elmira Gazette*, July 31, 1862
44. *Havana Journal*, Aug. 2, 1862
45. *Hornellsville Tribune*, July 31, 1862
46. *Elmira Gazette*, July 31, 1862
47. *Addison Advertiser*, July 23, 1862
48. Record Group 94, National Archives, Washington, D.C.
49. *Corning Democrat*, July 31, 1862
50. *Elmira Gazette*, July 31, 1862
51. *Elmira Advertiser*, July 26, 1862
52. *Addison Advertiser*, July 30, 1862
53. Arthur S. Fitch's Journal
54. *Elmira Advertiser*, Aug. 2, 1862
55. *Havana Journal*, Aug. 2, 1862
56. *Hornellsville Tribune*, July 31, 1862
57. *Elmira Gazette*, July 31, 1862
58. *Addison Advertiser*, July 16, 1862
59. *Addison Advertiser*, July 30, 1862
60. *Steuben Courier*, Aug. 6, 1862
61. *Steuben Courier*, July 30, 1862
62. A.S. Diven speech, 5th reunion 107th Reg't Assoc. Sept. 17, 1871
63. Arthur S. Fitch's Journal
64. *Addison Advertiser*, June 30, 1862
65. Arthur S. Fitch's Journal
66. *Steuben Courier*, Aug. 6, 1862
67. Arthur S. Fitch's Journal
68. Notes of Roger Sturcke, Chemung County Historical Society
69. Fox, William. *Slocum and His Men*, Page 156
70. Co. F initial issue of clothing and equipment, John Orr collection, NYS Historical Assoc.
71. *Steuben Courier*, July 30, 1862
72. *Addison Advertiser*, July 30, 1862
73. *Havana Journal*, Aug. 2, 1862
74. Arthur S. Fitch's Journal
75. *Steuben Courier*, Aug. 6, 1862
76. *Corning Journal*, Aug. 7, 1862
77. *Steuben Courier*, Aug. 13, 1862
78. Arthur S. Fitch's Journal

79. Record Group 94, National Archives
80. *The Advocate, Bath*, Aug. 13, 1862
81. Arthur S. Fitch's Journal
82. *Corning Democrat*, Aug. 14, 1862. The original letter is the property of the Montour Falls library.
83. Arthur S. Fitch's Journal
84. *Elmira Weekly Gazette*, Aug. 14, 1862
85. *Elmira Advertiser*, Aug. 23, 1862
86. *Havana Journal*, Aug. 16, 1862
87. *Corning Democrat*, Aug. 14, 1862
88. *New York in the War of the Rebellion* by Phisterer
89. *Havana Journal*, Nov. 6, 1869, Chapter I History of the 107th NY Vols. Regmt. by Harvey G. Denniston
90. *Elmira Advertiser*, Aug. 14, 1862
91. *Havana Journal*, Nov. 6, 1869, Chapter I History of the 107th NY Vols. Regmt. by Denniston
92. *Elmira Advertiser*, Aug. 14, 1862
93. *Havana Journal*, Nov. 6, 1869, Chapter I History of the 107th NY Vols. Regmt. by Denniston
94. *Elmira Advertiser*, Aug. 14, 1862
95. *Corning Journal*, Aug. 14, 1862
96. *Corning Journal*, July 24, 1862
97. 1903 NYS Adjutant-General Report, No. 34, 107th New York Volunteer Infantry Regiment

## Chapter 2

1. *Symbol, Sword and Shield* by B. Franklin Cooling
2. Arthur S. Fitch's Journal, member of the 107th
3. *Elmira Advertiser*, Aug. 23, 1862, letter from Sigma, pseudonym for a member of the 107th
4. History of the 107th by Harvey G. Denniston
5. *The Avenue of the Presidents* by Mary Cable
6. *History of the 107th* by Harvey G. Denniston
7. *Addison Advertiser*, Sept. 3, 1862, Aug. 27, letter from John Orr
8. *History of the 107th* by Harvey G. Denniston
9. *Elmira Advertiser*, Aug. 23, 1862, July 16, letter from Sigma
10. The banner may have been presented by Secretary of State Seward, History of the 107th
11. *Elmira Star-Gazette*, Pad and Pencil, Sept. 24, 1917
12. Constance Barone, Director of the Chemung County Historical Society
13. *Washington National Republican*, reprinted by Aug. 23, 1862, *Elmira Advertiser*
14. Arthur S. Fitch's Journal
15. *Elmira Advertiser*, Aug. 23, 1862
16. Arthur S. Fitch's Journal
17. *The Avenue of the Presidents*
18. Topographical Map of Washington Defenses, Lathel Duffield
19. *Elmira Advertiser*, Aug. 23, 1862, July 16 letter from Sigma
20. *Symbol, Sword, and Shield*
21. 107th Company Books, Record Group 94, National Archives

22. Capt. Brigham's address, 107th Reg. Assoc. 25th Reunion, Sept. 17, 1891
23. Elmira Advertiser, *Aug. 23, 1862*, July 17 letter from Sigma
24. Arthur S. Fitch's Journal
25. Capt. Brigham's address
26. *Addison Advertiser*, Aug. 27, 1862, letter from John Orr
27. Arthur S. Fitch's Journal
28. *Symbol, Sword and Shield*
29. *History of the 107th* by H.G. Denniston
30. *Addison Advertiser*, Aug. 27 letter from John Orr
31. Regiment Records
32. Andrew Brockway Letter Home August 24, 1862
33. Arthur S. Fitch's Journal
34. National Archives, Record Group 94, General Order 6
35. *Addison Advertiser*, Aug. 27 letter from John Orr
36. National Archives, Record Group 94, General Order 7
37. Elmira Advertiser, Aug. 24, letter from Sigma
38. Addison Advertiser, Aug. 27, letter from John Orr
39. *Addison Advertiser*, Sept. 10, 1862
40. *History of the 107th* by H.G. Denniston
41. *A Civil War Courtship*, The Letters of Edwin Weller
42. Arthur S. Fitch's Journal
43. *Elmira Advertiser*, Aug. 31, 1862, letter from Sigma
44. Arthur S. Fitch's Journal
45. Capt. Brigham's address
46. *Steuben Courier* Sept. 10, 1862, Aug. 31, letter from Harvey G. Denniston
47. *Elmira Advertiser*, Aug. 31, letter from Sigma
48. National Archives, Record Group 94, Order issued from 5th Brigade Hdqtrs, Whipples Division
49. Arthur S. Fitch's Journal
50. *The March to Antietam* by Capt. Wm. F. Fox
51. 1903 NYS Adjutant-General Report No. 34

## Chapter 3

1. Arthur S. Fitch's Journal, Chemung County Historical Society
2. *Fox Family News*, Mar. 1, 1915, "The March to Antietam" by Capt. Wm. Freeman Fox
3. *Havana Journal*, Nov. 13, 1869, Chap. III, *History of the 107th* by Denniston
4. *Elmira Gazette*, Oct. 16, 1862, J.J. Phelps letter
5. *Addison Advertiser*, Oct. 1, 1862, Letter from John Orr
6. Van Valkenburgh, Record Group 94, National Archives
7. Arthur S. Fitch's Journal, Chemung County Historical Society
8. *Fox Family News*, Mar. 1, 1915, by Capt. Wm. Freeman Fox

9. *The 27th Indiana* by E.R. Brown

10. *Addison Advertiser*, Oct. 1, 1862, Letter from John Orr

11. Arthur S. Fitch's Journal, Chemung County Historical Society

12. *Slocum and His Men*, page 138

13. Arthur S. Fitch's Journal, Chemung County Historical Society

14. *The 27th Indiana* by E.R. Brown

15. *Service with the 3rd Wisconsin Infantry* by J.W. Hinkley

16. Arthur S. Fitch's Journal

17. *Washington National Tribune*, June 25, 1925, Col. S.L. Pittman, 1st Mich. Cav.

18. *The 27th Indiana* by E.R. Brown

19. *Service with the 3rd Wisconsin Infantry* by J.W. Hinkley

20. Arthur S. Fitch's Journal

21. Letter from Capt. John Orr

22. Lt. Martin Bachman address at 18th Reunion of 107th Reg't Assoc., Sept. 17, 1884

23. *The 27th Indiana* by E.R. Brown

24. Letter from John W. Schildt, Oct. 16, 1994

25. *The 27th Indiana* by E.R. Brown

26. *Addison Advertiser*, Oct. 15, 1862, Letter from Major G.L. Smith

27. Theodore Smith's address at the 23rd reunion of the 107th Reg't Assoc., Sept. 17, 1887

28. Letter from John W. Schildt, Oct. 16, 1994

29. *Drums Along the Antietam* by John W. Schildt

30. *Battle of Antietam* by John Bresnahan, Co. A, 27th Indiana

31. Letter from Capt. N. Colby to his father, Oct. 9, 1862, Wm. E. Hughes

32. *Battle of Antietam* by John Bresnahan, Co. A, 27th Indiana

33. *Fox Family News*, Mar. 1, 1915, "The March to Antietam" by Capt. Wm. Freeman Fox

34. Arthur S. Fitch's Journal

35. Letter Capt. N. Colby to his father, Sept. 21, 1862

36. Battle of Antietam by John H. Bresnahan, 27th Indiana; Frank Frost's scrapbook, Chemung County Historical Society

37. Theodore Smith's address

38. *Addison Advertiser*, Oct. 15, 1862, Letter from Lt. G.L. Smith

39. Letter to his father, Capt. N. Colby, Sept. 21, 1862

40. Edward Kendall address to the 24th Annual reunion of the 107th Reg't Assoc., Sept. 21, 1890

41. *Fox Family News*, Mar. 1, 1915, "The March to Antietam" by Capt. Wm. Freeman Fox

42. *The Young Volunteer* by Joseph E. Crowell

43. *Corning Journal*, Oct. 2, 1862

44. *Elmira Daily Advertiser*, Sept. 29, 1885

45. Letter from Capt. Newton Colby to his father, Sept 21, 1862

46. Article by Capt. Wm. F. Fox, Fox Family News, Mar. 1, 1915

47. Letter from Capt. John Orr

48. Letter from Capt. Newton Colby to his father, Sept. 21, 1862

49. *Fox Family News*, Mar. 1, 1915, "The March to Antietam" by Capt. Wm. Freeman Fox

50. *Addison Advertiser*, Sept. 21, 1862, Letter from Capt. John Orr

51. *Corning Journal*, Oct. 10, 1862, Letter from Lt. Col. Diven to his son

52. *Elmira Advertiser*, Oct. 4, 1862, Letter from Sigma and John Orr

53. *Fox Family News*, Mar. 1, 1915, "The March to Antietam" by Capt. Wm. Freeman Fox

54. Story related by R.S. Ganoung, private Co. E from Seneca Falls newspaper, May 30, 1911

55. *Corning Journal*, Oct. 2, 1862, Letter from Lt. Col. Diven to his son

56. Letter from Capt. John Orr

57. Letter from Capt. Newton Colby

58. Letter from Angela Kirkham Davis to her nieces, Washington County Free Library, Hagerstown, Md.

59. *Elmira Daily Advertiser*, Sept. 29, 1884

60. *Antietam Hospitals* by John W. Schildt

61. *Elmira Daily Advertiser*, Sept. 29, 1884

62. *Elmira Sunday Tidings*, Oct. 4, 1885, Article by Arthur S. Fitch

63. Letter to his father, Capt. Newton Colby, Sept. 21, 1862

64. Letter to his father, Capt. Newton Colby, Oct. 9, 1862

65. Letter from Angela Kirkham Davis to her nieces, Washington County Free Library, Hagerstown, Md.

66. *Havana Journal,* Oct. 4, 1862

67. Letter home from Pvt. Patrick Traynor, Oct. 2, 1862

68. *Elmira Gazette,* Sept. 27, 1862, Letter from J.J. Phelps

69. *Fox Family News*, Mar. 1, 1915, "The March to Antietam" by Capt. Wm. Freeman Fox

70. Address by Adjutant Hull Fanton at the 5th annual reunion of the 107th Reg'l Assoc., Sept. 17, 1871

71. *Elmira Gazette*, Sept. 27, 1862, Letter from from J.J. Phelps

72. *History of the 107th* by Lt. H.G. Denniston; *Havana Journal*, Nov. 11, 1869

73. Letter to his father, Capt. N. Colby, Sept. 30, 1862

74. *From the Cannon's Mouth*, The Letters of Gen. A.S. Williams

75. *Fox Family News*, Mar. 1, 1915, "The March to Antietam" by Capt. Wm. Freeman Fox

76. Letters from Angela Kirkham Davis to her nieces, Washington County Free Library, Hagerstown, Md.

77. Address by Adjutant Hull Fanton at the 5th annual reunion of the 107th Reg'l Assoc., Sept. 17, 1871

78. Roll of Honor, burial places of the Union dead

79. *Elmira Weekly Gazette*, Oct. 16, 1862

80. Letter from Angela Kirkham Davis to her nieces, Washington County Free Library, Hagerstown, Md.

## Chapter 4

1. *Elmira Advertiser*, Oct. 1862, Thomas K. Beecher letter
2. Arthur S. Fitch's Journal
3. Arthur S. Fitch letter to his sister, Sept. 21, 1862
4. *History of the 107th* by Harvey Denniston
5. Arthur S. Fitch's Journal
6. *History of the 107th* by Harvey Denniston
7. Arthur S. Fitch's Journal
8. *History of the 107th* by Harvey Denniston
9. Arthur S. Fitch's journal
10. *Elmira Advertiser*, Sept. 24, 1862, letter to from Sigma
11. Sept. 30, 1862, letter home from Capt. N. Colby
12. Arthur S. Fitch's Journal
13. *From the Cannon's Mouth,* The Letters of Gen. A.S. Williams
14. *Elmira Advertiser*, Oct. 7, 1862, letter from Sigma
15. *Elmira Weekly Gazette*, Oct. 8, 1862, letter from Private S.
16. *Steuben Courier*, Oct. 6, 1862, letter from Lieut. Harvey Denniston
17. Sept. 30, 1862, letter home from Capt. N. Colby
18. Sept. 29, 1862, letter home from Arthur S. Fitch
19. Speech given at the 6th 107th regimental association reunion
20. Sept. 30, 1862, letter home from Capt. N. Colby
21. Oct. 11, 1862, letter home from Capt. N. Colby
22. *The Record Of the 2nd Massachusetts Infantry* by Alonzo H. Quint
23. *Addison Advertiser*, Oct. 14, 1862, letter from Lieut. J. Orr
24. Arthur S. Fitch's Journal
25. Oct. 1, 1862, letter to O.S. Whitmore from Private F.W. Young
26. Arthur S. Fitch's Journal
27. Sept. 29, letter from Arthur S. Fitch
28. Oct. 1, 1862, letter to O.S. Whitemore from Private F.W. Young
29. 1890, 107th Regimental Association reunion, speech by Edward Kendall
30. 1871, 107th Regimental Association reunion, speech by Hull Fanton
31. *Havana Journal*, Sept. 27, 1862
32. Arthur S. Fitch's Journal
33. *Elmira Advertiser*, Oct. 7, 1862, letter from Sigma
34. *Steuben Courier*, Oct. 6, 1862, letter from Harvey Denniston
35. *Elmira Advertiser*, Oct. 4, 1862, letter from Gabriel L. Smith
36. Arthur S. Fitch's Journal
37. *Elmira Advertiser*, Oct. 7, 1862, letter from Sigma
38. Oct. 10, 1862, letter home from Capt. N. Colby
39. Arthur S. Fitch's Journal
40. *Elmira Advertiser*, Oct. 7, 1862, letter from Sigma
41. Group 94, National Archives, Washington, DC
42. Oct. 11, 1862, letter home from Capt. N. Colby
43. Phisterer's Register of New York Regiments
44. Group 94, National Archives, Washington, DC
45. Arthur S. Fitch's Journal
46. *Addison Advertiser*, Oct. 14, 1862, letter from Lieut. J. Orr
47. *Elmira Advertiser*, Oct. 7, 1862, letter from Sigma
48. Addison Advertiser, Oct. 14, 1862, letter from Lieut. J. Orr
49. *Elmira Advertiser*, Oct. 7, 1862, letter from Sigma
50. *History of the 107th* by Harvey Denniston
51. Oct. 10, 1862, letter home from Capt. N. Colby
52. *The Young Volunteer*
53. *Slocum and His Men*
54. Arthur S. Fitch's Journal
55. *The Young Volunteer*
56. Arthur S. Fitch's Journal
57. *Elmira Advertiser*, Oct. 25, 1862, letter from Thomas K. Beecher
58. Oct. 21, 1862, letter home from Capt. N. Colby
59. Arthur S. Fitch's Journal
60. *Elmira Advertiser*, Oct. 25, 1862, letter from Thomas K. Beecher
61. Group 94, National Archives, Washington, DC
62. *Elmira Advertiser*, Nov. 1, 1862
63. *Havana Journal*, Nov. 1, 1862
64. *Corning Journal*, Oct. 30, 1862
65. *Addison Advertiser*, Nov. 5, 1862
66. Edward Kendall's speech, 1890 107th Regimental Association reunion
67. Group 94, National Archives, Washington, DC
68. New York State Adjutant's Report of 1903
69. Arthur S. Fitch's Journal
70. New York State Adjutant's Report of 1903
71. Arthur S. Fitch's Journal
72. *Slocum and His Men*
73. Arthur S. Fitch's Journal
74. *Slocum and His Men*
75. Arthur S. Fitch's Journal
76. New York State Adjutant's Report of 1903
77. Jim Sundman, *Emerging Civil War,* Jan. 12 and 16, 2012
78. Arthur S. Fitch's Journal
79. *Elmira Advertiser*, Nov. 8, 1862, letter from Sigma
80. Arthur S. Fitch's Journal
81. Group 94, National Archives, Washington, DC

82. Arthur S. Fitch's Journal
83. Group 94, National Archives, Washington, DC
84. Arthur S. Fitch's Journal
85. Group 94, National Archives, Washington, DC
86. *Havana Journal*, Nov. 22, 1862
87. *Elmira Weekly Advertiser*, Nov. 8, 1862
88. Group 94, National Archives, Washington, DC
89. *Elmira Advertiser*, Nov. 8, 1862, letter from Sigma
90. Speech given at 6th regimental assoc. reunion, Sept. 17, 1872
91. *Elmira Advertiser*, Nov. 8, 1862, letter from Sigma
92. *History of the 107th* by Harvey Denniston
93. *Elmira Advertiser*, Apr. 11, 1895, article by Mrs. G.L. Smith
94. *Elmira Weekly Advertiser*, Nov. 29, 1862, letter from Chaplain Crane
95. Group 94, National Archives, Washington, DC
96. Arthur S. Fitch's Journal
97. Group 94, National Archives, Washington, DC
98. New York Adjutant's Report of 1903
99. *Elmira Weekly Advertiser*, Nov. 29, 1862, letter from Chaplain Crane
100. Group 94, National Archives, Washington, DC
101. Arthur F. Fitch's Journal
102. *Elmira Weekly Advertiser*, Nov. 29, 1862, letter from Chaplain Crane
103. Arthur S. Fitch's Journal
104. Rare Book, Manuscript & Special Collections Library, Duke University
105. *Corning Journal*, Dec. 18, 1862
106. *Corning Journal*, Dec. 18, 1862, letter from Chaplain Crane

## *Chapter 5*

1. Arthur Fitch's Journal
2. Gen. A.S. Williams, Dec. 14, 1862, Letter to his daughter
3. Arthur Fitch's Journal
4. Gen. A.S. Williams, Dec. 14, 1862, Letter to his daughter
5. Arthur Fitch's Journal
6. Gen. A.S. Williams, Dec. 14, 1862, Letter to his daughter
7. Arthur Fitch's Journal
8. John Orr's Journal
9. Arthur Fitch's Journal
10. *History of the 107th Regt. NYV* by Harvey Denniston
11. Edw. Kendall, Dec. 26, 1862, Letter to his father
12. John D. Hill, Dec. 18, 1862, Letter to his mother
13. Arthur S. Fitch's Journal
14. *History of the 107th Regt. NYV* by Harvey Denniston
15. Arthur S. Fitch's Journal
16. *History of the 107th Regt. NYV* by Harvey Denniston
17. Arthur S. Fitch's Journal
18. John Hill, January 4, 1863, Letter to his sister
19. *A Civil War Courtship, The Letters of Edwin Weller*, Edited by Wm. Walton
20. Edwin Weller, Jan. 6, 1863, Letter, Near Fairfax Station, Va.
21. Edw. Kendall Jan. 13, 1863, Letter to his parents, Near Kelly's Ford, Va.
22. *History of the 107th Regt. NYV* by Harvey Denniston
23. John Orr's Journal
24. *History of the 107th Regt. NYV* by Harvey Denniston
25. Pvt. Andrew Brockway, Jan. 16, 1863, Letter home
26. 2nd Lt. John Hill, Jan. 16, 1863, Letter home
27. *History of the 107th Regt. NYV* by Harvey Denniston
28. Major C.J. Fox Sept. 17, 1872, Reunion Talk
29. Arthur Fitch's Journal
30. *History of the 107th Regt. NYV* by Harvey Denniston
31. Arthur Fitch's Journal
32. *History of the 107th Regt. NYV* by Harvey Denniston
33. Arthur Fitch's Journal
34. John Hill, Feb. 17, 1863, Letter to his sister and brother
35. Arthur Fitch's Journal
36. *History of the 107th Regt. NYV* by Harvey Denniston
37. Arthur Fitch's Journal
38. *History of the 107th Regt. NYV* by Harvey Denniston
39. John Orr's Journal
40. Arthur Fitch's Journal
41. Edw. Kendall, Jan. 30, 1863, Letter to his father
42. Arthur Fitch's Journal
43. Rufus Harnden, Jan. 31, 1863, Letter
44. *History of the 107th Regt. NYV* by Harvey Denniston
45. John Orr's Journal
46. Edw. Kendall, February 12, 1863, Letter to his father
47. Edw. Kendall, February 18, 1863, Letter to his father
48. John Orr's Journal
49. Dr. and Jane Marshall
50. Arthur Fitch's Journal
51. Duke University Library
52. National Archives
53. *Slocum And His Men*
54. John Hill, March 22, 1863, Letter to his sister
55. John Hill, March 28, 1863, Letter to his sister

56. *History of the 107th Regt. NYV* by Harvey Denniston
57. Arthur S. Fitch's Journal
58. Private Cornelius Murray, March 1, 1863, Letter to his brother and sister
59. John Hill, April 2, 1863, Letter to his sister
60. *History of the 107th Regt. NYV* by Harvey Denniston
61. Regimental records
62. Arthur S. Fitch's Journal
63. *History of the 107th Regt. NYV* by Harvey Denniston
64. *A Civil War Courtship* by Wm. Walton
65. *History of the 107th Regt. NYV* by Harvey Denniston
66. Private Rufus Harnden, April 12, 1863, Letter to his parents

## Chapter 6

1. *History of the 107th Regt. NYV* by Harvey Denniston
2. Arthur S. Fitch's Journal
3. Capt. John Orr's Journal
4. Arthur S. Fitch's Journal
5. Andrew Brockway, April 15, 1863, Letter
6. Capt. John Orr's Journal
7. Regimental Records
8. *History of the 107th Regt. NYV* by Harvey Denniston
9. Major C.J. Fox Sept. 17, 1872, Reunion Presentation
10. Arthur S. Fitch's Journal
11. *Slocum and His Men*
12. *History of the 107th Regt. NYV* by Harvey Denniston
13. Arthur S. Fitch's Journal
14. *History of the 107th Regt. NYV* by Harvey Denniston
15. Harnden's Chancellorsville Sketch
16. Arthur S. Fitch's Journal
17. Harnden's Chancellorsville Sketch
18. Major C.J. Fox Sept. 17, 1872, Reunion Presentation
19. Arthur S Fitch's Journal
20. Major C.J. Fox Sept. 17, 1872, Reunion Presentation
21. Arthur S. Fitch's Journal
22. *Slocum and His Men*
23. Arthur S. Fitch's Journal
24. *Slocum and His Men*
25. Arthur S. Fitch's Journal
26. *Slocum and His Men*
27. Arthur S. Fitch's Journal
28. *History of the 107th Regt. NYV* by Harvey Denniston

## Chapter 7

1. Chemung County Historical Society

2. *History of the 107th Regt. NYV* by Harvey Denniston
3. Capt. John Orr's Journal
4. *Havana Journal*
5. *History of the 107th Regt. NYV* by Harvey Denniston
6. Edward Kendall, June 24, 1863, Letter
7. John Orr's Journal
8. Arthur Finch's Journal
9. *History of the 107th Regt. NYV* by Harvey Denniston
10. Arthur Fitch's Journal
11. *Slocum and His Men*
12. John Orr's Journal
13. Arthur Fitch's Journal
14. *History of the 107th Regt. NYV* by Harvey Denniston
15. John Orr's Journal
16. *The Left Attack at Gettysburg*, Capt. E. Whittier, Feb. 10, 1891
17. Medical and Surgical History of the Civil War, Vol. X
18. "107th NY at Gettysburg" Paper by G. Farr
19. Arthur Fitch's Journal
20. *History of the 107th Regt. NYV* by Harvey Denniston
21. Edward Kendall, Letter
22. John Orr's Journal
23. *Slocum and His Men*
24. Edward Kendall, Letter
25. *Slocum and His Men*
26. Edward Kendall, Letter
27. *Slocum and His Men*

## Chapter 8

1. *Mr. Lincoln's Military Railroads*, Roy Meredith & Arthur Meredith
2. *History of the 107th Regt. NYV* by Harvey Denniston
3. Hadley Beal, Oct. 5, 1863, Letter
4. *Slocum and His Men*
5. Hadley Beal, Oct. 5, 1863, Letter
6. John D. Hill, Oct. 6, 1863, Letter, Carlisle Institute
7. Gen. Joseph Wheeler Report, Oct 6, 1863
8. Mark M. Boatner, III. *The Civil War Dictionary NY*
9. *History of the 107th Regt. NYV* by Harvey Denniston
10. John D. Hill, Oct. 6, 1863, Letter
11. *History of the 107th Regt. NYV* by Harvey Denniston
12. John Orr's Journal, Oct. 7, 1863
13. E. Kendall, Oct. 10, 1863, Letter
14. *History of the 107th Regt. NYV* by Harvey Denniston
15. E. Kendall, Oct. 11, 1863, Letter
16. Hadley Beal, Oct. 12, 1863, Letter
17. *History of the 107th Regt. NYV* by Harvey Denniston
18. Multiple Letters Oct. 1863, 107th NY

19. E. Kendall, Oct. 16, 1863, Letter
20. H. Beal, Oct. 17–18, 1863, Letter
21. E. Kendall, Nov. 1, 1863, Letter
22. E. Kendall, Nov. 15, 1863, Letter
23. General Williams, Nov 11, 1863, Letter
24. *History of the 107th Regt. NYV* by Harvey Denniston
25. Hadley Beal, Nov. 4, 1863, Letter
26. John Hill, Nov. 12–15, 1863, Letters
27. Hadley Beal, Nov. 16, 1863, Letter
28. *History of the 107th Regt. NYV* by Harvey Denniston
29. National Archives Records Group 94
30. Hornell, NY Public Library
31. E. Kendall, Jan. 15, 1864, Letter
32. National Archives, Washington, DC, Records Group 94
33. *Slocum and His Men*
34. *History of the 107th Regt. NYV* by Harvey Denniston
35. E. Kendall, Dec. 15, 1863, Letter
36. E. Kendall, Dec. 27, 1863, Letter
37. National Archives, Washington, DC, Records Group 94
38. J.D. Hill, Jan. 28, 1864, Letter
39. John Orr's Journal
40. J.D. Hill, Jan. 28, 1864, Letter
41. John Orr's Journal
42. *Mr. Tubb's War* by Nat Brandt, Chap. 19 pg. 143
43. John Orr's Journal
44. National Archives, Washington, DC, Records Group 94
45. NYS Military History Museum
46. Arthur Finch's Journal
47. National Archives, Washington, DC, Records Group 94
48. Wm Graham, Feb. 13, 1864, Letter
49. National Archives, Washington, DC, Records Group 94
50. Weller, Mar. 22, 1864, Letter
51. National Archives, Washington, DC, Records Group 94
52. John Orr's Journal
53. Frost Scrapbook, CCHS
54. *Slocum and His Men*
55. *Mr. Tubb's Civil War*
56. E. Kendall, Apr. 26, 1864, Letter
57. National Archives, Washington, DC, Records Group 94
58. E. Kendall, May 5, 1864, Letter
59. NY History Military Museum
60. National Archives, Washington, DC, Records Group 94

## Chapter 9

1. John Orr's Journal
2. Lt. Edwin Weller's Journal
3. Graham, May 21, 1864, Letter
4. *Historical Times Illustrated Encyclopedia of the Civil War* Vol. 5
5. Daniel Scott May 20, 1864, Letter
6. *The Evolution of Skirmish Tactics in the U.S. Civil* War by Kent J. Goff
7. John Orr's Journal
8. Edward Kendall, May 20, 1864, Letter
9. Lt. Edwin Weller's Journal
10. John Orr's Journal
11. *Slocum and His Men*
12. John Orr's Journal
13. Lt. A.S. Fitch, *National Tribune*, Nov. 15, 1883
14. Lt. Edwin Weller's Journal
15. Edward Kendall, June 7, 1864, Letter
16. Lt. Edwin Weller Journal
17. Edward Kendall, June 11, 1864, Letter
18. Lt. Edwin Weller's Journal
19. Edward Kendall, July 14, 1864, Letter
20. Lt. Edwin Weller's Journal
21. Edward Kendall, June 20, 1864, Letter
22. *Slocum and His Men*
23. Lt. Edwin Weller's Journal
24. Edward Kendall, June 29, 1864, Letter
25. Lt. Edwin Weller's Journal
26. *Slocum and His Men*
27. Edward Kendall, July 6, 1864, Letter
28. Edward Kendall, July 23, 1864, Letter

## Chapter 10

1. Edward Kendall, July 30, 1864, Letter
2. Edward Kendall, Aug. 7, 1864, Letter
3. *Slocum and His Men*
4. Lt. Edwin Weller's Journal
5. Edward Kendall, July 23, 1864, Letter
6. *Slocum and His Men*
7. Edward Kendall, July 30, 1864, Letter
8. Wm. R. Perkins Library, Duke University
9. Edward Kendall Aug. 6, 1864, Letter
10. Edward Kendall, Aug. 12, 1864, Letter
11. Edward Kendall, Aug. 20,1864, Letter
12. Edward Kendall, Aug. 24, 1864, Letter
13. *Slocum and His Men*
14. Lt. Edwin Weller, Aug. 29, 1864
15. National Archives, Washington, DC
16. Lt. Edwin Weller's Journal
17. *Elmira Star Gazette*, Steele Memorial Library
18. Wm Graham, Sept. 7, 1864, Letter
19. *History of the 107th Regt. NYV* by Harvey Denniston
20. Report of Lt. Col. Allen Sill, 107th NY Operations Sept. 2–Dec. 23, 1864
21. Edward Kendall, Sept. 11, 1864, Letter
22. Mayor James M Calhoun of Atlanta
23. Edward Kendall, Sept. 23, 1864, Letter
24. Lt. Edwin Weller's Journal
25. Capt. John Orr's Journal
26. Lt. Edwin Weller's Journal
27. E.A. Bator, Mar. 16, 2000, Letter
28. The Annual Report of the NYS Adjutant General, 1904
29. Lt. Edwin Weller's Journal

30. *Ontonagon Herald*, Manistique, Michigan, Aug. 10, 1930, Obituary of John McCanna
31. Capt. John Orr's Journal
32. Arthur Fitch's Journal
33. Wm. Graham, Oct. 12, 1864, Letter
34. Lt. Edwin Weller, Oct. 15, 1864, Letter
35. Edward Kendal, Oct. 23, 1864, Letter
36. Capt. John Orr's Journal
37. Edward Kendall, Oct. 23, 1864
38. Capt. John Orr's Journal
39. Wm. Graham, Oct. 12, 1864, Letter, Schuyler County Historical Society
40. Edward Kendall, Nov. 6, 1863, Letter
41. *Slocum and His Men*

## Chapter 11

1. *History of the 107th Regt. NYV* by Harvey Denniston
2. Capt. John Orr's Journal
3. *The Story of the Great March*, George Ward Nichols
4. Capt. John Orr's Journal
5. Records 107th NY
6. *History of Shannon's Scouts*
7. Edward Kendall, Dec. 17, 1864, Letter
8. Chemung County, NY Historical Society
9. Regimental Report
10. Capt. John Orr's Journal
11. Speech by Lt. Arthur Fitch, 107th 16 Reunion, Sept 17, 1882
12. Manley Crane's Diary
13. *The Story of the Grand March*, George Ward Nichols
14. *Service with the Third Wisconsin*, Julian Wisner Hinkley
15. *A Civil War Courtship*, William Walton
16. Official Records Milledgeville, Ga., Hawley's Report of Property Seized and Destroyed
17. Capt. John Orr's Journal
18. Montour Falls, NY Public Library
19. *Service with the 3rd Wisconsin*, Julian Wisner Hinkley
20. *Milledgeville, Georgia's Antebellum Capital*, James C. Bonner
21. *Service with the 3rd Wisconsin*, Julian Wisner Hinkley
22. *Slocum and His Men*
23. *Milledgeville, Georgia's Antebellum Capital*, James C. Bonner
24. Capt. John Orr's Journal
25. Arthur Fitch's Journal
26. Edw. Kendall, Dec. 17, 1864, Letter
27. *History of the 107th Regt. NYV* by Harvey Denniston
28. Russell Tuttle, Dec. 16, 1864, Letter
29. Arthur Fitch's Journal
30. *Civil War Courtship*, William Walton
31. Russell Tuttle, Dec. 26, 1864, Letter
32. Edw. Kendall, Dec. 10, 1864, Letter
33. *History of the 107th Regt. NYV* by Harvey Denniston

34. *Maps and Mapmakers of the Civil War*, Earl B. McElfresh
35. *History of the 107th Regt. NYV* by Harvey Denniston
36. Capt. John Orr's Journal
37. *Slocum and His Men*

## Chapter 12

1. *Slocum and His Men*
2. *History of the 107th Regt. NYV* by Harvey Denniston
3. Capt. John Orr Journal
4. *History of the 107th Regt. NYV* by Harvey Denniston
5. Capt. John Orr's Journal
6. Edward Kendall, Mar. 10, 1865, Letter home
7. Charles von Wagoner's Journal
8. Capt. John Orr's Journal
9. Wm. R Hammond, Letter to his daughter Alice
10. *History of the 107th Regt. NYV* by Harvey Denniston
11. *Miracle at Rockingham*
12. Annual Report Adjutant General of the State of NY 1903
13. Capt. John Orr's Journal
14. Lt. Edwin Weller Mar. 12, 1865, Letter
15. Capt. John Orr's Journal
16. Journal of Captain Robert McDowell, 141st NY
17. Capt. John Orr's Journal
18. Lt. Edwin Weller, Mar. 25, 1865, Letter
19. *History of the 107th Regt. NYV* by Harvey Denniston
20. Capt. John Orr's Journal

## Chapter 13

1. Edwin Weller's journal
2. *History of the 107th Regt. NYV* by Harvey Denniston
3. Edwin Weller's Journal
4. Captain John Orr's Journal
5. Edwin Weller's Journal
6. Captain John Orr's Journal
7. *A Civil War Courtship*, William Walton
8. *History of the 107th Regt. NYV* by Harvey Denniston
9. *Reminiscences of the 13th NJ*, Samuel Toombs
10. Captain John Orr's Journal
11. *History of the 107th Regt. NYV* by Harvey Denniston
12. Copy of the pass written by Col. Newton P. Colby
13. Pension General Affidavit by his mother, Schuyler County 1884
14. Edwin Weller's Journal
15. *History of the 107th Regt. NYV* by Harvey Denniston
16. *Elmira Daily Advertiser*, June 9, 1865

17. *Havana Journal*, June 9, 1865

18. *Havana Journal*, June 17, 1865

19. *History of the 107th Regt. NYV* by Harvey Denniston

## *Chapter 14*

1. *Canisteo Times*, Dec. 20, 1867, 107th NY Veterans, Organizational Meeting

2. *Havana Journal*, Sept. 18, 1868, First 107th NY Reunion, Havana, NY

3. *Elmira Daily Advertiser*, Oct. 22, 1869, Second 107th NY Reunion, Elmira, NY

4. *Elmira Daily Advertiser*, Sept. 17, 1870, Third 107th NY Reunion and Banquet

5. Fox, C.J. and Fitch, A.S. Addresses, *Elmira Daily Advertiser*, Sept. 18, 1872

6. Diven, Col. A.S., July 4th Presentation, *Elmira Daily Advertiser*, July 5, 1873

7. *Elmira Daily Advertiser*, Sept. 18, 1878, "Statue, Memorial Statue Planning"

8. *Elmira Daily Advertiser*, Sept. 22, 1882, "Statue, Memorial Dedication"

9. Smith, Theodore at Antietam, *Elmira Daily Advertiser*, Sept. 29, 1884

10. Diven, Col. A.S. Address at Reg't Monument Dedication Gettysburg, *Elmira Star-Gazette*, Sept. 18, 1888

11. Crane, Col. Nirom, Address at Reg't Monument Dedication at Gettysburg, *Elmira Star-Gazette*, Sept. 18, 1888

12. Invitation to the 24th Reunion in 1890, Frost Scrapbook, Chemung County Historical Society

13. Brigham, Capt. H. G., Address at 25th Annual Reunion, *Elmira Star-Gazette*, Sept. 18, 1891

14. *Elmira Star-Gazette*, September 18, 1898, "Grant's Tomb Visit"

15. *Elmira Star-Gazette*, September 18, 1908, "107th NY Veteran's Deaths"

16. *Elmira Sunday Telegram*, Sept. 14, 1912, "50th 107th NY Anniversary"

17. *Elmira Star-Gazette*, Sept. 24, 1917, "Banner of the 107th NY"

18. Frost, Frank, *Elmira Sunday Telegram*, September 20, 1931

# Bibliography

## Newspapers

*Addison (NY) Advertiser*
*Advocate* (Bath, NY)
*Corning (NY) Democrat*
*Corning (NY) Journal*
*Elmira (NY) Advertiser*
*Elmira (NY) Advertiser & Republican*
*Elmira (NY) Star-Gazette*
*Elmira (NY) Weekly Gazette*
*Elmira Daily Gazette*
*Havana Journal* (Montour Falls, NY)
*Hornellsville Tribune* (Hornell, NY)
*Steuben Courier* (Corning, NY)
*Washington (DC) National Republican*
*Washington (DC) National Tribune*

Boatner, Mark M., III. *The Civil War Dictionary.* New York: David McKay, 1959.

Brandt, Nat. *Mr. Tubb's Civil War.* Syracuse, NY: Syracuse University Press, 1996.

Bresnahan, John H. *Battle of Antietam.* Frank Frost Scrapbook. Chemung County Historical Society, Elmira, NY.

Brown, E. R. *The Twenty-Seventh Indiana.* Butternut Press, 1899.

Burt, Col. Silas W. Memoirs, issued as *NY War of the Rebellion Series* Bulletin No. 1.

Crowell, Joseph E. *The Young Volunteer.* Paterson, NJ: self-published, 1906.

Denniston, Harvey G. *History of the 107th New York. Havana Journal,* microfilm, November 1869-May 1870, Montour Falls (NY) Library. Originally published in the *Canesteo Valley Times.*

Dyer, John Percy. "The Tennessee Raid, The Civil War Career of General Joseph Wheeler." *Georgia Historical Quarterly,* March 1935.

Fox, William F. *Slocum and His Men.* Albany, NY: J.B. Lyon, 1904.

Hinkley, J.W. *Service with the 3rd Wisconsin Infantry,* Wisconsin History Commission, 1912.

Hoar, Victor M. "Sketches of Elmira's 107th Infantry Regiment," *The Chemung County Historical Society Journal,* March 1960.

Keller, S. Roger. *Crossroads of War.* Burd Street Press, 1997.

Lamans, J. J. *Rare Book, Manuscript & Special Collections Library,* Duke University, Durham, NC.

McCanna, John. Obituary, *Ontonagon Herald,* Manistique, Michigan, August 10, 1930.

*Medical and Surgical History of the Civil War,* Volume X, War of the Rebellion, Barnes, Washington Print Office 1870–1888.

Meredith, Roy and Arthur. *Mr. Lincoln's Military Railroads,* W. W. Norton and Co. 1979.

*New York State Adjutant General Report No. 34* on 107th NY Vol. Infantry Regiment.

*New York State Asst. Adjutant General,* Report (1862) on raising troops for the Civil War.

107th NY Official Correspondence and Reports, Record Group 94, National Archives, Washington, D.C.

Quaife, Milo M. *From the Cannon's Mouth, The Civil War Letters of A. S. Williams.* Garden Springs Publication, 2015.

Quint, Alonzo H. *The Record of the 2nd Mass. Infantry.* Biblio Life, 2009.

Ross, Steve. Pass for Washington, D.C., after Grand Review by Col. N. P. Colby.

Schildt, John W. *Antietam Hospitals,* Antietam Publications, 1987.

Sill, Lt. Col. Allen. *Report 107th NY Operations 9/2/64–12/23/64* National Archives Grp 94

Smith, Mrs. G.L. Letter to the *Elmira Advertiser,* April 11, 1895.

Sturcke, Roger. *Chemung County Historical Society Collection.* Elmira, NY.

Toombs, Samuel. *Reminiscences of the 13th NJ.* Longstreet House, Reprint 1994.

Towner, Ausborn. *History of Chemung County 1892.* CCHS.

Walton, William. *A Civil War Courtship, The Letters of Edwin Weller.* New York: Doubleday 1980.

Whittier, Capt. E. *The Left Attack at Gettysburg,* MOLLUS Feb. 10, 1891.

## Letters Written by 107th New York Soldiers, 1862–1865

Baldwin, L. *Elmira Daily Advertiser,* May 27, 1864.

Bator, E.A. Chemung County Historical Society, Elmira, NY Society.

Beal, Hadley. Chemung County Historical Society, Elmira, NY.

Beecher, Thomas K. (141st NY), *Elmira Advertiser*, Elmira, NY.

Brockway, Andrew. Wm. L. Clements Library, Univ. of Michigan, NYS Library, Albany, NY.

Colby, N. Letter to his father, September 21,1862, *Havana Journal*, Montour Falls, NY.

Crane, Ezra F. *Elmira Daily Advertiser*, Elmira, NY.

Denniston, Harvey, *Havana Journal*, Montour Falls, NY.

Diven, A. S., *Elmira Daily Advertiser*, Elmira, NY.

Fitch, A. S. *National Tribune*, Nov. 15, 1883, Chemung County Historical Society, Elmira, NY.

Harnden, R. Chancellorsville Sketch, Library of Virginia (online source).

Hill, John D. Carlisle Military Institute, Carlisle, PA.

Hammond, Wm. R., Alice Harnden (daughter). January 23, 1915, Chemung County Historical Society.

Kendall, Edward. Letter Collection, Chemung County Historical Society, Elmira, NY.

Lamans, J. J. Special Collections Library, Duke University.

Lockwood, Dunning K. U.S. Army Military Institute, Carlisle, PA.

Murray, Cornelius, Bob Kilpatrick. Middleport, NY.

Orr, John. *Addison (NY) Advertiser*, March 4, 1863.

Phelps, J. J. Captured Social Circle, GA. *Elmira Daily Advertiser*, Nov. 11, 1864.

Reniff, Solomon. Hannibal, NY Town Historian, Lowell C. Newvine.

Scott, Daniel. *Addison (NY) Advertiser*, July 30, 1864.

Sigma (Pseudonym for 107th New York member). *Addison (NY) Advertiser*, August 23, 1862.

Smith, G. L. *Addison (NY) Advertiser*, October 15, 1862.

Traynor, Patrick, Bob Kilpatrick, Middleport, NY.

Van Valkenburg, R. B. *Corning Journal*, Corning, NY, October 2, 1862.

## Journals Kept by 107th New York Soldiers

Fitch, Arthur. Chemung County Historical Society, Elmira, NY.

McDowell, Captain Robert. 141st NY, Chemung Cunty Historical Society.

Orr, John. New York State Military History Museum, Cooperstown, NY.

Weller, Lt. Edwin. Held by Sue Ann Hackett-Earnst, Lyons, CO.

Von Wagoner, Charles. Chemung County Historical Society, Elmira, NY.

## Speeches and Material Relating to the 107th NY Regimental Assoc. Reunions

Bachman, Martin. "Antietam," *Elmira Star-Gazette*, September 18, 1884,

Brigham, H. G. *Elmira Star-Gazette*, September 17, 1891.

Diven, Alexander S. *Elmira Daily Advertiser*, Elmira, NY, September 17, 1871.

Fanton, Hull. "Raising the Regiment," *Elmira Daily Advertiser*, Elmira, NY, September 18, 1883.

"50th Anniversary," *Elmira Star-Gazette*, September 14, 1912.

Fitch, Arthur. "Gettysburg, Pennsylvania," *Elmira Daily Advertiser*, Elmira, NY, September 18, 1872.

Fitch, Arthur and Alexander Diven. *Elmira Daily Advertiser*, Elmira, NY, September 17, 1870.

Fitch, Arthur and Dallas Woods. *Elmira Daily Advertiser*, Elmira, NY, September 18, 1883.

Fox, C. J. Chancellorsville, *Elmira Daily Advertiser*, Elmira, NY. September 18, 1872.

"Frank Frost, Last Living Member," *Elmira Sunday Telegram*, September 20, 1931.

"Grant's Tomb," *Elmira Star-Gazette*, September 18, 1898.

Kendall, Edward. *Elmira Star-Gazette*, September 17, 1890.

"Members' Deaths," *Elmira Star-Gazette*, September 18, 1908.

"Organizational Meeting," *Canisteo Times*, Canisteo, NY, December 20, 1867.

"Regimental Banner," *Elmira Star-Gazette*, September 24, 1917.

"Second Reunion, Montour House," *Havana Journal*, Montour Falls, NY, September 17, 1868.

Smith, Theodore. *Elmira Star-Gazette*, September 17, 1887.

"Third Reunion, Rathbun House," *Elmira Daily Advertiser*, Elmira, NY, September 17, 1869.

# Index

Numbers in **_bold italics_** indicate pages with figures

Index 357

defended by Logie during a war meeting held in Coopers Plains 36; medical inspection of the regiment 92; need of more troops 10; replaced by Lincoln for inactivity 95; Special Order No. 3 issued by 55; veteran troops of 50
McCullough, J. (Pvt.) 114
McCumber, A.C. 21
McDonald, S.M. 13, 22, 23, 25, 28, 31, 33
McDowell, A.H. 30, 218
McDowell, R. (Capt.) 218
McGuire, M. 172
McKay, J. (Pvt.) 215
McKee, W. 133
McKeel, A.V. 21
McMillen, G. (Pvt.) 220
McMillen, M. 16
McPhearson, J.B. (Maj. Gen.) 182
McPherson, G. 263
McWilliams, J.A. 8
Meade, G.G. (Maj. Gen.) 129, 135, 161
Meagher, T, F. (Gen.) 81
Mekell, A.V. 232
Mellen, H. (Pvt.) 189
Middleton, I. (Pvt.) 181, 183
Miles, J.H. (Capt.) 20, 32, 33–34, 36, 90, 237
Millen Prison 264
Miller, A. (Pvt.) 85
Miller, D. 62
Minier, C. 35
Mitchell, J. (Pvt.) 65, 74
Mitchell, S.M. 9
Mitchell, W.A. (Pvt.) 57
Monocacy River 57, 135
Montgomery County 55
Montour Falls 81
Montour Falls Public Library 199
Mooers, Edward T. 42
Moore, J. 34
Moranville, D.P. (Pvt.) 116
Morgan, A.B. (Pvt.) 220
Morgan, A.C. 29, 30
Morgan, E.D. 42
Morgan, J. (Pvt.) 26, 219, 220
Morgan, W.L. (Capt.) 8, 9, 65–66, 82, 90, 114, 115, 121
Morgenson, J. 262
Morris, T.F. (Pvt.) 126, 127
Morrow, J. 232
Mosher, A. 63, 75
Mosher, J.B. 21
Mower, J.A. (Gen.) 222
Mowers, E.J. (Pvt.) 101, 184, 185
Murray, C. (Cpl.) 220

Nancy's Creek 180
New Hope Church 171, 248; battle of 5, 173, 188
New River 225
New York City 109, 231
*New York City Military Critic* 155
*New York Herald* 139
*New York Tribune* 202

Newman, B.F. 9
Nichols, N. 33
Nickajack Creek 180
Nicks, J.I. 15, 22, 23
North Anna River 225
North Carolina 224
Nottaway River 224

Occoquan River 259
Oconee Mill 199
Oconee River 200
Oelschlaeger, G. (Pvt.) 219
Oguache River 201, 202, 264
Ohio River 145
Olcott, A. 29
Old Alexandria 43
Oostanaula River 262
Orange Plank Road 124
Orr, J. (Lt.) 134, 159, 176, 188, 190, 191, 198, 234
Osburn, L. 74
Osmer, J.H. 21
Osmere, E.H. 30
Ostrander, J. 34
*Owego Gazette* 29

Paddock, H. (Pvt.) 114
Palmer, S.H. 32
Palmer, W.J. (Maj. Gen.) 166
Paris, T. 63, 75
Parks, D. 30
Parks, W. 115
Partridge, S. 22
Paterson, D. (Pvt.) 110
Paxton, L. 79
Peach Tree Creek 184, 263; battle of 182
Pee Dee River 212
Peninsula Campaign 49
Personius, W. (Sgt.) 189
Philip Pry Farm 59
Phoenix, S. (Pvt.) 85
Pickering, D.F. 8, 22
Pickett's Charge 4–5
Pinch, J.W. (Cpl.) 154
Pinch, S. 154
Pine Hill 178
Pitman, C.H. (Col.) 58
Pleasant Valley 77, 141
Poffenberger, S. 67
Polk, L. (Gen.) 178
Pomeroy, T. 252
Porter, F.H. (Gen.) 93
Post, W.T. 15
Post Barracks 9
Potomac River 4, 47–48, 52, 53, 78, 82, 110, 141
Potter, C. 45
Preswick, C. 25
Pulaski, C. (Gen.) 206
Pumpkin Vine Creek 171
Putnam, T. 160, 220

Quantico Creek 132

Raccoon Ford 142
"Rally Round the Flag Boys" 237
Ransom, R.H. 8

Rapidan River 123, 142
Rasco, H.H. (Pvt.) 115
Rathbone, G. (Cpl.) 208
Rathbun, J.T. 15, 22, 23
Rathbun, M.M. 24
Rathbun Barracks 9, 20
Rathbun Hotel *see* Brainard House
Reader, L. (Sgt.) 172
"The Rebel Flags" 16
"The Red, White, and Blue" 16, 29
Reid, G.W. (Capt.) 195
Reniff, S. 156
Resaca, battle of 168, 261
*Resolute* 202
reunions 236–267
Reynolds, E.M. (Pvt.) 99
Reynolds, I.H. 38
Reynolds, O.D. (Lt.) 121
Reynolds, S. 95
Richardson, C. (Pvt.) 127
Rickey, S. (Pvt.) 105
Rinker, E. (Pvt.) 219, 220
Roanoke River 224
Robertson, A. 13, 30
Robinson, J.M. 23
Robinson, N.A. (Pvt.) 63, 75, 104
Robinson Barracks 9
Rock Creek 136, 139, 211
Rodburn, J. 21, 30
Rogers, A. (Sgt.) 66, 74, 83, 141
Rogers, D. 29
Rood, S.I. 19
Root, S.L. 33
Rosecrans, W.S. (Gen.) 143, 144
Rosencrans, D. (Pvt.) 85
"Roslyn Castle" 240
Ross, J. 21
Ruger, T.A. (Gen.) 259
Ruger, W. (Col.) 79, 97, 116–118, 129, 138, 147, 149, 154, 161, 185, 244
Rumsey, B.D. 34
Rutter, J.H. (Lt.) 24, 25, 66, 69, 79, 242
Rutter, N.E. (Capt.) 124, 126, 127, 259

Sage, M. (Pvt.) 82
Saltzman, J. (Lt.) 204, 220
*Sampson* 202
Sandy Hook 78, 141
Sanford, D. 101, 265
Savannah River 207–208
Sawyer, S.R. 156
Sayler, L.O. 20
Sayles, H. 24
Saylor, L.O. (Lt.) 89, 232
Schuyler County 7–8, 16, 20, 21, 24, 81, 90
Scott, D. 114
Second Bull Run/2nd Bull Run 50, 232
Seibert, H. (Pvt.) 215
Seward, W.H. 2, 4, 12, 16, 41–42, 252
Sexton, J. 22